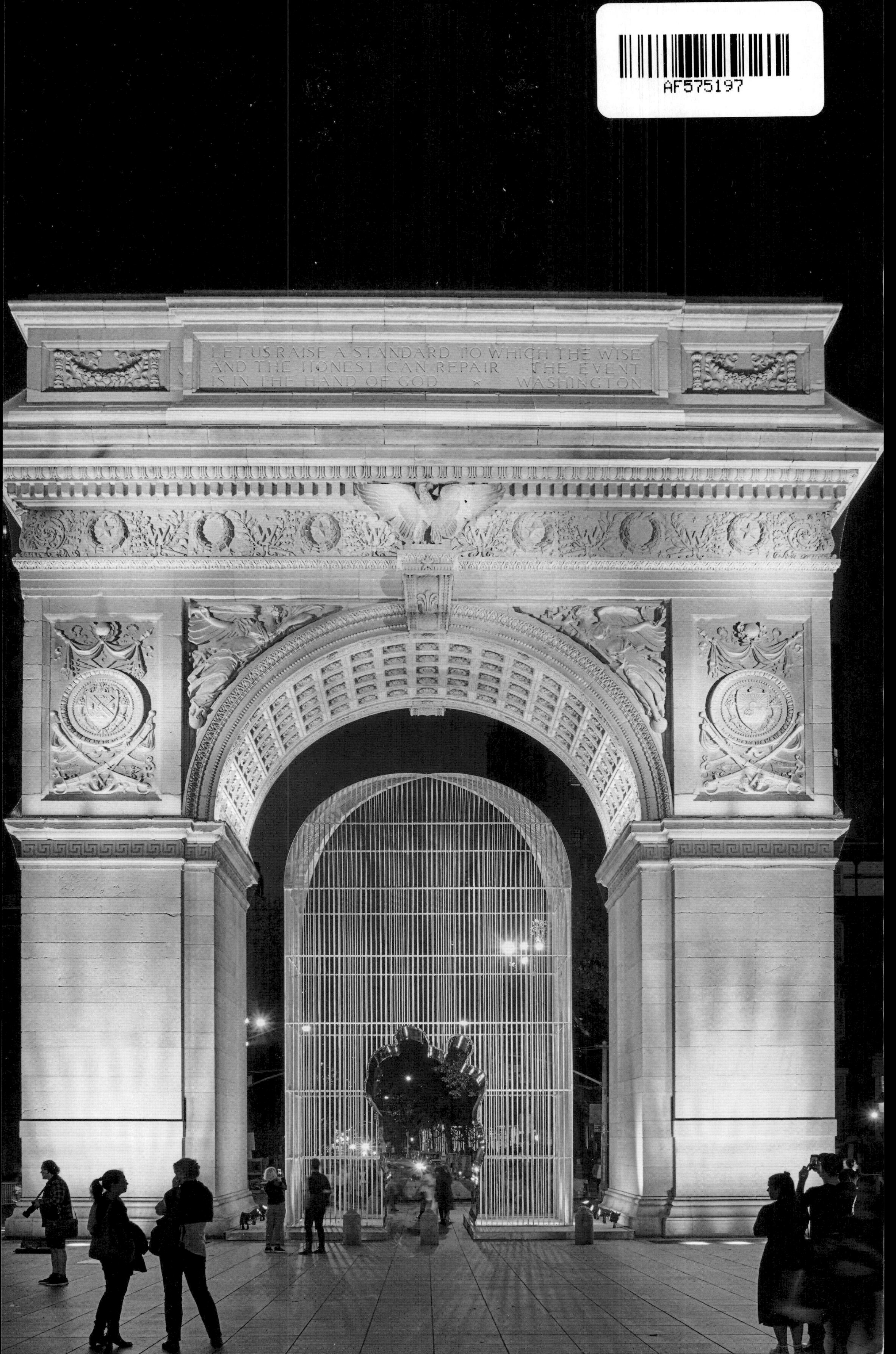
LET US RAISE A STANDARD TO WHICH THE WISE
AND THE HONEST CAN REPAIR THE EVENT
IS IN THE HAND OF GOD × WASHINGTON

AI WEIWEI

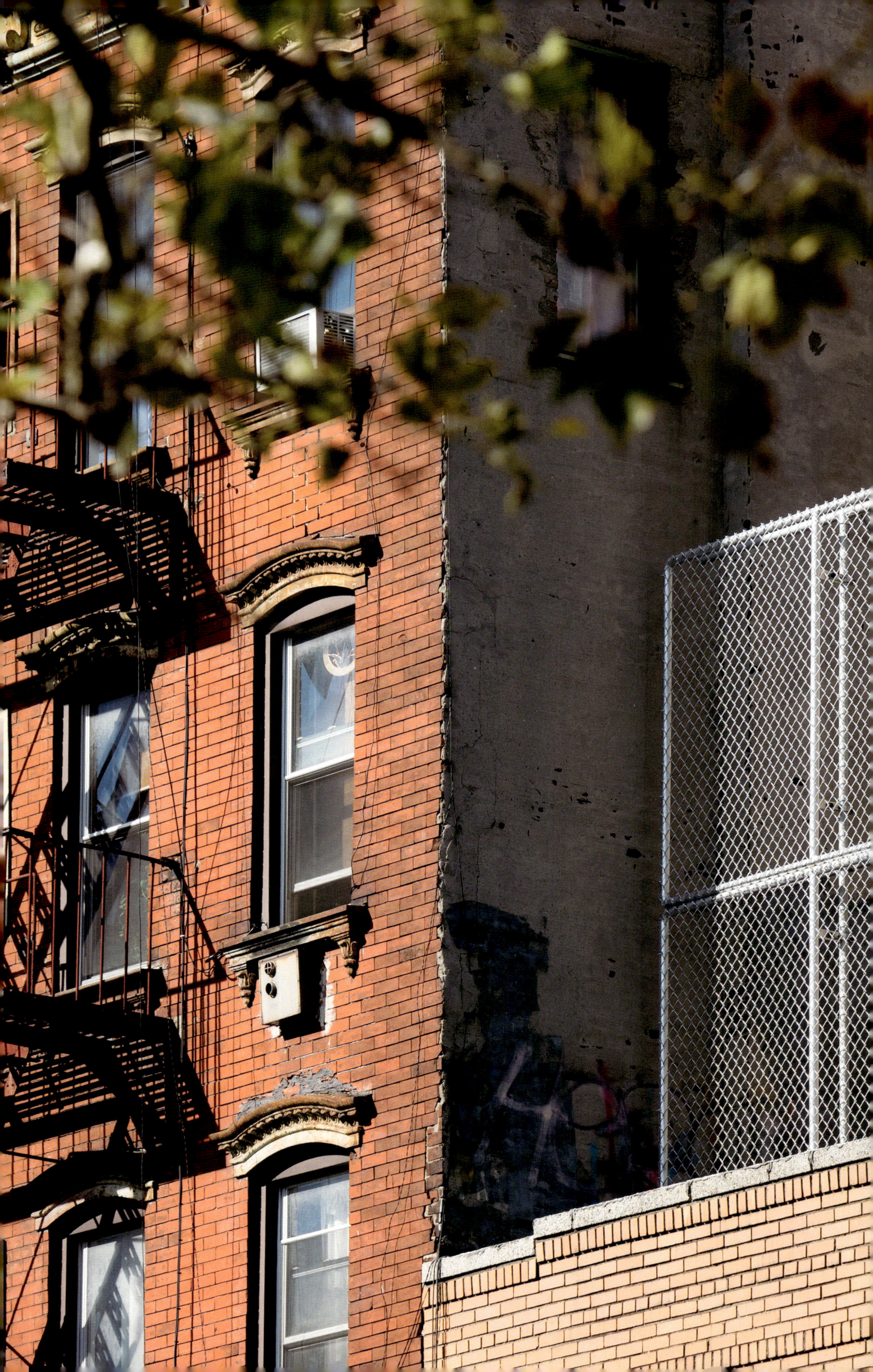

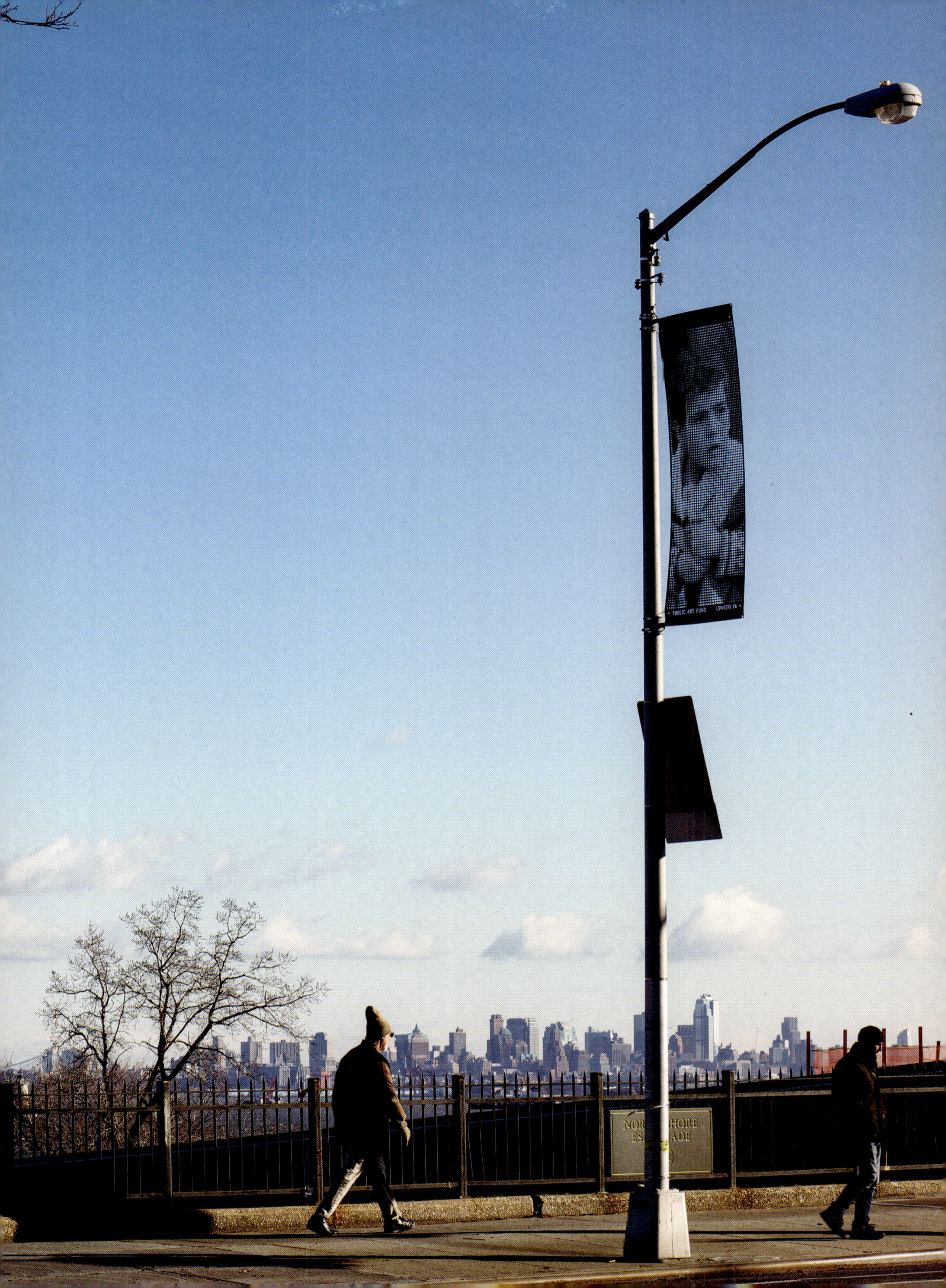
PUBLIC ART FUND

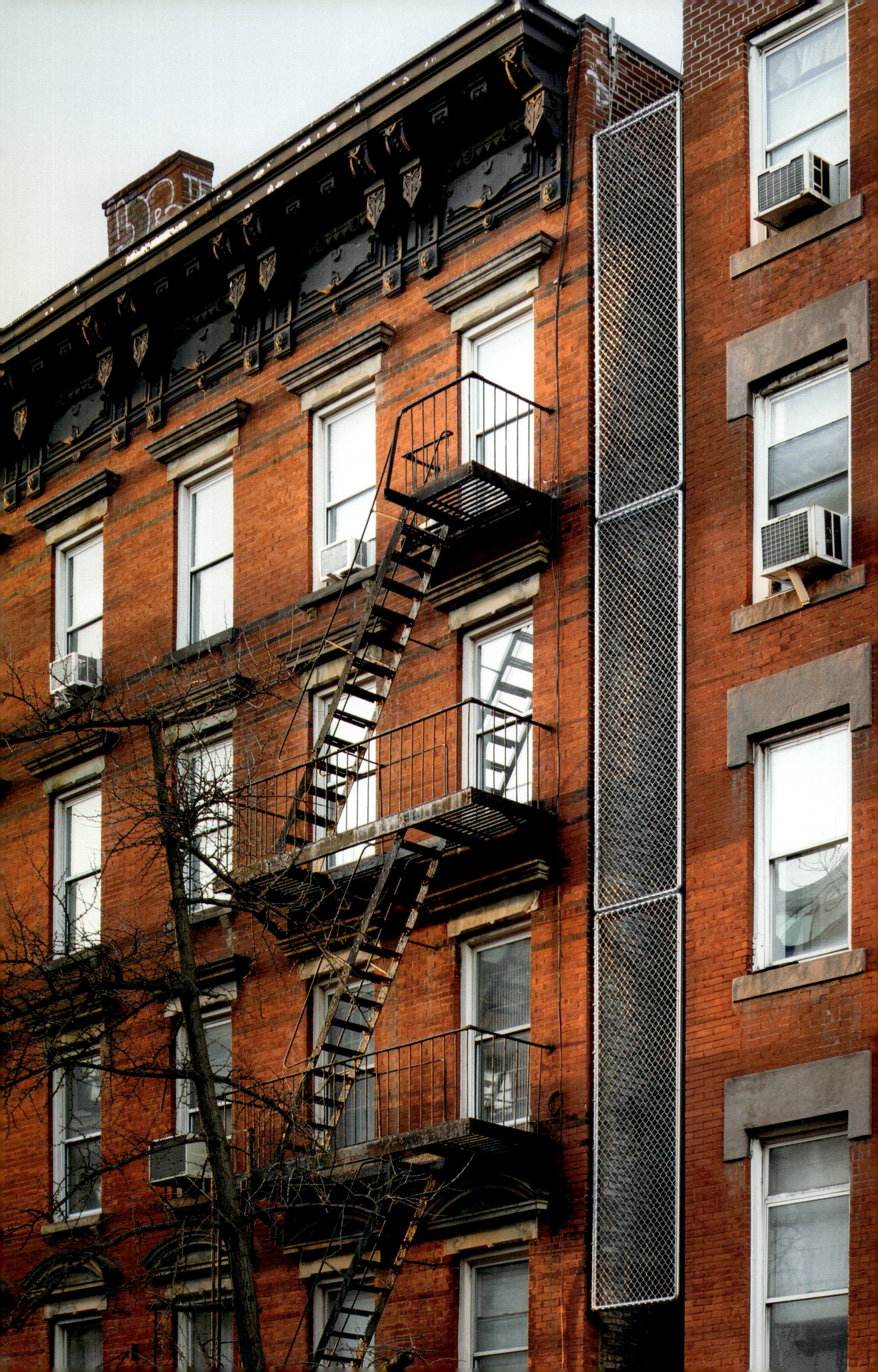

AI WEIWEI

GOOD FENCES MAKE GOOD NEIGHBORS

Nicholas Baume

Foreword by
Susan K. Freedman

With texts by
Daniel S. Palmer and Katerina Stathopoulou

Commentaries by
Richard Armstrong, Carol Becker, Bill de Blasio, Sandra Bloodworth,
Gale A. Brewer, Melissa Chiu, Coral Juárez Ard Dawson, Olafur Eliasson,
Jason Farago, Tom Finkelpearl, Ryan Gander, Elizabeth Goldstein,
Agnes Gund, Rick Jacobs, Letitia James, Corey Johnson, Ninette Kelley,
Chirlane McCray, Joseph V. Melillo, David Miliband, Bitta Mostofi,
Regina Myer, Hans Ulrich Obrist, Bernard Parisot, Jorge Ramos,
David Rockwell, Mitchell J. Silver, Andrew Solomon, Nader Tehrani,
Hank Willis Thomas, Billie Tsien, Larry Warsh, Devin Wenig

Public Art Fund, New York
Distributed by Yale University Press, New Haven and London

Contemporary public sculpture presents a new visual and emotional experience, a challenge to our senses and sensibilities. Sculpture that confronts us on our way to work, or on our daily errands, is no longer the remote object belonging to the world of galleries and museums, but a special component of our daily lives.

Doris C. Freedman (1928–1981), Founder, Public Art Fund

When my mother founded Public Art Fund in 1977, she envisioned an organization that would bring art of the highest caliber to the people of New York City and enable artists to work in the urban landscape in unexpected and powerful ways. Today our work holds true to her vision. Public Art Fund presents contemporary art in varied mediums, free of charge, on view 24/7, and available to anyone and everyone who lives, works, and visits this great city. Our projects surprise, delight, challenge, and inspire the public, while offering artists unique opportunities to respond to the city's ever-changing physical landscape and engaging the viewer in a dialogue that public art so naturally invites.

Last year marked our fortieth anniversary and my thirty-second as Public Art Fund's President. Contemporary art, like our world, is inherently dynamic, and our history and program are as multifaceted as the remarkable artists who have worked with us to captivate the city. Art changes, but the core values that my mother believed in endure: that art should be inclusive, that art is vital to our civic discourse, and that art will inspire new ideas and connections. Ai Weiwei's *Good Fences Make Good Neighbors* was a proclamation—a remarkable citywide exhibition that served as the capstone to our anniversary. It embodied the most important qualities of great public art, and I can imagine no other artist or project that would have provided the aesthetic, emotional, intellectual, and political impact of Ai Weiwei's monumental New York City project. Given the size and scale of this exhibition—more than 320 works throughout all five boroughs—it was nearly impossible to experience the exhibition in its entirety. So breathtaking, moving, significant, and extensive an exhibition clearly deserved to be memorialized, and I am thrilled that this volume will stand as the definitive historical reference for generations to come.

A work of this scope and complexity could have been realized only through the hard work, creativity, and support of countless individuals. Our full thanks can be found on pages 298–99, but I want to make special mention of Public Art Fund's lean, nimble, and remarkably talented team led by Nicholas Baume, our Director and Chief Curator; our Board of Directors, chaired by Jill Kraus; our broad network of dedicated partners; and our extraordinarily generous donors, all of whom supported us and this exhibition in countless ways.

I know my mother would be extremely proud that one of the exhibition's signature works, *Gilded Cage*, was installed (as well as *Banner 14* and *Banner 107*) at the plaza that bears her name, located at the southeast entrance to Central Park. As this comprehensive book on Ai Weiwei's extraordinary exhibition attests, more than forty years after our founding, we continue to present arresting artworks that are at once beautiful and provocative and that challenge how we see ourselves and our relationships with others.

Susan K. Freedman
President, Public Art Fund

The Art of Political Landscaping

Nicholas Baume

Accessible public space—very literally, our common ground—is increasingly recognized and valued as essential to a vibrant society. As we now reckon with tectonic shifts that have greatly impacted the global economy, the myriad effects of digital technologies are felt in virtually every aspect of our lives, including how we perceive the world. Ideological conflict, characterized by polarization and extremism, now defines our politics. In this contentious environment, how can artists actively contribute to impactful civic dialogue? How can art provide powerful individual and collective experiences? How can public art enrich communities while challenging artists to extend their own work in ways that are new, unexpected, and profound? *Good Fences Make Good Neighbors*, Ai Weiwei's landmark, citywide exhibition, commissioned for and presented in New York City to mark Public Art Fund's fortieth anniversary in 2017, offers a compelling model for how we might begin to answer these important questions.

Ai's expansive multidisciplinary exhibition was physically woven into the fabric of the city, conceptually linked to both New York's past and its present, inextricably connected to the most pressing global issues of our time. The artist deployed a broad range of materials to create prominent immersive and interactive installations at a monumental architectural scale, as well as more discrete works, often in unexpected and even obscure locations. In a mash-up characteristic of contemporary urban experience, he brought together the sculptural and the functional, the legible and the ambiguous, image and text, inviting a rich combination of aesthetic and intellectual engagement.

In its documentation and interpretation of Ai's work, this publication is intended to provide a complementary path and experience, bringing together in one volume all the many strands of a project that was installed in more than 300 different locations across the five boroughs of New York. Through this book, we hope readers gain an understanding of how these ideas came to fruition and an in-depth sense of this ambitious exhibition's scope and impact.

An important aspect of Ai's originality is his ability to turn an idea on its head and to see any problem from new angles. He is a contrarian, and as an artist and activist in China, he had activated his creativity, generosity of spirit, and strength of personality toward resisting and combating oppression. It would seem almost absurd to imagine an individual person amounting to anything that might attempt to approximate a force of opposition to the all-powerful Chinese state, yet Ai's determined and uncompromising challenges to state ideology have garnered him unprecedented national and international attention for the many aspects of his life and work.

Having grown up in China, where self-expression and originality were regarded by the state with suspicion if not hostility, Ai's path inevitably led him away from his homeland in 1981. In the years following his return in 1993, he became a successful artist and prominent blogger on nascent social media channels and was met with even more brutal censorship and, eventually, imprisonment at a secret location for eighty-one days. He knew the risks of independent thought and action firsthand, having grown up as the son of one of the country's most famous modernist poets, Ai Qing. In 1957, the year Ai Weiwei was born, his father was sent into exile for twenty years, purged together with other intellectuals under the Anti-Rightist Campaign. In this context, the simplest form of self-expression takes on the moral force of a basic human right. Of course Ai's self-expression, including above all his art, has always been

Circle Fence, 2017. Flushing Meadows Corona Park, Queens

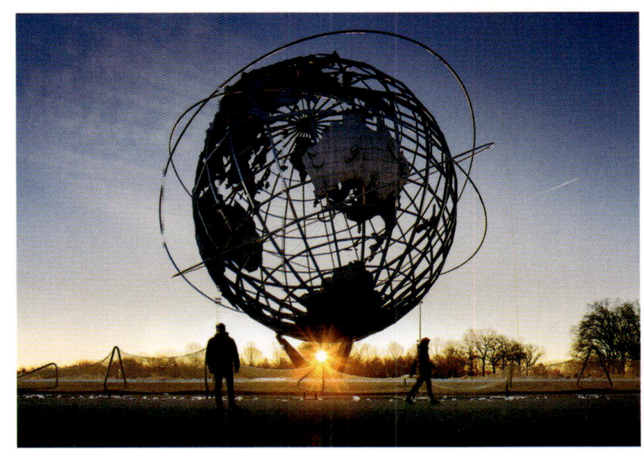

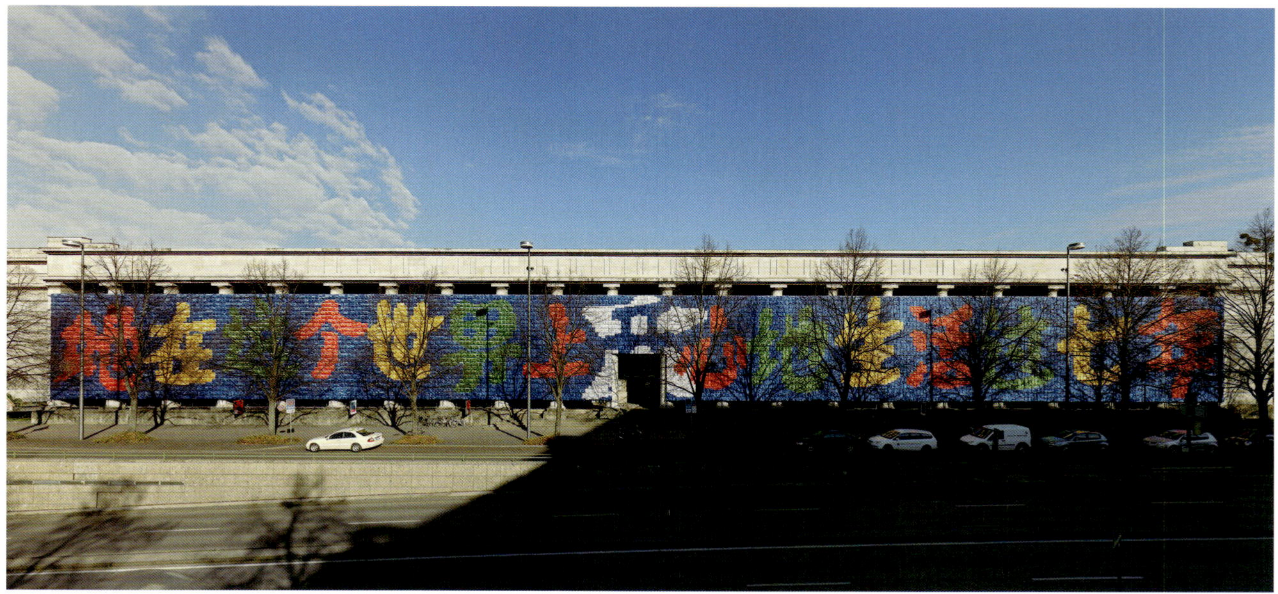

Remembering, 2009. 9,000 children's backpacks, 4,160 × 368 inches. Haus der Kunst, Munich

anchored in his unflinching insights into the personal, social, and political realities of his context: there is nothing more threatening to a totalitarian regime than a person speaking the truth—or demanding it.

Public art has long been established as a uniquely potent force for individual expression in the social sphere. In the context of Ai's background, having been denied that freedom and the ability to participate in civic dialogue, it is not surprising that public-facing activities—especially public art—should hold a place of particular significance for him. The power of Ai's engagement with art and activism was sharply foregrounded following the devastating 2008 Sichuan earthquake, with its particularly heavy death toll among students inside schools that were inadequately constructed due to government corruption (twelve thousand school buildings, according to UNICEF). He doggedly compiled and listed the names of the deceased children—5,196 in total—and produced his own documentary film on the subject.[1] His artwork *Remembering* (2009) covered the facade of Munich's Haus der Kunst with thousands of colorful children's backpacks forming the phrase written to Ai by the mother of one of the thousands of children killed: "She lived happily in this world for seven years." Site specific and epic in scale, with a nod to the colorful graphics of US corporate marketing (think Toys"R"Us), *Remembering*'s Chinese script contradicted the apparent familiarity of its bold presentation. Generous yet demanding, playful yet truly devastating, this work showed Ai's ability to process intensely serious subject matter in ways that were both sophisticated and accessible.

In my heart it felt so sweet to think that you're in detention but some of your work is still being shown in public. It seems you have wings outside of the cage.

×

Ai's long history with New York City began in the 1980s when he was an art student at Parsons School of Design. My intuition was that he would have something interesting to offer back to the city that had first welcomed him as a young, unknown immigrant. I met Ai socially in Miami in December 2009 and, after briefly chatting with him, suggested a further meeting. That took place the following March in New York, when he was in town to prepare for the exhibition of his first public sculpture, a series of bronze heads of zodiac figures titled *Circle of Animals/Zodiac Heads*. It was installed at the Pulitzer Fountain, Grand Army Plaza, in 2011, beginning what would

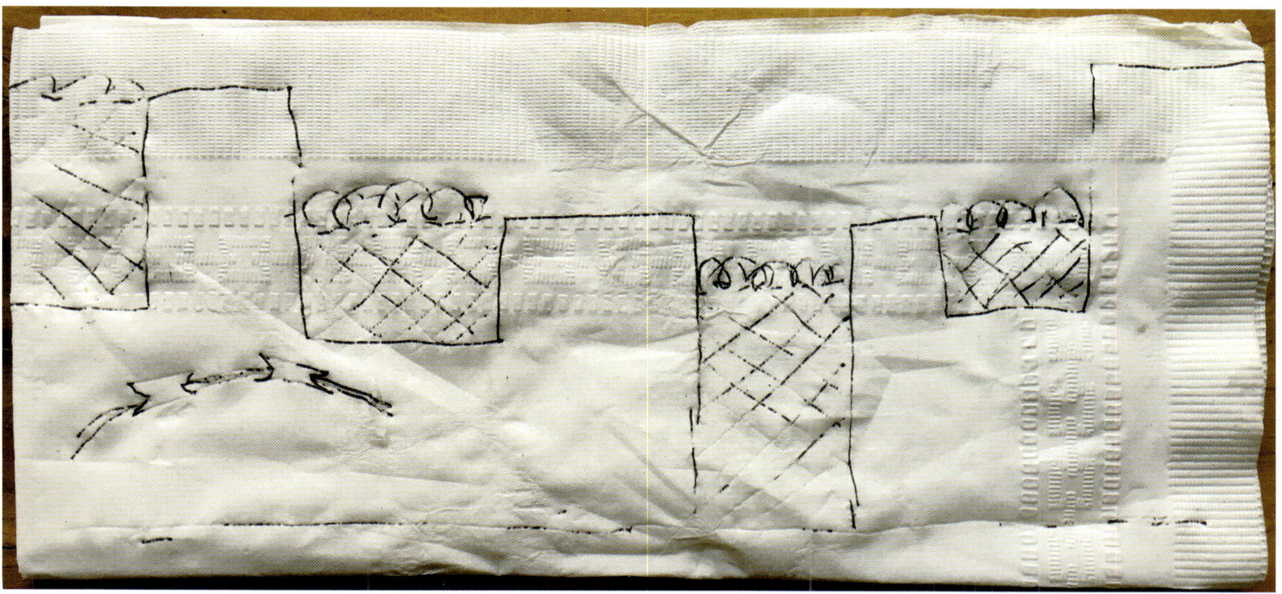

he wrote to describe the project: “the fence has always been a tool in the vocabulary of political landscaping.”[8]

Preparatory sketch of the fence motif, made by Ai Weiwei during his first site visit, New York, May 2016 (top)

Peter Moore, performance view of Trisha Brown's *Man Walking Down the Side of a Building*, 80 Wooster Street, New York, 1970 (bottom)

Thus, the fence became the primary motif and organizing concept of our exhibition, providing the basis for a unique and project-specific sculptural language. He did not want fences to obstruct or divert people but rather wanted to find ways of inserting them seamlessly into the built environment, calling attention to both our freedom and its vulnerability. He gestured at the typical Lower East Side tenement streetscape visible through the café window: a series of brick facades of varying height. His initial idea, which he immediately sketched for me on a paper napkin, was to fill in the undulating roofline with chain link or wire mesh fencing, creating a series of oddly functionless fences related to architecture around the city. They could be on buildings, between buildings, even on the ground, and Ai would design them to be subtly different from everyday fences. These ideas were strong and relevant, and we began to investigate the feasibility. As Ai talked about his concept I was reminded of American modernist poet Robert Frost's iconic poem “Mending Wall,” with its ironic refrain “good fences make good neighbors.” He didn't know the poem, so I shared it with him, and he admired both its economical expression and pointed wit (see p. 287).

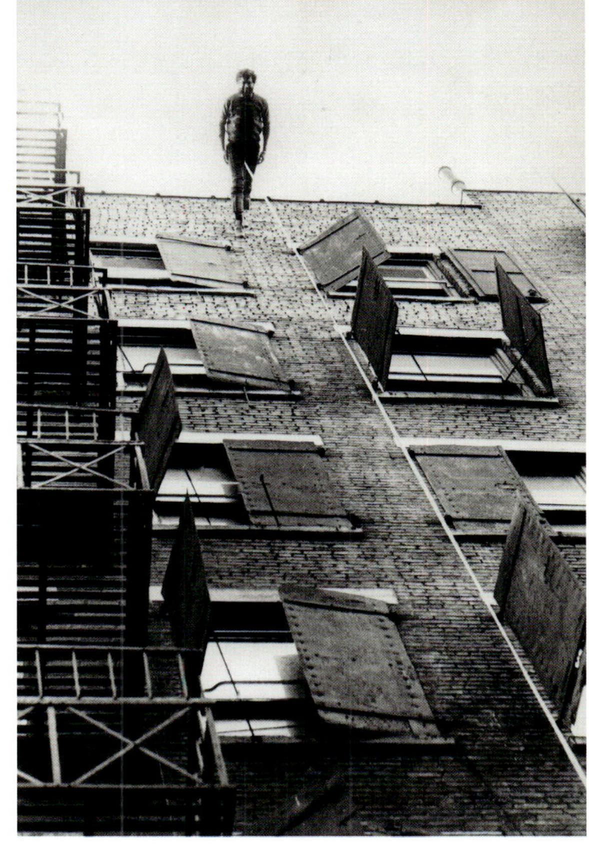

Ready to further explore for the project, we took to the pavement. Entire streetscapes suddenly became potential installation sites. Details of cornices and eaves, slivers of space between lots, shifts of scale from one structure to the next all seemed ripe with possibility. We discussed fences and borders of different kinds. Larry Warsh, an old friend of the artist's who accompanied us, pointed out an eruv, the wire suspended above a street to indicate the symbolic border within which Orthodox Jews may conduct activities otherwise confined to indoors on the Sabbath. The now fashionable Lower East Side neighborhood was once the site of the city's most overcrowded slums, where tens of thousands of immigrants had found their first US home. This history, together with its architectural character, made the area an important focal point. Ai was also keen to identify other locations, including sites beyond Manhattan, particularly areas with large immigrant populations.

With the refugee crisis established as a thematic focus for Ai, his aesthetic interests and visual language also related strongly to his understanding of the physical, psychological, and artistic character of New York. For Ai, the city grid represents a democratic ideal, in both spatial and ethical terms. He sees this embodied in a number of the defining artistic impulses of recent art history: "Since the 1960s," he wrote, "these democratic ideas have been reflected in many important conceptual and minimalist artworks."[9] In some ways, the ultimate realization of Ai's New York City project pays quiet tribute to that earlier generation of artists, including Trisha Brown, Richard Serra, and Gordon Matta-Clark, who first began to explore the city itself as a medium.

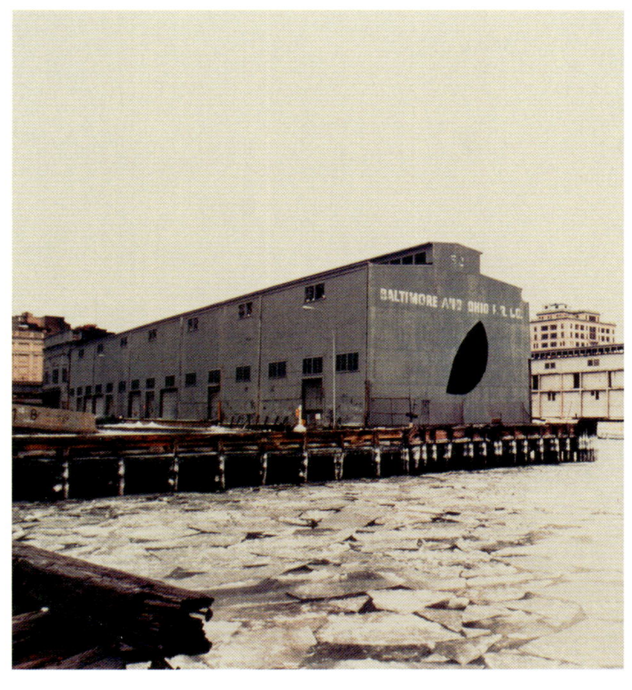

Gordon Matta-Clark, *Day's End (Pier 52), (Exterior with Ice)*, 1975. Chromogenic color print, 40½ × 31¼ inches (top)

Richard Serra, *To Encircle Base Plate Hexagram, Right Angles Inverted*, 1970, 183rd and Webster Avenues, Bronx. Hot-rolled steel, 304 inches diameter, 8 inches wide rim. Documentation by Peter Moore (bottom)

×

Barely seventeen months after this first site visit, we would stand at the foot of Washington Square Arch and celebrate the launch of *Good Fences Make Good Neighbors*. It could not have happened without a colossal, coordinated, and relentless international effort on the part of scores of people and the organizations, agencies, and companies they represent. The complex development, logistics, and expedited execution of this project would have probably been impossible in an earlier period. That is, of course, a reflection of the tools now available in our digital era. It is also a result of the support and cooperation of city government, donors, fabrication partners, and stakeholders. Above all, it required an artist able to rapidly develop a general overall concept into multiple detailed, realizable designs in a range of materials who at the same time could quickly and constructively respond and adapt to limitations and feedback.

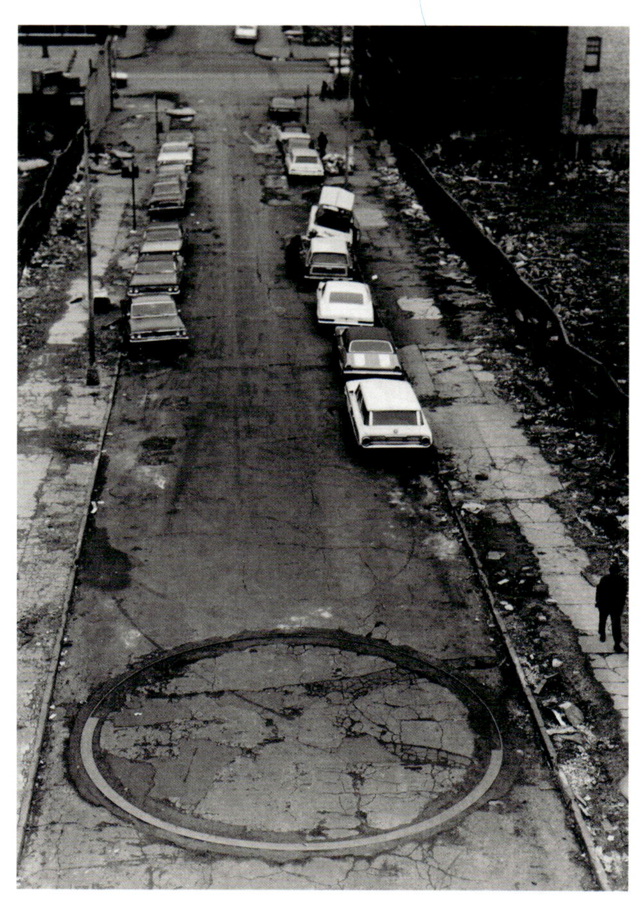

Great public art is not easy to create, and the court of public opinion can be harsh. Conceptual clarity, strength, and originality; effective and robust execution; legibility and accessibility are all basic requirements for success—but they are not enough. Health and safety regulations, height and weight limitations, myriad permits and permissions, not to mention time and money, are also considerations. Given the unconventional nature of all of the works conceived by Ai, and their unusual locations, those factors became an even greater challenge.

Two things astonished me as the process of realizing *Good Fences Make Good Neighbors* unfolded. First, how fast and prolific Ai was in generating ambitious proposals for new works (in fact, it soon became clear that we would never be able to realize all of his proposals). The second was the way he developed these proposals,

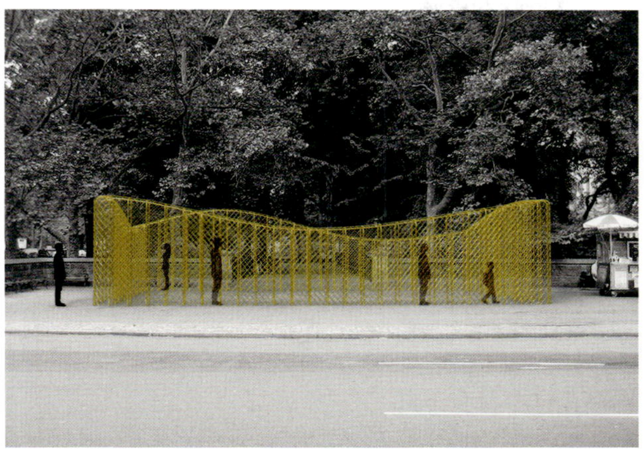
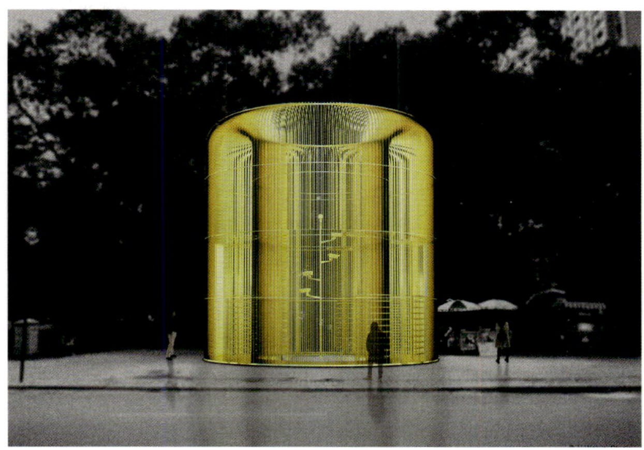

Gilded Cage, unrealized early concept (left) and final design (right), Doris C. Freedman Plaza, Central Park, Manhattan, 2017

which required extensive aesthetic, technical, and regulatory review. Artists are often so attached to ideas that any change can be very difficult. Ai, in contrast, seemed to relish the challenge of revising an idea in ways that would both accommodate feedback and make it stronger. Several proposals evolved so radically that they became unrecognizable as the original formations. He accomplished all of this with notable efficiency and lack of drama. I found this surprising, perhaps because as an artist, Ai's vision is always clearly defined and his approach determined. How could an artist be so clear about what he wants and yet so adaptable?

The answer to this question, at least in part, must be understood in relation to his experience as an artist in China. Ai's creative life has been shaped by an administrative culture of refusal, censorship, limitation, regulation, and restriction, all with no accountability whatsoever. His ability to survive as an artist without compromising his integrity relied on his skill in responding to habitual refusals, turning limitations into opportunities. That inventiveness and creative agility are evident in his work and are key to understanding how he has achieved so much in so many different and difficult contexts. As he remarked during our public conversation at Cooper Union, "All my creativity comes from problems."[10]

The process rapidly moved forward following his visit. Ensuing months would see a series of further site visits by Ai and studio members to scout locations, develop designs, and work with our team in New York (we also met several times in Berlin and elsewhere in Europe). And ever prolific, he was also shooting *Human Flow*, his first feature-length documentary, in more than twenty-six countries, as well as mounting several large-scale museum and gallery exhibitions around the world while the development of our exhibition was under way. It seemed that after being prevented from traveling for so long, the artist was suddenly everywhere.

The initial rooftop fence concept quickly evolved into a sculptural language of theme and variations, in which the fence motif took on different forms and materials, ranging from architectural interventions on existing buildings to freestanding immersive sculptures. From the beginning, Ai wanted to work with the city as a "readymade."[11] In addition to architecture, he was interested in infrastructure, such as public transportation and communication platforms, including advertising. He spoke about the city as a kind of body, with key installation sites (organs) linked by infrastructure networks (arteries). If we could find a way to access them, these different contexts would also require different kinds of works.

Given the scale and ambition of the project, it was clear that we needed the support and enthusiasm of City Hall (Public Art Fund is an independent nonprofit organization, not a government agency, as many people assume). At the same time, given the nature of our mission, we regularly work closely with city government and its departments in securing permissions and access to public sites. A number of the rooftop locations of interest to Ai were privately owned, but without access to major civic sites and urban infrastructure, the exhibition would not be viable. Happily, the city administration embraced the exhibition, and First Lady Chirlane McCray, an admirer of Ai's art and activism, became an early advocate.

Once an understanding of the types of sites Ai was looking for was established, we worked with a variety of city agencies to identify potential locations and partners. Through this process, in collaboration with agencies such as NYC Parks, Department of Transportation, Economic Development Corporation, and NYC & Company, we settled on a number of key sites that Ai had selected for major installations. We secured access to two hundred city lampposts, normally used for paid banner advertising, for displaying works of art. We were introduced to JCDecaux, the world's largest outdoor advertising company, which manages bus shelters and other street fixtures in every borough. JCDecaux responded positively to the project, agreeing to let us use of a number of its bus shelters for sculptural installations as well as advertising space on one hundred bus shelters and a selection of newsstand kiosks around the city. LinkNYC also agreed to place artworks in the regular ad cycle of its digital kiosks, the newest addition to the city's street advertising platforms.

Not every location was publicly owned. Cooper Union, for example, appealed to Ai because of its history, mission, and Astor Place location, which he had often passed through when living in the East Village. (He joked that although he attended Parsons, briefly, he wished he had gone to Cooper Union for the free tuition.[12]) The school was very receptive to Ai's proposal and hosted a major installation, *Five Fences*, on the facade.

The Lower East Side, given its historic association with immigration, would be the focus of a series of rooftop installations and related works. The East Village would include a work adjacent to the artist's former apartment, as well as at Cooper Union, while nearby Washington Square Park would host a major freestanding sculpture underneath the historic arch. For the entrance to Central Park, Ai would create *Gilded Cage*. Bus shelter sculptures were designed for Harlem and the Bronx, as well as downtown Brooklyn. In Queens, Ai surrounded the iconic Unisphere in Flushing Meadows Corona Park with *Circle Fence*. Staten Island hosted banner portraits on lampposts and photographic works on bus shelters; the banners were also installed elsewhere around the city, augmenting the other key locations. These important locations and partnerships ensured that we would be able to meet our goal of installing works in every borough—both significant sculptural installations in prominent locations and clusters of lamppost banners and bus shelter images nearby—for critical mass and maximum impact.

Good Fences Make Good Neighbors exhibition poster, bus shelter, Queens

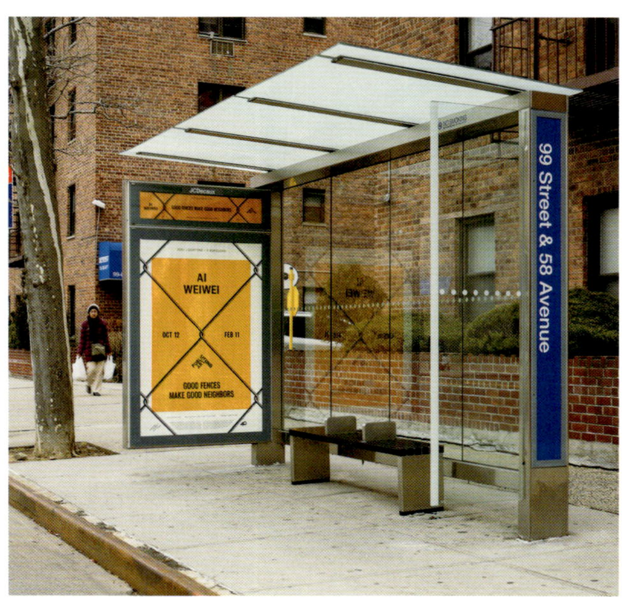

Ai's initial proposition about security fences had now evolved into a suite of related works in different materials, each conceived for a specific site and context. This language of fencing—chain link, expanded steel mesh, rope netting, barred metal cages, and perforated vinyl banners—became expansive. In addition, for street-level advertising spaces, Ai created *Good Neighbors*, a series of photo and text-based images of refugees, and for newsstand kiosks, he adapted his graphic narrative of refugee flight, *Odyssey*. One of the most striking successes of the project was that despite the wildly varied material nature of the works, the exhibition maintained its formal and conceptual coherence as a whole, while a strong graphic identity for the exhibition reinforced its legibility across print and digital platforms, including an interactive digital map to help people navigate the citywide installation.

Ai's lamppost banners introduced a powerful human element into the architectural language of fences, translating photographs of two hundred individuals into striking eight-foot-tall portraits. With these, the artist created an apt synergy between subject matter and form, extending the exhibition's historic context from present-day refugees whom he had photographed all over the world, outward to prominent exiles throughout history, and back to nineteenth-century Ellis Island immigrants. The banners were made from industrial black vinyl, a material that is often used for the boats that have carried countless refugees to uncertain futures. Rather than print onto the material, Ai digitally etched each image into the vinyl, creating a negative portrait that could be viewed from both sides. These faces—known and unknown, past and present, local and global—would appear and disappear depending on vantage point and background. For Ai, the human image possesses an unrivaled level of power. "It's time to put their faces into our normal daily environment. They deserve to be seen right in front of Trump Tower or some Chinese restaurant or somewhere in Harlem or on the streets of Queens or Brooklyn; their faces are so beautiful to me."[13]

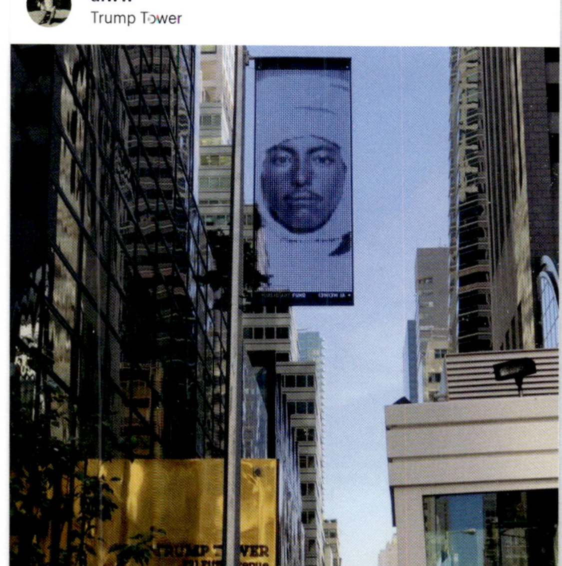

683 likes

aiww @publicartfund #goodfences #humanflow

michael_pfenning ...trumps guardian angel? ;-)

myprdiaries

bobinedesign Great pic, @aiww!

michael_pfenning ...or maybe just a flag in the wind? *lol*

fakejerrysaltz I knew you were going to trump tower

artbyequivocation Beautiful

OCTOBER 4, 2017

Social media post, *Banner 2*, Algerian Man, ca. 1905–1914

Given the global breadth of Ai's themes, it would stand to reason that production of the exhibition itself would be a complex international effort. To meet our tight deadlines, fabrication was expedited, though with no compromise whatsoever in quality. Coordinated between our New York office and the artist's Berlin studio, artworks were simultaneously fabricated in Shanghai, Queens, New Jersey, and Berlin. Engineers, fencing contractors, fine art metal fabricators, digital printing houses, rope and rigging specialists, permit expeditors, and numerous other professionals took on the daunting challenges inherent in producing and installing works for which there was generally no precedent.

It would be impossible to anticipate every obstacle with a project of this scale; problem solving is always a consequential aspect of our work, and the fact that public art can generate controversy is hardly breaking news. During the summer leading up to our fall opening, a potentially damaging controversy erupted around the installation conceived for Washington Square Park. We were well aware that the politically charged content of Ai's work would likely be met with strong reactions. For example, one of the difficulties it presented was attracting corporate sponsorship. Corporations, generally wary of contemporary art and certainly anything with a whiff of politics, grew positively allergic if they had business in China (and these days, who doesn't?). To our surprise, however, there was virtually no pushback from the public about the themes of the exhibition. In fact, it drew an almost universally positive response. The exception was an independent neighborhood group, the Washington Square Association, which took exception to our plan to install a major

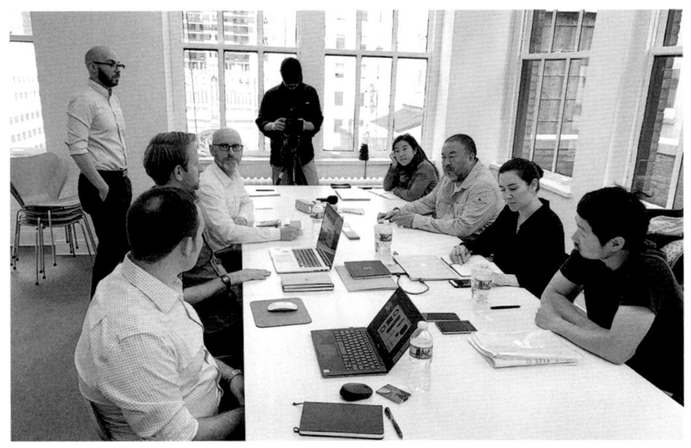

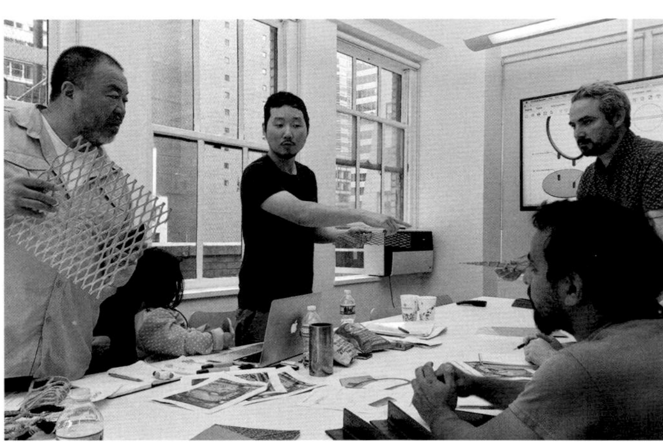

Project meetings with Ai Weiwei's studio and art fabricators, Public Art Fund offices, Manhattan, June 2017

work in dialogue with the historic Washington Square Arch.

Public parks and monuments are treasured and indispensable components of our civic life. All of us feel a sense of ownership and investment in them, particularly in our own neighborhoods. Washington Square has a strong history of community activism, having resisted attempts by Robert Moses to extend Fifth Avenue through the park in the 1950s and with eminent local resident Jane Jacobs having led the fight to prevent construction of the Lower Manhattan Expressway in the 1960s. Ai's temporary installation was hardly akin to the demolition of historic buildings, but passions do run high on Washington Square. Aside from objections on aesthetic grounds, the association's major complaint was that the holiday tree, a long-standing tradition, would have to be relocated to a nearby position in the park during the festive period. As reported in the *West Village Patch* headline: "Ai Weiwei Art Would Politicize Washington Square and Ruin Holiday Tree, Group Says."[14]

This complicated what had already become the most complex work in the exhibition to develop and realize. Ai had immediately gravitated to the site. He spent a lot of time in the park when he lived in the East Village, often walking through it on his way to West Fourth Street, where he made street portraits for fifteen dollars per drawing. He loved the park for its diversity, its youthful energy, its rebelliousness (from protests to pot smoking), and its artistic legacy (in 1917, Marcel Duchamp and friends took over the arch, declaring their own republic). By any measure, the arch is an icon. As a triumphal symbolic entrance to New York City, Ai felt, it would be the perfect location for a work on the theme of fences and exclusion.

As a major historic monument, the site had numerous limitations on how it could be used. Any sculpture would have to respect the integrity of the arch, be freestanding and noninvasive (no fixing into masonry, no touching, leaning, or hanging, no foundations). ADA-compliant public access through it would need to be maintained; the design had to follow building code and be approved by the Landmarks Preservation Commission as well as NYC Parks. Disused water mains underground limited the weight load, which had to be evenly distributed over the footprint.

Ai's initial idea for the site was a barred fence, sized to the arch's opening, pivoted horizontally and cantilevered in an open position. Amidst the exhibition's vertical fences, the optimism of this work added an important dimension. It was, however, not possible to realize satisfactorily in a way that was entirely freestanding, so it was quickly rejected. Several further iterations of possible designs followed, leading, after an exhaustive review process, to the final, officially approved proposal. Although this site was the most complex, some version of this process took place, concurrently, with every major work in the exhibition. As Ai later wryly commented, "This work really comes out not from creativity but from regulations—like most of my work."[15]

With a viable proposal now in hand, we consulted with community representatives, including elected officials and leadership of the local community

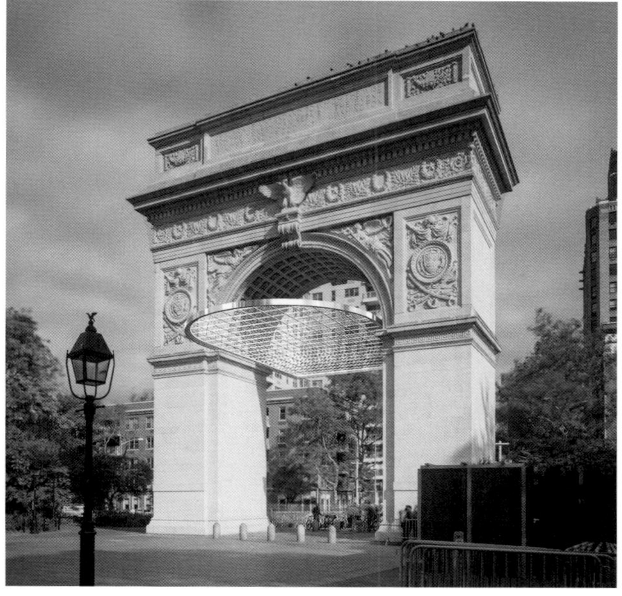

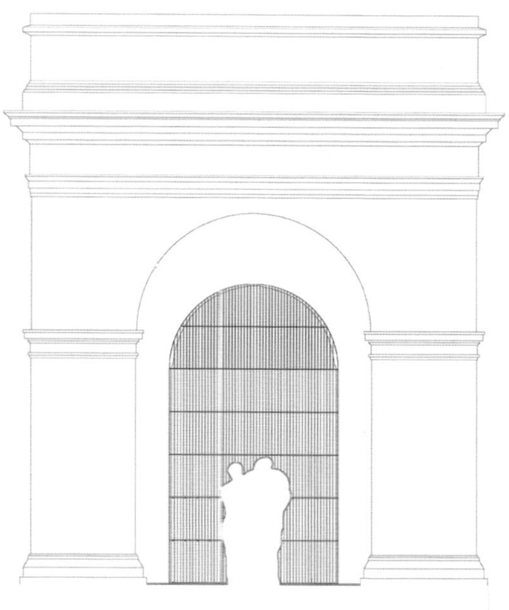

Arch, unrealized early concept rendering (left) and final design (right), Washington Square Park, Manhattan, 2017

board and the Washington Square Association. Initially, all were enthusiastic about Ai's work and participating in this citywide project. After meeting as a group, however, the Washington Square Association was upset about not having been consulted earlier and by the temporary relocation of the holiday tree. We learned of its objections only when it issued a letter to the press, demanding that the project be stopped. We suddenly had a real controversy on our hands, with online, print, and television journalists all eager to pick up the story.

Faced with a public relations crisis, we had to respond quickly, marshaling support and endorsements and responding clearly to mischaracterizations. Fortunately, we were in a strong position to defend and advocate for the project. A series of community meetings and presentations ensued; ultimately, the community board voted resoundingly in support of the project. The controversy resulted in widespread awareness of Ai's project in the lead-up to our opening, and Ai's *Arch* went on to become the signature work in the exhibition, widely admired for its sculptural power and conceptual eloquence. Fully realized on its own terms, it also honored the historic monument and renewed its relevance. Given scale, material character, the effects of light, shade, and other environmental variables, public art is particularly hard to imagine in advance, and even supporters of the project were unprepared for just how brilliantly this sculpture would inhabit its site.

Opportunities to place prominent signage were often limited given the nature of the sites, including Washington Square. Our online resources supplemented on-site signage, but many people experienced the work without reading any introductory labels. Remarkably, Ai's sculpture was able to function and communicate its themes successfully even without didactic support. *Arch* offered visitors an immersive, visceral experience, as did several of the major installations. People responded to the work in different ways, but its thematic content was highly legible—on some level, people "got it" without having to read an explanation. That is a hard thing to pull off, and one of the great challenges in making conceptually based public art.

Arch, together with *Gilded Cage* at the entrance to Central Park and *Circle Fence* at the Unisphere in Queens, managed to convey the prohibition inherent in the idea of a fence while also inviting the public to engage and interact with a generosity of spirit. Each of these sites holds civic significance as a democratic public space. Shared by New Yorkers and visitors alike, they are places of recreation, community, entertainment, self-expression, and activism. For the majority of the public, Ai's works were seen not as intrusions

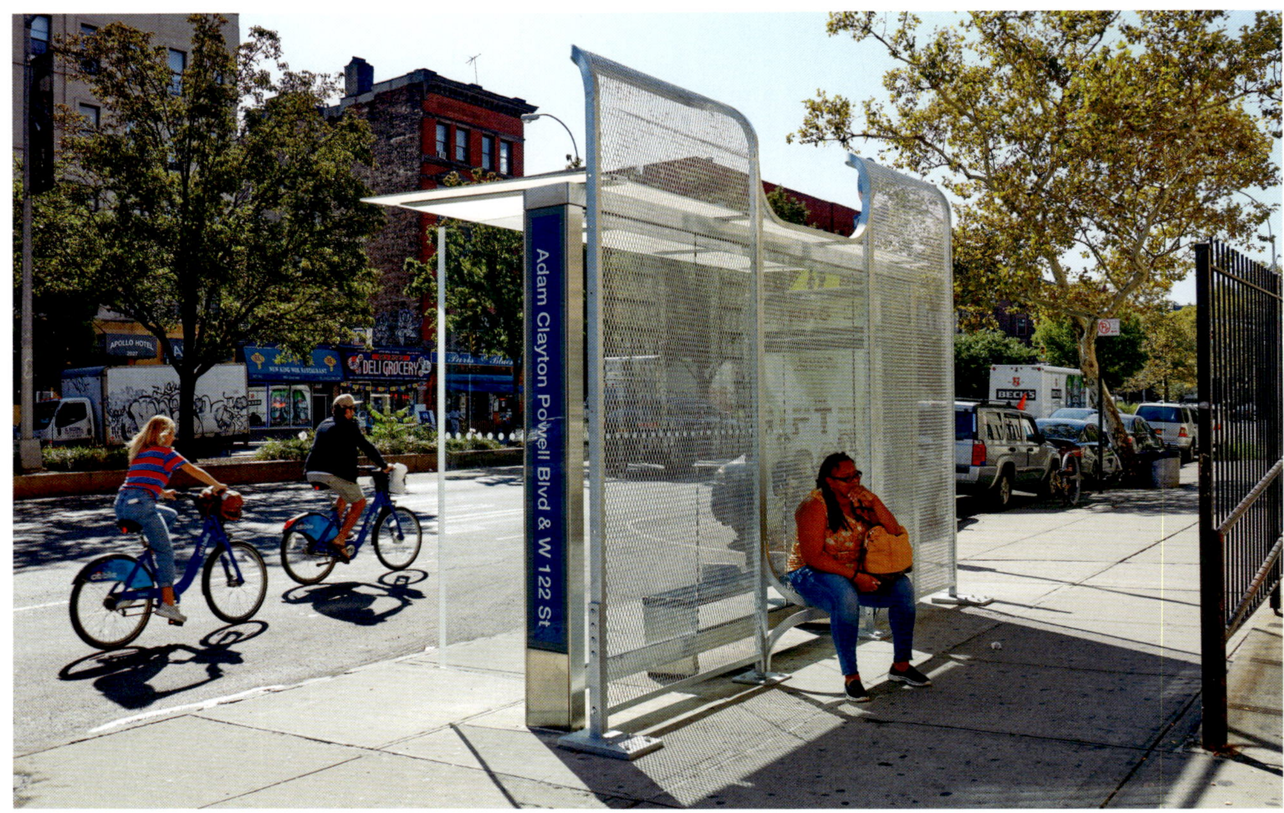

Harlem Shelter 2, 2017.
W. 122nd Street and Adam Clayton Powell Jr. Boulevard, Manhattan

but as important articulations of shared values. They were also monumental, beautiful, and interactive, giving pleasure even while raising difficult themes. Not surprisingly, *Good Fences Make Good Neighbors* quickly became the most posted Public Art Fund exhibition ever on social media.

More unconventional platforms such as rooftops, bus shelters, lampposts, and digital screens, in combination with the prominent civic locations, came to define the character of the exhibition and Ai's approach. He wanted to make the exhibition relevant to different kinds of people in diverse locations going about their daily lives. "I tried to make a work that functions on multiple levels and talks to different kinds of people, makes people feel something is different, that something has been touched or changed."[16] For example, his bus shelter sculptures incorporated a seat facing away from the street, adding both utility and an element of ambiguity as to the nature of the structure.

Ai wanted to communicate broadly in a way that did not rely on the framing of "art"; whether or not it would be recognized as a work of art was unimportant to him. The bus shelter sculptures and, in lieu of regular advertising, one hundred different images with texts depicting the lives and conditions of refugees represent this kind of infrastructural integration. These photographs and texts attempt to call attention to some of the stark realities of the contemporary refugee experience. Reflecting on how New York commuters might experience the work, Ai observed, "People are tired; they have to wait there for a certain moment. They may pay attention, or not even pay attention, but it is there. It's prepared to structure our city's life in a highly political, intellectual way."[17] With *Good Neighbors*, *Odyssey*, and his *Banner* portraits, he may have borrowed the spaces of advertising, but he refused its commercial strategy of repetition. Each image, design, and portrait was a different artwork, distributed so widely throughout the city that actually viewing all of them, along with the all the major sculptural installations, would have been a mammoth undertaking. In a sense, the overwhelming proliferation of these images was far more important than the ability to experience every one of them in person; massive in scale and scope, like the refugee crisis itself,

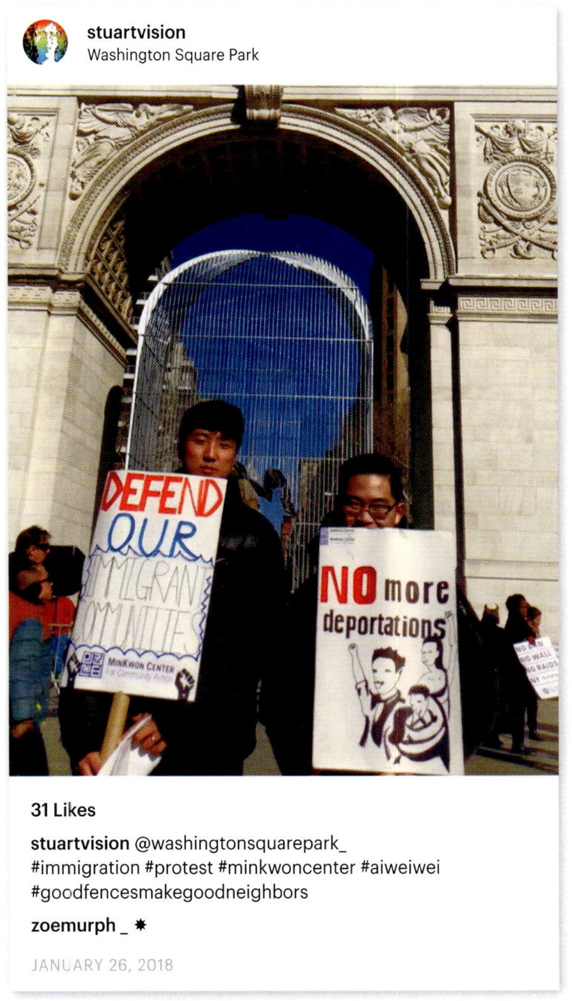

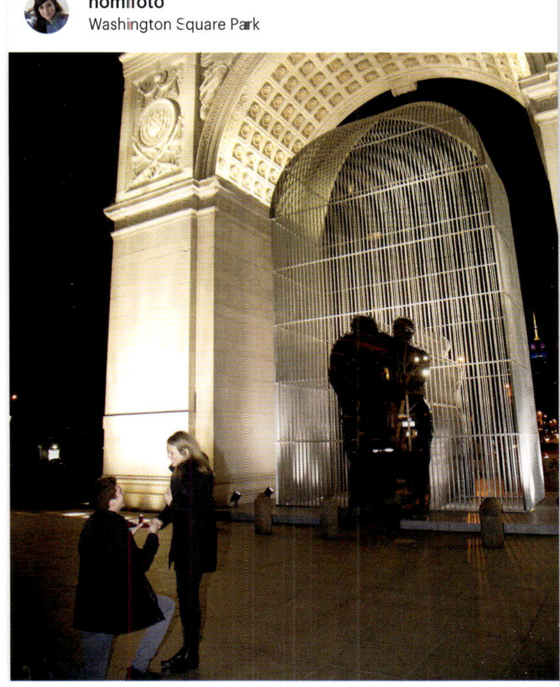

123 Likes

nomifoto As the daughter of two rabbis, sentimental moments get to me. When my friend of 15 years asked me to document him proposing at @washingtonsquarepark_ I was excited. Additionally, because of the @publicartfund #GoodFences instillation by artist #Aiweiwei, the proposal captured our city at this special moment. #PAF40 #PublicArt #PublicArtFund #PAFpicoftheweek

NOVEMBER 29, 2017

Social media posts, *Arch* (left and right)

NB: How do you feel about the response to the exhibition? Was it what you expected? Did anything surprise you?

AW: A good exhibition always has two parts: a fixed concept and its reception by viewers, which can't be imagined in advance. It is this challenge that makes an exhibition unique and irreplaceable. My exhibitions are not just about producing something familiar but about exploring unknown experiences. Those new experiences can enable a viewer to feel the strength of others, or even their own. In the case of *Good Fences Make Good Neighbors*, this might appear in the excitement of children, the interest of a tourist passing by, or the reactions of those who happen upon the works and discover their environment has fundamentally changed.

NB: This exhibition could not have happened in a museum or gallery. Are there challenges involved with making public art that interest you?

AW: The challenge of making public art is like cooking a meal for family or friends; it is unlike taking them to a nice restaurant.

NB: What makes for a successful public art exhibition?

AW: Public art is successful when the public doesn't see the art as foreign but as something deeply rooted. It is successful when they can see it as something that tells their story and not as something alien appearing in their neighborhood. When it reflects the meaning of their struggle.

MIDTOWN MANHATTAN

	Banners	20
	Good Neighbors	1
	Odyssey	2
	Structures	1

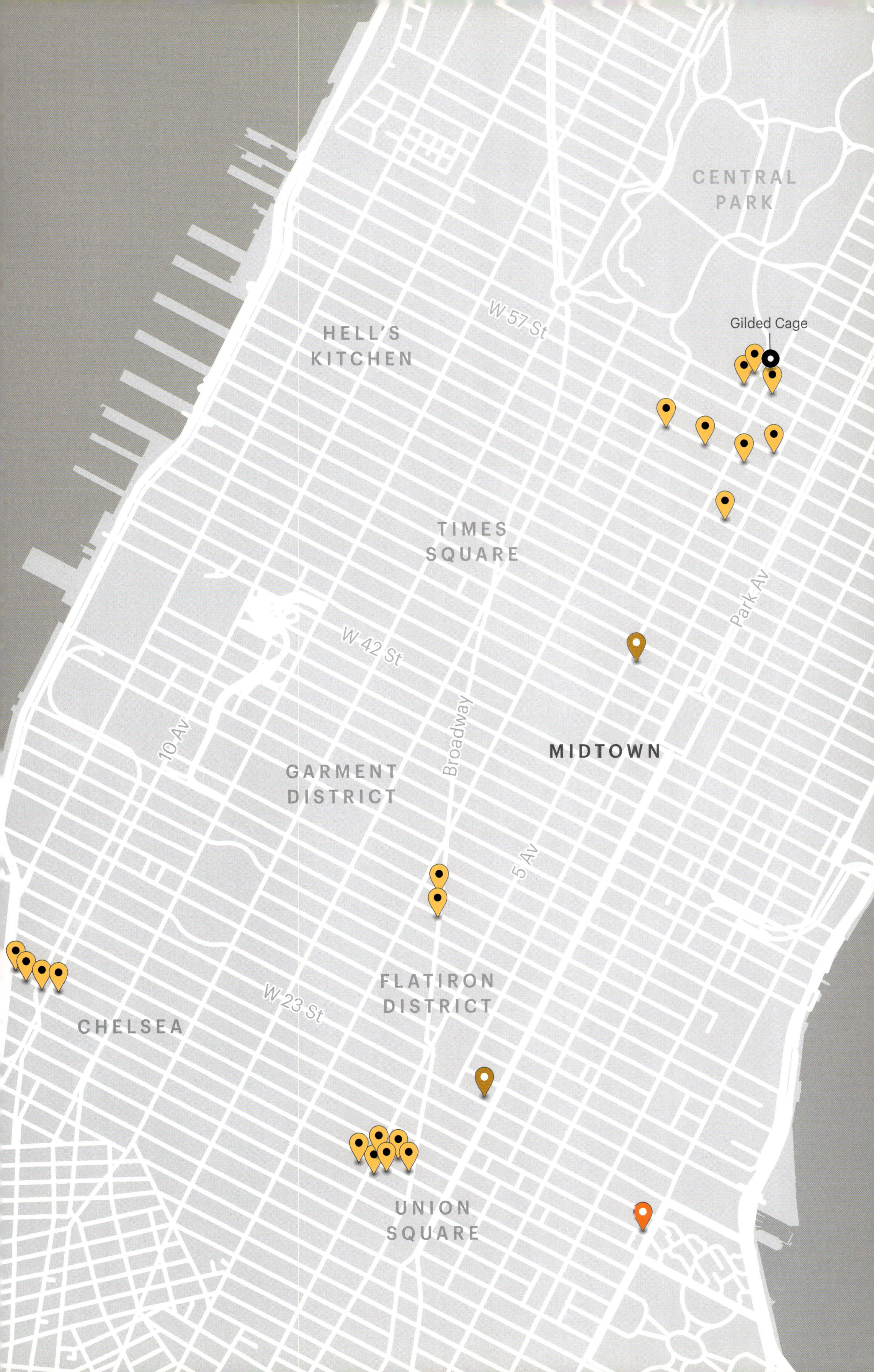

CENTRAL PARK
Gilded Cage
W 57 St
HELL'S KITCHEN
TIMES SQUARE
Park Av
W 42 St
10 Av
Broadway
MIDTOWN
GARMENT DISTRICT
5 Av
FLATIRON DISTRICT
W 23 St
CHELSEA
UNION SQUARE

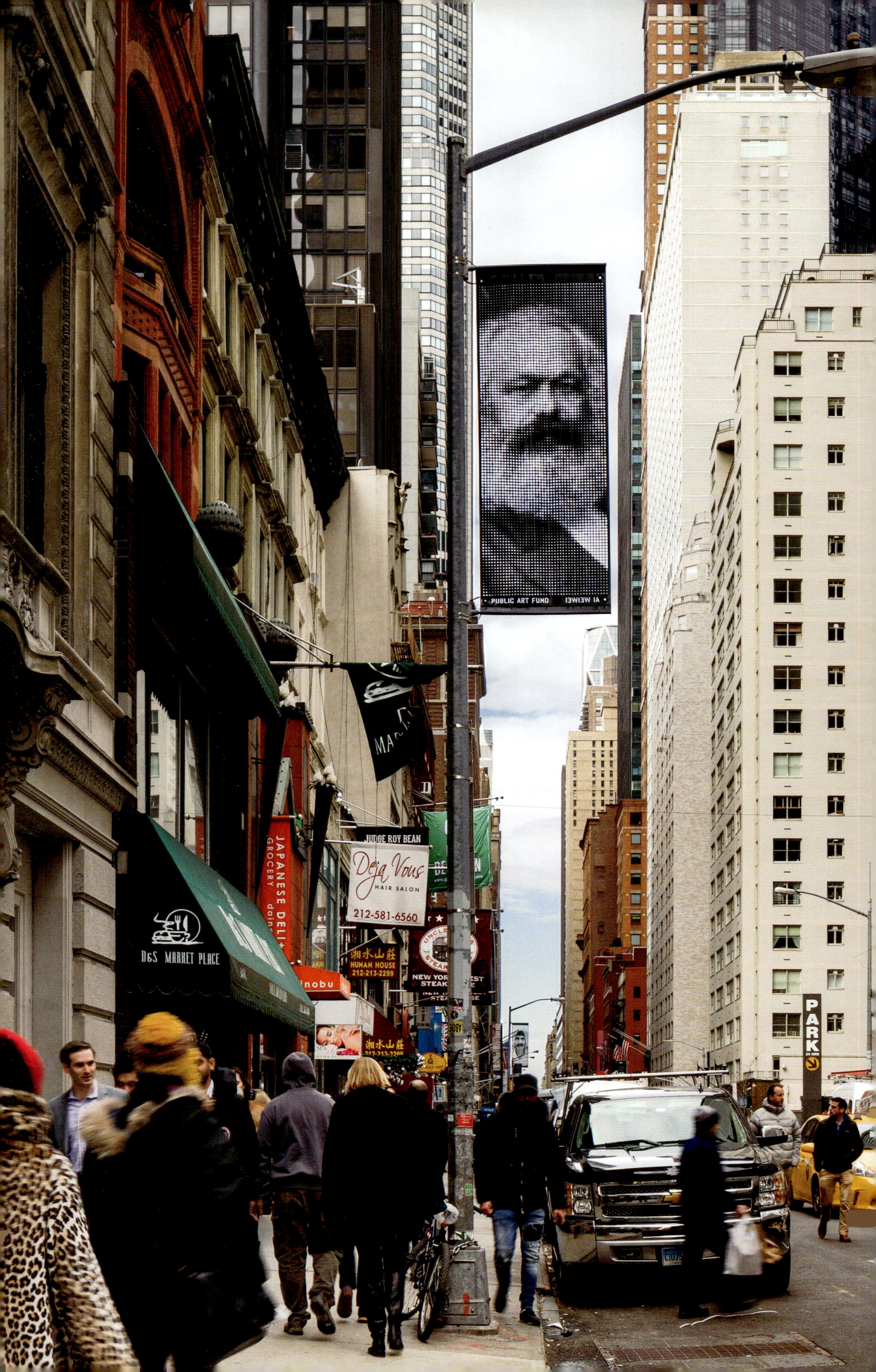
PUBLIC ART FUND
JUDGE ROY BEAN
Deja Vous
HAIR SALON
212-581-6560
JAPANESE DELI
GROCERY
D&S MARKET PLACE
HUNAN HOUSE
212-213-2299
PARK

Midtown Manhattan

Midtown Manhattan is more intertwined with the history of Public Art Fund than any other part of the city. In 1977, two pioneering art organizations, City Walls and the Public Arts Council, merged to become Public Art Fund, led by Doris C. Freedman, who was also New York City's first director of cultural affairs. Freedman's groundbreaking accomplishments contributed to a more expansive understanding of art making and viewing—now well established—through commissioning a broad range of artists to create significant large-scale public artworks for city spaces. Her efforts led to legislation requiring eligible city-funded construction projects to spend at least one percent of their budgets on public art. In honor of her pioneering work, in 1981 the corner of Fifth Avenue and Sixtieth Street at the southeast entrance to Central Park was named Doris C. Freedman Plaza. It has become a landmark site for rotating art installations and is one of the primary exhibition sites for Public Art Fund; to date, more than sixty projects have been presented at this location.

With strategic precision, Ai Weiwei chose Doris C. Freedman Plaza in Midtown—the very center of commerce, wealth, and power in New York—as the site for *Gilded Cage.* He also installed a number of his refugee and immigrant portrait banners on lampposts that flank surrounding streets (among them, the portrait of an Algerian man who arrived through Ellis Island was prominently placed next to the residential entrance to Trump Tower, south of Central Park).

In 2017 alone, the city welcomed a record 62.8 million visitors—the highest number to date—many of whom are drawn to destinations such as Times Square, the Empire State Building, and Rockefeller Center. When *Good Fences Make Good Neighbors* opened in October 2017, *Gilded Cage* immediately became a prominent feature of the area, with throngs of viewers flocking to Ai's enormous birdcage-like sculpture. While retaining references often associated with structures of division, such as bars and turnstiles, this monumental artwork was juxtaposed to Central Park, one of the most visited and celebrated urban public parks in the world. Designed as a democratic oasis for city dwellers, its vast open areas, lush forests, and monuments to heroes and explorers stood in strong contrast to Ai's formally minimal yet metaphorically powerful work.

Banner 57
Karl Marx, ca. 1875
W. 56th Street and 5th Avenue, Manhattan (opposite)

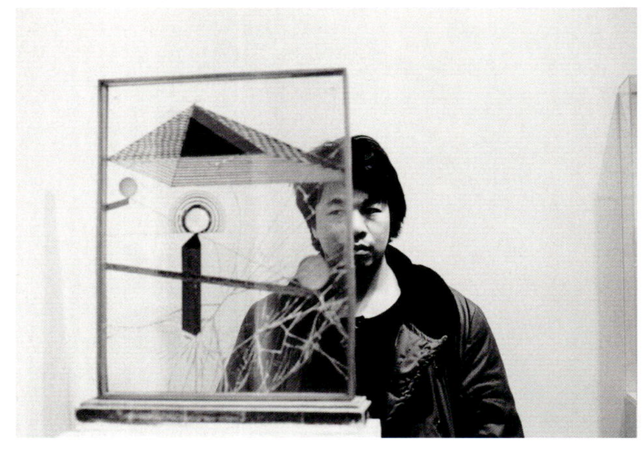

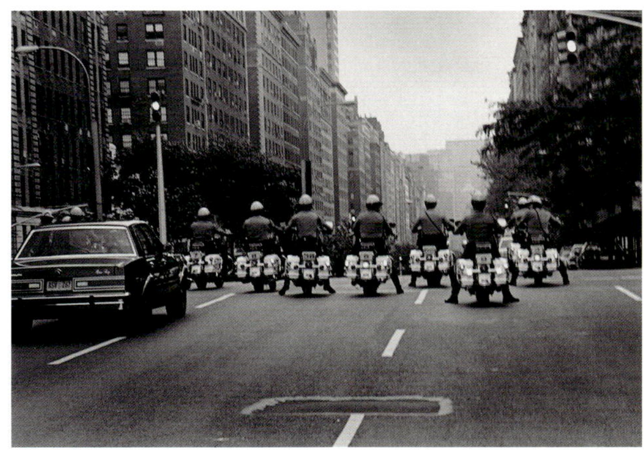

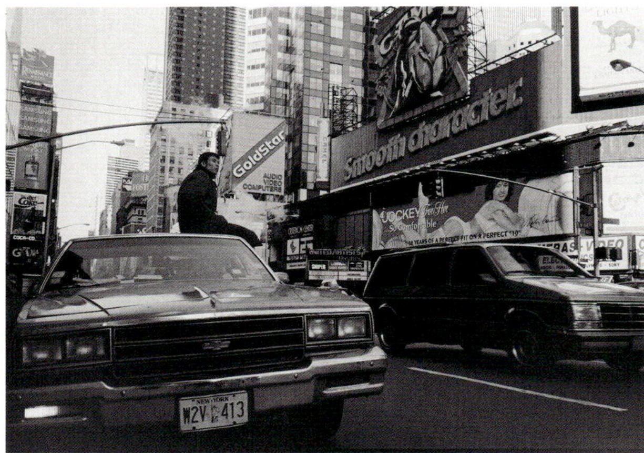

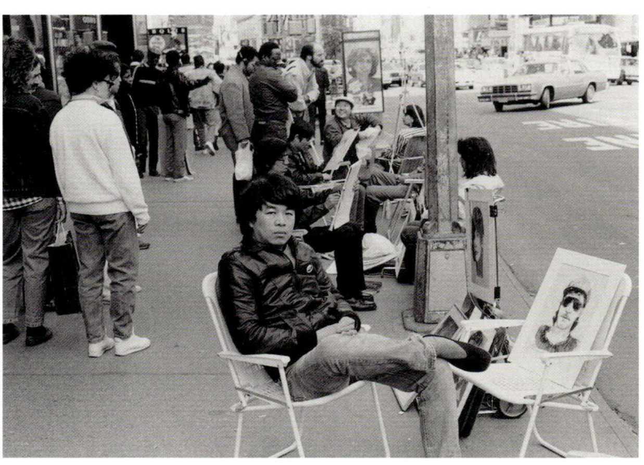

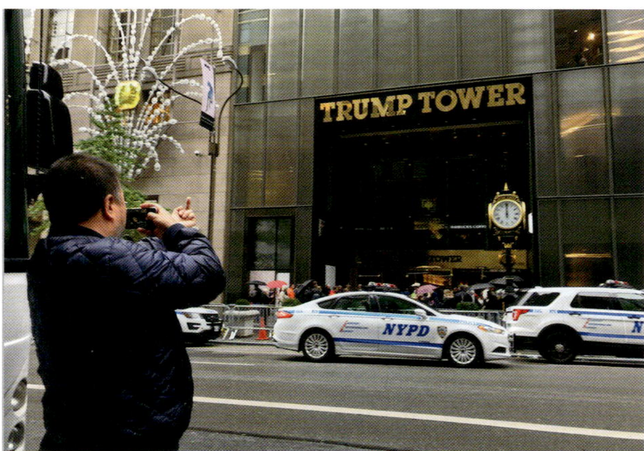

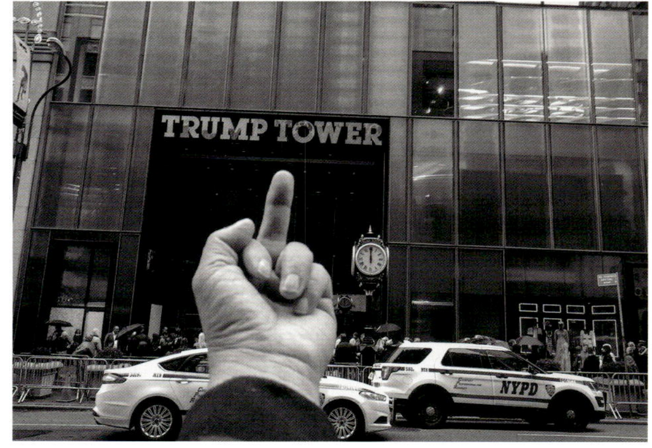

In Front of Duchamp's Work, Museum of Modern Art, 1987, from the series New York Photographs 1983–1993. Black-and-white photograph (top left)

Park Avenue, 1988, from the series New York Photographs 1983–1993. Black-and-white photograph (top right)

Feng Xiaogang on Top of a Rented Taxi, Times Square, 1993, from the series New York Photographs 1983–1993. Black-and-white photograph (middle left)

Portrait Artist in Times Square, 1987, from the series New York Photographs 1983–1993. Black-and-white photograph (middle right)

Ai Weiwei photographing Trump Tower, an image that would become part of his Study of Perspective series, October 22, 2016 (bottom left)

Study of Perspective—Trump Tower, 2016. Black-and-white photograph (bottom right)

I have had the great privilege of seeing Ai Weiwei's work in locations all around the world. What sticks out the most in his work to me is an extraordinary sensibility to intimacy, humor, and materiality. *Good Fences Make Good Neighbors* is both timely and timeless. While simultaneously caging us in, we are also welcomed into a collective experience. The material both alienates us and brings us together. At a time when what it means to be American is being put into question, Ai Weiwei's work reminds us of how we can find ourselves in each other.

Hank Willis Thomas, artist

×

In this project, Ai Weiwei reconceives what public art can be. This is not a monument remaining fixed to a particular context or locality but rather a project that forms a network of artworks all over New York. This act of artistic expression throughout the fabric of the city creates a connectedness across boroughs; it is an archipelago of public intervention that extends across time and space. The connective threads of this archipelago result in a certain in-betweenness. Ai Weiwei's project chimes with Édouard Glissant's proclamation that "we need to put an end to the idea of a border that defends and prevents. Borders must be permeable; they must not be weapons against migration or immigration processes."

Hans Ulrich Obrist, Artistic Director, Serpentine Galleries, London

×

At a time when borders and minds are being slammed shut on the more than 68 million souls across the globe who are desperately seeking refuge, Ai Weiwei's *Good Fences Make Good Neighbors* is a prophetic cry for a more tolerant and humane world. At sites across New York City, Ai Weiwei's work powerfully reminded us who we are at the core of our humanity. Walking through the city, the banners and sculptures may have surprised us, but they never failed to make us stop and think, inspiring us to fight to tear down the barriers that keep us from the enlightened world in which we want to live.

The overwhelming majority of us who encountered Ai Weiwei's inspired art are immigrants or refugees—or our forebearers were—so how dare we fail to empathize with those suffering in today's global refugee crisis? My faith tradition commands me to love the stranger; Ai Weiwei's work helps me to do so. There can be no doubt that *Good Fences Make Good Neighbors* has had a profound impact on those of us who live and work in New York City. As great art often does, his has changed us for the better.

Rabbi Rick Jacobs, President, Union for Reform Judaism

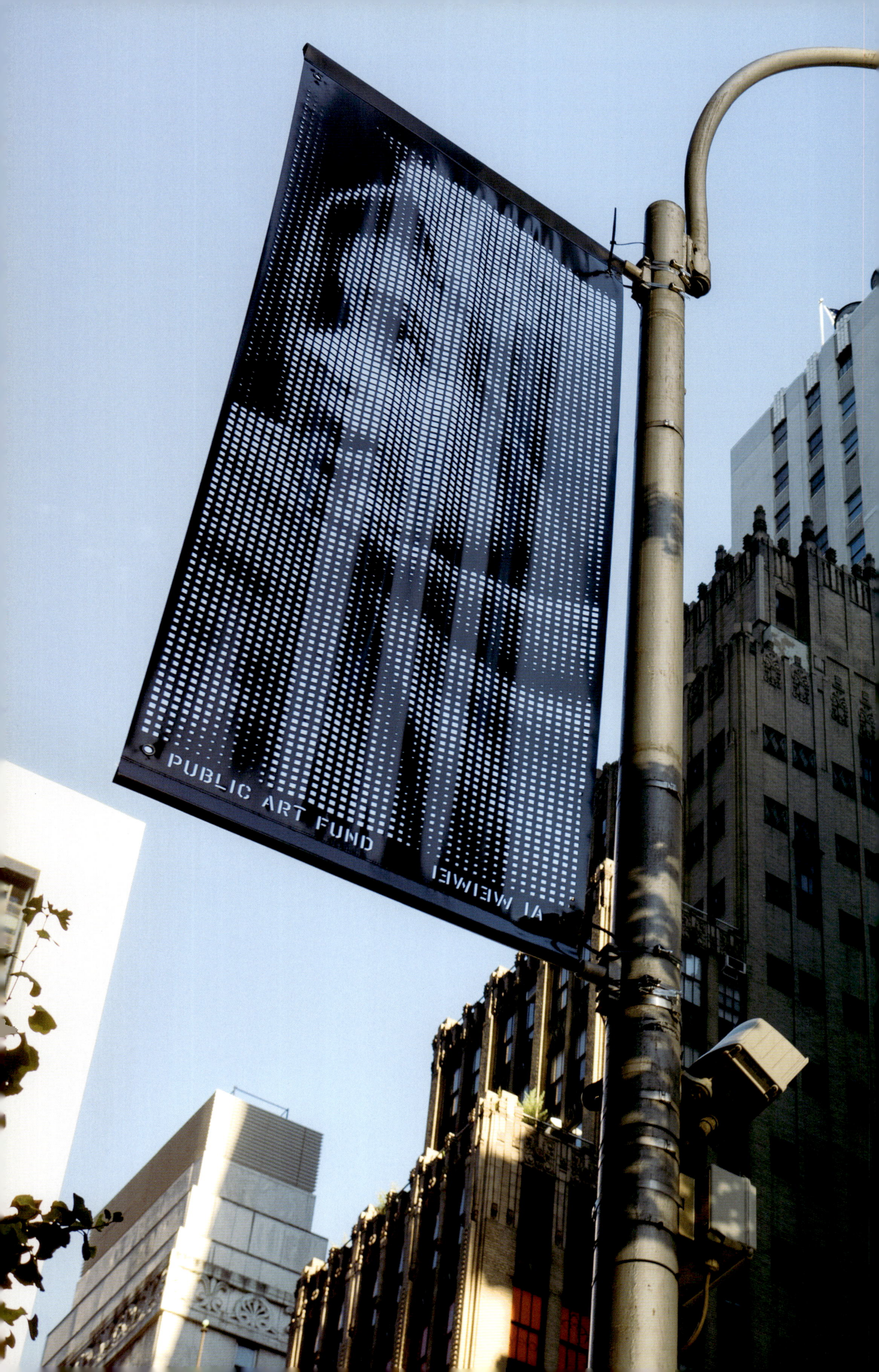
PUBLIC ART FUND

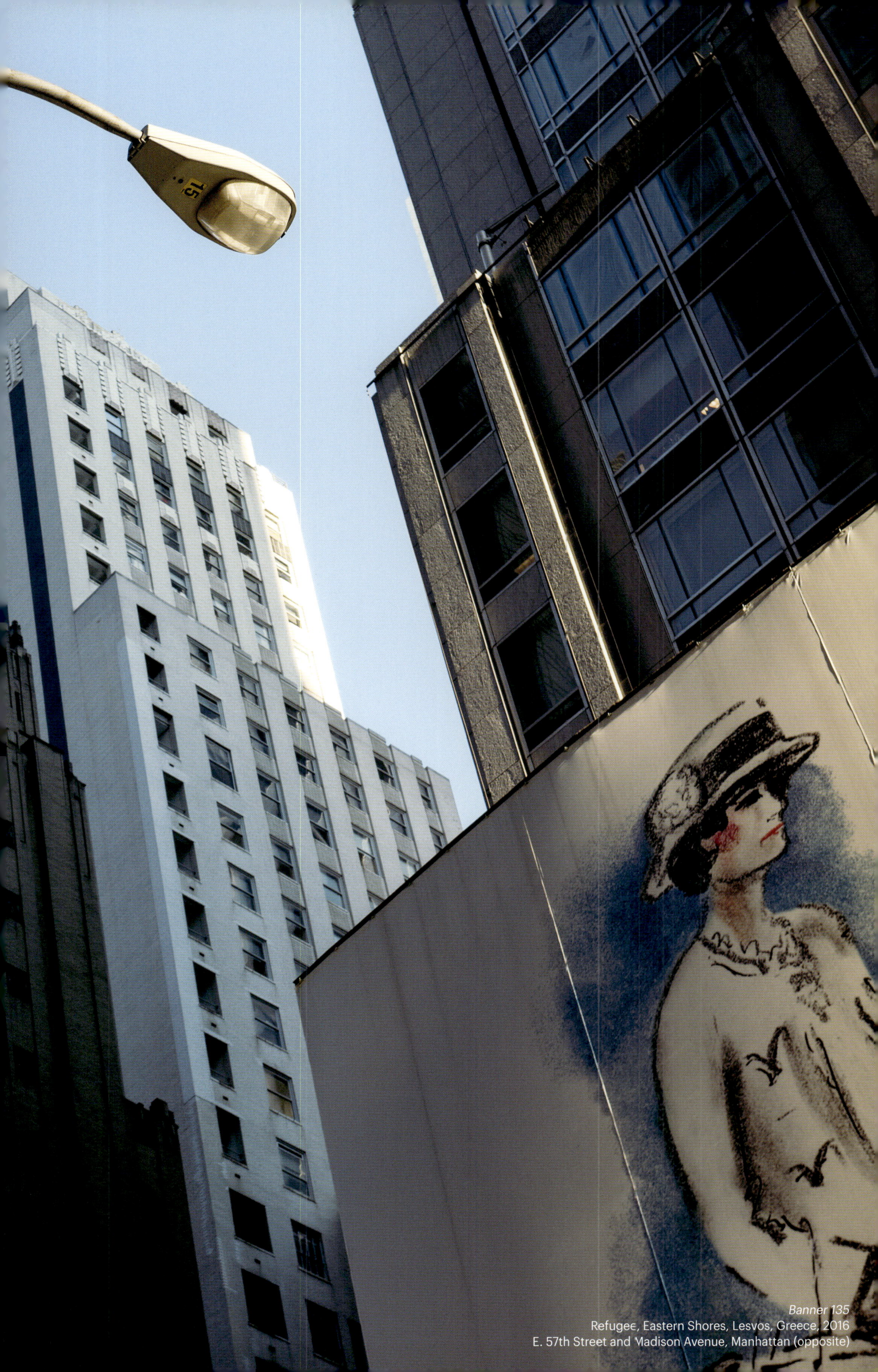

Banner 135
Refugee, Eastern Shores, Lesvos, Greece, 2016
E. 57th Street and Madison Avenue, Manhattan (opposite)

Good Neighbors 36
Makeshift Camp, Idomeni, Greece, 2016 (bottom)

Banner 2
Algerian Man, ca. 1905–1914 (opposite)

1 AVE & E 20 ST

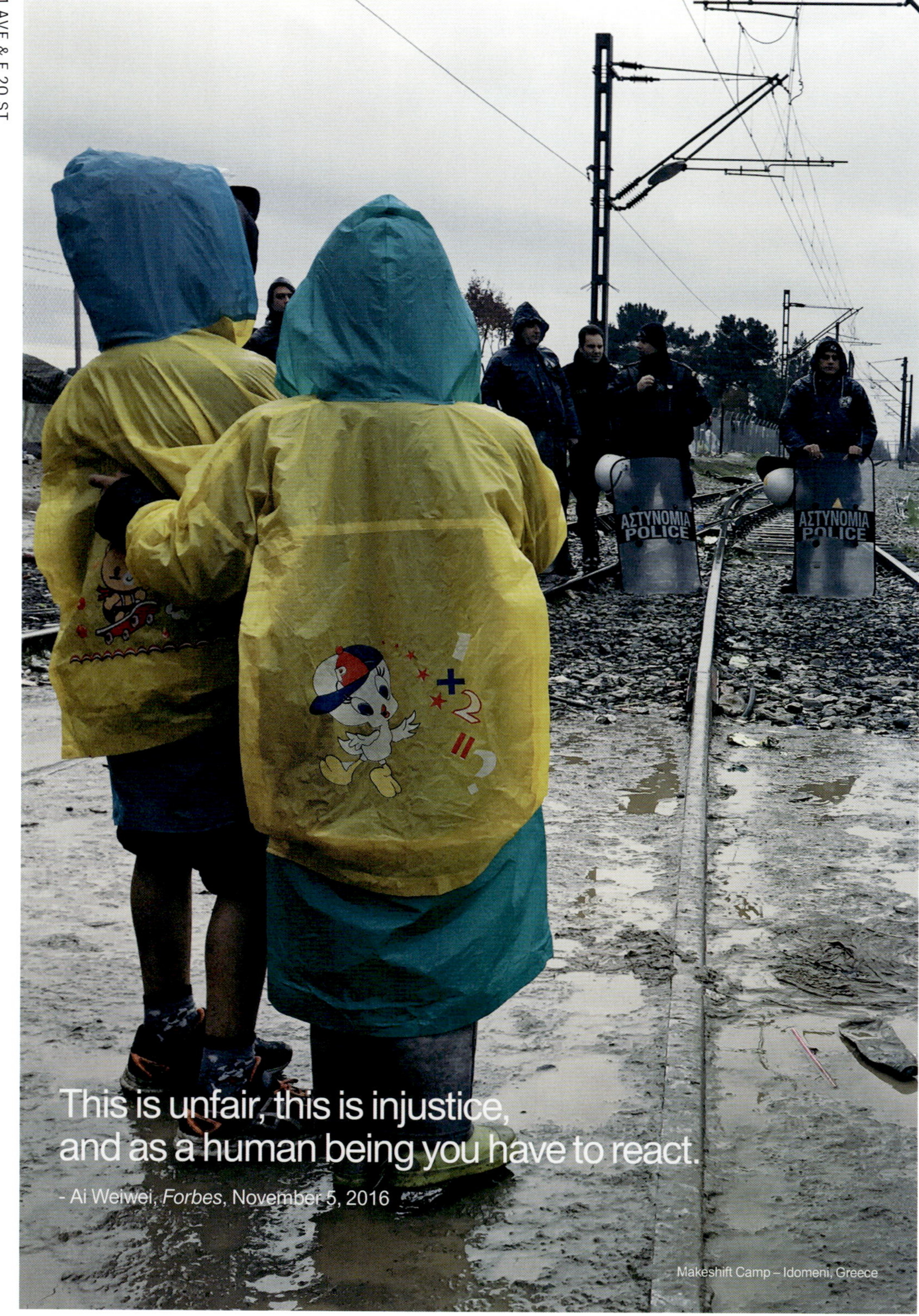

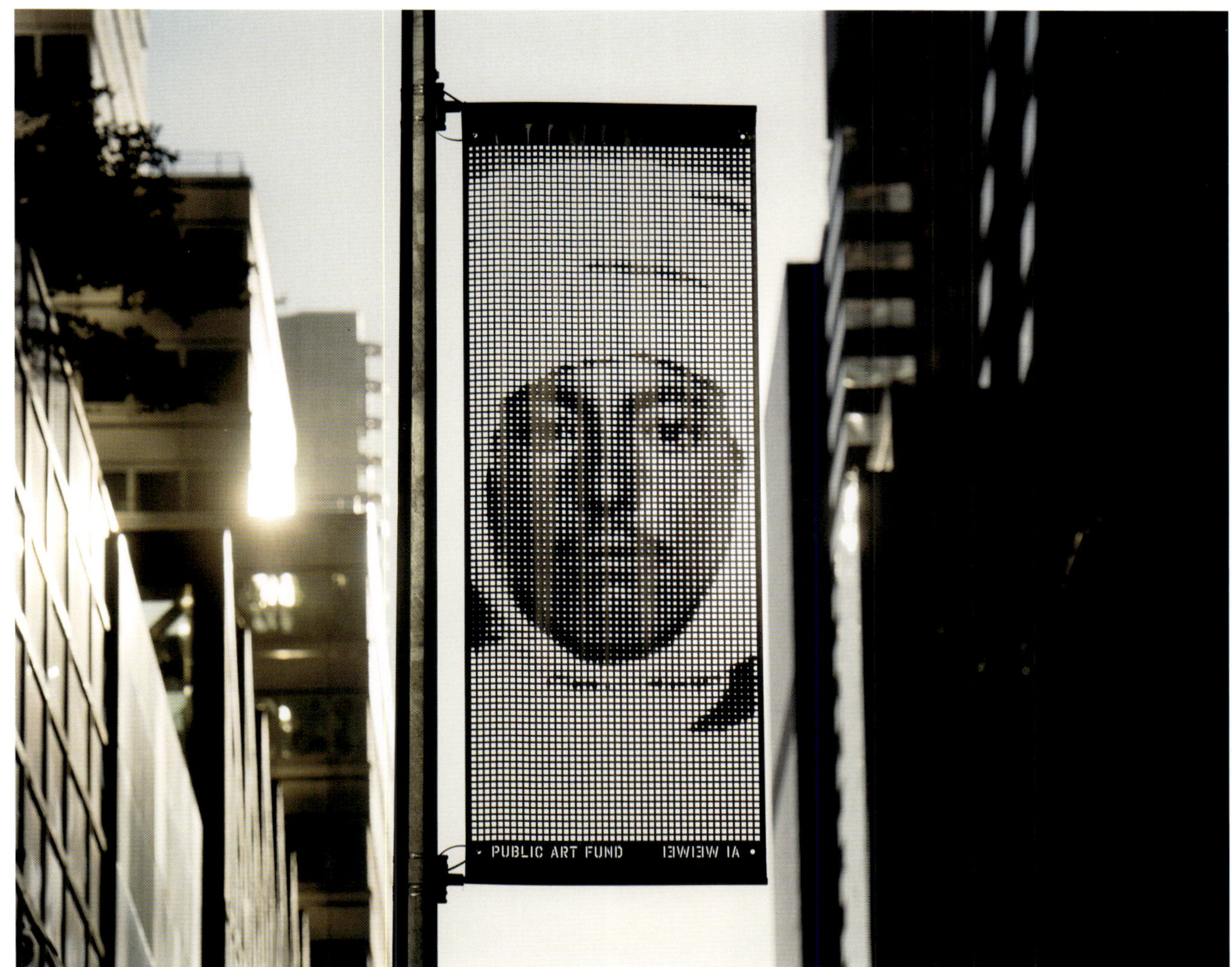

Ai Weiwei's installations in New York arrive at a time when our American government has chosen to torture refugees it could easily help. *Good Fences Make Good Neighbors* is elegant in its construction and appearance, but dark in its message that the refugee crisis is a humanitarian disaster unfolding all around our fragile oasis of privilege and order. It could not have come at a more critical moment for the United States. In aestheticizing what is very nearly a genocide, it unsettles those who choose to remain unaware of how fenced in we are, at what cost to those inside and outside the barricade.

Andrew Solomon, writer

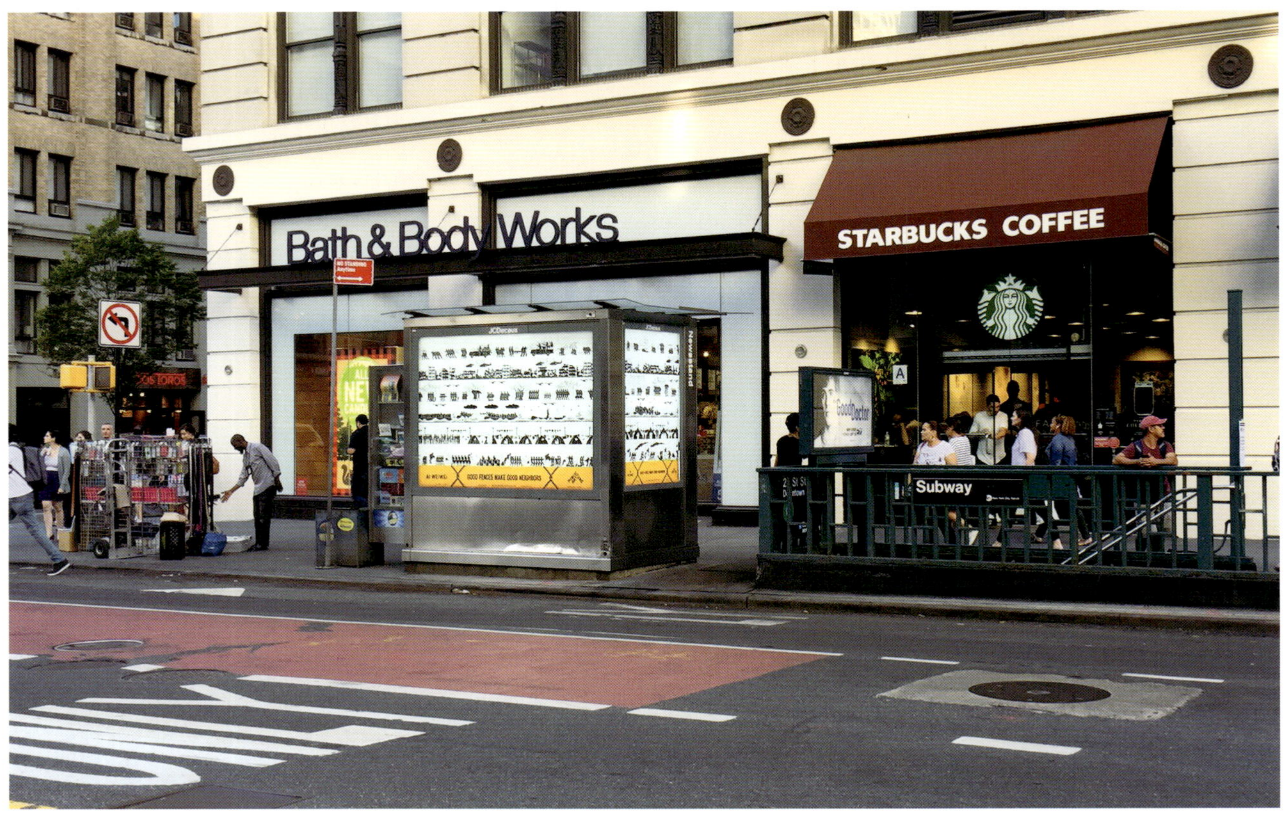

Natural signs and signifiers, not the conventional ones.
Interpretable interventions, not readable ones.
Ambiguity and the oblique, not forcefully driven content.
Increasing the complexity of our experiential narratives, not simplifying them.
Art for the public, not public art.

Ryan Gander, artist

Odyssey 2 (top)

Social media post, *Gilded Cage* (opposite, top)

Gilded Cage and *Banner 14*, Finnish Family, ca. 1905–1914 (opposite, bottom)

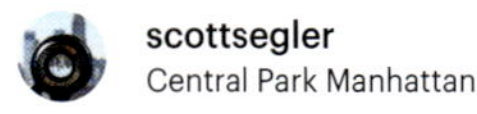

scottsegler
Central Park Manhattan

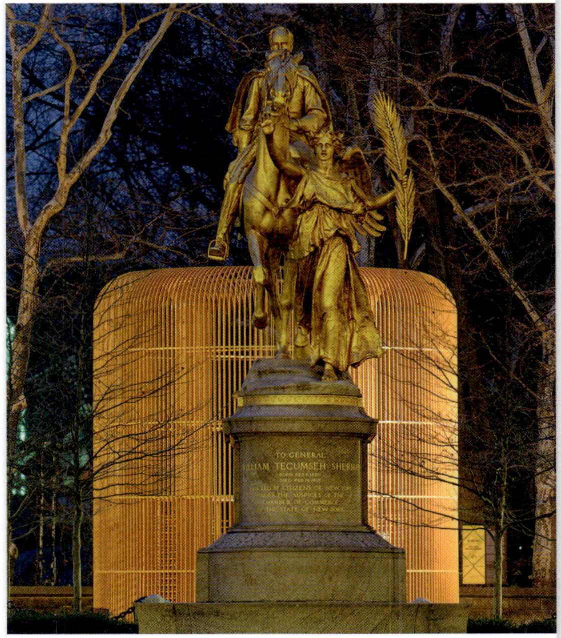

84 likes

scottsegler The twice-reguilded 23.75-karat gold General William Tecumseh Sherman on horseback (depicted walking over a Georgia pine branch) with the allegorical figure Peace in front of the Ai Weiwei "Good Fences Make Good Neighbors" temporary art exhibit at the entrance of Central Park in Grand Army Plaza, Manhattan, New York, NY

JUNE 21, 2018

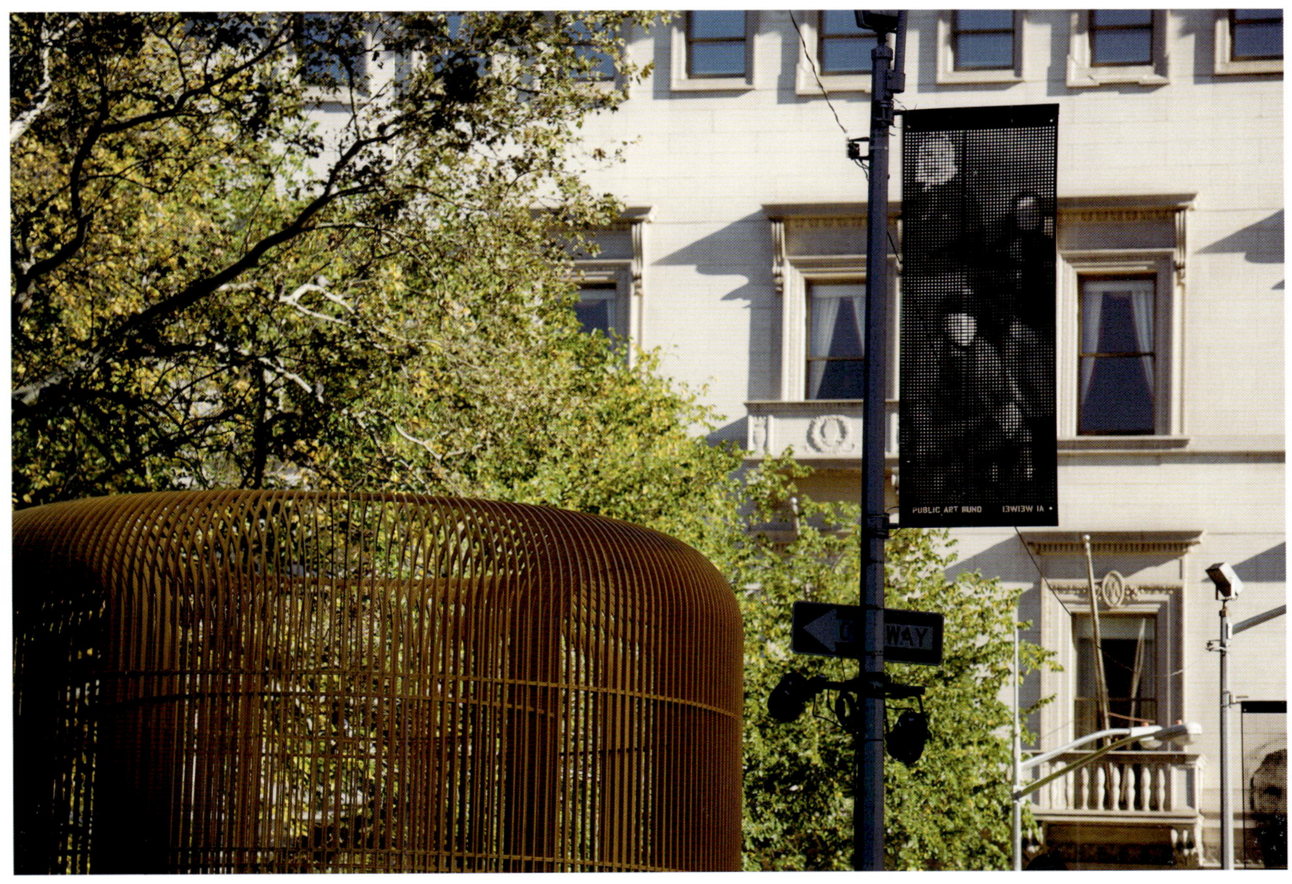

W 60 ST & 5 AVE

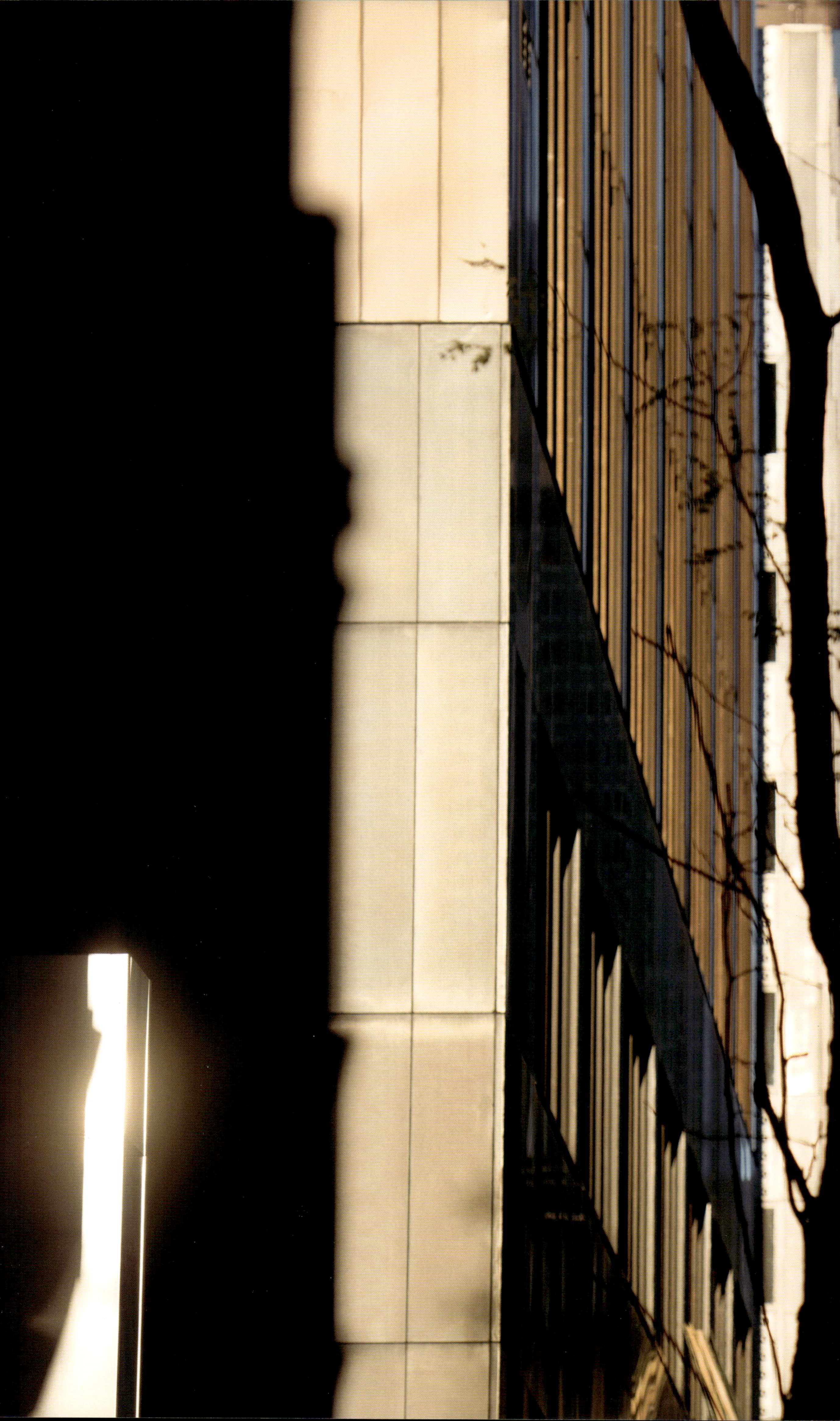

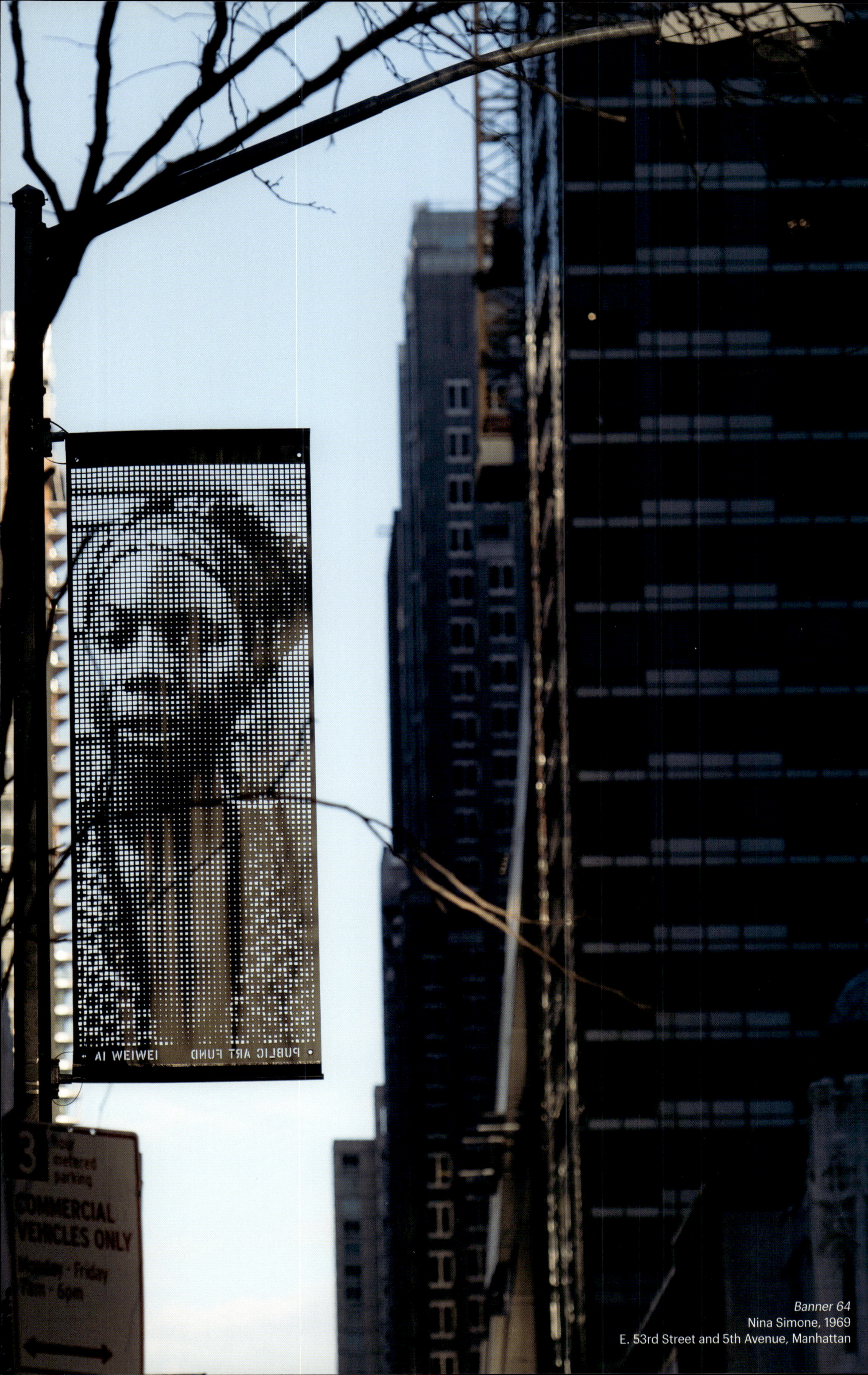

Banner 64
Nina Simone, 1969
E. 53rd Street and 5th Avenue, Manhattan

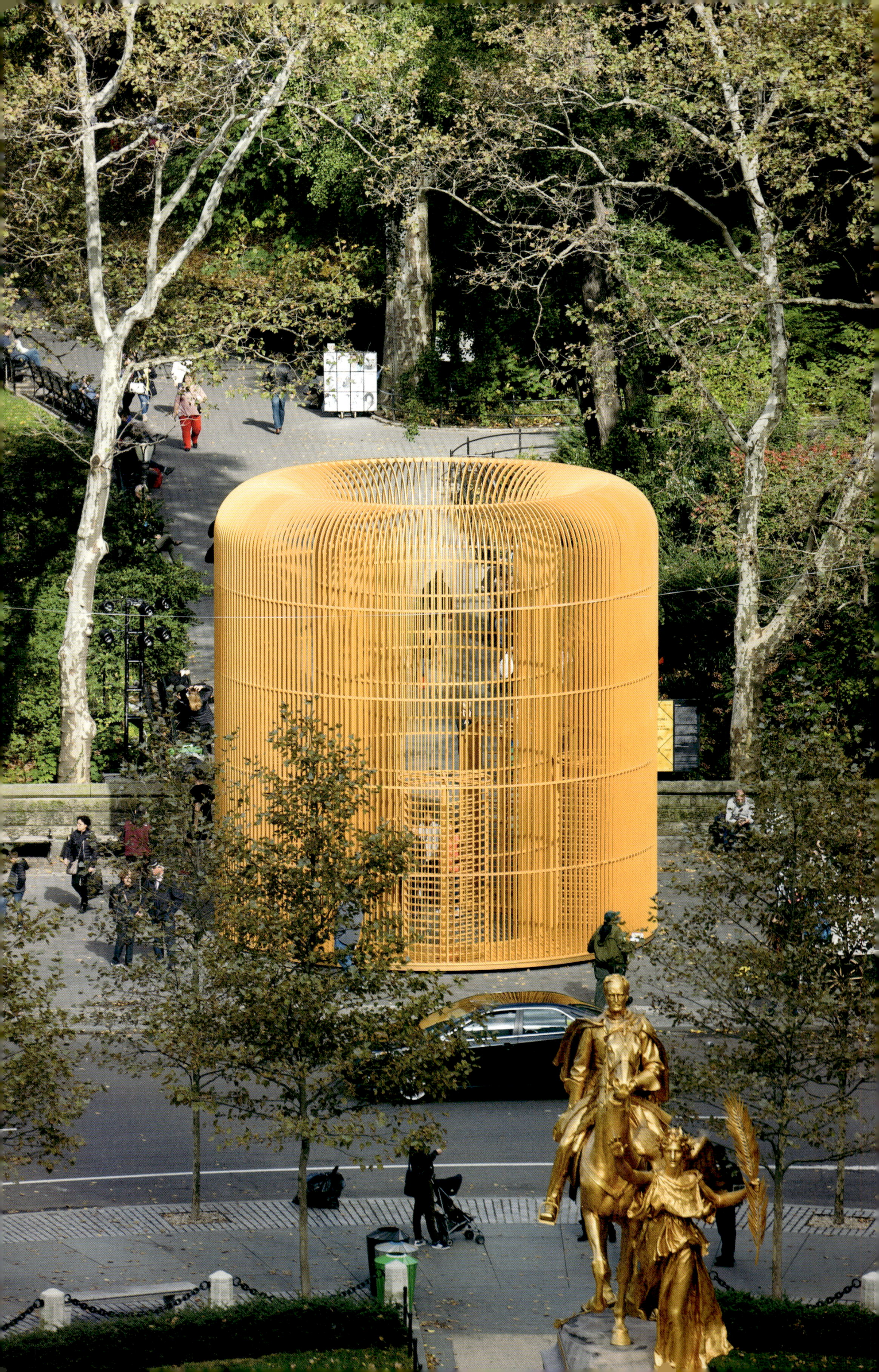

Gilded Cage

Doris C. Freedman Plaza

I know our president likes gold, so this is really for his appreciation.

Ai Weiwei on *Gilded Cage*, speaking on *Democracy Now*

At the entrance to Central Park, Ai Weiwei created a giant gold-hued structure that simultaneously suggests the exclusivity of Fifth Avenue and the privations of confinement. For this large-scale, freestanding sculpture, Ai transforms the fence motif into an abstract, cage-like installation. With Trump Tower only blocks away, the pointed intentions of this sculpture's gilded color are clear. (On numerous occasions during the exhibition, the artist made coy references to Donald Trump's predilection for gilded environments and claimed he hoped the sculpture would please the president.) Likewise, the artist's chosen title for this piece metaphorically suggests superficially attractive situations that might be constraining or confining at the same time, perhaps inviting First World audiences to consider their privilege and what other types of freedoms it may keep them from. To further suggest reflective engagement, visitors were drawn into the artwork's central space to find themselves in an open-top cylinder surrounded by bars and turnstiles—a direct reference to checkpoints and other barriers that refugees encounter. Functioning as a structure of both control and display, the work reveals the complex power dynamics of repressive architecture that the artist has encountered throughout the world at border checkpoints, "temporary" detention centers, and prisons.

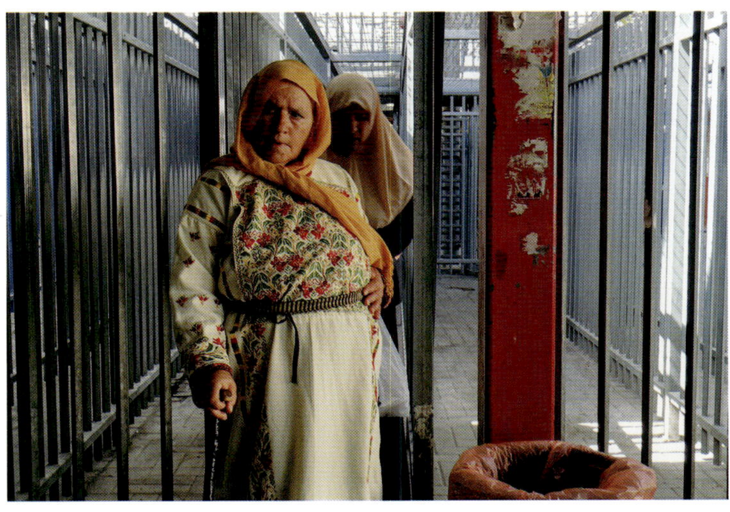

Qalandia Checkpoint, West Bank, 2016

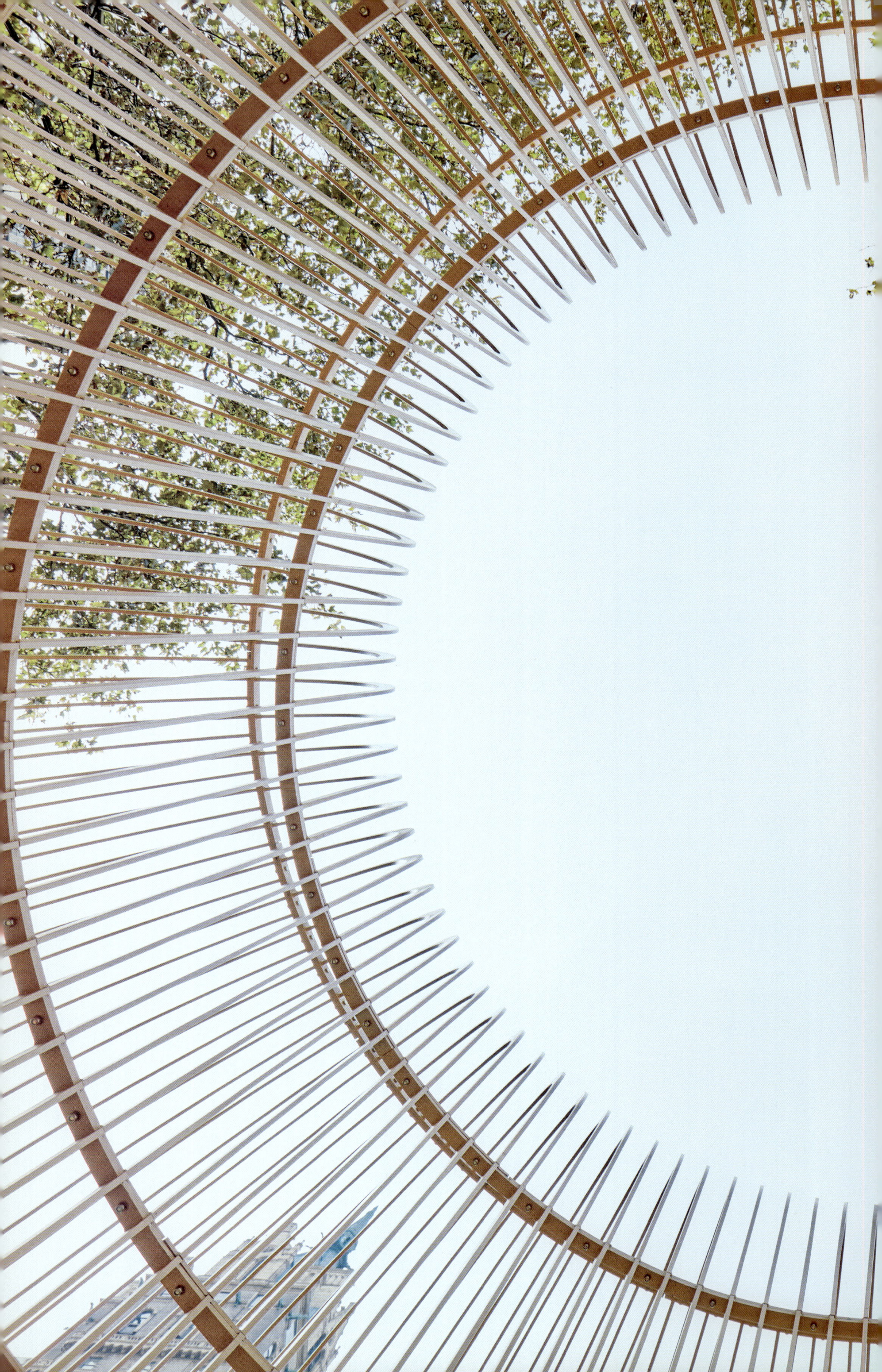

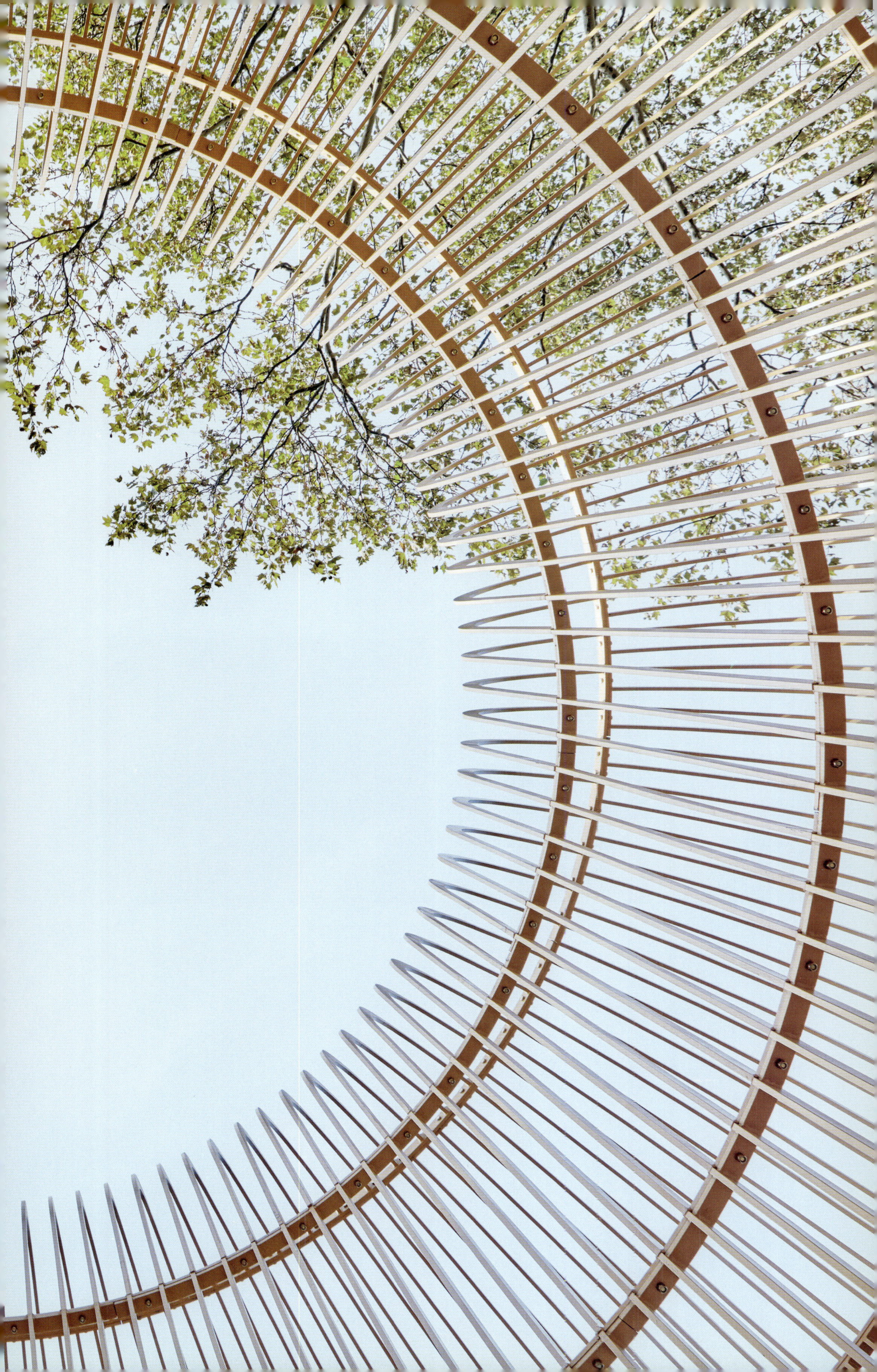

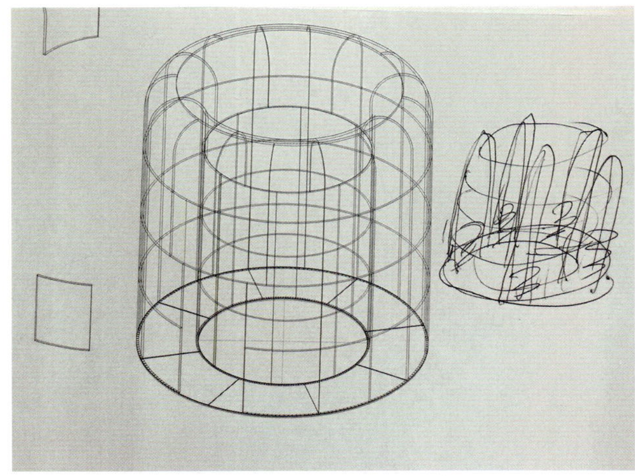

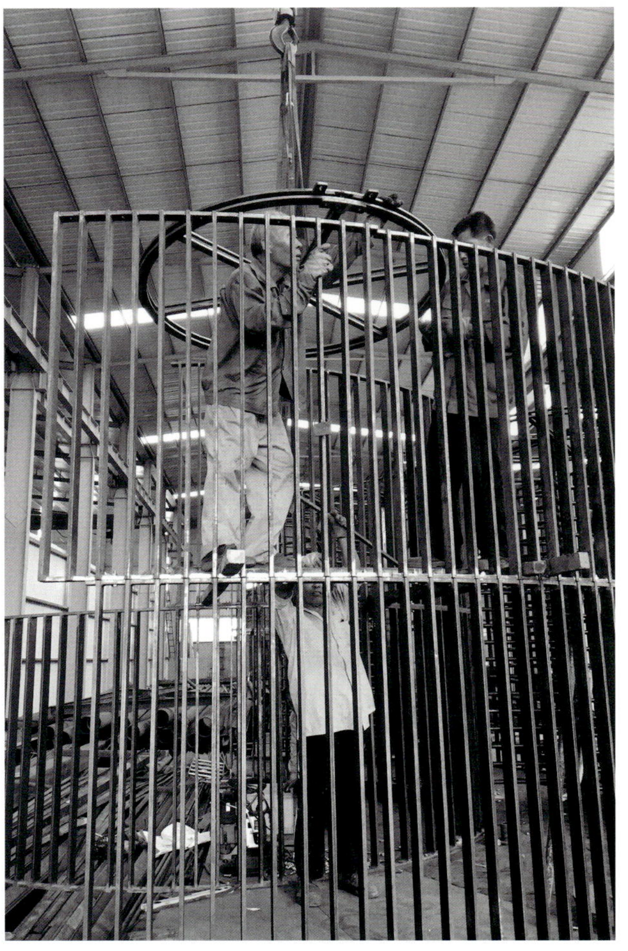

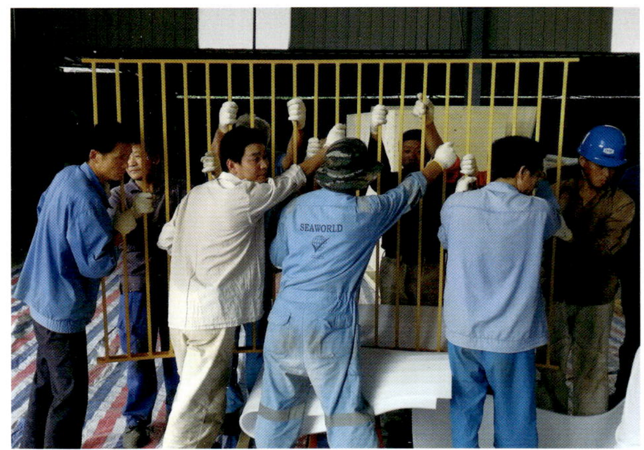

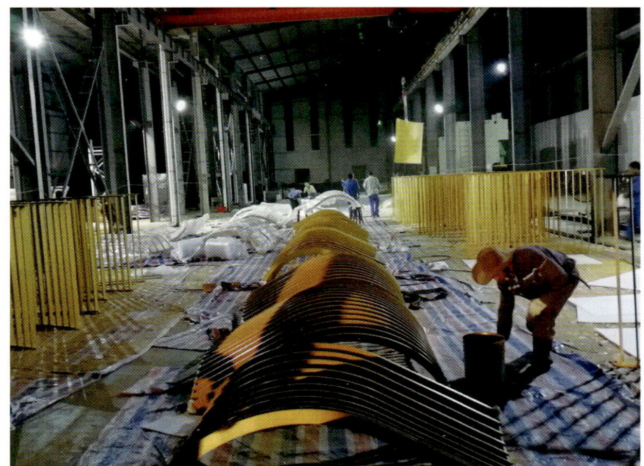

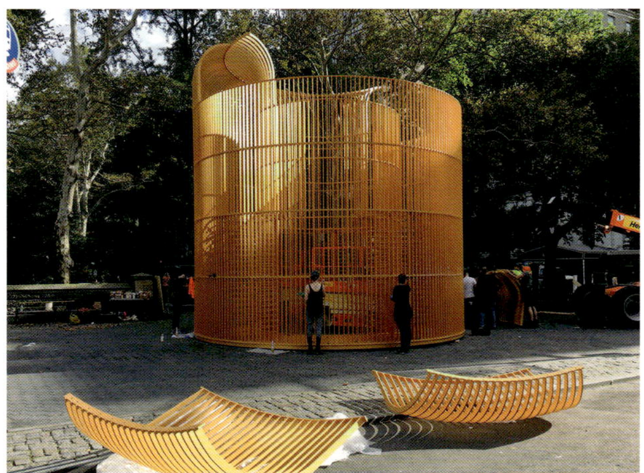

Computer-generated drawing and Ai Weiwei's hand-drawn sketch of *Gilded Cage* (top left)

Fabrication of steel components for *Gilded Cage* in UAP's workshop in Shanghai (top right, center left, and bottom left)

Installation of *Gilded Cage* at Doris C. Freedman Plaza, Manhattan (bottom right)

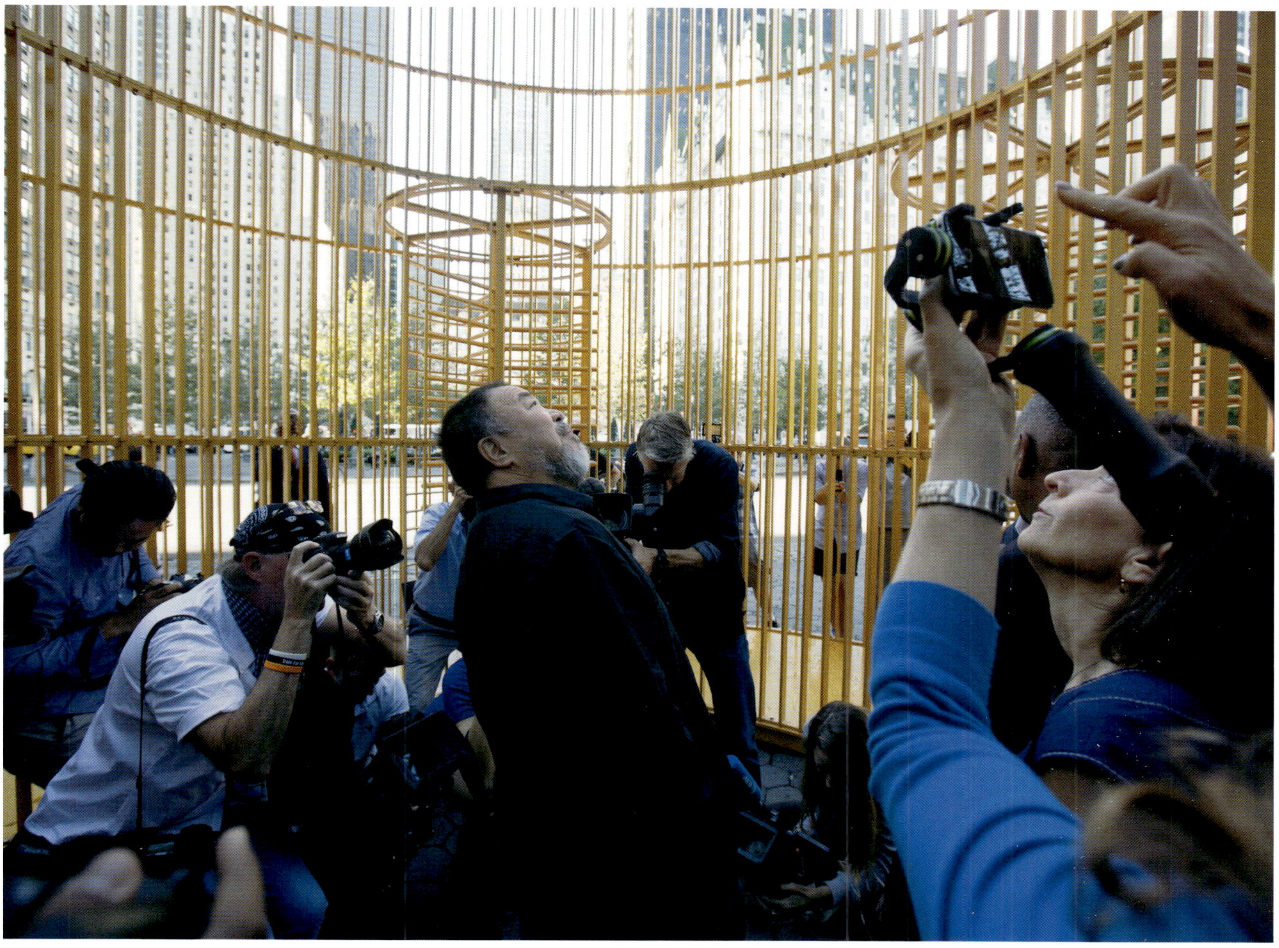

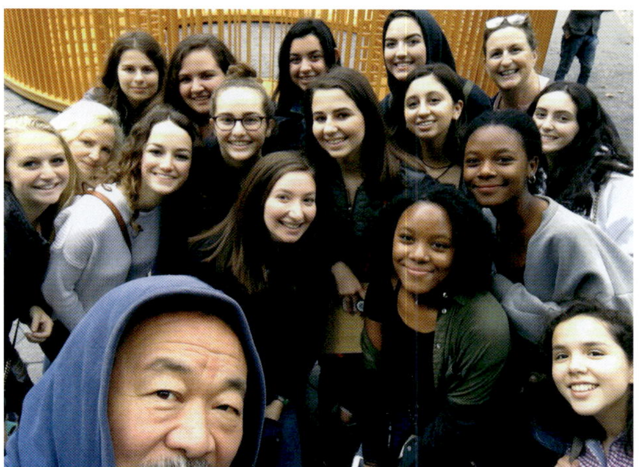

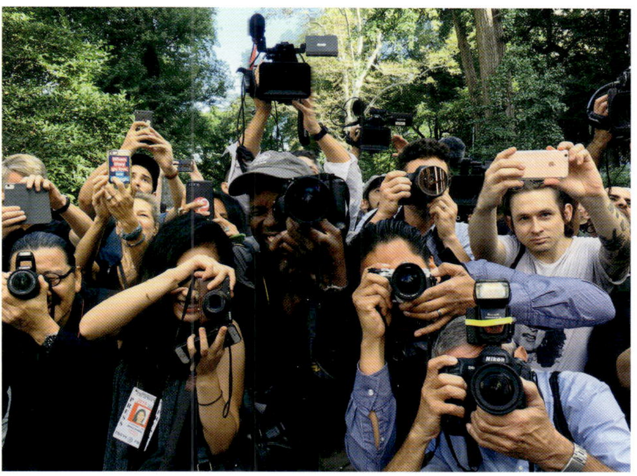

Press opening for *Good Fences Make Good Neighbors*, October 10, 2017

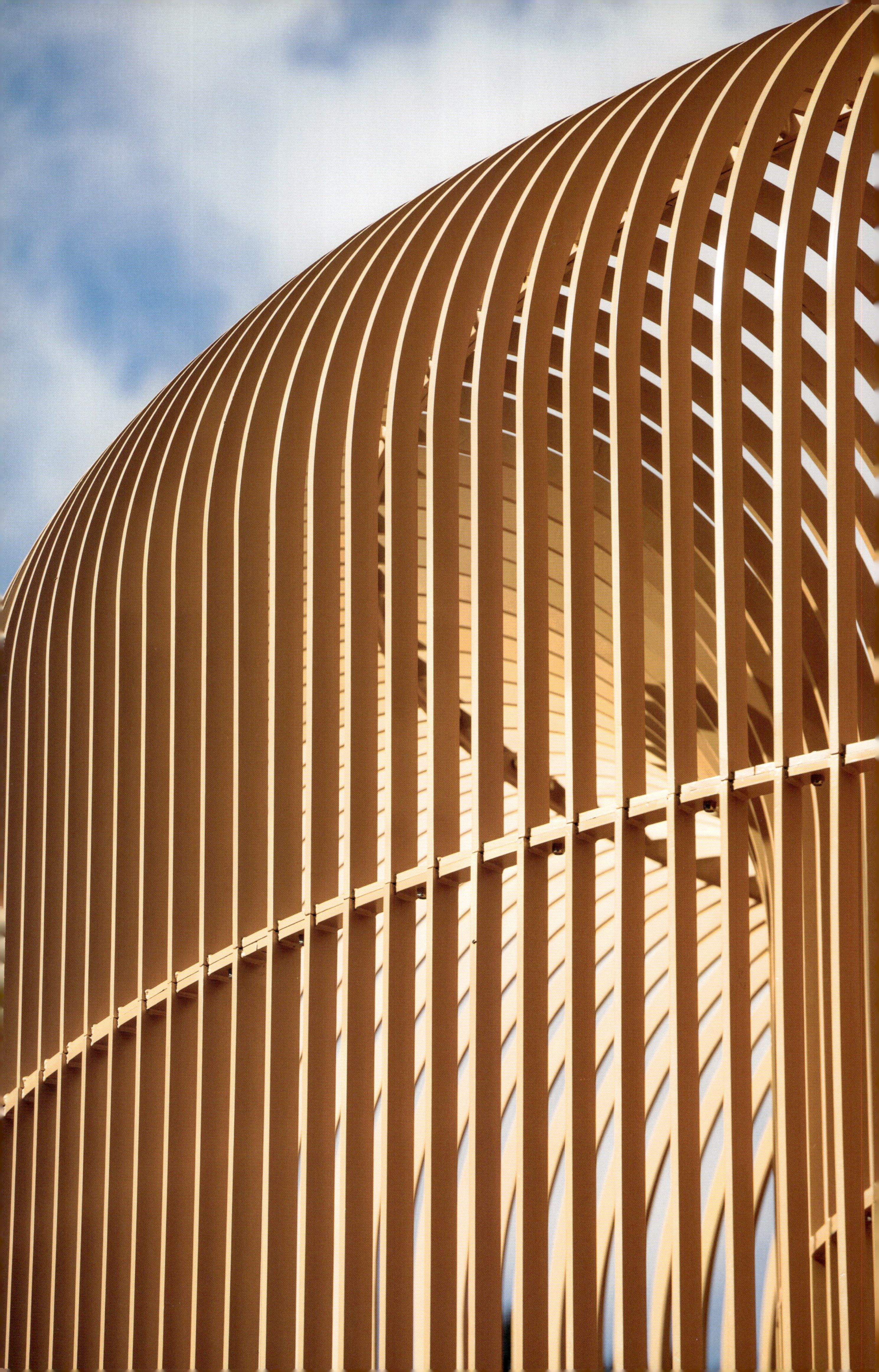

Good Fences Make Good Neighbors by world-renowned artist Ai Weiwei is the perfect exhibition at the right time and in the right places. What I find compelling is the timing of the exhibition, given the international climate on immigration, the refugee crisis, and border control. Rather than fanning the flames of division, the exhibition embraces inclusiveness and diversity. Borders are virtually broken by embracing all five New York City boroughs in the exhibition with stand-alone sculptures and banners that represent the incredible and vibrant diversity of our planet. The piece I enjoy the most is the golden cage sculpture located at Doris C. Freedman Plaza in Central Park. At one of the main entrances to the most democratic and visited park in the world, the cage-like structure is transparent and accessible. The viewer experiences the piece by walking in and around the art. But what I find most memorable is standing in the middle of the sculpture and looking up to the sky. Why? Because the sky has no borders, and everyone has access to it regardless of who you are as a global citizen. I personally thank Ai Weiwei for his creativity and humanity that has resulted in this profound exhibit from his heart and soul.

Mitchell J. Silver, FAICP, Hon. ASLA, Commissioner, City of New York Parks & Recreation

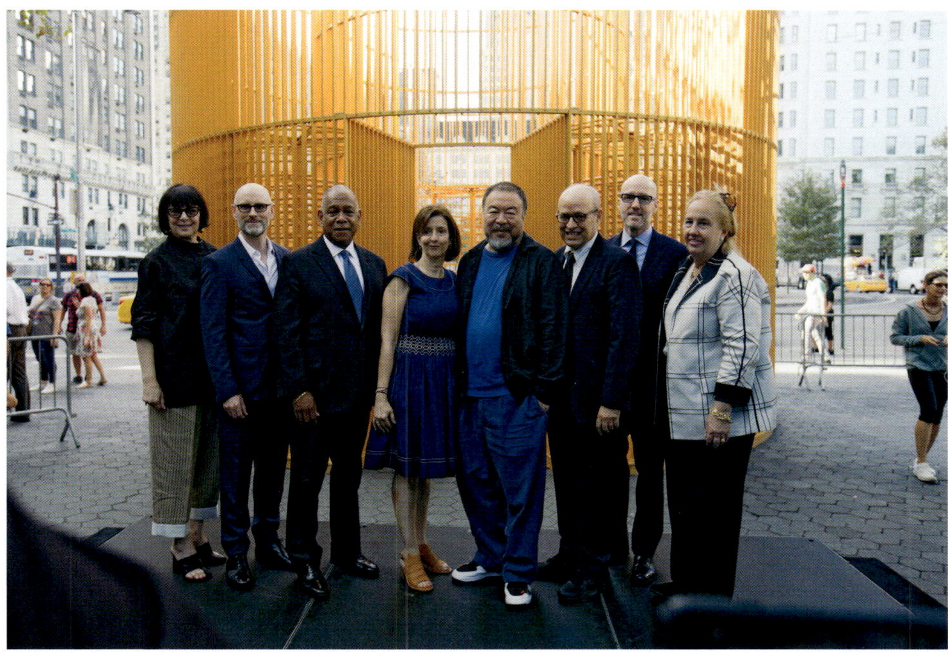

Left to right: Jill Kraus, Nicholas Baume, Mitchell J. Silver, Susan K. Freedman, Ai Weiwei, Tom Finkelpearl, Peter Hatch, and Gale A. Brewer at the press opening for *Good Fences Make Good Neighbors*, October 10, 2017

Social media post, *Gilded Cage*

jcgarcialavin
Central Park Manhatan

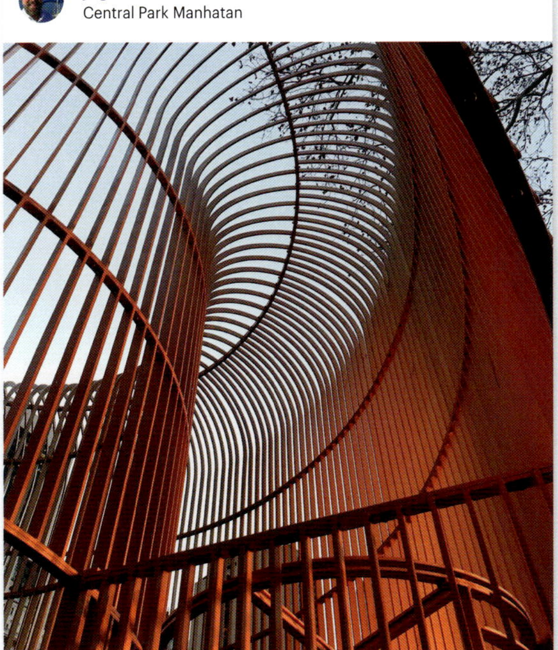

242 Likes

jcgarcialavin Ai WeiWei, "Good fences make good neighbors", NYC

jcgarcialavin #aiweiwei #sculpture #goodfencesmakegoodneighbors #nyc #newyork #newyorkcity #manhattan #urban #art #metal #steel #centralpark #sunset #uptown

NOVEMBER 27, 2017

New York City, the epicenter of art and culture, is the perfect canvas for Ai Weiwei's work. Ambitious projects such as *Good Fences Make Good Neighbors* foster vital cultural discourse, challenge us, and can bring about real social progress. We are thrilled to share our iconic public spaces with these bold installations.

Bill de Blasio, New York City Mayor

×

New York wouldn't be what it is without public art that inspires, challenges, and teaches us. Ai Weiwei's powerful exhibition makes New Yorkers and visitors think about how space can be shared and the beauty that comes when we don't put up walls between us and the rest of the world.

Gale A. Brewer, Manhattan Borough President

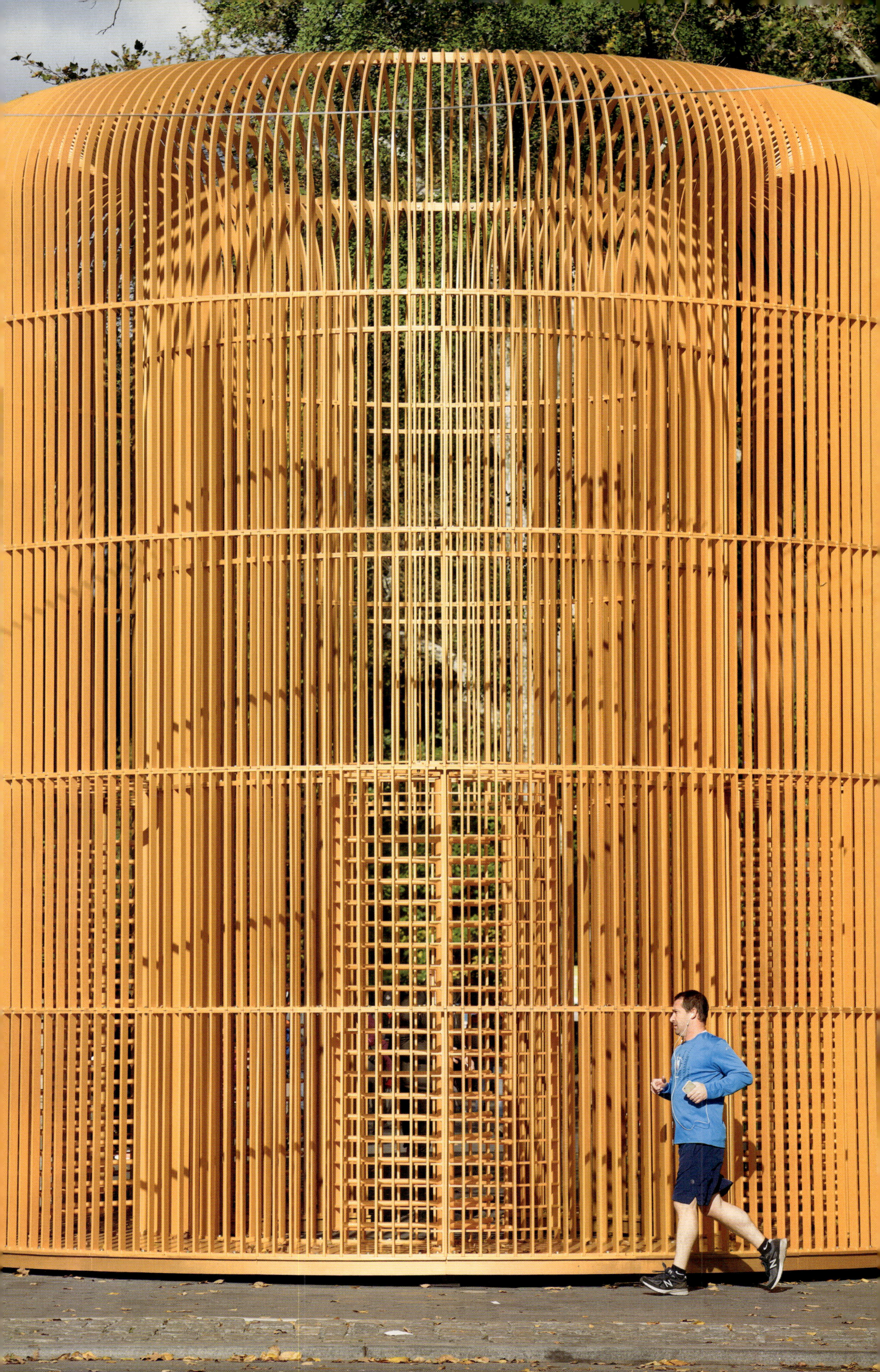

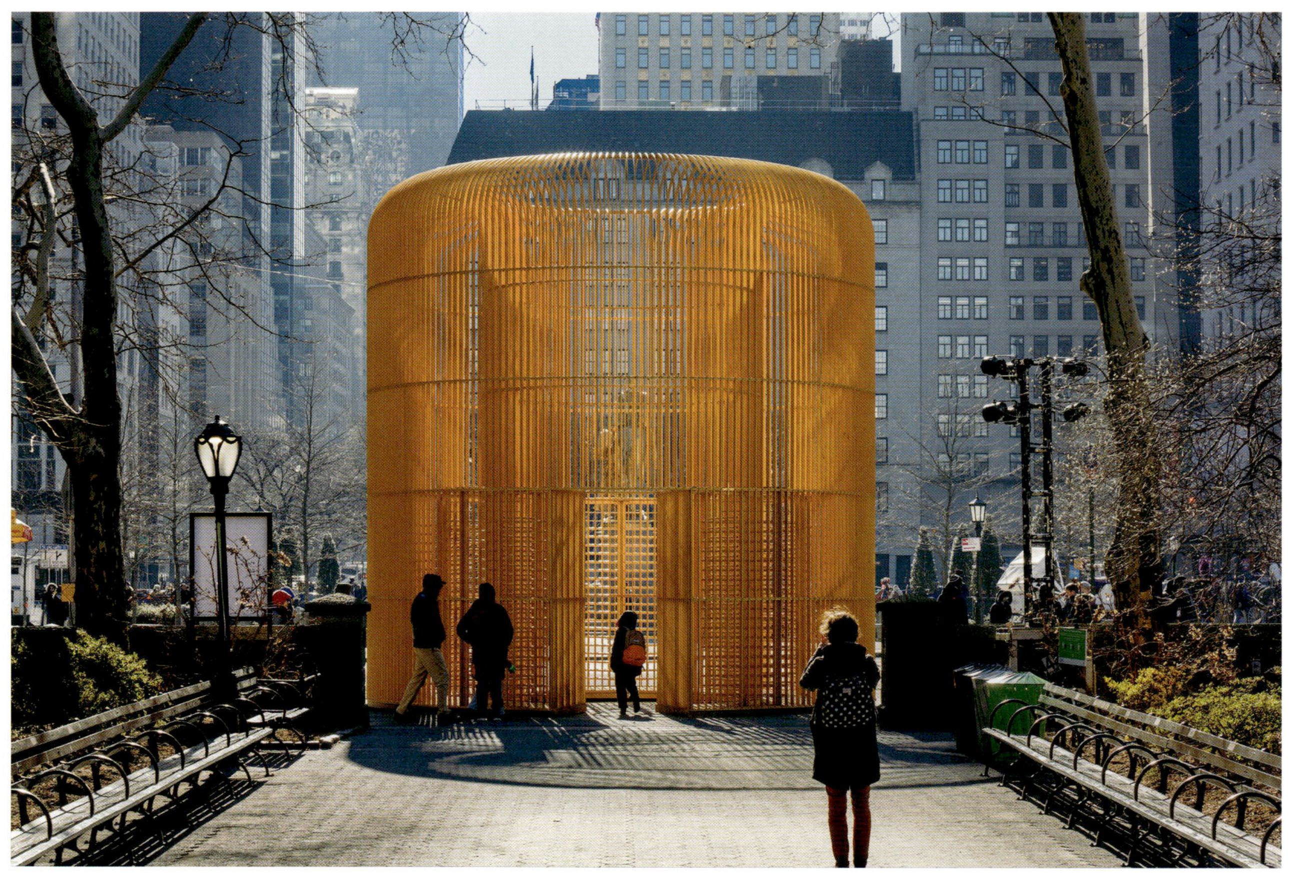

This is a piece related to refugee conditions. Related to migrants, related to borders, fences, territory, nationalism, and the ways our society becomes more divided.

Ai Weiwei on *Gilded Cage*, in *Vice*

×

I was overwhelmed by how sad and tragic it feels to be inside this beautiful gilded cage.

Viewer comment on *Gilded Cage*

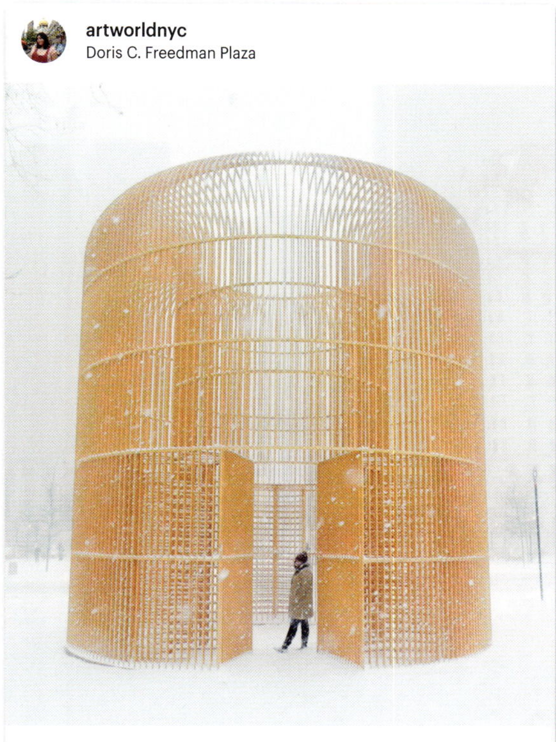

737 likes

artworldnyc#artworldnyc
Photographer✌ @nickshotit
What:GOOD FENCES MAKE GOOD NEIGHBORS
"Ai Weiwei conceived this multi-site, multi-media exhibition for public spaces, monuments, buildings, transportation sites, and advertising platforms throughout New York City.

JANUARY 5, 2018

Social media post, *Gilded Cage* (left)

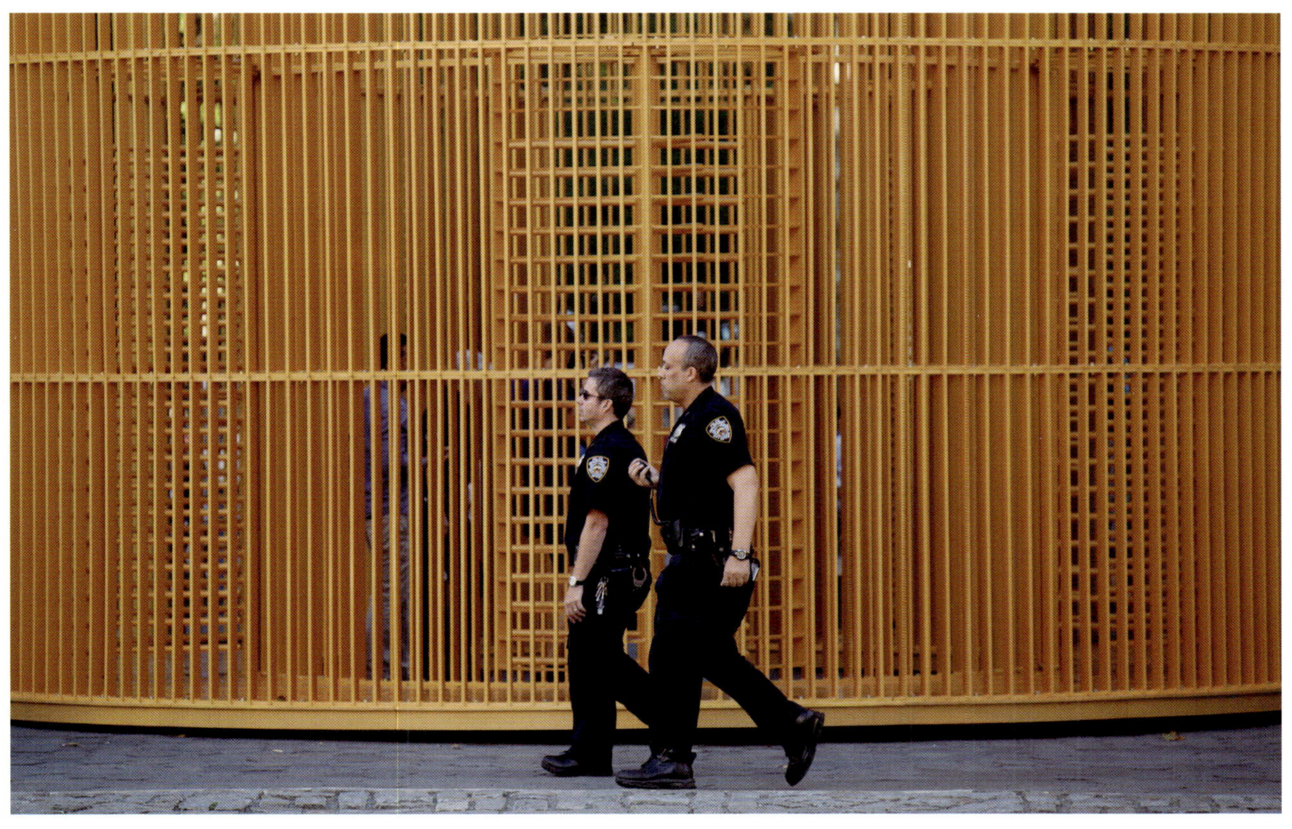

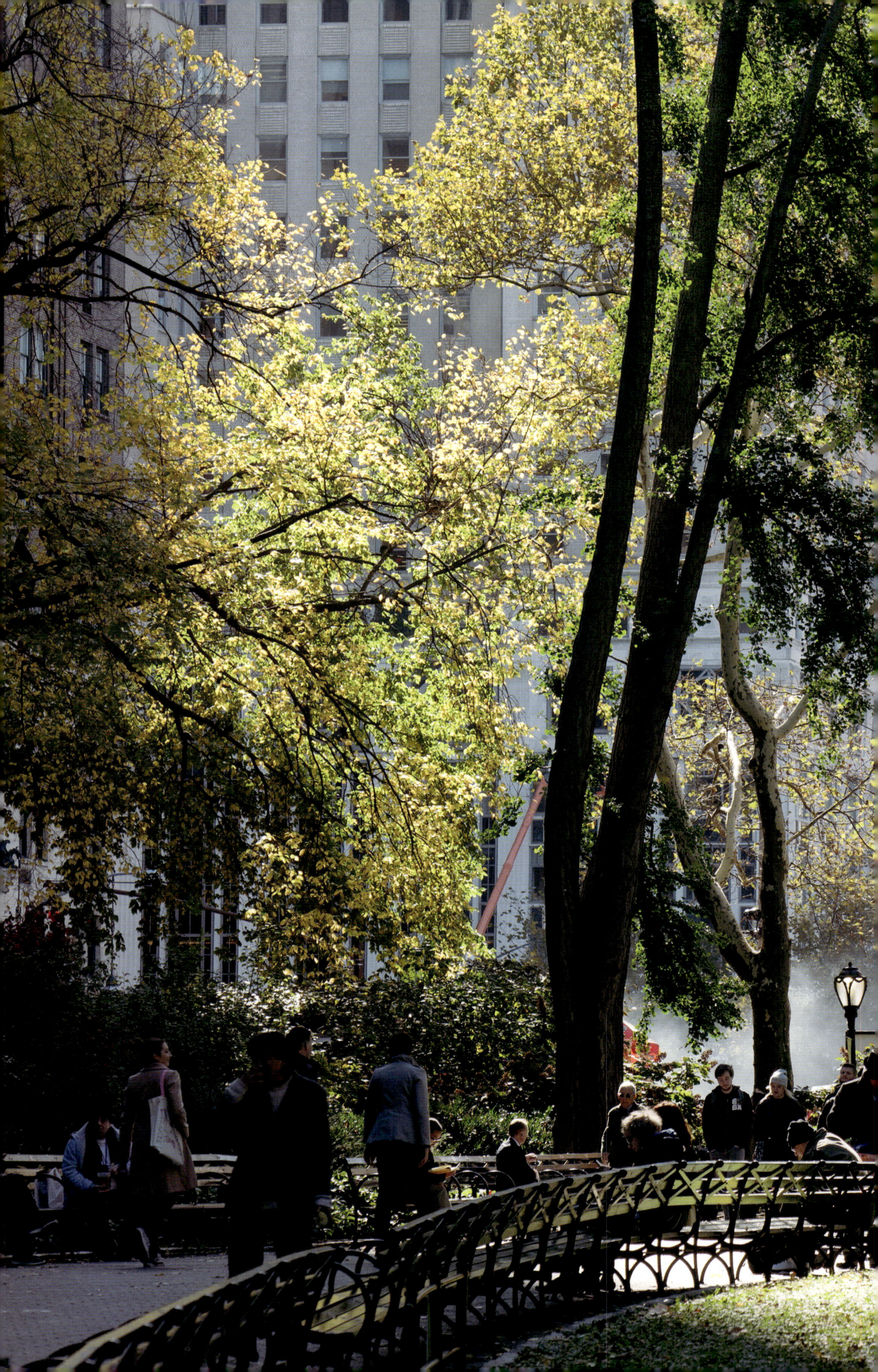

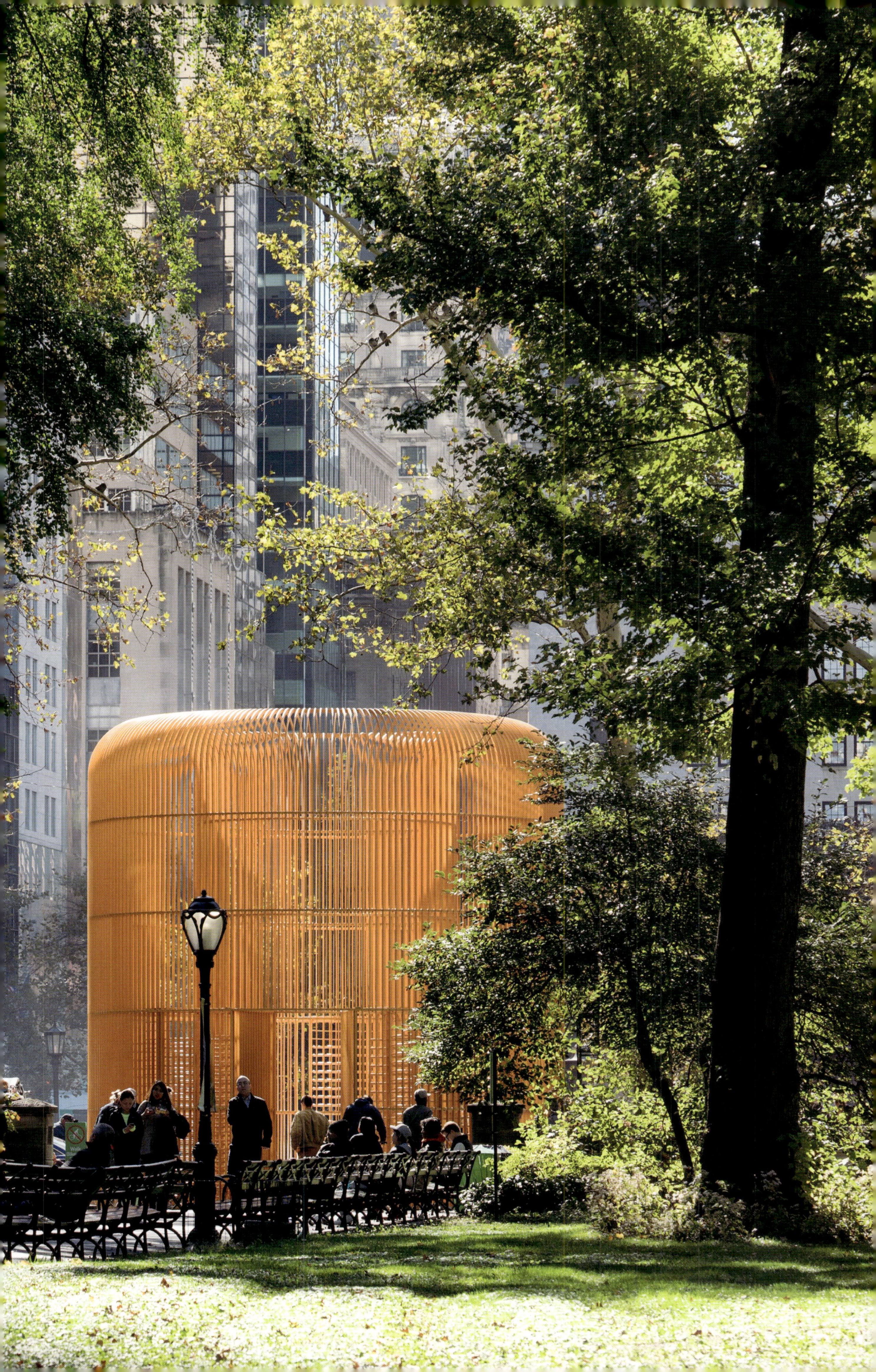

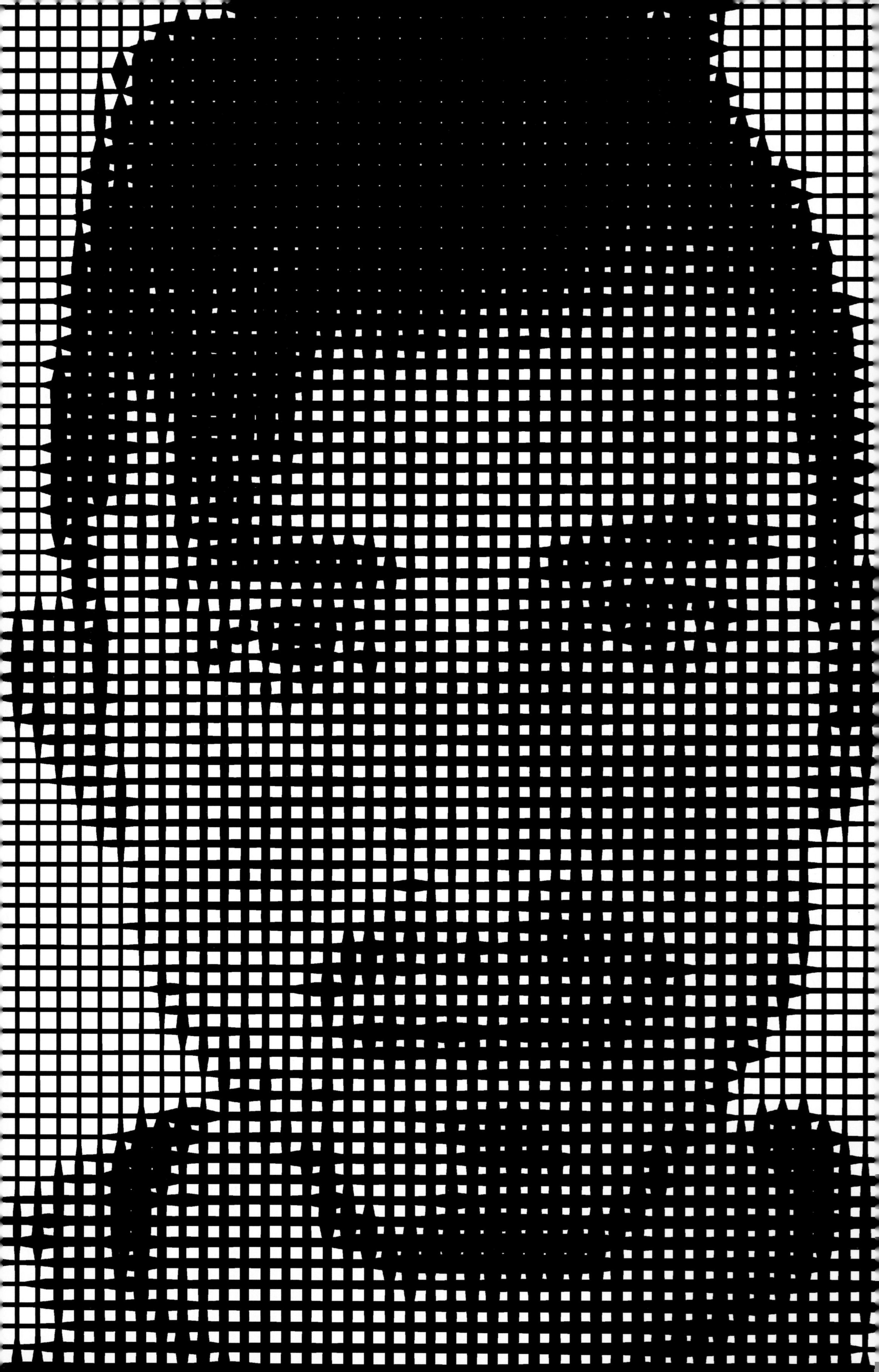

Banners

200 Lampposts Citywide

Ai Weiwei's citywide exhibition used elements of existing urban infrastructure as platforms for his public art. Lampposts displayed a series of two hundred banner portraits of refugees and immigrants in all five boroughs. Instead of the advertisements usually found on these posts, Ai created his unique, double-sided banner portraits with laser-cut, industrial black vinyl (the portrait images remain after the cuts were made). The artist's choice of this commercially available vinyl material is a very specific reference: it is the same vinyl used for the truck tarps that cover the large cargo containers where refugees often stow away in desperate attempts to flee their home countries in search of a better life abroad. In this way, the play of positive and negative space in the banners, and in the shadows they cast, is analogous to the often ambiguous status of refugees and migrants.

Today, more than sixty-eight million people worldwide have been displaced as a result of persecution, conflict, violence, or human rights violations (the highest number since World War II). According to the UN Refugee Agency, just three countries plagued by conflict—Syria, Somalia, and Afghanistan—are responsible for more than half of the world's current refugees (this figure excludes five million Palestinians registered by the UN Relief and Works Agency). Nations closest to conflict zones, such as Turkey, Greece, Lebanon, and Kenya, face overwhelming challenges due to the enormous influx of fleeing populations and struggle to accommodate the displaced. The humanitarian crisis is exacerbated by wealthier nations who are slow to respond with badly needed aid, the closing of international border crossings, and delays caused by layers of governmental bureaucracy. Ai's portraits of refugees from all corners of the world pay tribute to their personal identities, while poignantly honoring their resilience and humanity.

The series encompasses many groups by spanning several periods and locales, including historic images from Ellis Island, photographs of notable refugees, formal portraits taken by Ai's studio at the Shariya Camp in Iraq, and the artist's cell phone photographs made at camps and national borders around the world. While the sites for their installation were carefully selected in partnership with the New York City Department of Transportation, the various groups of images were randomly distributed throughout the city in reference to the fluidity of human movement and the integration of people from all backgrounds into communities. Indeed, these portraits have a monumental, even celebratory quality to them, and each was presented in this egalitarian manner, emphasizing the refugees' shared humanity and equal value to our society.

Banner 90
Refugee, Shariya Camp, Iraq (detail), 2015 (opposite)

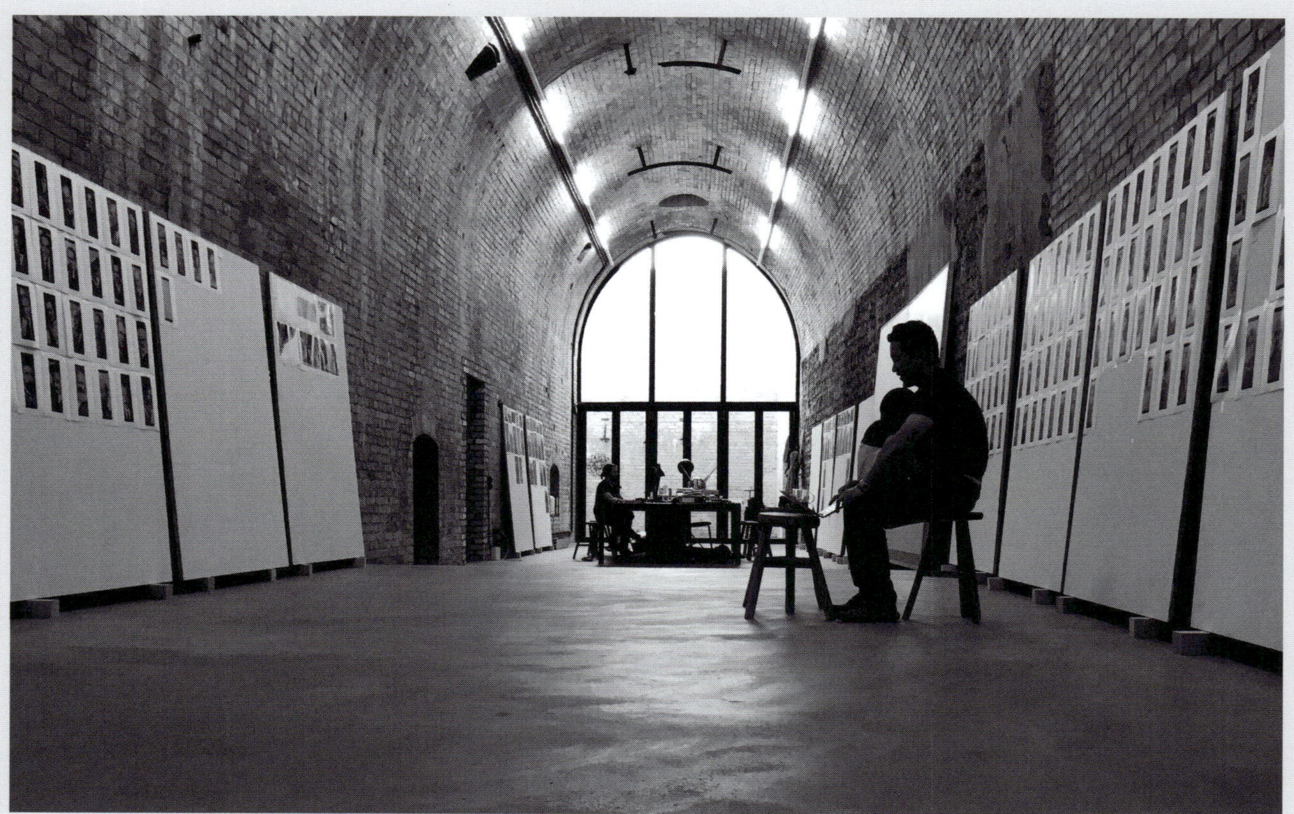

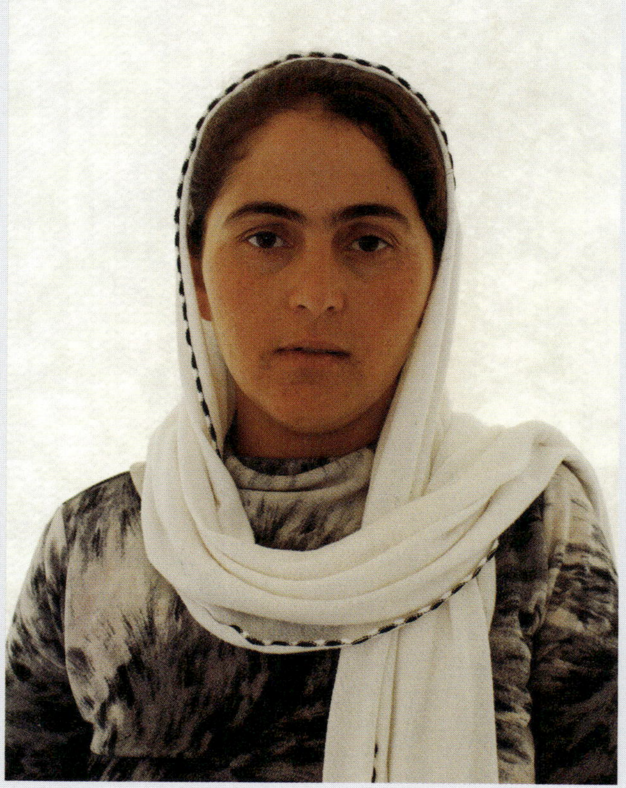

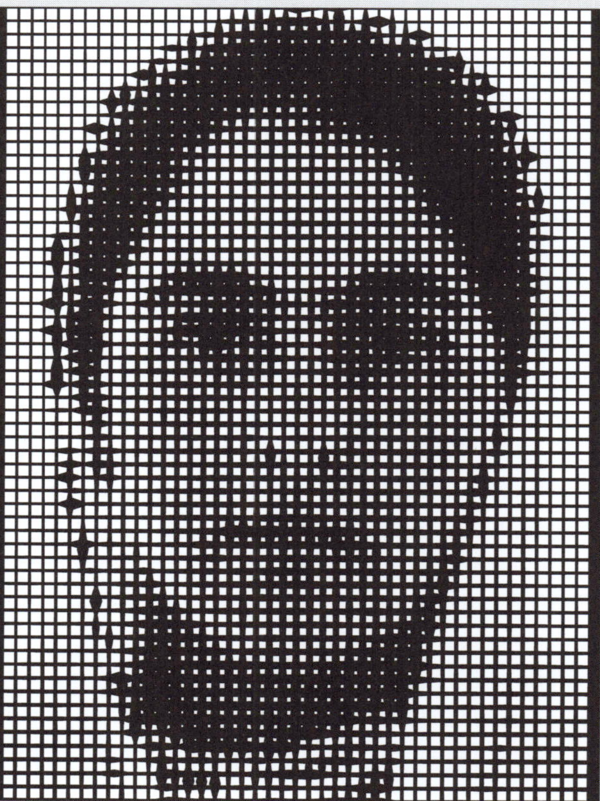

Much like Ai Weiwei, New York City's immigrant communities have had to tap deep from wells of resilience to overcome obstacles and fight for place and belonging. These works stop New Yorkers in their paths and invite reflection on the barriers that divide us and, in turn, the immensity of what unites us as humans.

Bitta Mostofi, Commissioner, Mayor's Office of Immigrant Affairs

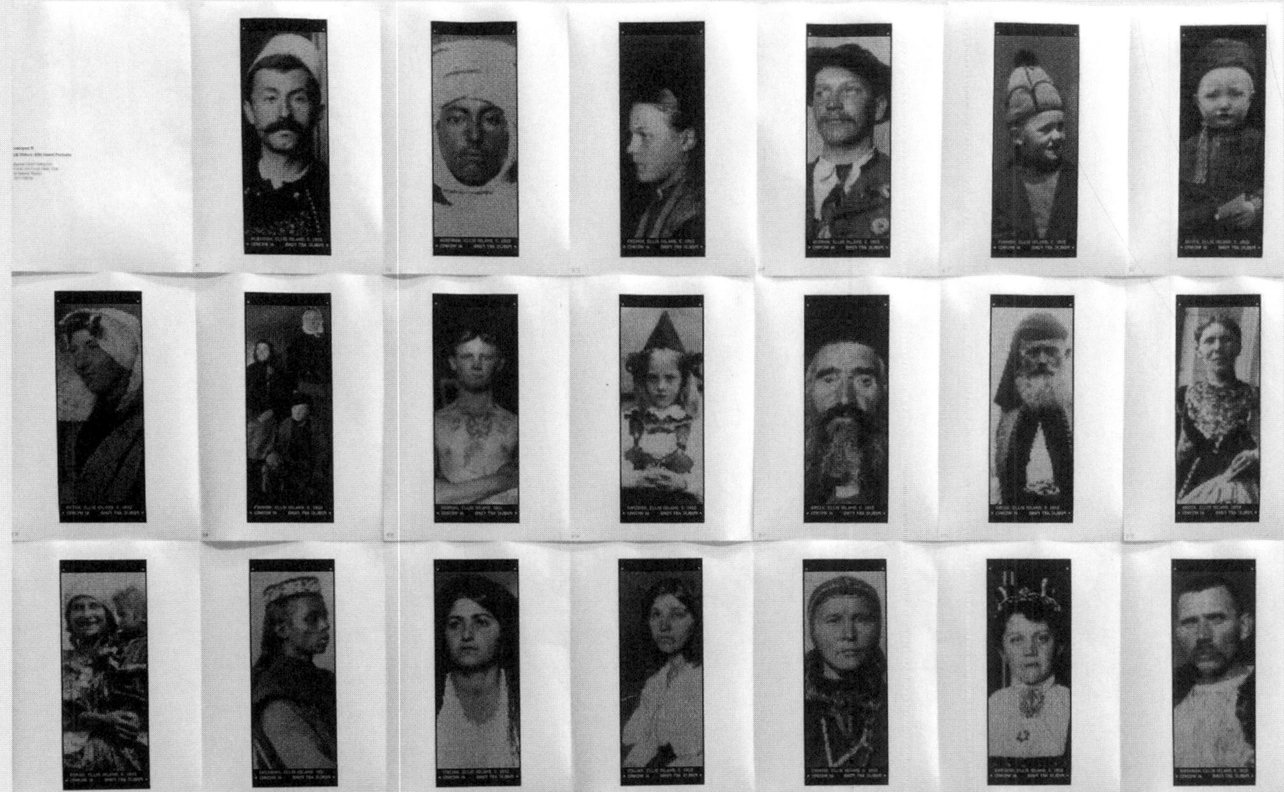

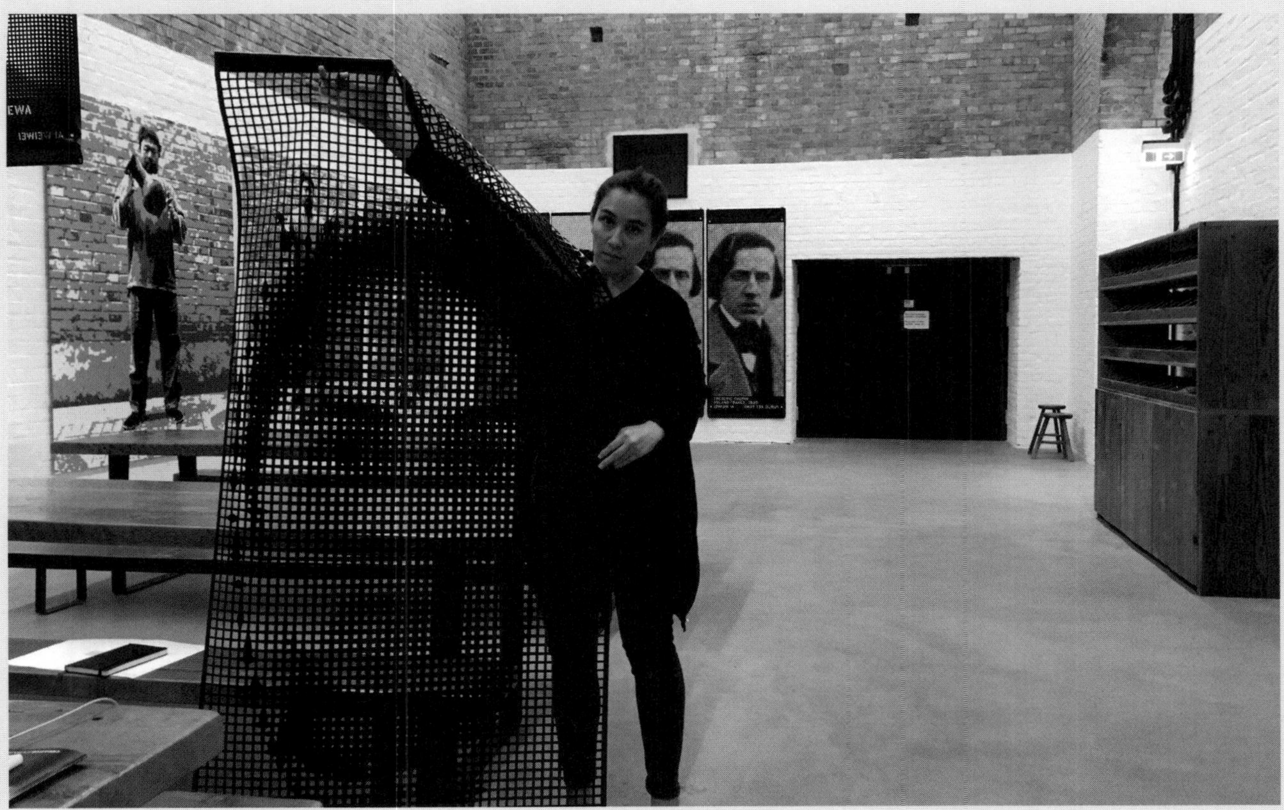

Preparing portraits for *Banners*, Ai Weiwei studio, Berlin, August 2017 (opposite, top)

Refugee, Shariya Camp, Iraq, 2015. Source photograph for *Banner 73* and *Banner 73* (detail) (opposite, bottom)

Bulletin board with Augustus Sherman portraits used for *Banners*, Ai Weiwei studio, Berlin, August 2017 (top)

Jennifer Schmachtenberg with a prototype for *Banner 73*, Ai Weiwei studio, Berlin, August 2017 (bottom)

Augustus Sherman

A group of thirty-six banners that Ai Weiwei created for this exhibition was derived from a suite of approximately 250 images made by Augustus Sherman (1865–1925, b. Lynn, Pennsylvania), an amateur photographer and bureau of immigration clerk who worked at Ellis Island between 1892 and 1925. Sherman was interested in the diverse origins of the individuals he processed, so he took it upon himself to make photographic portraits of them, often in their traditional clothing. He used a large-format camera (requiring long exposures) to document these recent arrivals to the United States' main port of immigration at the time, which processed nearly twelve million newcomers between 1892 and 1954.

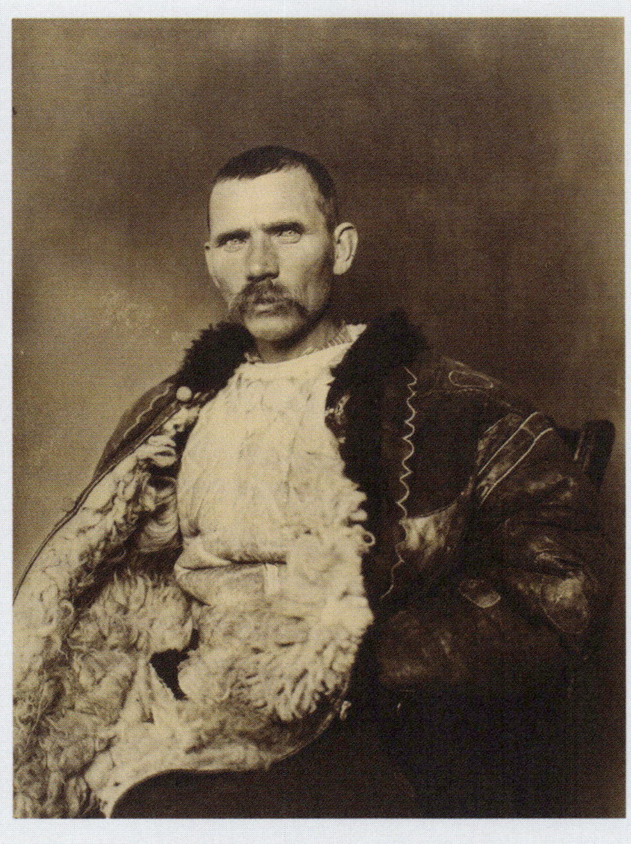

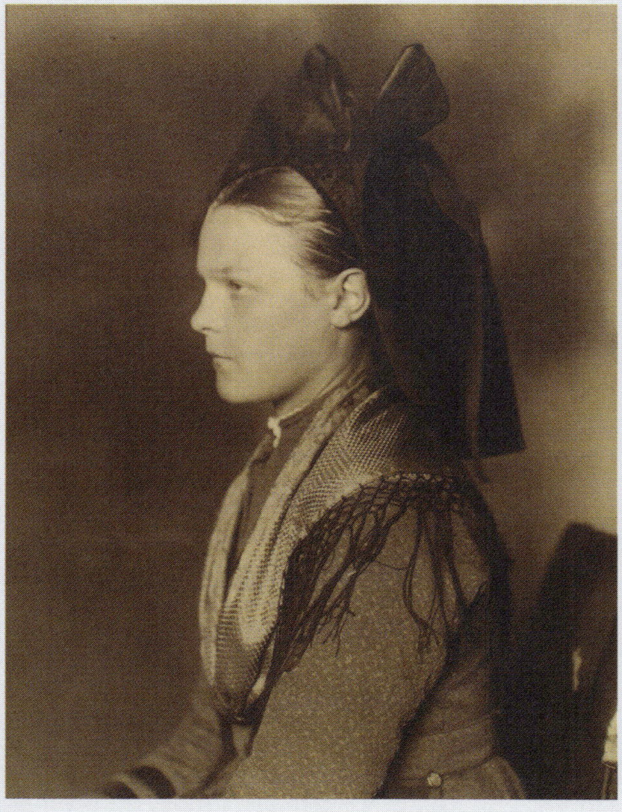

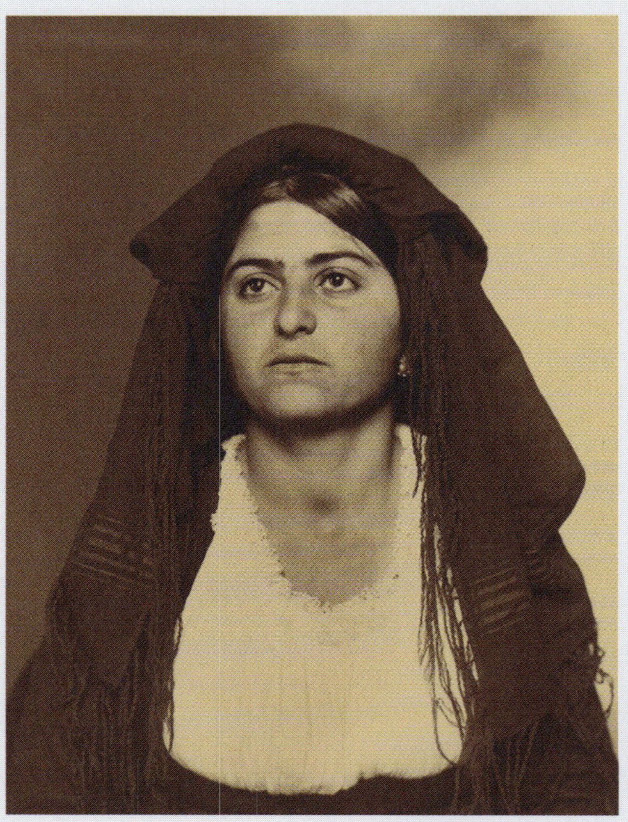

Romanian Shepherd, 1906. Source photograph for *Banner 28* (top)

Girl from Alsace-Lorraine, 1906. Source photograph for *Banner 3* (bottom left)

Italian Woman, ca. 1905–1914. Source photograph for *Banner 23* (bottom right)

Thumbu Sammy, 1911. Source photograph for *Banner 21* and *Banner 21* (opposite, top, left and right)

Laplander, 1910. Source photograph for *Banner 25* and *Banner 25* (opposite, bottom, left and right)

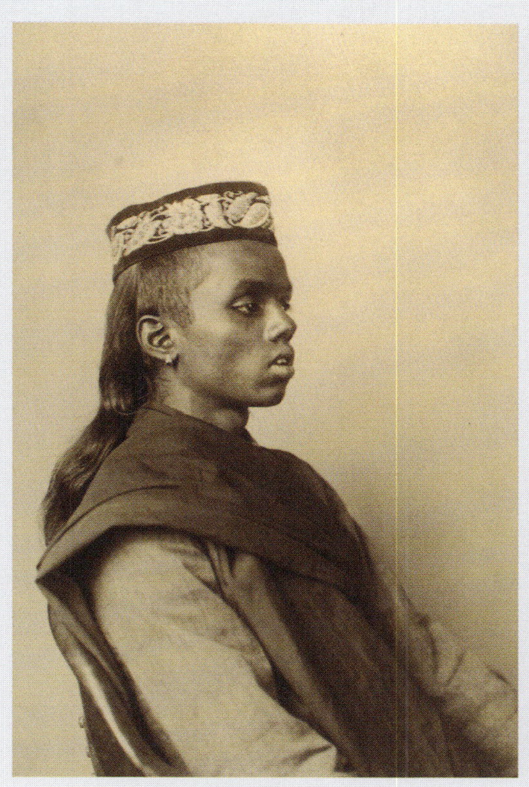

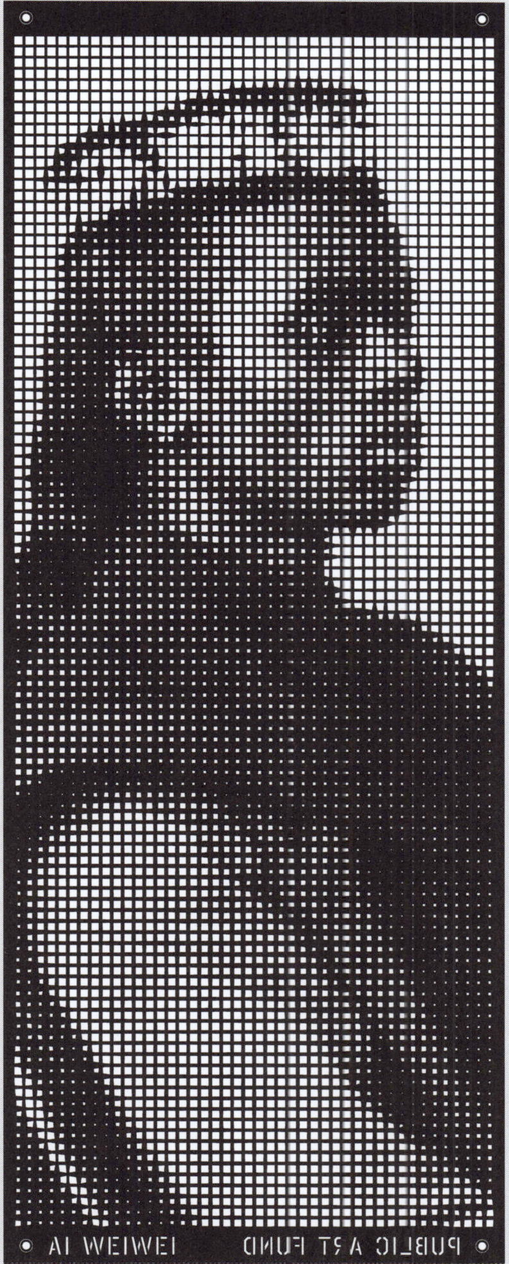

AI WEIWEI
PUBLIC ART FUND

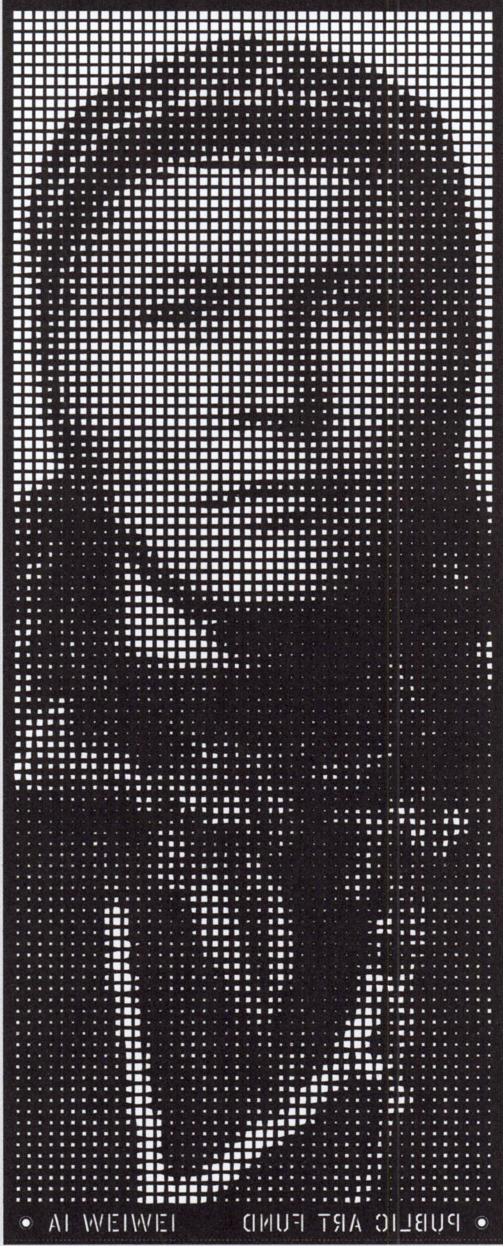

AI WEIWEI
PUBLIC ART FUND

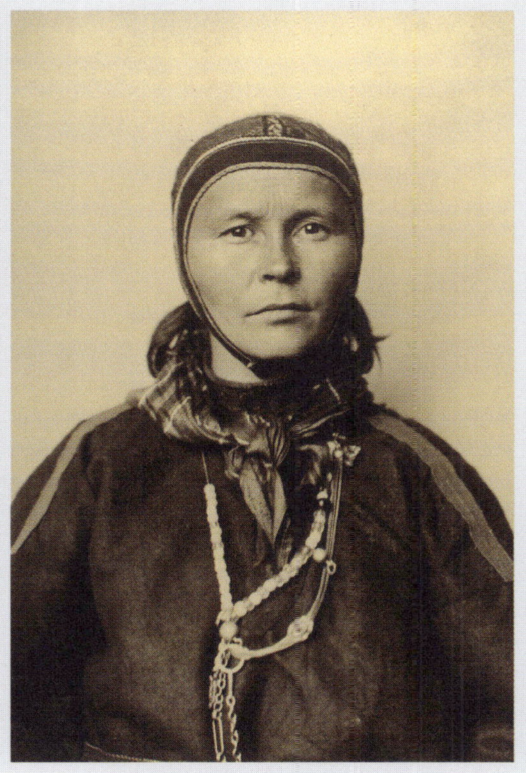

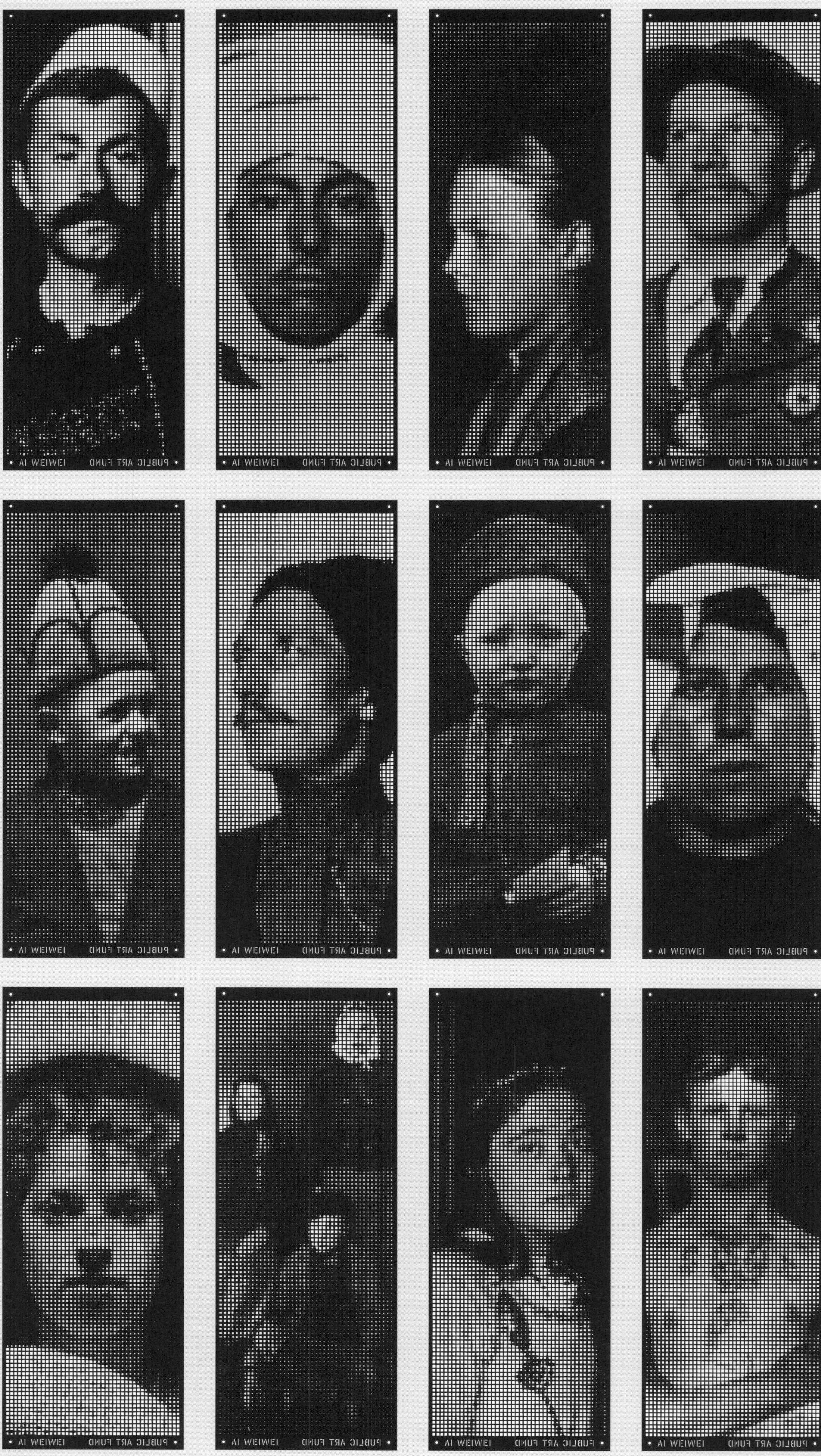
AI WEIWEI
PUBLIC ART FUND

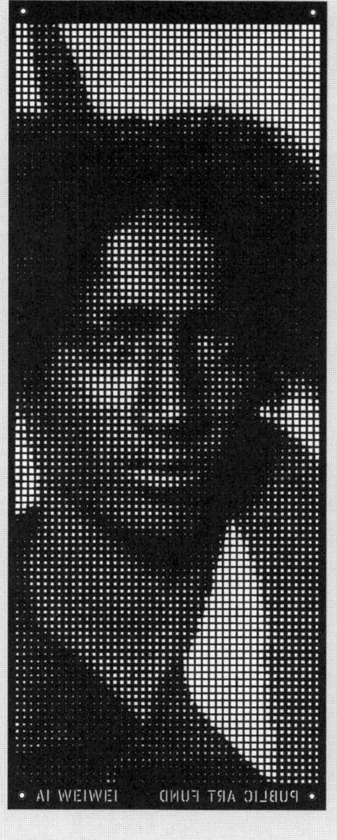

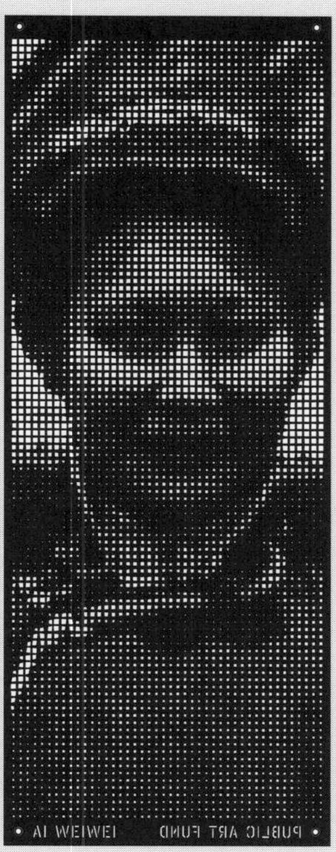

Banner 1
Albanian Soldier,
ca. 1905–1914

Banner 2
Algerian Man, ca. 1905–1914

Banner 3
Girl from Alsace-Lorraine,
1906

Banner 4
Bavarian Man, ca. 1905–1914

Banner 5
Borana Family from Southern Ethiopia (detail),
ca. 1905–1914

Banner 6
Cantonese Woman,
ca. 1905–1914

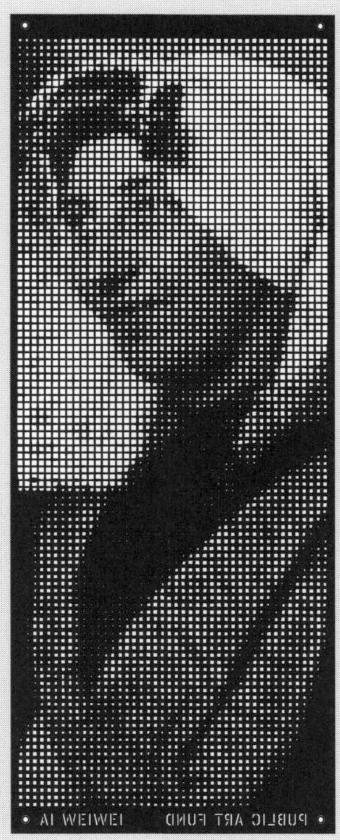

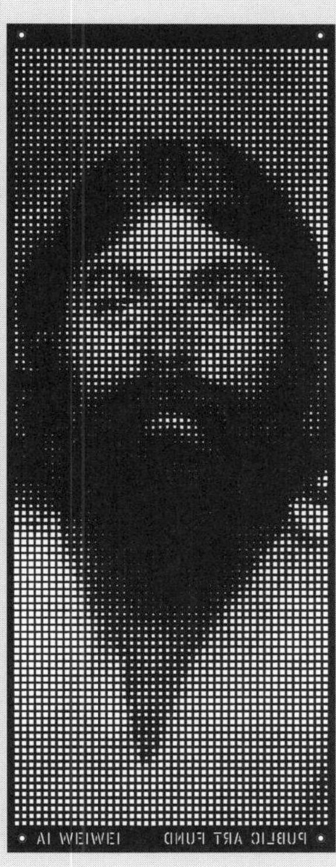

Banner 7
Lapland Children (detail),
ca. 1905–1914

Banner 8
Cossack Immigrants (detail),
ca. 1905–1914

Banner 9
Dutch Siblings from the Island of Marken Holding Religious Tracts (detail),
ca. 1905–1914

Banner 10
Mother from the Netherlands,
ca. 1905–1914

Banner 11
Protestant Woman from the Netherlands, ca. 1905–1914

Banner 12
Eleazar Kaminetzko, Russian Hebrew, Hamburg, 1914

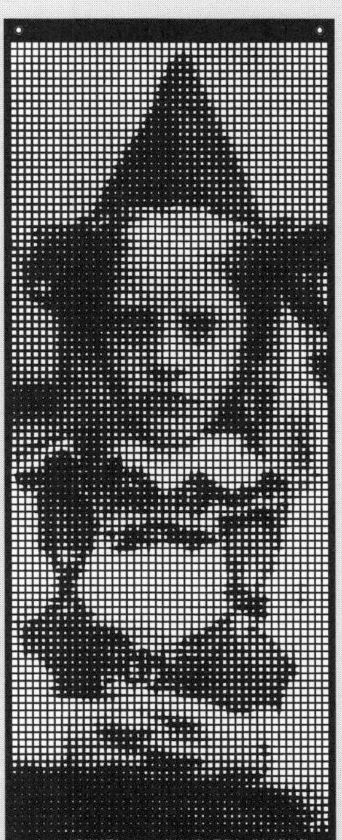

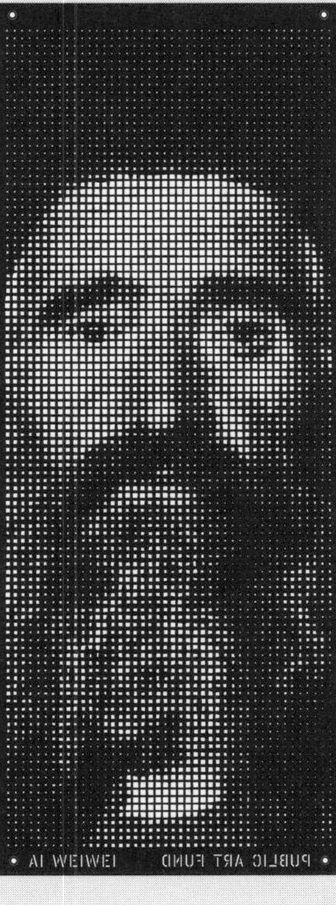

Banner 13
English Jew, ca. 1905–1914

Banner 14
Finnish Family, ca. 1905–1914

Banner 15
Finnish Girl, ca. 1905–1914

Banner 16
German Stowaway, 1911

Banner 17
Swedish Girl, ca. 1905–1914

Banner 18
Reverend Joseph Valison,
ca. 1905–1914

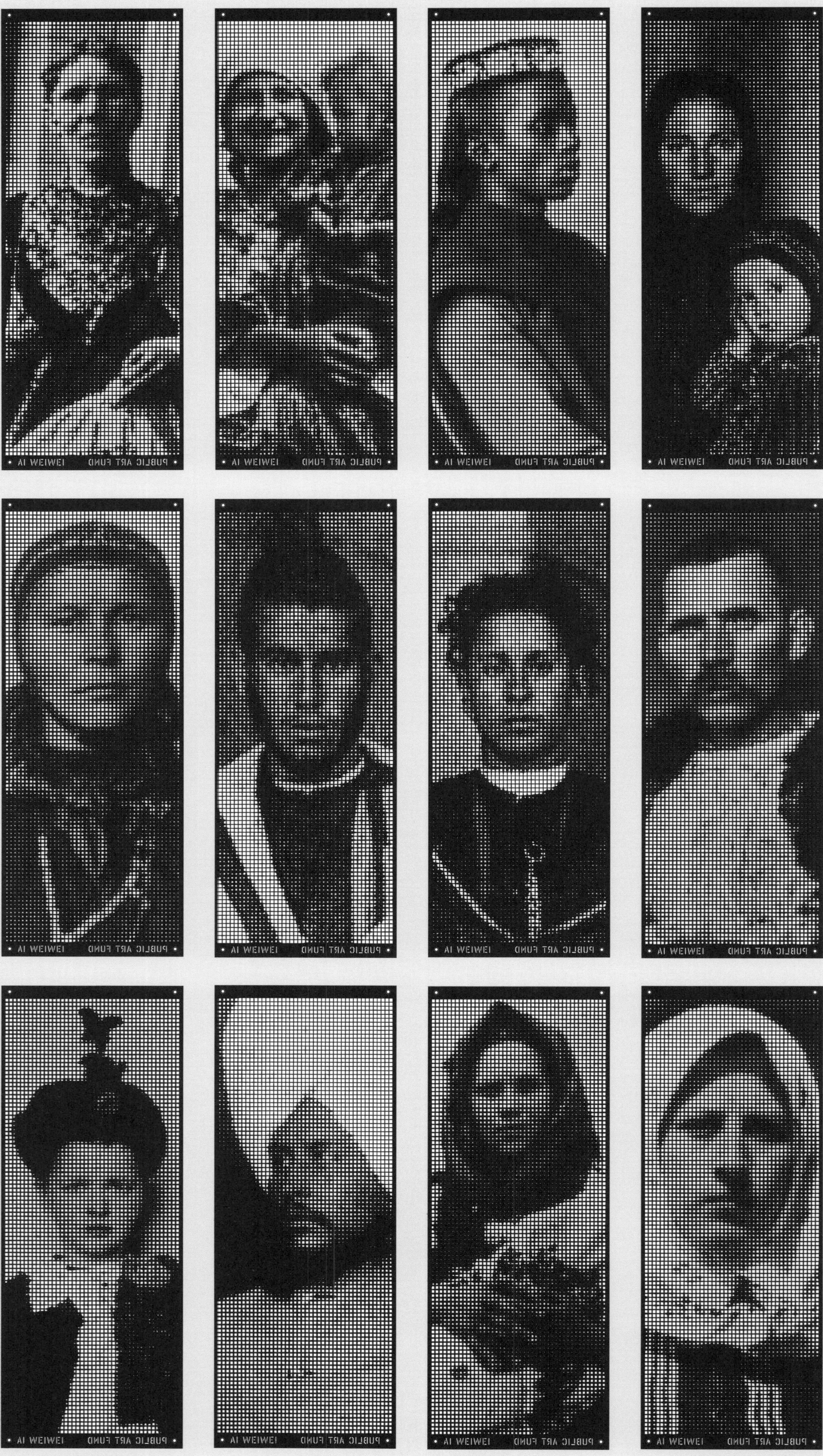

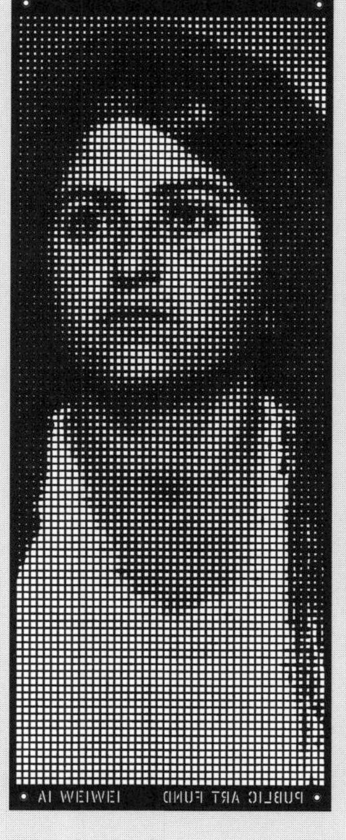

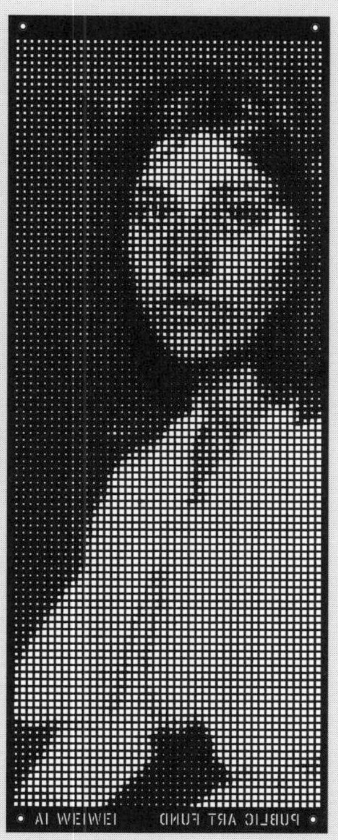

Banner 19
Greek Woman, 1909

Banner 20
Roman Family (detail), ca. 1905–1914

Banner 21
Thumbu Sammy, 1911

Banner 22
Hungarian Family (detail), ca. 1905–1914

Banner 23
Italian Woman, ca. 1905–1914

Banner 24
Italian Woman, ca. 1905–1914

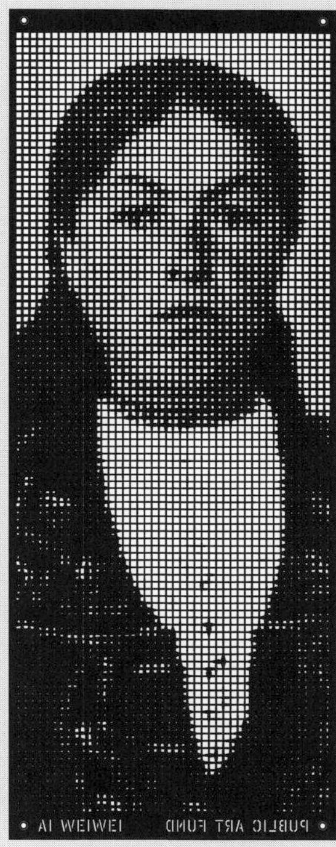

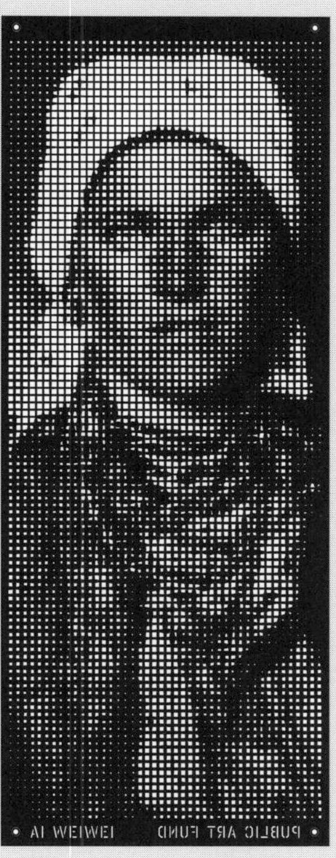

Banner 25
Laplander, ca. 1910

Banner 26
Moroccan Men and Boy (detail), ca. 1905–1914

Banner 27
Moroccan Men and Boy (detail), ca. 1905–1914

Banner 28
Romanian Shepherd, 1906

Banner 29
Romanian Woman, ca. 1905–1914

Banner 30
Ruthenian Woman, 1906

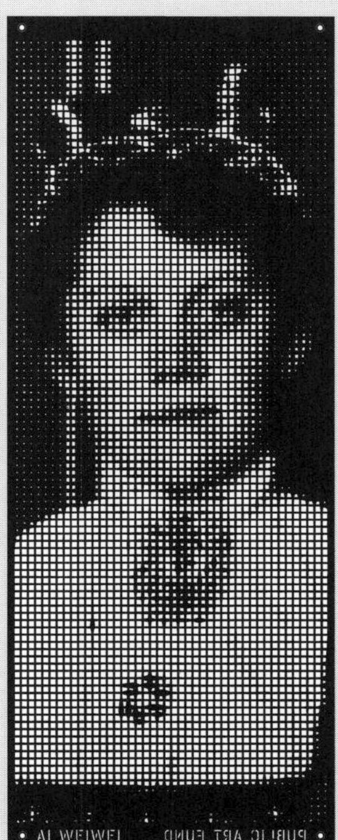

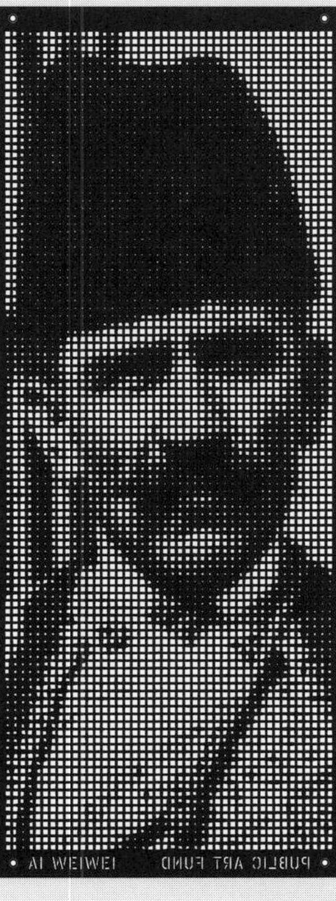

Banner 31
Scottish Girls in Kilts (detail), ca. 1905–1914

Banner 32
Sikh from India, ca. 1905–1914

Banner 33
Slovakian Mother and Her Children (detail), ca. 1905–1914

Banner 34
Slovakian Woman, ca. 1905–1914

Banner 35
Swedish Woman, ca. 1905–1914

Banner 36
Turkish Bank Guard, John Postanzi, 1912

Notable Refugees

Ai Weiwei created a selection of thirty-one banners derived from images of prominent historical figures who were displaced or persecuted for political, racial, or religious reasons. Personalities from a diverse range of fields, such as activism (Emma Goldman), art (Wassily Kandinsky), entertainment (Josephine Baker), literature (Ai Qing), philosophy (Karl Marx), religion (Dalai Lama), and science (Albert Einstein), are all linked by their shared status as refugees. Ai's distinctive banner portraits of these notable individuals, dispersed throughout the city, remind us that some of the most historically significant contributions to world culture have been made by refugees. A further two blank banners stood for unnamed refugees.

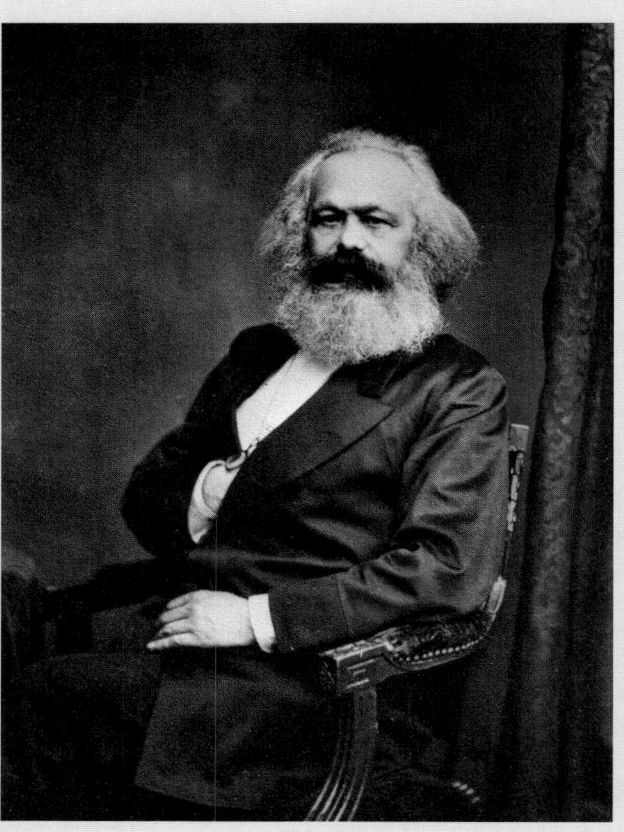

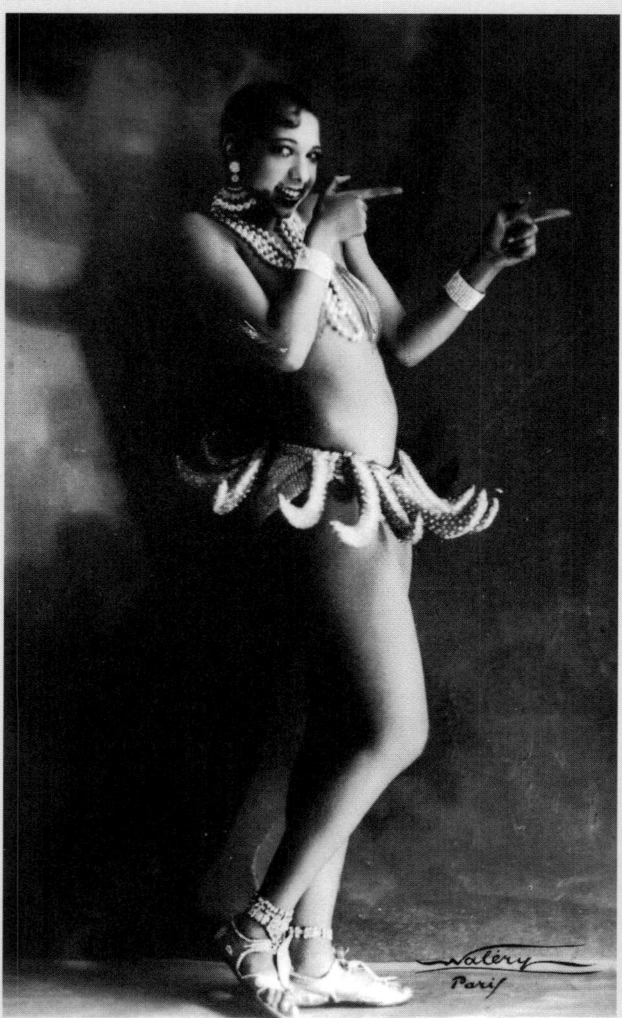

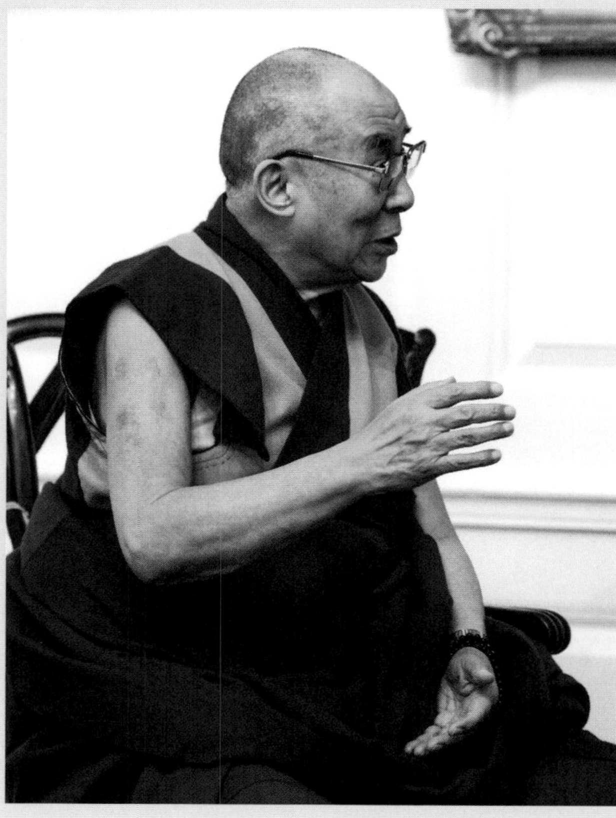

Josephine Baker, 1927. Source photograph by Lucien Waléry for *Banner 38* (bottom left)

Karl Marx, ca. 1875. Source photograph by John Jabez Edwin Mayall for *Banner 57* (top right)

The Dalai Lama, 2014. Source photograph by Pete Souza for *Banner 46* (bottom right)

Sigmund Freud, ca. 1921. Source photograph by Max Halberstadt for *Banner 50* and *Banner 50* (opposite, top left and right)

Marlene Dietrich, 1932. Source photograph by Don English for *Banner 47* and *Banner 47* (opposite, bottom left and right)

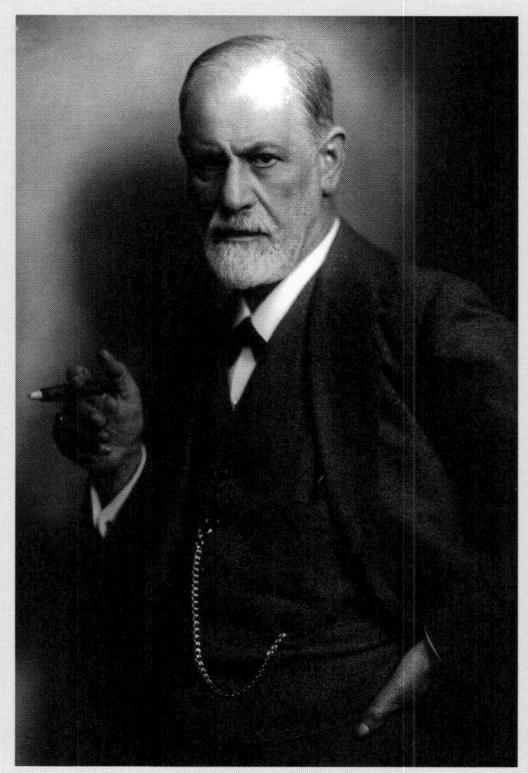

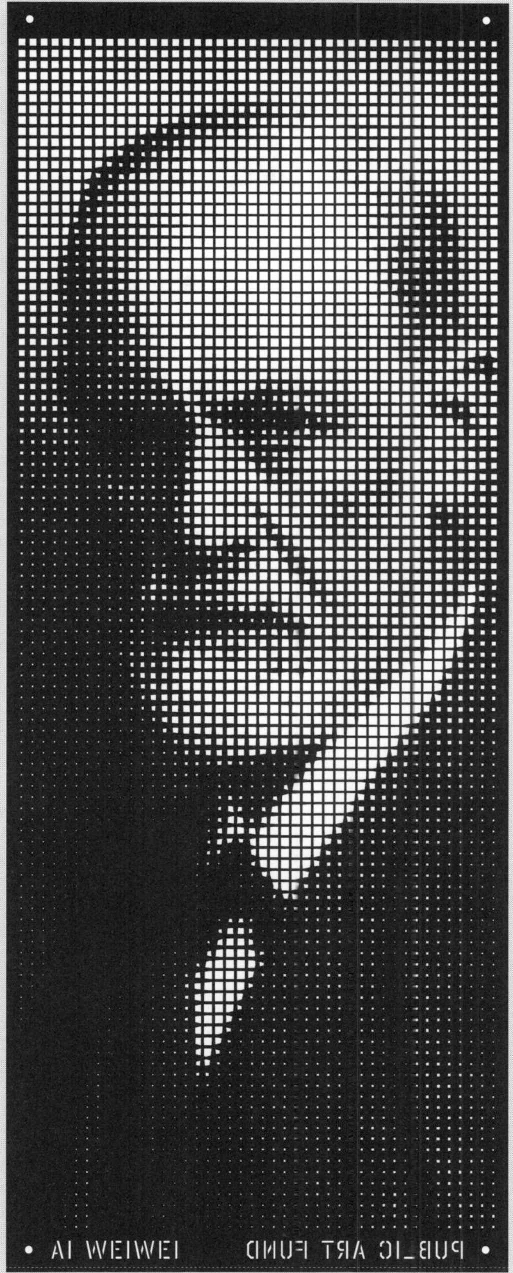
AI WEIWEI
PUBLIC ART FUND

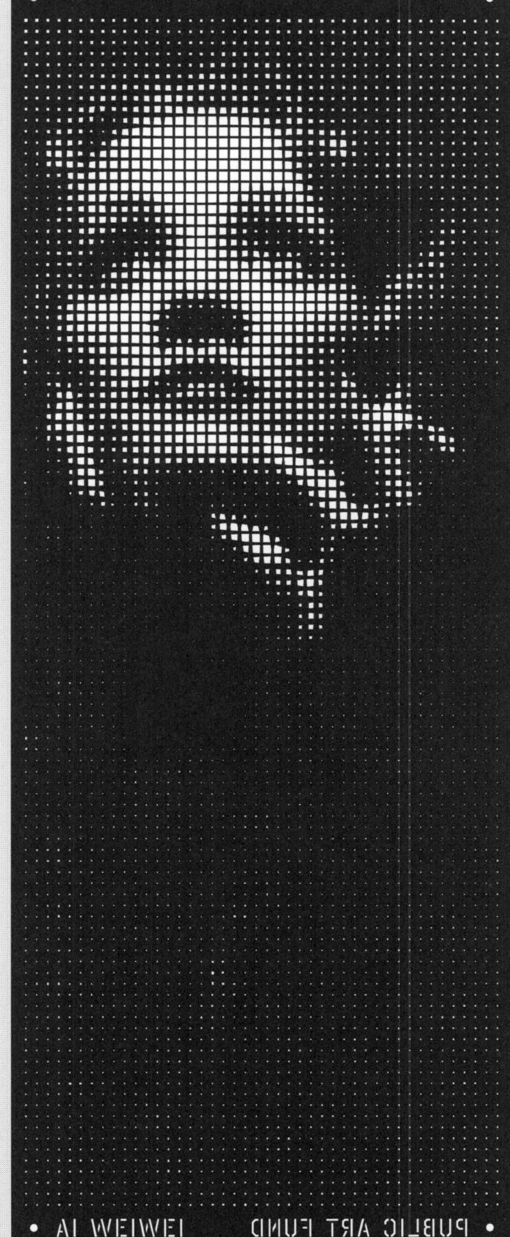
AI WEIWEI
PUBLIC ART FUND

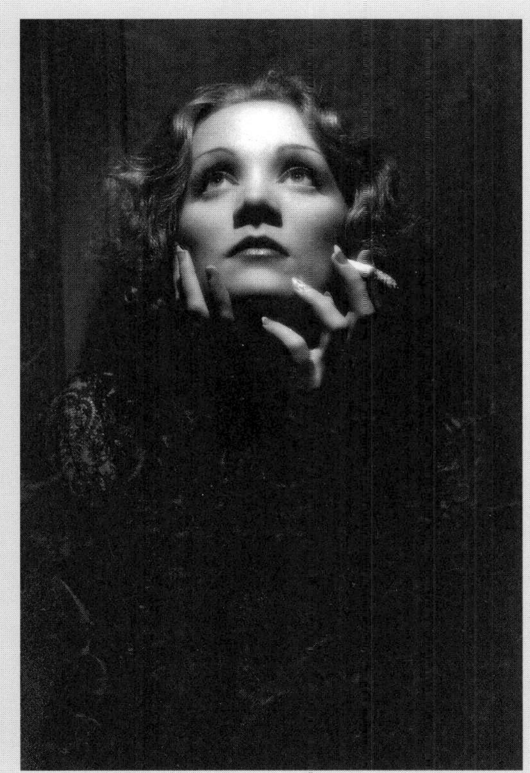

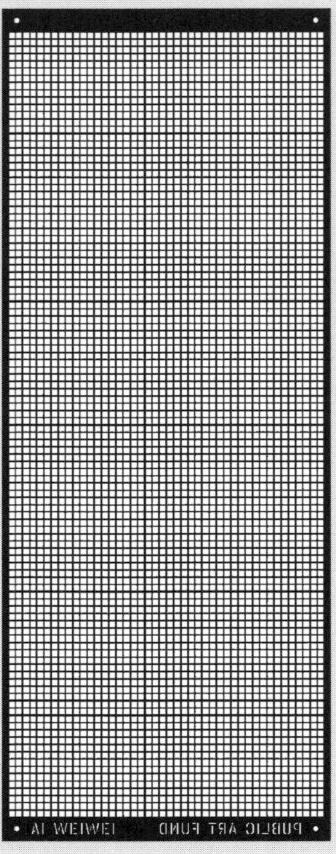

Blank

Banners 37 and 65

The exhibition included two blank banners to signify refugees who could not be named. These works also remind us that many refugees suffer political repression, censorship, and persecution, even to the point of the erasure of their identities.

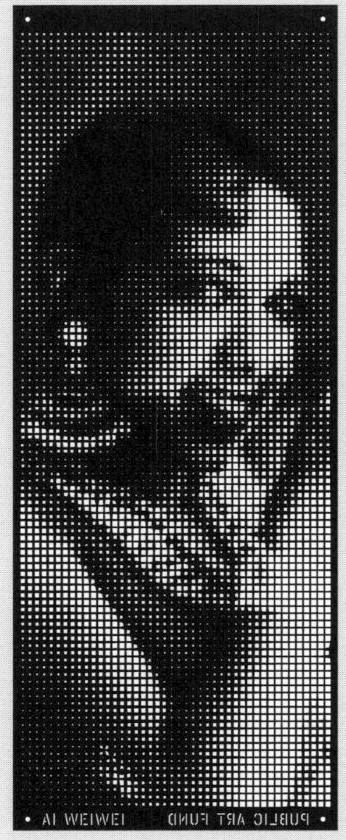

Josephine Baker, 1927

Banner 38

African American performer Josephine Baker (1906–1975, b. Saint Louis, Missouri) emigrated from the United States to Paris in the 1920s at the age of nineteen because she desired to live and work in a more integrated society than that of the early twentieth-century United States. In France, she quickly gained success and became renowned for her remarkable singing and dancing.

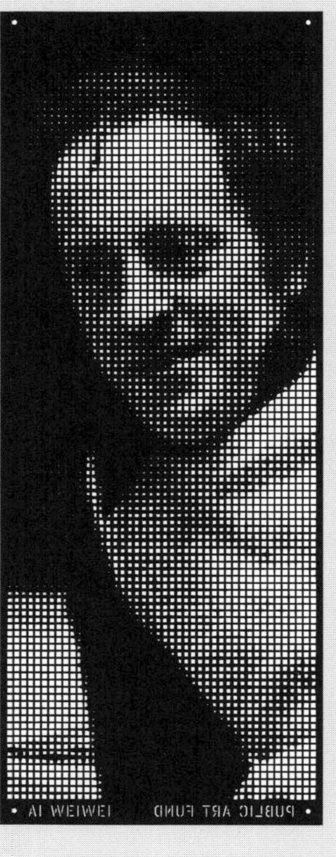

Joseph Brodsky, 1972–1973

Banner 41

Poet Joseph Brodsky (1940–1996, b. Saint Petersburg, Russia) was convicted of "social parasitism" by the Soviet authorities for his politically charged poetry and sentenced to hard labor. Though he was released after eighteen months, the government continued to persecute him. Despite mass protests in support of the author, he was forced into exile in 1972. Shortly thereafter, he moved to the United States, never to return to his home country.

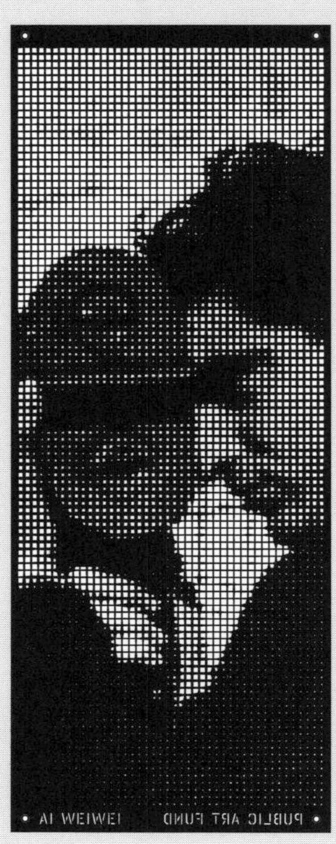

Robert Capa, 1937

Banner 42

Robert Capa (1913–1954, b. Budapest, Hungary), a Jewish photojournalist who was first exiled from Hungary at age eighteen for harboring communist sympathies, was later forced to flee Germany when the Nazis rose to power. He immigrated to Paris before settling permanently in the United States.

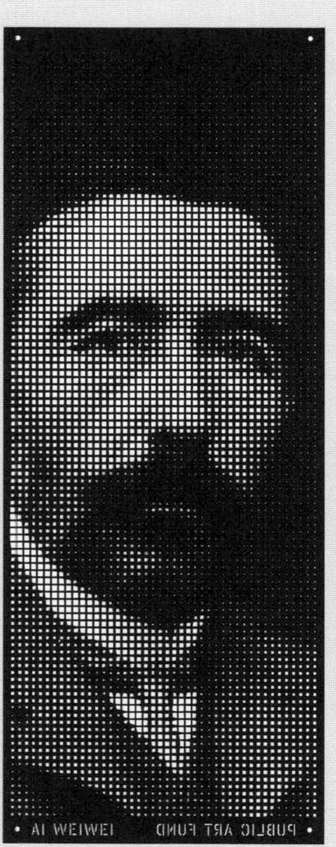

Joseph Conrad, 1904

Banner 45

Joseph Conrad (1857–1924, b. Berdychiv, Ukraine) was an early modernist novelist and author of *The Heart of Darkness*, a novella set on the Congo River that explores themes of imperialism and racism. He was an advocate for Polish independence and was exiled as a child because of his father's involvement in the November Rebellion against the Russian Empire. As an adult, Conrad chose to leave Russia and gained citizenship in England, where he turned his attention to themes of colonialism in his work.

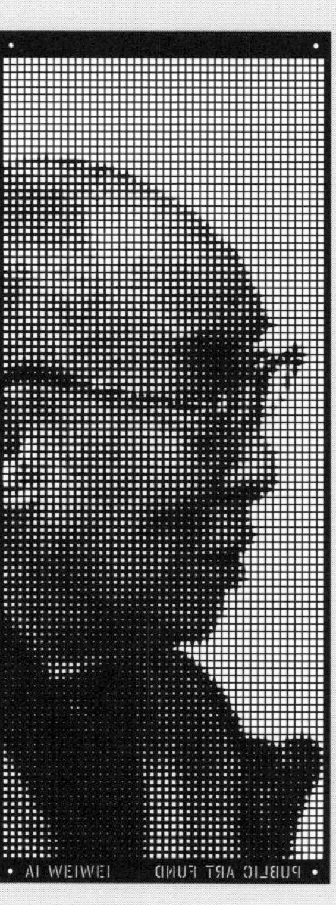

The Dalai Lama, 2014

Banner 46

His Holiness the 14th Dalai Lama (b. 1935, Taktser, Amdo, Tibet), the Nobel Peace Prize–winning spiritual leader of the Tibetan Buddhist people, was forced to flee his homeland in 1959 after the Tibetan uprising against the People's Republic of China. He sought refuge in India, where he established the Government of Tibet in Exile, and has remained in exile ever since.

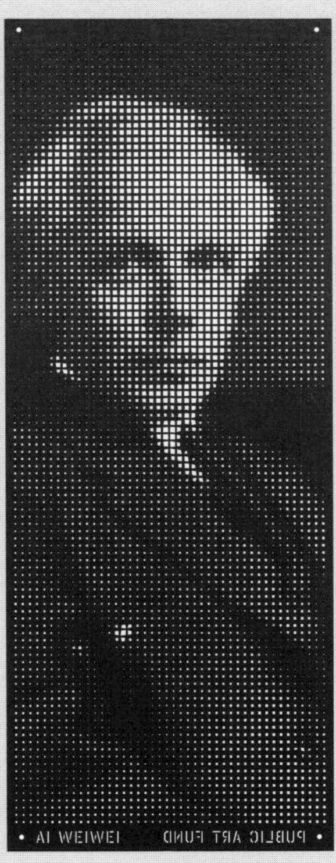

Béla Bartók, 1927

Banner 39

Béla Bartók (1881–1945, b. Nagyszentmiklós, Kingdom of Hungary, Austria-Hungary), pianist and composer, created music that is considered some of the most important of the twentieth century. Bartók's anti-fascist political views placed him in strong opposition to Hungary's alliance with Germany when the Nazis came to power, and he refused to give concerts there. His continued opposition to Hungary's government eventually led him to immigrate to the United States. He settled in New York where he remained for the rest of his life.

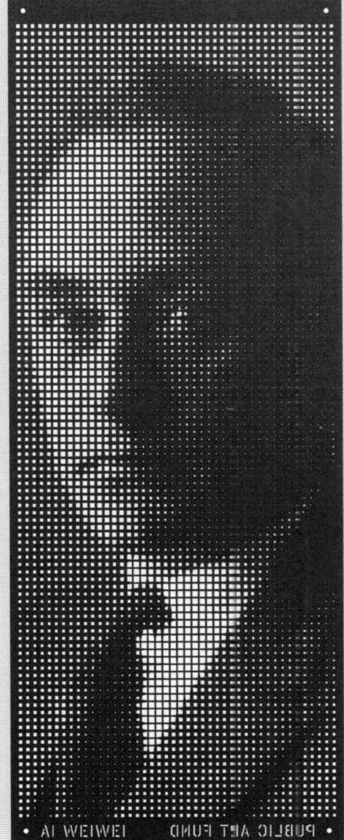

Max Born, date unknown

Banner 40

Max Born (1882–1970, b. Wrocław, Poland), Nobel Prize–winning German physicist and mathematician, was instrumental in the development of quantum mechanics. Born was forced to flee Germany when Hitler dismissed all Jews from their academic appointments and revoked their credentials in 1933. He found refuge in England, teaching at Cambridge University, and became a British citizen in 1939.

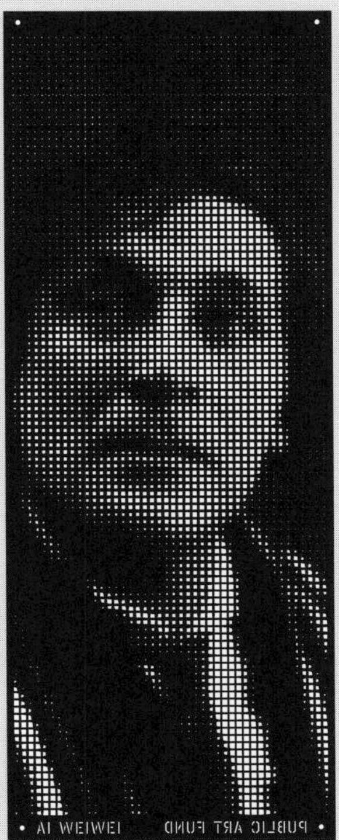

Marc Chagall, 1920

Banner 43

Marc Chagall (1887–1985, b. Liozna, Belarus), a Jewish-Russian artist famed for integrating folk culture into his art, escaped from the Soviet Union and immigrated to France in 1923. In 1941, he fled Nazi-occupied France for the United States.

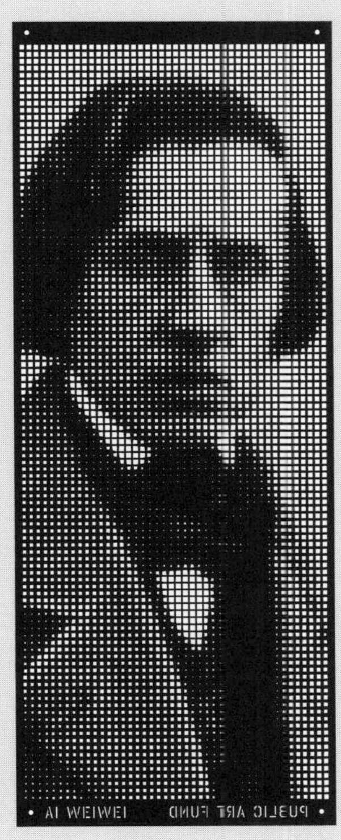

Frédéric Chopin, 1849

Banner 44

One of the leading musicians of his time, Frédéric Chopin (1810–1849, b. Żelazowa Wola, Poland) was forced to flee Poland after the 1830 November Uprising against the Russian Empire. Although he did not participate in the rebellion, he immigrated to France, fearing arrest due to his prominent position as a Polish nationalist.

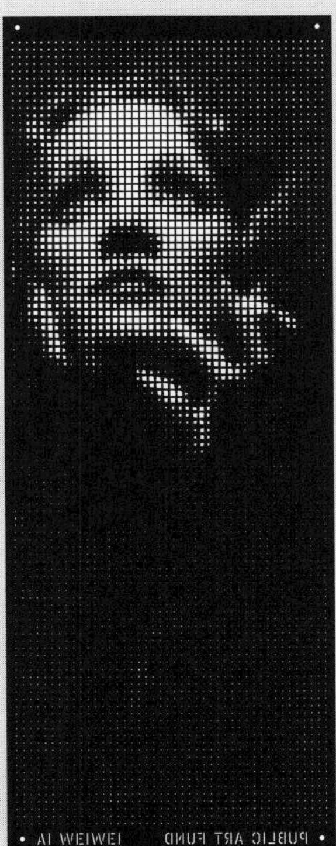

Marlene Dietrich, 1932

Banner 47

Marlene Dietrich (1901–1992, b. Schöneberg, Germany) was a German actress and singer, famed for femme fatale roles that challenged traditional notions of femininity. In 1930, Dietrich emigrated from Germany to the United States under contract with Paramount Pictures. When Nazi officials requested that she return to Germany to work on propagandist films, she refused and actively opposed the Third Reich. During World War II, Dietrich became an American citizen and contributed to the war effort by establishing a fund to aid Jewish refugees and helping the US government sell war bonds.

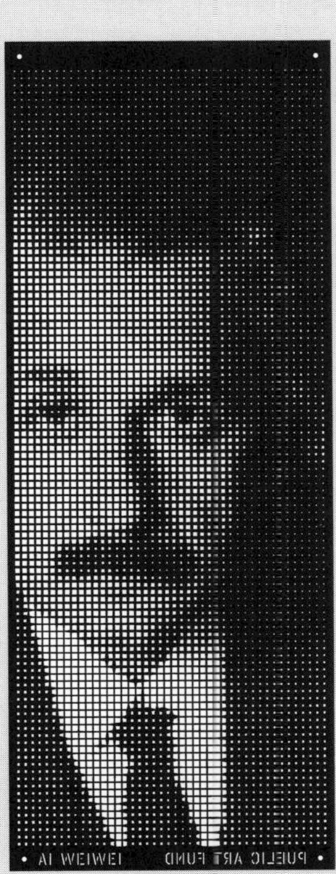

Albert Einstein, 1920

Banner 48

Albert Einstein (1879–1955, b. Ulm, Germany), the Nobel Prize–winning German theoretical physicist famed for his theory of relativity, was stripped of his academic appointment by Hitler in 1933. Forced to immigrate to the United States, he gained citizenship in 1940.

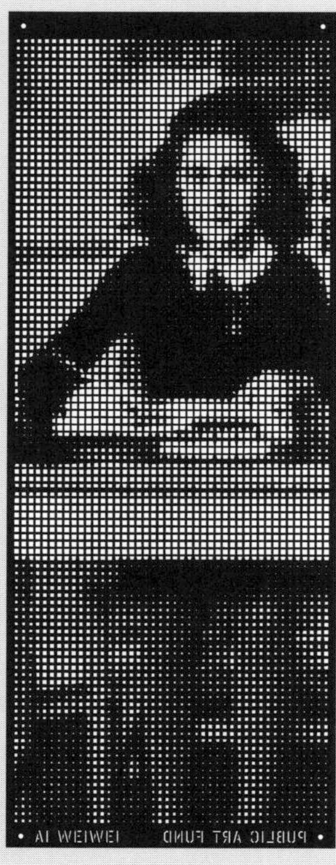

Anne Frank, 1940

Banner 49

Anne Frank's (1929–1945, b. Frankfurt, Germany) childhood diary documented her family's time in hiding in Nazi-occupied Amsterdam before they were discovered by the Gestapo and transported to concentration camps.

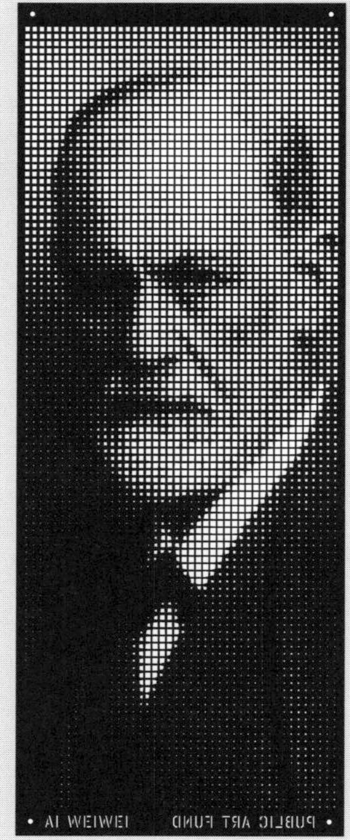

Sigmund Freud, ca. 1921

Banner 50

The founder of psychoanalysis, Sigmund Freud (1856–1939, b. Freiberg, Moravia, Austrian Empire, now Příbor, Czech Republic) was one of the most influential thinkers of the twentieth century. After years of working in Austria, he fled Vienna when the Nazis came to power. Fearing anti-Semitic persecution, Freud immigrated to London in 1938 and remained there until his death.

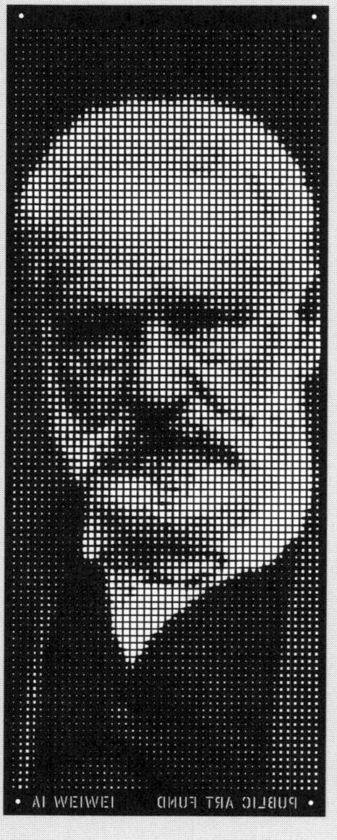

Victor Hugo, 1876

Banner 53

French novelist Victor Hugo (1802–1885, b. Besançon, France) was the author of such masterpieces as *Les Misérables* and *The Hunchback of Notre Dame*. Due to his outspoken political views, Hugo was exiled from France by Napoleon III; he remained in exile for nearly twenty years, returning to his native country only later in life.

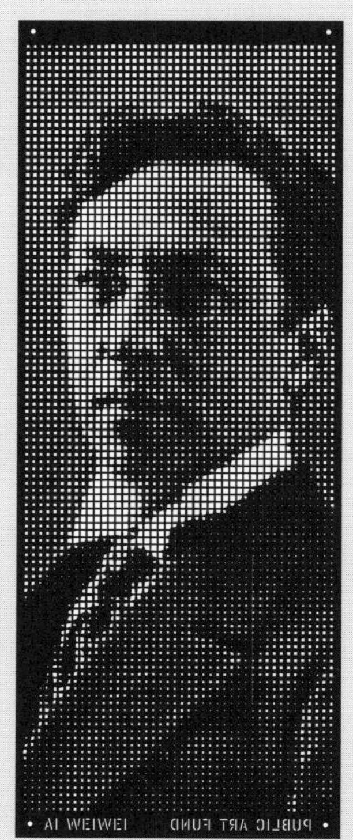

Wassily Kandinsky, 1913

Banner 54

Wassily Kandinsky (1866–1944, b. Moscow, Russia), pioneering Russian abstract painter, worked in Germany until Nazi persecution drove him to France, where he spent the remainder of his life.

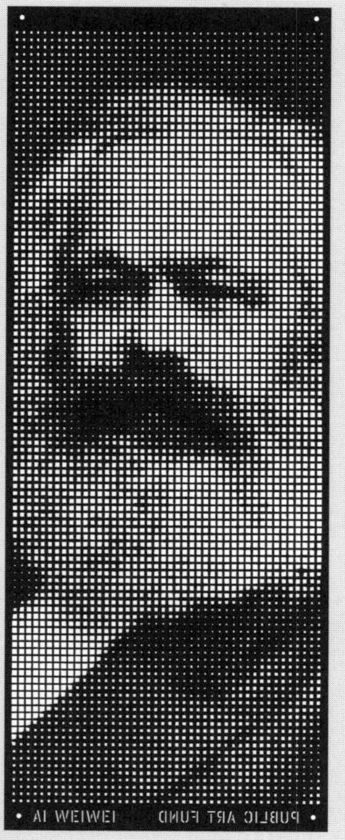

Karl Marx, ca. 1875

Banner 57

One of the most influential thinkers of the nineteenth century, Karl Marx (1818–1883, b. Trier, Germany) was a Prussian political and economic theorist and author of *The Communist Manifesto*. Despite this (or perhaps because of it), he was exiled numerous times and was stateless for most of his life. He sought refuge in Paris, Brussels, and Cologne before finally settling in London.

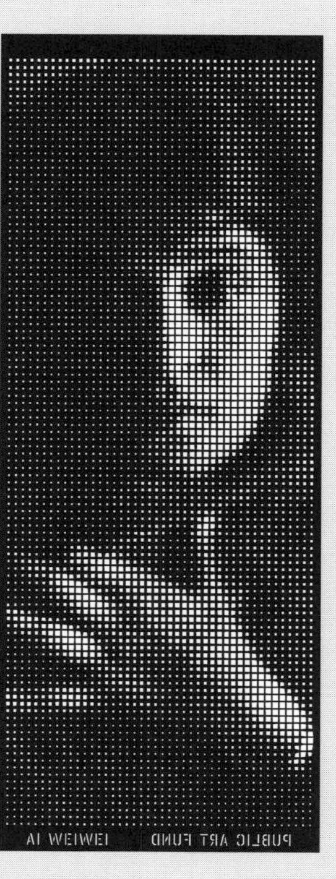

Tina Modotti, 1921

Banner 58

Tina Modotti (1896–1942, b. Udine, Italy) was a photographer, model, actress, and revolutionary. She immigrated to the United States as a teenager from Italy and later moved to Mexico City with her partner, Edward Weston, to join the artistic community centered around Frida Kahlo and Diego Rivera. An outspoken member of the Mexican Communist Party, she was exiled from Mexico, first to Berlin, next to Moscow, and then to Spain during the Spanish Civil War. She returned to Mexico in 1939 under a false identity.

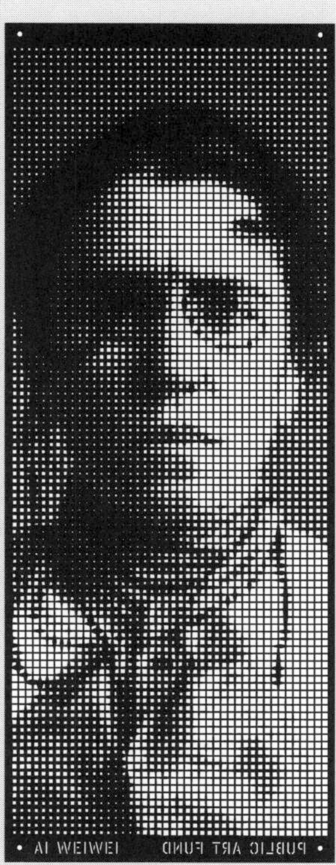

Emma Goldman, 1901

Banner 51

Emma Goldman (1869–1940, b. Kaunas, Lithuania), an anarchist and feminist political activist, immigrated to the United States from Russia in 1885 but was arrested for her outspoken condemnation of the US military draft and later deported back to Russia. While there, she grew increasingly critical of the Soviet Union and eventually left to live in England, Canada, and France.

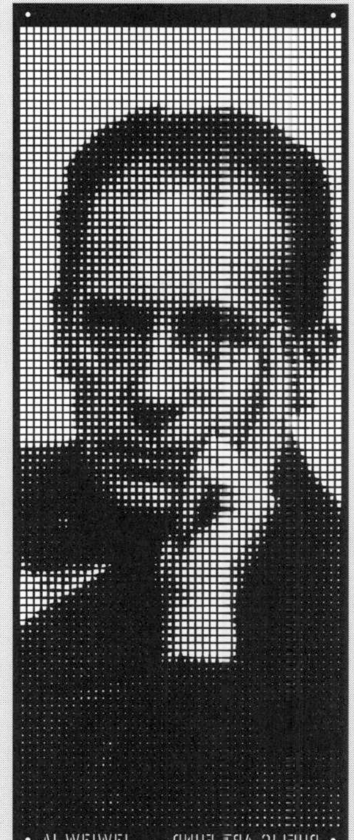

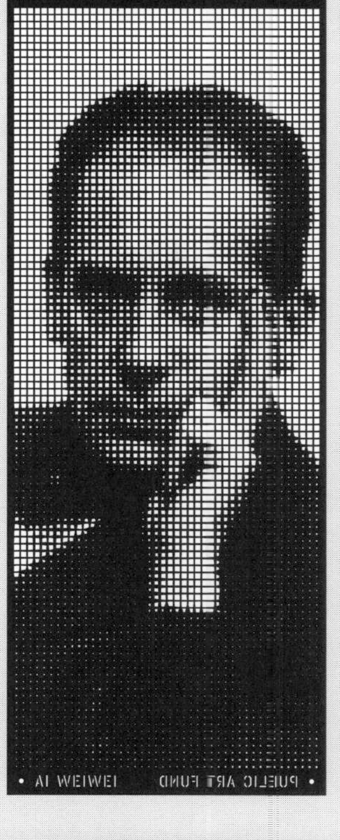

Walter Gropius, 1919

Banner 52

Walter Gropius (1883–1969, b. Berlin, Germany), groundbreaking modernist architect and founder of the interdisciplinary Bauhaus School, fled Nazi Germany and resettled in the United States, where he taught at Harvard Graduate School of Design.

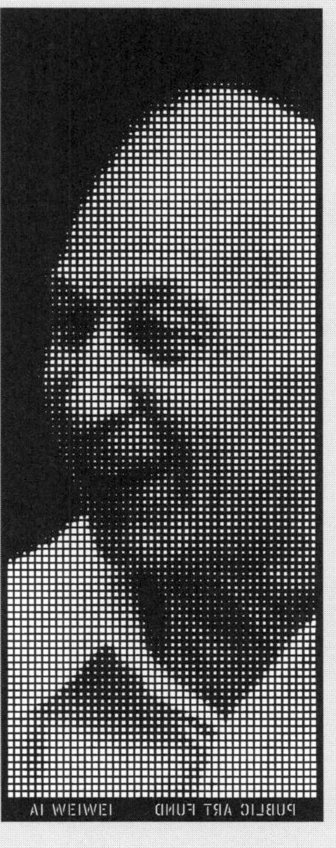

André Kertész, 1975

Banner 55

Hungarian photojournalist André Kertész (1894–1985, b. Budapest, Austria-Hungary) moved to Paris in the 1920s to join the French avant-garde artistic community. As a Jew, he feared for his safety during the Nazis' rise to power and fled to the United States in 1936.

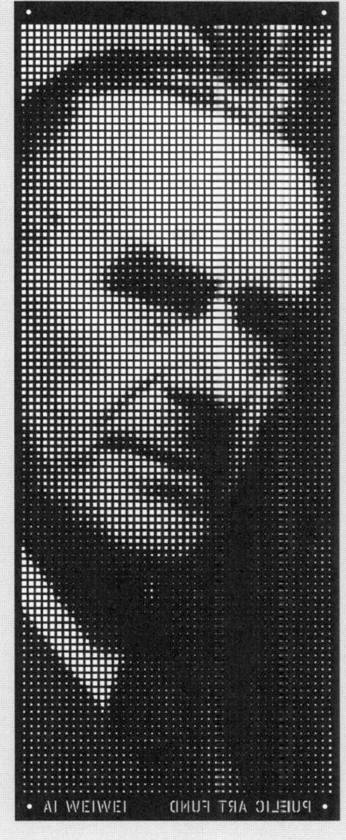

Thomas Mann, 1937

Banner 56

Thomas Mann (1875–1955, b. Free City of Lübeck, German Empire) was a Nobel Prize–winning author who fled from Germany to Switzerland and then to the United States after the Nazis came to power. During his time in exile, Mann made monthly radio broadcasts to speak out against Nazi atrocities.

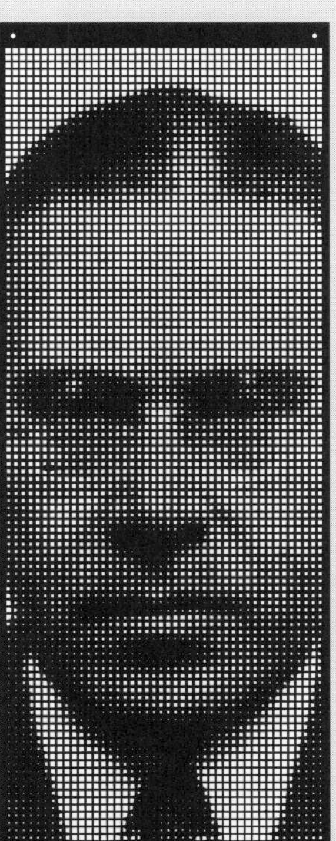

László Moholy-Nagy, 1938

Banner 59

László Moholy-Nagy (1895–1946, b. Bácsborsód, Hungary) was an artist and Bauhaus instructor who integrated art and technology. As a foreign national living in Germany when the Nazis came to power, Moholy-Nagy was stripped of his right to work. He fled first to the Netherlands and then to London. In 1937, he relocated to Chicago, where he lived until his death.

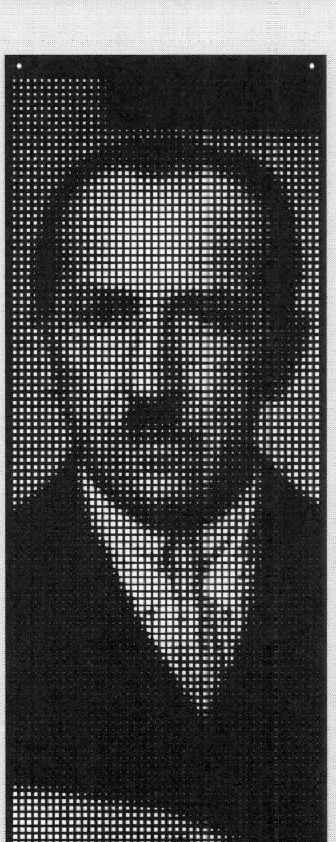

Piet Mondrian, 1926

Banner 60

Dutch De Stijl artist Piet Mondrian (1872–1944, b. Amersfoort, Netherlands) moved to Paris in 1911 to pursue his artistic career but fled to London in 1938 and then New York when the specter of World War II loomed over Europe.

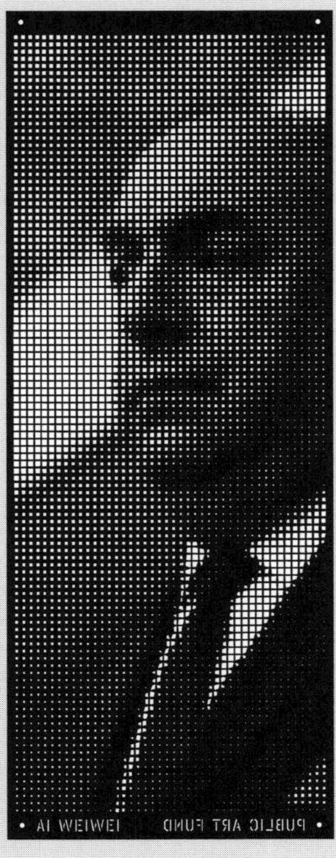

Pablo Neruda, 1936

Banner 61

The Nobel Laureate Chilean poet and politician Pablo Neruda (1904–1973, b. Parral, Chile) was forced to go into hiding before fleeing to Argentina due to his prominent role in the Communist Party. He was able to return to Chile under Socialist rule, but circumstances surrounding his death after Augusto Pinochet's coup raise questions about whether Neruda's death might have been the result of his political views.

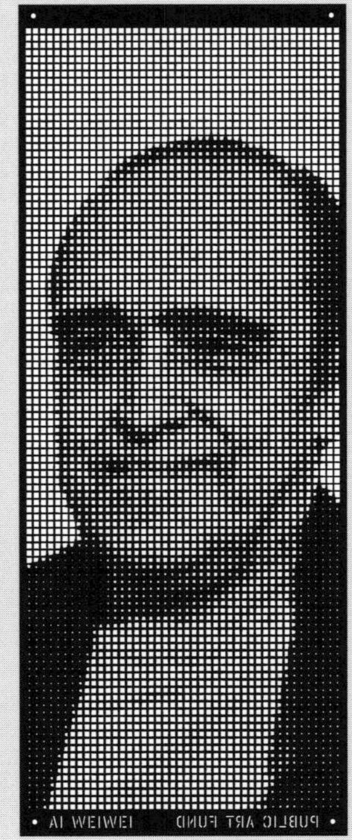

Oscar Niemeyer, ca. 1950

Banner 62

Oscar Niemeyer (1907–2012, b. Rio de Janeiro, Brazil), the Pritzker Prize–winning Brazilian architect, was forced to live in exile in Paris for nearly twenty years because of his outspoken support of the Communist Party. Niemeyer was able to return to his home country after the restoration of civil government.

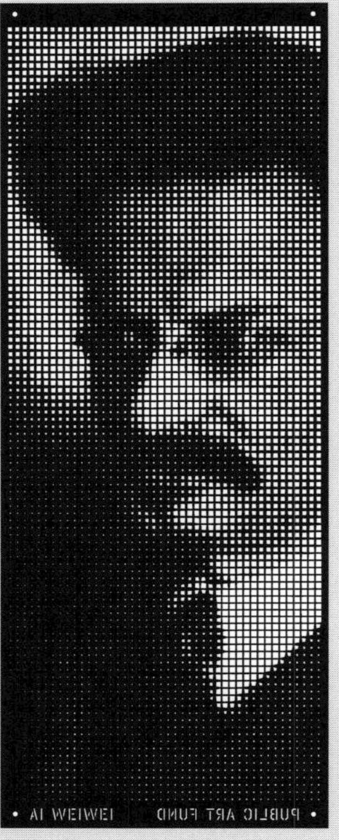

Leon Trotsky, 1920

Banner 66

Leon Trotsky (1879–1940, b. Bereslavka, Ukraine), Marxist revolutionary and Communist politician, was exiled from the Soviet Union by Joseph Stalin after attempting to lead an oppositional faction against Stalin's authority. He sought refuge in Turkey, France, Norway, and finally Mexico, where he was assassinated by the NKVD, or Soviet secret police, in 1940.

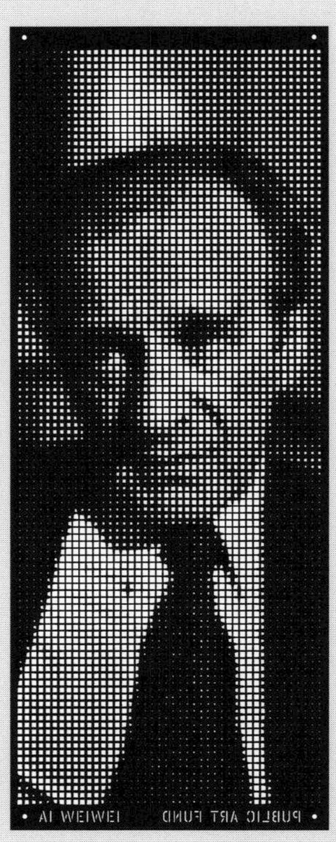

Elie Wiesel, 1987

Banner 67

The writer, activist, professor, and Nobel Laureate Elie Wiesel (1928–2016, b. Sighet [now Sighetu Marmaţiei], Romania) survived Nazi persecution and Buchenwald concentration camp and fled to France after liberation. Wiesel eventually immigrated to the United States where he shared with the public his experiences during the Holocaust and advocated for tolerance and justice in the postwar period.

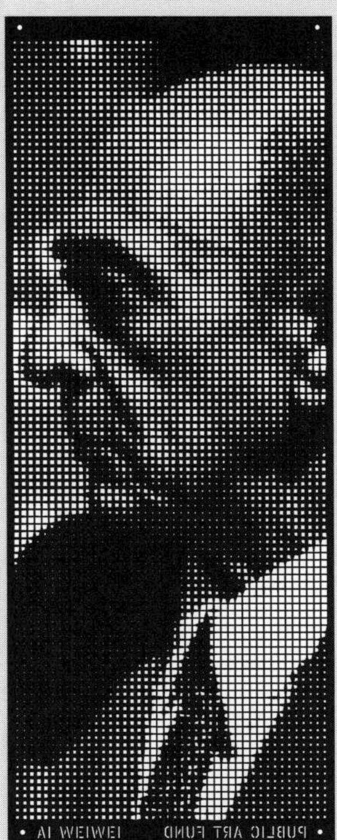

Arnold Schoenberg, 1948

Banner 63

Austrian modernist composer, musician, and painter Arnold Schoenberg (1874–1951, b. Vienna, Austria) taught at the Prussian Academy of Arts in Berlin. However, when the Nazis came to power and his twelve-tone-technique compositions were labeled "degenerate music," Schoenberg fled to the United States.

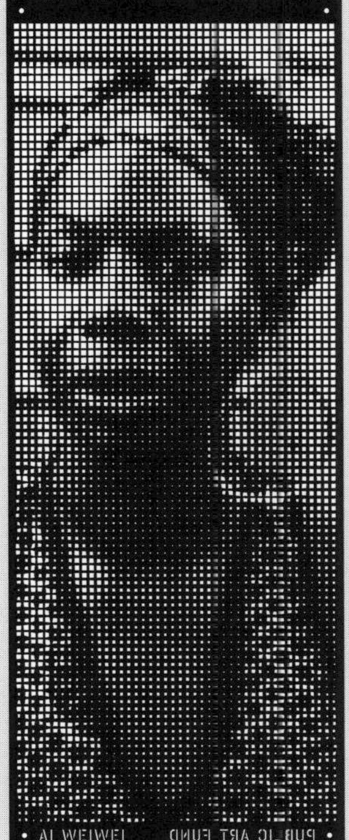

Nina Simone, 1969

Banner 64

Nina Simone (1933–2003, b. Tryon, North Carolina) was an American singer, pianist, and civil rights activist. Her experiences of racism in her home country led her to emigrate from the United States to Barbados, England, Liberia, Switzerland, and the Netherlands. She finally settled in France to escape a US arrest warrant for tax evasion—her form of protest against the Vietnam War.

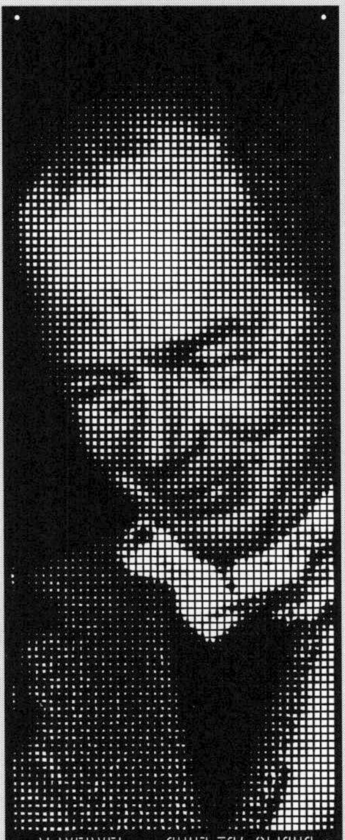

Billy Wilder, ca. 1950

Banner 68

Billy Wilder (1906–2002, b. Sucha Beskidzka, Poland) was a director, producer, and screenwriter who created such memorable films as *The Seven Year Itch*, *Some Like It Hot*, and *Sunset Boulevard*. Wilder, fearing anti-Semitism, fled Berlin, where he was working as a screenwriter, for Paris during the Nazis' rise to power. He then immigrated to the United States in 1933, seeking further refuge and opportunities to advance his career as a filmmaker in Hollywood.

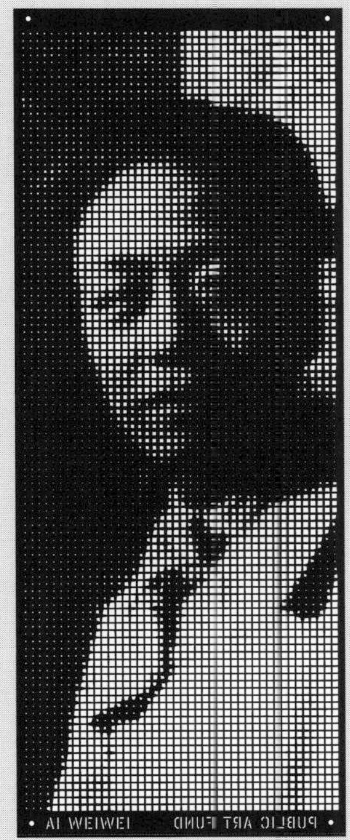

Ai Qing, 1929

Banner 69

One of the foremost Chinese modernist poets, Ai Qing (1910–1996, b. Jiang Zhenghan) was exiled with his family (including his son, Ai Weiwei) to Shihezi, Xinjiang Province, in northwestern China. During the Cultural Revolution (1966–1976), Ai Qing was forced to perform hard labor and clean public toilets.

Contemporary Refugees

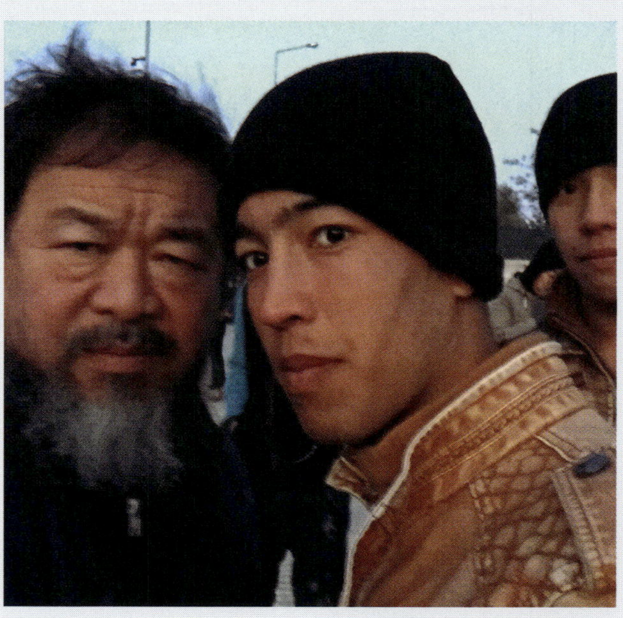

Ai Wewei with refugees in Moria Camp, Lesvos, Greece, 2015 (above)

Refugees, Dadaab Camp, Kenya, 2016. Source image for *Banner 200* and *Banner 200* (opposite, top, left and right)

Refugee, Shariya Camp, Iraq, 2015. Source image for *Banner 77* and *Banner 77* (opposite, bottom, left and right)

Ai Weiwei created 131 banners derived from images taken during his team's visits to refugee camps and national borders over a two-year period during preparations for *Human Flow*, his acclaimed documentary film on the severity of the global refugee crisis. Ai's team traveled to more than twenty countries, recording living conditions for refugees with a variety of technologies including cameras, iPhones, and drones. The extensively researched project underscores the fact that wars between states, ethnic conflicts, economic hardships, and flights from repression have all led to the displacement of more sixty-eight million people globally. Photographs that Ai and his studio took on these travels were used as source material for his banners.

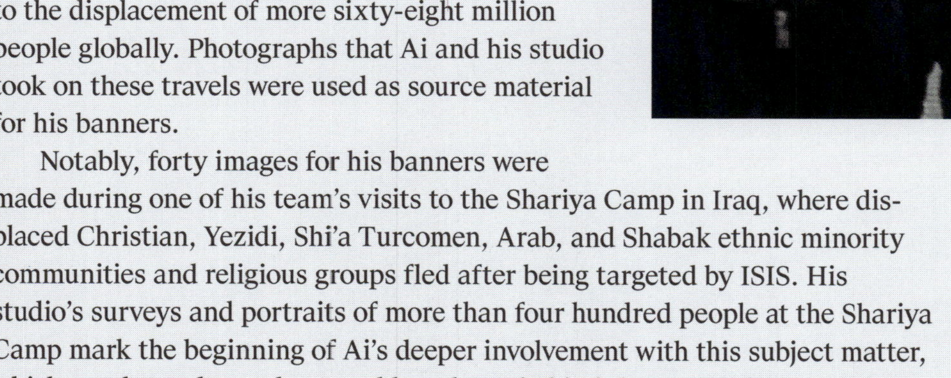

Notably, forty images for his banners were made during one of his team's visits to the Shariya Camp in Iraq, where displaced Christian, Yezidi, Shi'a Turcomen, Arab, and Shabak ethnic minority communities and religious groups fled after being targeted by ISIS. His studio's surveys and portraits of more than four hundred people at the Shariya Camp mark the beginning of Ai's deeper involvement with this subject matter, which accelerated once he was able to leave behind the oppressive conditions he faced in China.

Fifty banners are portraits that depict refugees in camps in Greece. The island of Lesvos has served as the entry point into Europe for hundreds of thousands of refugees fleeing Afghanistan, Iraq, Pakistan, Senegal, Syria, Somalia, Cameroon, and elsewhere. Most of those who reach Lesvos, after making the perilous journey across the narrow strait that separates the island from Turkey, end up at the Moria Camp, where their asylum paperwork is processed. Formerly a detention center, Moria Camp was turned into an official refugee camp in March 2015 and was intended to accommodate only 1,500 people; at its most crowded, the camp's population grows to approximately 5,000 refugees awaiting asylum. Other banners feature refugees from Greece's largest unofficial refugee camp in Idomeni, located at the informal pedestrian border crossing on the Greek-Macedonian border, established in 2014. After Macedonia closed its border to immigrants in March 2016, the camp's population peaked at more than 14,000 refugees before closing later that year.

Other banner portraits depict refugees from the Dadaab Camp in Garissa County, Kenya, the world's largest refugee camp. This camp, established in 1991, has a population of 350,000, far exceeding its planned capacity of 90,000. These refugees are primarily from Somalia and the Democratic Republic of the Congo. Citing reasons of national security, authorities have threatened to close the camp, which would displace hundreds of thousands of individuals and families, forcing many to return to war-torn Somalia. Additional source photographs were taken in Germany, Jordan, Lebanon, Palestine, and Turkey.

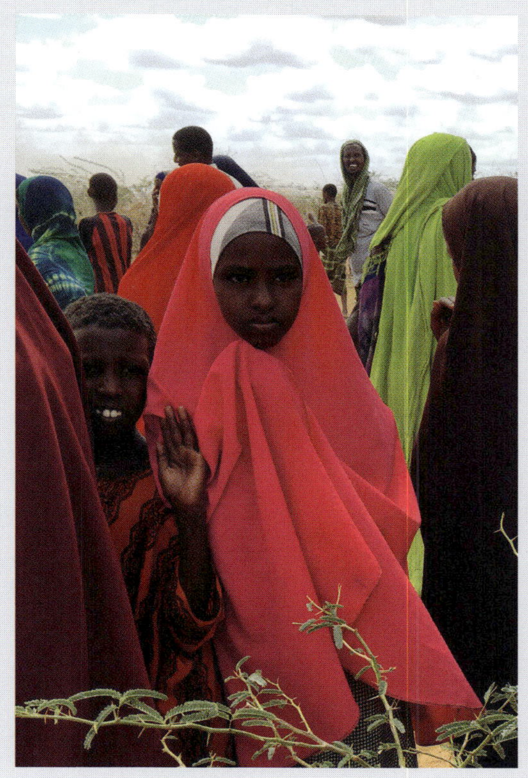

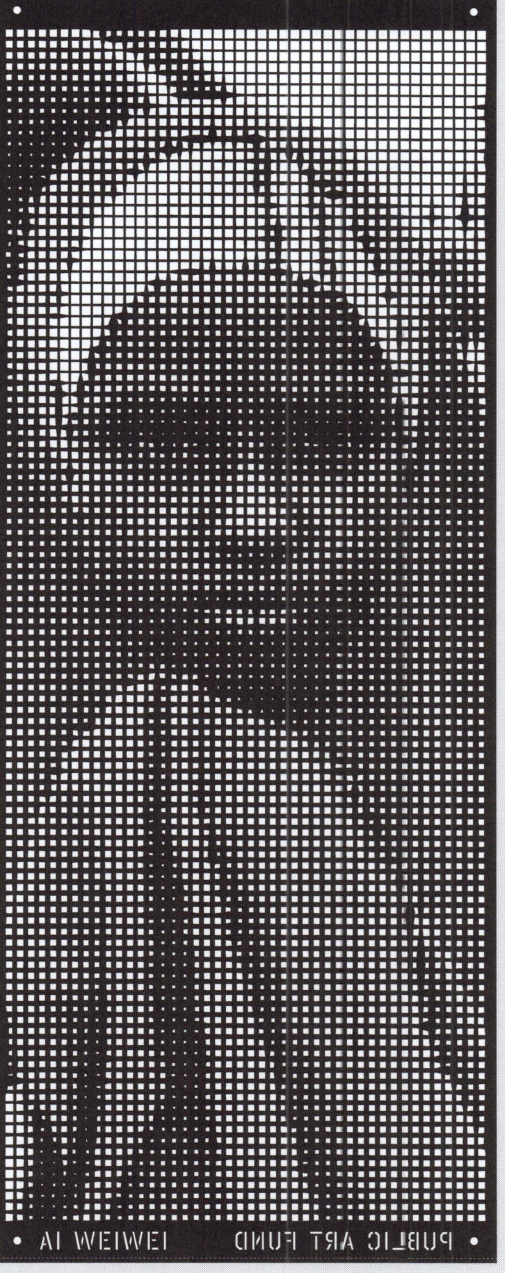
AI WEIWEI
PUBLIC ART FUND

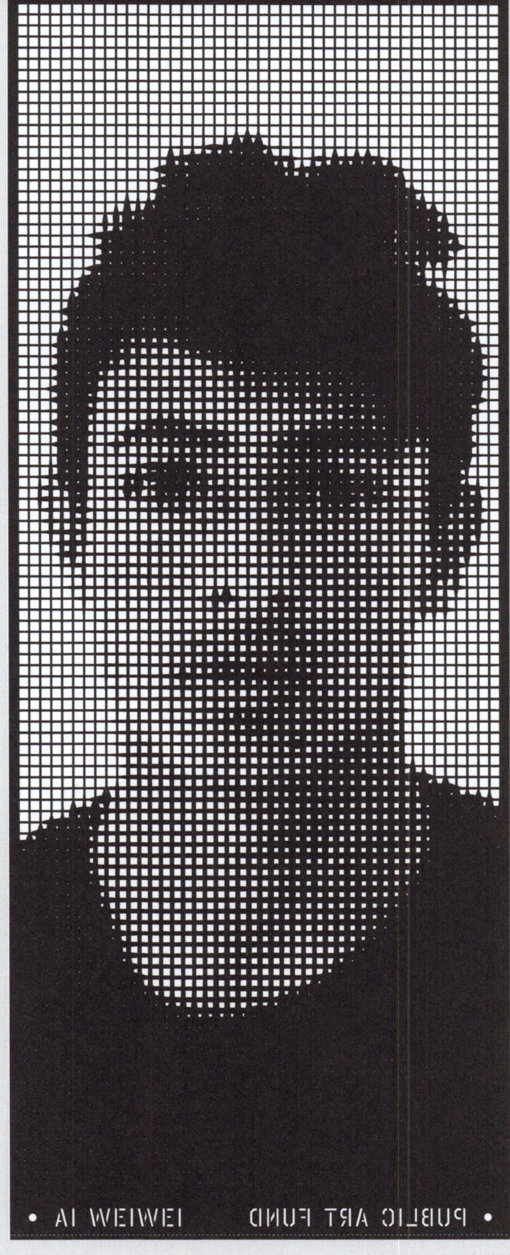
AI WEIWEI
PUBLIC ART FUND

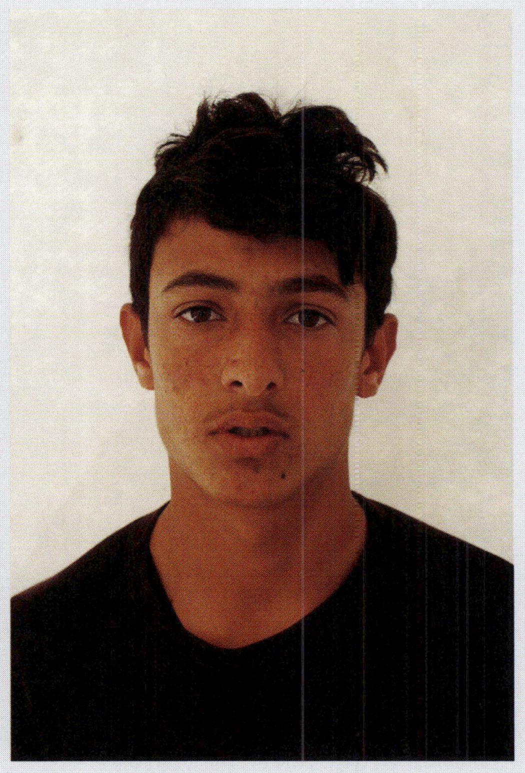

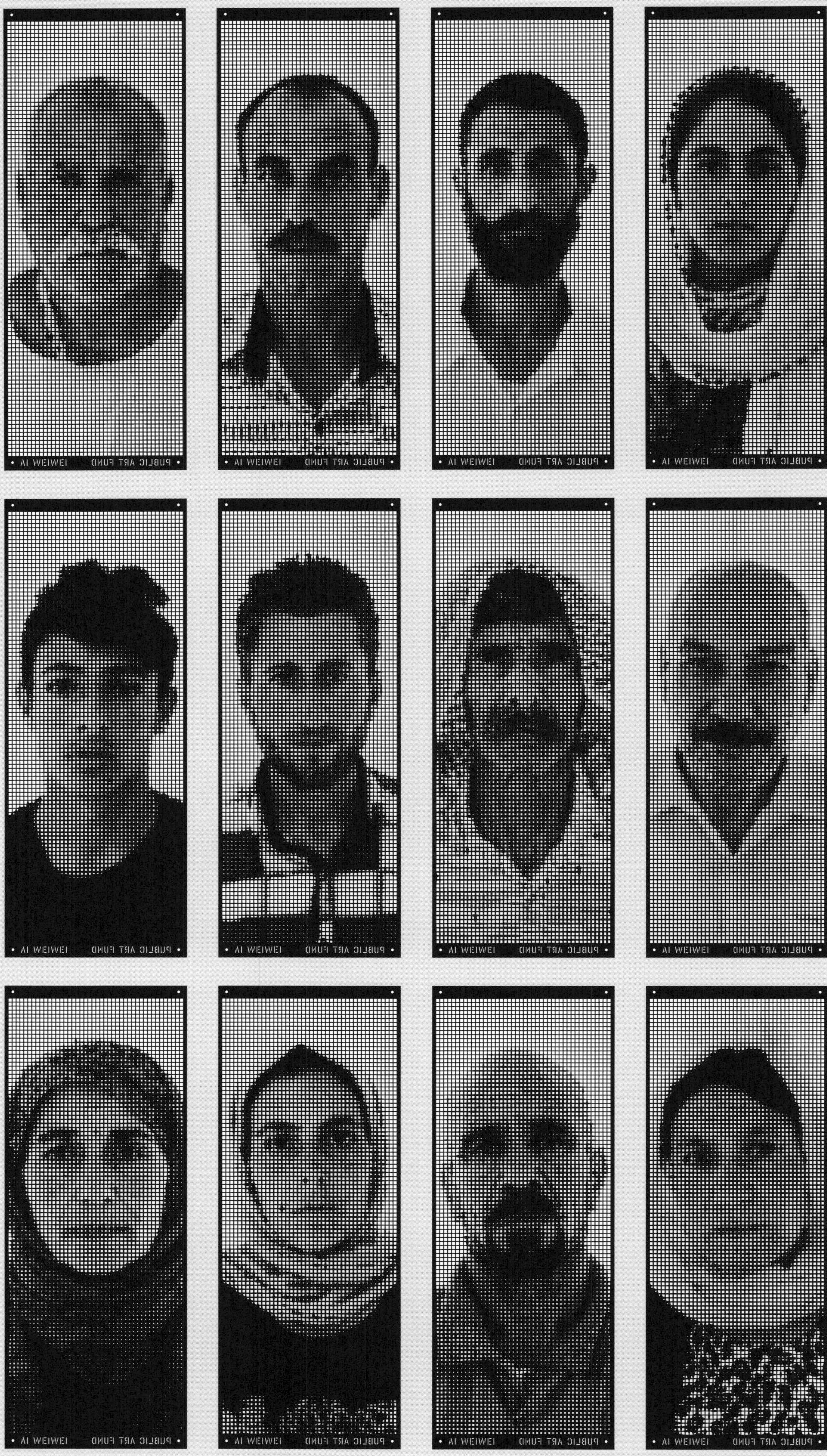
PUBLIC ART FUND

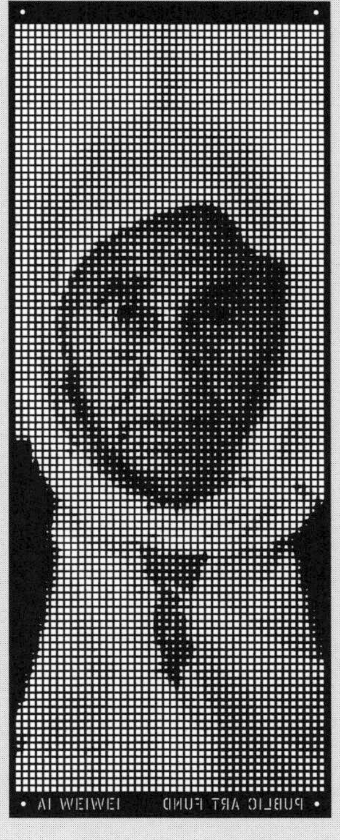

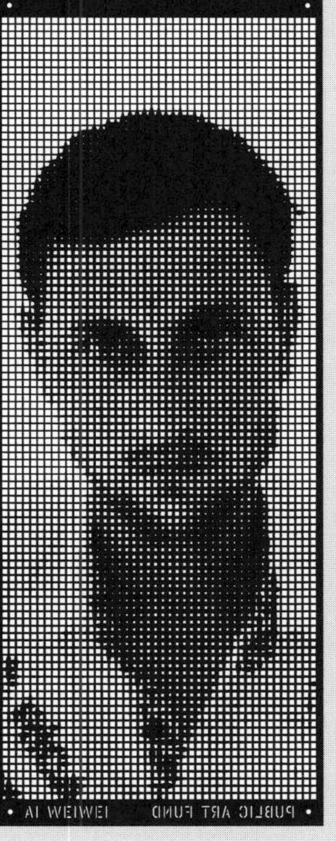

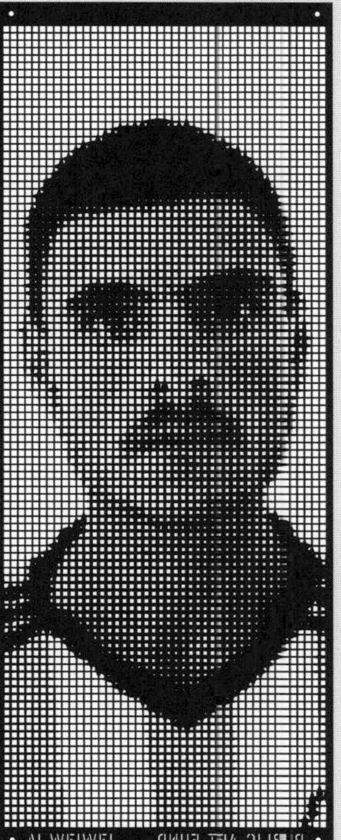

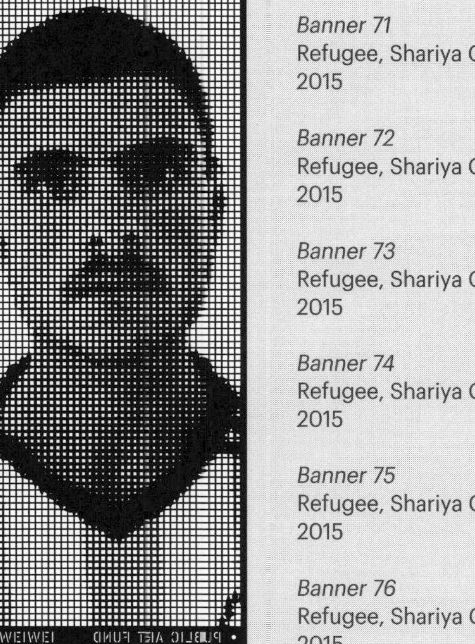

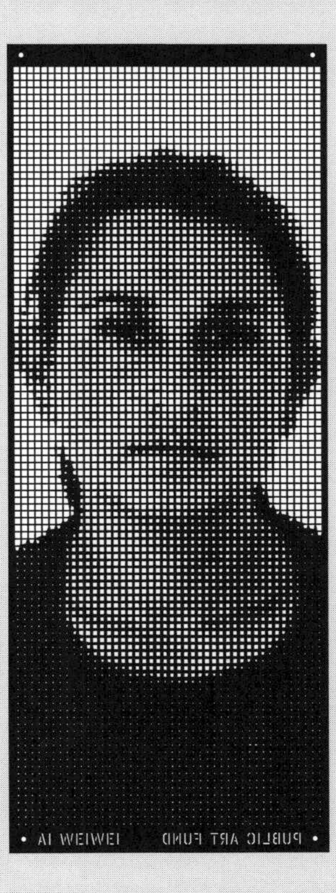

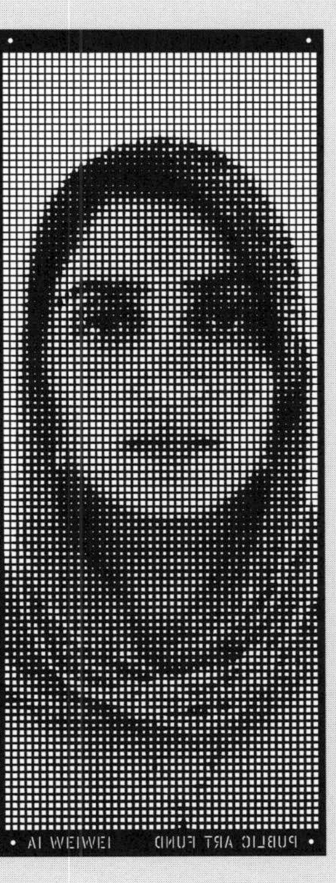

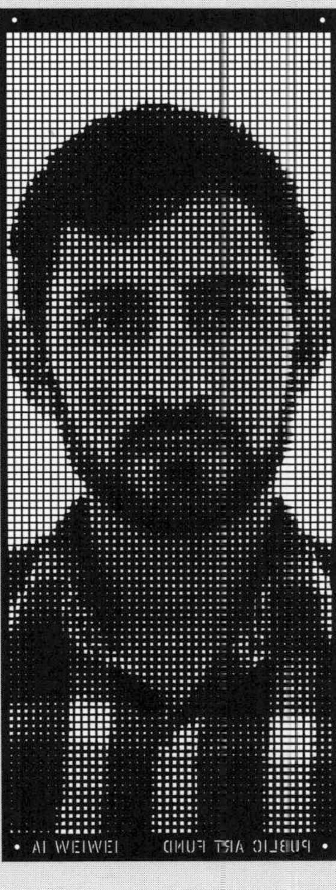

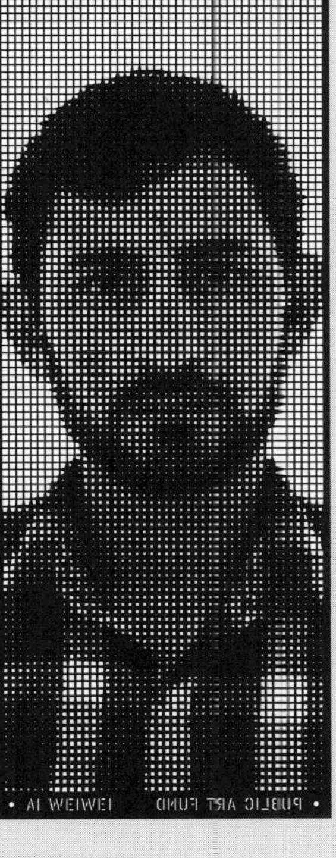

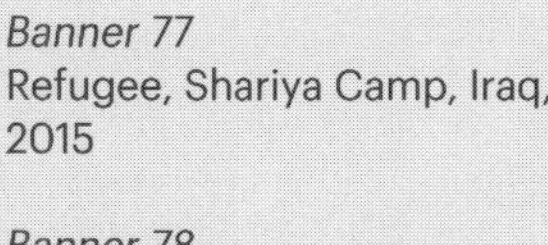

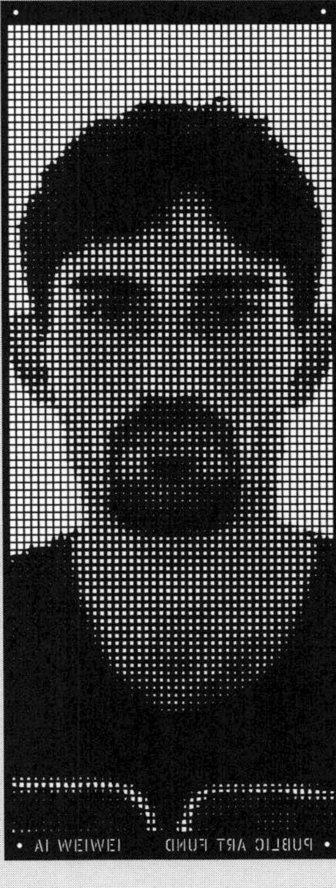

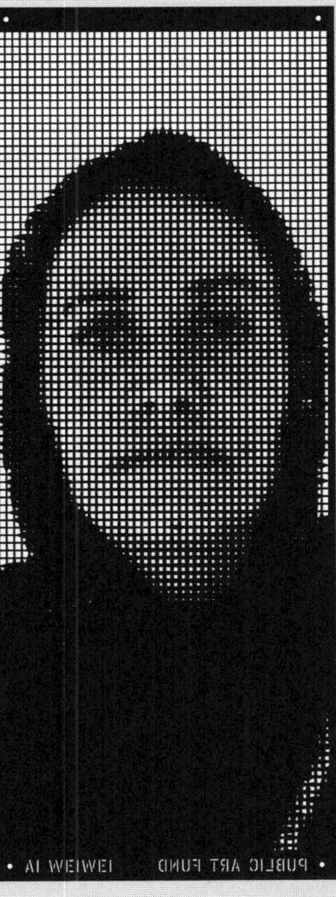

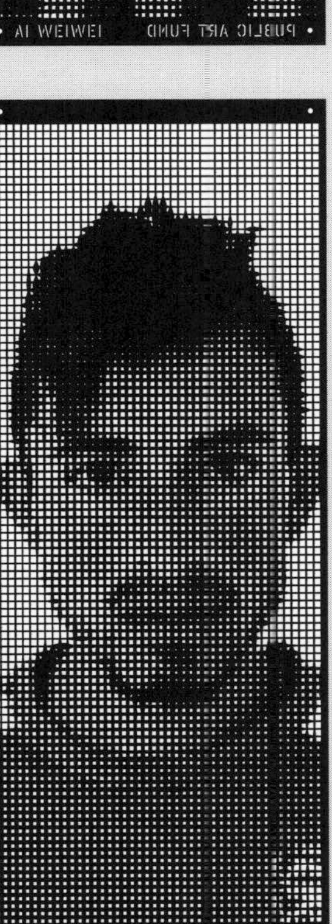

Banner 70
Refugee, Shariya Camp, Iraq, 2015

Banner 71
Refugee, Shariya Camp, Iraq, 2015

Banner 72
Refugee, Shariya Camp, Iraq, 2015

Banner 73
Refugee, Shariya Camp, Iraq, 2015

Banner 74
Refugee, Shariya Camp, Iraq, 2015

Banner 75
Refugee, Shariya Camp, Iraq, 2015

Banner 76
Refugee, Shariya Camp, Iraq, 2015

Banner 77
Refugee, Shariya Camp, Iraq, 2015

Banner 78
Refugee, Shariya Camp, Iraq, 2015

Banner 79
Refugee, Shariya Camp, Iraq, 2015

Banner 80
Refugee, Shariya Camp, Iraq, 2015

Banner 81
Refugee, Shariya Camp, Iraq, 2015

Banner 82
Refugee, Shariya Camp, Iraq, 2015

Banner 83
Refugee, Shariya Camp, Iraq, 2015

Banner 84
Refugee, Shariya Camp, Iraq, 2015

Banner 85
Refugee, Shariya Camp, Iraq, 2015

Banner 86
Refugee, Shariya Camp, Iraq, 2015

Banner 87
Refugee, Shariya Camp, Iraq, 2015

Banner 88
Refugee, Shariya Camp, Iraq, 2015

Banner 89
Refugee, Shariya Camp, Iraq, 2015

Banner 90
Refugee, Shariya Camp, Iraq, 2015

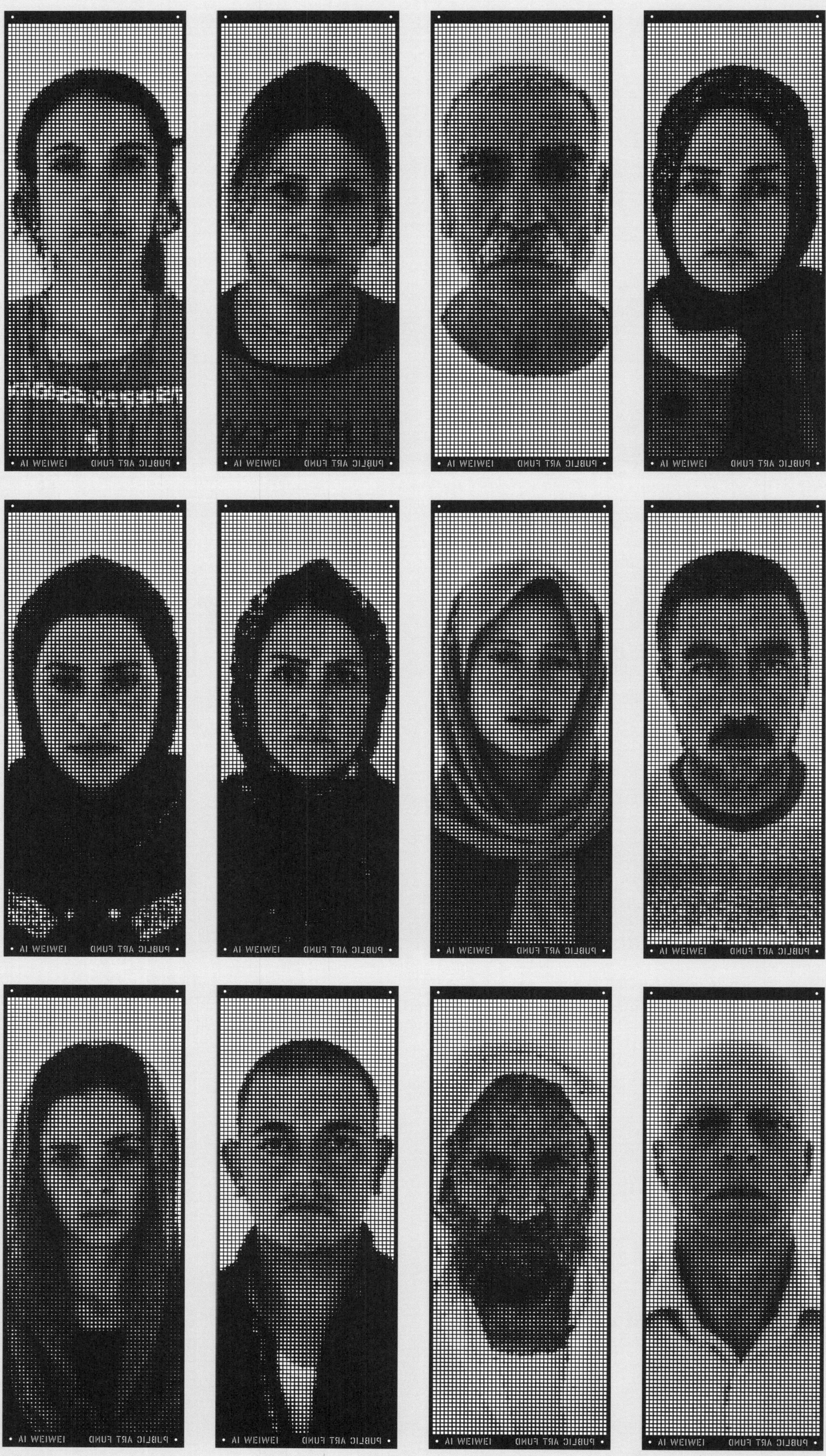
AI WEIWEI
PUBLIC ART FUND
AI WEIWEI
PUBLIC ART FUND
AI WEIWEI
PUBLIC ART FUND
AI WEIWEI
PUBLIC ART FUND
AI WEIWEI
PUBLIC ART FUND
AI WEIWEI
PUBLIC ART FUND
AI WEIWEI
PUBLIC ART FUND
AI WEIWEI
PUBLIC ART FUND
AI WEIWEI
PUBLIC ART FUND
AI WEIWEI
PUBLIC ART FUND
AI WEIWEI
PUBLIC ART FUND
AI WEIWEI
PUBLIC ART FUND

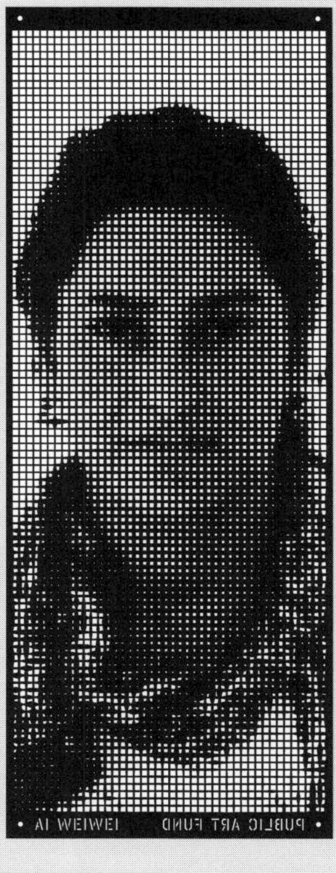

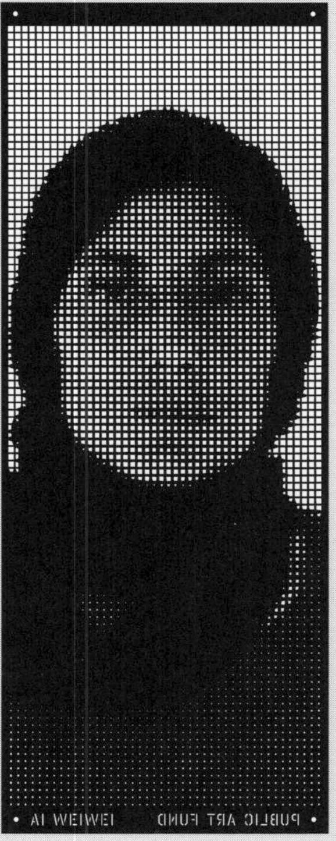

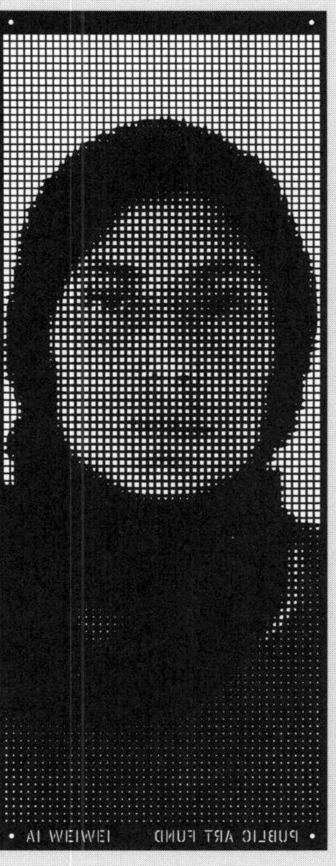

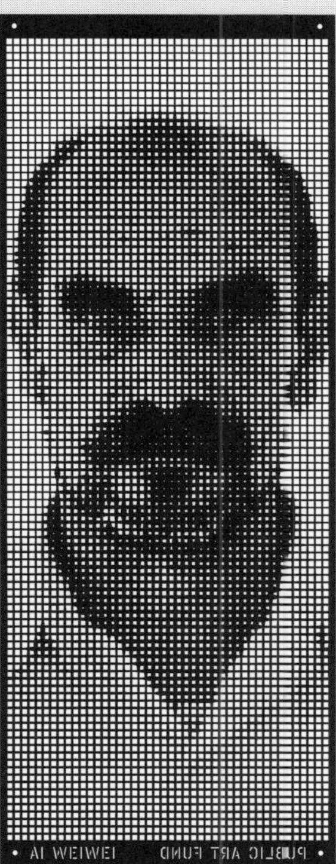

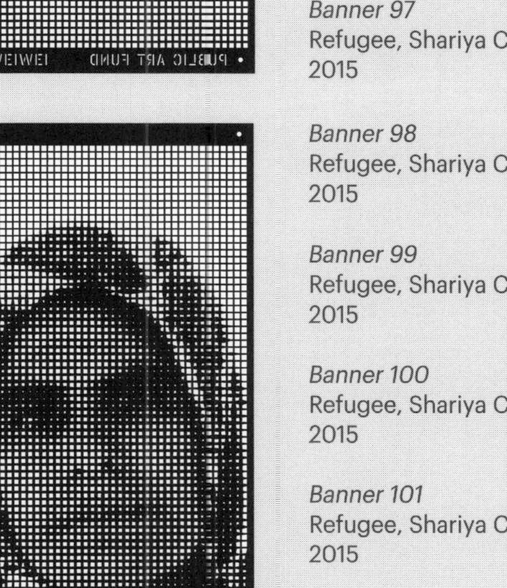

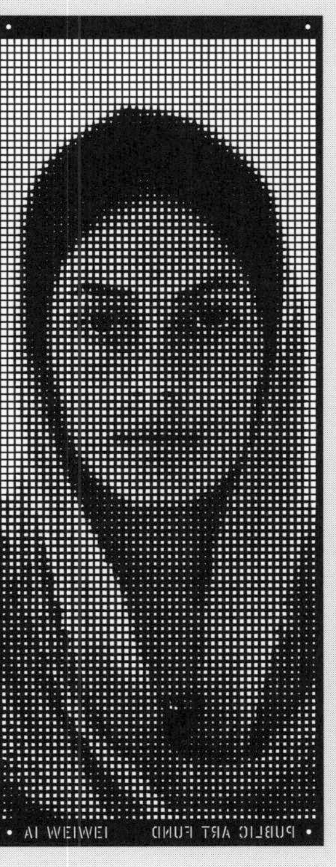

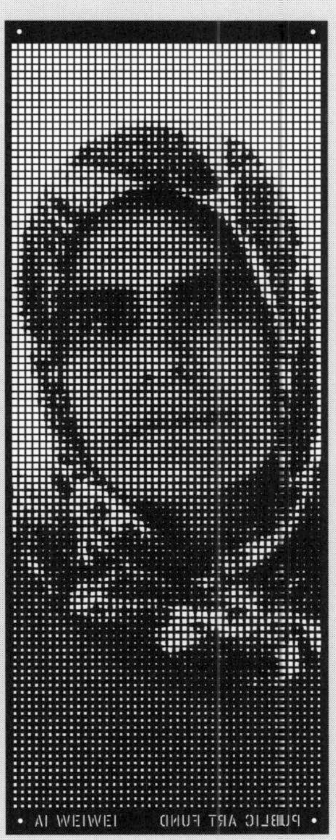

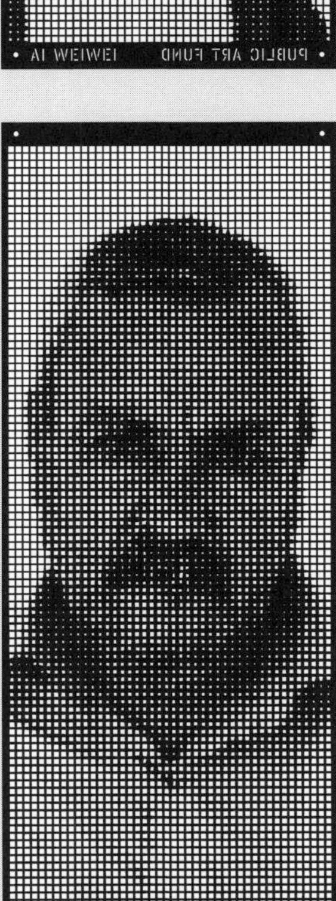

Banner 91
Refugee, Shariya Camp, Iraq, 2015

Banner 92
Refugee, Shariya Camp, Iraq, 2015

Banner 93
Refugee, Shariya Camp, Iraq, 2015

Banner 94
Refugee, Shariya Camp, Iraq, 2015

Banner 95
Refugee, Shariya Camp, Iraq, 2015

Banner 96
Refugee, Shariya Camp, Iraq, 2015

Banner 97
Refugee, Shariya Camp, Iraq, 2015

Banner 98
Refugee, Shariya Camp, Iraq, 2015

Banner 99
Refugee, Shariya Camp, Iraq, 2015

Banner 100
Refugee, Shariya Camp, Iraq, 2015

Banner 101
Refugee, Shariya Camp, Iraq, 2015

Banner 102
Refugee, Shariya Camp, Iraq, 2015

Banner 103
Refugee, Shariya Camp, Iraq, 2015

Banner 104
Refugee, Shariya Camp, Iraq, 2015

Banner 105
Refugee, Shariya Camp, Iraq, 2015

Banner 106
Refugee, Shariya Camp, Iraq, 2015

Banner 107
Refugee, Shariya Camp, Iraq, 2015

Banner 108
Refugee, Shariya Camp, Iraq, 2015

Banner 109
Refugee, Shariya Camp, Iraq, 2015

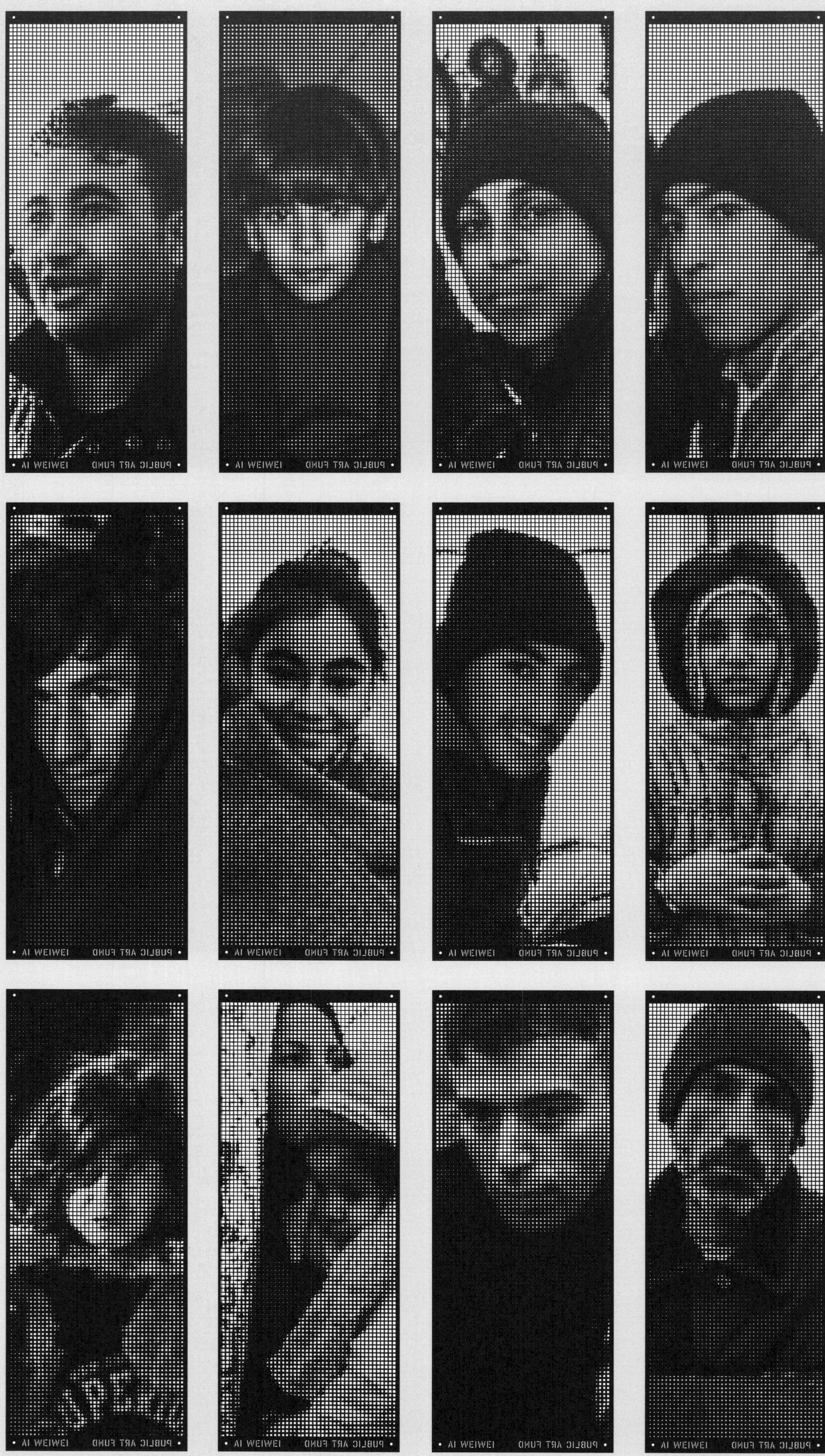
AI WEIWEI
PUBLIC ART FUND

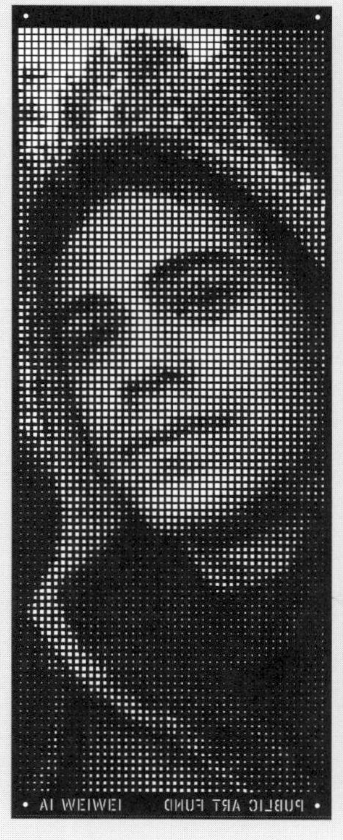

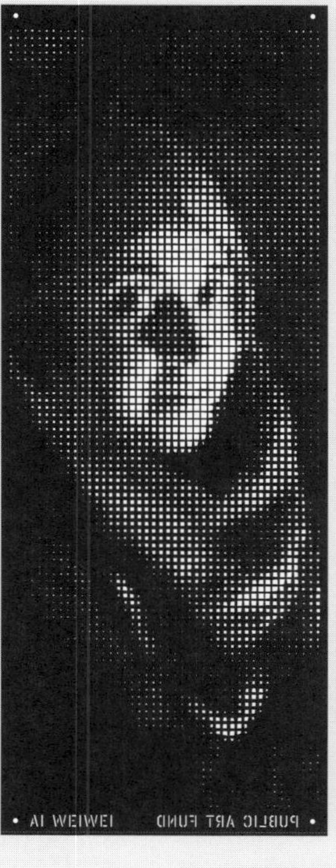

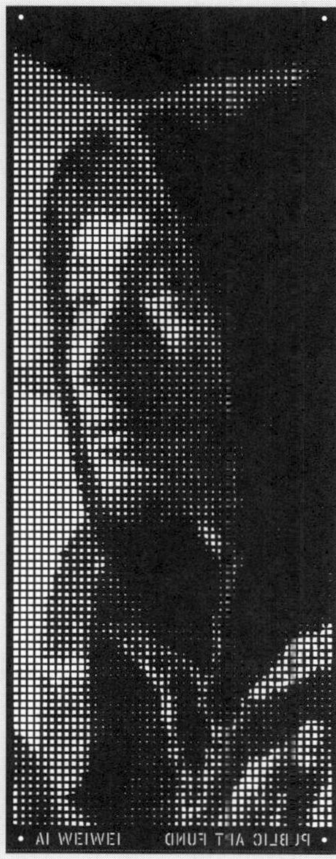

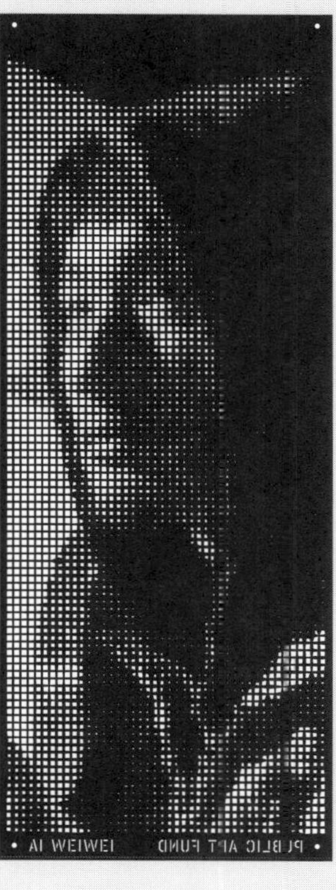

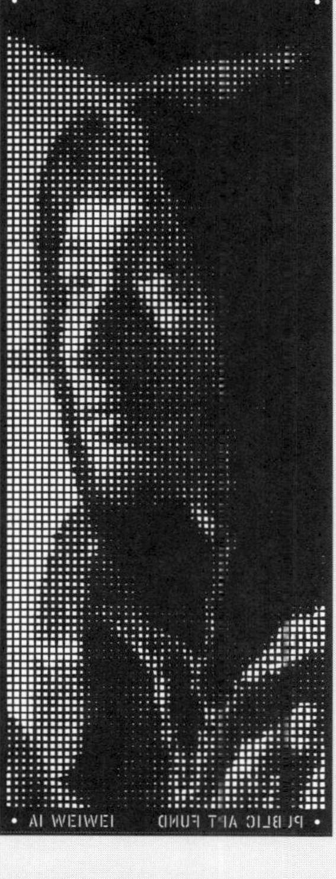

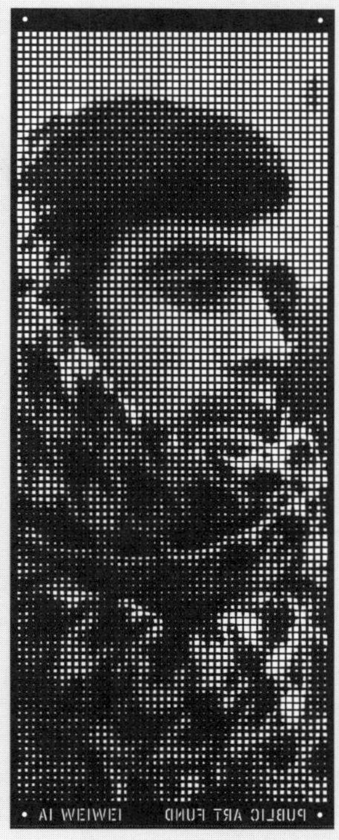

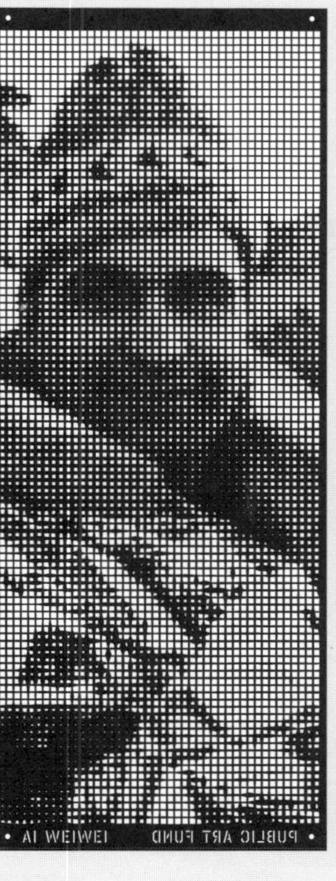

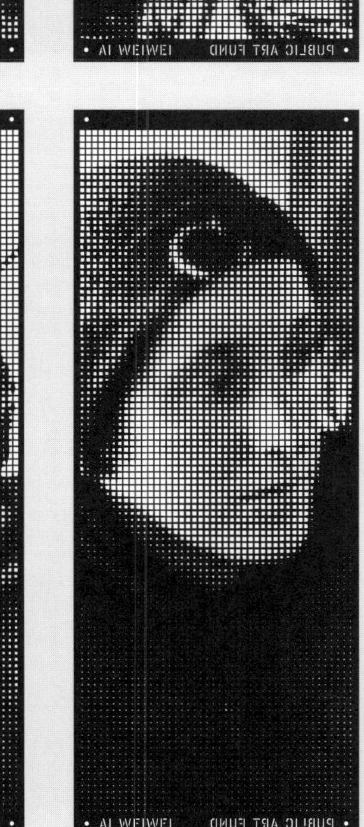

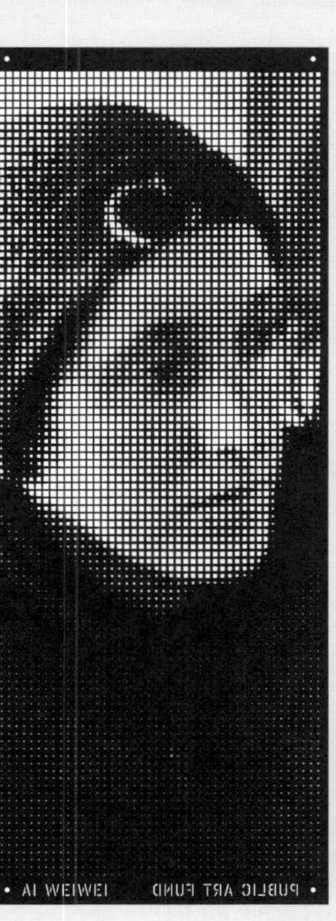

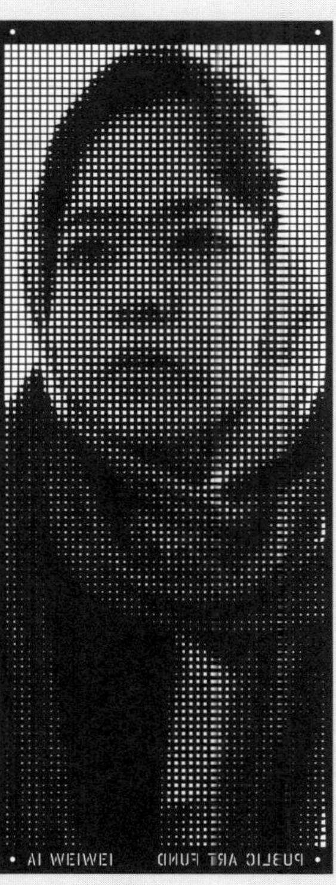

Banner 110
Refugee, Moria Camp, Lesvos, Greece, 2015

Banner 111
Refugee, Moria Camp, Lesvos, Greece, 2015

Banner 112
Refugee, Moria Camp, Lesvos, Greece, 2015

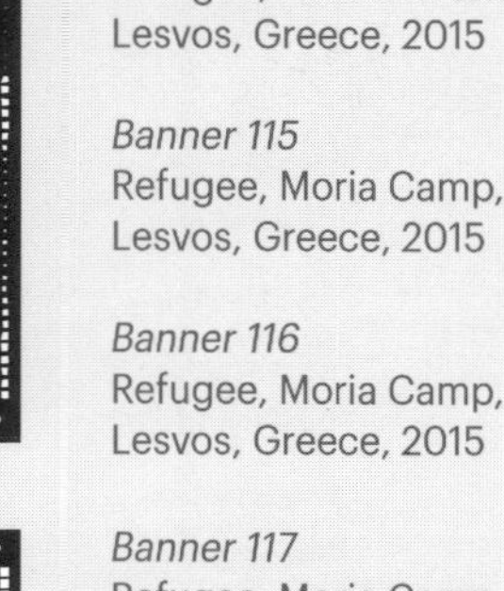

Banner 113
Refugee, Moria Camp, Lesvos, Greece, 2015

Banner 114
Refugee, Northern Shores, Lesvos, Greece, 2015

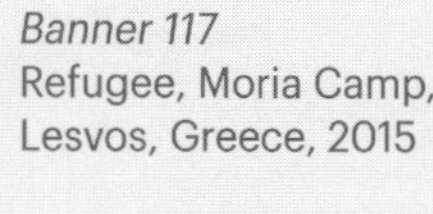

Banner 115
Refugee, Moria Camp, Lesvos, Greece, 2015

Banner 116
Refugee, Moria Camp, Lesvos, Greece, 2015

Banner 117
Refugee, Moria Camp, Lesvos, Greece, 2015

Banner 118
Refugee, Moria Camp, Lesvos, Greece, 2015

Banner 119
Refugee, Moria Camp, Lesvos, Greece, 2015

Banner 120
Refugee, Moria Camp, Lesvos, Greece, 2015

Banner 121
Refugee, Moria Camp, Lesvos, Greece, 2015

Banner 122
Refugee, Molyvos, Lesvos, Greece, 2015

Banner 123
Refugee, Northern Shores, Lesvos, Greece, 2015

Banner 124
Refugee, Port of Mytilene, Lesvos, Greece, 2015

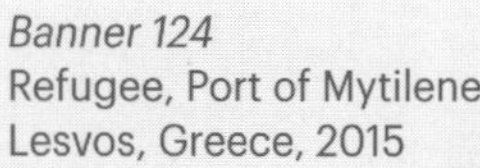

Banner 125
Refugees, Northern Shores, Lesvos, Greece, 2016

Banner 126
Refugee, Northern Shores, Lesvos, Greece, 2016

Banner 127
Refugee, Lesvos, Greece, 2016

Banner 128
Refugee, Northern Shores, Lesvos, Greece, 2016

Banner 129
Refugee, Eastern Shores, Lesvos, Greece, 2016

Banner 130
Refugee, Eastern Shores, Lesvos, Greece, 2016

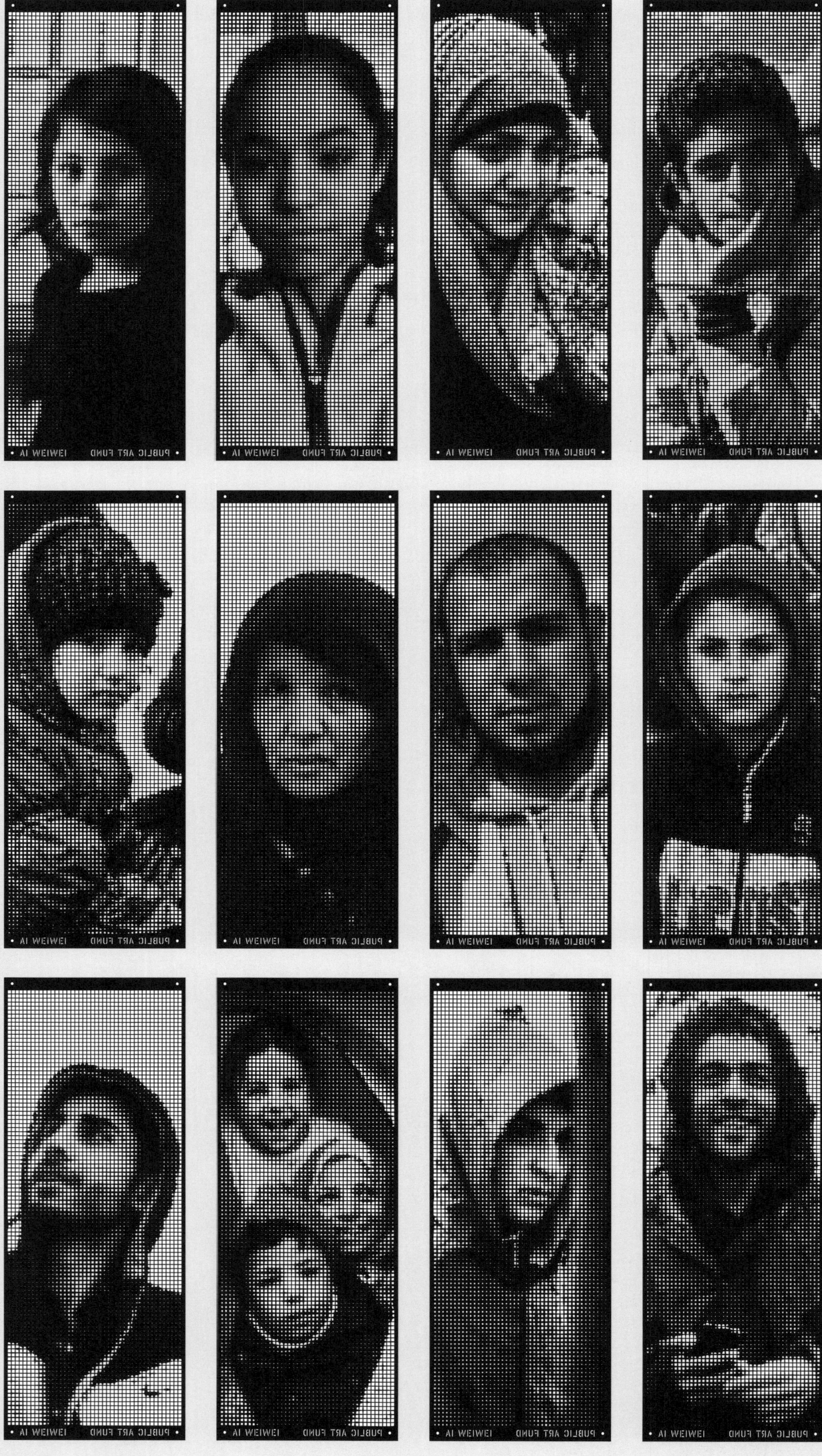
PUBLIC ART FUND

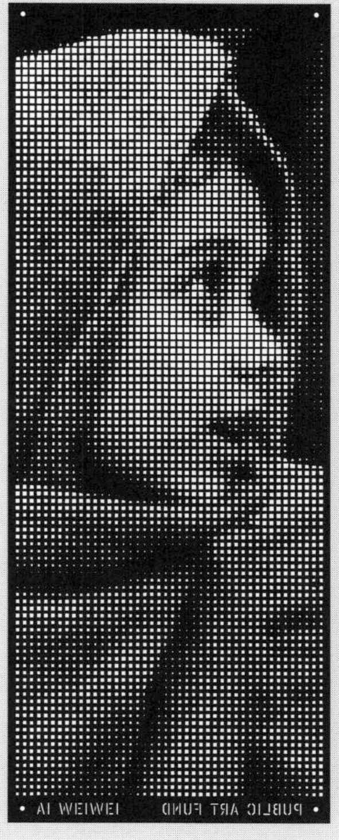
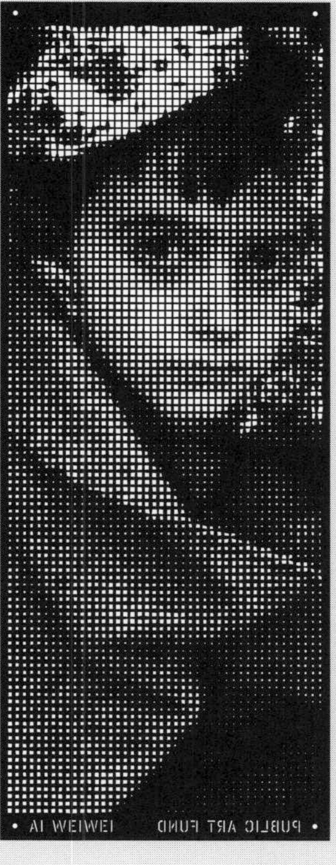
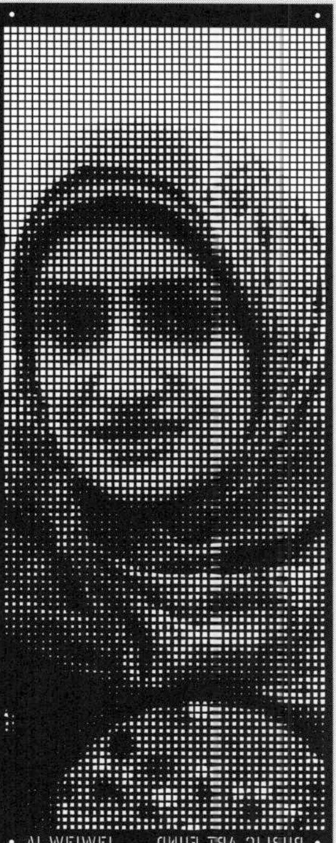
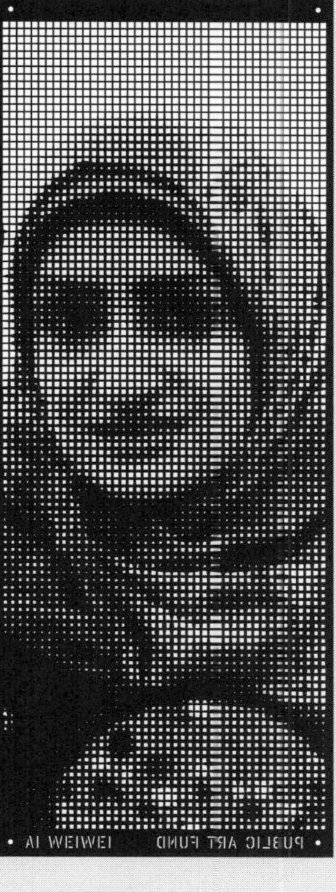
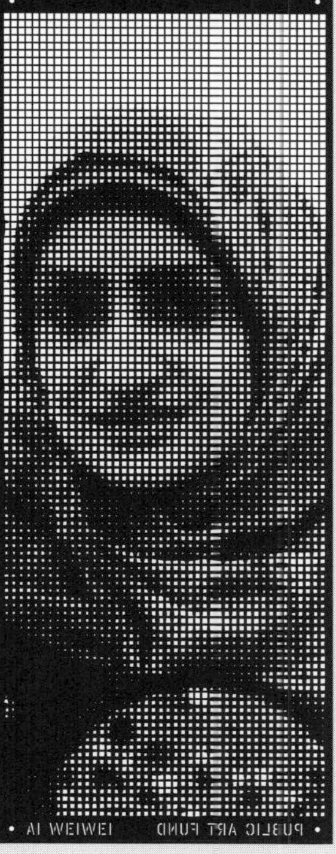
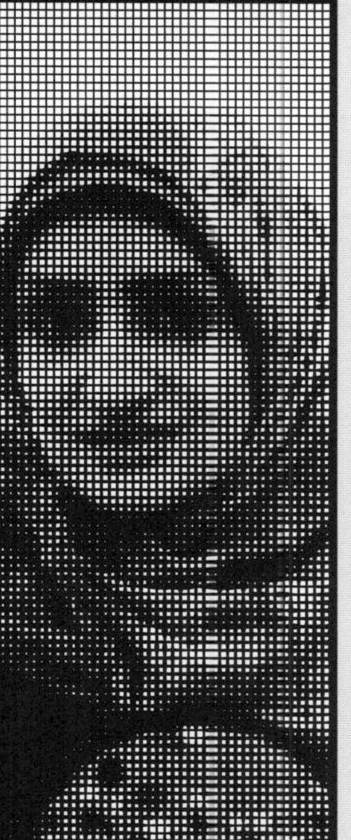
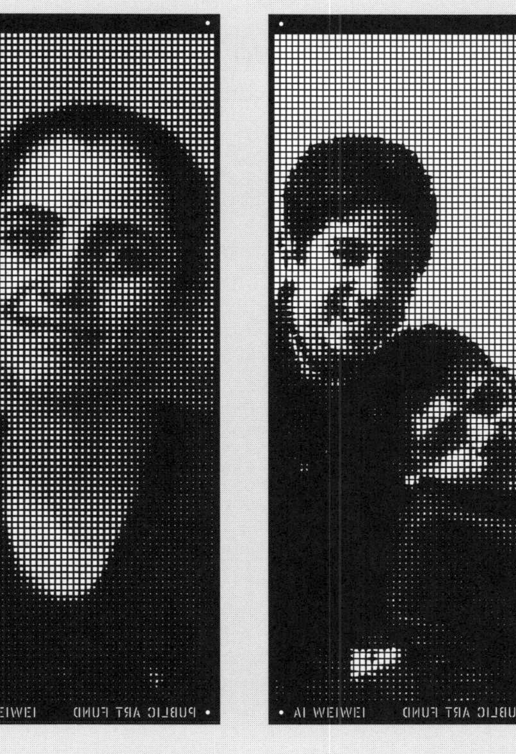
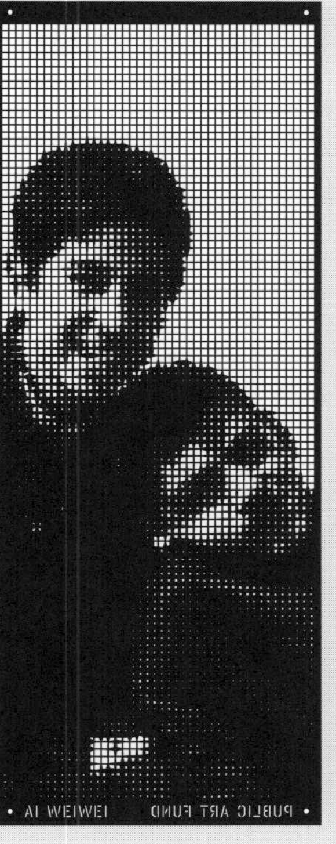
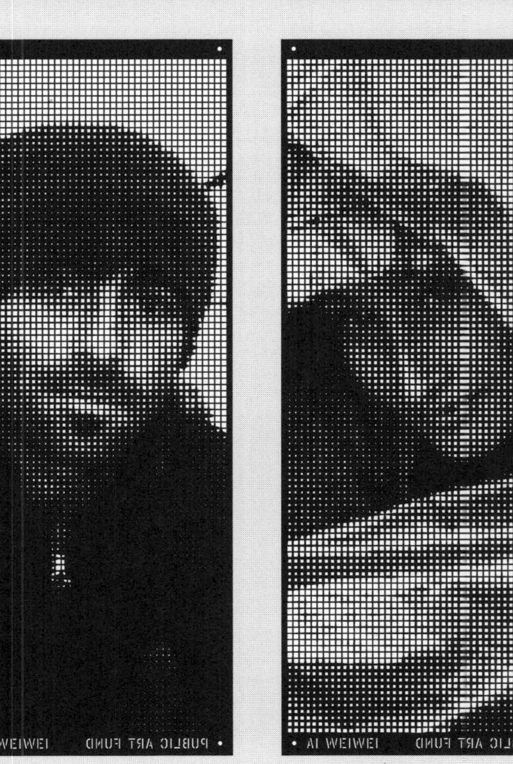
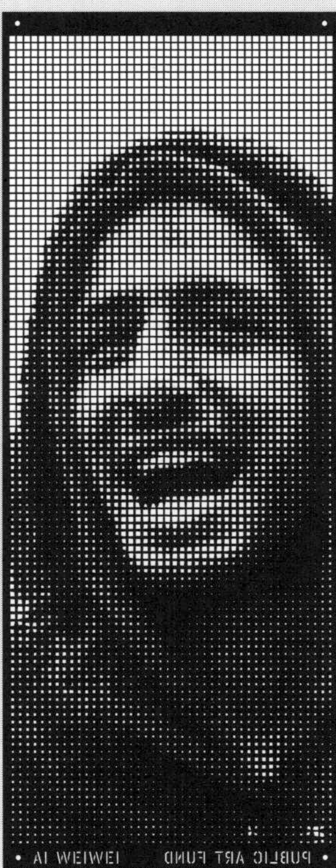
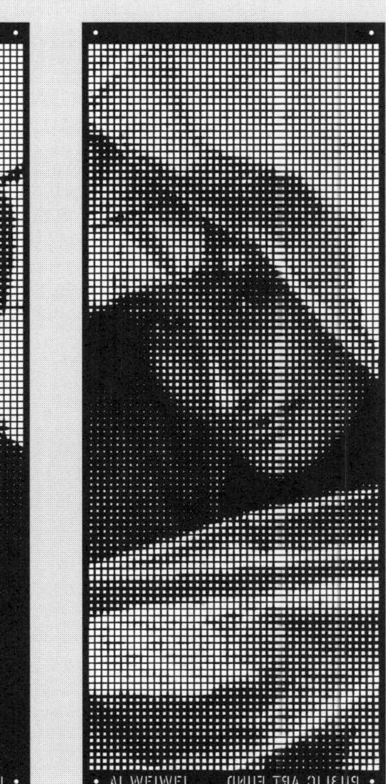

Banner 131
Refugee, Tempelhof Airport, Berlin, Germany, 2016

Banner 132
Refugee, Tempelhof Airport, Berlin, Germany, 2016

Banner 133
Refugee, Eastern Shores, Lesvos, Greece, 2016

Banner 134
Refugee, Port of Mytilene, Lesvos, Greece, 2016

Banner 135
Refugee, Eastern Shores, Lesvos, Greece, 2016

Banner 136
Refugee, Eastern Shores, Lesvos, Greece, 2016

Banner 137
Refugee, Eastern Shores, Lesvos, Greece, 2016

Banner 138
Refugee, Eastern Shores, Lesvos, Greece, 2016

Banner 139
Refugee, Eastern Shores, Lesvos, Greece, 2016

Banner 140
Refugee, "Refugee Graveyard," Lesvos, Greece, 2016

Banner 141
Refugee, Port of Mytilene, Lesvos, Greece, 2016

Banner 142
Refugee, Ferry from Lesvos to Athens, Aegean Sea, 2016

Banner 143
Refugees, Ferry from Lesvos to Athens, Aegean Sea, 2016

Banner 144
Refugee, Ferry from Lesvos to Athens, Aegean Sea, 2016

Banner 145
Refugee, Ferry from Lesvos to Athens, Aegean Sea, 2016

Banner 146
Refugees, Idomeni Makeshift Camp, Idomeni, Greece, 2016

Banner 147
Refugee, Idomeni Makeshift Camp, Idomeni, Greece, 2016

Banner 148
Refugee, Idomeni Makeshift Camp, Idomeni, Greece, 2016

Banner 149
Refugee, Idomeni Makeshift Camp, Idomeni, Greece, 2016

Banner 150
Refugee, Idomeni Makeshift Camp, Idomeni, Greece, 2016

Banner 151
Refugee, Idomeni Makeshift Camp, Idomeni, Greece, 2016

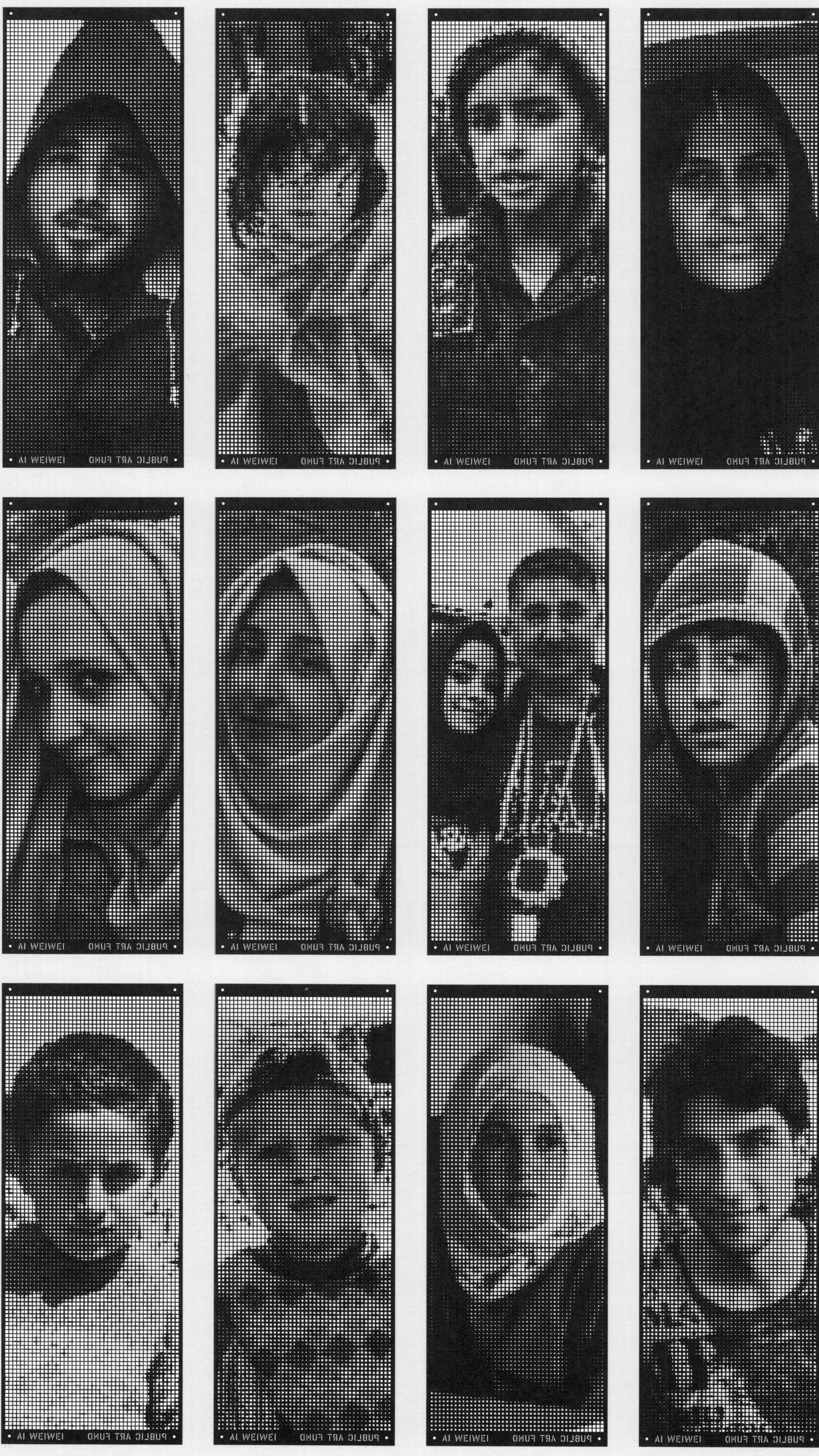
AI WEIWEI
PUBLIC ART FUND

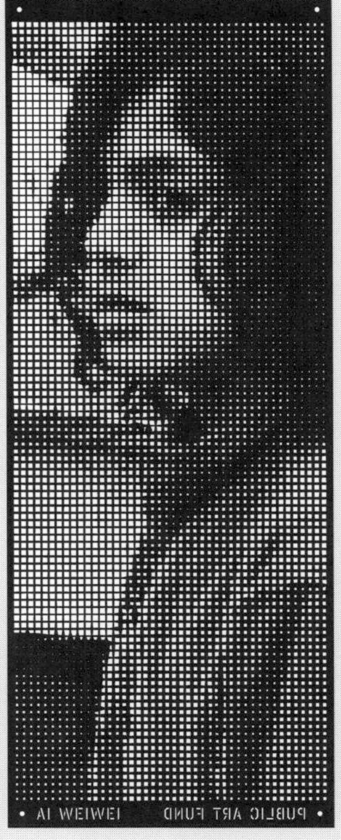

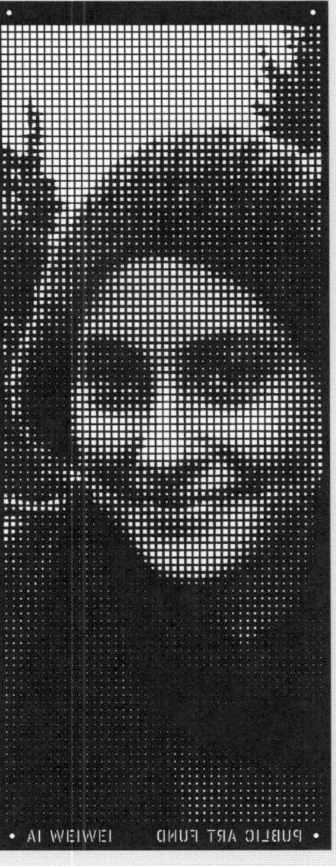

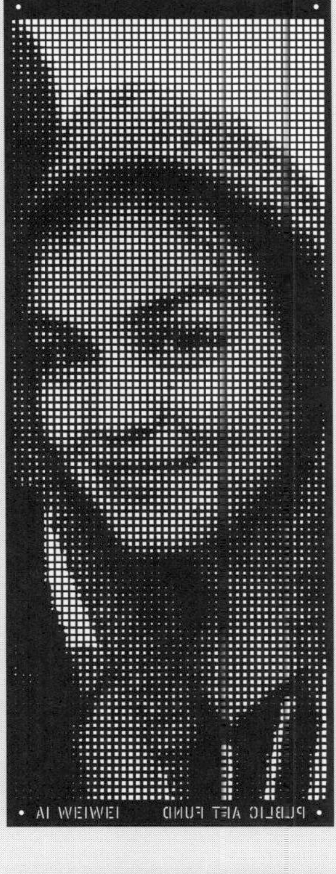

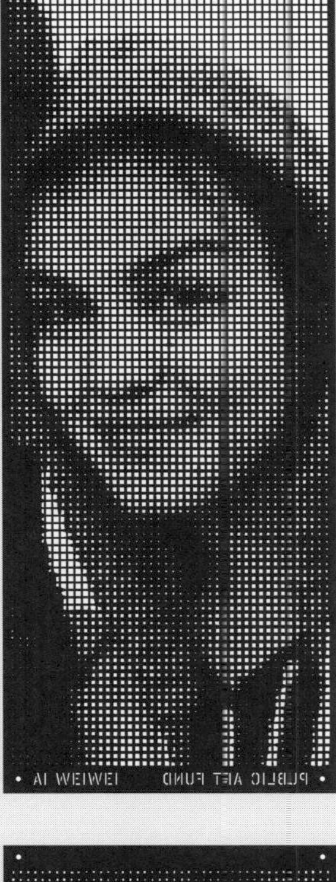

Banner 152
Refugee, Idomeni Makeshift Camp, Idomeni, Greece, 2016

Banner 153
Refugee, Idomeni Makeshift Camp, Idomeni, Greece, 2016

Banner 154
Refugee, Idomeni Makeshift Camp, Idomeni, Greece, 2016

Banner 155
Refugee, Idomeni Makeshift Camp, Idomeni, Greece, 2016

Banner 156
Refugee, Idomeni Makeshift Camp, Idomeni, Greece, 2016

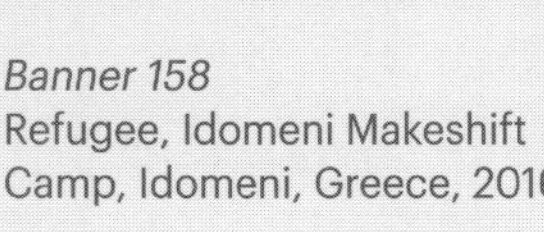

Banner 157
Refugee, Idomeni Makeshift Camp, Idomeni, Greece, 2016

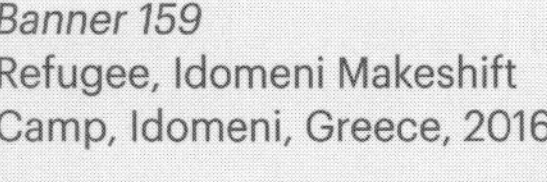

Banner 158
Refugee, Idomeni Makeshift Camp, Idomeni, Greece, 2016

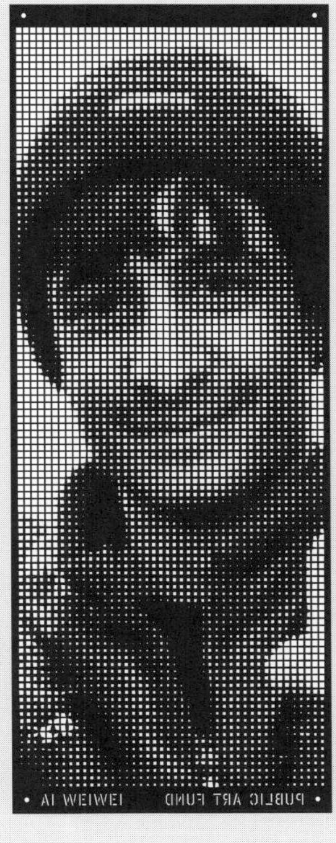

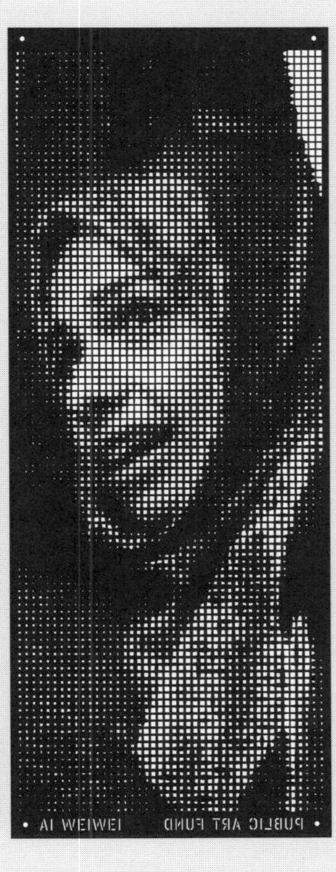

Banner 159
Refugee, Idomeni Makeshift Camp, Idomeni, Greece, 2016

Banner 160
Refugee, Idomeni Makeshift Camp, Idomeni, Greece, 2016

Banner 161
Refugees, Kara Tepe Camp, Lesvos, Greece, 2016

Banner 162
Refugee, Port of Mytilene, Lesvos, Greece, 2016

Banner 163
Refugee, Shariya Camp, Iraq, 2016

Banner 164
Refugee, Idomeni Makeshift Camp, Idomeni, Greece, 2016

Banner 165
Refugee, Idomeni Makeshift Camp, Idomeni, Greece, 2016

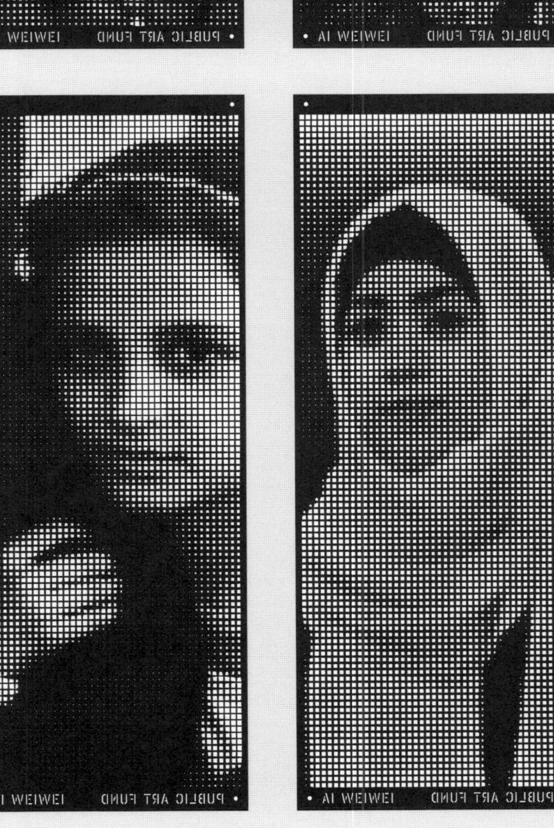

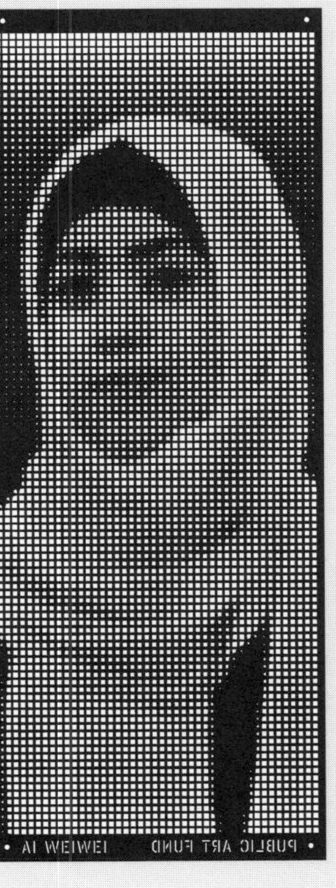

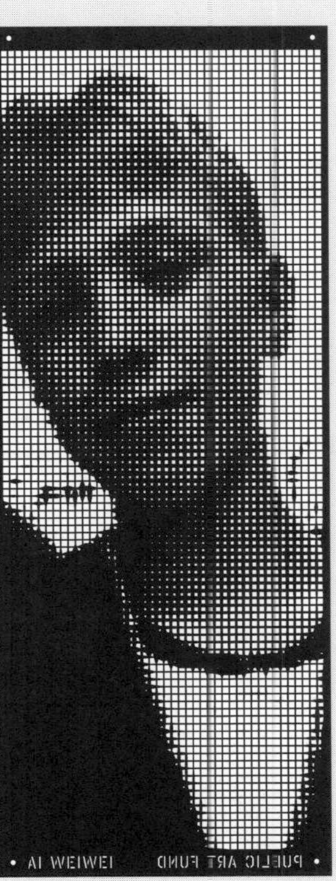

Banner 166
Refugee, Istanbul, Turkey, 2016

Banner 167
Refugee, Makeshift Camp, Torbali, Izmir, Turkey, 2016

Banner 168
Refugee, Nizip Camp, Gaziantep, Turkey, 2016

Banner 169
Refugee, Nizip Camp, Gaziantep, Turkey, 2016

Banner 170
Refugee, Nizip Camp, Gaziantep, Turkey, 2016

Banner 171
Refugee, Nizip Camp, Gaziantep, Turkey, 2016

Banner 172
Refugee, Nizip Camp, Gaziantep, Turkey, 2016

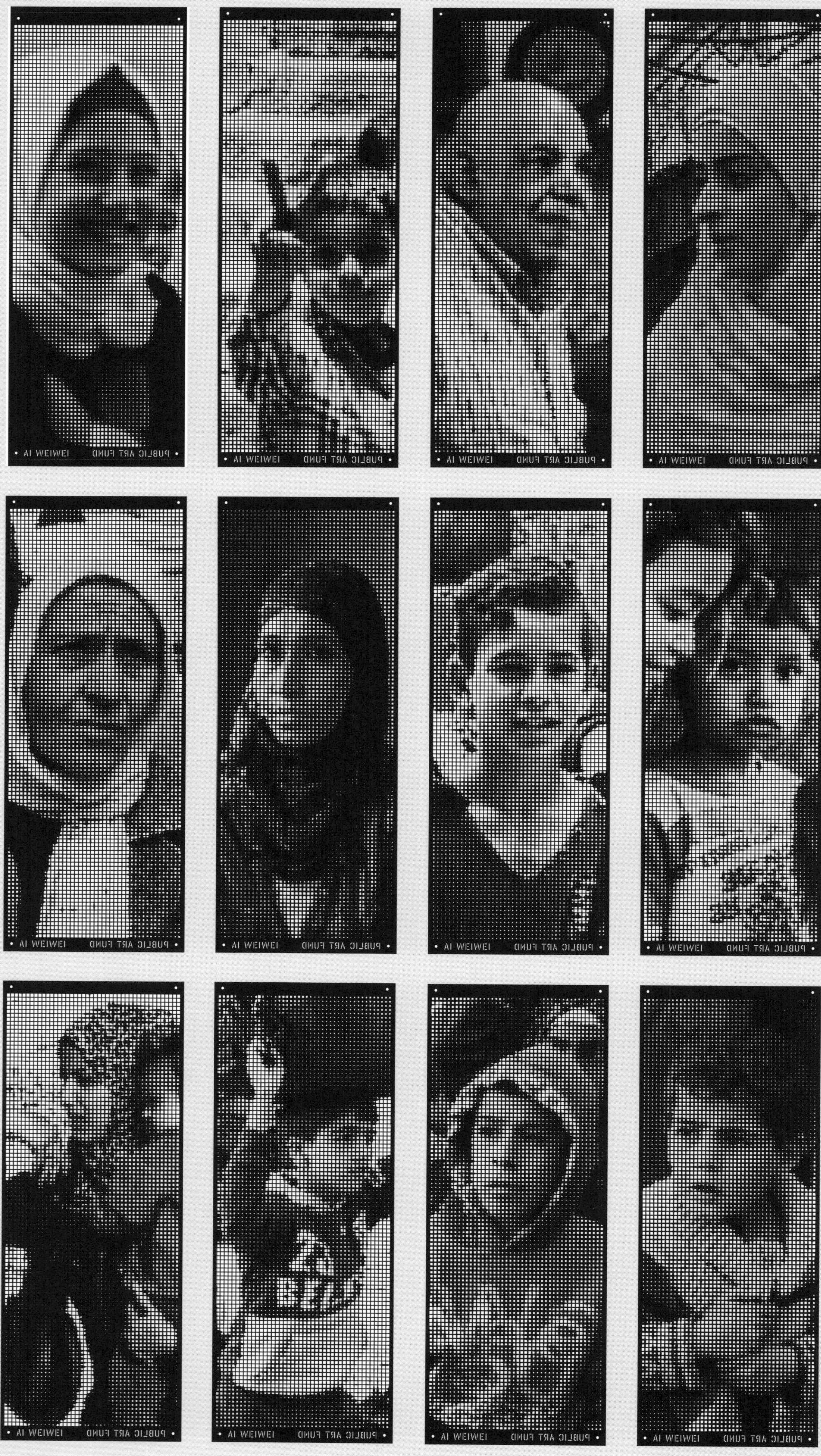
AI WEIWEI
PUBLIC ART FUND

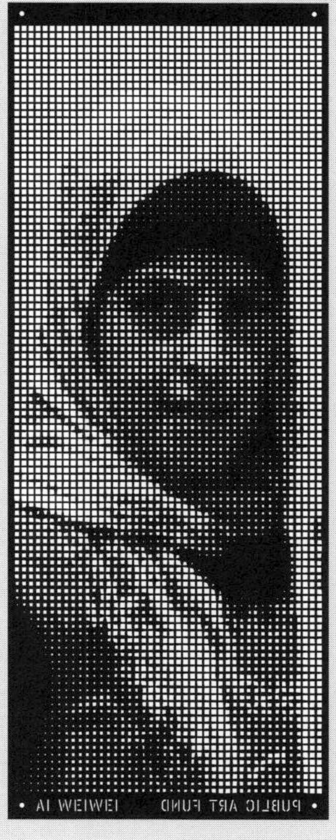
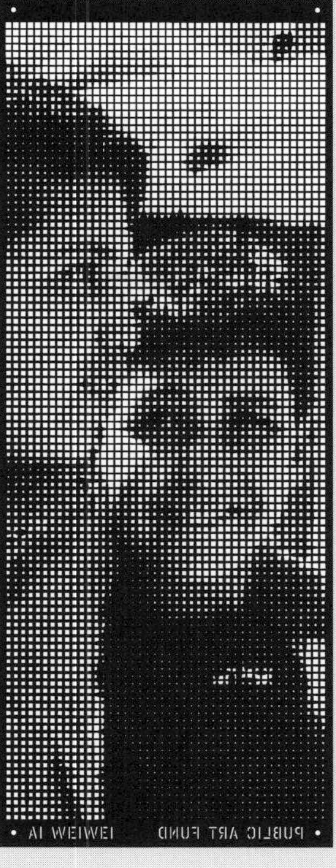
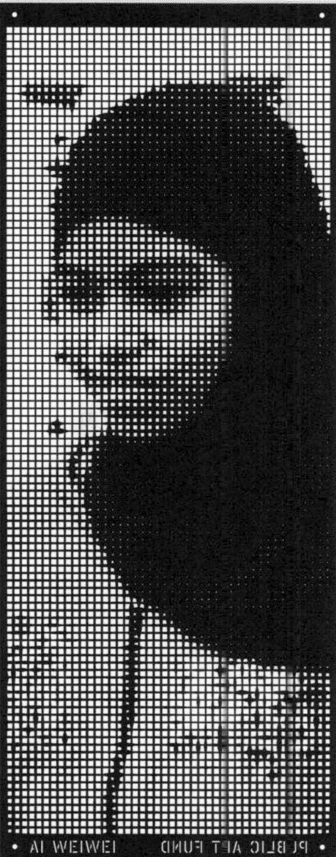
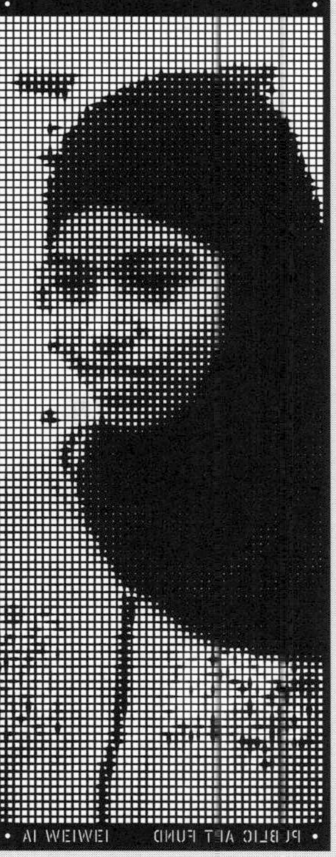
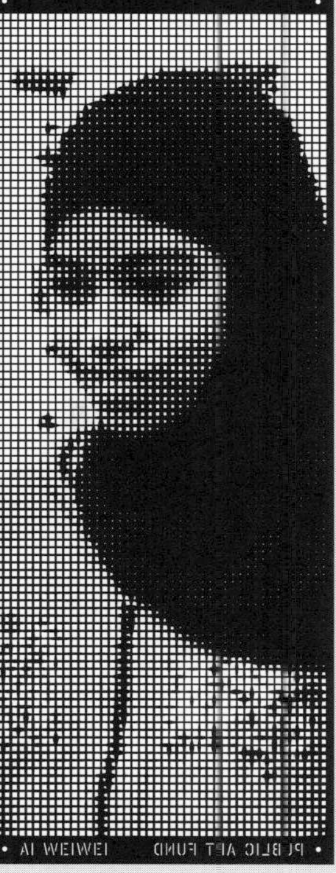
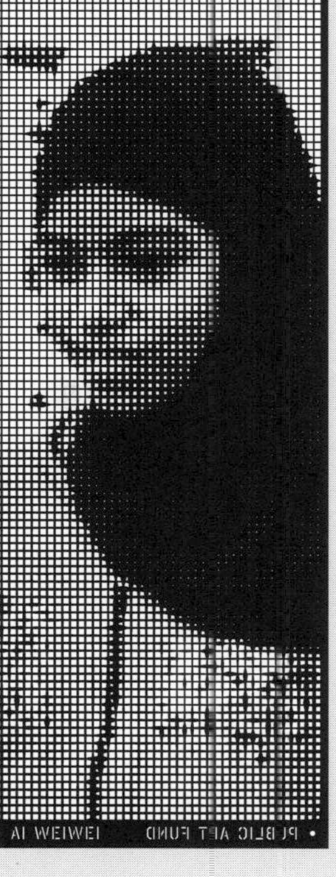
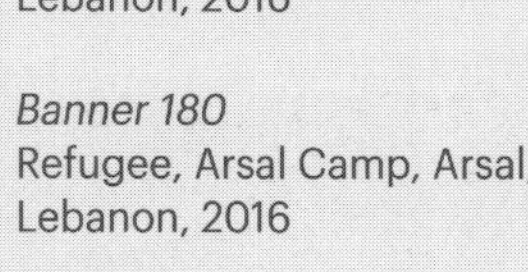
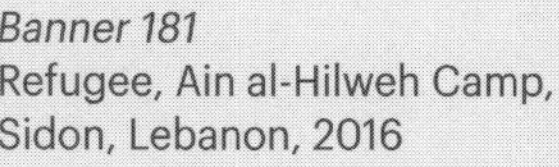
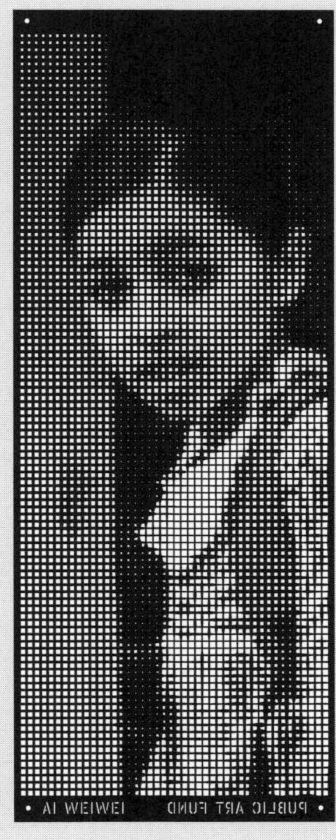
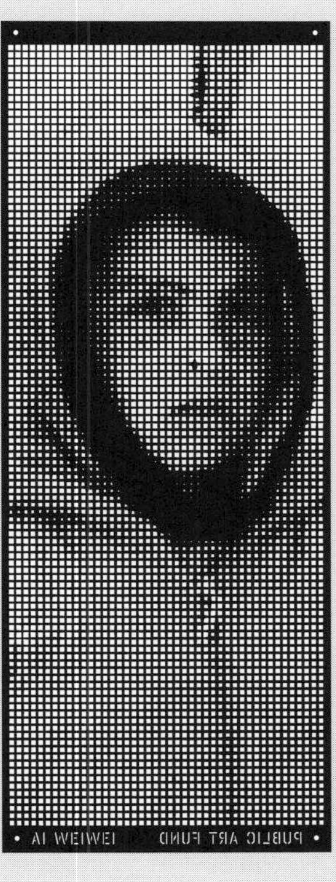
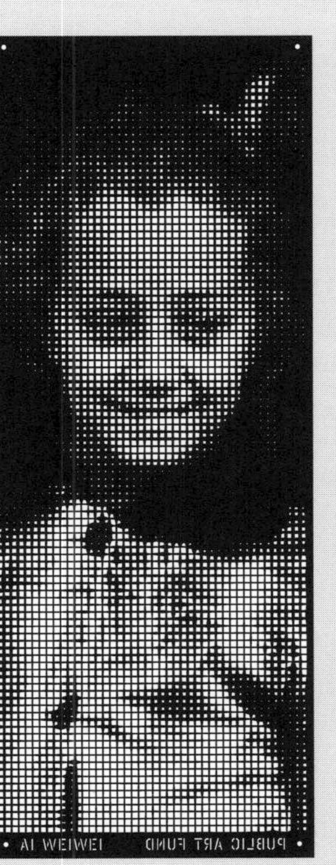
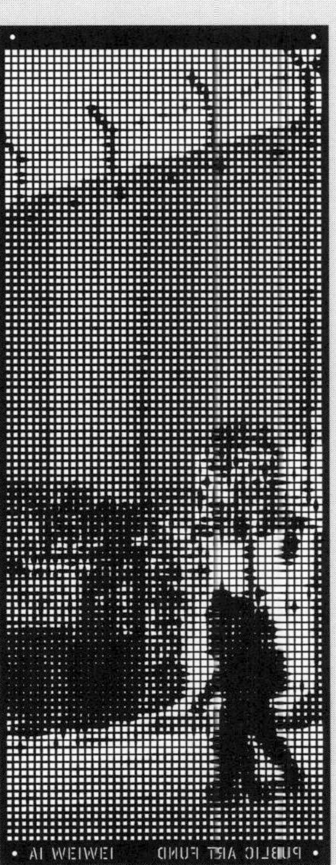
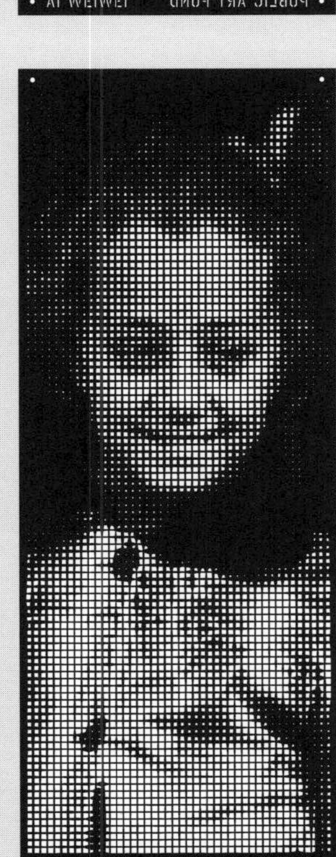

Banner 173
Refugee, Nizip Camp, Gaziantep, Turkey, 2016

Banner 174
Refugee, Shatila Camp, Beirut, Lebanon, 2016

Banner 175
Refugee, Shatila Camp, Beirut, Lebanon, 2016

Banner 176
Refugee, Shatila Camp, Beirut, Lebanon, 2016

Banner 177
Refugee, Arsal Camp, Arsal, Lebanon, 2016

Banner 178
Refugees, Arsal Camp, Arsal, Lebanon, 2016

Banner 179
Refugee, Arsal Camp, Arsal, Lebanon, 2016

Banner 180
Refugee, Arsal Camp, Arsal, Lebanon, 2016

Banner 181
Refugee, Ain al-Hilweh Camp, Sidon, Lebanon, 2016

Banner 182
Refugee, Ain al-Hilweh Camp, Sidon, Lebanon, 2016

Banner 183
Refugees, Makeshift Camp, Beqaa Valley, Lebanon, 2016

Banner 184
Refugee, Makeshift Camp, Beqaa Valley, Lebanon, 2016

Banner 185
Refugee, Syrian-Jordanian Border, 2016

Banner 186
Refugee, Syrian-Jordanian Border, 2016

Banner 187
Refugees, Syrian-Jordanian Border, 2016

Banner 188
Refugee, Syrian-Jordanian Border, 2016

Banner 189
Refugee, Syrian-Jordanian Border, 2016

Banner 190
Refugee, Syrian-Jordanian Border, 2016

Banner 191
Refugee, Syrian-Jordanian Border, 2016

Banner 192
Refugee, Syrian-Jordanian Border, 2016

Banner 193
Refugees, Israeli West Bank Barrier, 2016

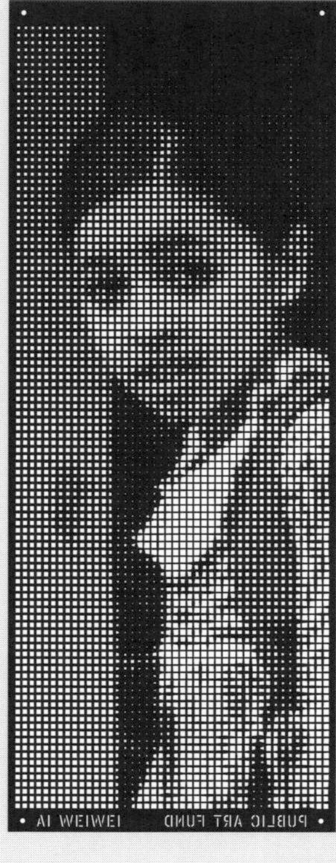

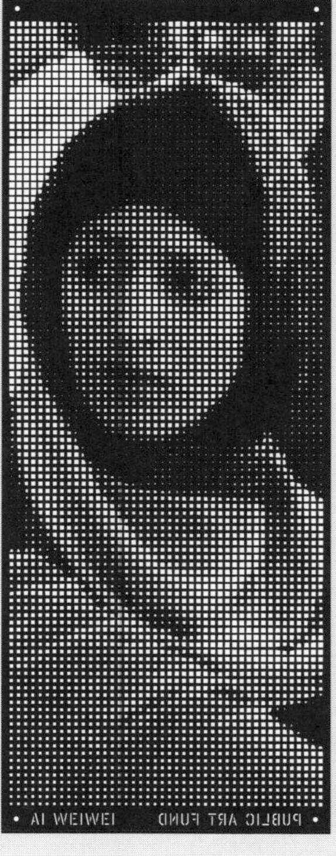

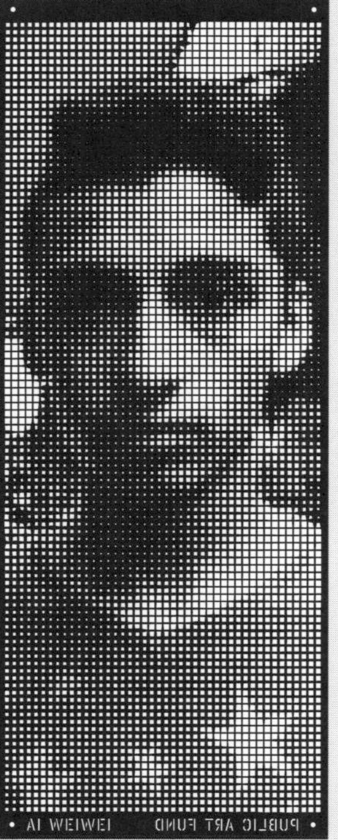

Banner 194
Refugee, Khan Yunis, Gaza Strip, 2016

Banner 195
Refugee, Rafah Crossing, Gaza Strip, 2016

Banner 196
Refugee, Gaza Strip, 2016

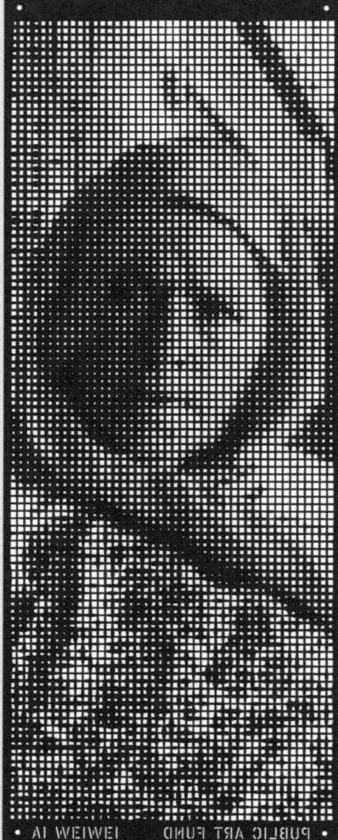

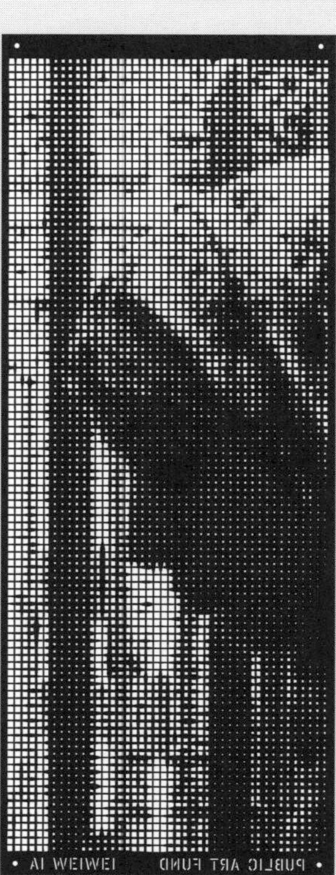

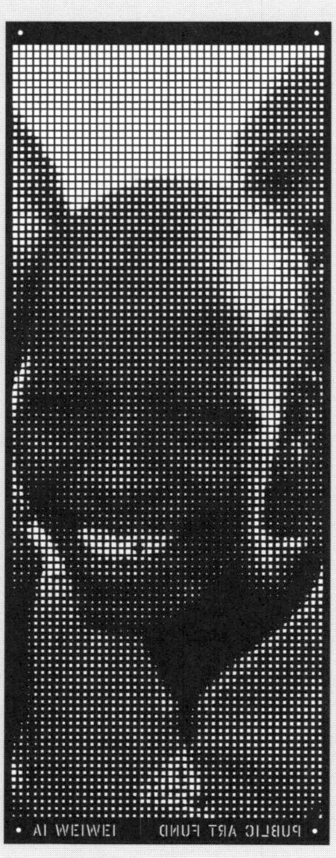

Banner 197
Refugee, Qalandiya Checkpoint, West Bank, 2016

Banner 198
Refugee, Qalandiya Checkpoint, West Bank, 2016

Banner 199
Refugee, Dadaab Camp, Kenya, 2016

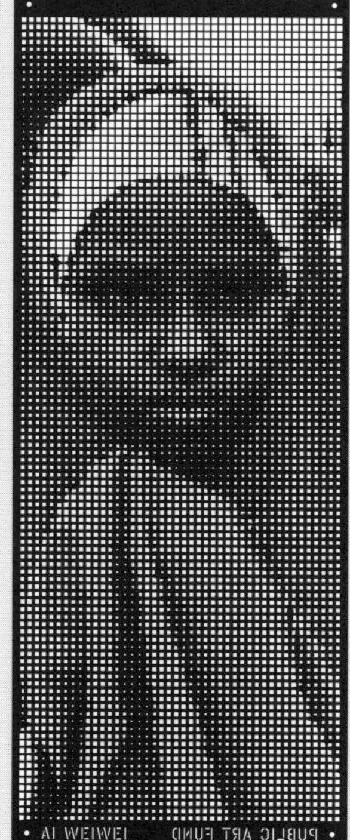

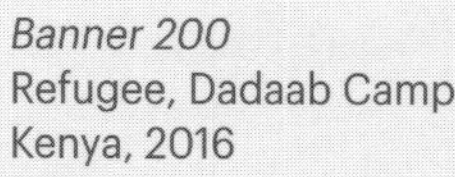

Banner 200
Refugee, Dadaab Camp, Kenya, 2016

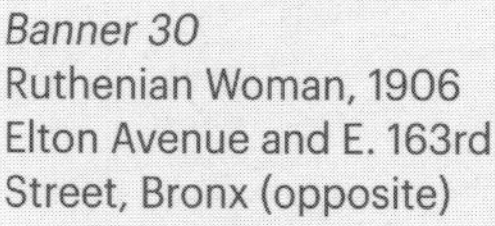

Banner 30
Ruthenian Woman, 1906
Elton Avenue and E. 163rd Street, Bronx (opposite)

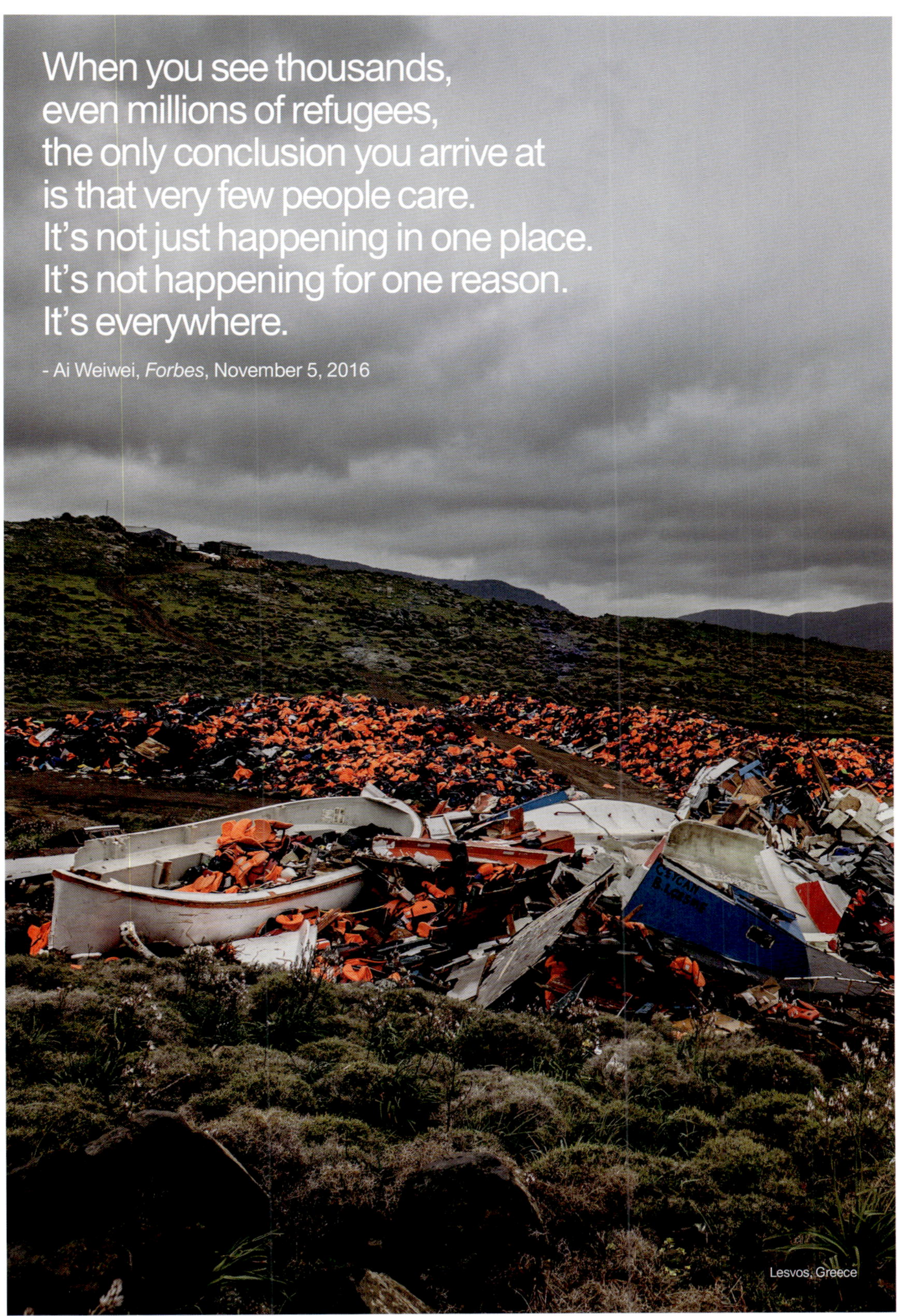

Social media post, *Banner 171*, Nizip Camp, Gaziantep, Turkey (opposite)

Good Neighbors 52
Lesvos, Greece, 2016 (above)

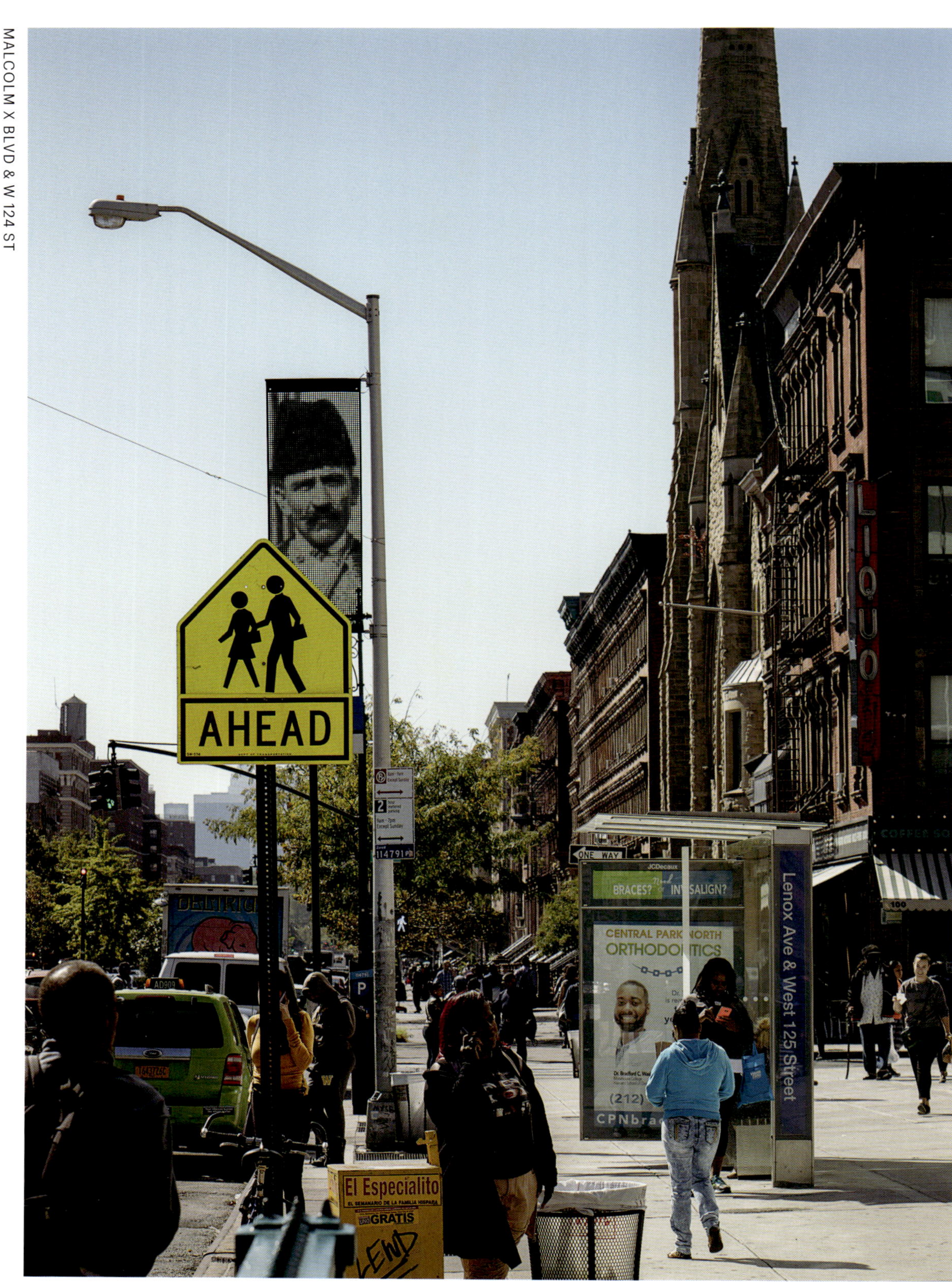

Banner 36
Turkish Bank Guard John Postanzi, 1912 (top)

Good Neighbors 95, MTA Subway platform exhibition advertisement (opposite, top)

Social media post, *Banner 75*, Refugee, Shariya Camp, Iraq, 2015 (opposite, bottom)

77 ST SUBWAY STATION

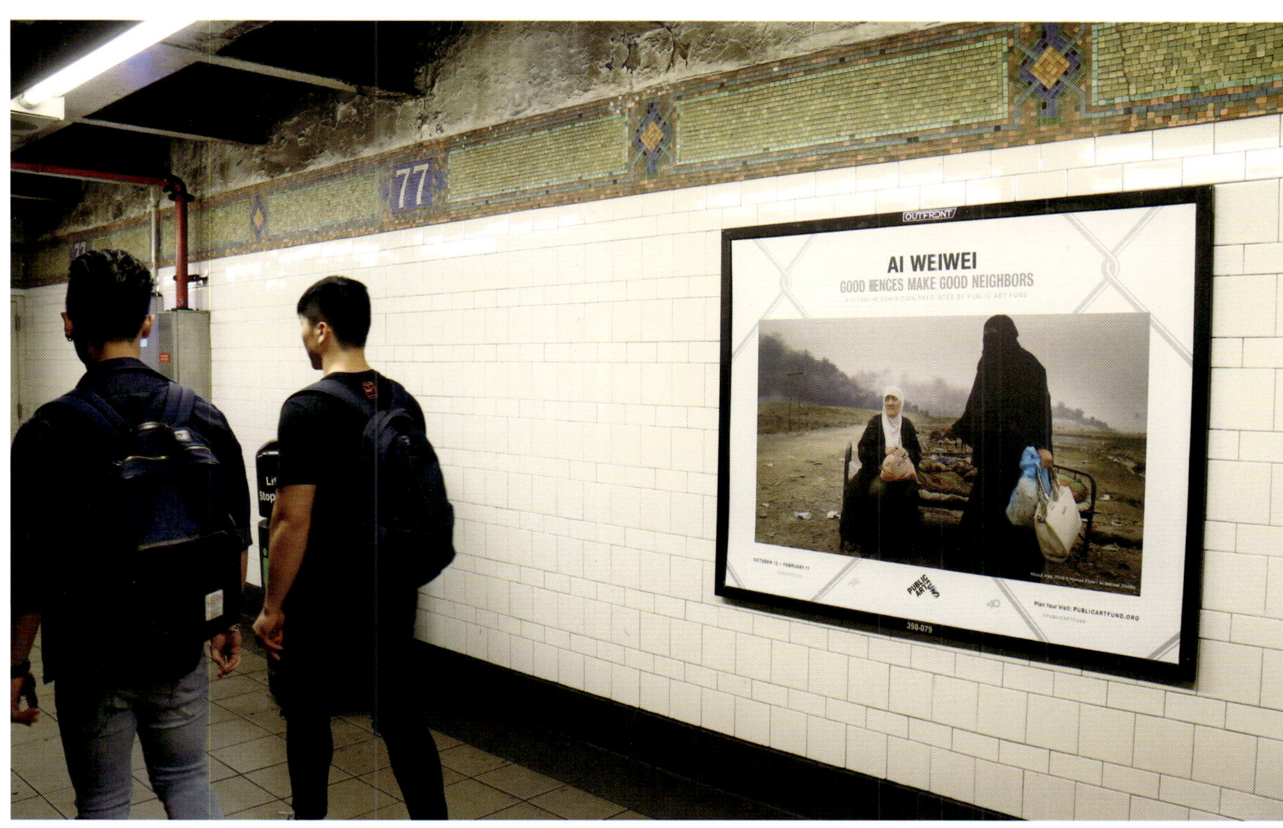

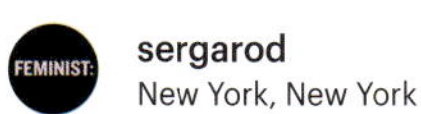

sergarod
New York, New York

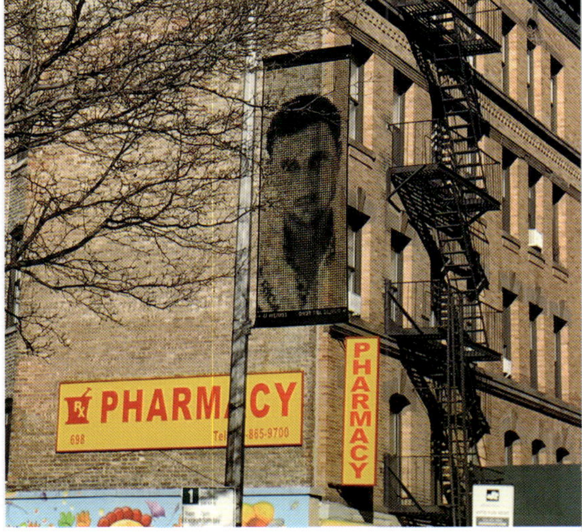

26 likes

sergarod This banner caught my eye as I was crossing the street. It was mesmerizing. Then I saw there were a handful more along Amsterdam Ave. Knowing nothing upon first view, you can tell this is art. It's special. It's sad. And it's important. Then I researched. There are 200 lamppost banners around the city! They're a part of Ai Weiwei's "Good Fences Make Good Neighbors" exhibit going on around #NYC (thank you @publicartfund!). You've probably seen images of the gilded cages at Central Park and Washington Park. I really think this is public art at its best. Beautiful, integrated, meaningful. Can't wait to go hunting for the rest.

DECEMBER 21, 2017

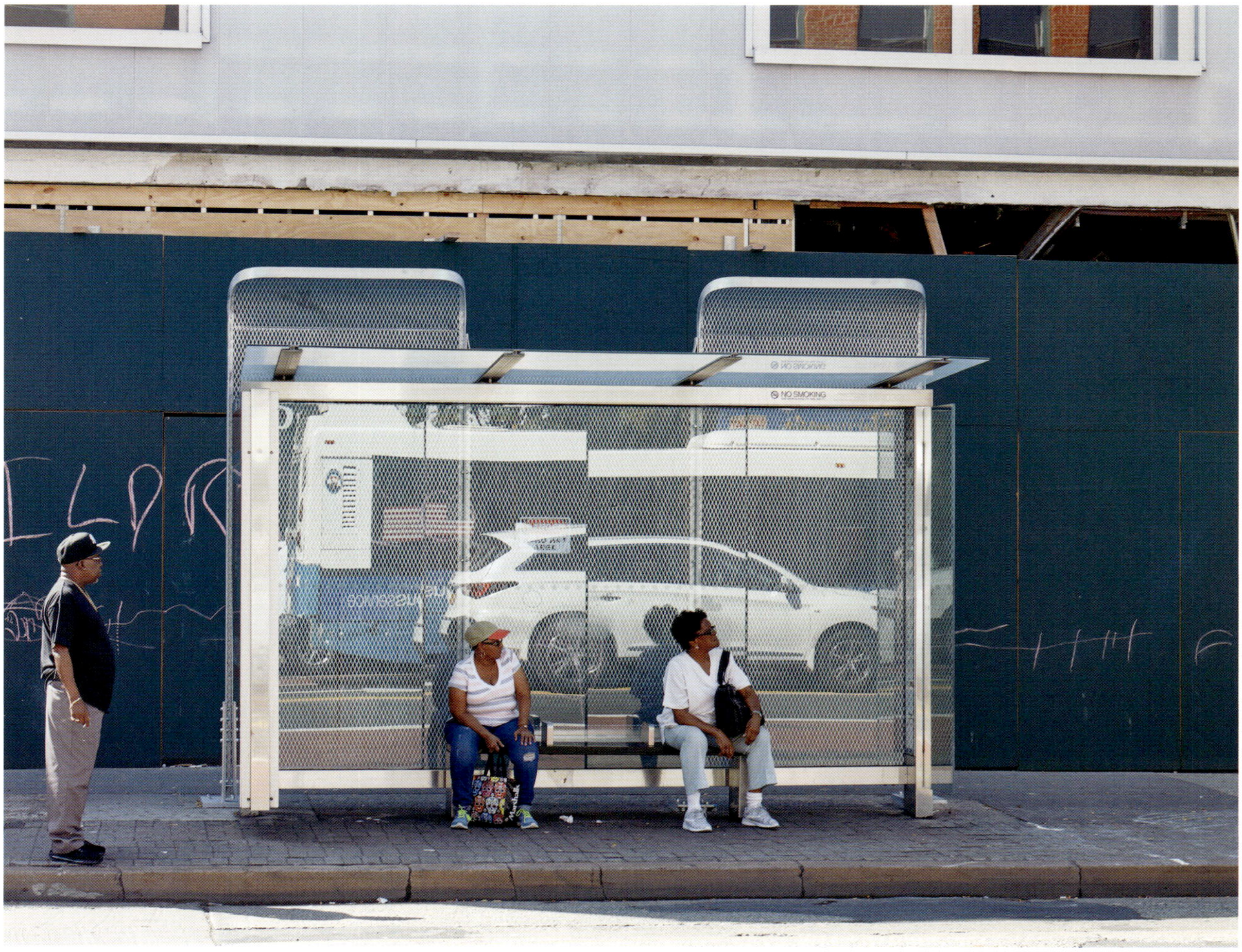

W 125 ST & FREDERICK DOUGLASS BLVD

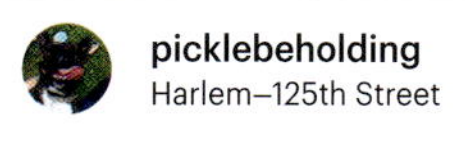

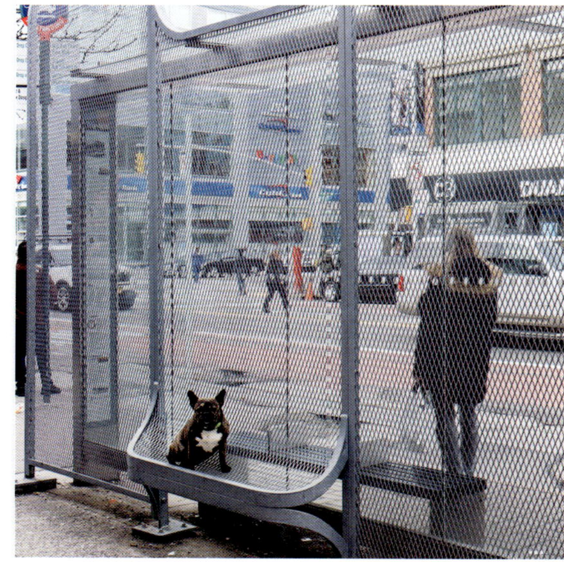

400 likes

picklebeholding I'm sitting on the art. This is making me very nervous. Please get me off the art. @aiww @publicartfund #goodfencesmakegoodneighbors #harlem #aiweiwei #publicartfund#PickleBeholding #PickleDog #frenchie #frenchbulldog #bulldog #artdog #gallerydog

MARCH 3, 2018

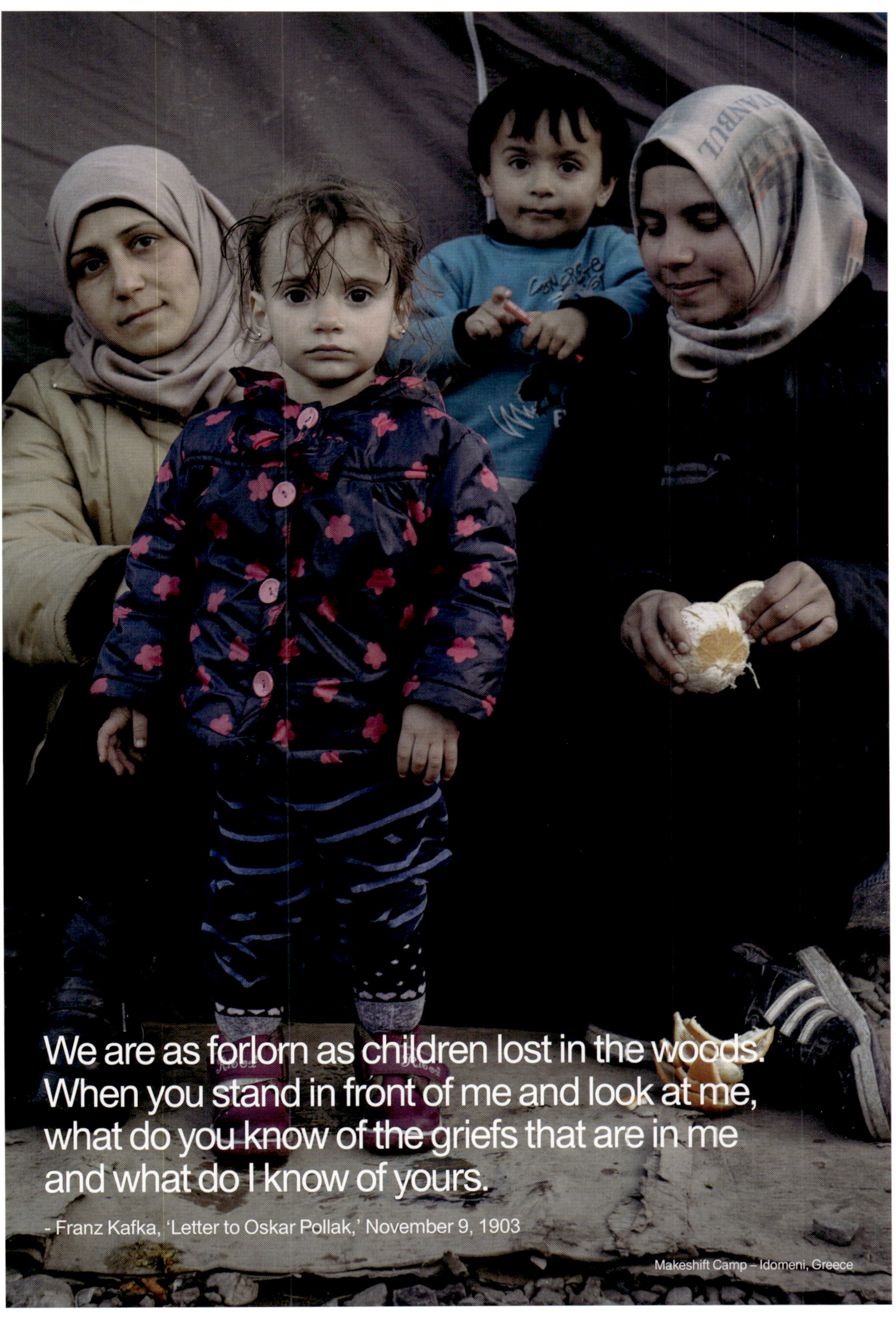

Harlem Shelter 3 (opposite, top)

Social media post, *Harlem Shelter 3* (opposite, bottom)

Good Neighbors 63
Makeshift Camp, Idomeni, Greece, 2016
(top)

BRONX & QUEENS

	Banners	26
	Bus Shelters	2
	Good Neighbors	21
	Structures	1

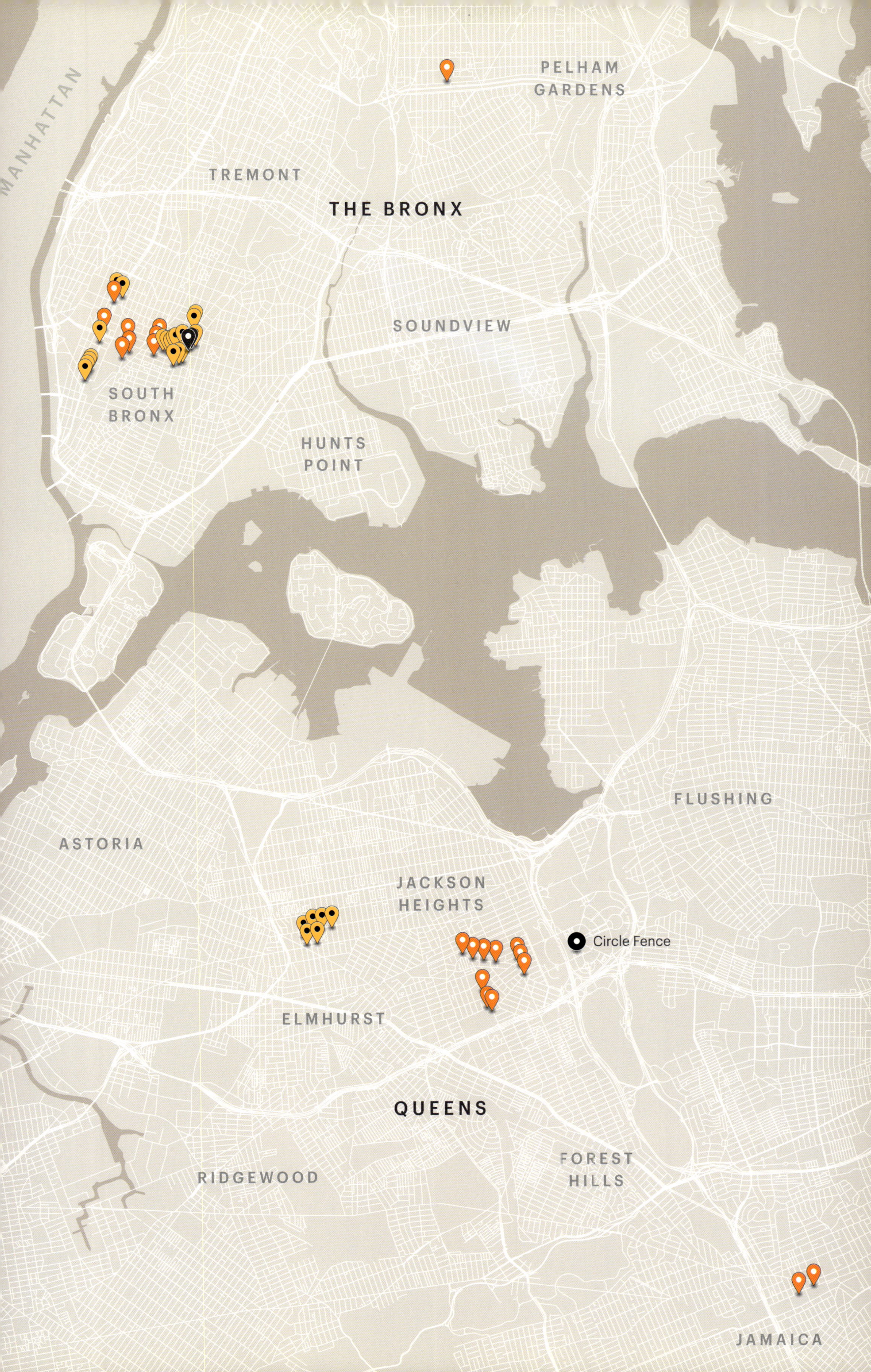
MANHATTAN
PELHAM GARDENS
TREMONT
THE BRONX
SOUNDVIEW
SOUTH BRONX
HUNTS POINT
FLUSHING
ASTORIA
JACKSON HEIGHTS
Circle Fence
ELMHURST
QUEENS
RIDGEWOOD
FOREST HILLS
JAMAICA

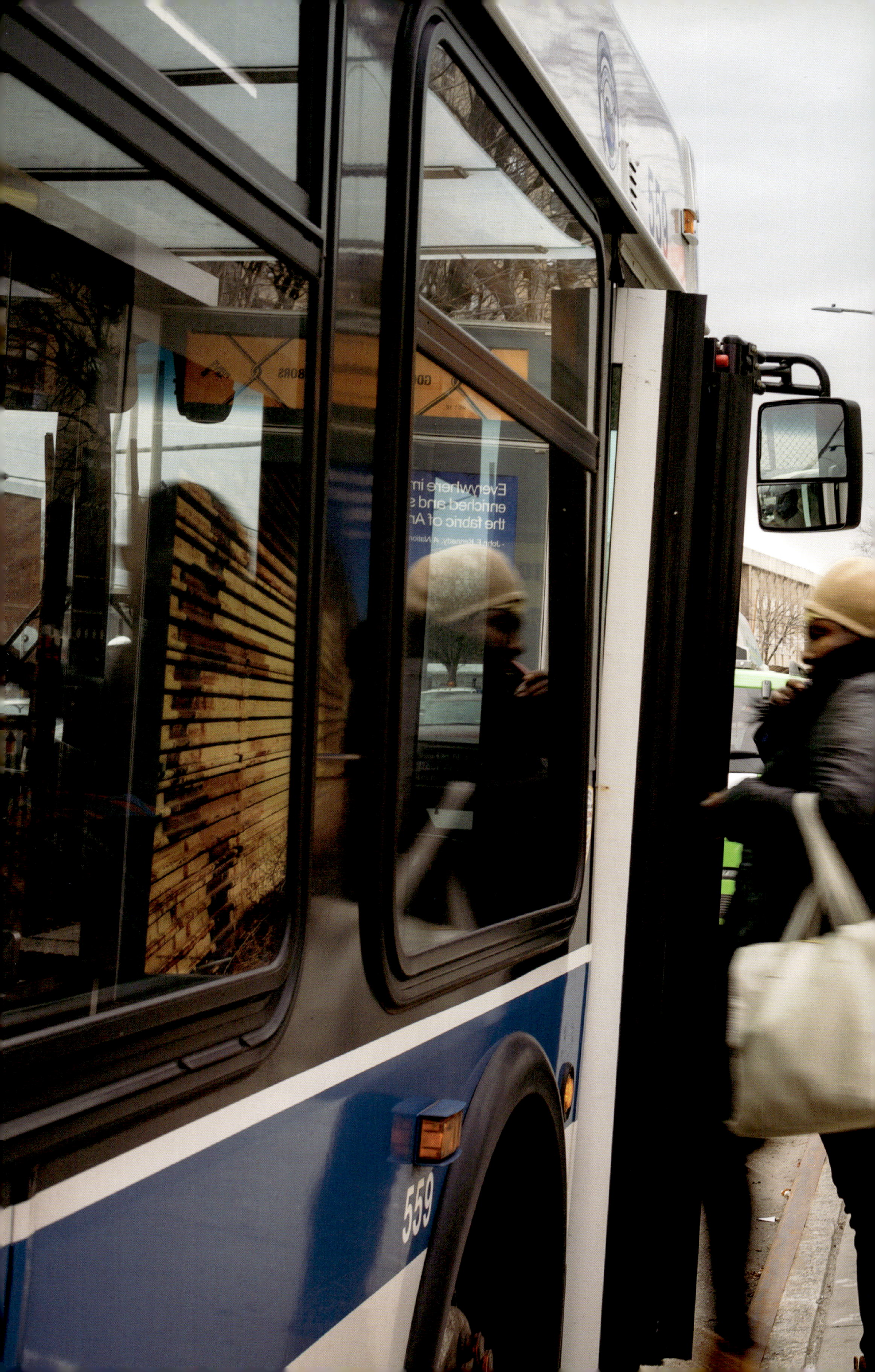
559

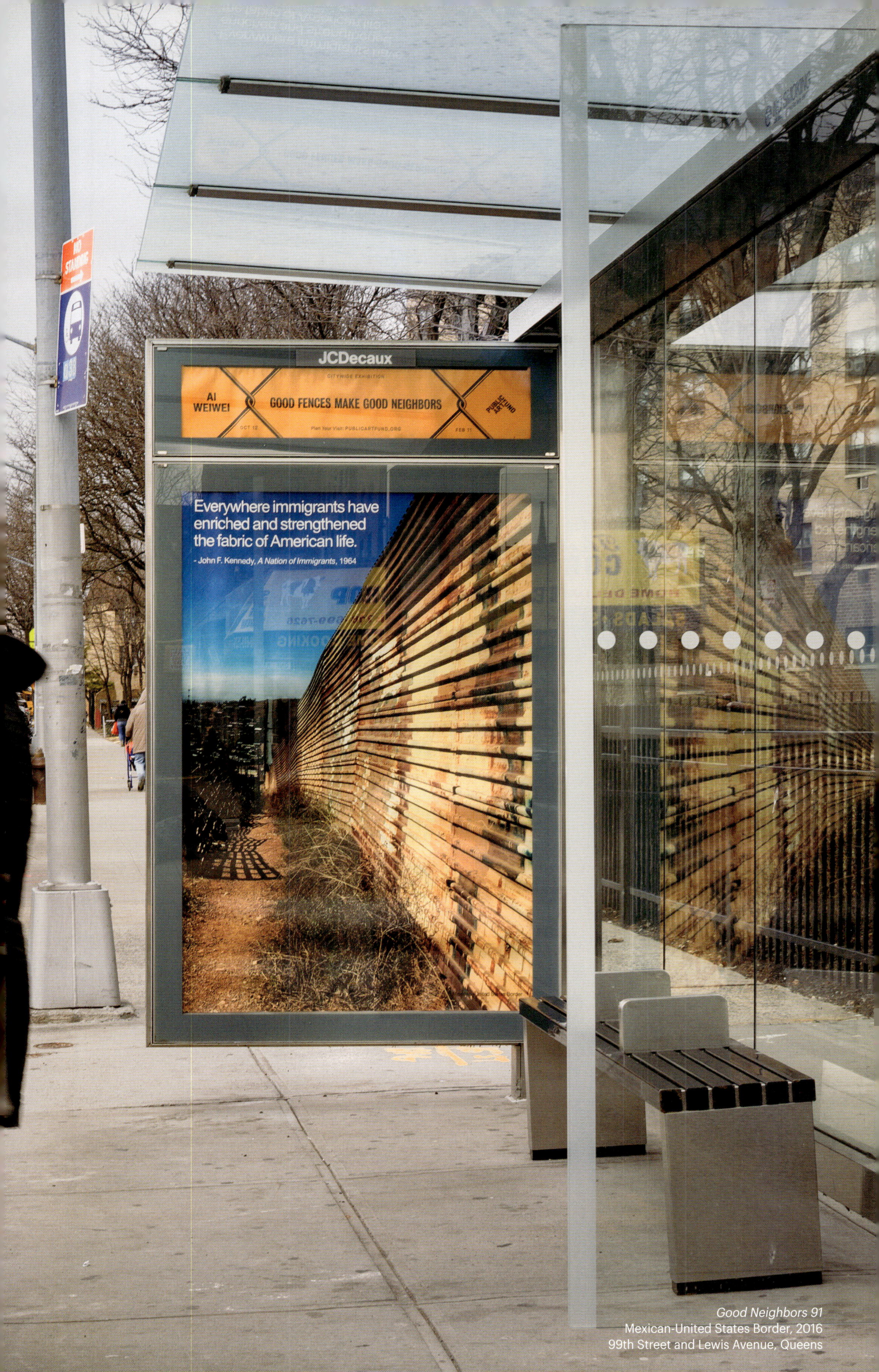

Good Neighbors 91
Mexican-United States Border, 2016
99th Street and Lewis Avenue, Queens

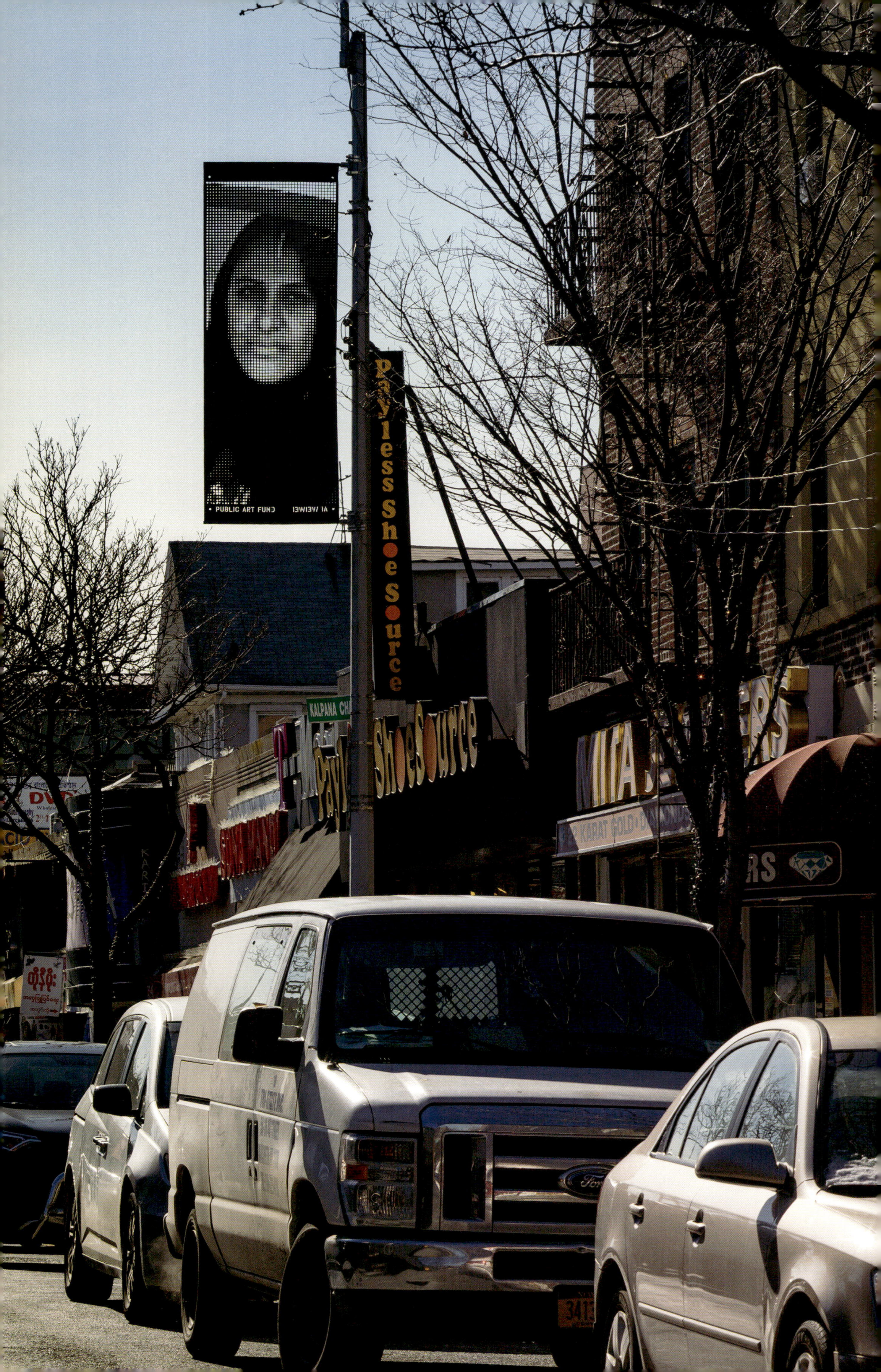
PUBLIC ART FUND
Payless ShoeSource
ShoeSource

Bronx & Queens

With the passage of the 1965 amendments to the Immigration and Nationality Act and the abolition of restrictive quotas, the countries from which waves of immigrants predominantly arrived shifted from southern and eastern Europe to Latin America, Asia, and the Caribbean. As a result, New York City's foreign-born population is currently at an all-time high and reflects cultures from every corner of the world. The heterogeneity of the city is evident in Queens, the most polyglot region globally, with more than 160 languages spoken, where nearly half its residents are foreign-born. In recent years, the borough has grown to be one of the largest ethnic Chinese enclaves outside Asia, and Flushing's Chinatown is one of the fastest-growing Chinatowns in the world. New Yorkers and tourists alike flock to the terminus of the 7 Flushing Local train for authentic cultural experiences, including cuisine that is known to be the best in the city. For the exhibition, Queens hosted works from Jackson Heights to Jamaica (the eastern boundaries of the project). Clustered between Broadway and Thirty-Seventh Avenue, banners marked the area's cultural concentration and tradition of hosting immigrants. Widely dispersed in Corona, *Good Neighbors* images met commuters at eye level while they waited at bus shelters. Anchored to the north in Flushing Meadows Corona Park, *Circle Fence* surrounded the landmark Unisphere sculpture created for the 1964 World's Fair to represent the theme of global interdependence. Ai Weiwei's 1,040-foot-long netted installation in the park became a pilgrimage site for the exhibition, the same park where Ai sold T-shirts as a young artist in the 1980s.

At present, the Bronx is the only New York City borough with a white minority—more than half the population is of Latin American origin. The Grand Concourse in the southern Bronx, a major thoroughfare connecting Manhattan to the northern Bronx, designed in the 1890s and modeled on the Champs-Élysées in Paris, marks the entry point into the borough. When the New York City subway opened a few blocks west of the Grand Concourse in 1917, it initiated a housing boom, with Jewish and Italian families looking to escape Manhattan tenements. The area is still home to some of the best remaining Art Deco and Art Moderne buildings in the city. South Bronx's main artery was flanked by the portraits of immigrants and images of refugee camps. Bordering on the east, twenty of Ai's works densely inhabited a ten-block radius in the neighborhood of Morrisania, with two *Bronx Shelter* sculptures flanking Third Avenue almost directly opposite each other, where bus routes connect the Bronx to Manhattan.

Banner 89
Refugee, Shariya Camp, Iraq, 2015
37th Avenue and 74th Street, Queens (opposite)

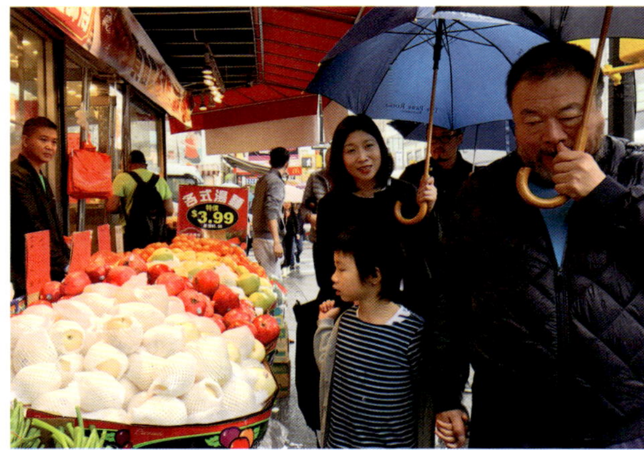

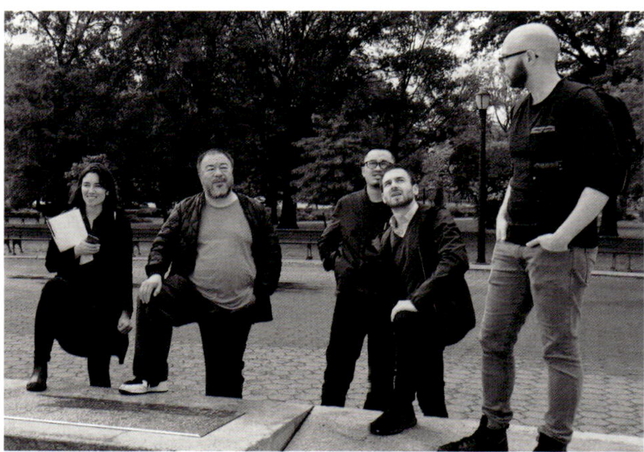

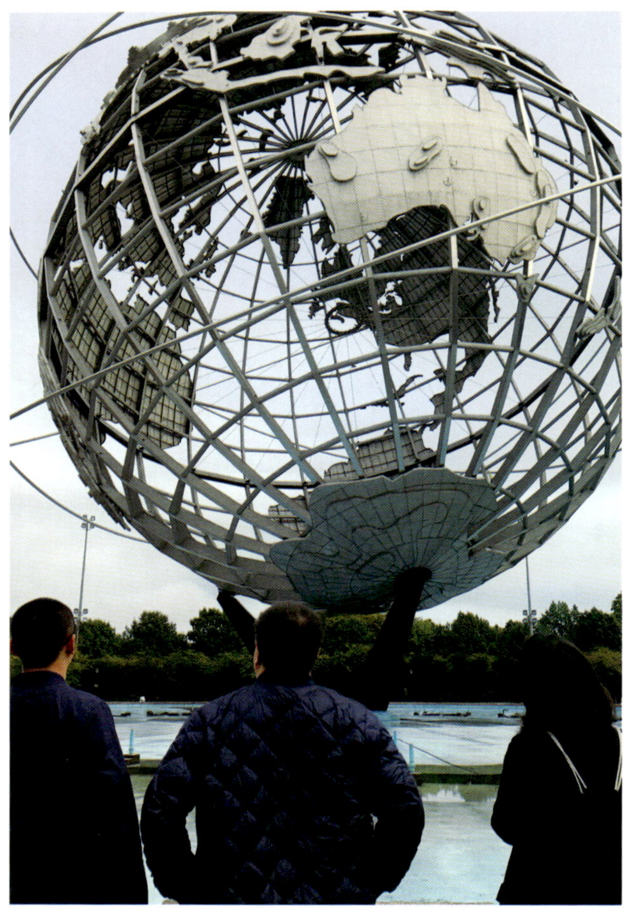

Ai Weiwei's art emerges from his deep humanism. When looking at his work or speaking with him, you sense that his every act, everything he does, is rooted in a fundamental commitment to improving the well-being of the people on this planet.

Olafur Eliasson, artist

Ai Weiwei and family explore Flushing's Chinatown during a site visit to Queens, October 21, 2016 (top left)

Jennifer Schmachtenberg, Ai Weiwei, Gui Nuo, Daniel S. Palmer, and Sam Rauch at the Unisphere during a location scouting visit, October 21, 2016 (bottom left)

Gui Nuo, Ai Weiwei, and Jennifer Schmachtenberg examine the Unisphere during a location scouting visit, October 21, 2016 (right)

Social media post, *Circle Fence* (opposite)

Forty percent of New Yorkers are foreign-born. There is no New York City without the millions of immigrants—past and present—who have come here in search of better lives for themselves and their families. Our neighbors are people from all across the globe—people who brought their dreams here and have helped make New York one of the greatest, most diverse cities in the world. It is no surprise then that Ai Weiwei's Public Art Fund project, *Good Fences Make Good Neighbors*—inspired by the international migration crisis and current geopolitical landscape—resonates so deeply across our five boroughs.

Corey Johnson, Speaker, New York City Council

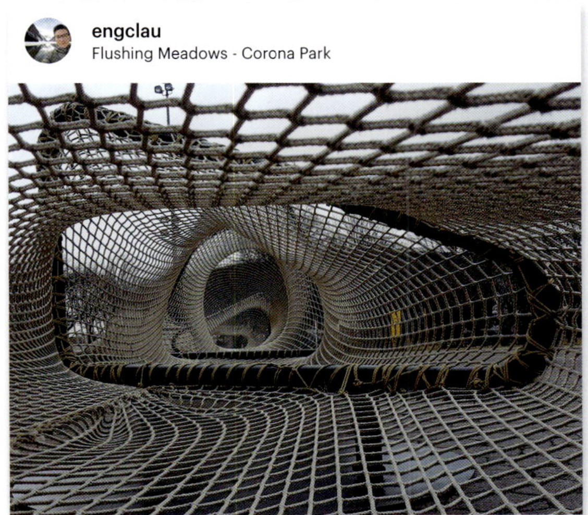

230 likes

engclau 1,000-foot-long #circlefence #goodfencesmakegoodneighbors

fraiche_boutique_toronto Where is it ?in Toronto

cqaronfor for cats?

cherimacleod Neato

adrianmcld Stunning ☺

engclau Yippee!! 😀☺😀

DECEMBER 23, 2017

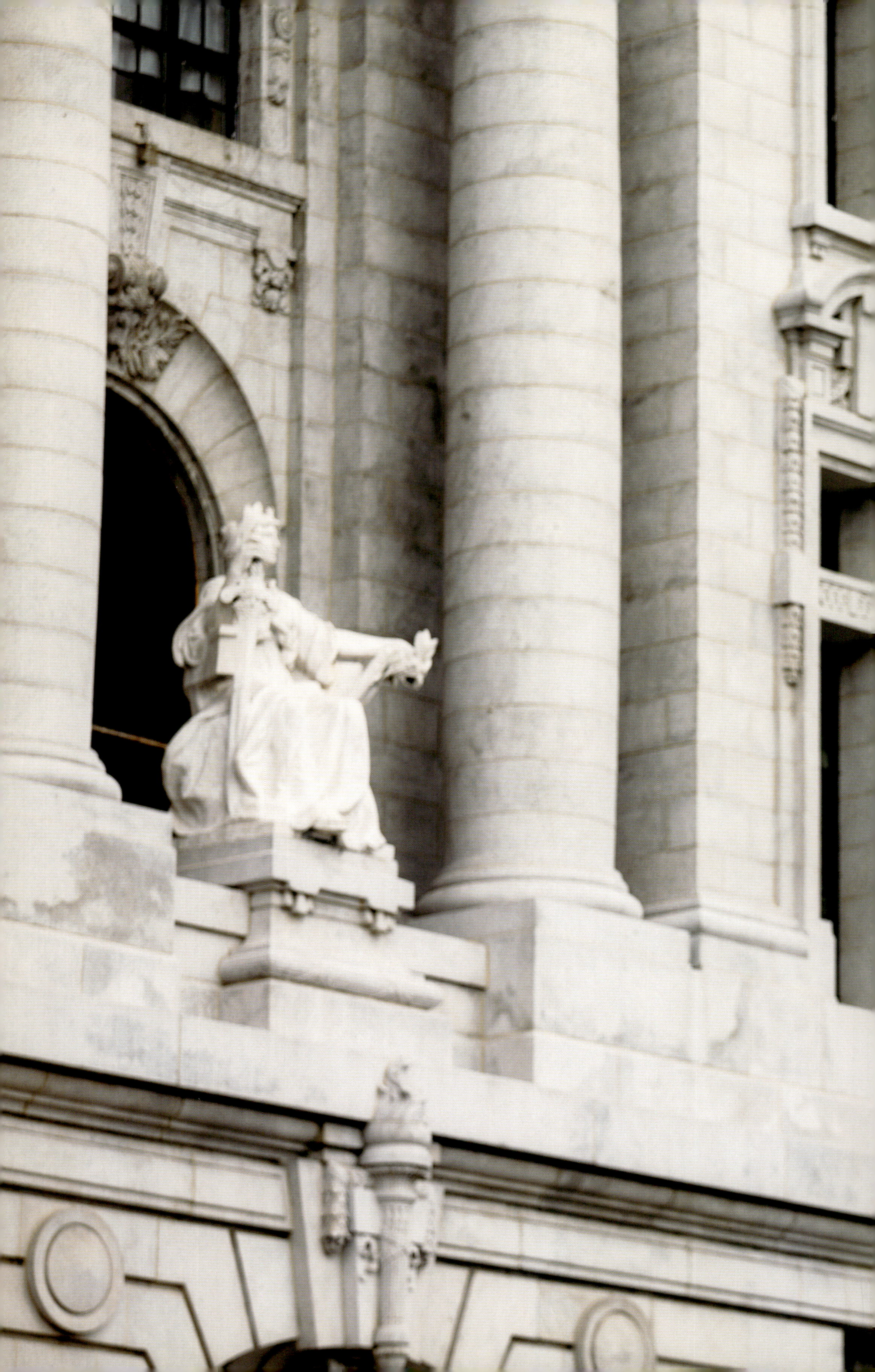

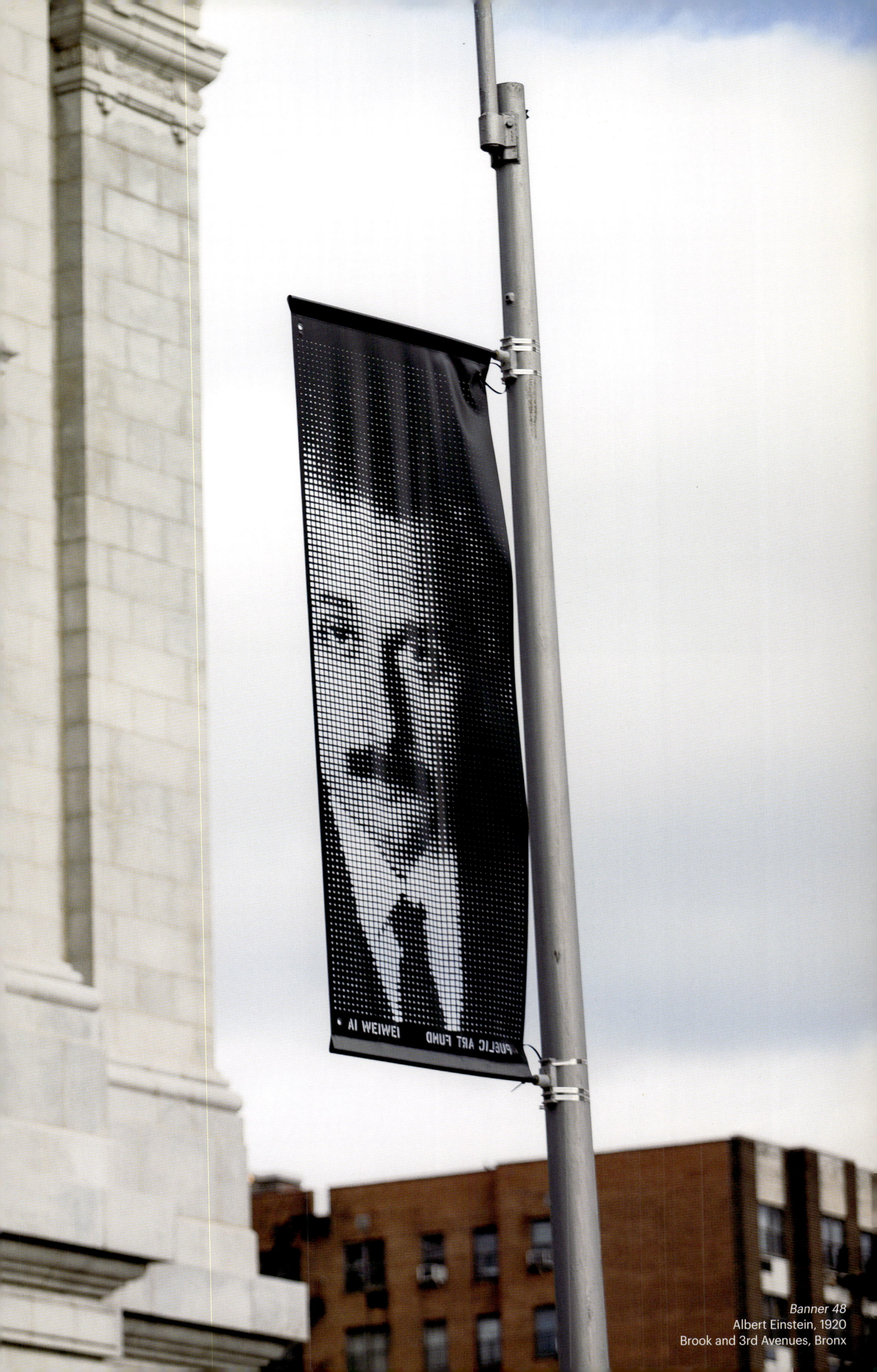

Banner 48
Albert Einstein, 1920
Brook and 3rd Avenues, Bronx

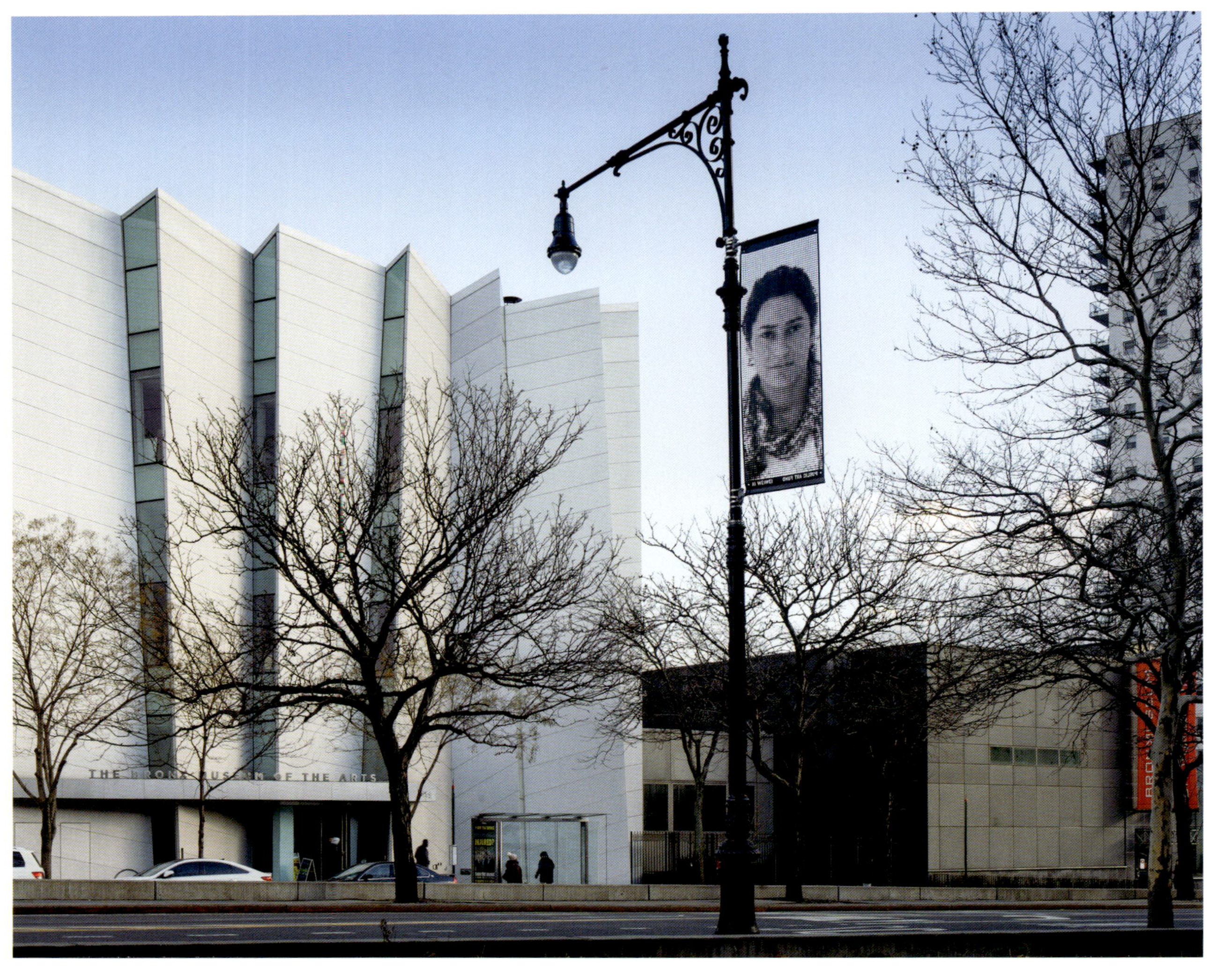

Surprising to some, Ai Weiwei's photos show that refugees look very much like New Yorkers. Taken up front and personal, they portray men, women, and children who resemble those we cross in our daily encounters. And this is important—especially at a time when refugees are often perceived as threats to security rather than victims of brutal conflicts well beyond their control. Ai Weiwei's focus on them as individuals with compelling personal histories and potential calls on us to take notice and challenges our assumptions.

Ninette Kelley, United Nations High Commissioner for Refugees (UNHCR), The UN Refugee Agency

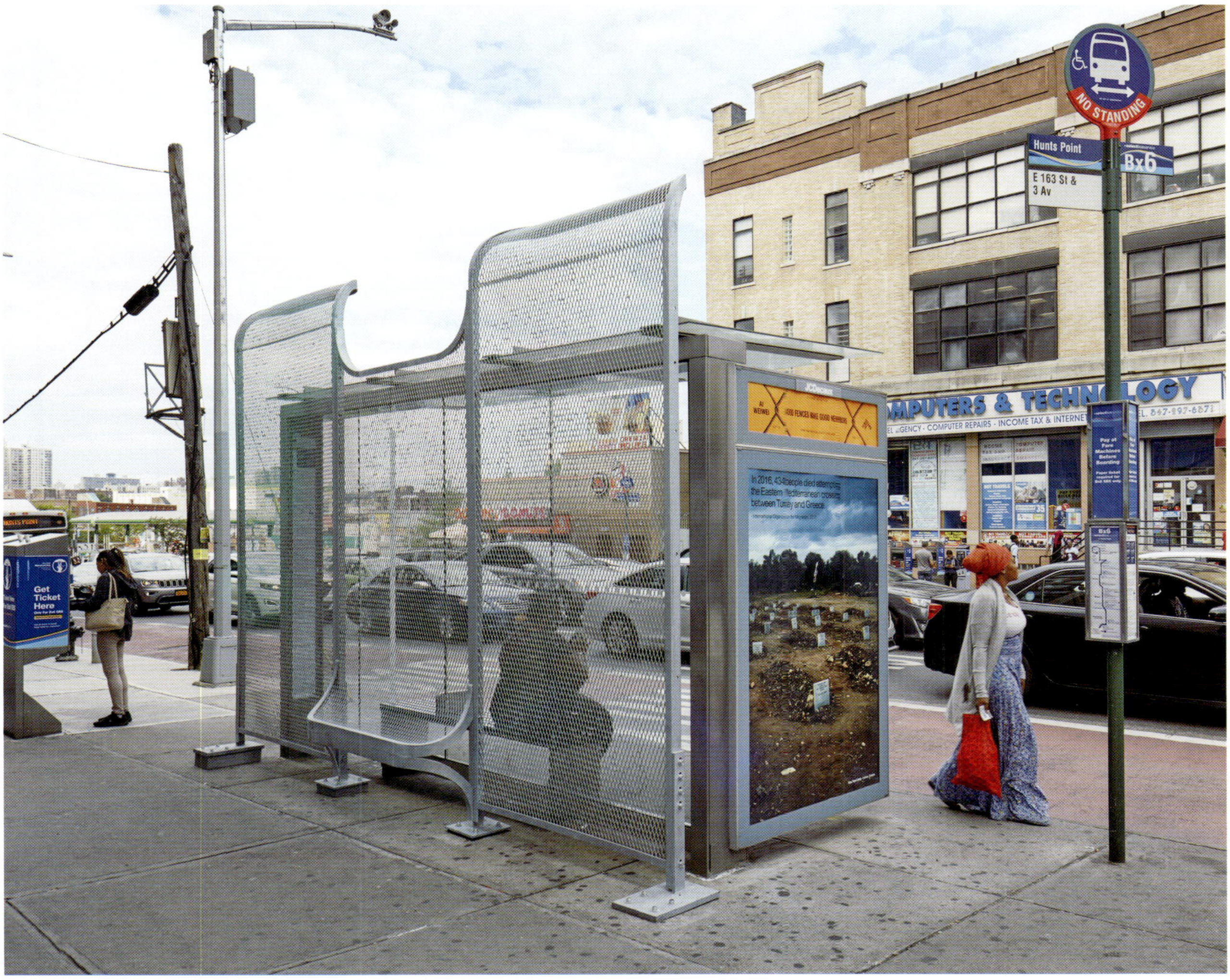

photos_by_ignacio_soltero

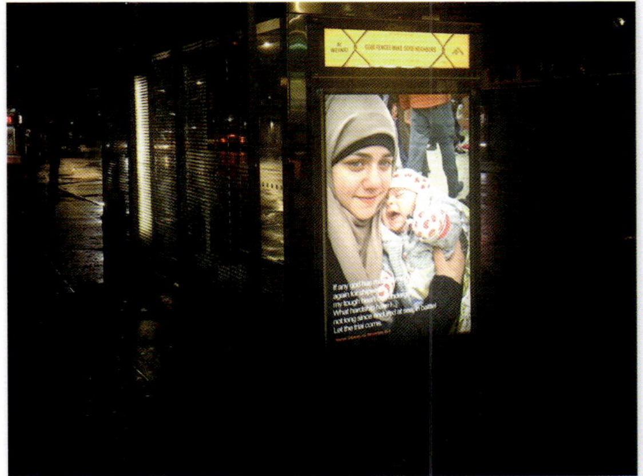

16 likes

photos_by_ignacio_soltero 163rd St & 3rd Ave
#goodfences #aiweiwei #southbronx
#photosbyignaciosoltero

OCTOBER 24, 2017

Banner 95
Refugee, Shariya Camp, Iraq, 2015
(opposite)

Bronx Shelter 1 with *Good Neighbors 26*,
Kara Tepe Camp, Lesvos, Greece, 2016
(top)

Social media post, *Bronx Shelter 2* with
Good Neighbors 28, Lesvos, Greece,
2016 (bottom)

ELTON AVE & E 161 ST, BRONX

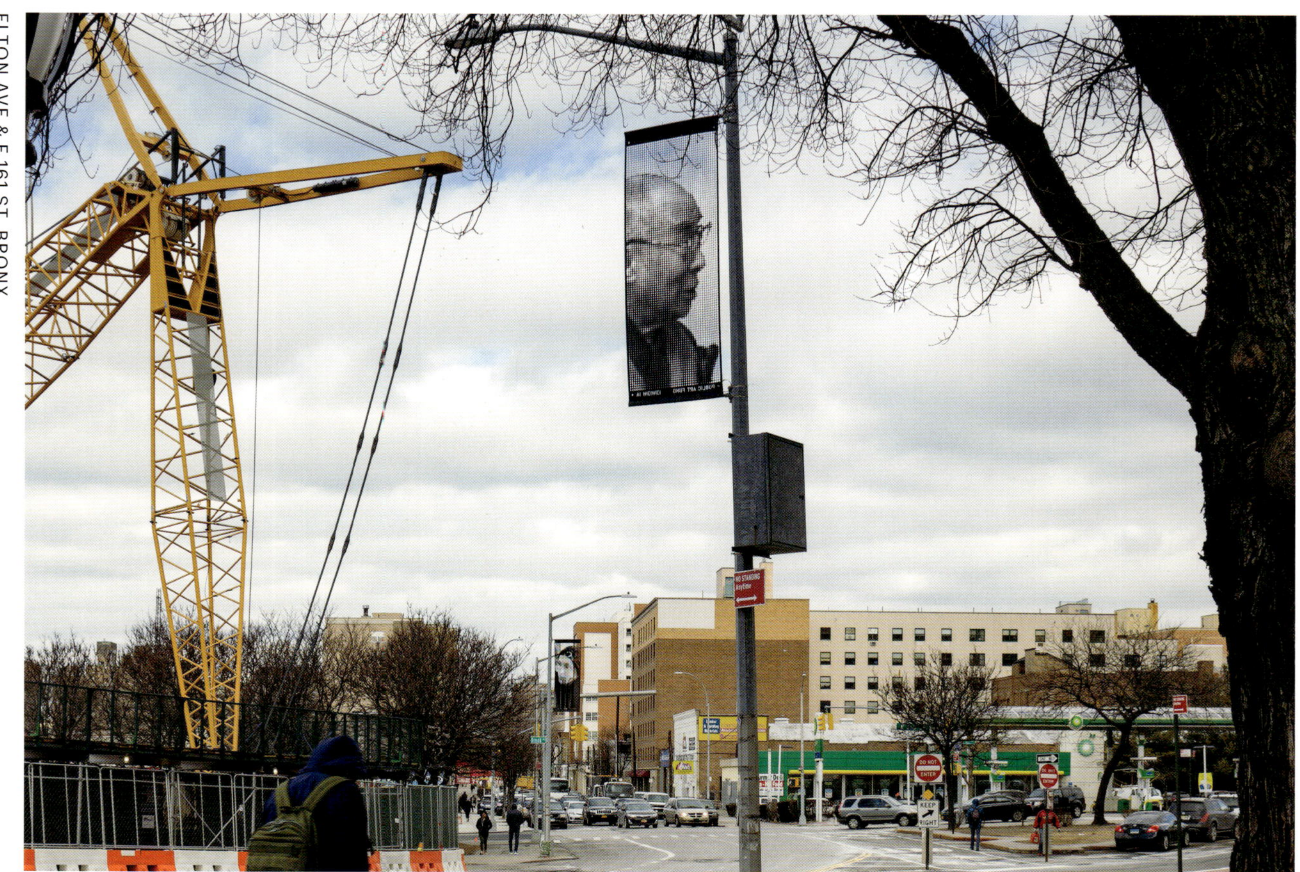

GRAND CONCOURSE & E 161 ST, BRONX

I kept falling, like an object thrown into a limitless sea, without shores and without a bed, slashed by the waters when it starts to sink, and by the wind if it starts to float. Forever sinking and rising, sinking and rising between the sea and the sky, with nothing to hold on to except the two eyes.

- Nawal El Saadawi, *Woman at Point Zero*, 1975

Lesvos, Greece

Banner 46
The Dalai Lama, 2014 (top)

Good Neighbors 23
Lesvos, Greece, 2016 (bottom)

Good Neighbors 3
Lesvos, Greece, 2015 (opposite)

As the world continues to face the greatest humanitarian crisis of our lifetime—68.5 million people displaced due to conflict and persecution—it's essential that there are platforms to engage individuals and keep the crisis—and what must be done to address it—at the center of national discourse. *Good Fences Make Good Neighbors* interjects elements of the refugee crisis into our everyday lives and forces us to examine our collective human response. I am inspired by its beauty, authenticity, and ability to start a dialogue. And even more, the 200 banners featured across the city put faces to the crisis, reminding us all that behind that 68.5 million figure are real human beings who need our support now more than ever.

David Miliband, President and CEO, International Rescue Committee

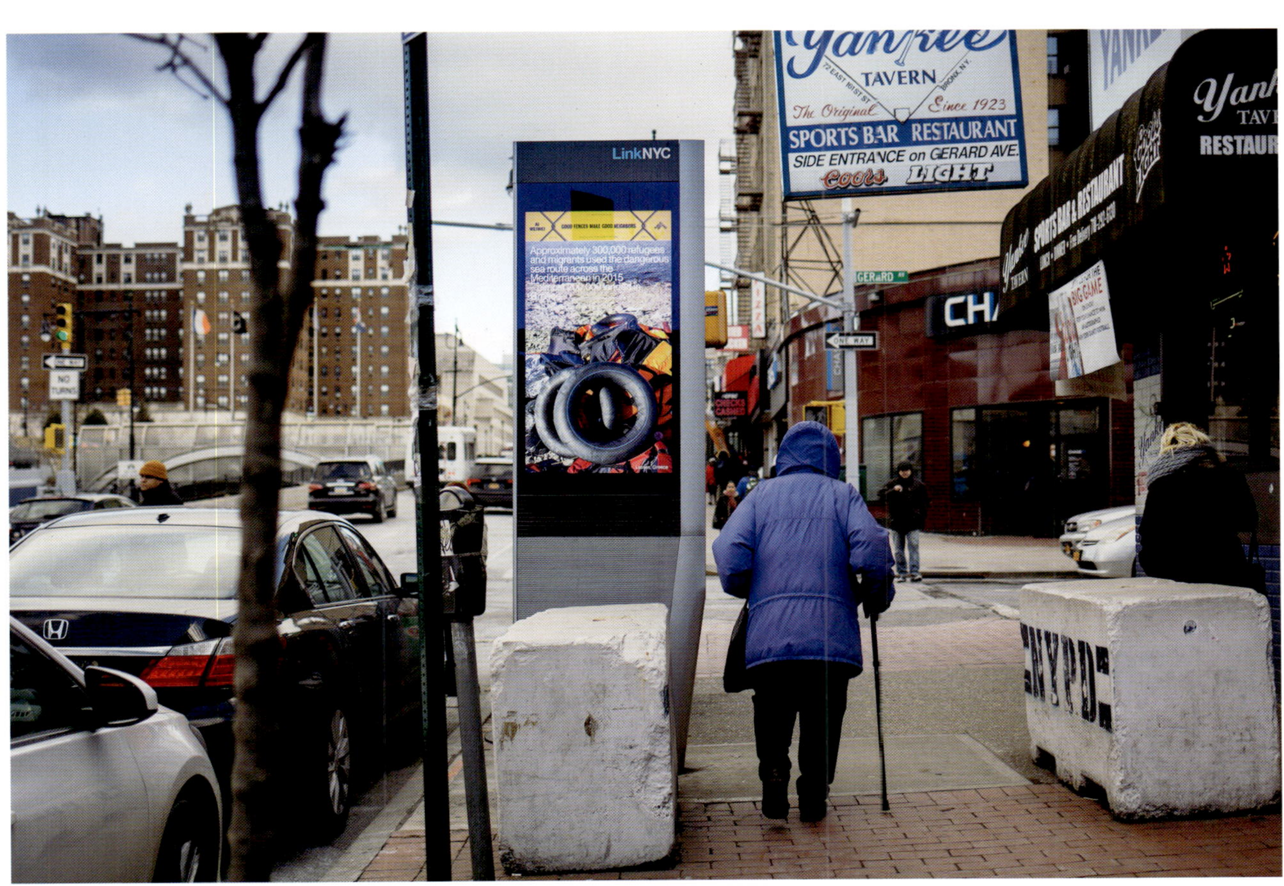

E 161 ST & GERARD AVE, BRONX

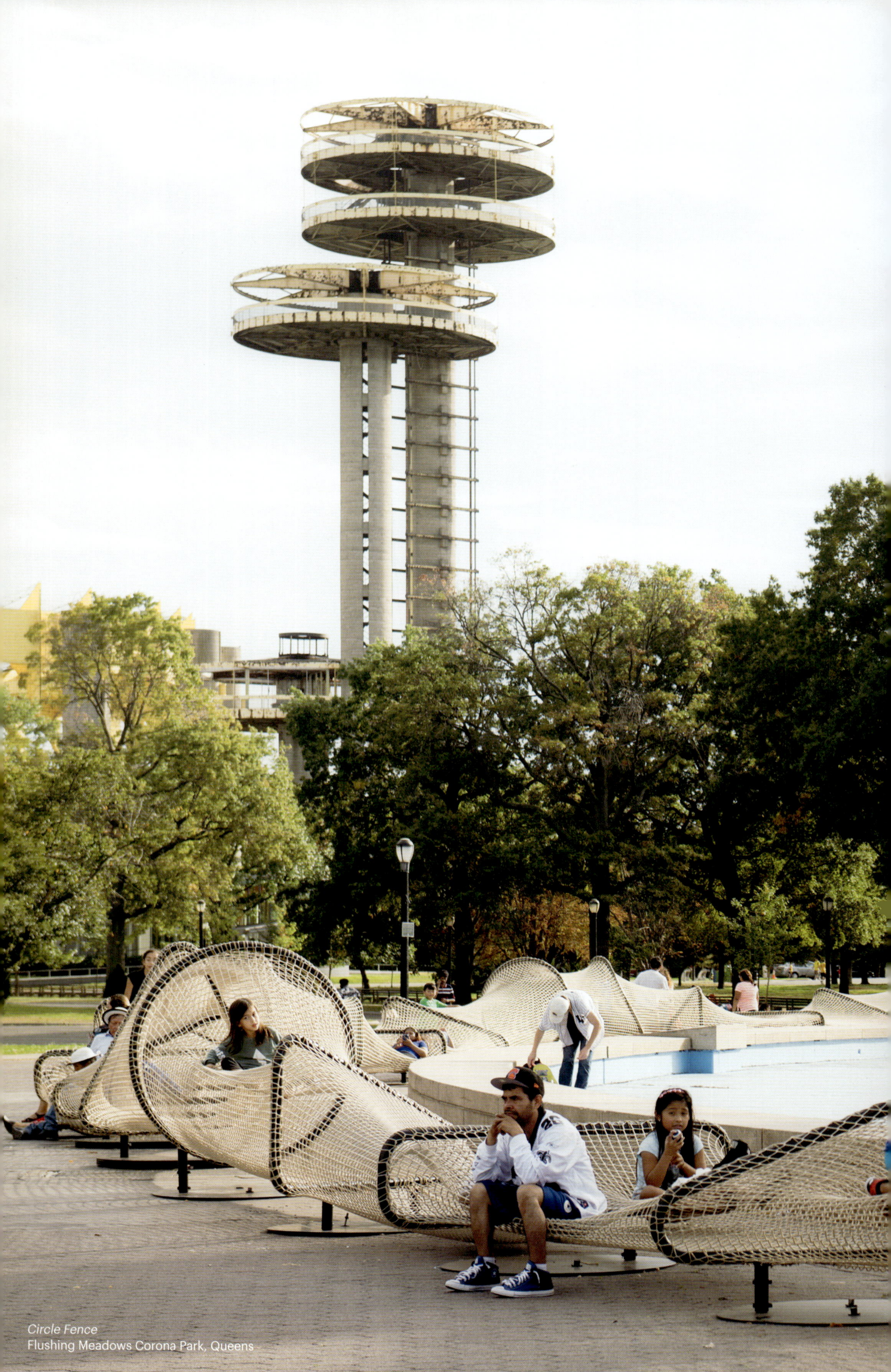

Circle Fence
Flushing Meadows Corona Park, Queens

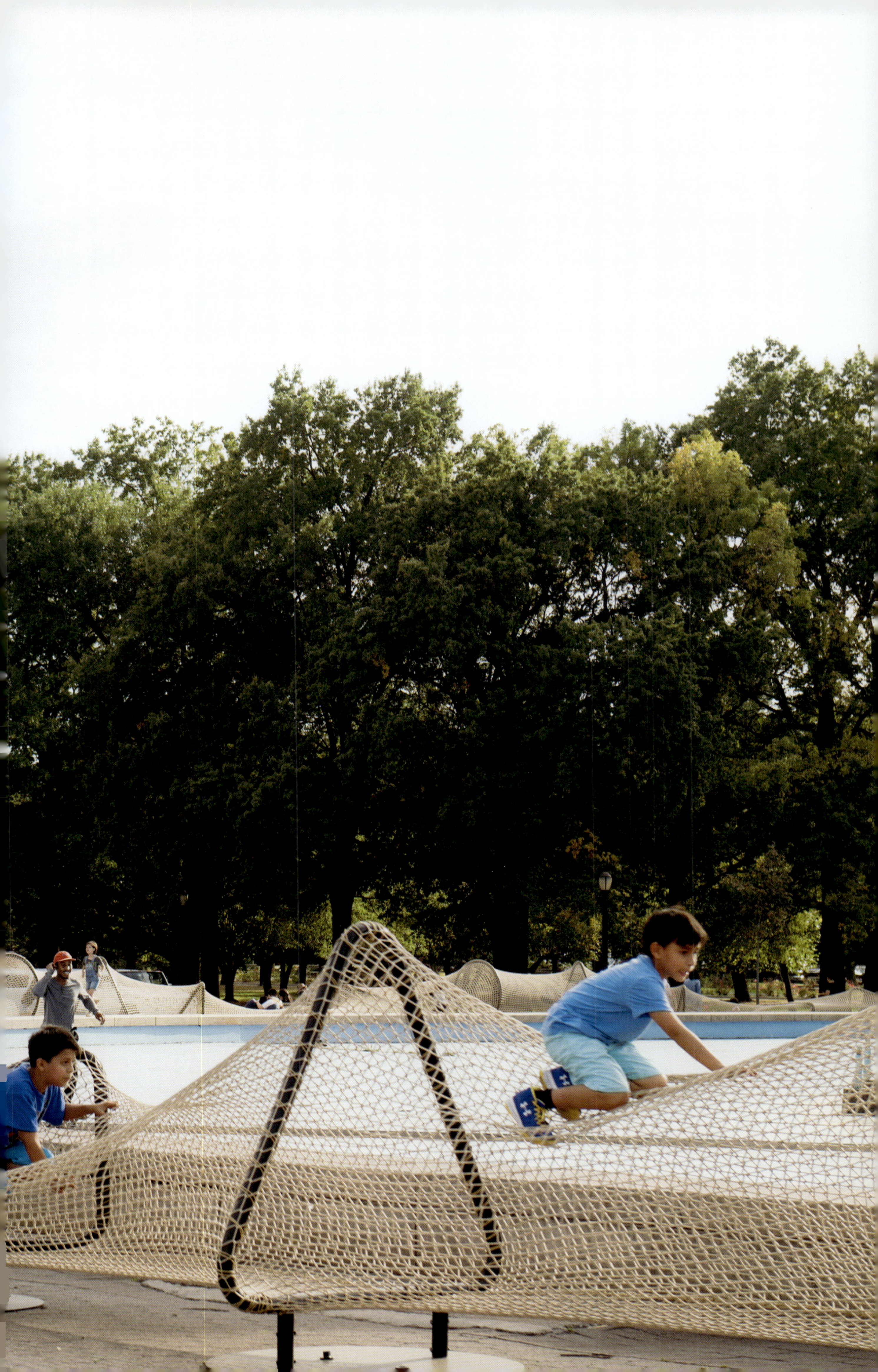

My parents came to New York City from Colombia in the 1970s. They met at work, fell in love, and started a family. They loved the city from day one for both its diversity and the comfort of being able to hear their native tongue in so many neighborhoods. In spite of some hardships, they have always believed they were living the American dream. In the past year, that belief has been challenged in our current social and political climate. While I sometimes lose hope—it's they who do not.

Viewer comment

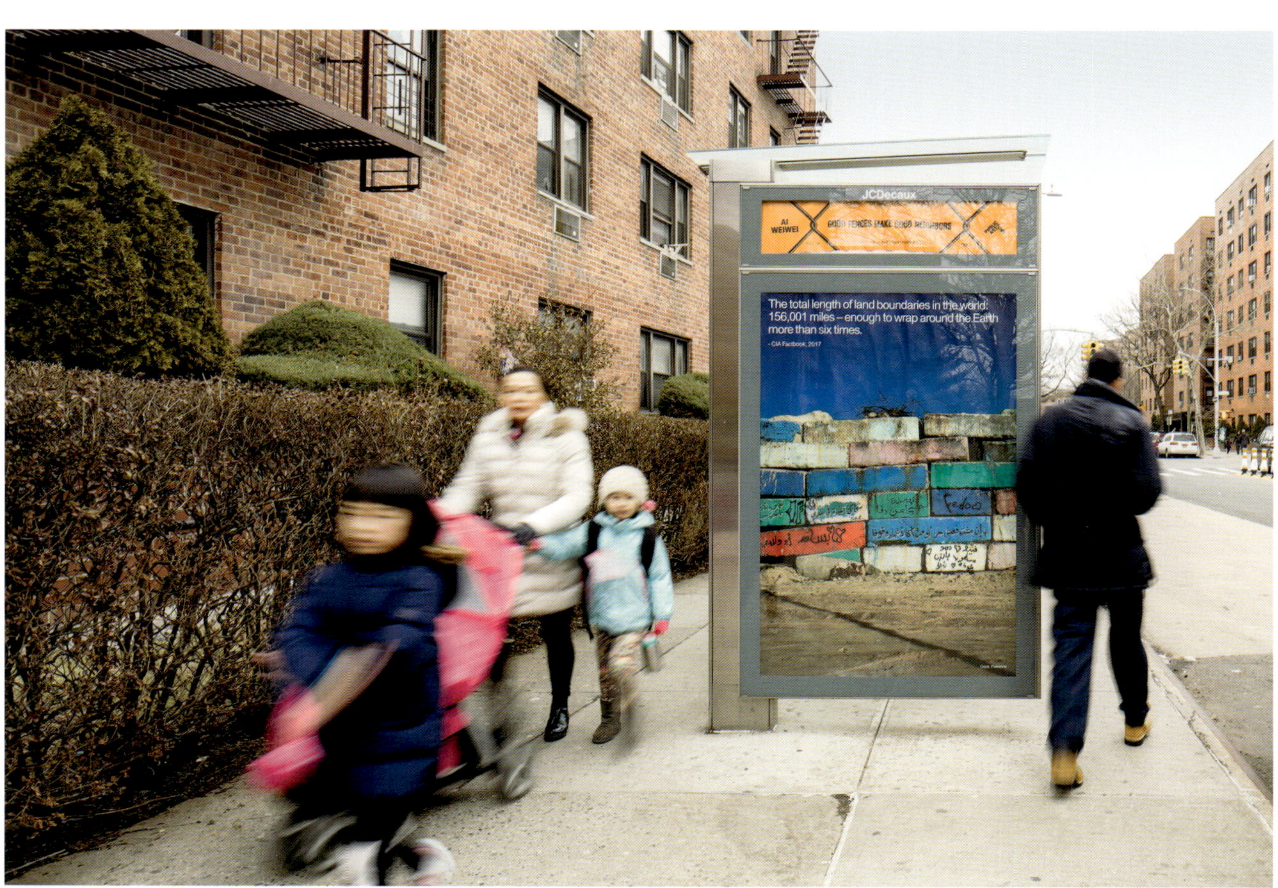

57 AVE & 99 ST, QUEENS

37 RD & 75 ST, QUEENS

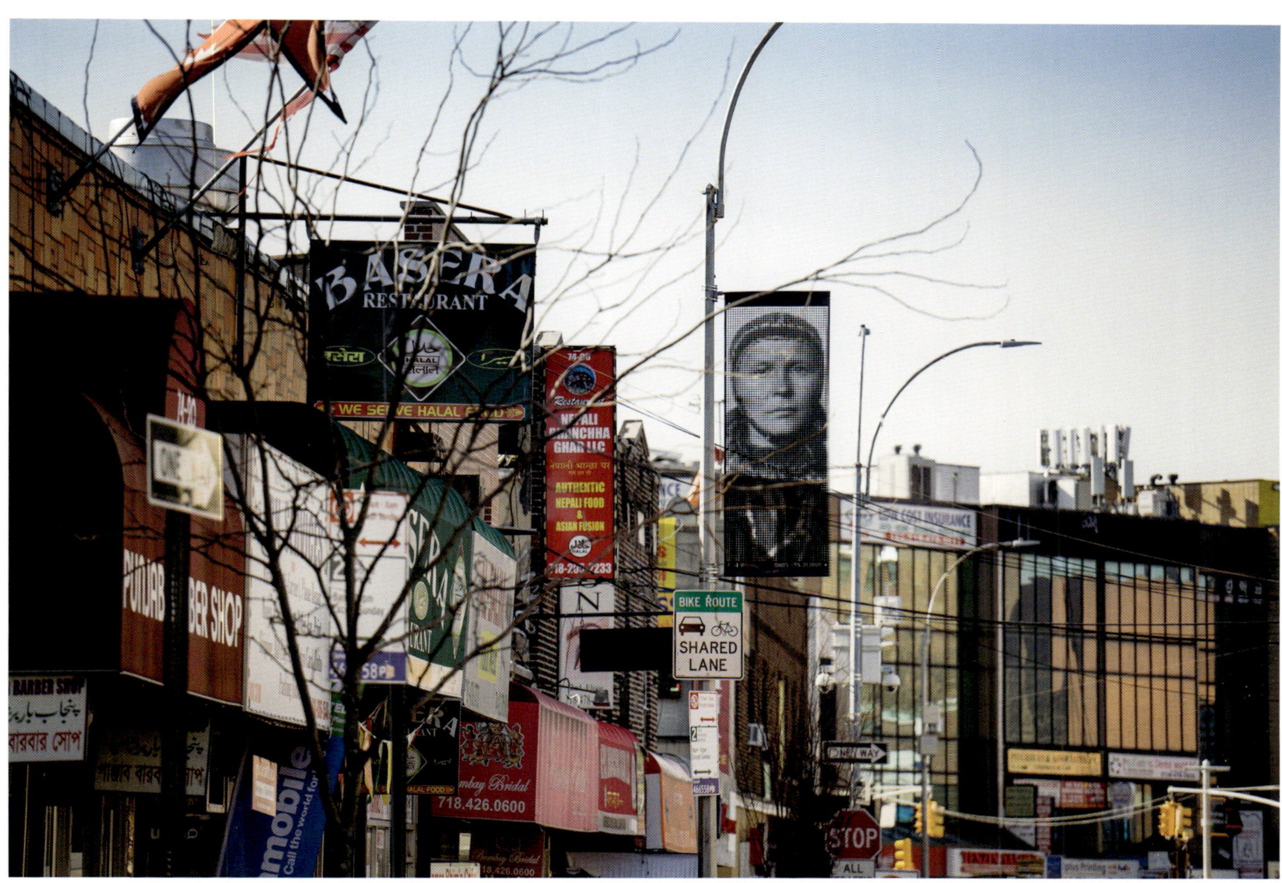

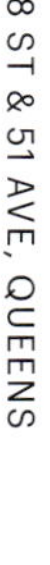
108 ST & 51 AVE, QUEENS

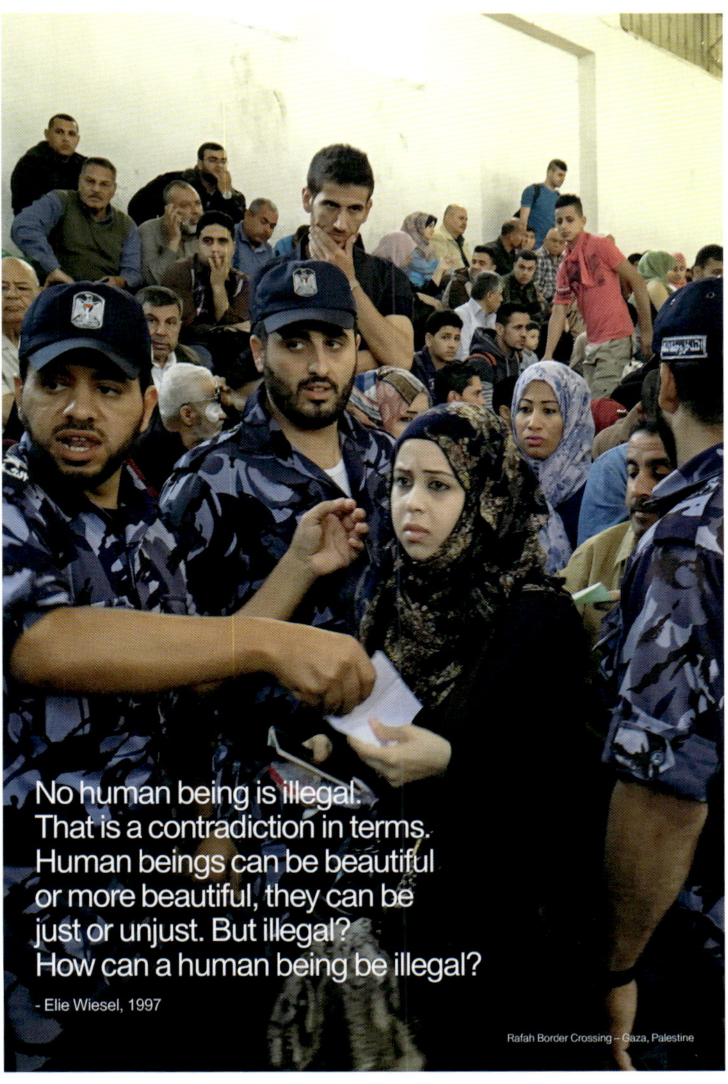

Good Neighbors 85
Gaza, Palestine, 2016
(opposite)

Banner 25
Laplander, 1910 (top)

Good Neighbors 84
Rafah Border Crossing, Gaza,
Palestine, 2016 (bottom)

CORONA AVE & 104 ST, QUEENS

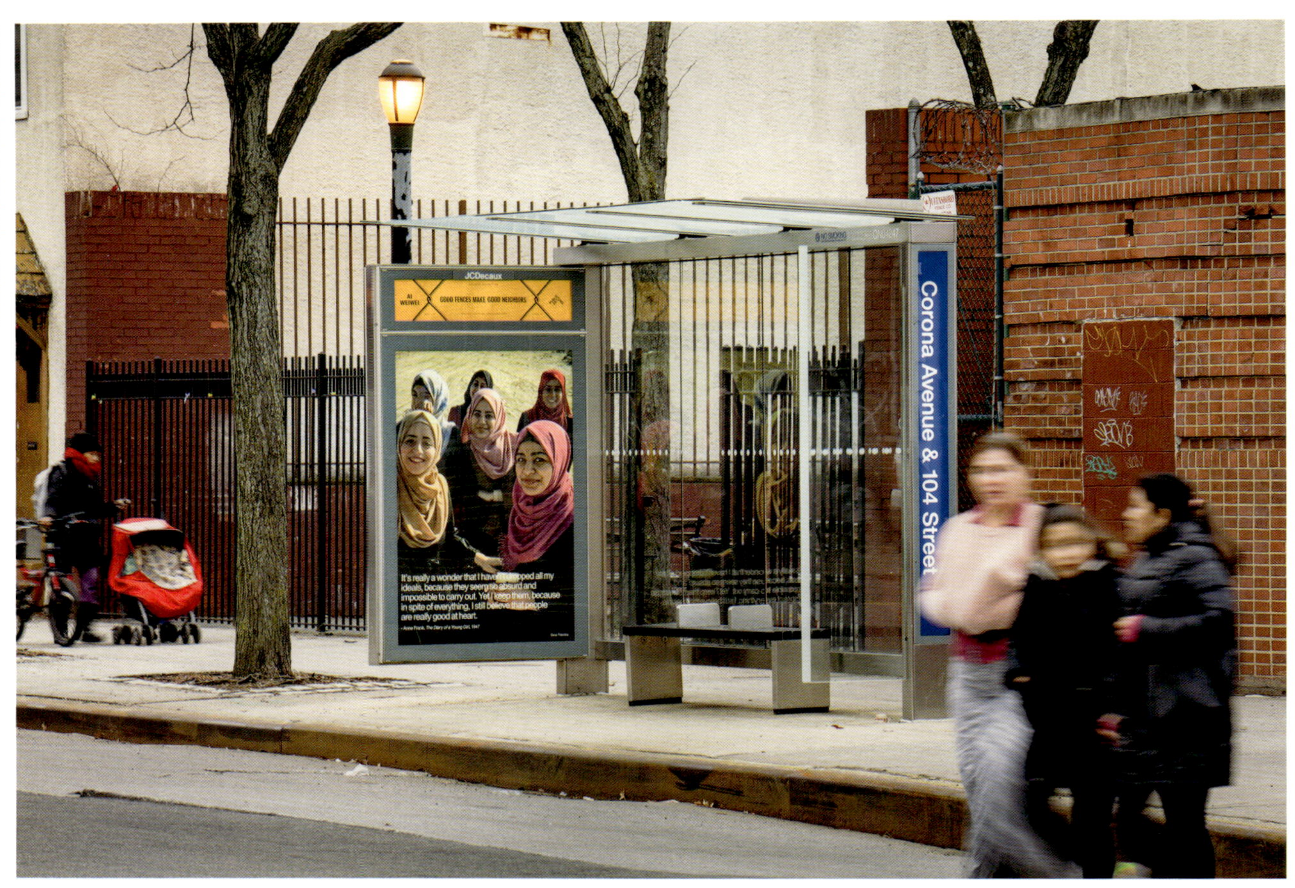

brooklynarchitect
Unisphere

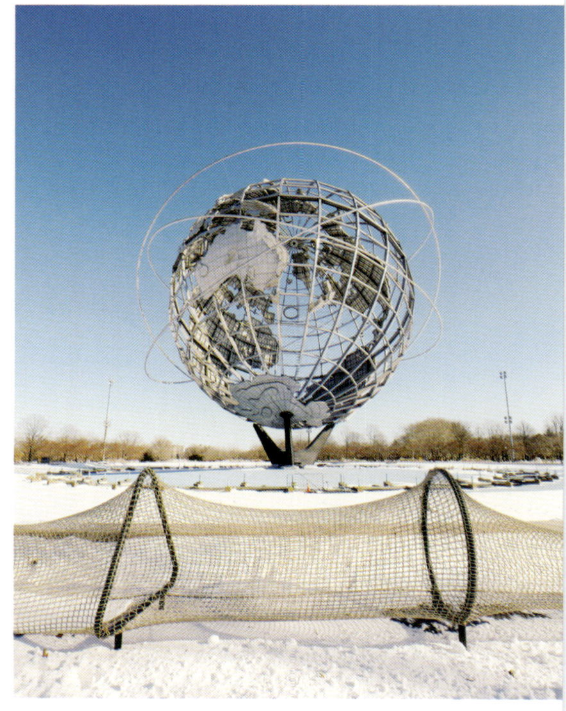

167 likes

brooklynarchitect #GoodFences @aiww @PublicArtFund

publicartfund 👏❄

brooklynarchitect @publicartfund 👌

JANUARY 7, 2018

Good Neighbors 86
Gaza, Palestine, 2016 (top)

Social media post, *Circle Fence* (bottom)

Good Neighbors 82
Kuba District, Gaza, Palestine, 2016 (opposite)

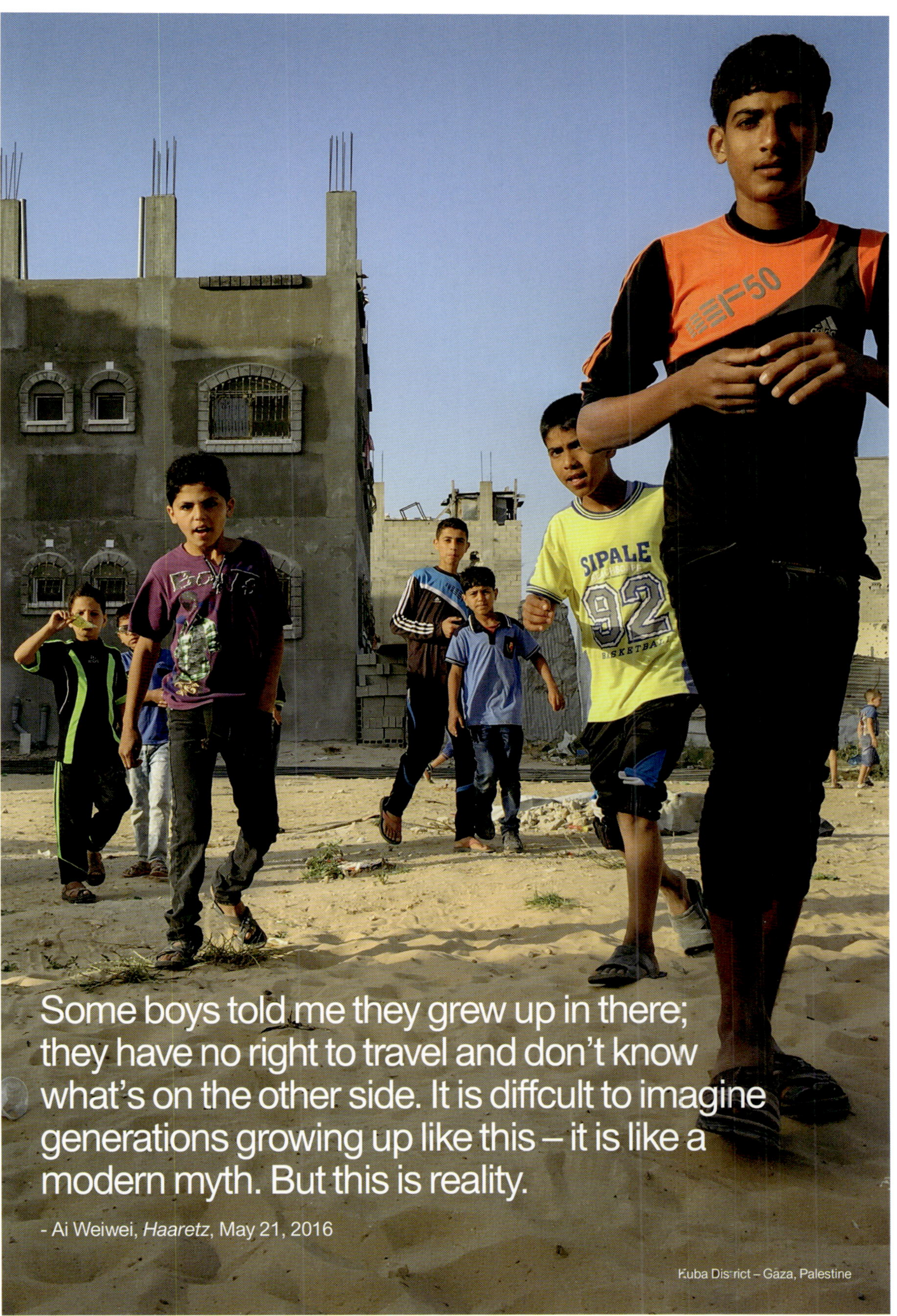

> Some boys told me they grew up in there; they have no right to travel and don't know what's on the other side. It is diffcult to imagine generations growing up like this – it is like a modern myth. But this is reality.
>
> - Ai Weiwei, *Haaretz*, May 21, 2016

Kuba District – Gaza, Palestine

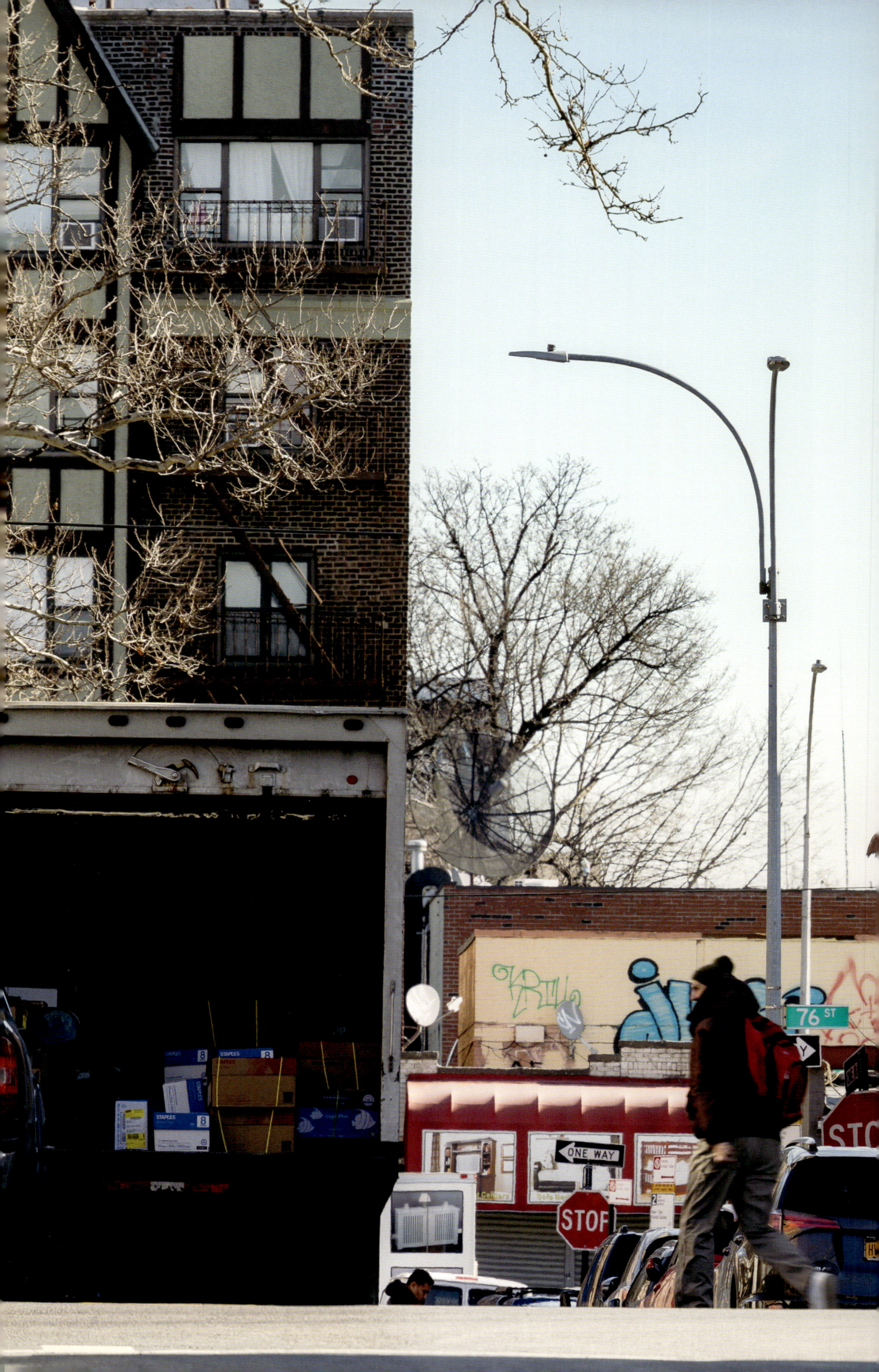
76 ST
ONE WAY
STOP

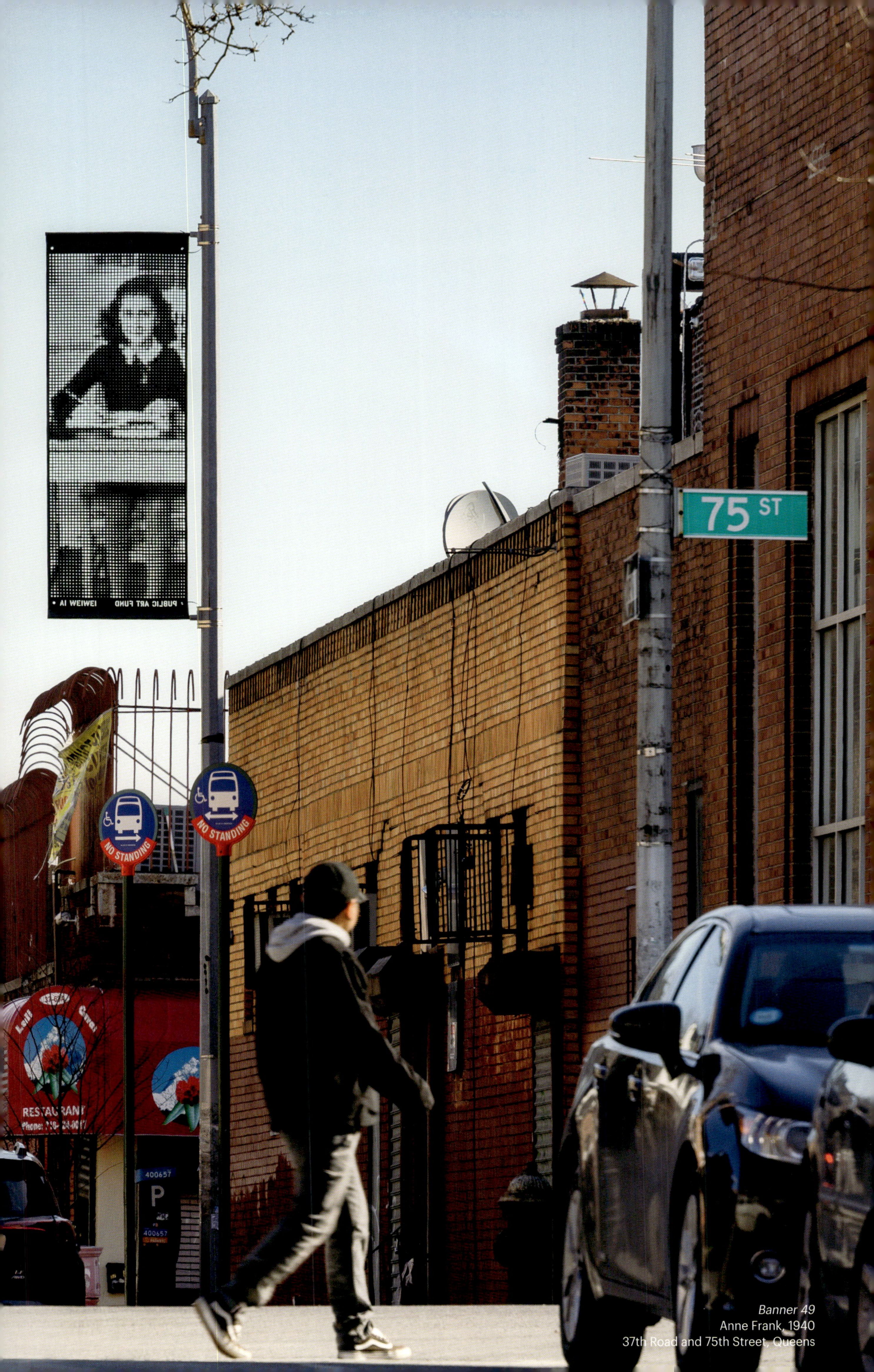

Banner 49
Anne Frank, 1940
37th Road and 75th Street, Queens

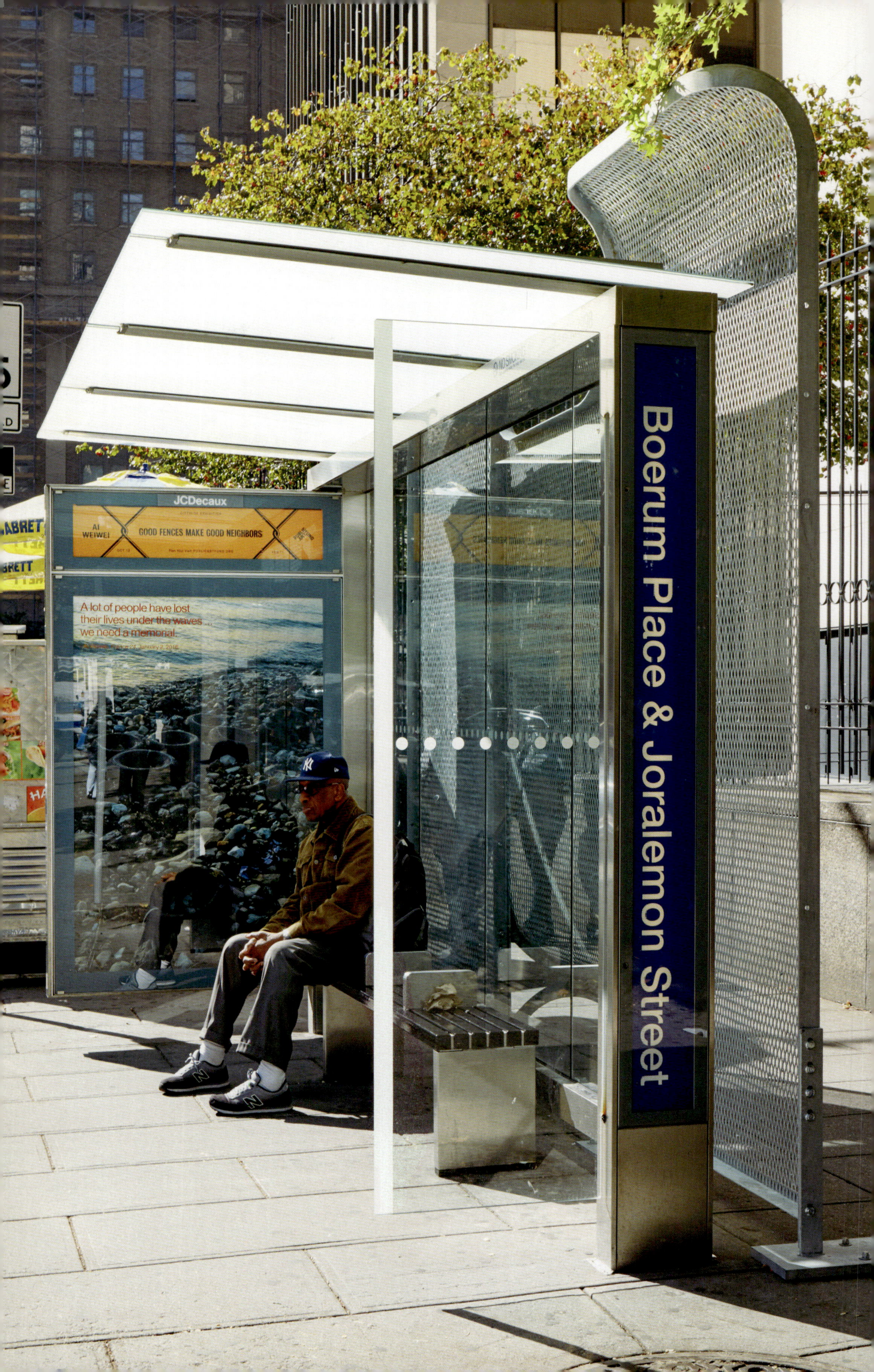
Boerum Place & Joralemon Street
JCDecaux
AI WEIWEI
GOOD FENCES MAKE GOOD NEIGHBORS
A lot of people have lost
their lives under the waves...
we need a memorial.

Bus Shelters

Ten Locations in Brooklyn, Harlem, and the Bronx

In New York City, the construction of the transportation infrastructure has played a vital role in the American immigrant story. It was the immigrant workforce that constructed the city's roads, bridges, and tunnels, and that same infrastructure continues to be essential to the flow of millions of people each day. Ai Weiwei's structures installed around ten bus shelters in downtown Brooklyn, Harlem, and the Bronx drew attention to the fundamental human right of free movement. With subtle references to the Art Nouveau curves of Hector Guimard's famous Paris Metro entrances, the artist brings a new aesthetic to the utilitarian language of metal fencing while incorporating additional public seating for passersby. As a complement to the sculptural installations surrounding this urban street furniture, Ai also created a series of *Good Neighbors* artworks from documentary images for display on these and other bus shelters across the city.

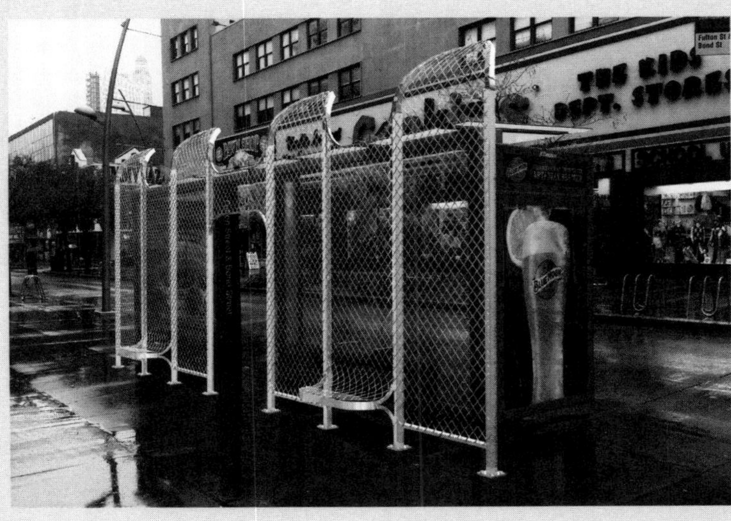

Brooklyn Shelter 1 with *Good Neighbors 19*, Lesvos, Greece, 2016
Boerum Place and Joralemon Street, Brooklyn (opposite)

Rendering of *Bus Shelter* prototype design (left)

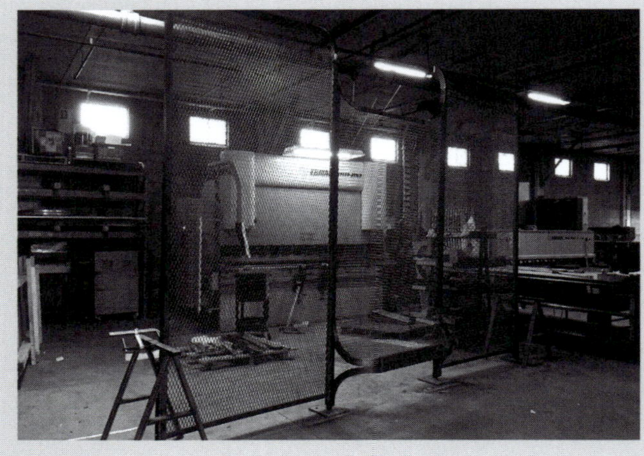

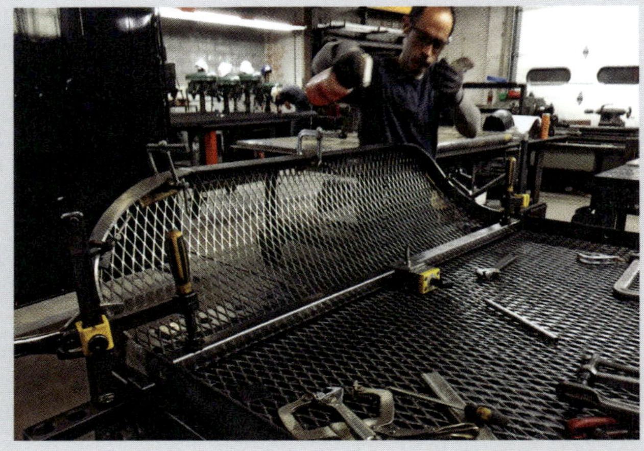

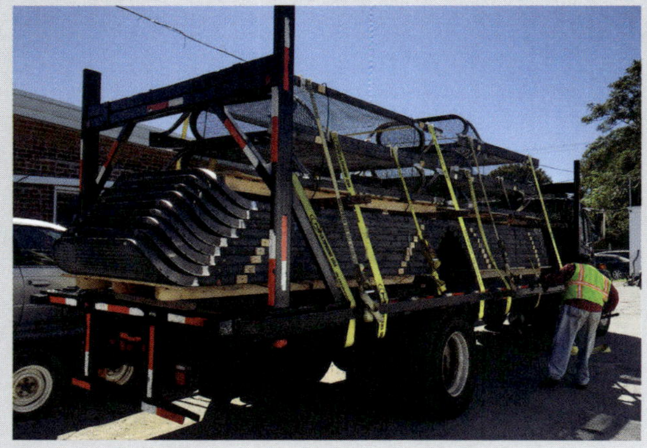

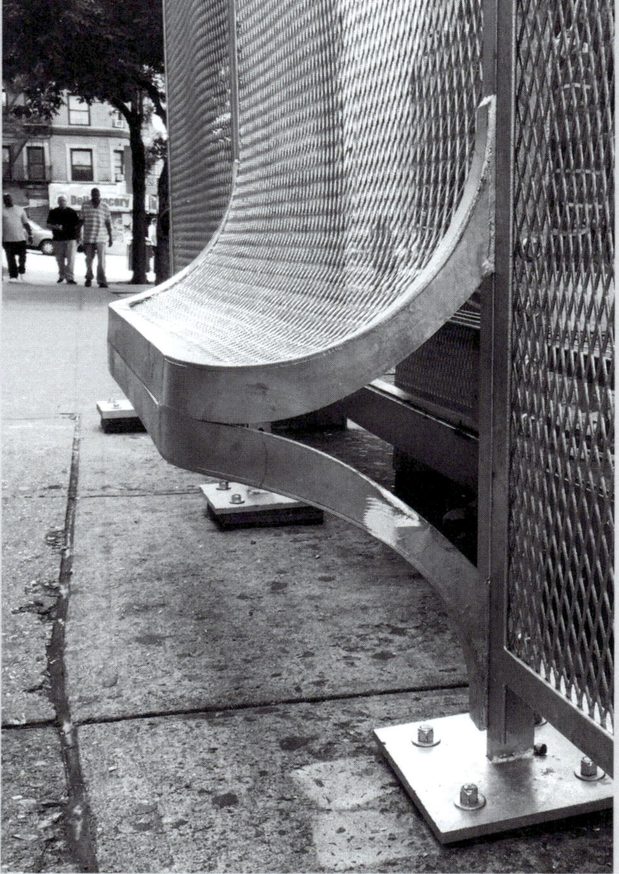

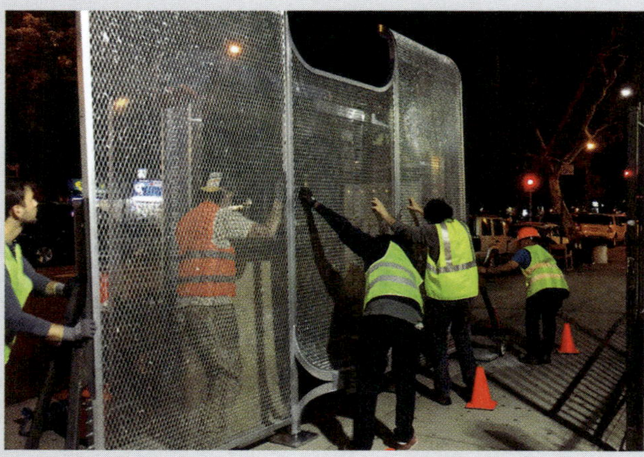

Fabrication of *Bus Shelters*, 4th State Metal workshop, Poughkeepsie, New York, September 2017 (top left and right)

Transportation of steel components and installation of *Harlem Shelter 3*, 125th Street and Frederick Douglass Boulevard, Manhattan, October 2017 (center left and bottom left)

Bus Shelter seat (detail) (bottom right)

Harlem Shelter 4
E. 125th Street and 5th Avenue, Manhattan (opposite)

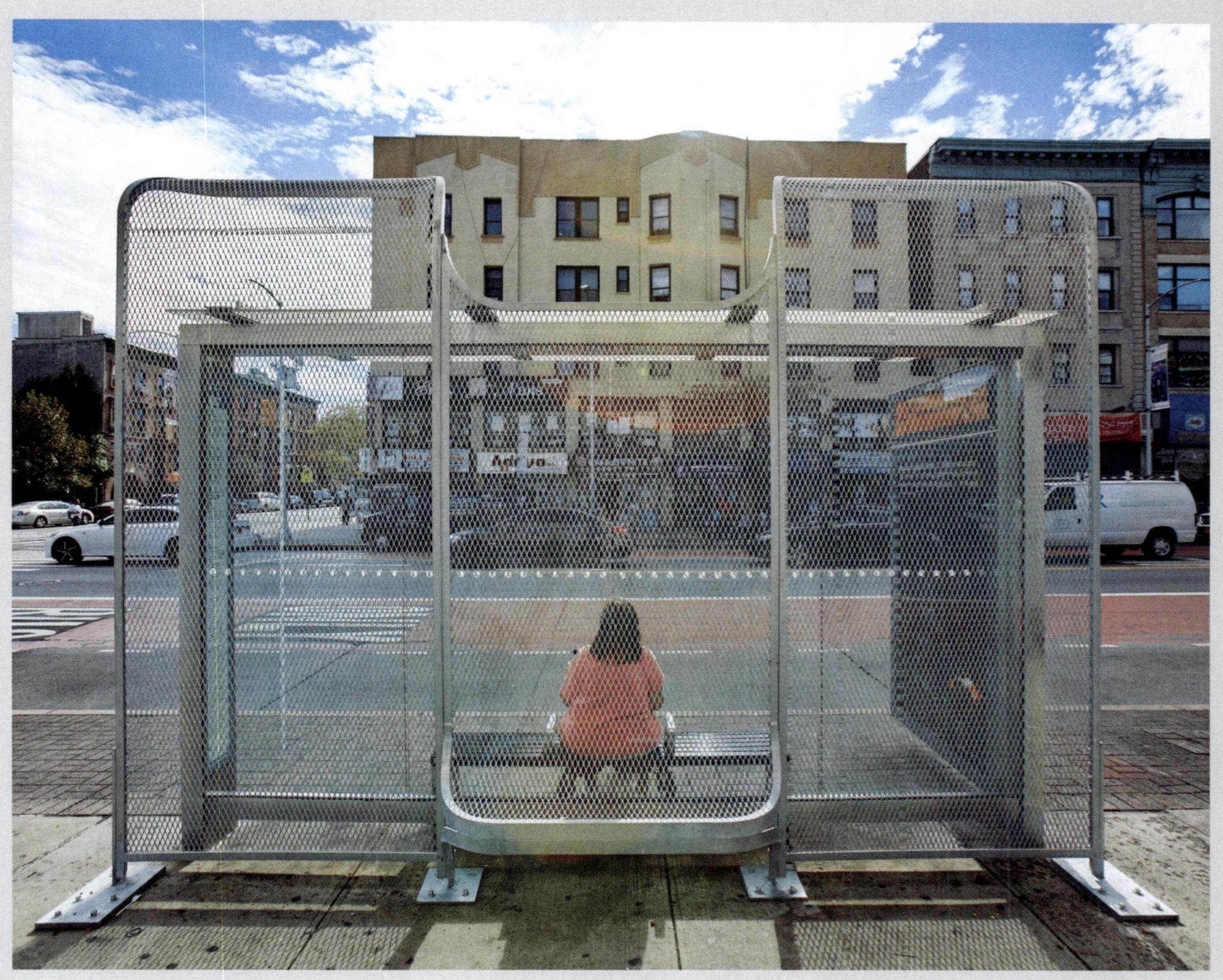

Ai Weiwei's *Good Fences Make Good Neighbors* invites us to question the role of barriers in our national political discourse by bringing the conversation to our local public spaces in New York City. His architectural designs engage us physically with civic structures, at times challenging their purpose as places of order and regulation. His personal experience with government oppression suggests he is mindful of the joy that comes when walls are torn down, freeing us from fear and hate. It is the genius of Ai Weiwei to make us think, feel, and care about the agony our political architecture can cause to those who live outside a perceived protected zone.

Sandra Bloodworth, Director, MTA Arts & Design

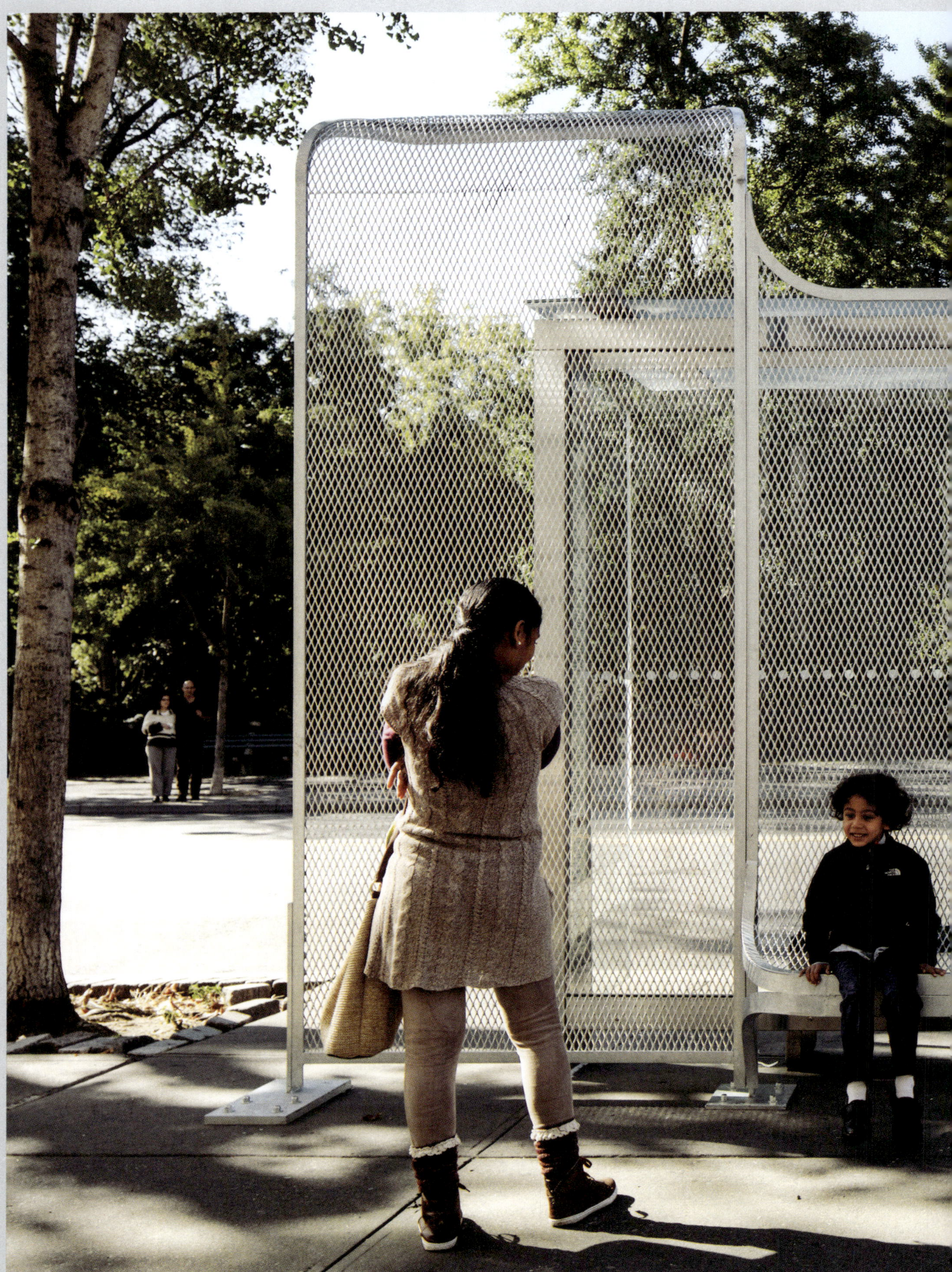

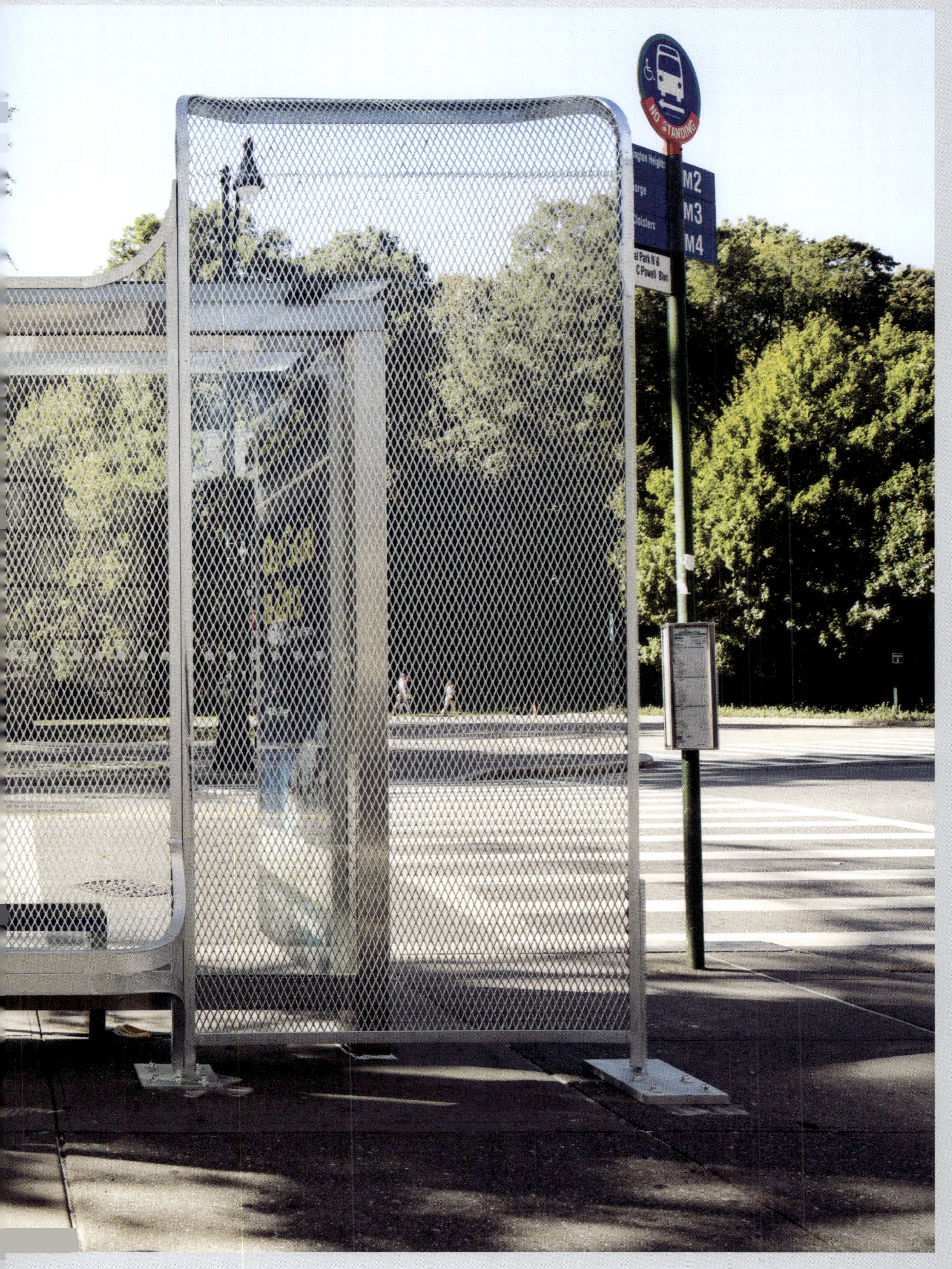

Harlem Shelter 1
Central Park N. and Adam Clayton Powell Jr. Boulevard, Manhattan

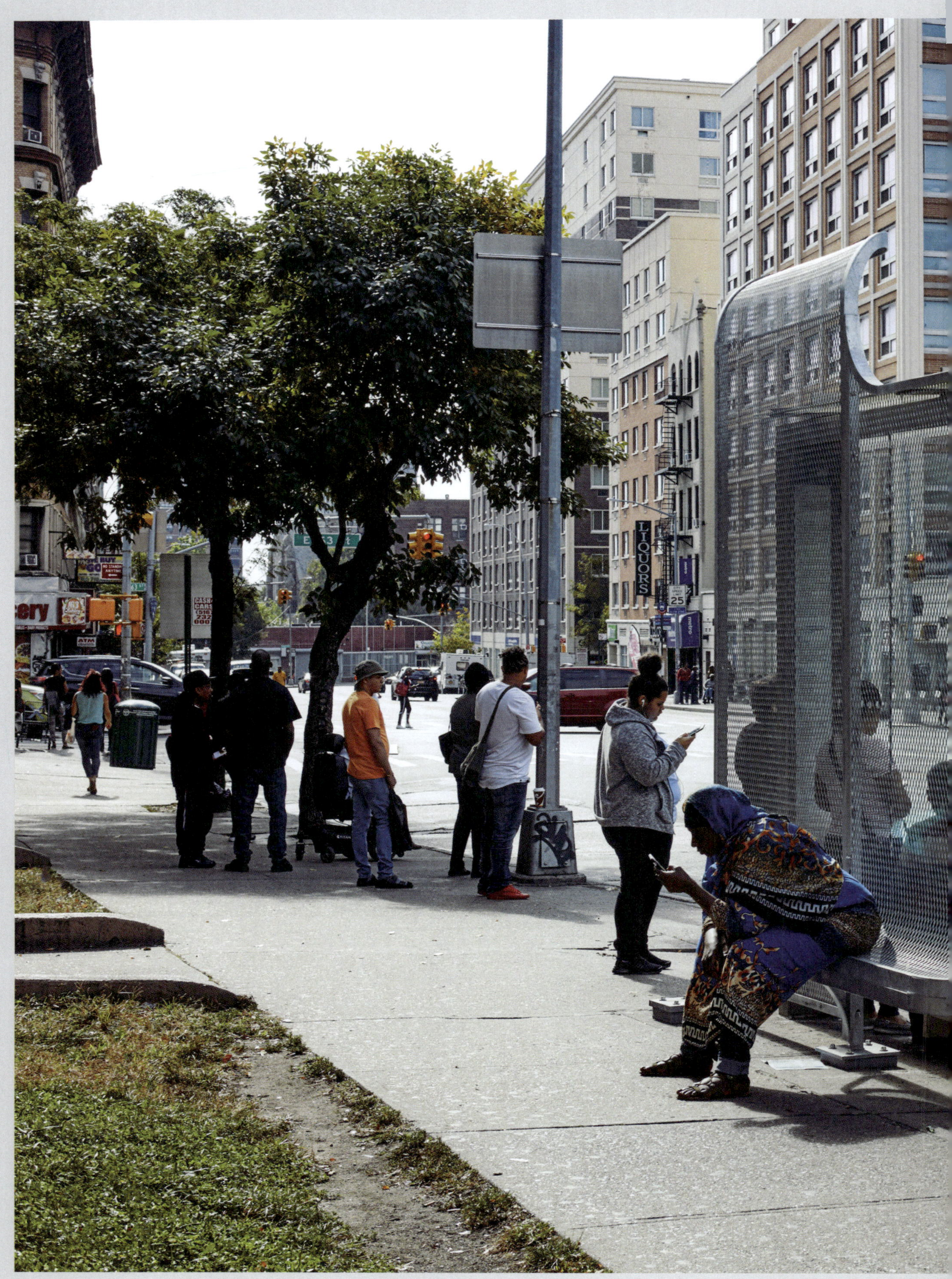
LIQUORS

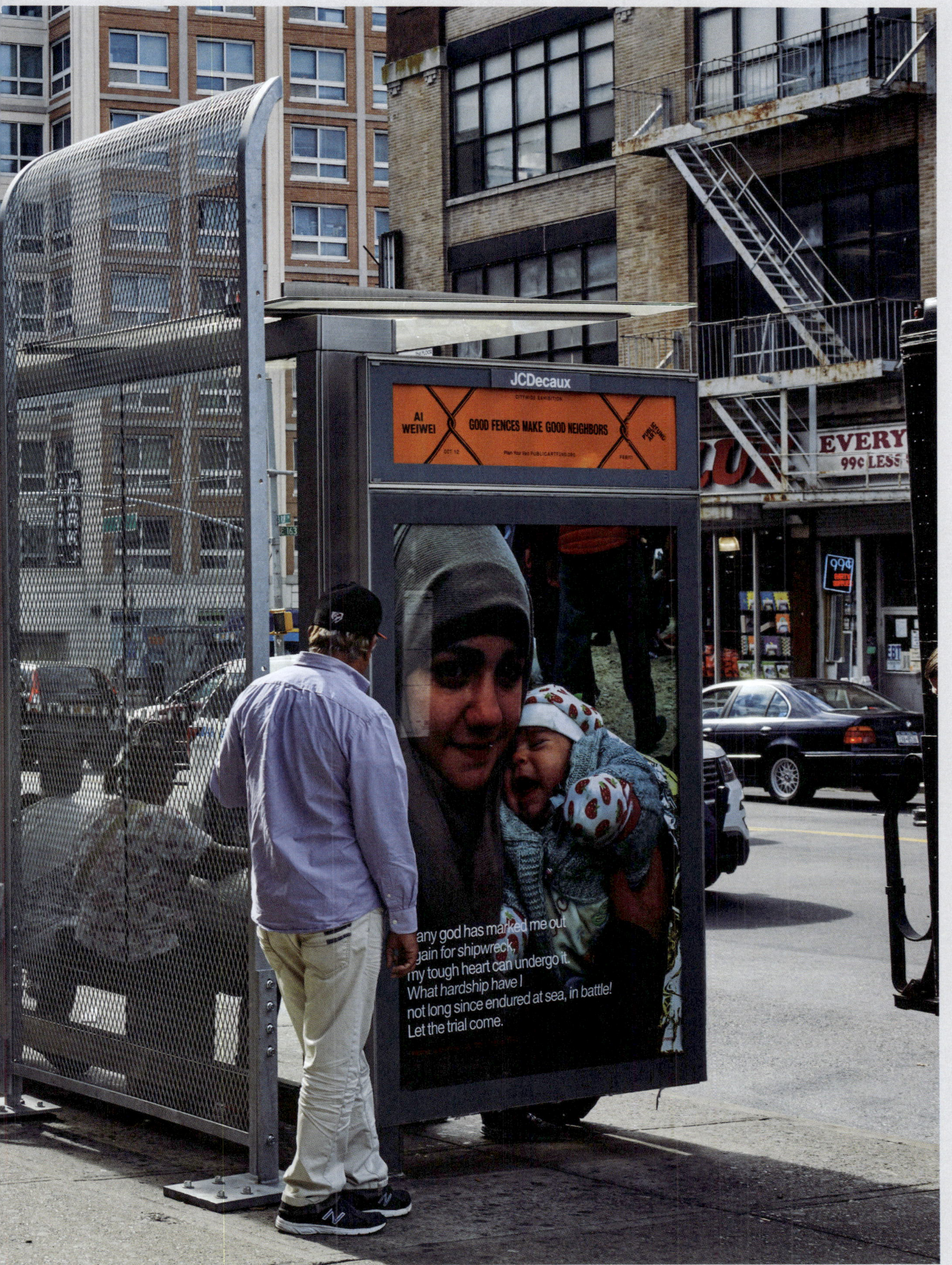

Bronx Shelter 2 with *Good Neighbors 28*,
Lesvos, Greece, 2016
E. 163rd Street and 3rd Avenue, Bronx

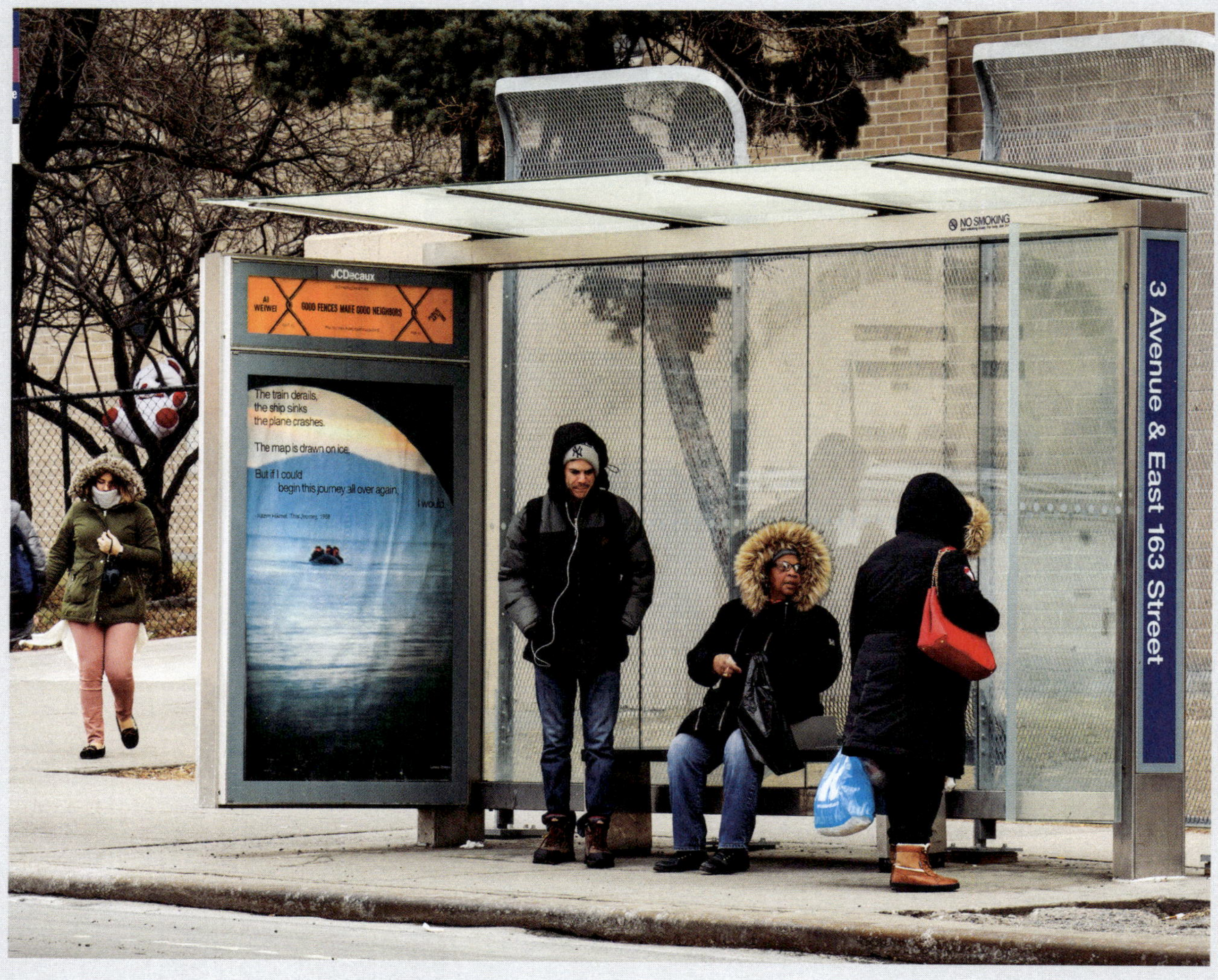

When visiting some of our bus shelters during the exhibition, I was struck by how these city services became true instruments of art, completely aligned with Ai Weiwei's vision of art as "the instrument of real life."

Bernard Parisot, President and Co-CEO, JCDecaux

Bronx Shelter 2 with *Good Neighbors 27*, Lesvos, Greece, 2016
E. 163rd Street and Third Avenue, Bronx (top)

Daniel S. Palmer and Fotene Demoulas, *Brooklyn Shelter 1* with *Good Neighbors 20*, Lesvos, Greece, 2016, October 12, 2017, Boerum Place and Joralemon Street, Brooklyn (opposite)

At no time in recent world history or US history has there been a greater need to see the humanity of those who are on the other side of the fence from us. Ultimately, the parks and the public realm are the places that we can all rely on for that outlet and opportunity.

Elizabeth Goldstein, President, Municipal Arts Society

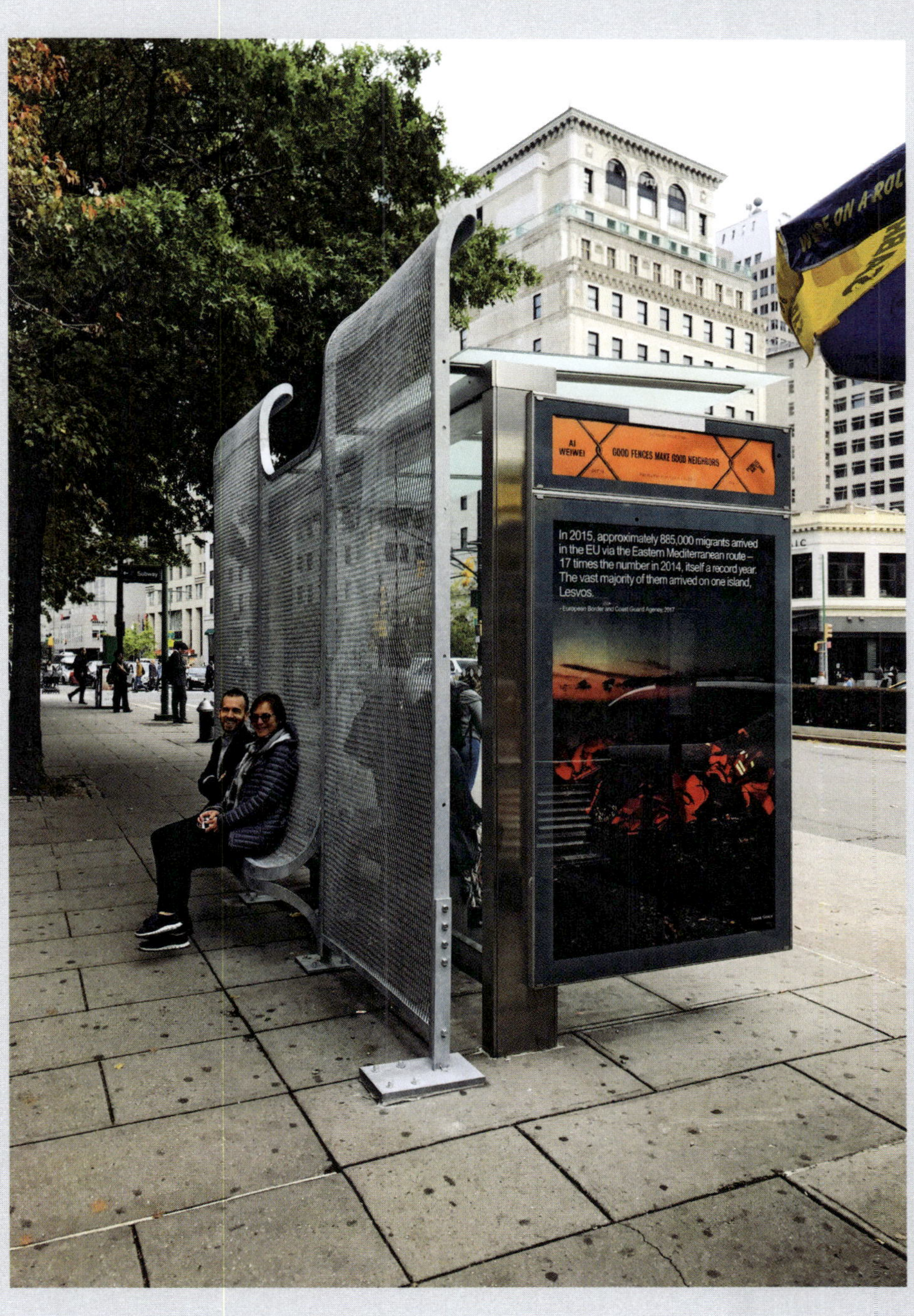

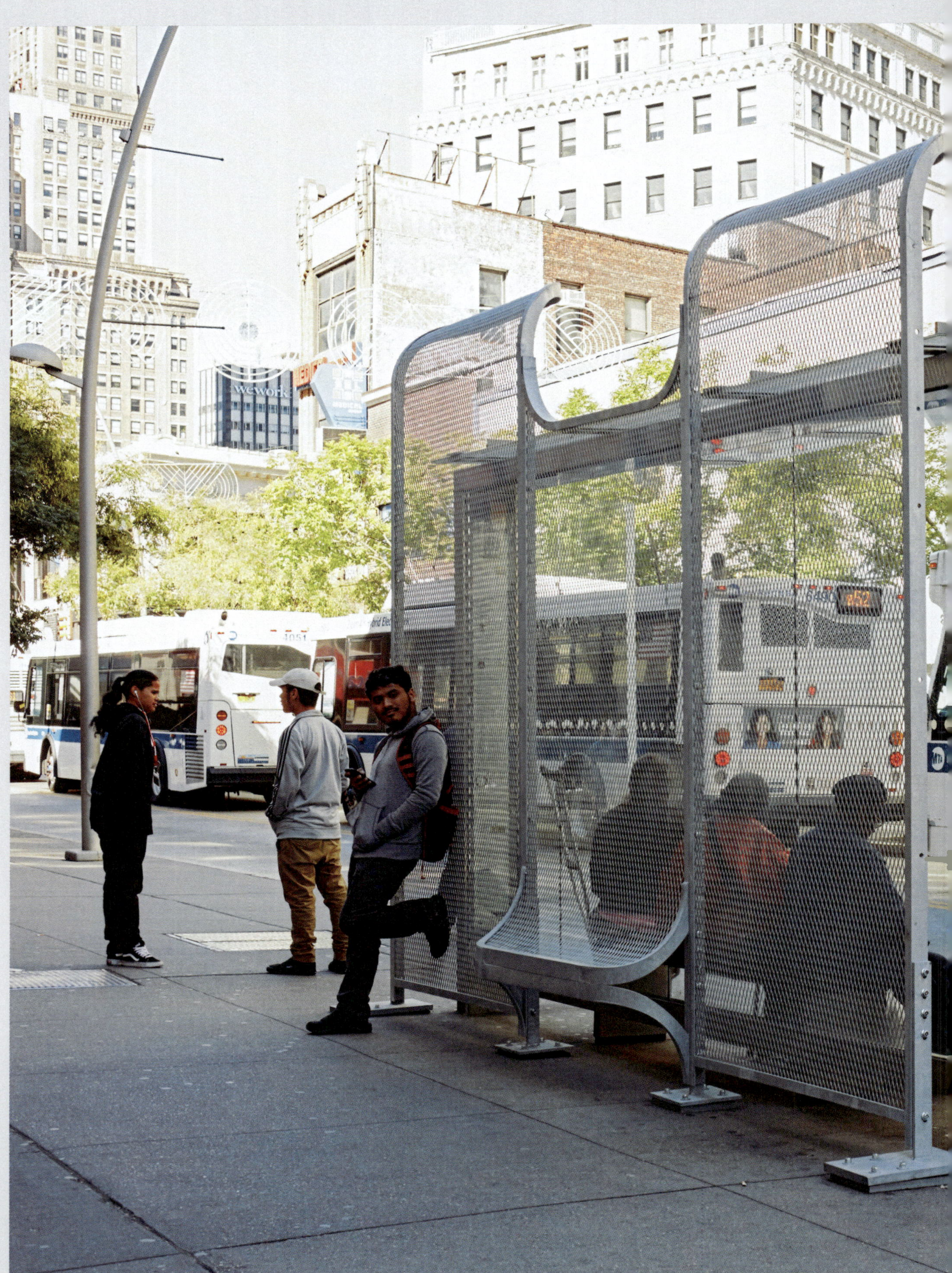

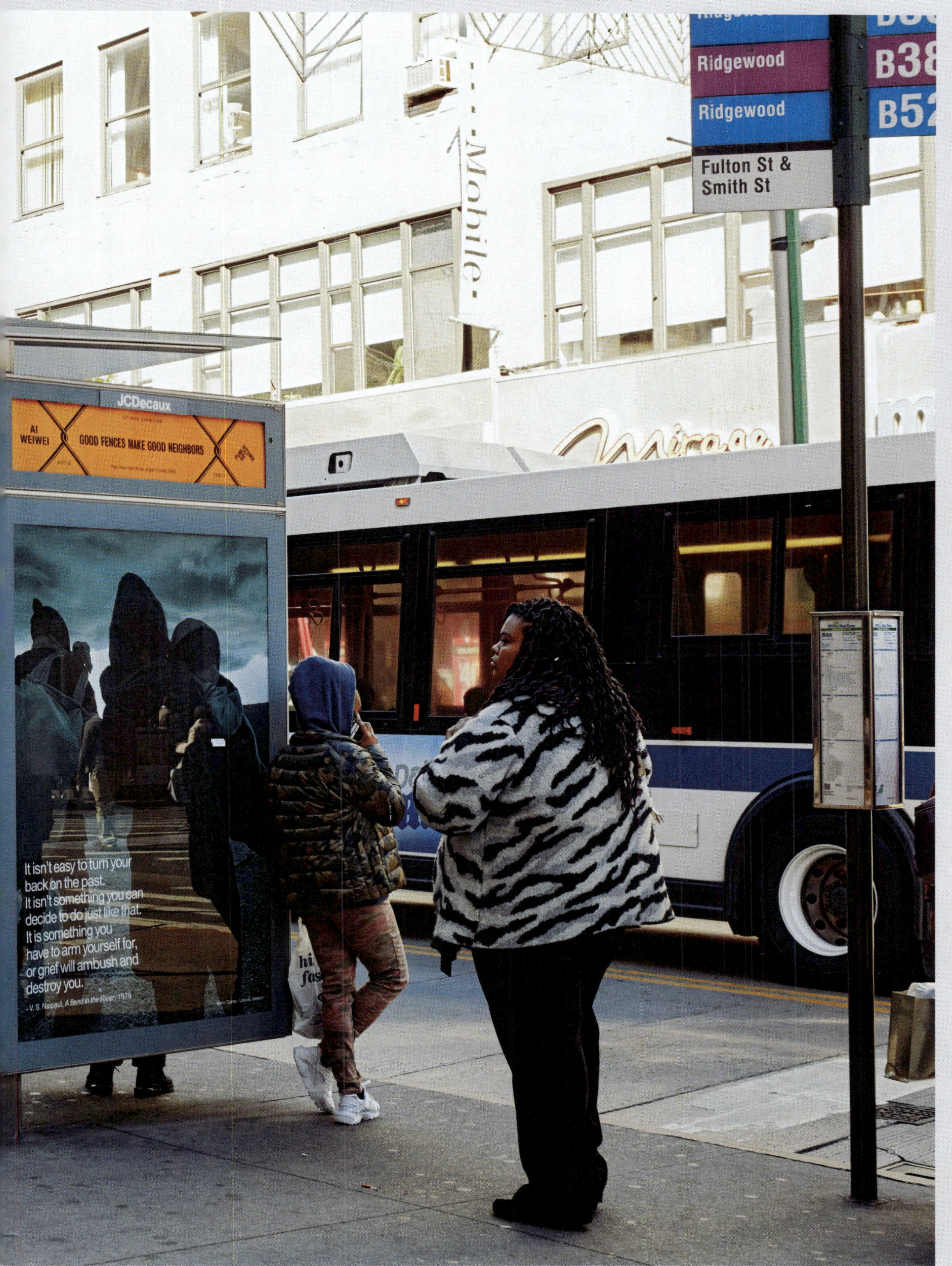

Brooklyn Shelter 2 with *Good Neighbors 15*, Moria Camp, Lesvos, Greece, 2015
Fulton and Smith Streets, Brooklyn

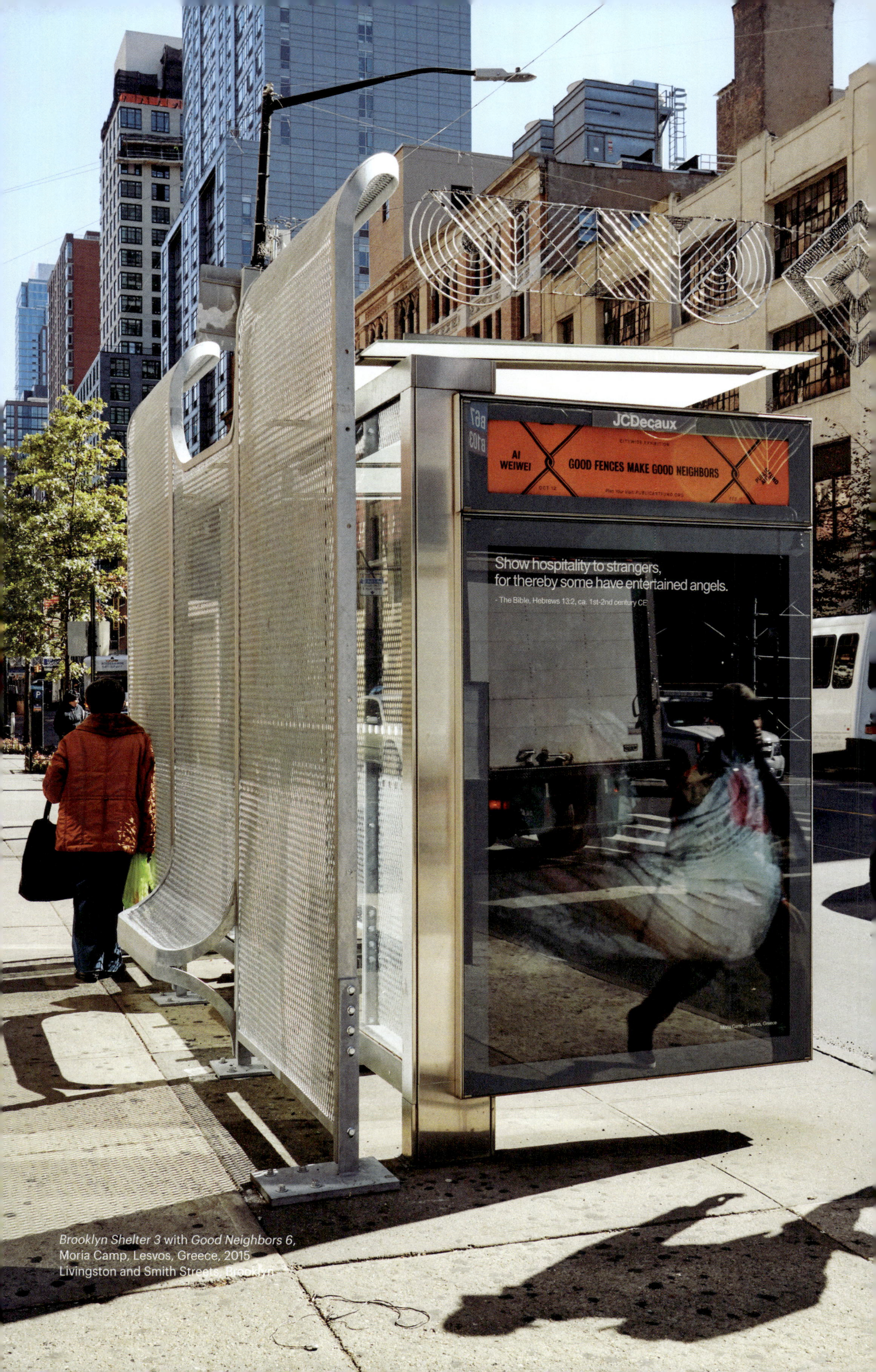

Brooklyn Shelter 3 with *Good Neighbors 6*,
Moria Camp, Lesvos, Greece, 2015
Livingston and Smith Streets, Brooklyn

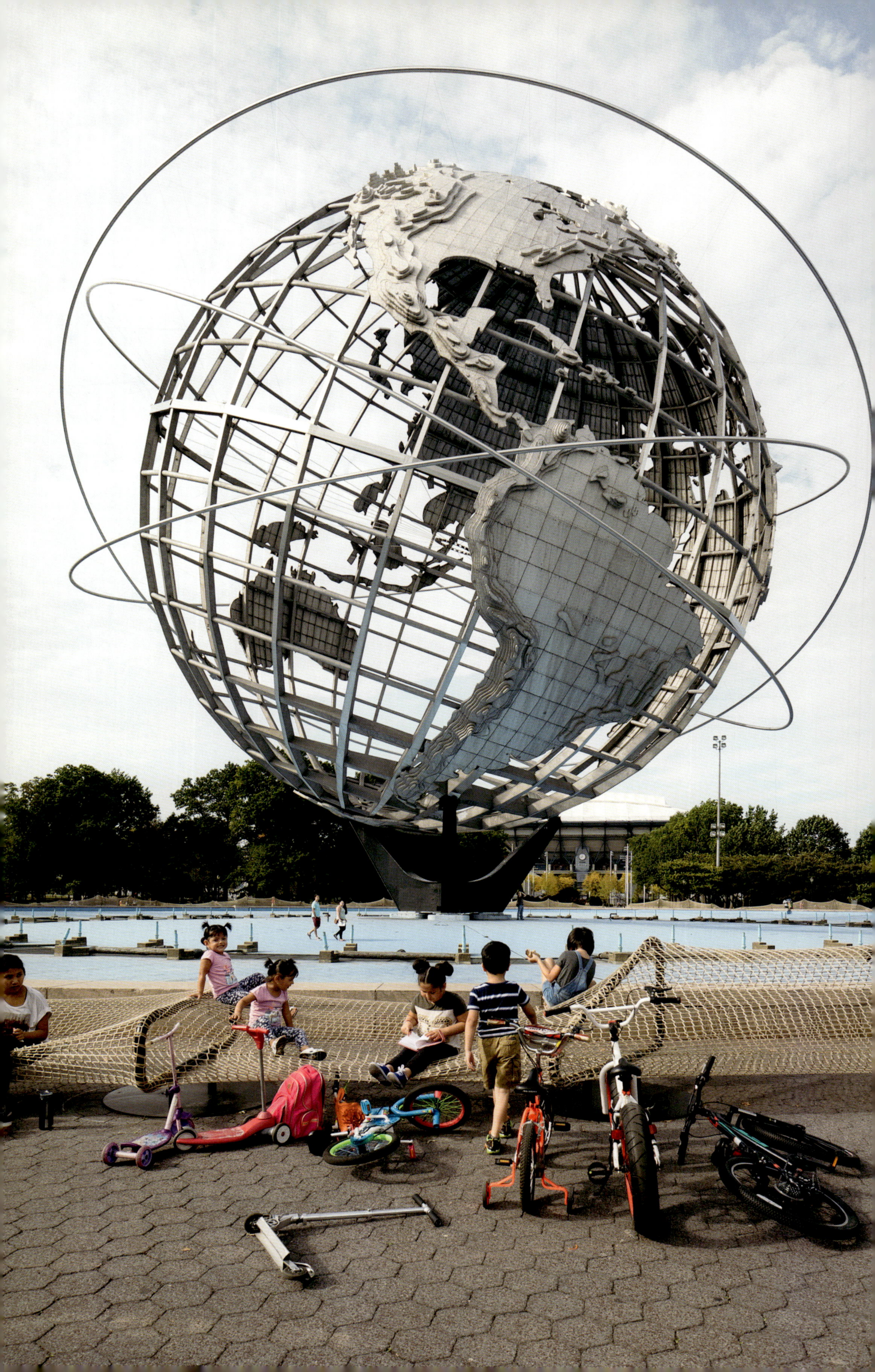

Circle Fence

Flushing Meadows Corona Park

Given the global increase in nationalism and anti-immigrant sentiment, Ai Weiwei's *Circle Fence* drew renewed attention to the symbolism of Corona Flushing Meadows Corona Park's Unisphere (1964). Measuring over one thousand linear feet, the artist's sculptural installation was composed of a series of metal frames with interconnected netting that surrounded the site, creating a metaphorical border that was at once playful and sobering. Rather than impeding views of the landmark site, the piece emphasized the Unisphere's form and emblematic meaning.

The Unisphere was created for the 1964 World's Fair, to embody the theme of "Peace through Understanding" and to serve as an aspirational image of global unity at the height of the Cold War. This site, which had also been used for the 1939 World's Fair, is located just in front of the New York City Building (today used as the Queens Museum of Art) and also housed the United Nations General Assembly from 1946–1950. Here, nearly every important world leader came to participate in post–World War II governance in order to assure maintenance of international peace and security, and it was on this site that world-changing decisions such as the partition of Palestine and the creation of UNICEF were enacted. The massive steel representation of the globe has become a proud icon for Queens, now one of the world's most ethnically diverse urban areas.

Ai designed the shapes of the sculpture's black metal stanchions and netting to reference the barricade structures of crowd control; however, his elemental shapes offered an almost childlike simplicity, while the extended netting produced undulating, rhythmic changes in height that made an oblique reference to the waves of the many oceans refugees often cross as they seek safety and their future homes. Moreover, *Circle Fence* encouraged visitors to recline on this netting as a modified hammock, offering respite but also demonstrating how each section of net connected and responded to its neighboring sections.

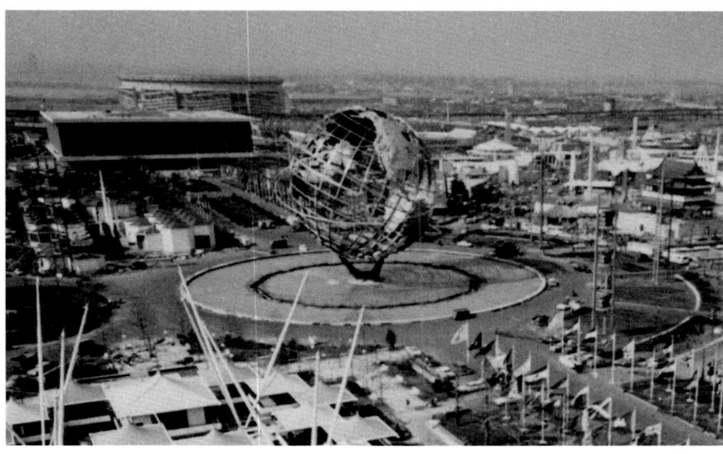

Panoramic view of 1964 World's Fair, Flushing Meadows Corona Park, Queens

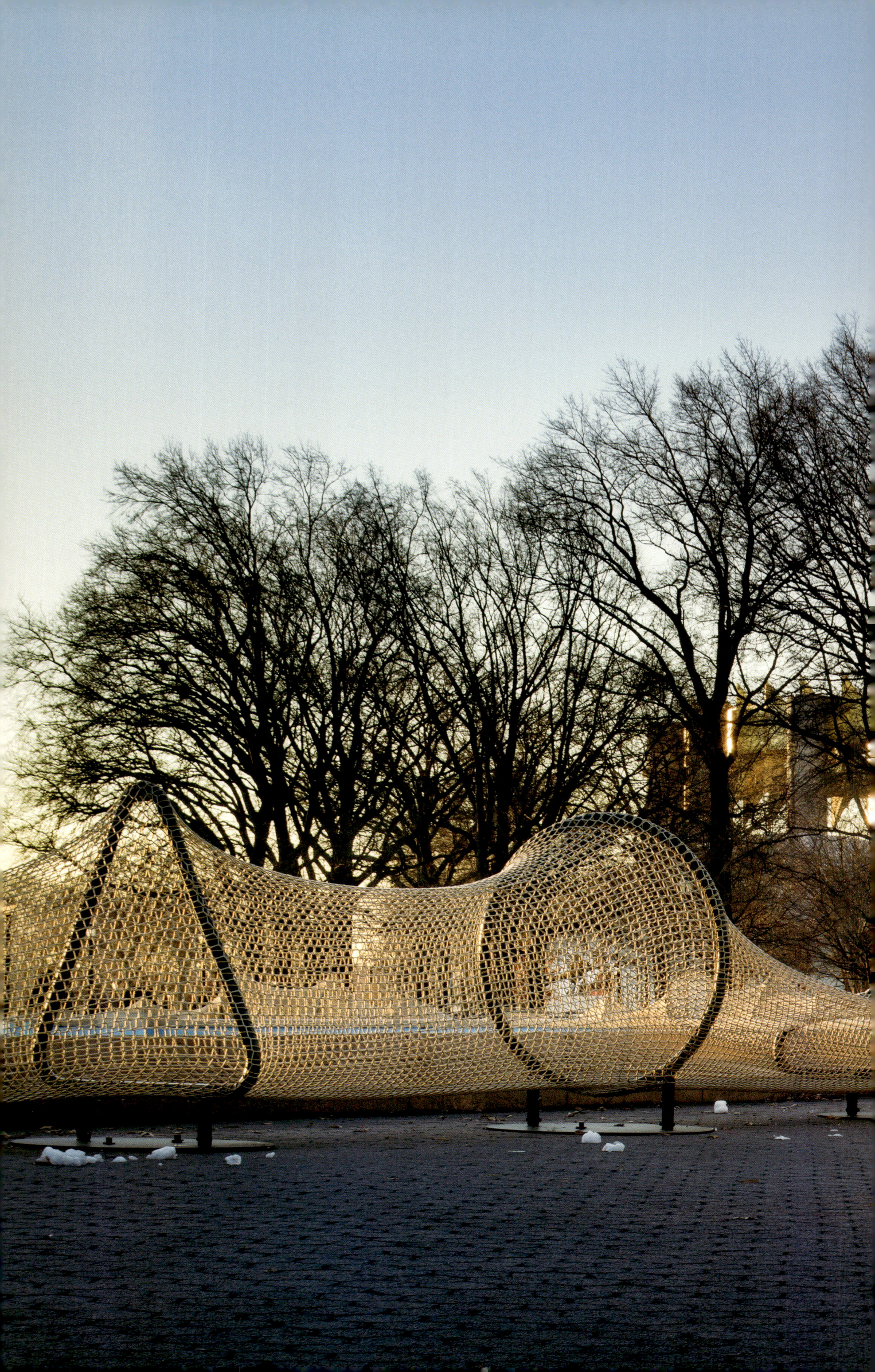

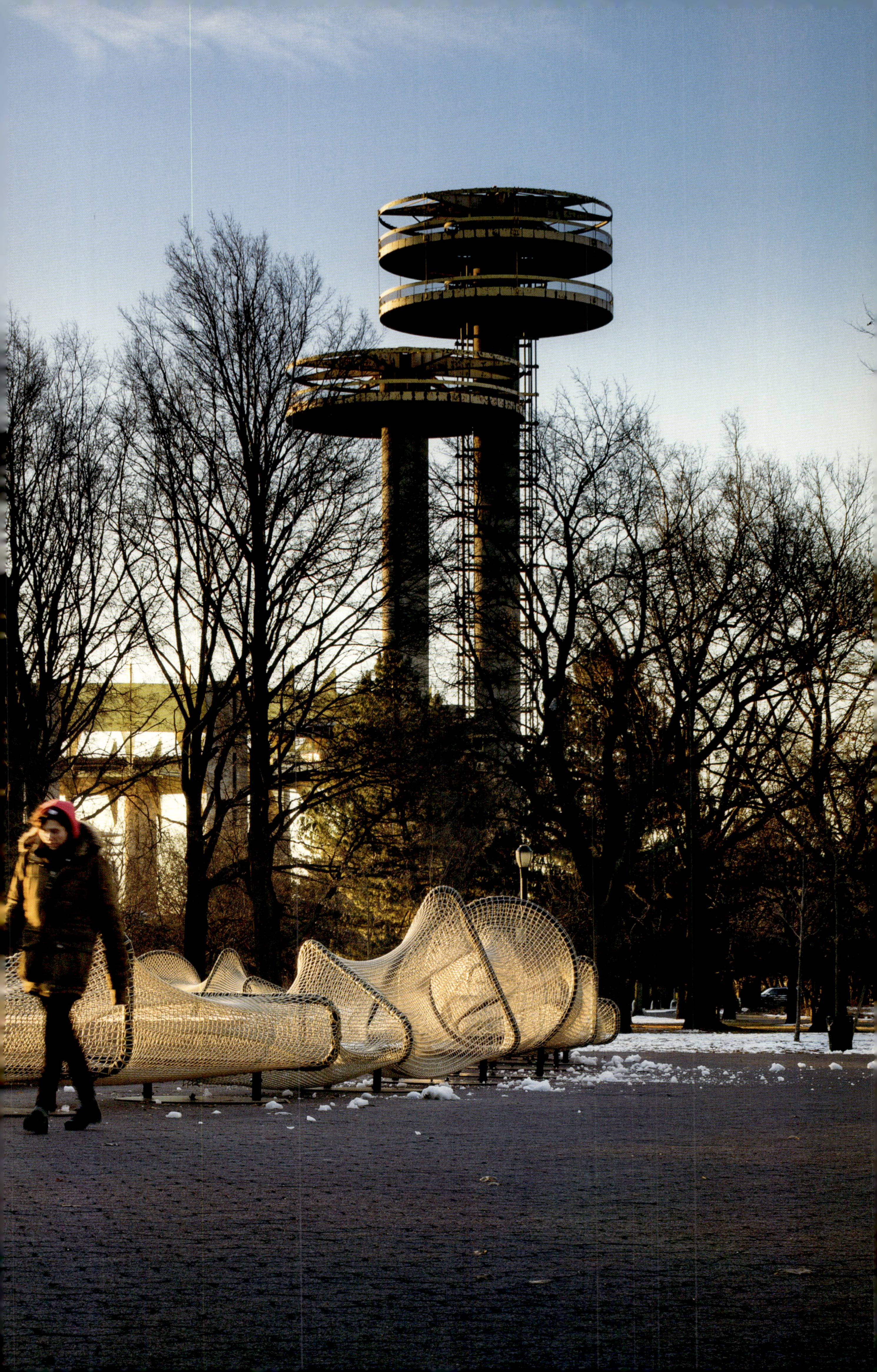

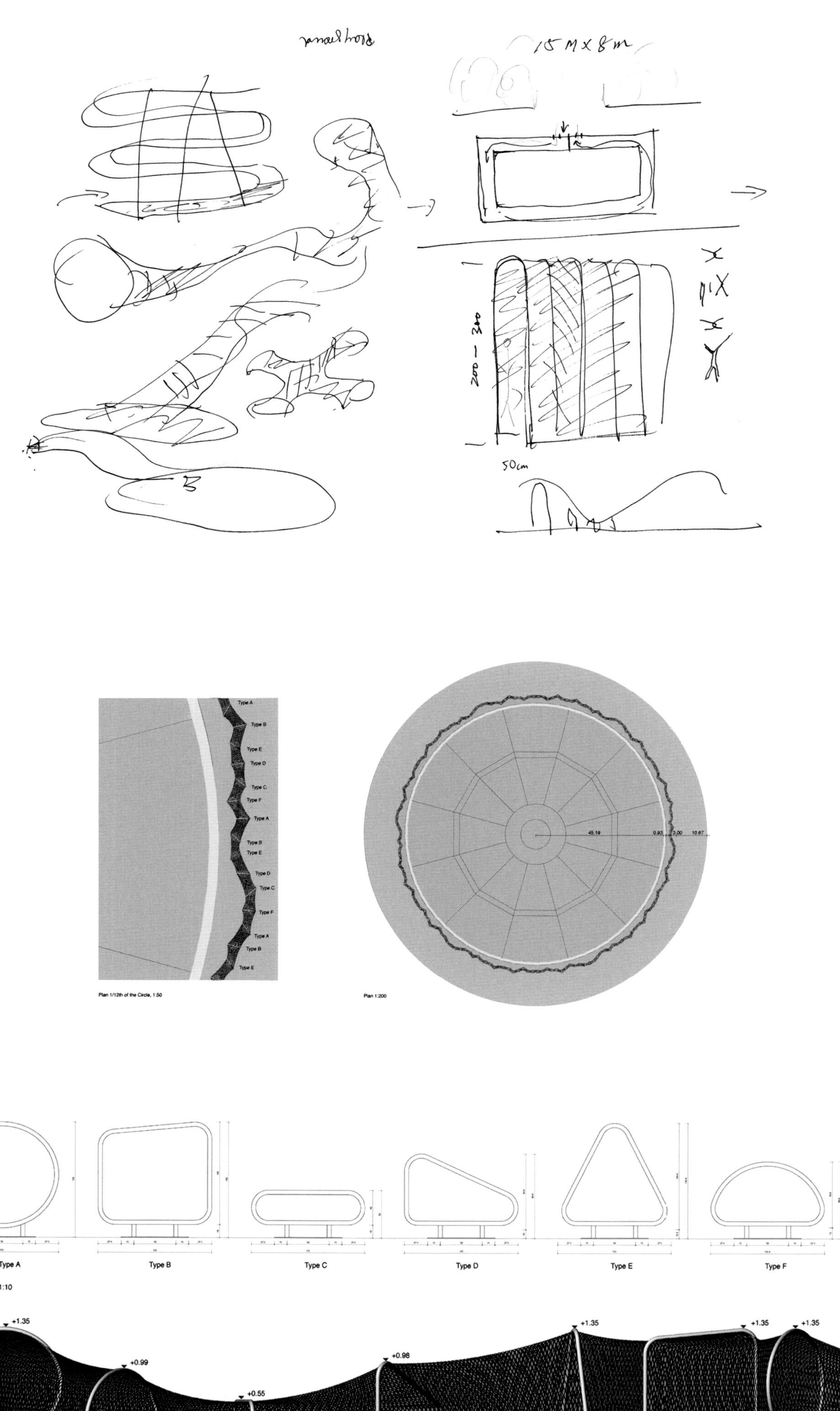

Plan 1/12th of the Circle, 1:50

Plan 1:200

Type A

Type B

Type C

Type D

Type E

Type F

Types of Frames 1:10

Elevation 1/24th of the Circle 1:10

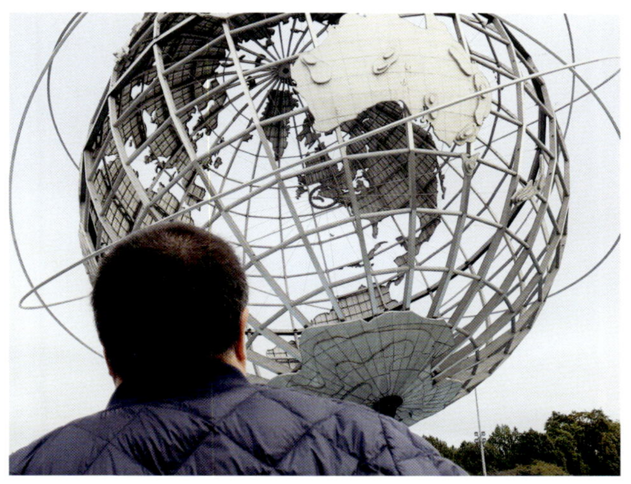

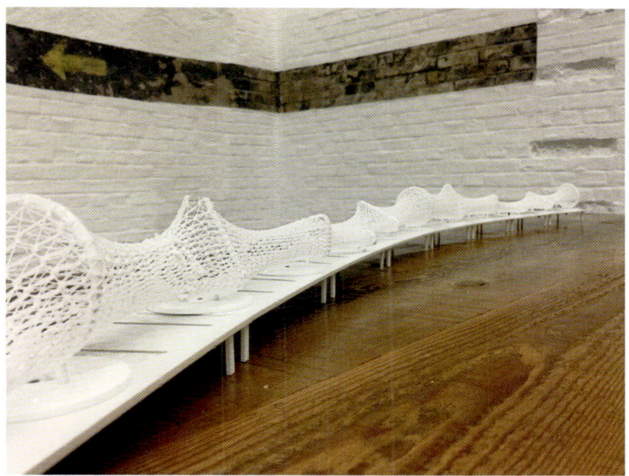

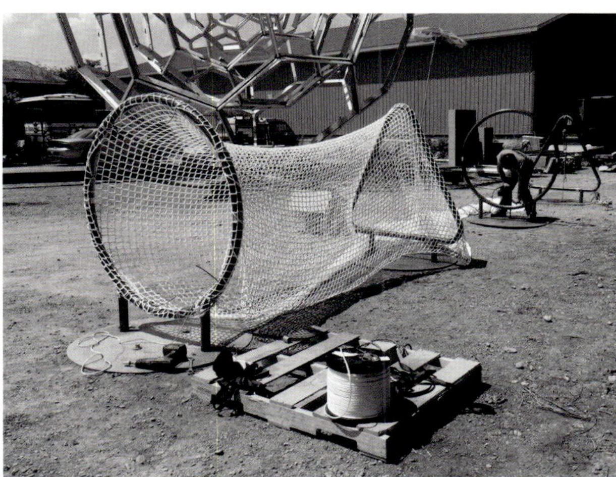

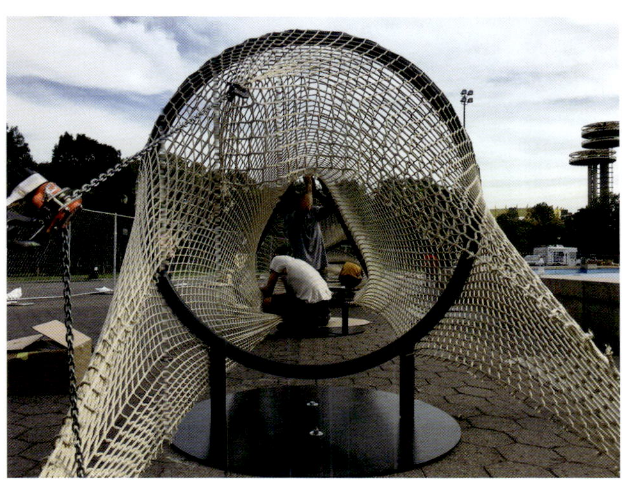

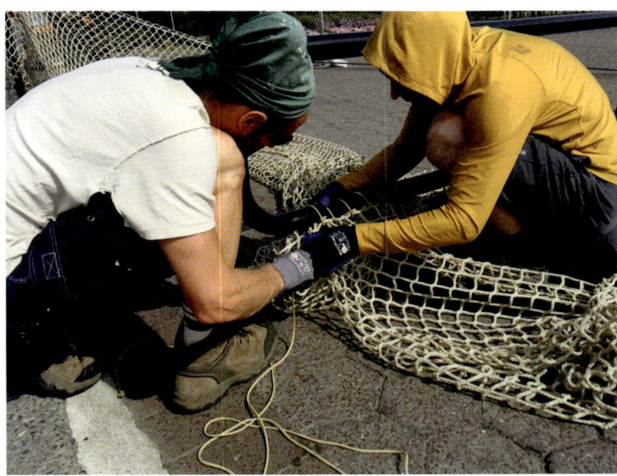

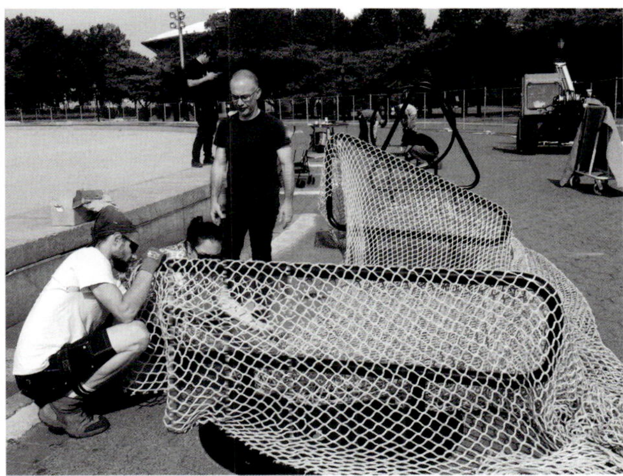

Ai Weiwei's preparatory sketches (opposite, top)

Technical drawings for *Circle Fence* (opposite, bottom)

Ai Weiwei examines the Unisphere during a site visit, October 21, 2016 (top left)

Maquette of *Circle Fence*, Ai Weiwei studio, Berlin, June 2017 (top right)

Dry fit of *Circle Fence*, 4th State Metal workshop, Poughkeepsie, New York, August 10, 2017 (center left)

Installation of *Circle Fence*, Flushing Meadows Corona Park, September 2017 (center right and bottom)

Ai Weiwei's *Good Fences Make Good Neighbors* builds on a rich history of public art in New York City—connecting, questioning, sparking dialogue, and encouraging people to engage with their environment in new ways. This remarkable uniting of all five boroughs and dozens of diverse communities harnesses the power of art to challenge borders of all kinds, physical and imagined.

Tom Finkelpearl, NYC Department of Cultural Affairs Commissioner

×

Just get people thinking. About what a fence can or cannot do.

Viewer comment

Social media posts, *Circle Fence* (opposite, bottom)

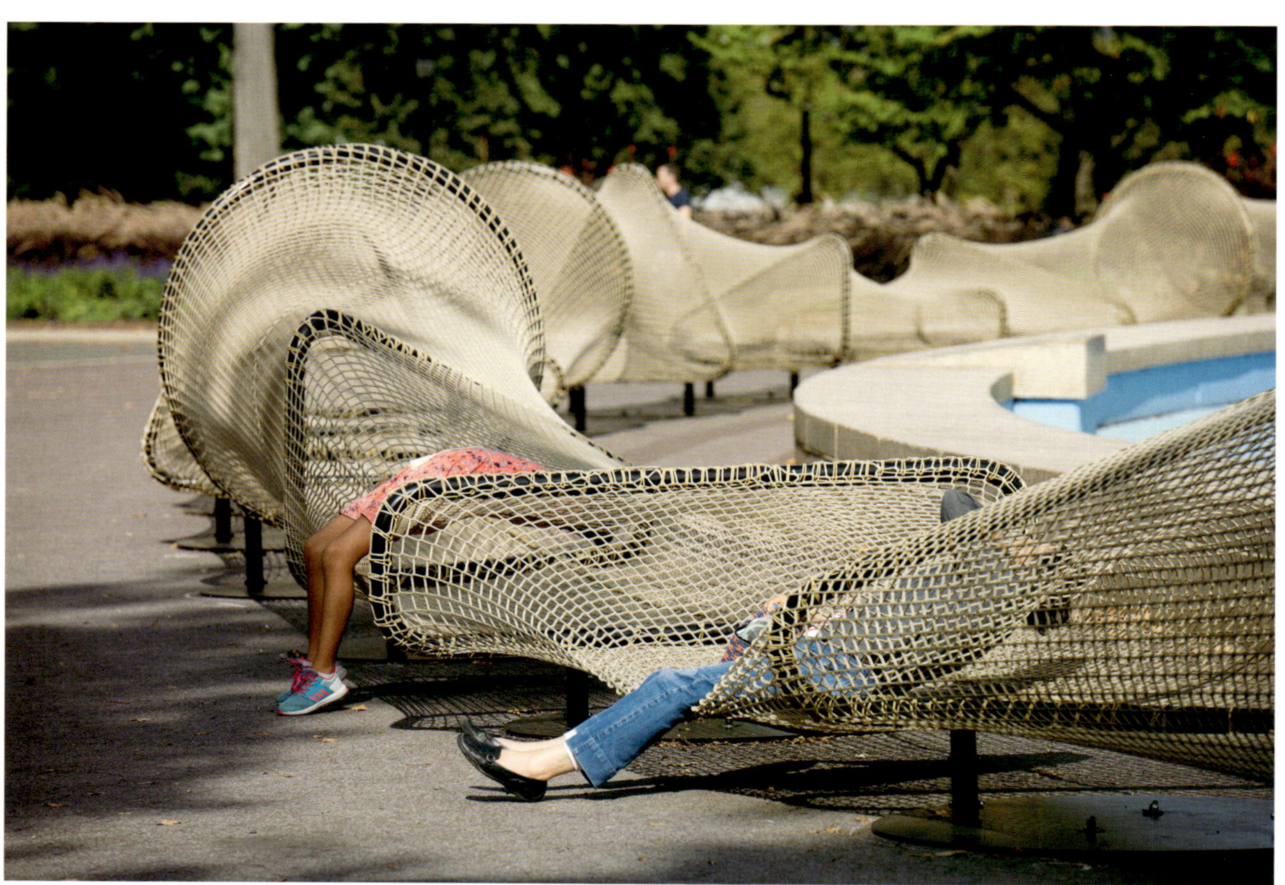

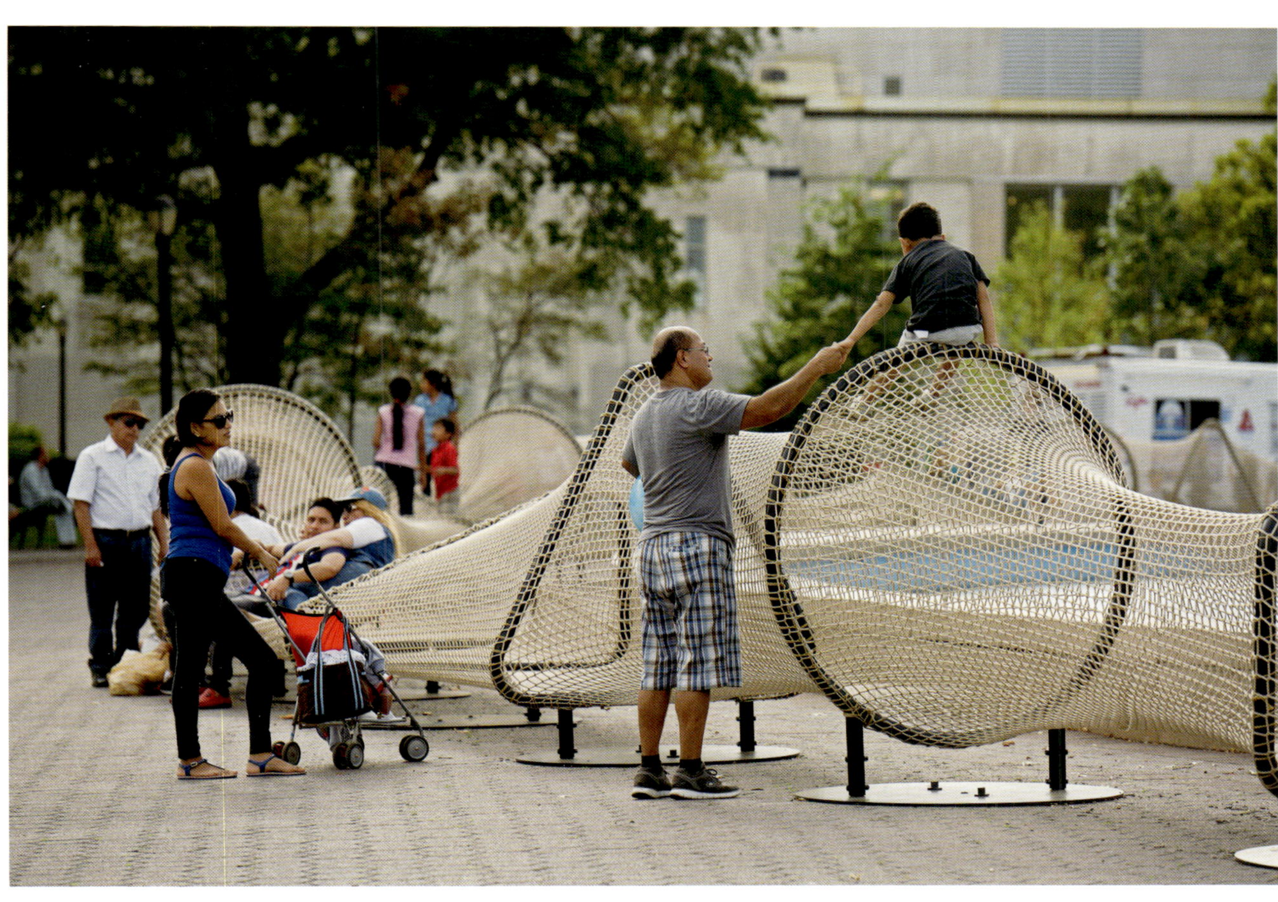

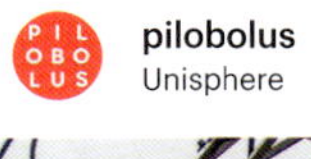

pilobolus
Unisphere

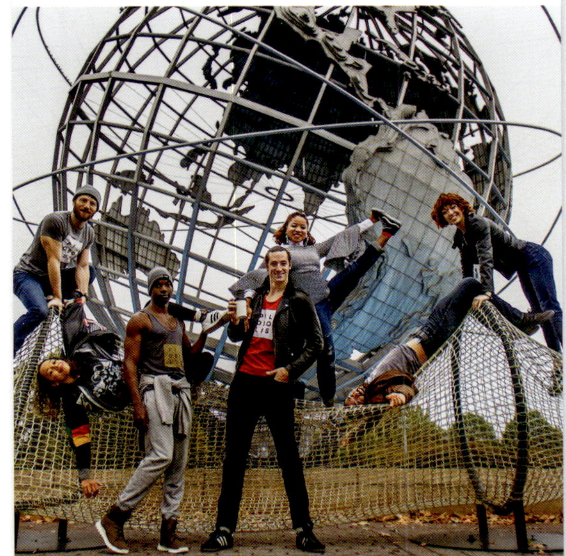

249 likes

pilobolus It's been real, Queens!! See you next time!

publicartfund love! thanks for visiting

litpixx ✶

NOVEMBER 5, 2017

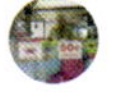

brooklynphoto2

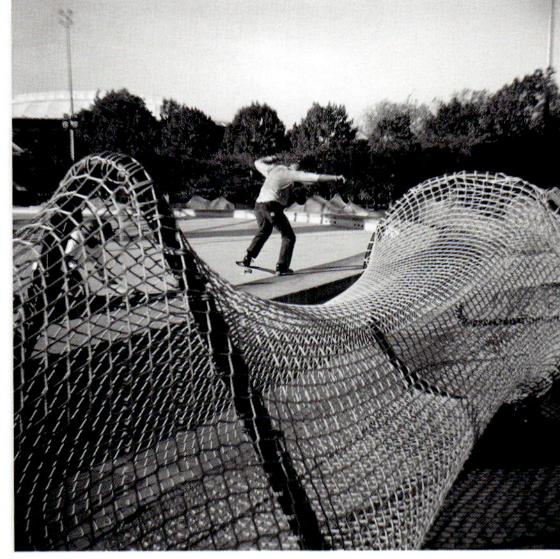

25 likes

brooklynphoto2 #streetphotography #blackandwhitephotography #dianaf #kodakfilm #flushingcoronapark #goodfencesmakegoodneighbors #aiweiwei #skateboarding #mediumformatphotography #unisphere

tlai_ 👍👍👍

NOVEMBER 13, 2017

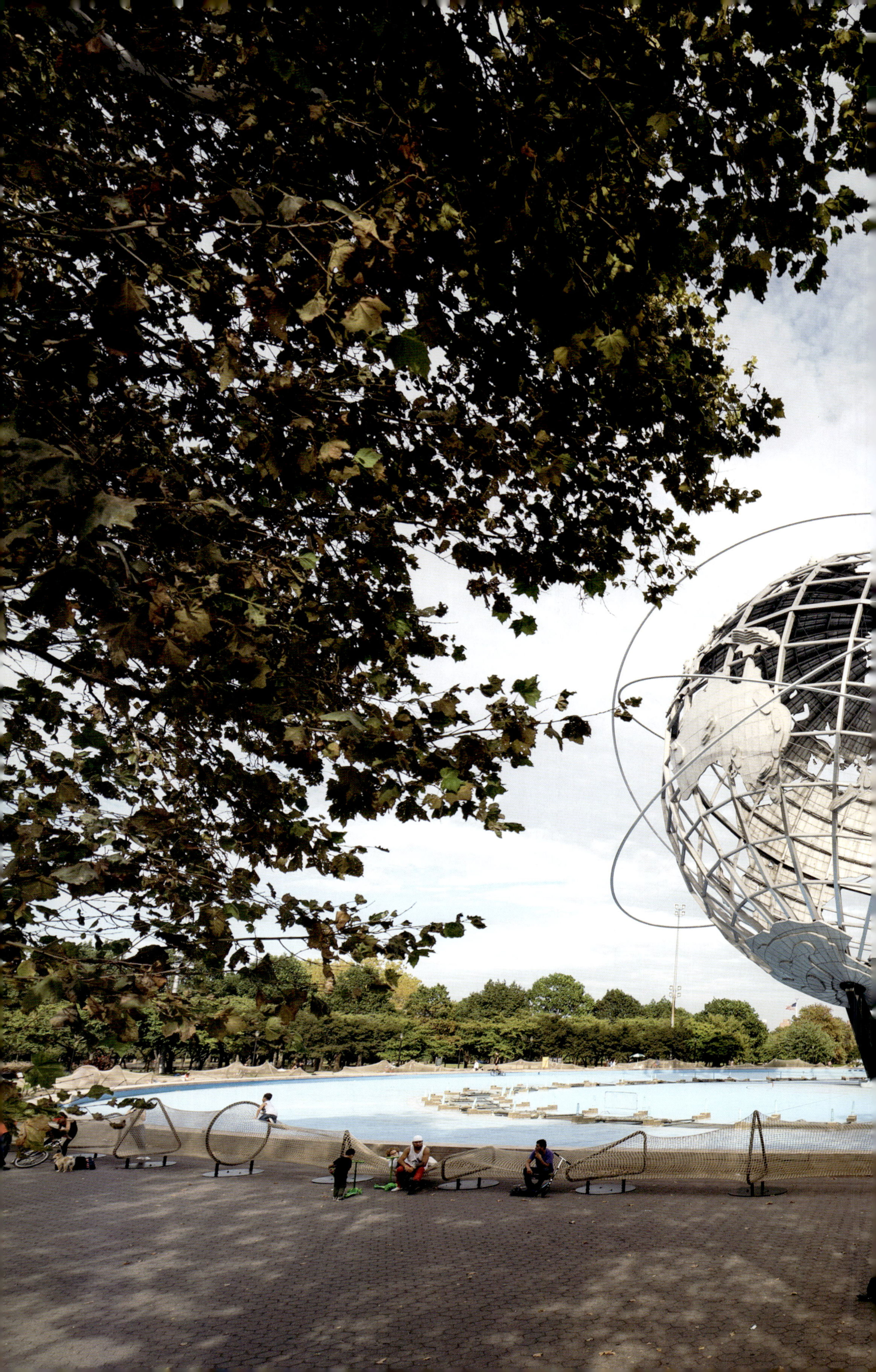

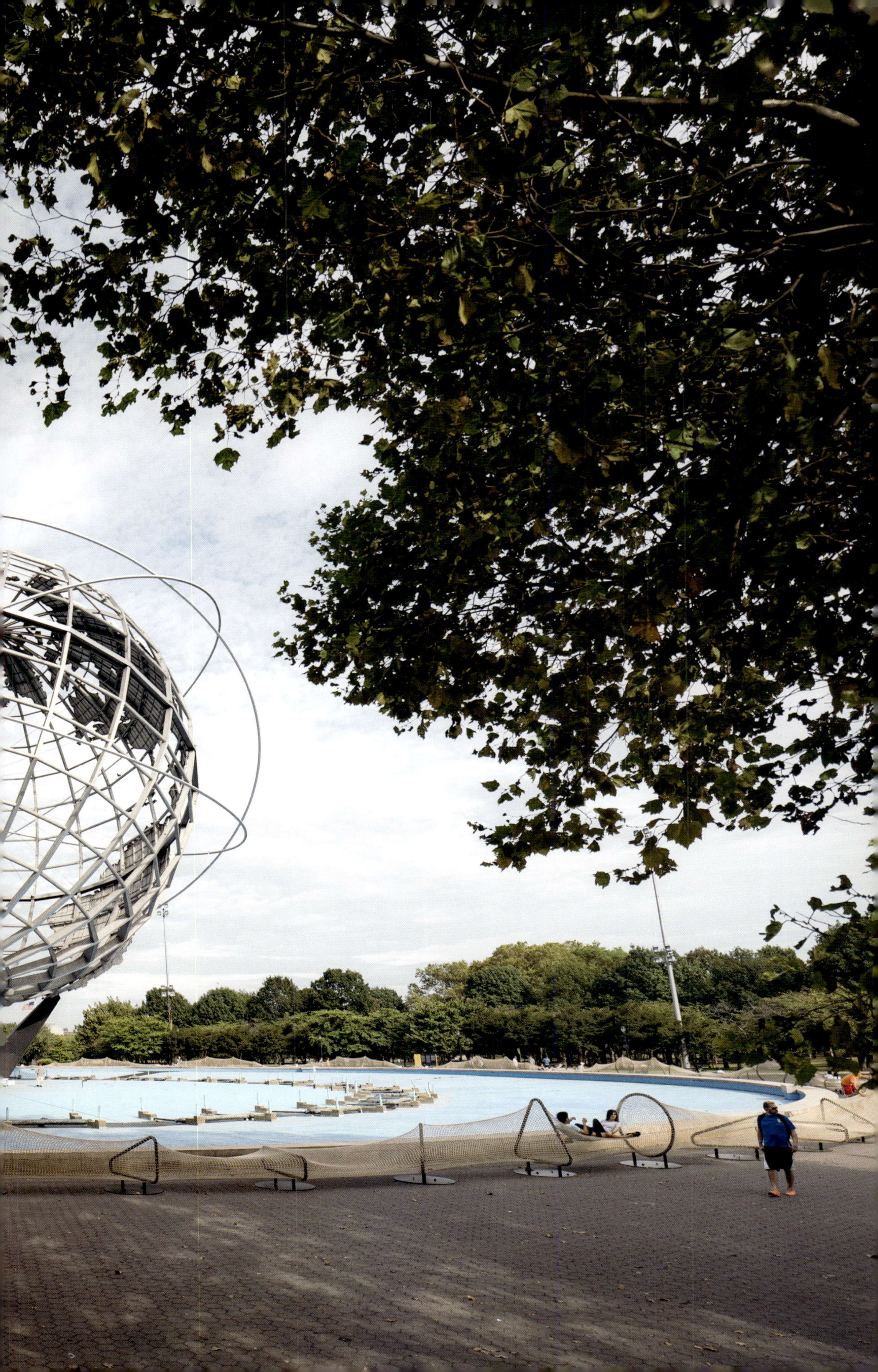

BROOKLYN & STATEN ISLAND

	Banners	23
	Bus Shelters	4
	Good Neighbors	31

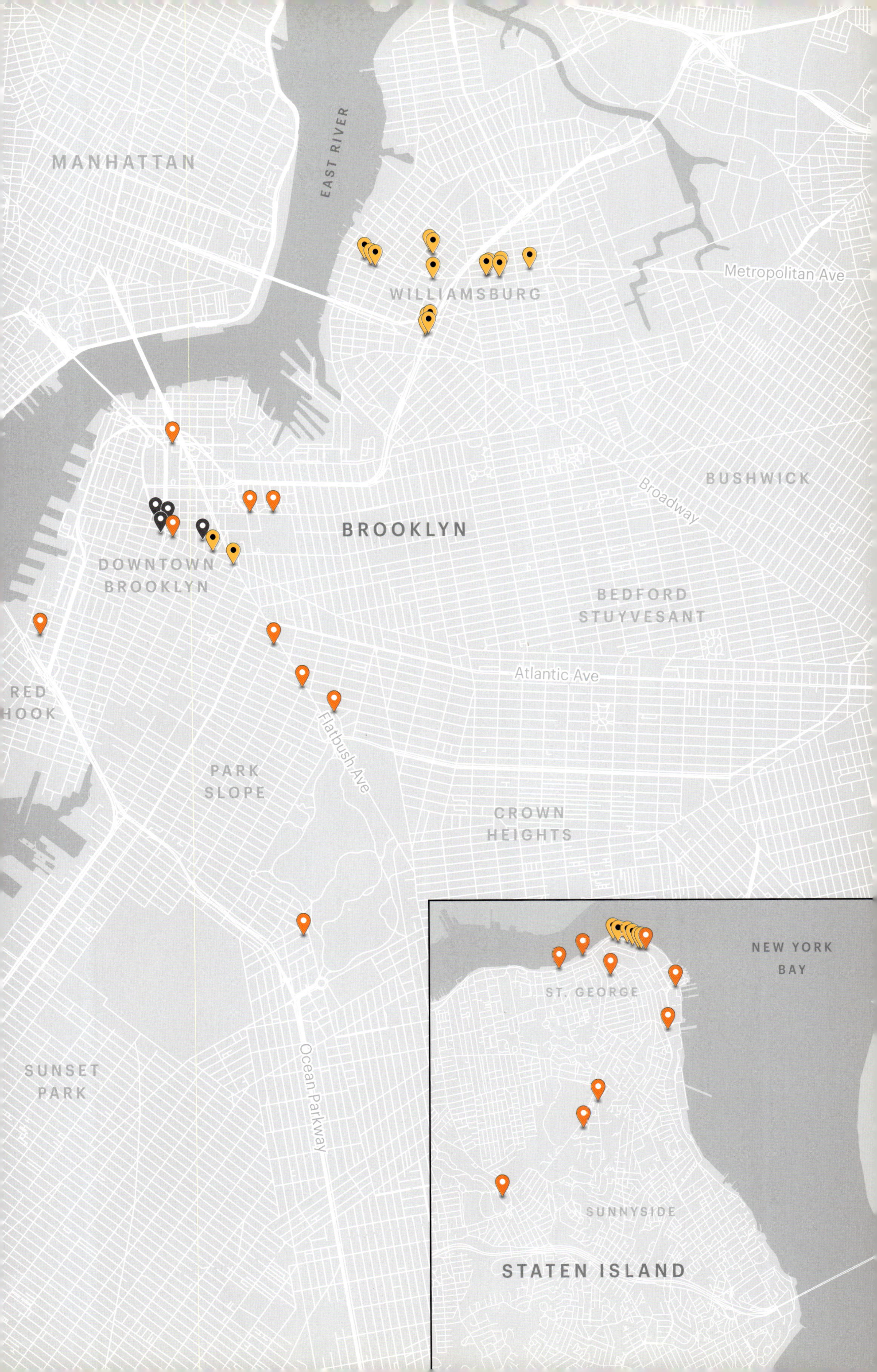
MANHATTAN
EAST RIVER
WILLIAMSBURG
Metropolitan Ave
BUSHWICK
Broadway
BROOKLYN
DOWNTOWN
BROOKLYN
BEDFORD
STUYVESANT
Atlantic Ave
RED
HOOK
Flatbush Ave
PARK
SLOPE
CROWN
HEIGHTS
SUNSET
PARK
Ocean Parkway
NEW YORK
BAY
ST. GEORGE
SUNNYSIDE
STATEN ISLAND

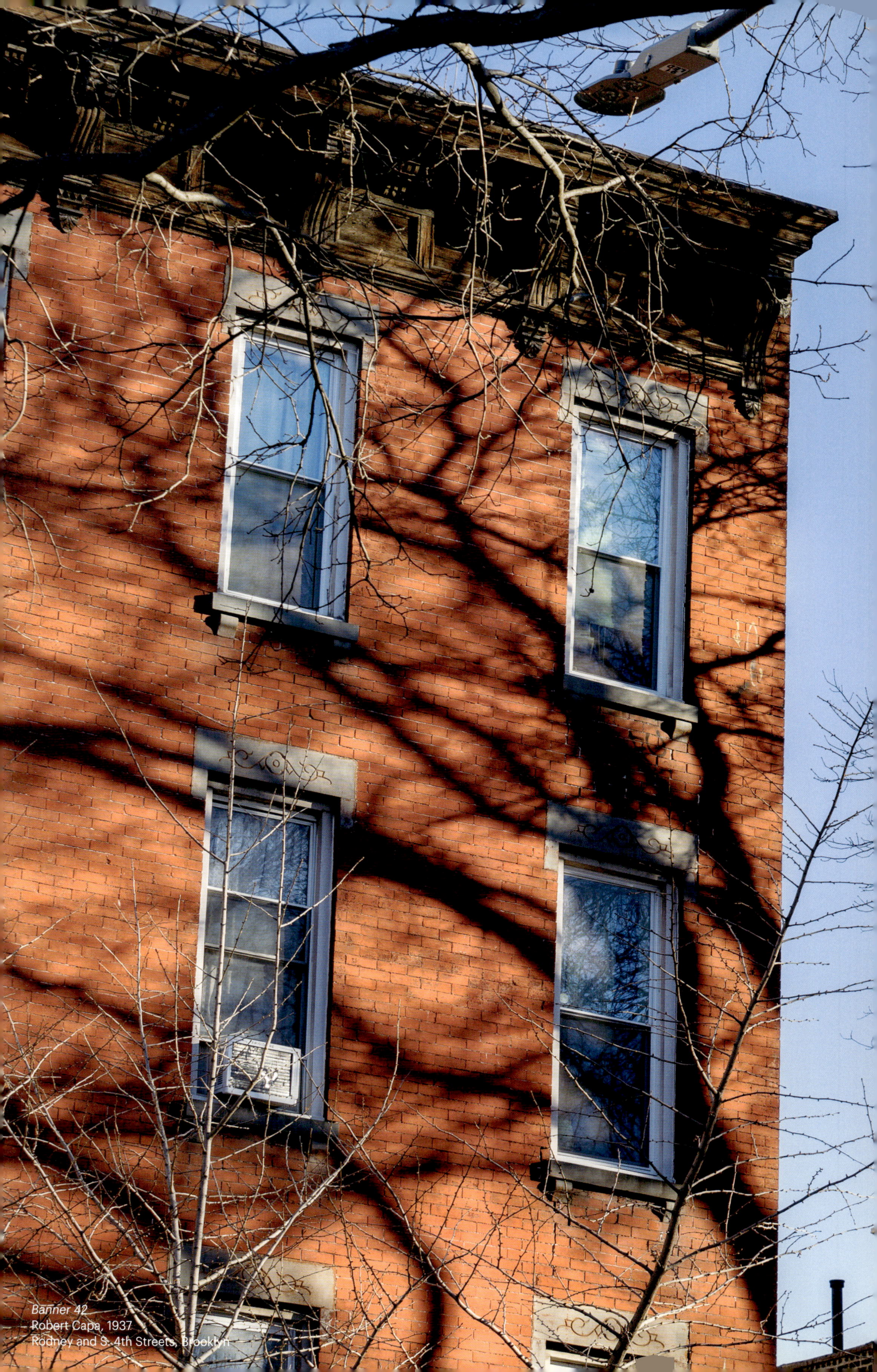

Banner 42
Robert Capa, 1937
Rodney and S. 4th Streets, Brooklyn

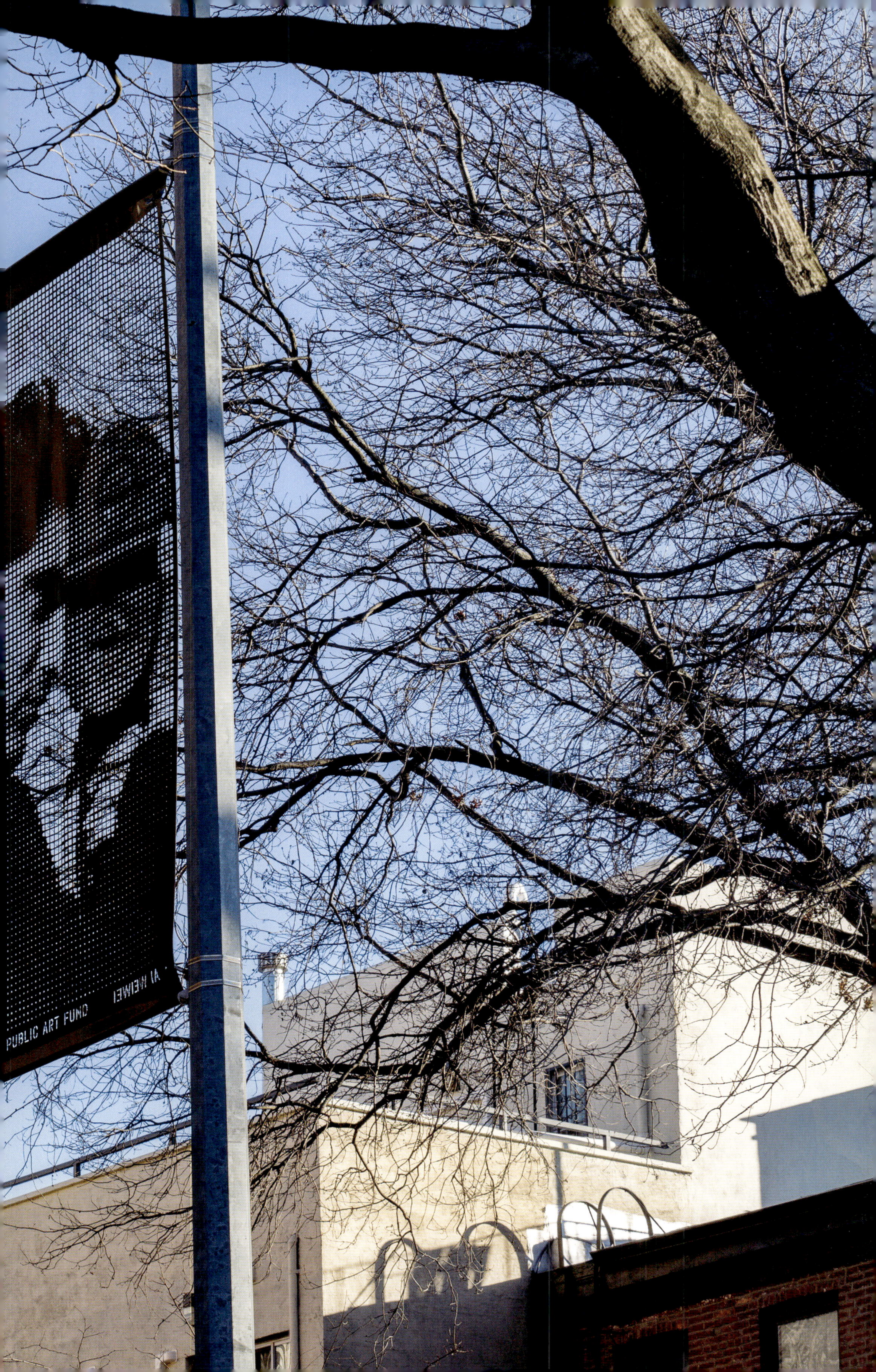
PUBLIC ART FUND

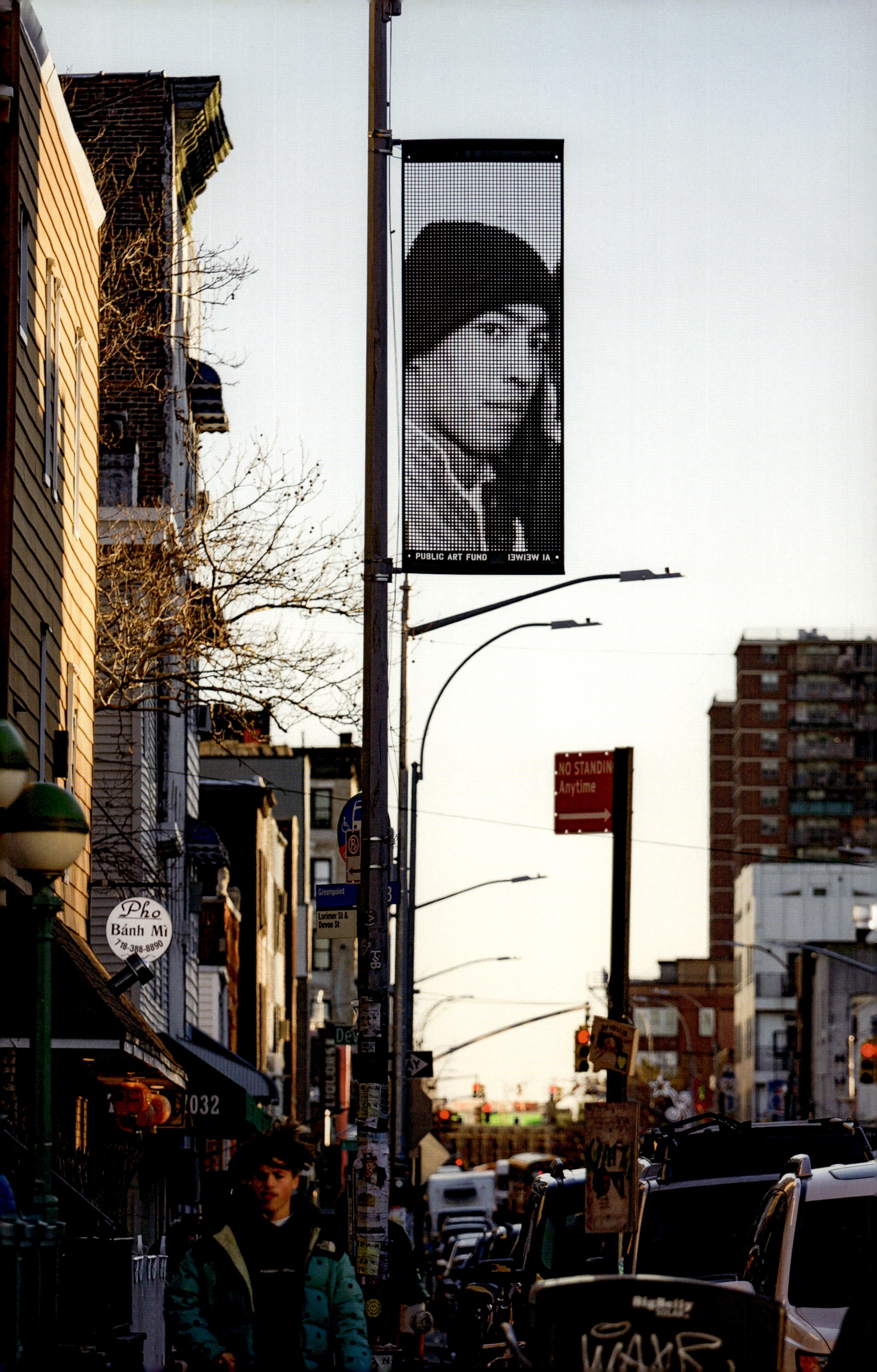
PUBLIC ART FUND
NO STANDING
Anytime
Pho
Bánh Mì
718-388-8890
Greenpoint
Lorimer St &
Devoe St

Brooklyn & Staten Island

Brooklyn and Staten Island are linked via the Verrazzano-Narrows Bridge, a massive double-deck suspension bridge named after Giovanni da Verrazzano, the Italian explorer who first encountered the indigenous Lenape people around New York Bay. This bridge spans the tidal strait known as the Narrows—the point that marks the entrance from the Atlantic Ocean into Upper New York Bay and the principal channel to the Hudson River. It is the gateway to New York City and the harbor that allowed the nascent city to thrive after Henry Hudson sailed up the river in 1609 and set in motion first Dutch, then British, colonial settlements.

But this strait also divides the two boroughs, which in many ways could not be more different. Staten Island is the least populated of the boroughs, with a very low population density, and Brooklyn is the most populous borough in New York City and one of the most densely inhabited counties in the United States. If Brooklyn were its own city, it would have the third-highest population in the country, after Los Angeles and Chicago. Brooklyn is intensely urban, with many high-rise buildings, avenues of brownstones, and large paved expanses, with multiple bridges connecting it to Manhattan's central core, and fancies itself the street-culture capital of the city. The borough of Staten Island, in contrast, is based on a more suburban residential plan, though it has seen the largest percentage increase of immigrants in recent years. The borough contains thousands of acres of parkland, including "greenbelt" and "blue belt" park systems, all accessible by the iconic Staten Island Ferry. Brooklyn and Staten Island were unified in 1898 when the five boroughs consolidated to form the City of New York.

Moreover, both of these boroughs are organized with strong transportation corridors. For this exhibition, the entry to Staten Island from the ferry became a main thoroughfare lined with *Banner* portraits running along Richmond Terrace, with breathtaking views of the Statue of Liberty and Ellis Island off its north shore, as well as *Good Neighbors* artworks on bus shelters running farther inland toward Interstate 278, which bisects the borough. Downtown Brooklyn featured three *Brooklyn Shelter* sculptures around existing bus shelters in the Borough Hall area. This included one on a double-length shelter and other *Good Neighbors* installations on shelters running down Flatbush Avenue toward Prospect Park. Elsewhere in Brooklyn, a cluster of banners was located in Williamsburg, the shores of which have long been a destination for new arrivals, from seventeenth-century settlers up through the young professionals of today.

Banner 113
Refugee, Moria Camp, Lesvos, Greece, 2015
Lorimer Street and Metropolitan Avenue, Brooklyn (opposite)

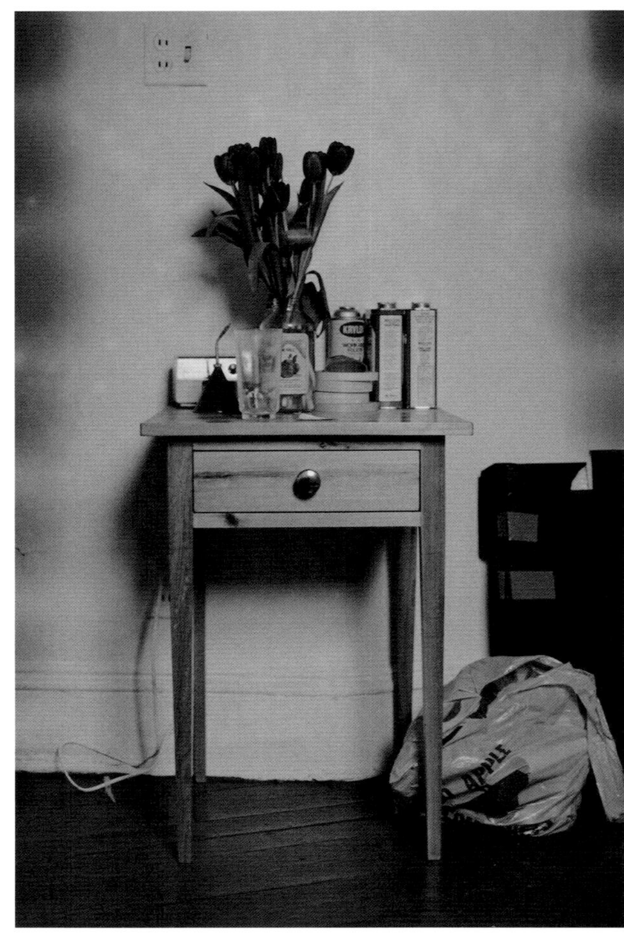

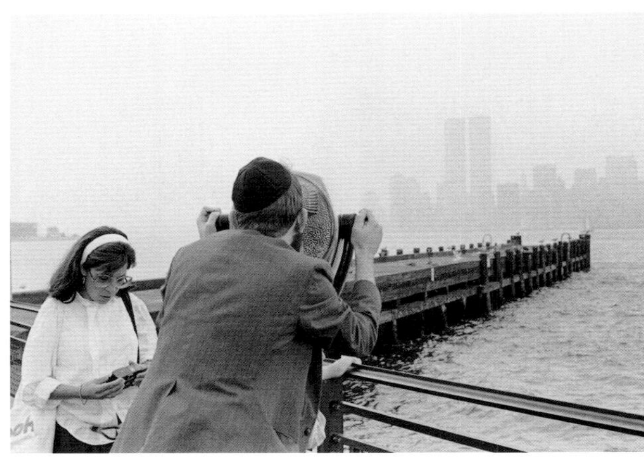

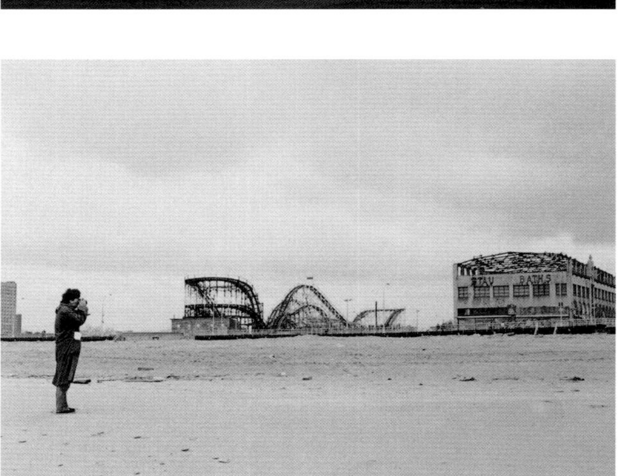

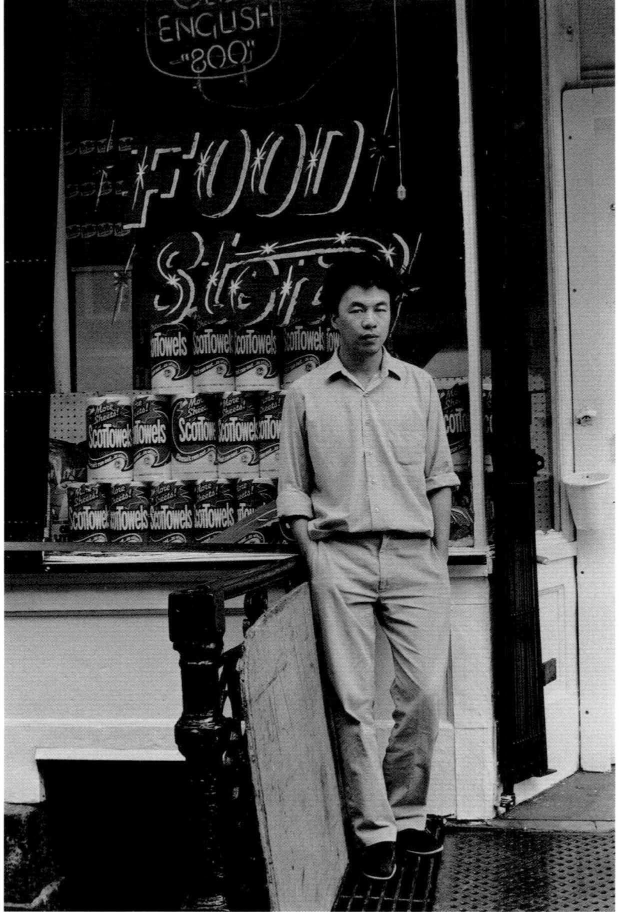

Lorimer Avenue Apartment, Brooklyn, 1983, and *A Jewish Family*, 1988, from the series New York Photographs 1983–1993. Black-and-white photographs (top left and right)

Ai Dan. Coney Island, 1987, and *Ai Weiwei. Williamsburg, Brooklyn*, 1983, from the series New York Photographs 1983–1993. Black-and-white photographs (bottom left and right)

Good Neighbors 10
Moria Camp, Lesvos, Greece, 2015
Devoe Street and Graham Avenue, Brooklyn (opposite)

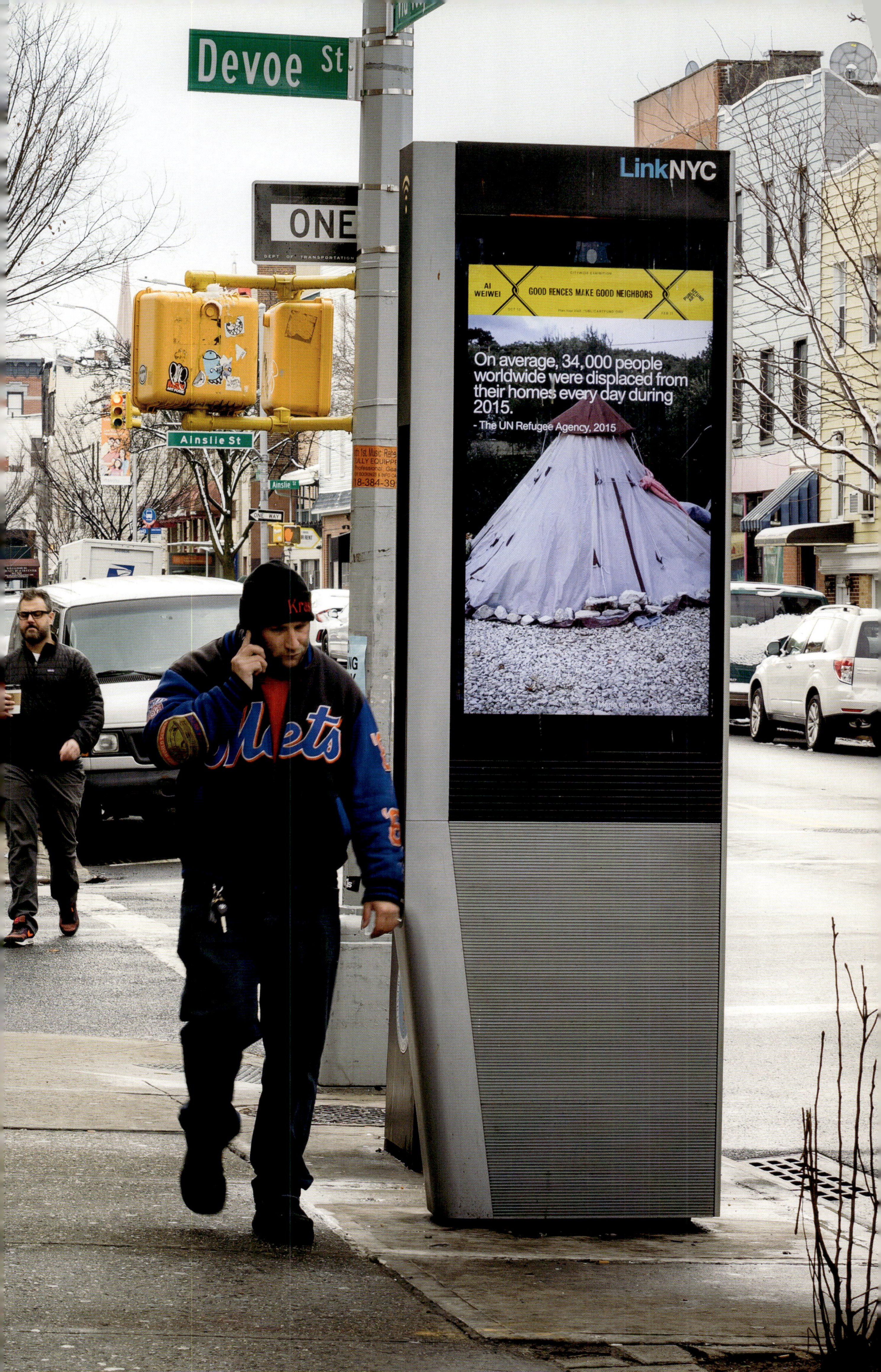
Devoe St
ONE
Ainslie St
LinkNYC
AI WEIWEI
GOOD FENCES MAKE GOOD NEIGHBORS
On average, 34,000 people worldwide were displaced from their homes every day during 2015.
- The UN Refugee Agency, 2015
Mets

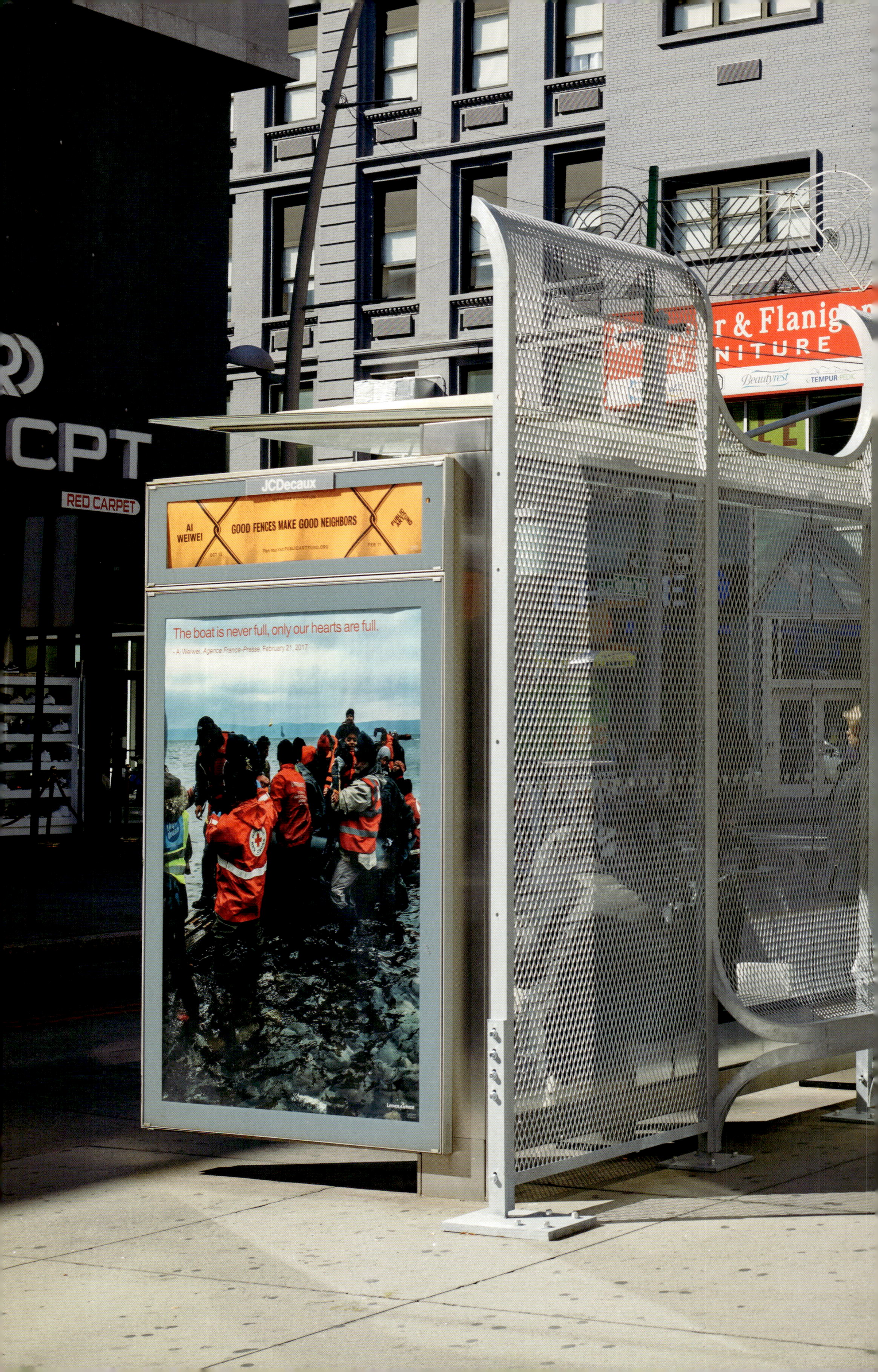
CPT
RED CARPET
& Flanig
NITURE
Beautyrest
TEMPUR
JCDecaux
AI
WEIWEI
GOOD FENCES MAKE GOOD NEIGHBORS
PUBLIC ART FUND
OCT 12
Plan Your Visit PUBLICARTFUND.ORG
FEB 11
The boat is never full, only our hearts are full.
- Ai Weiwei, Agence France-Presse, February 21, 2017

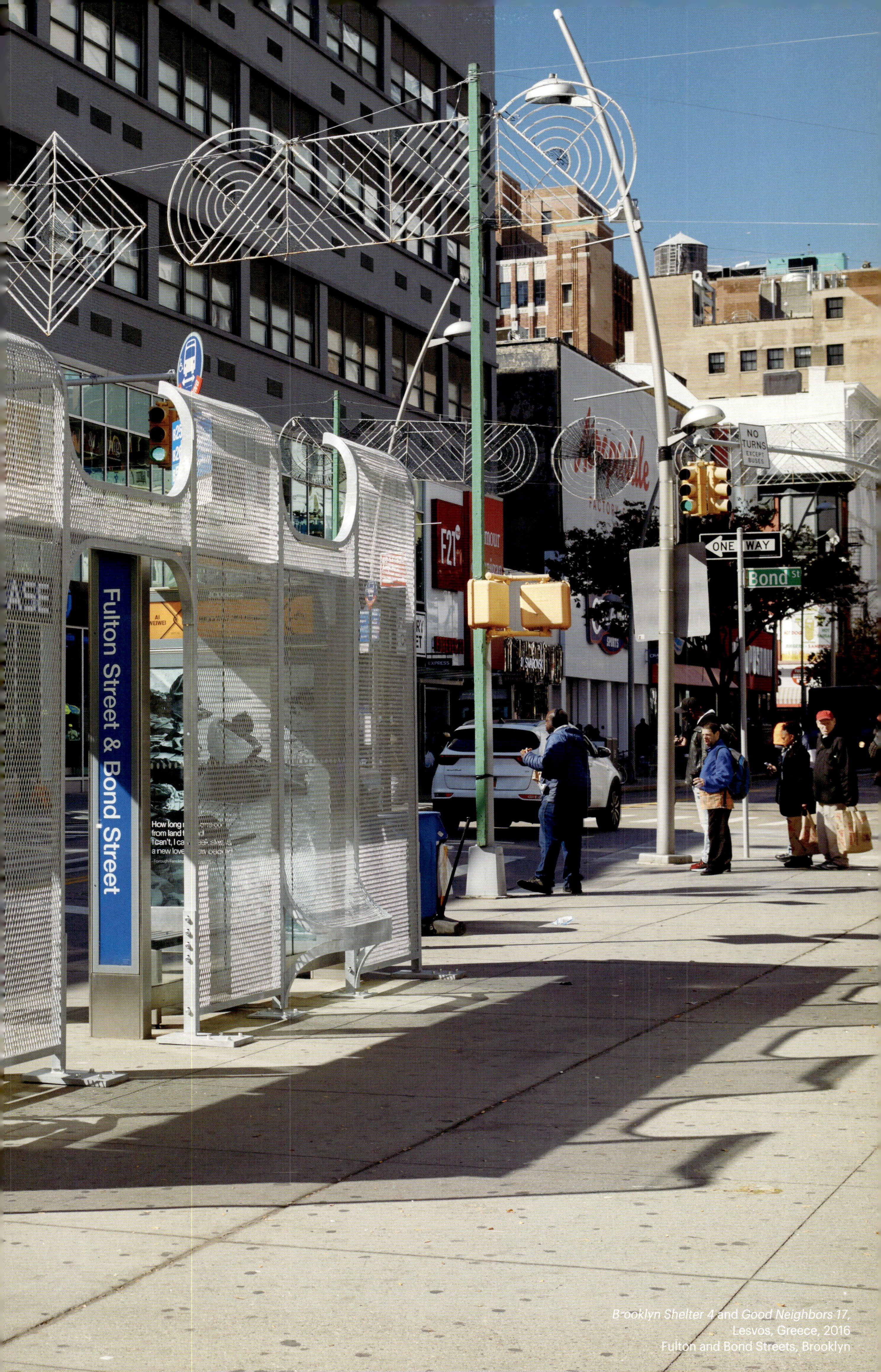

Brooklyn Shelter 4 and *Good Neighbors 17*,
Lesvos, Greece, 2016
Fulton and Bond Streets, Brooklyn

LIVINGSTON ST & NEVINS ST, BROOKLYN

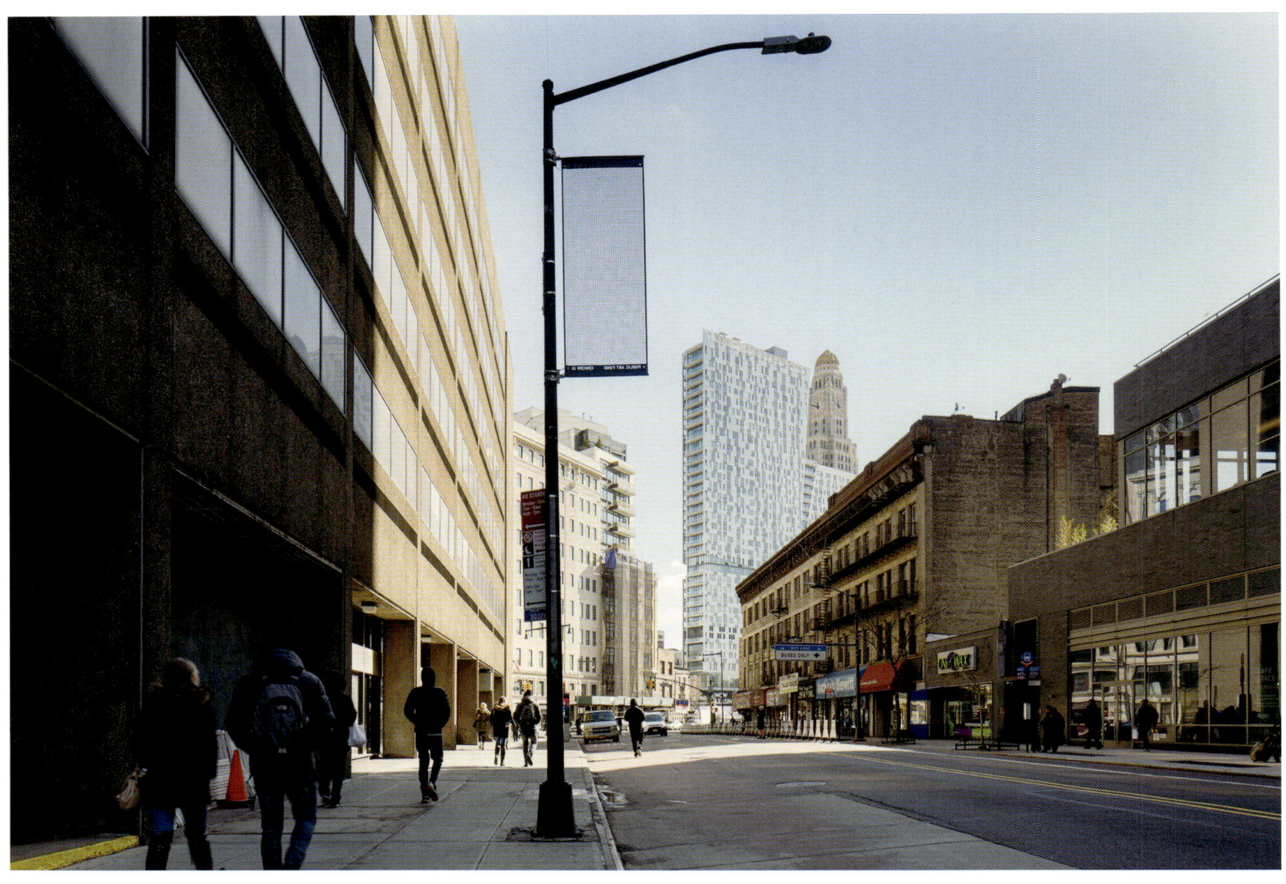

It is truly an honor to be aligned with Ai Weiwei as a close friend and collaborator. Of all the amazing installations that he has done around the globe, I think *Good Fences Make Good Neighbors* in New York City represents one of his most powerful and sincere engagements with the public. Ai's focus on the plight of refugees has been the impetus for several incredible projects, including his documentary film, publications, large-scale sculptures, photos, and other creative interpretations that reference this worldwide crisis that haunts all of humanity.

Larry Warsh

Banner 37, Blank (top)

Social media post, *Good Neighbors 10,* Moria Camp, Lesvos, Greece (opposite, top)

Good Neighbors 92
Nizip Camp, Gaziantep, Turkey, 2017
(opposite, bottom)

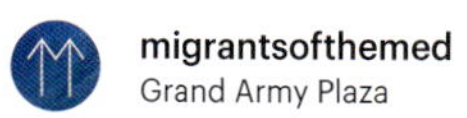

migrantsofthemed
Grand Army Plaza

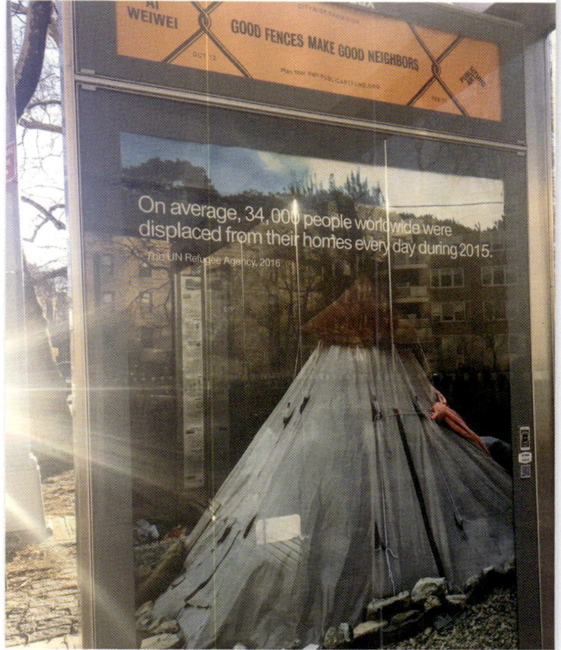

23 likes

migrantsofthemed It's Monday! Move through it knowing there is something you are a part of that depends on your active support to survive: humanity. Here is a bus shelter installment from @publicartfund & @aiww to remind us that even across a commute to work we can stay aware of the people who need our consciousness and love.

#goodfencesmakegoodneighbors

JANUARY 29, 2018

RICHMOND TER & SHUYLER ST, STATEN ISLAND

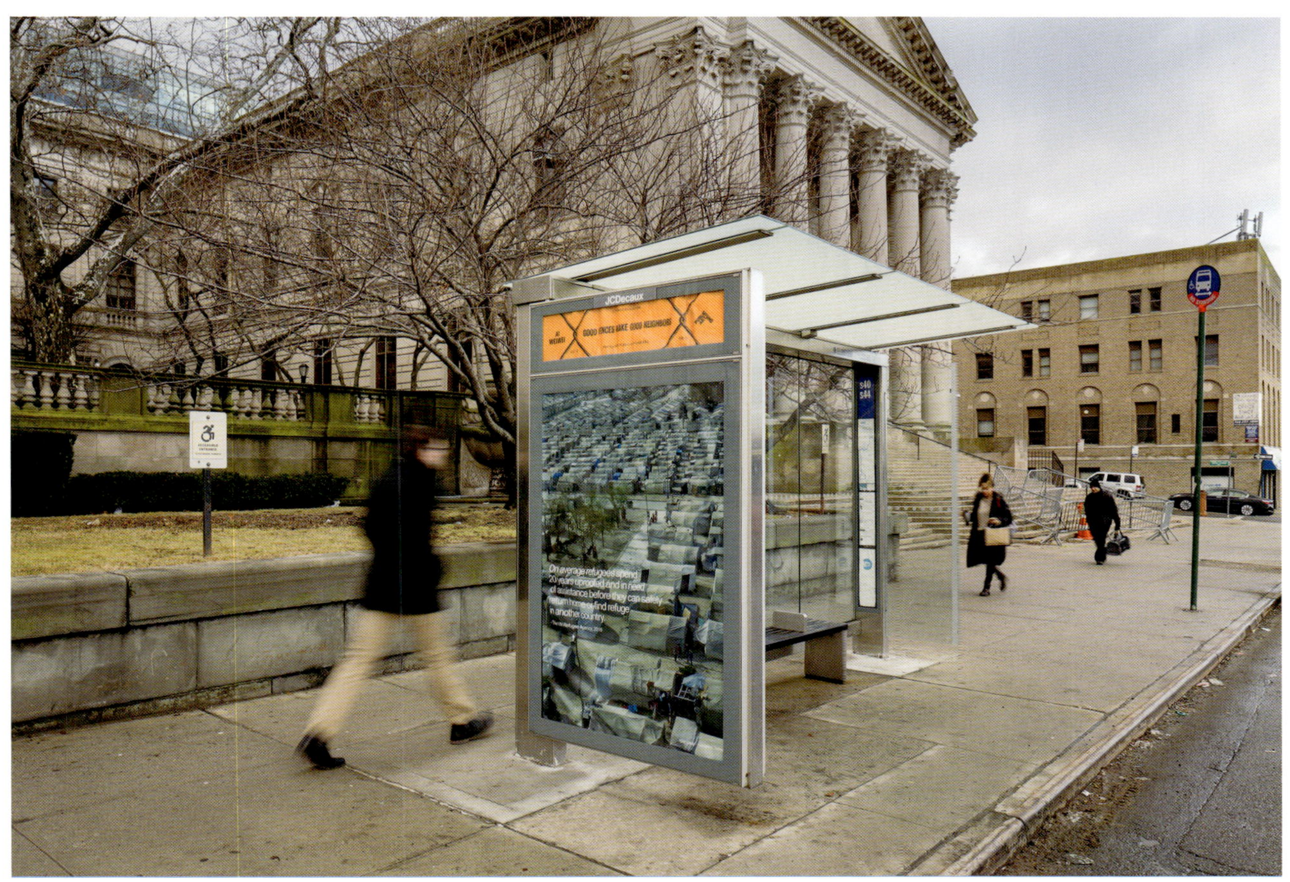

FULTON ST & BOND ST, BROOKLYN

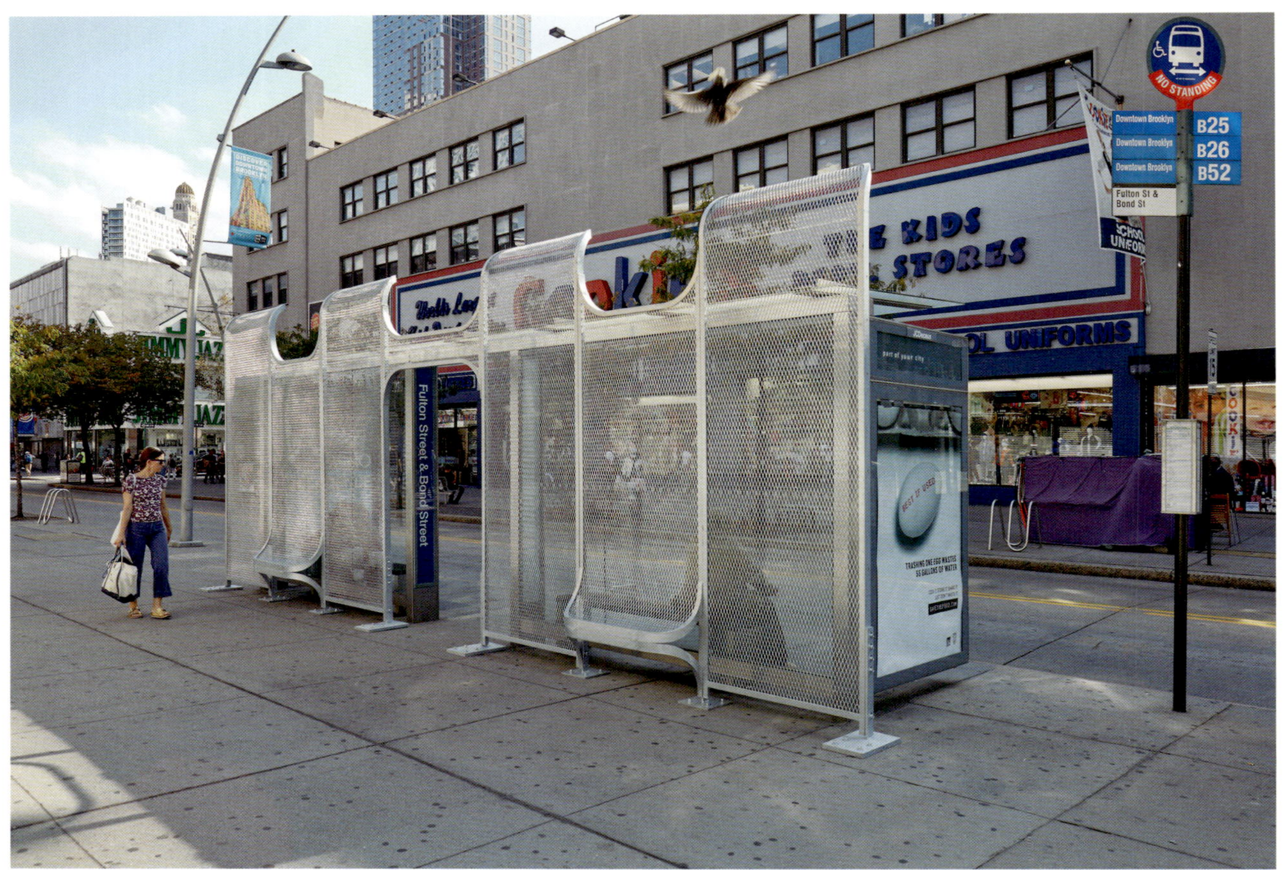

COLUMBIA ST & CARROLL ST, BROOKLYN

you and I
can say we loved
each other
and the people's greatest cause
— we fought for it —
we can say
'We lived'.

Nazim Hikmet, 'On Death Again,' 1939

Lesvos, Greece

Brooklyn Shelter 4 (top)

Good Neighbors 4
Refugee wallet found on the beach, Lesvos, Greece, 2015 (bottom)

Good Neighbors 11
Moria Camp, Lesvos, Greece, 2015 (opposite)

With *Good Fences Make Good Neighbors*, Ai Weiwei draws attention to the unprecedented divisions in our political system, the controversies over immigrants, and the pain and perils of fleeing refugees. Ai Weiwei confronts xenophobia inspired by his own lived experiences and uses art to encourage inclusiveness and understanding. I salute him for his bold creativity and activism.

Chirlane McCray, New York City First Lady

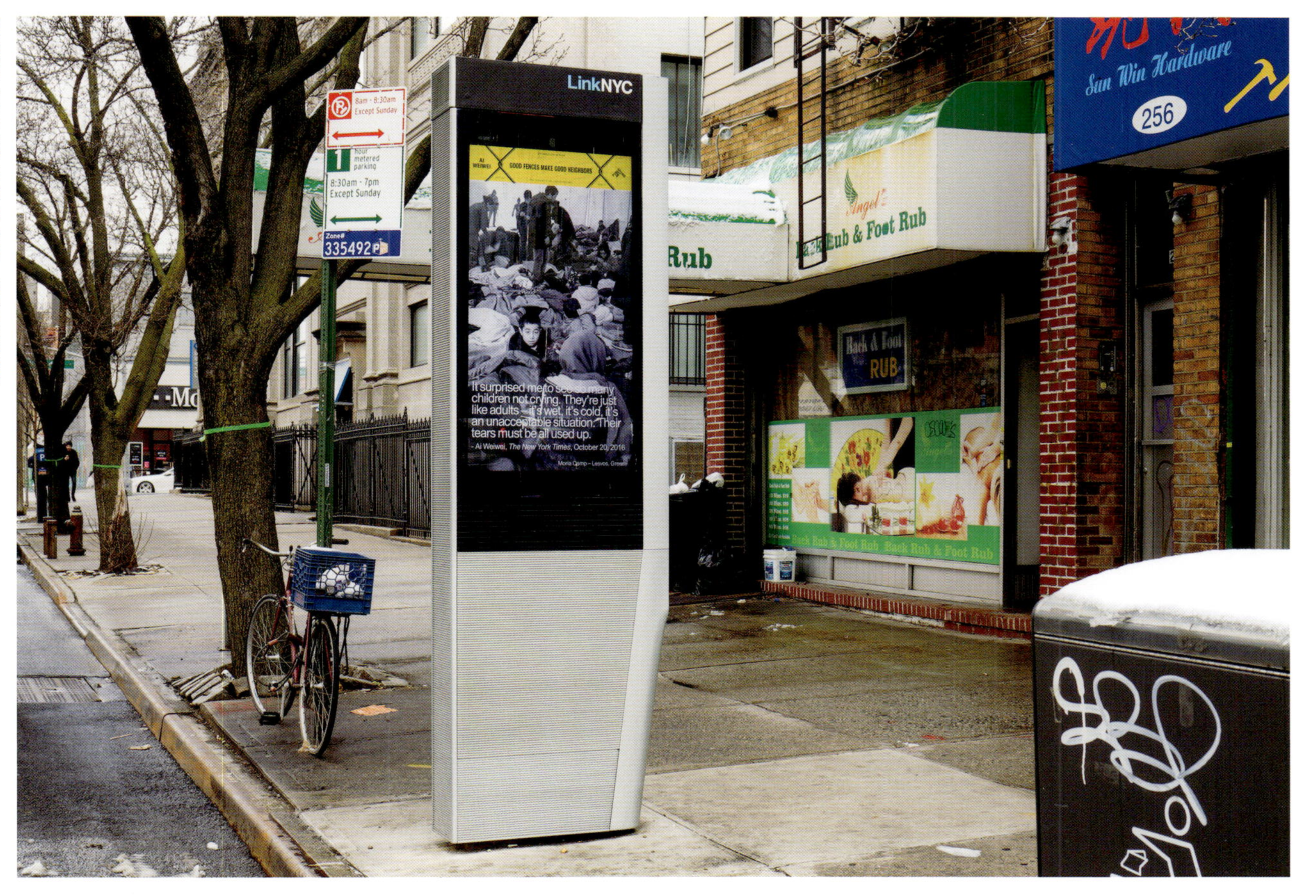

DEVOE ST & GRAHAM AVE, BROOKLYN

Who belongs on what side of which border and who we should stop or prevent or allow. I think the artist is questioning whether anyone has the authority to make those decisions.

Viewer comment

×

Good Fences Make Good Neighbors embraces the people of New York City, reminding us all that there should be no boundaries to our humanity for others.

Regina Myer, President, Downtown Brooklyn Partnership

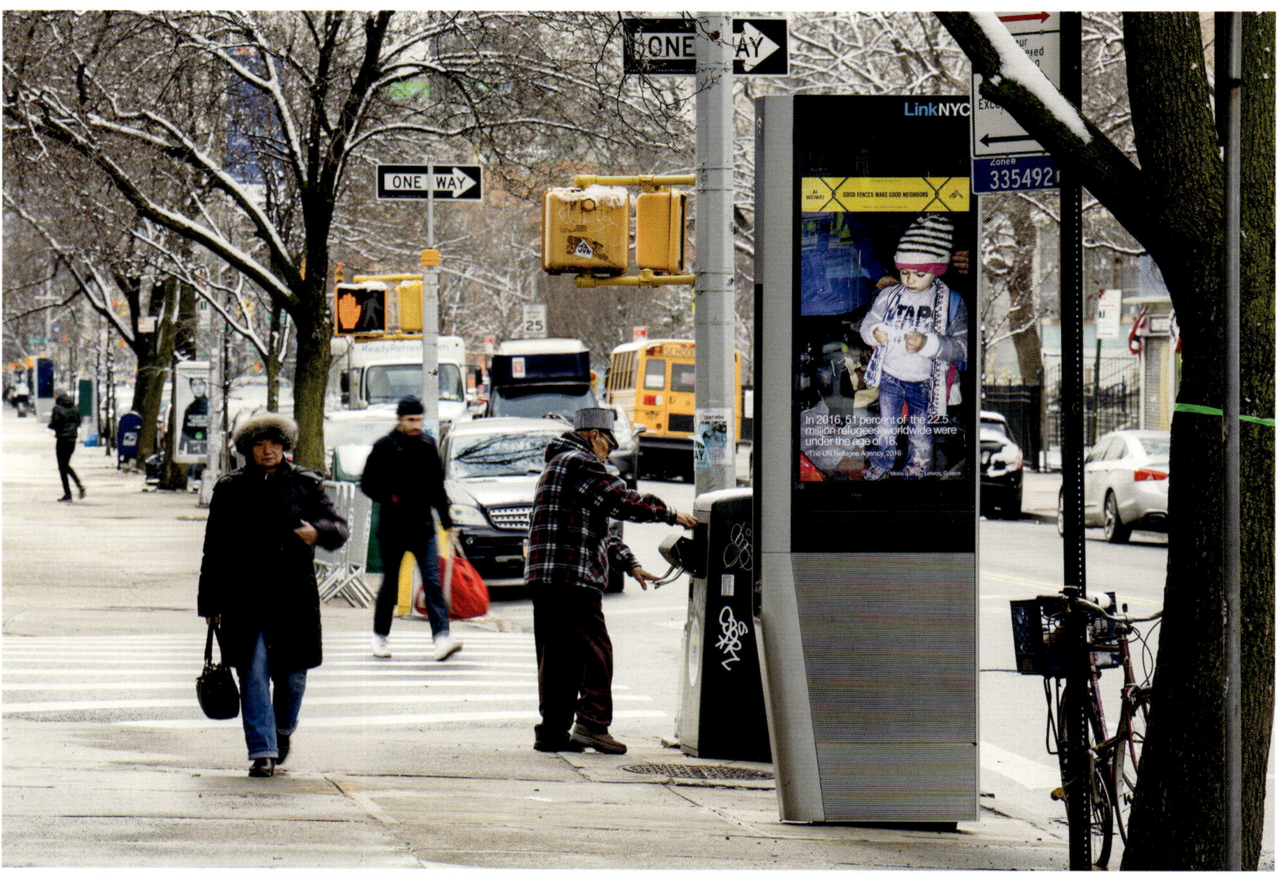

PROSPECT PARK & WINDSOR PL, BROOKLYN

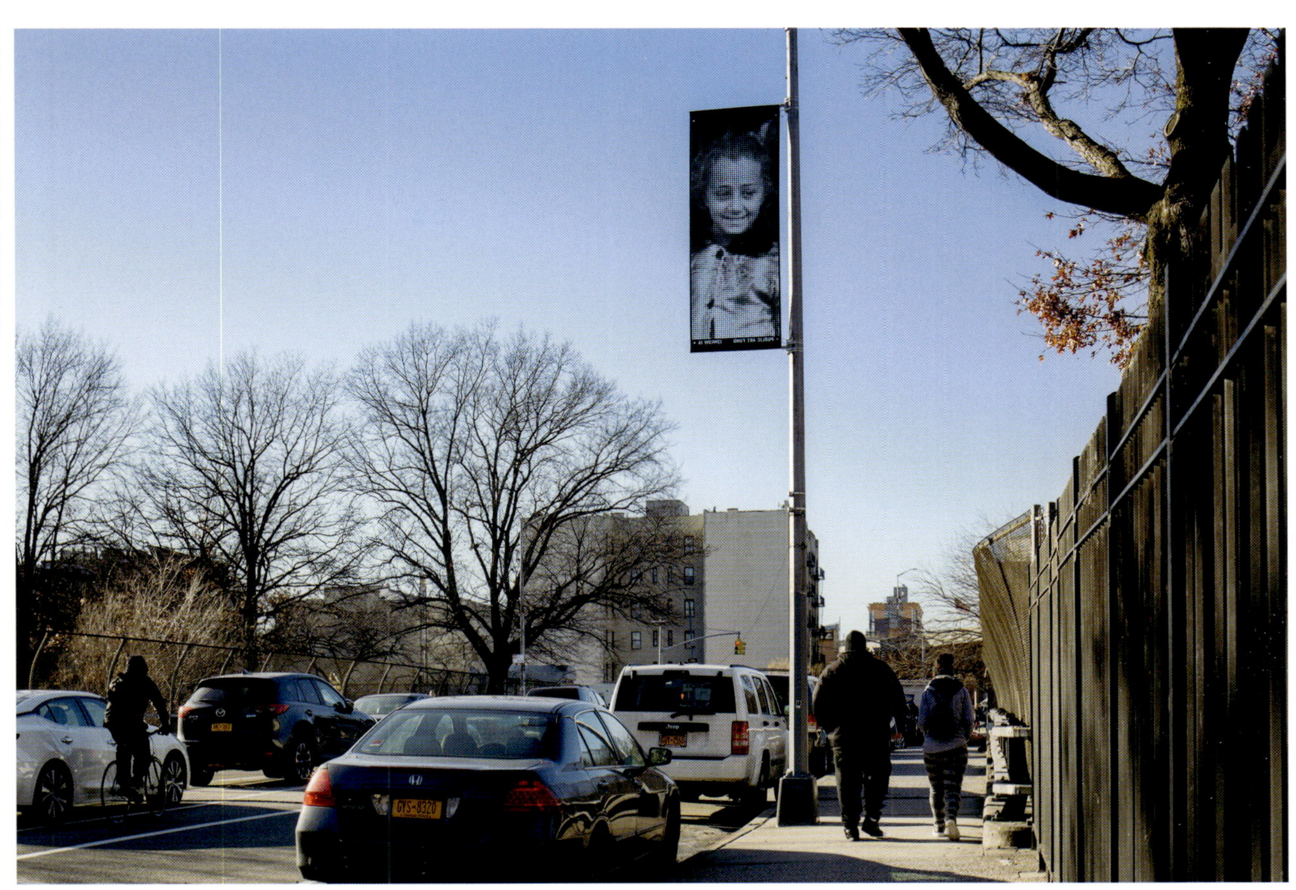

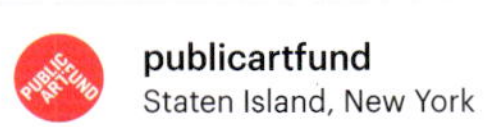

publicartfund
Staten Island, New York

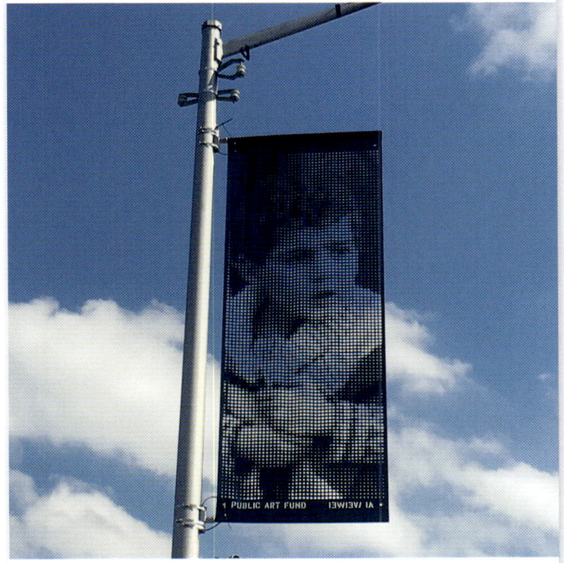

664 likes

publicartfund 200 portraits on lampposts dot the city as part of @aiww's #GoodFences Make Good Neighbors. Banner 190, located in Staten Island, depicts a refugee from the Syrian-Jordanian Border, where nearly 60,000 Syrian refugees have encamped in the middle of the desert. Read more at publicartfund.org/goodfences.

georgesbergesgallery ✱✱✱✱

NOVEMBER 6, 2017

Good Neighbors 8
Moria Camp, Lesvos, Greece, 2015 (opposite)

Banner 192
Refugee, Syrian-Jordanian Border, 2016 (top)

Social media post, *Banner 190*, Refugee, Syrian-Jordanian Border, 2016 (bottom)

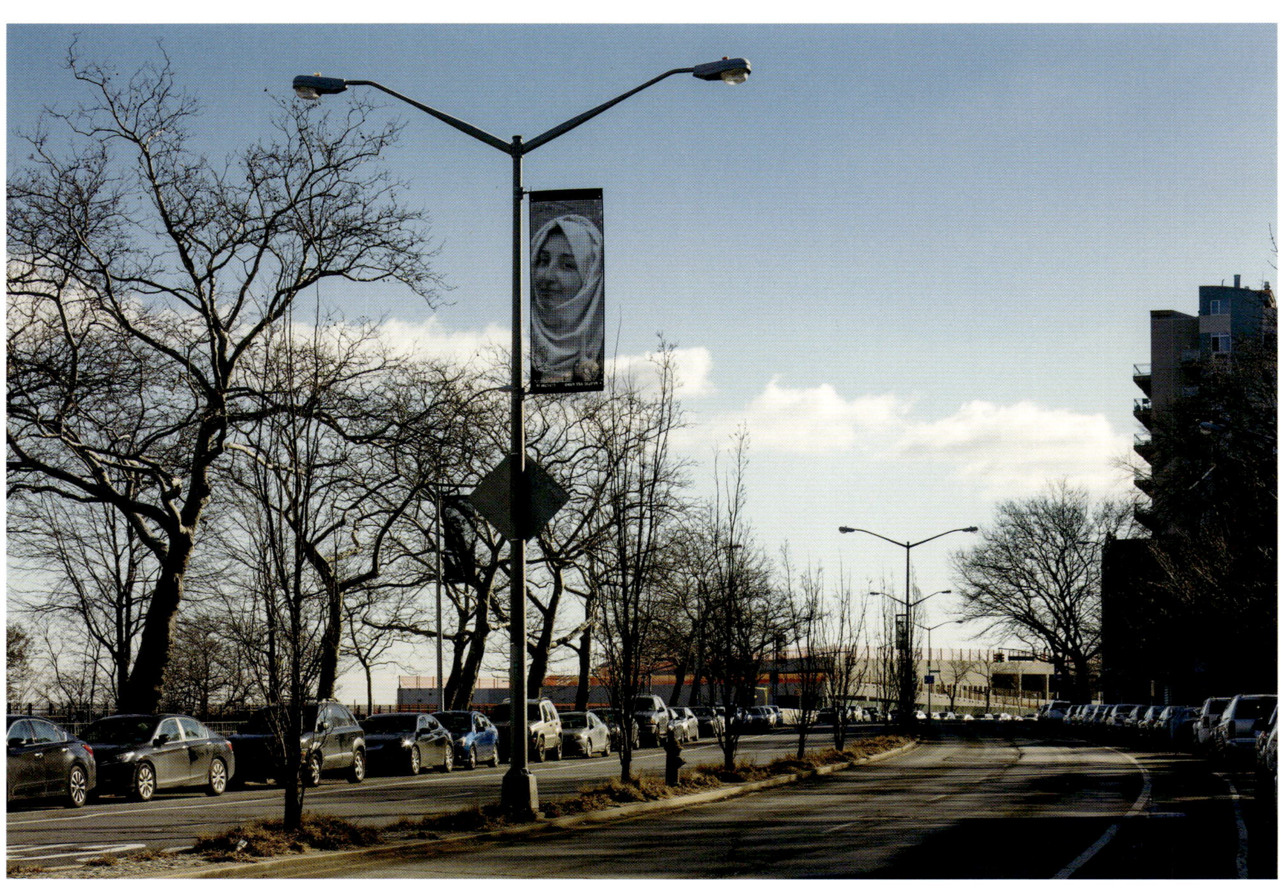

Ai Weiwei's thoughtful, creative way of framing those questions is a welcome change from a discourse that can often be reactive and sometimes downright hateful. My belief is that New York City is, and will always remain, a beacon of inclusion and diversity. In fact, I think that is exactly why this exhibition fits so well into all five boroughs.

Corey Johnson, Speaker, New York City Council

Banner 160
Refugee, Idomeni Makeshift Camp, Idomeni, Greece, 2016 (top)

Good Neighbors 94
Mediterranean Sea, 2017 (opposite, top)

Good Neighbors 97
Near Idomeni, Greece, 2017 (opposite, bottom)

VICTORY BLVD & MONTGOMERY AVE, STATEN ISLAND

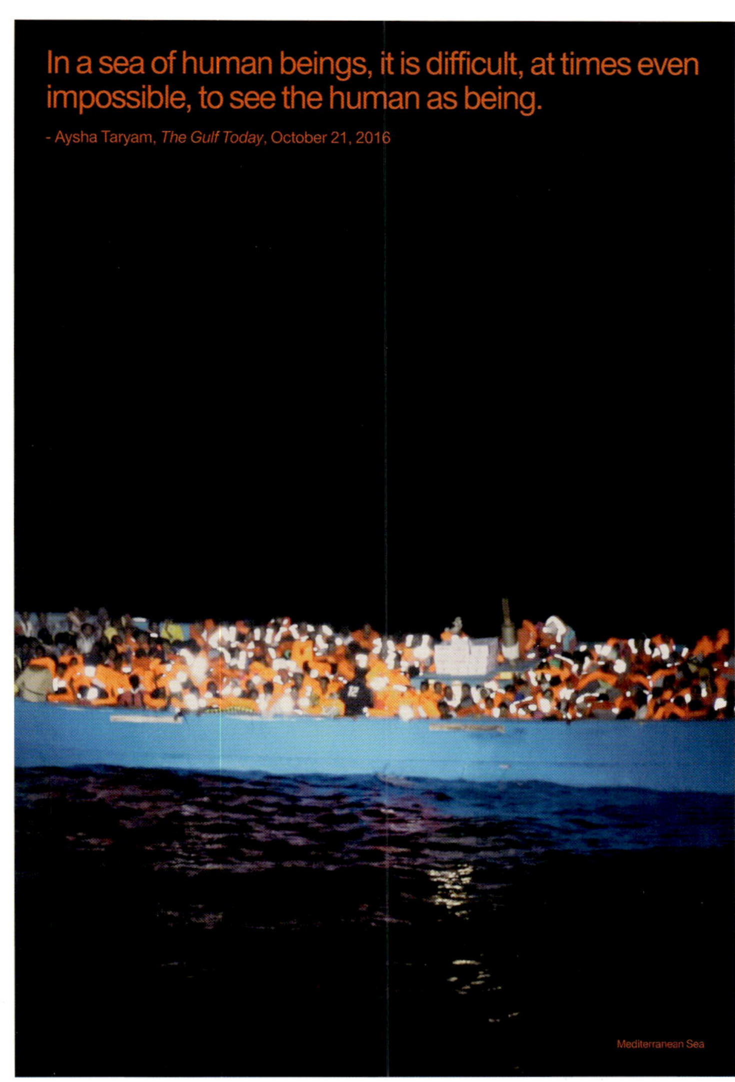

RICHMOND TER & JERSEY ST, STATEN ISLAND

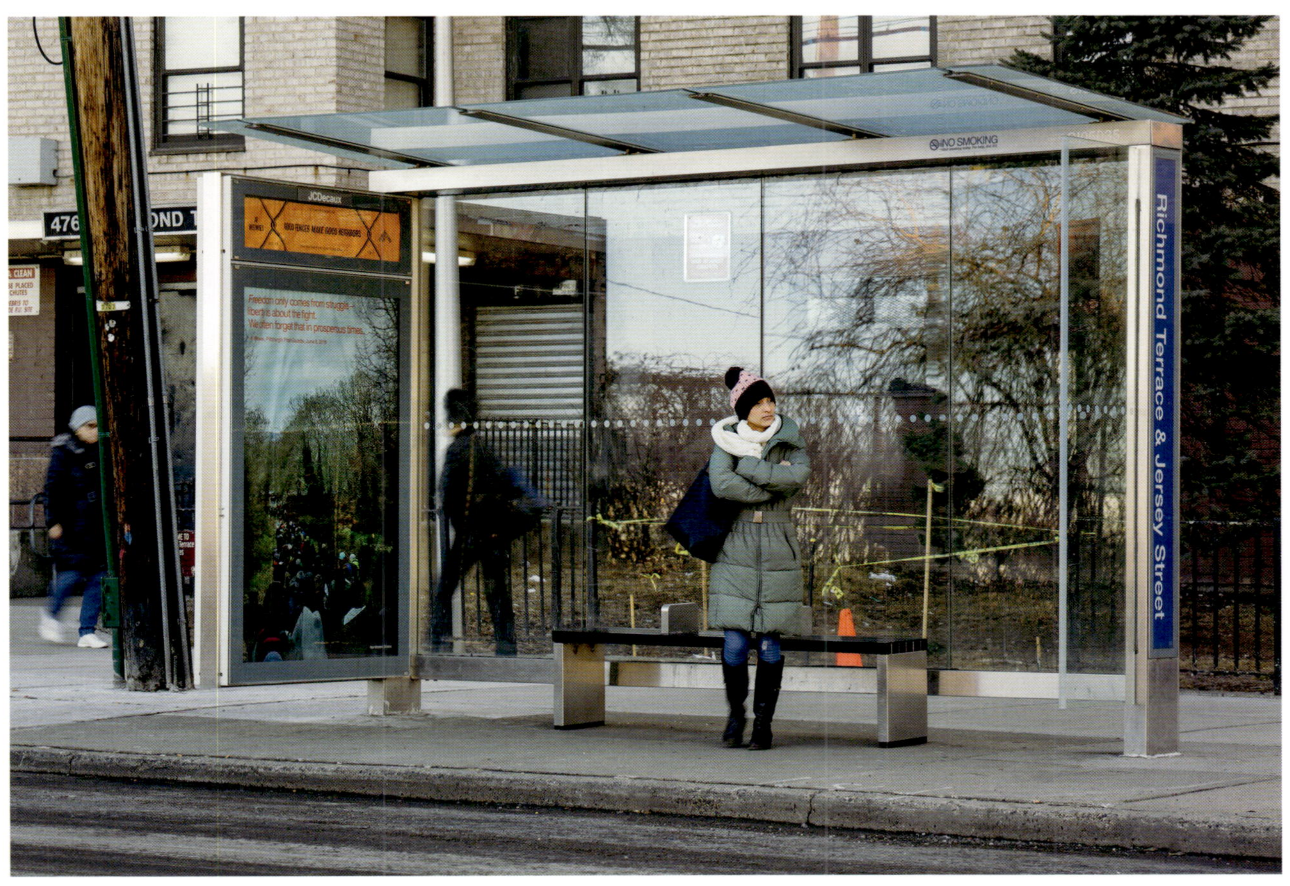

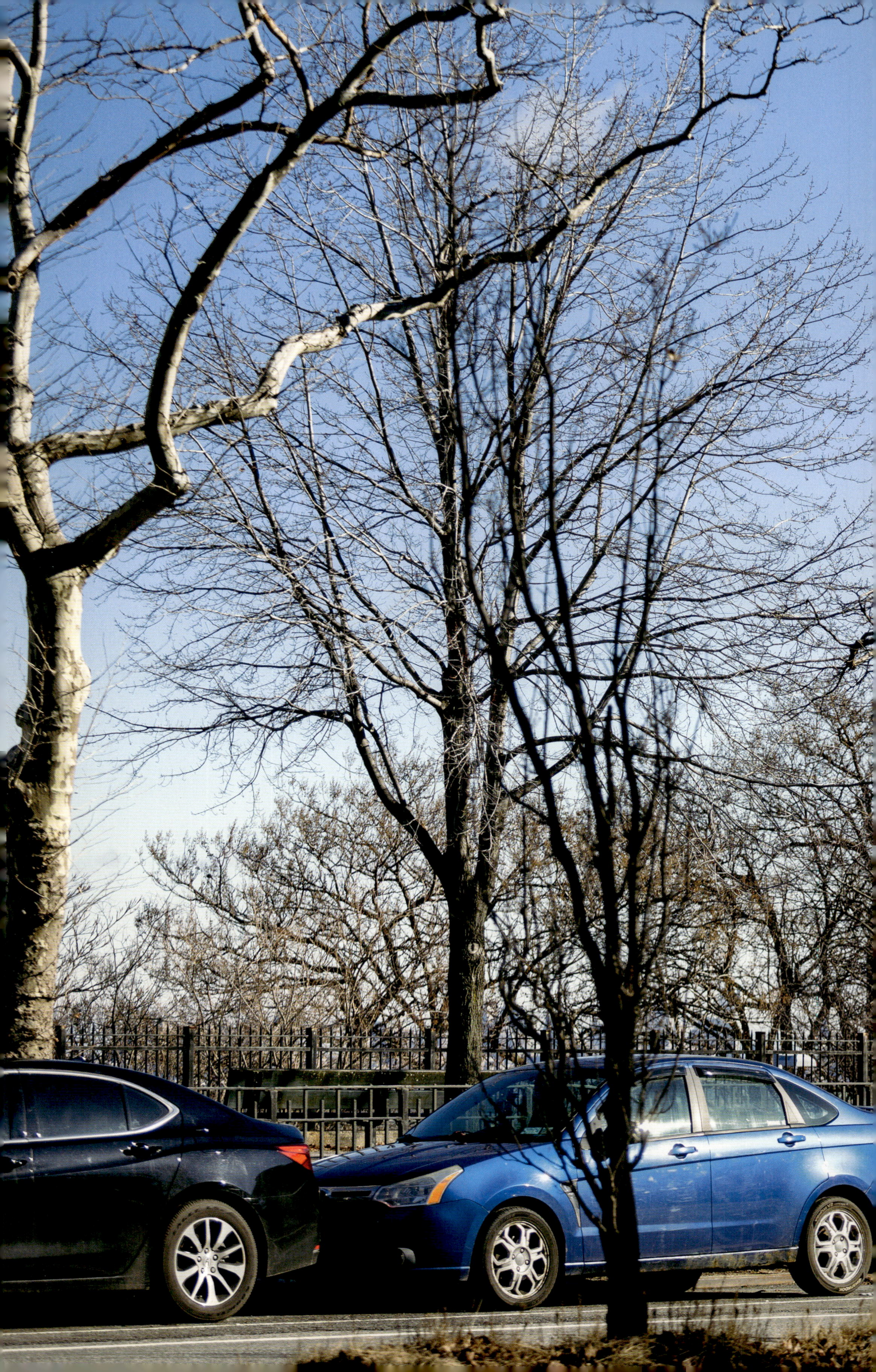

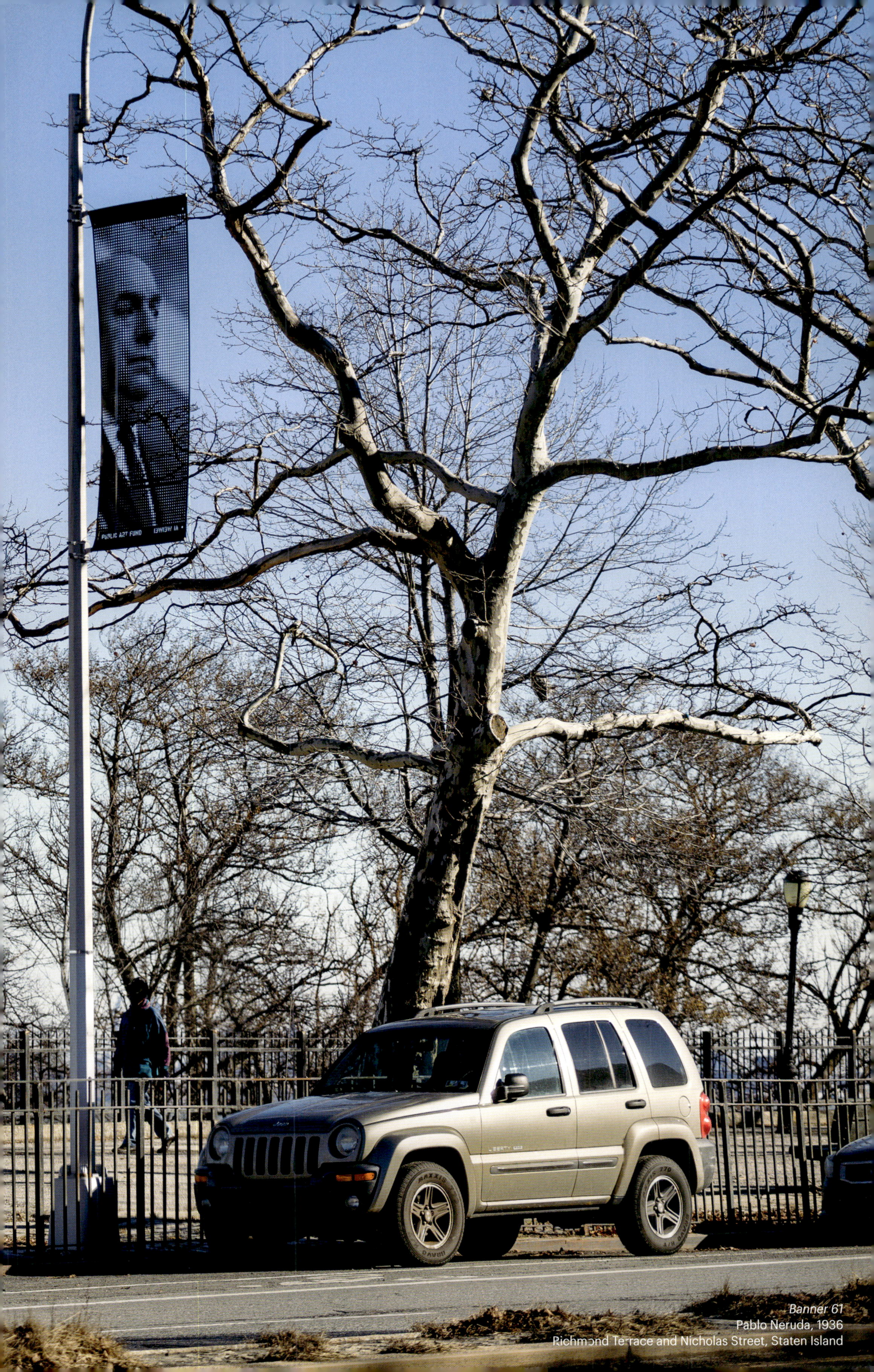

Banner 61
Pablo Neruda, 1936
Richmond Terrace and Nicholas Street, Staten Island

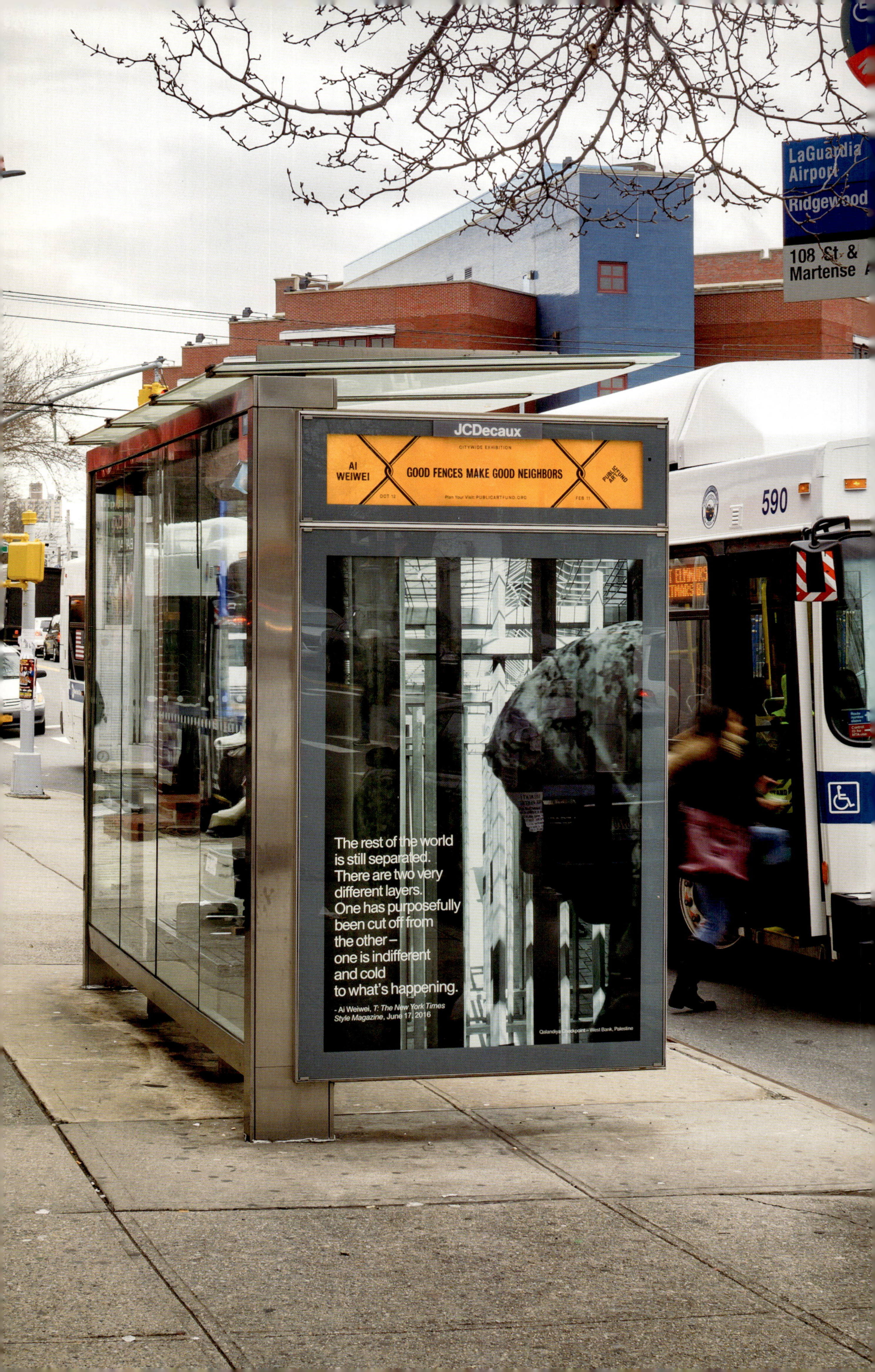
LaGuardia Airport
Ridgewood
108 St &
Martense
JCDecaux
CITYWIDE EXHIBITION
AI WEIWEI
GOOD FENCES MAKE GOOD NEIGHBORS
PUBLIC ART FUND
OCT 12
Plan Your Visit: PUBLICARTFUND.ORG
FEB 11
590
The rest of the world
is still separated.
There are two very
different layers.
One has purposefully
been cut off from
the other –
one is indifferent
and cold
to what's happening.
- Ai Weiwei, *T: The New York Times Style Magazine*, June 17, 2016
Qalandiya Checkpoint – West Bank, Palestine

Good Neighbors

On JCDecaux Bus Shelters and LinkNYC Kiosks

Ai Weiwei engaged with urban spaces that are ordinarily occupied by advertising on bus shelters and electronic LinkNYC kiosks. Here, he displayed one hundred works from the photographic series *Good Neighbors*, made during his visits to refugee camps and national borders, where fences are used to confine people and define them as different. These striking images were paired with related information from prominent humanitarian organizations, poetic excerpts on the subject of immigration, or quotes from the artist himself, to call our attention to the plight of the millions of displaced people across the globe. They were distributed throughout the city's five boroughs in ordinary spaces where they spoke directly to their communities at street level. Their evocative images and texts created an arresting injunction that was integrated into the fabric of daily life, urging citizens of the city to reflect on current dire conditions and to recognize their shared humanity.

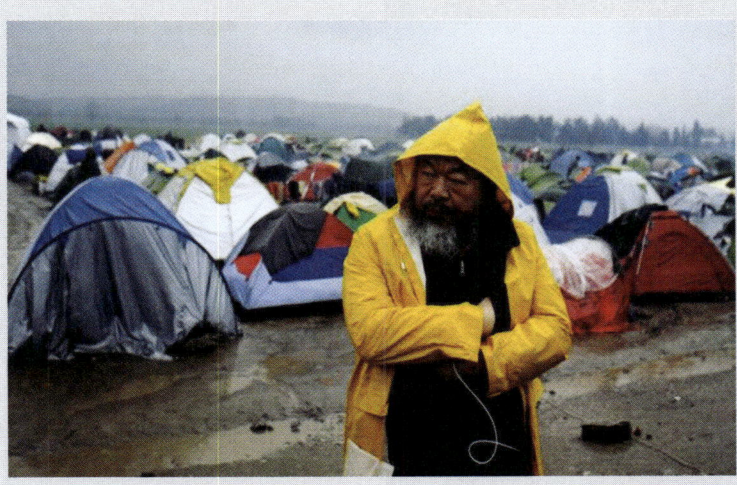

Good Neighbors 88
Qalandiya Checkpoint, West Bank, Palestine, 2016
108th Street and Martense Avenue, Queens (opposite)

Ai Weiwei at the Makeshift Camp, Idomeni, Greece, 2016 (left)

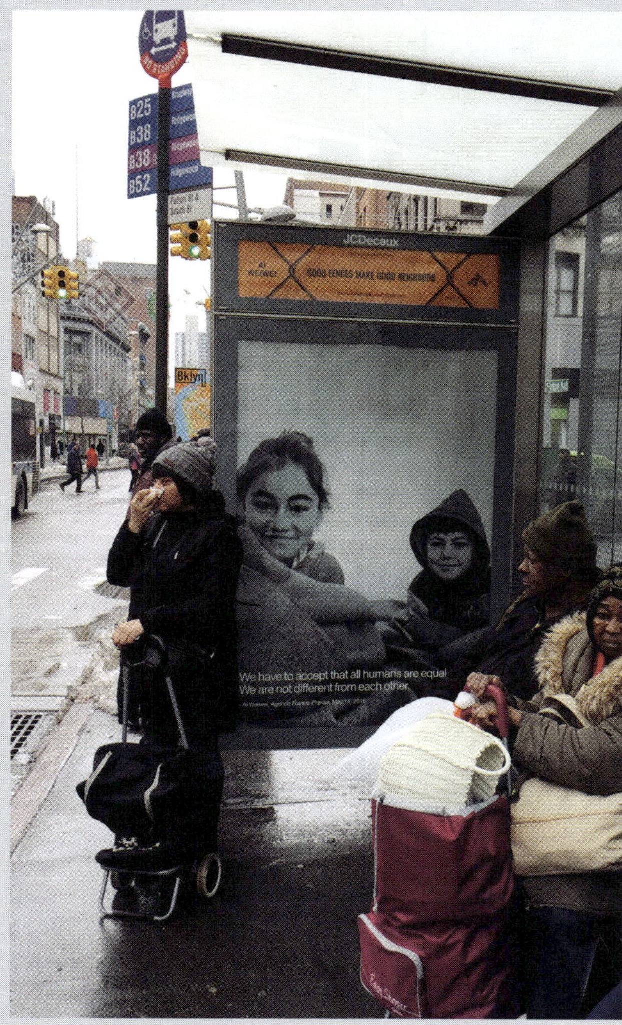

Good Neighbors 14, Moria Camp, Lesvos, Greece, 2015. Fulton and Smith Streets, Brooklyn

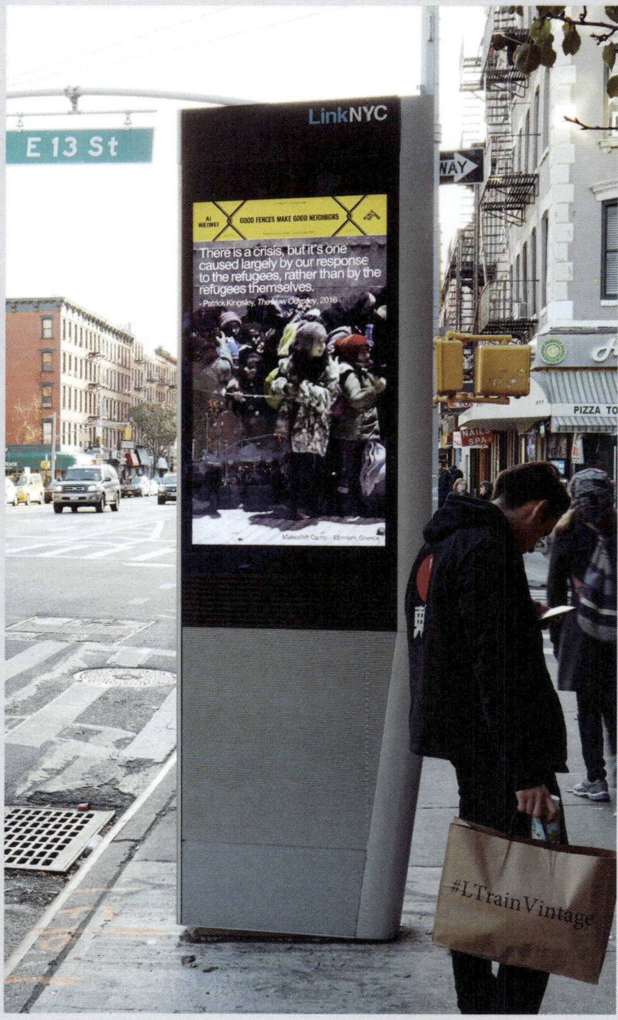

Good Neighbors 2, Moria Camp, Lesvos, Greece, 2015. E. 13th Street and 1st Avenue, Manhattan

I personally find Ai Wewei's work to be both beautiful and provocative. As an aesthetic proposition, the work stands alone, and *Good Fences Make Good Neighbors* continues his string of projects that are stunning in their scope, scale, balance, and beauty. But what really elevates him is his strong moral compass, his backstory, and his frankly bad-ass way of going deep with his critique of injustice.

Devin Wenig, CEO, eBay

Ai Weiwei, Makeshift Camp, Idomeni, Greece, 2016 (opposite, top)

Board showing sections of image details for *Good Neighbors*, Ai Weiwei studio, Berlin, August 2017 (opposite, bottom left)

Good Neighbors 26 and *Good Neighbors 48* (opposite, middle right)

Lucas Lai and Kang Sunkoo review texts for *Good Neighbors*, Ai Weiwei studio, Berlin, August 2017 (opposite, bottom right)

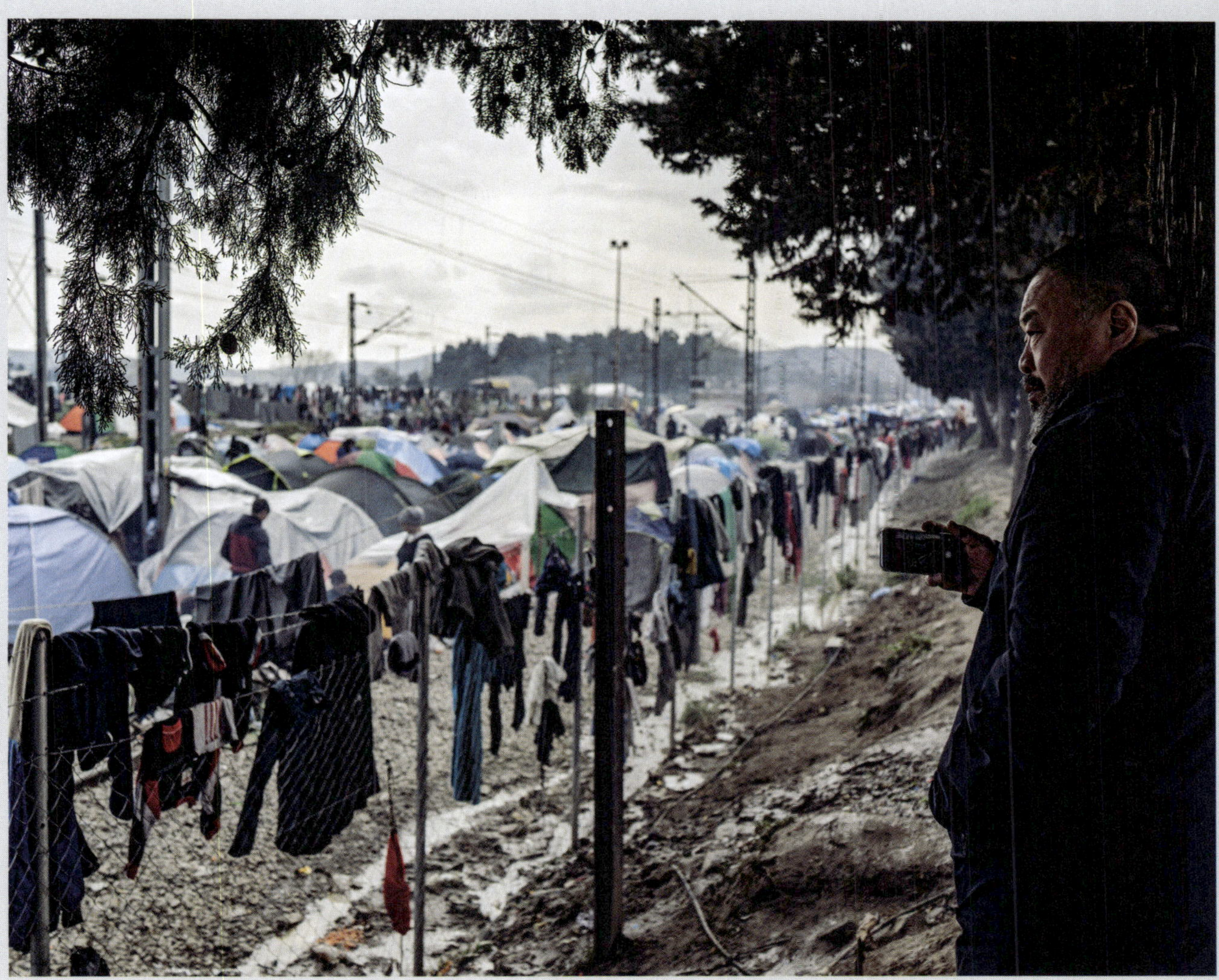

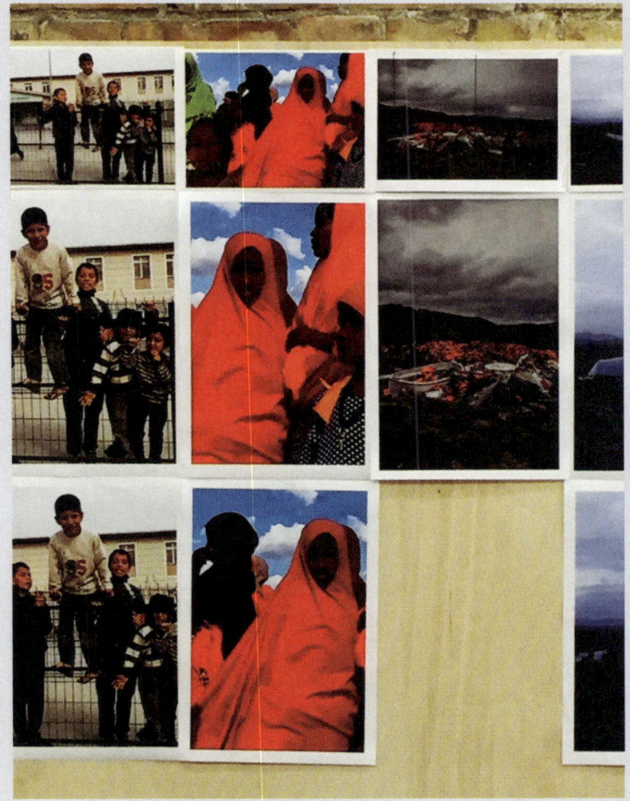

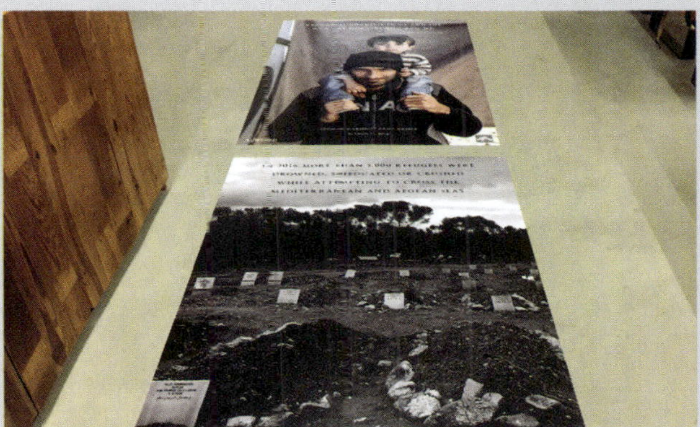

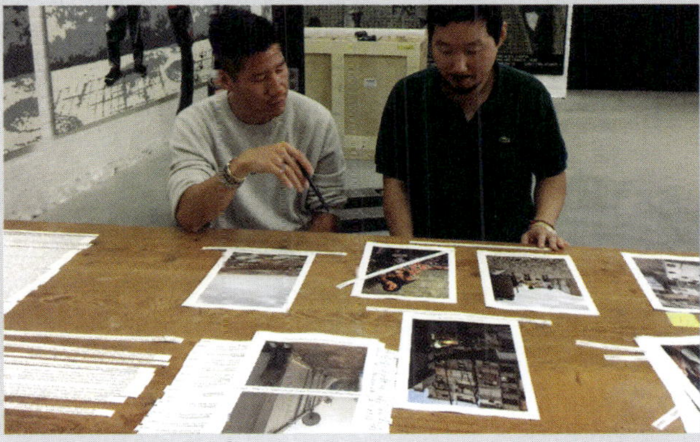

Lesvos, Greece

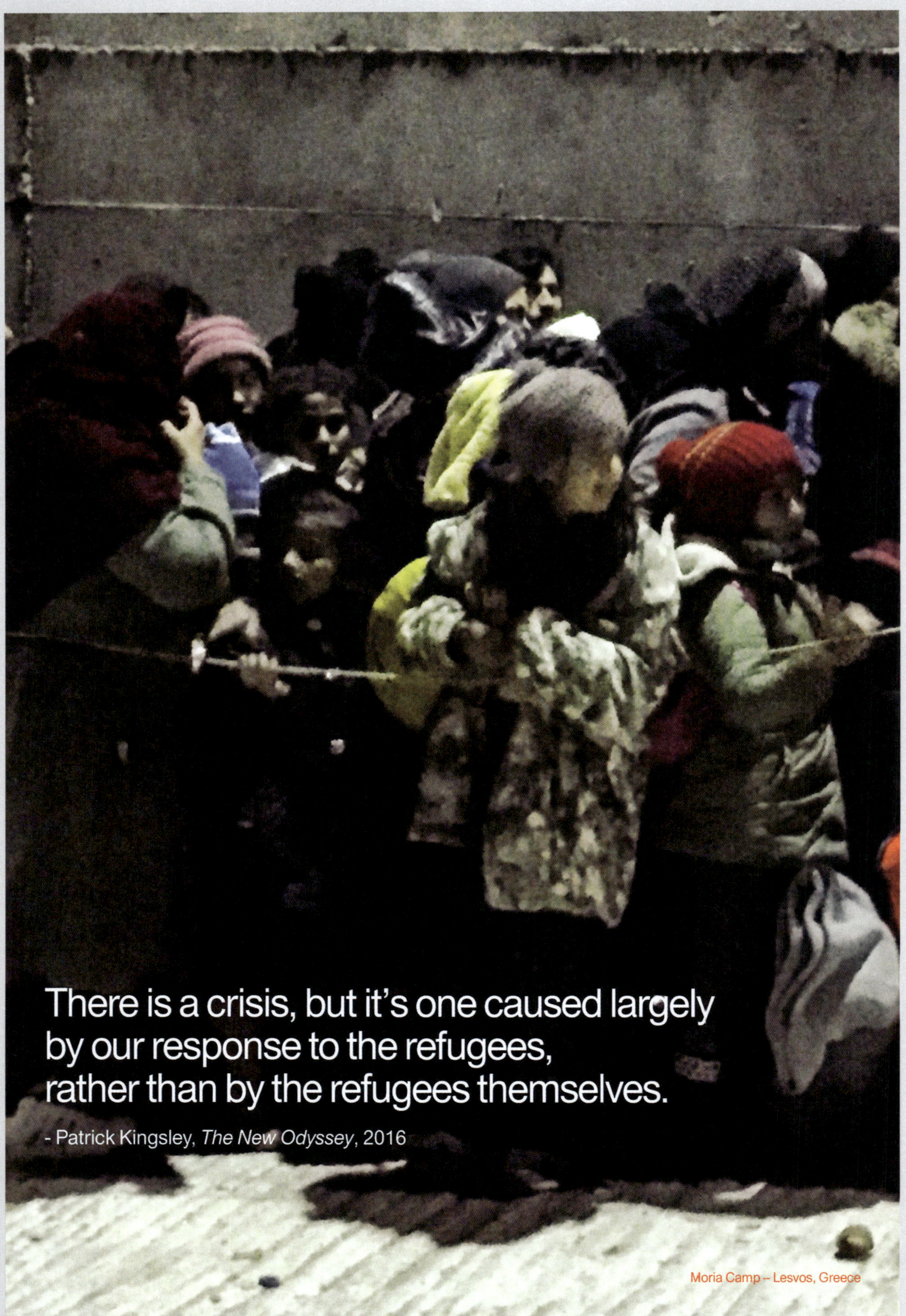

Good Neighbors 2, Moria Camp, Lesvos, Greece, 2015

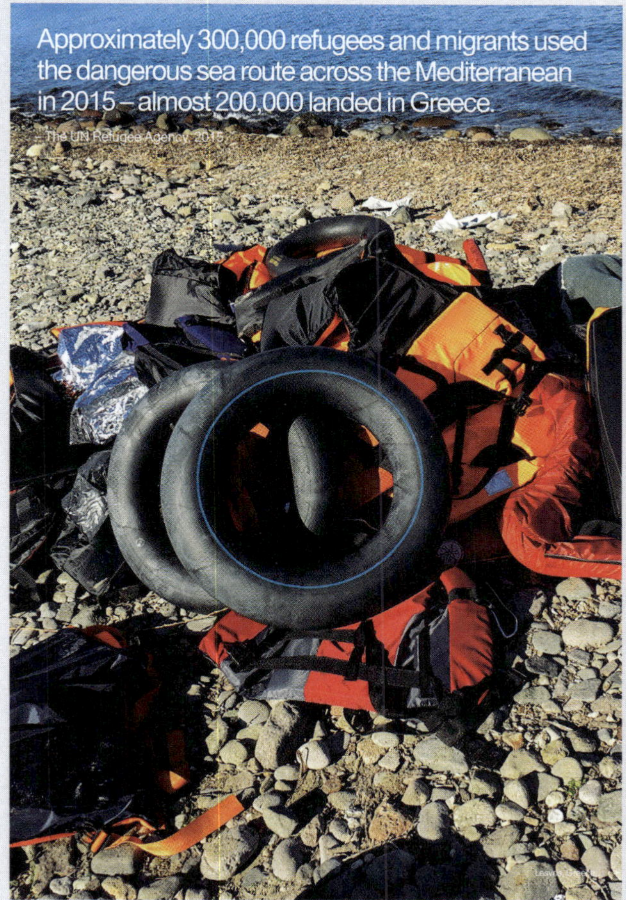

Good Neighbors 3, Lesvos, Greece, 2015

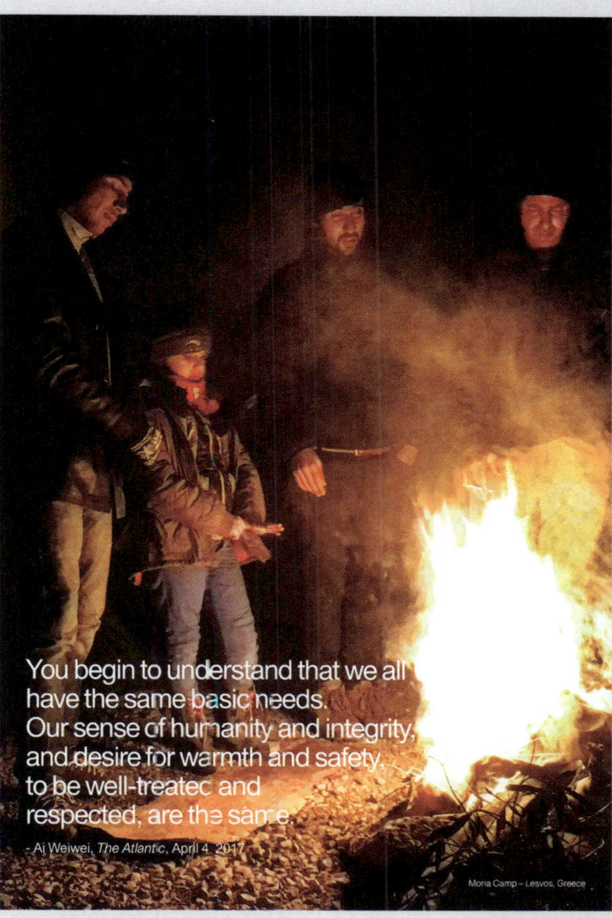

Good Neighbors 5, Moria Camp, Lesvos, Greece, 2015

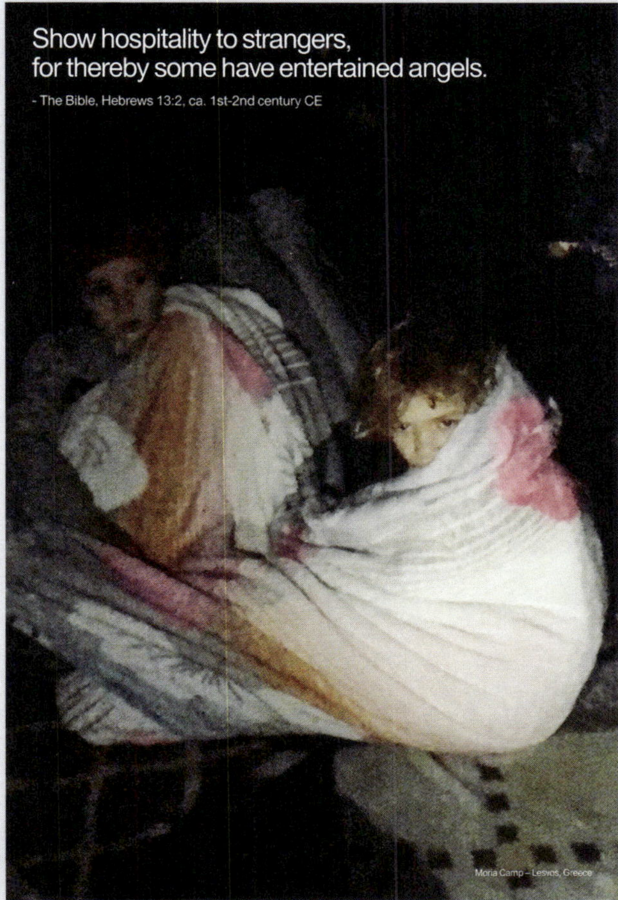

Good Neighbors 6, Moria Camp, Lesvos, Greece, 2015

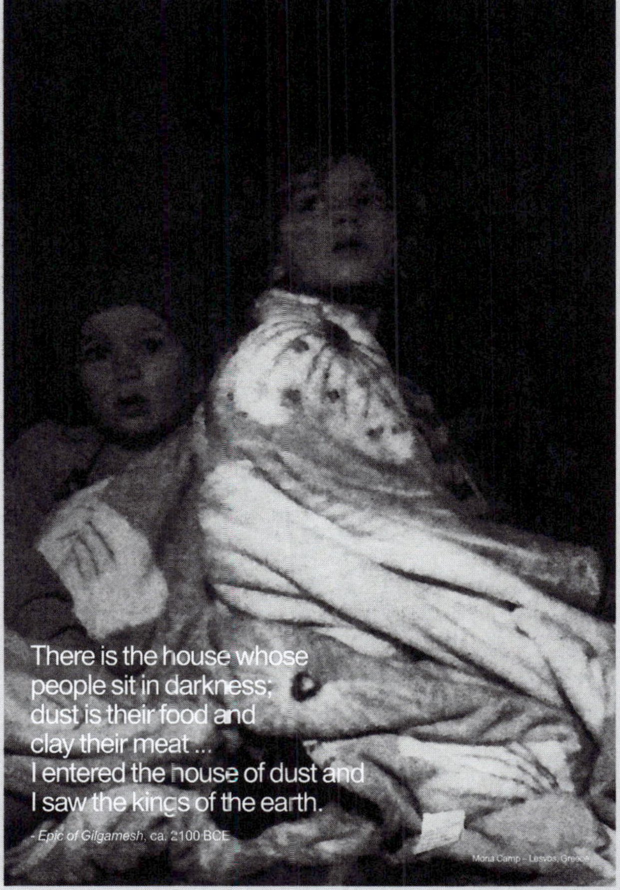

Good Neighbors 7, Moria Camp, Lesvos, Greece, 2015

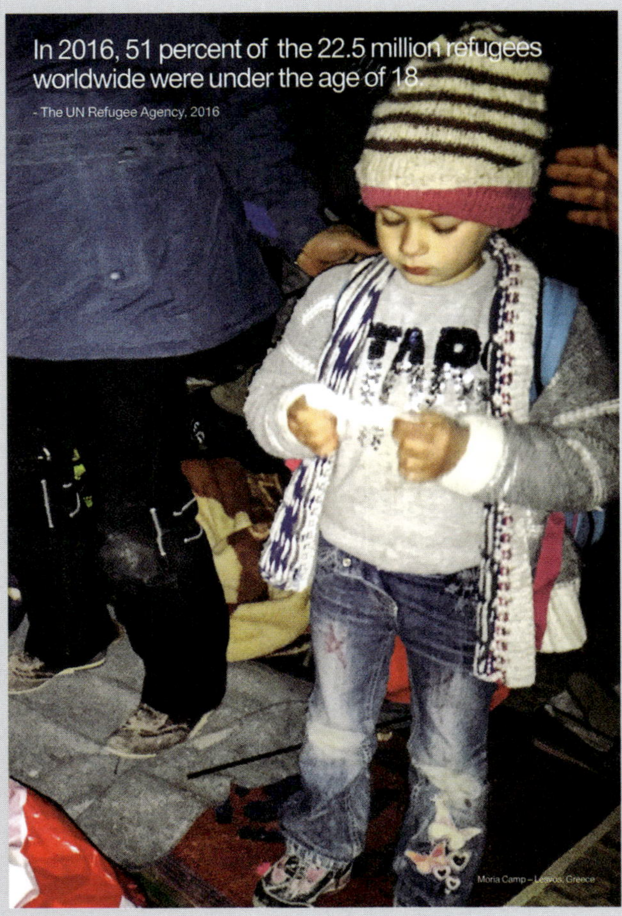

Good Neighbors 8, Moria Camp, Lesvos, Greece, 2015

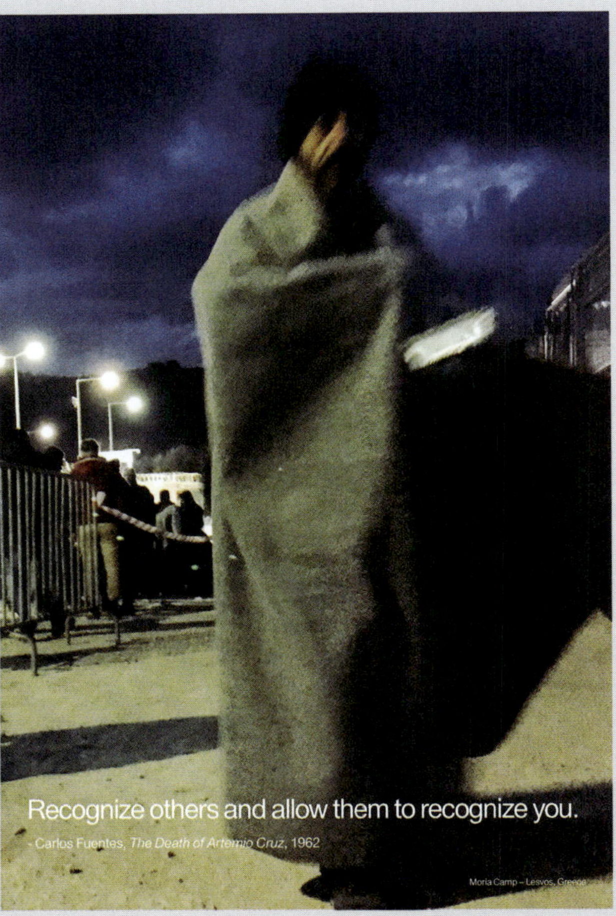

Good Neighbors 9, Moria Camp, Lesvos, Greece, 2015

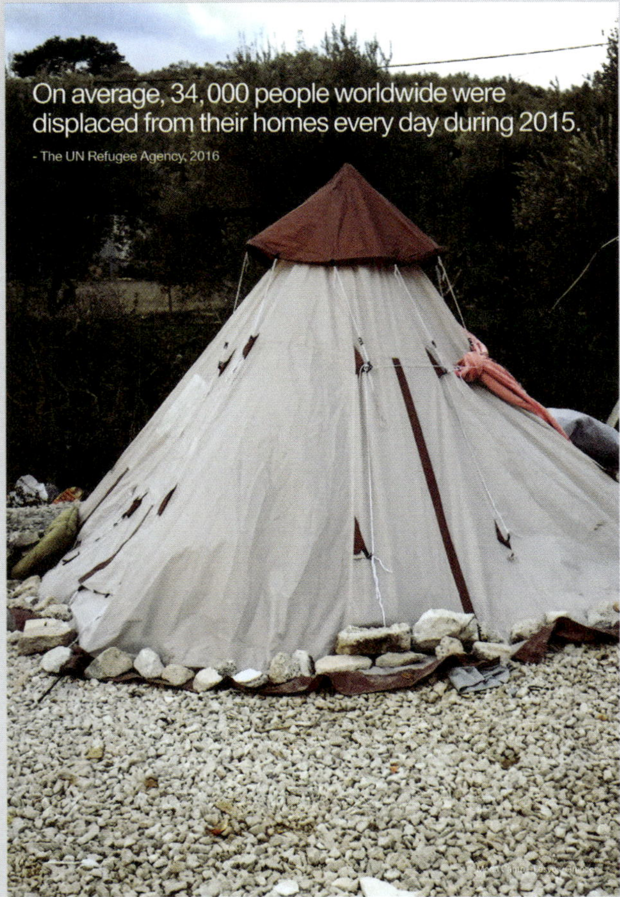

Good Neighbors 10, Moria Camp, Lesvos, Greece, 2015

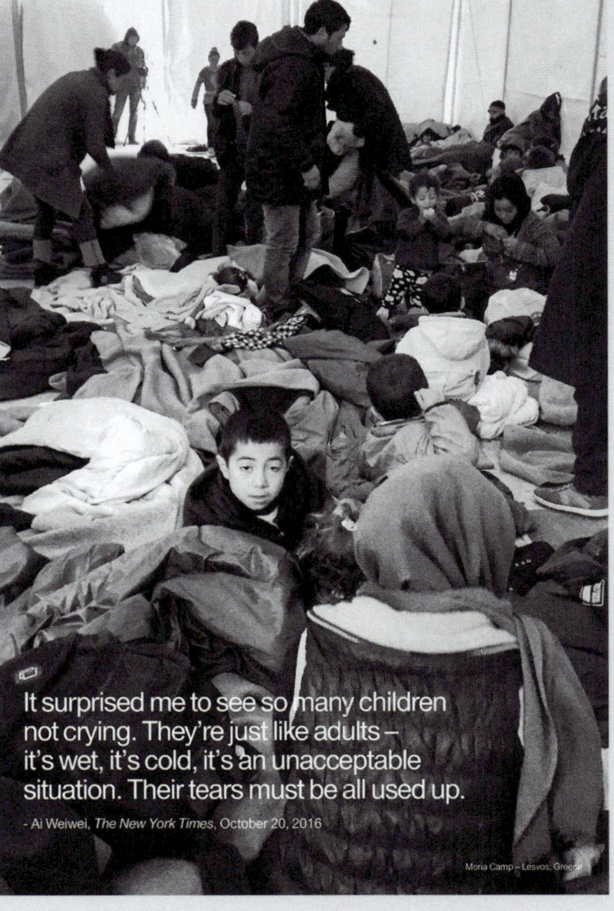

Good Neighbors 11, Moria Camp, Lesvos, Greece, 2015

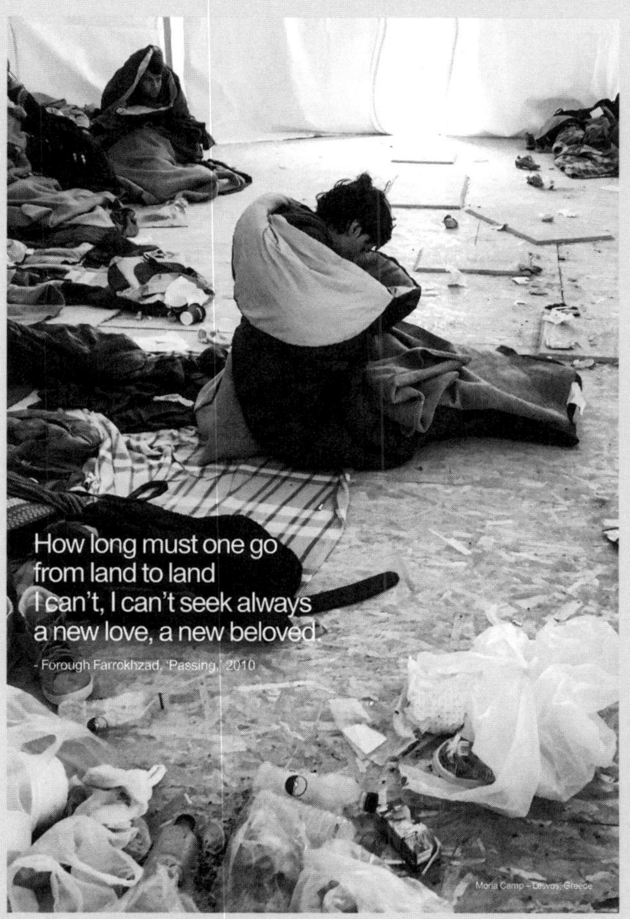

Good Neighbors 12, Moria Camp, Lesvos, Greece, 2015

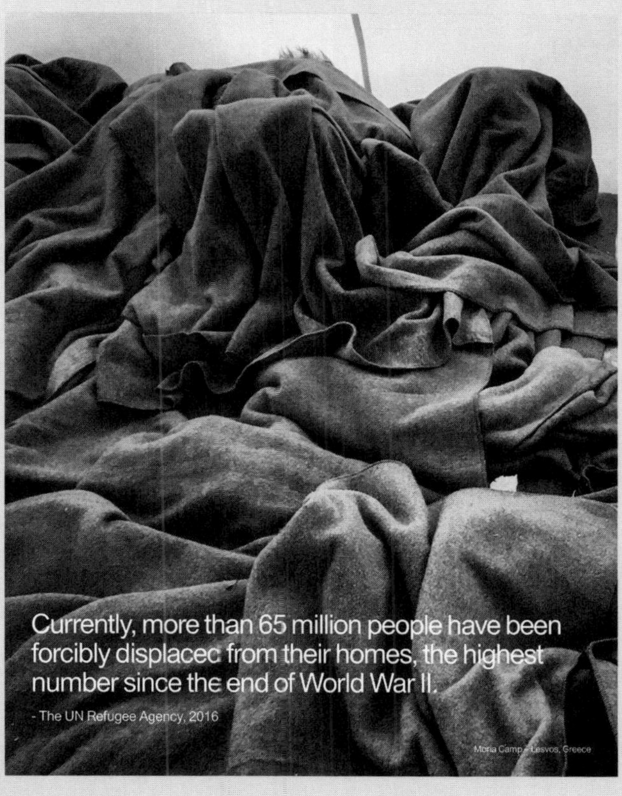

Good Neighbors 13, Moria Camp, Lesvos, Greece, 2015

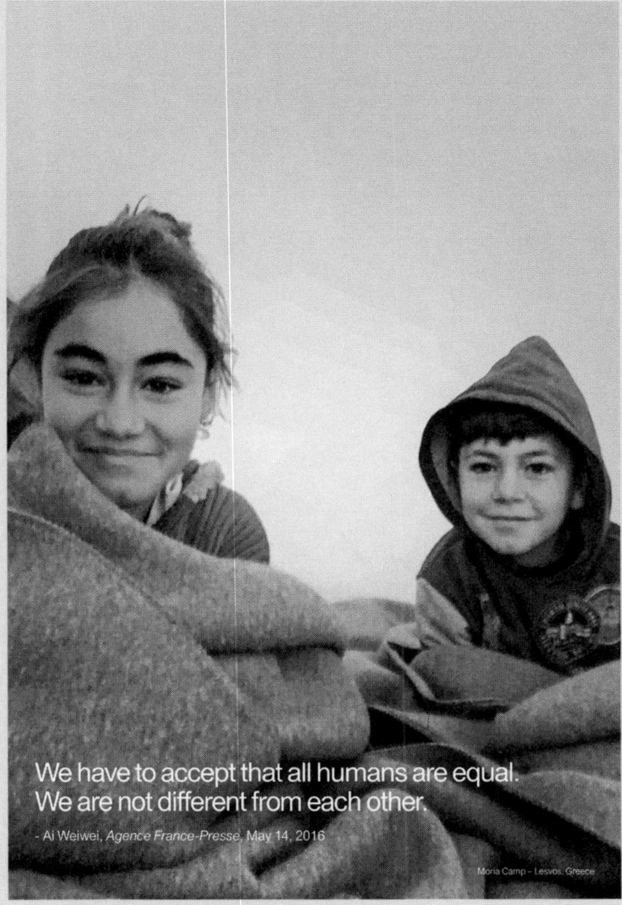

Good Neighbors 14, Moria Camp, Lesvos, Greece, 2015

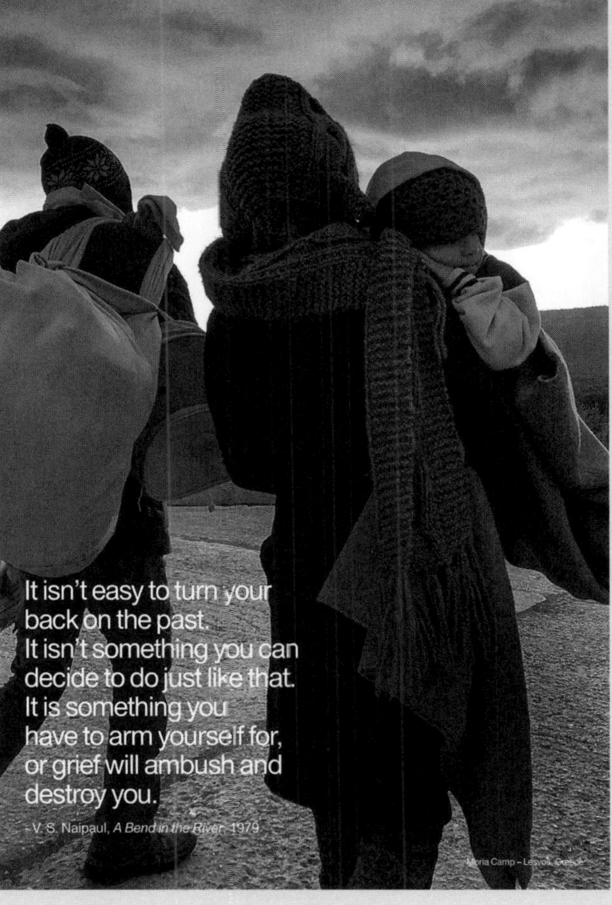

Good Neighbors 15, Moria Camp, Lesvos, Greece, 2015

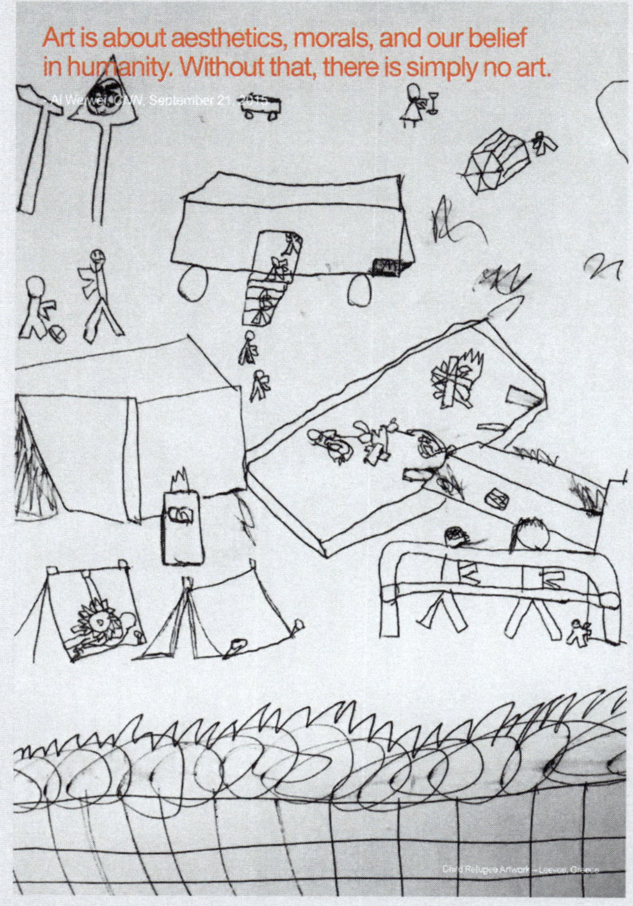

Good Neighbors 16, Child Refugee Artwork, Lesvos, Greece, 2016

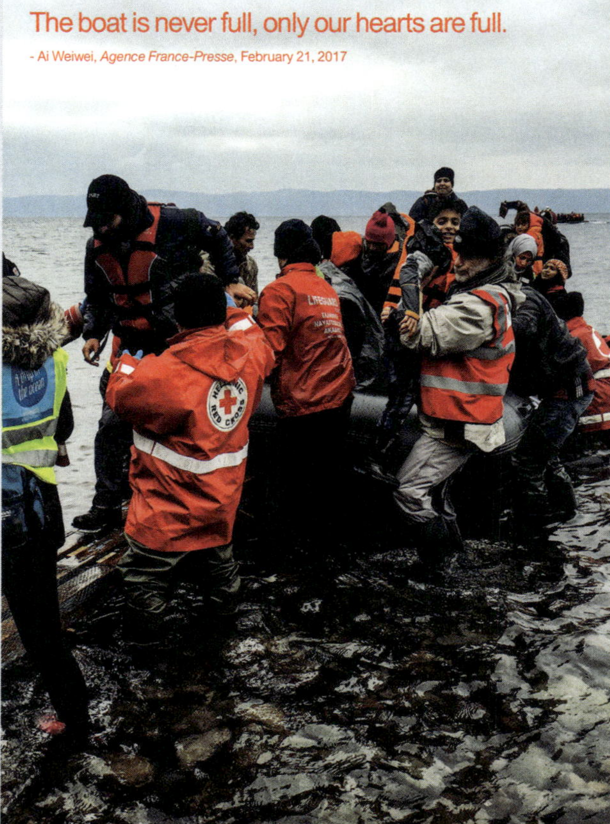

Good Neighbors 17, Lesvos, Greece, 2016

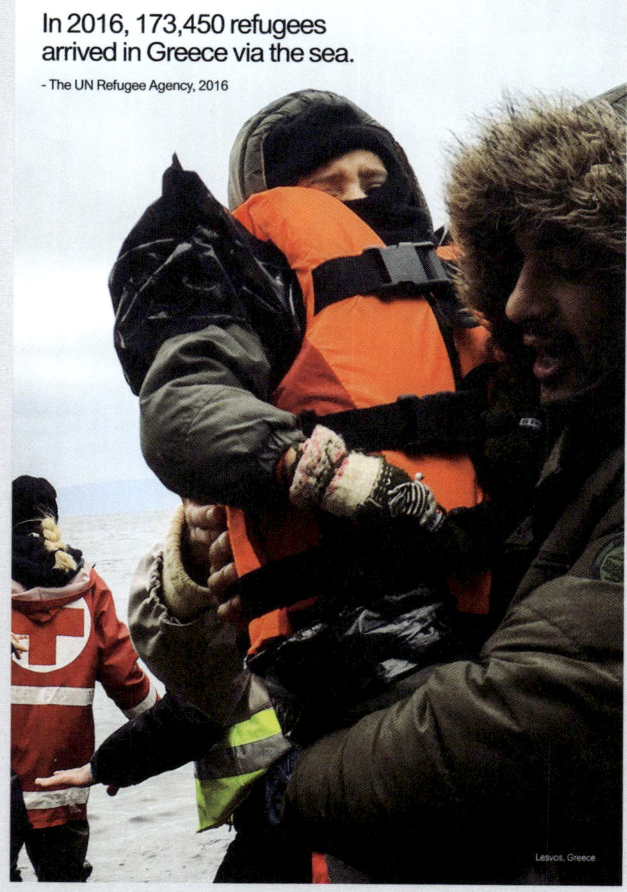

Good Neighbors 18, Lesvos, Greece, 2016

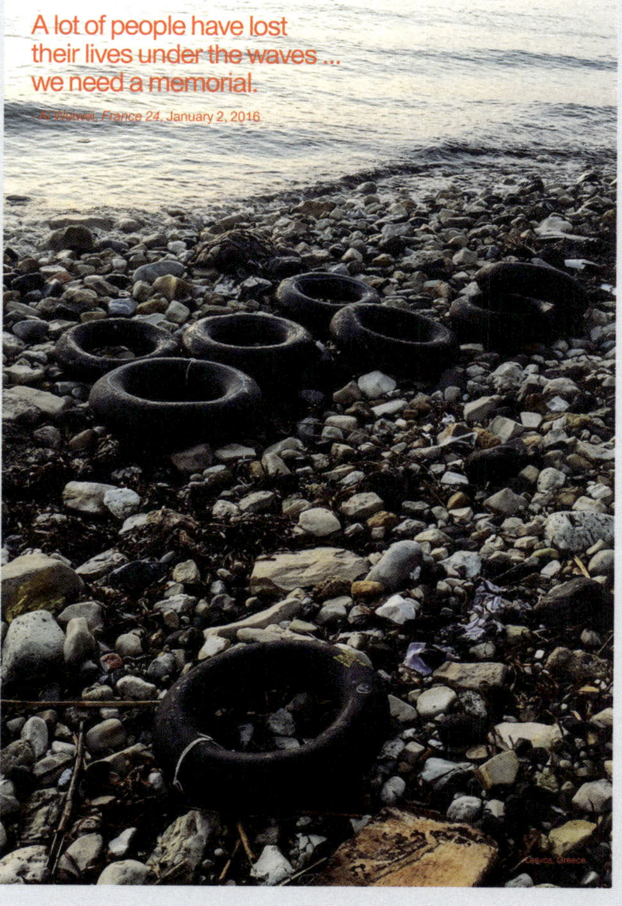

Good Neighbors 19, Lesvos, Greece, 2016

In 2015, approximately 885,000 migrants arrived in the EU via the Eastern Mediterranean route – 17 times the number in 2014, itself a record year. The vast majority of them arrived on one island, Lesvos.

- European Border and Coast Guard Agency, 2017

Lesvos, Greece

Good Neighbors 20, Lesvos, Greece, 2016

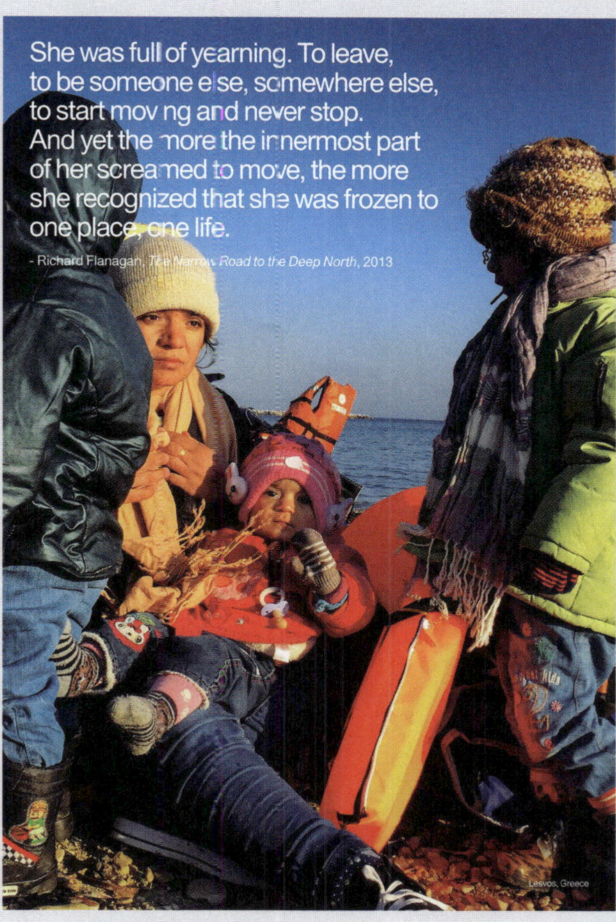

Good Neighbors 21, Lesvos, Greece, 2016

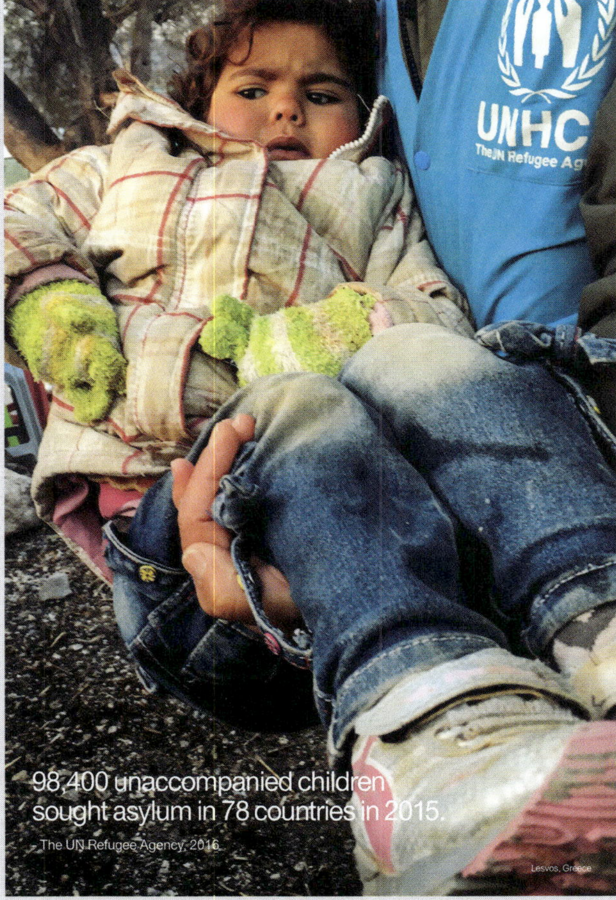

Good Neighbors 22, Lesvos, Greece, 2016

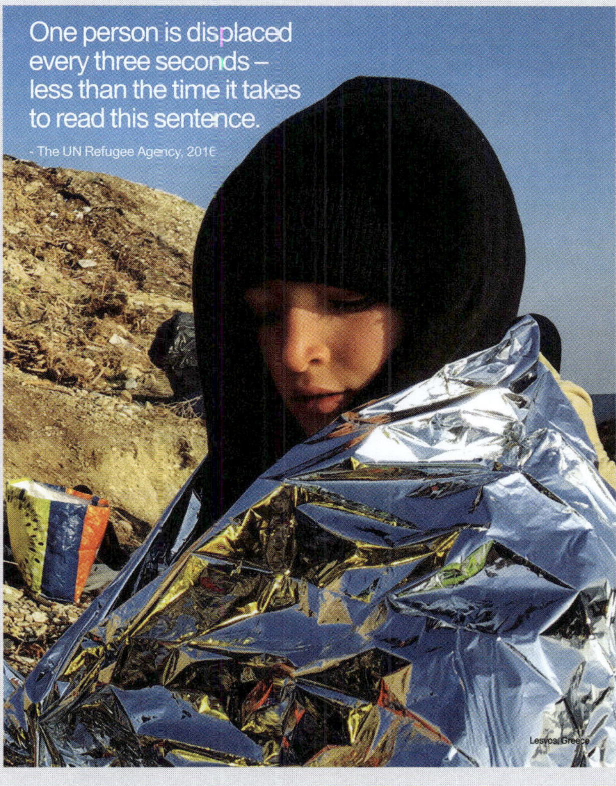

Good Neighbors 24, Lesvos, Greece, 2016

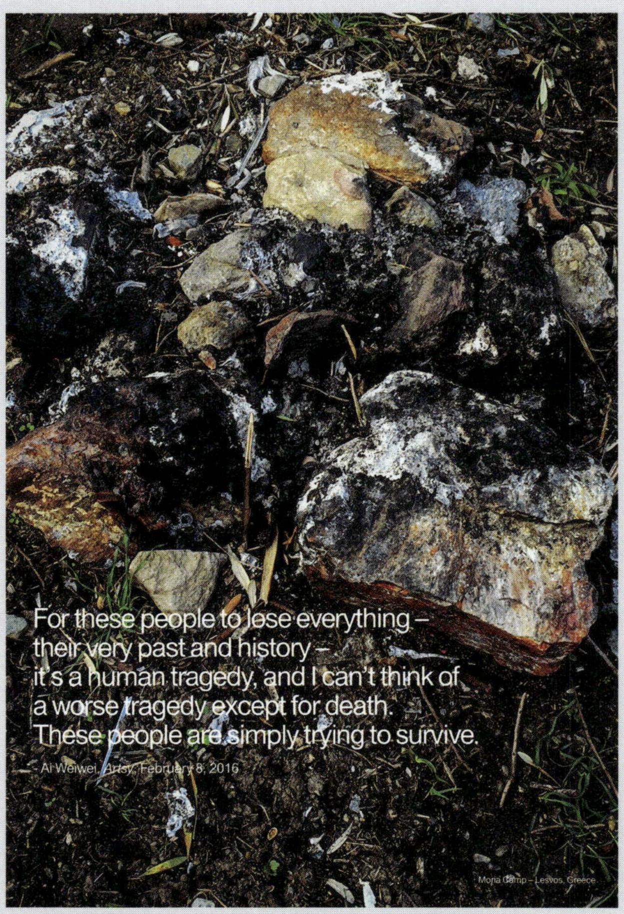

Good Neighbors 25, Moria Camp, Lesvos, Greece, 2016

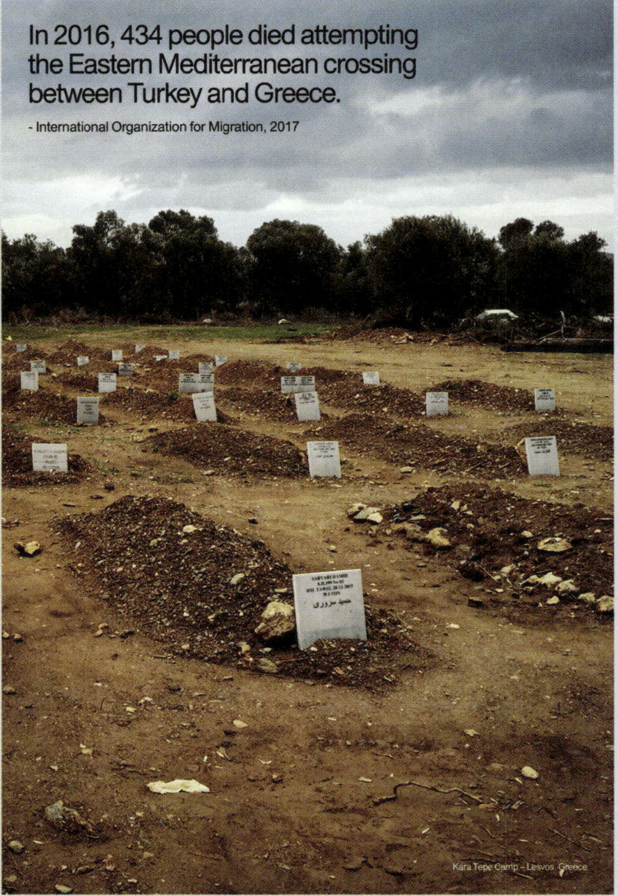

Good Neighbors 26, Kara Tepe Camp, Lesvos, Greece, 2016

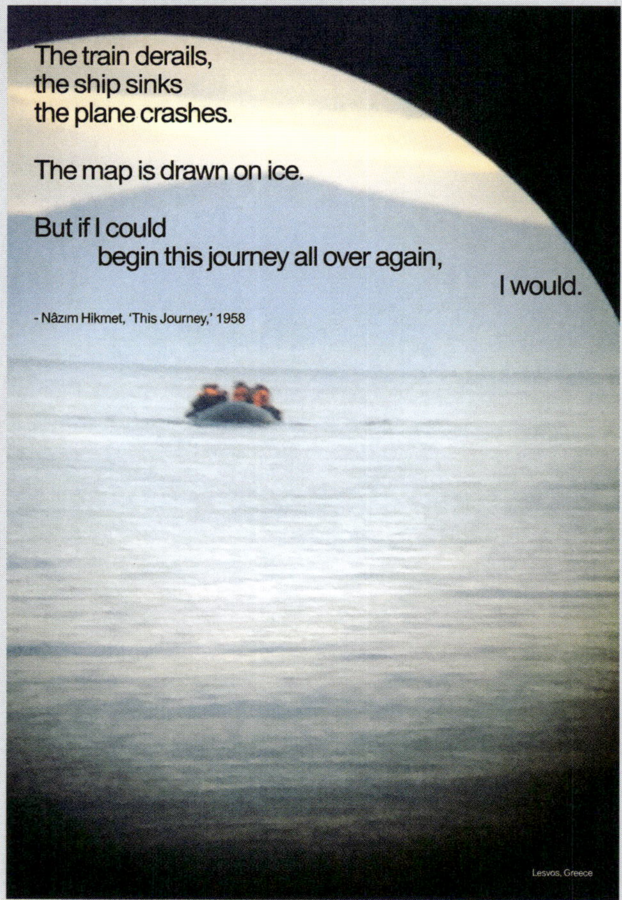

Good Neighbors 27, Lesvos, Greece, 2016

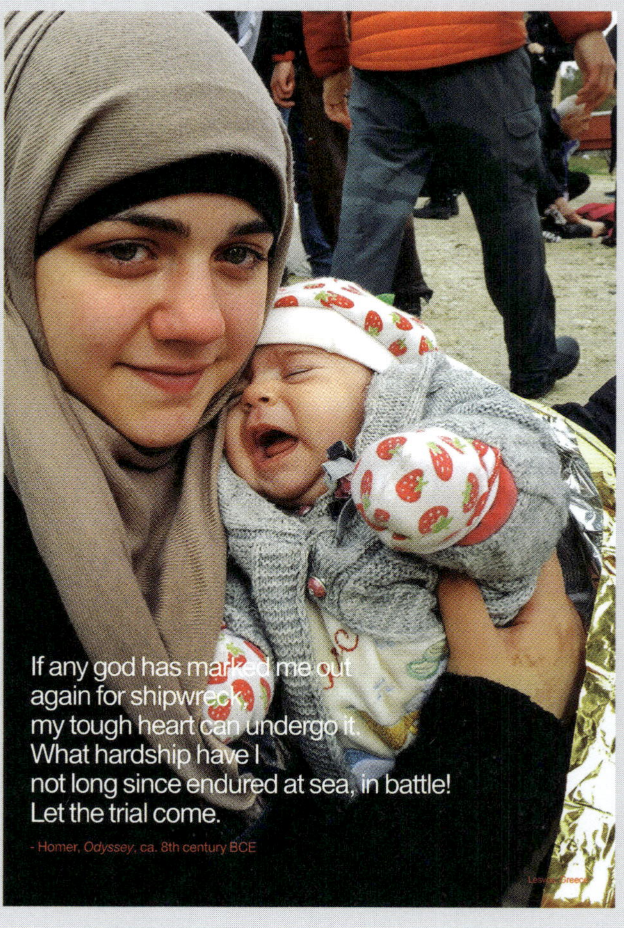

Good Neighbors 28, Lesvos, Greece, 2016

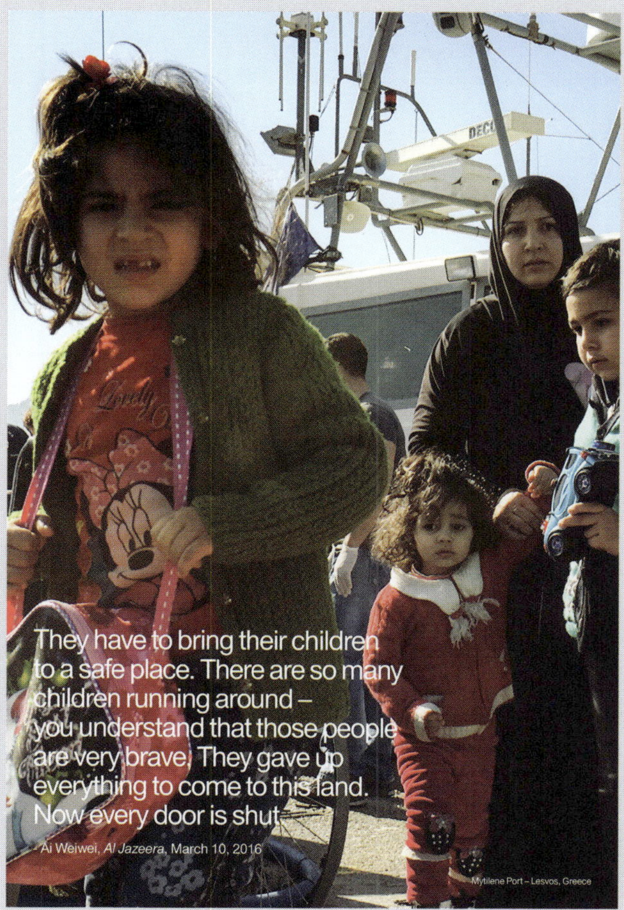

Good Neighbors 29, Mytilene Port, Lesvos, Greece, 2016

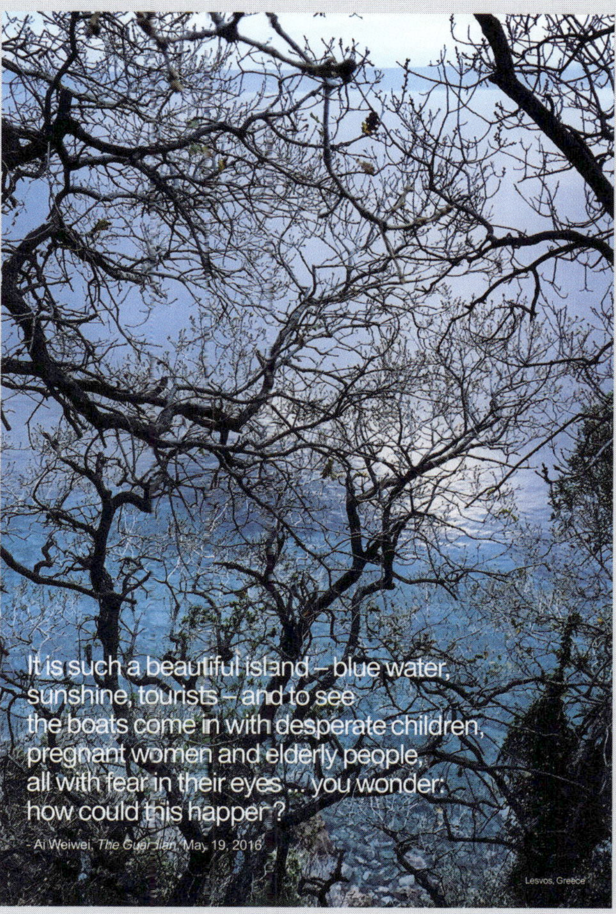

Good Neighbors 30, Lesvos, Greece, 2016

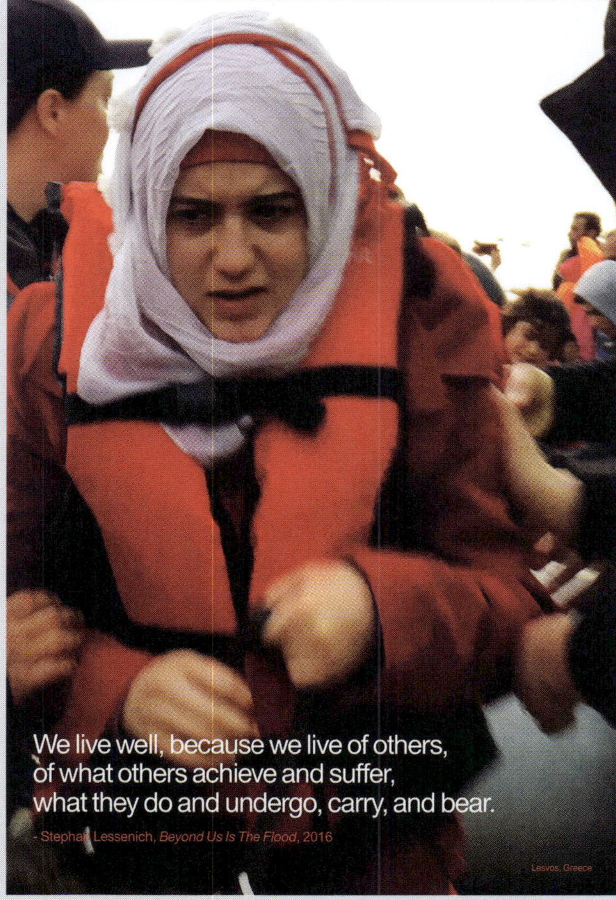

Good Neighbors 31, Lesvos, Greece, 2016

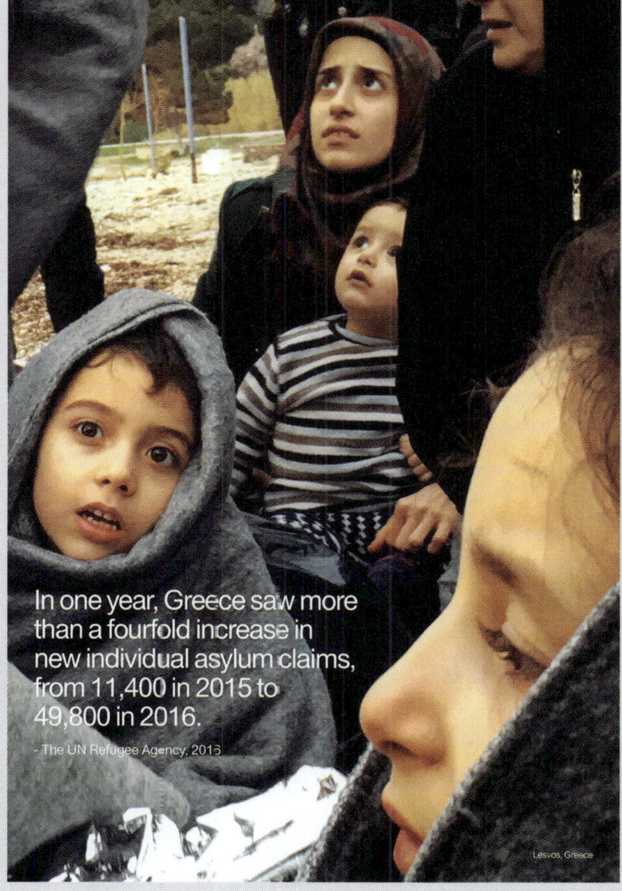

Good Neighbors 32, Lesvos, Greece, 2016

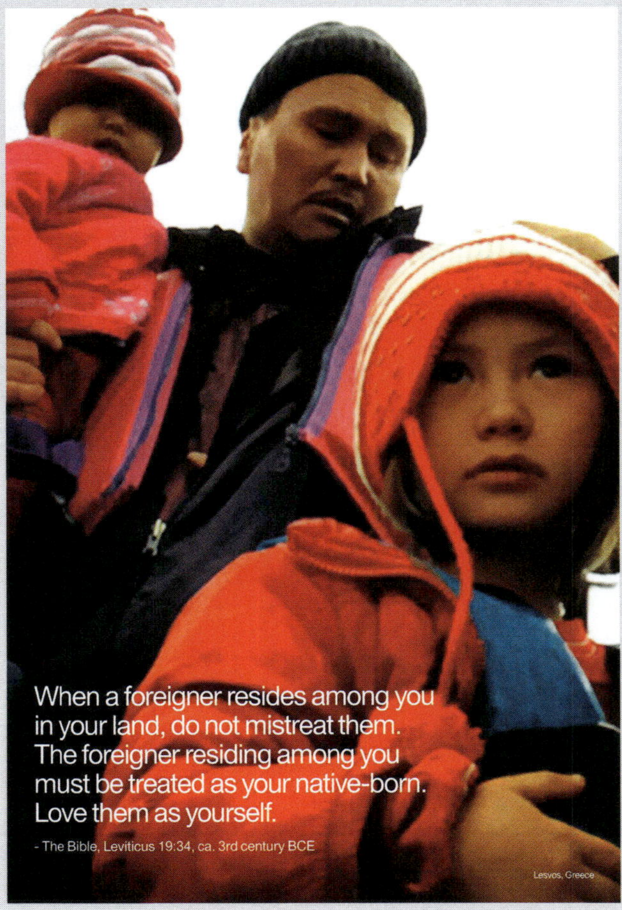

Good Neighbors 33, Lesvos, Greece, 2016

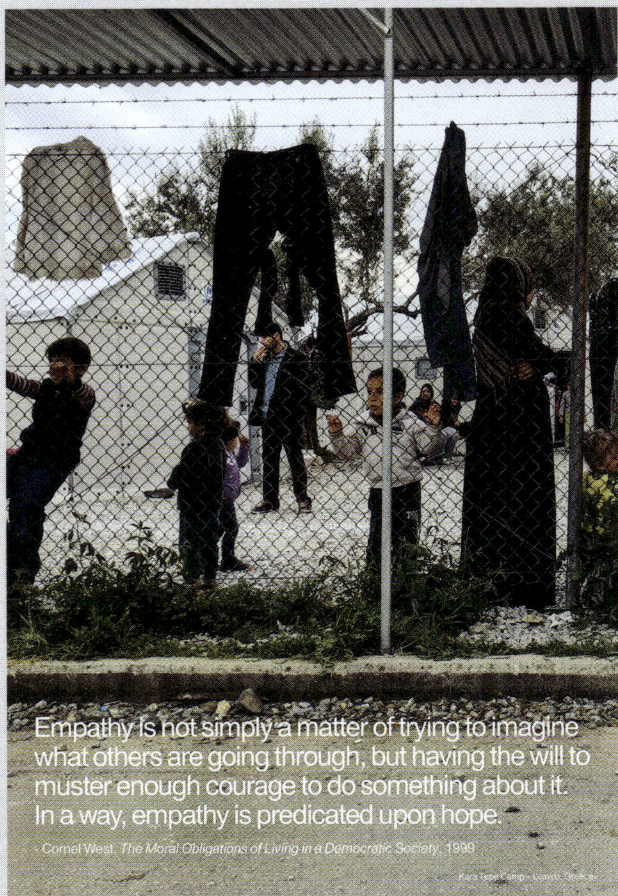

Good Neighbors 50, Kara Tepe Camp, Lesvos, Greece, 2016

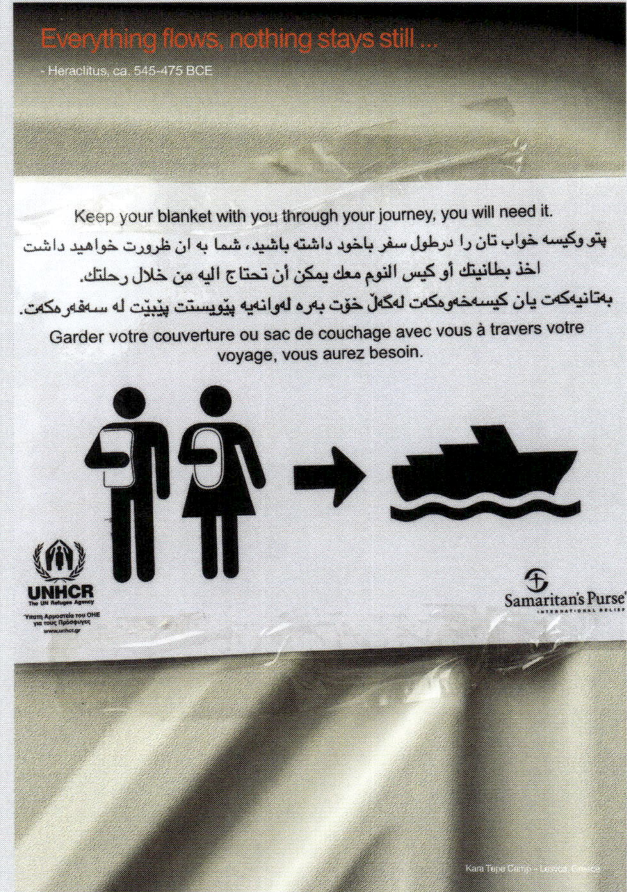

Good Neighbors 51, Kara Tepe Camp, Lesvos, Greece, 2016

Idomeni, Greece

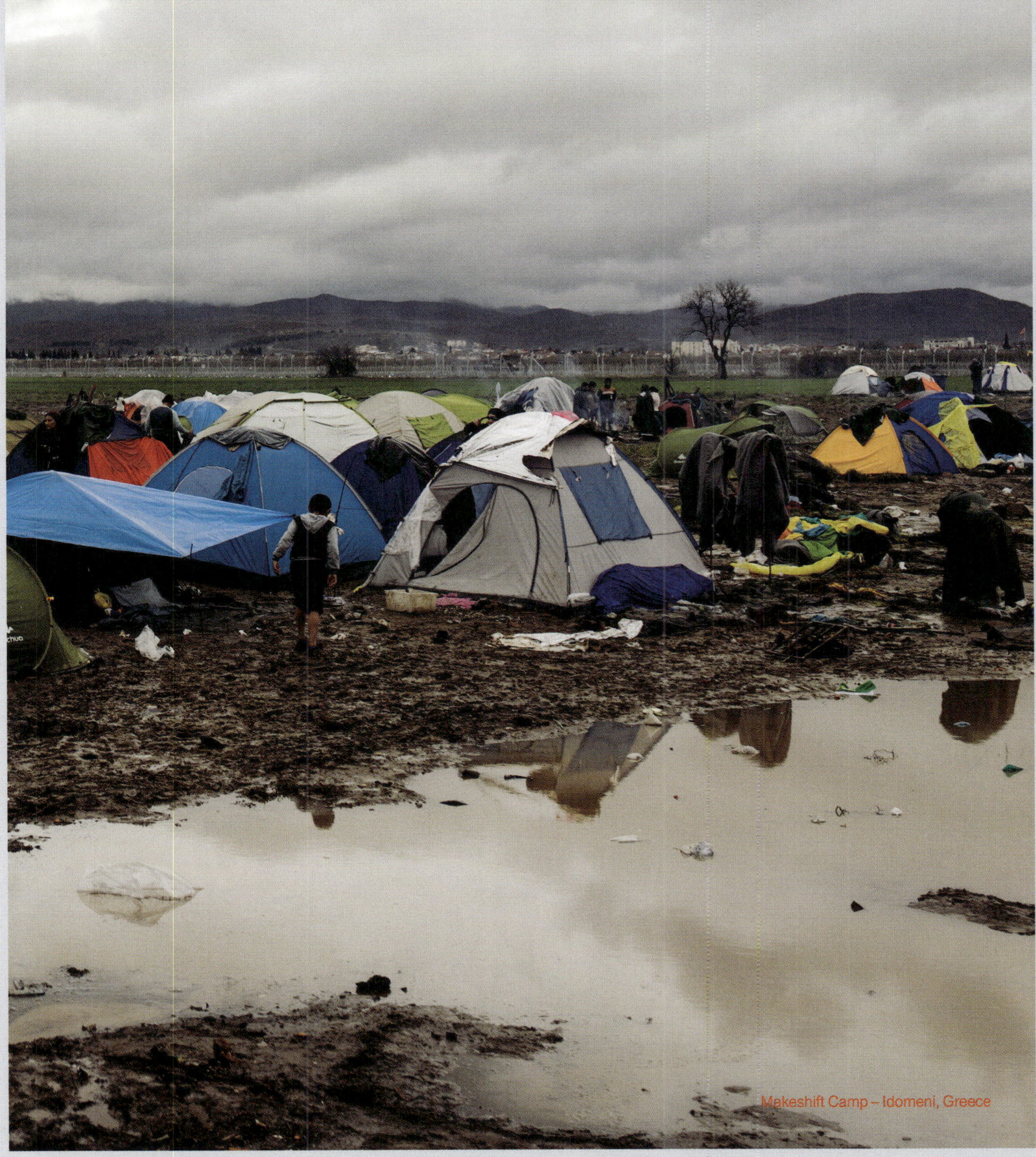

Good Neighbors 37, Makeshift Camp, Idomeni, Greece, 2016

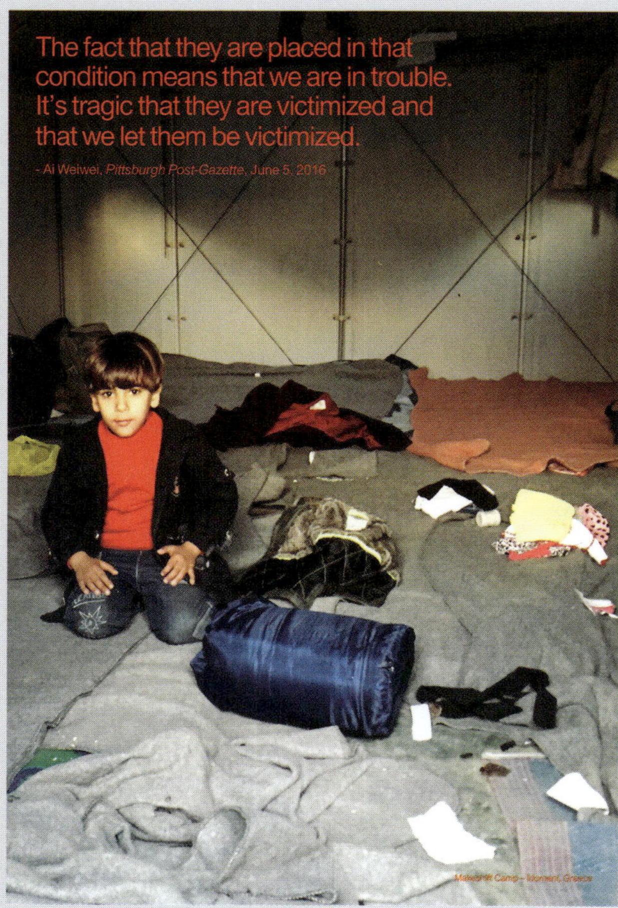

Good Neighbors 1, Makeshift Camp, Idomeni, Greece, 2016

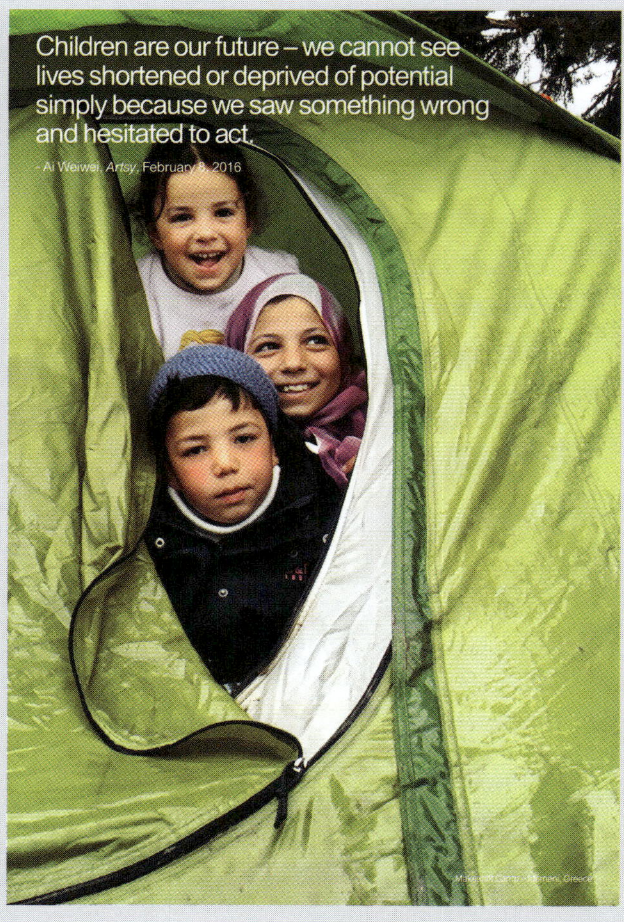

Good Neighbors 34, Makeshift Camp, Idomeni, Greece, 2016

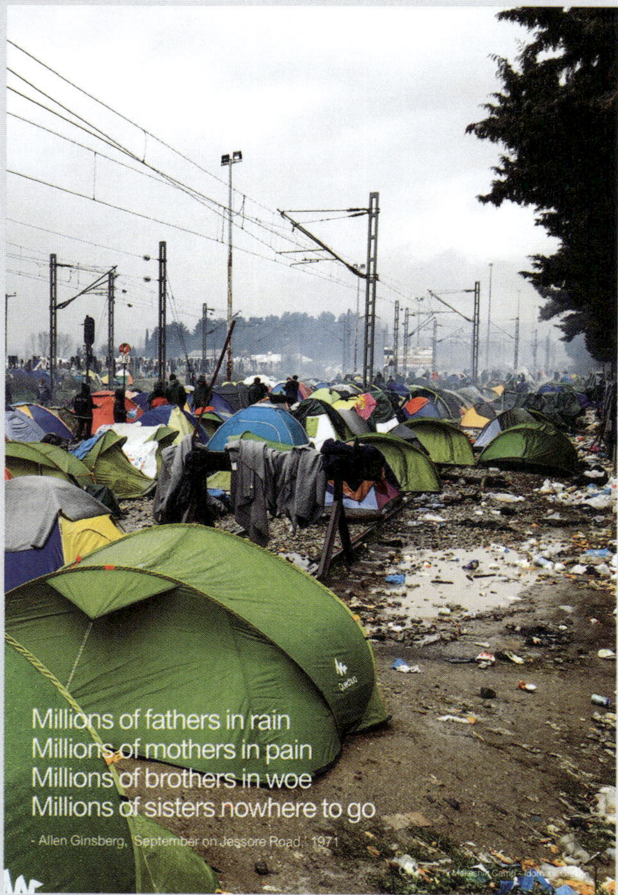

Good Neighbors 35, Makeshift Camp, Idomeni, Greece, 2016

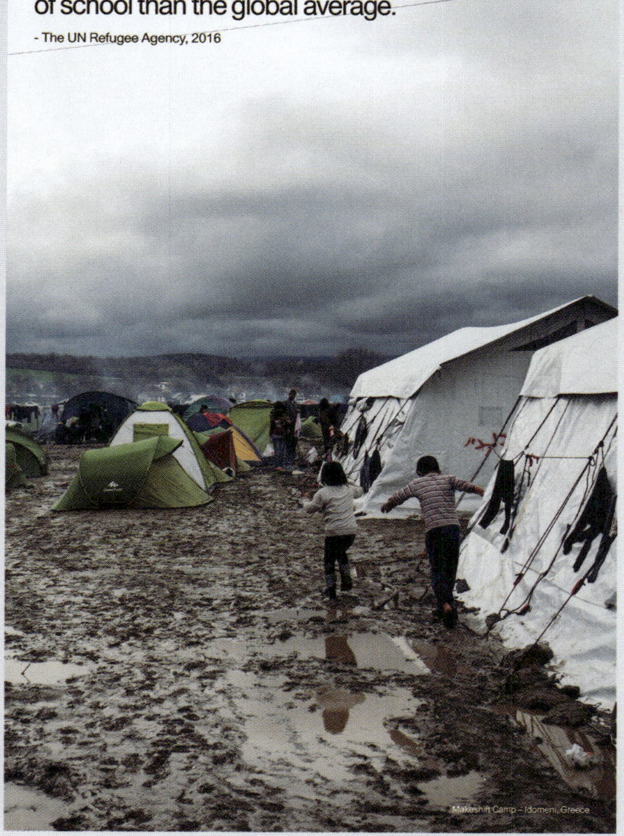

Good Neighbors 38, Makeshift Camp, Idomeni, Greece, 2016

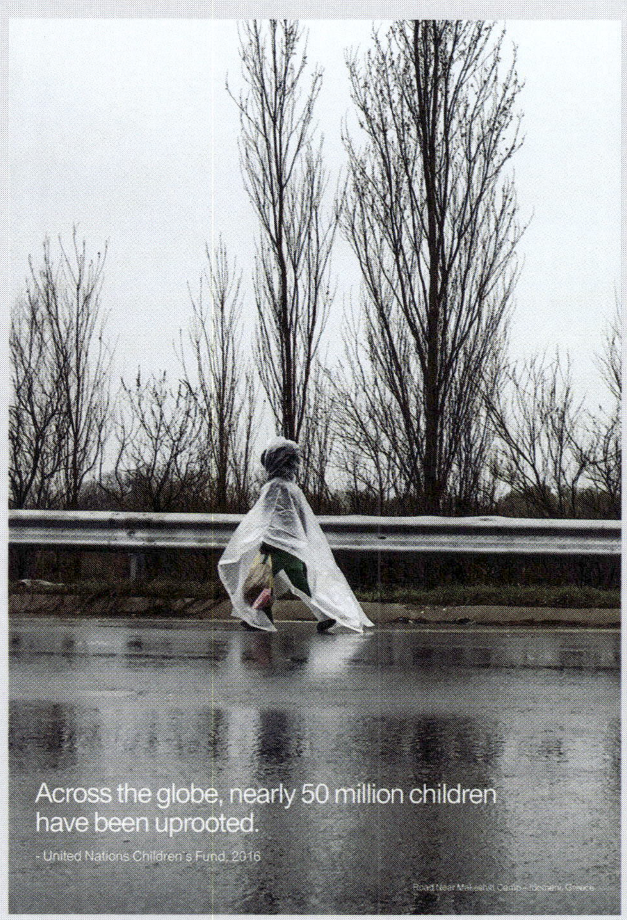

Good Neighbors 39, Road near Makeshift Camp, Idomeni, Greece, 2016

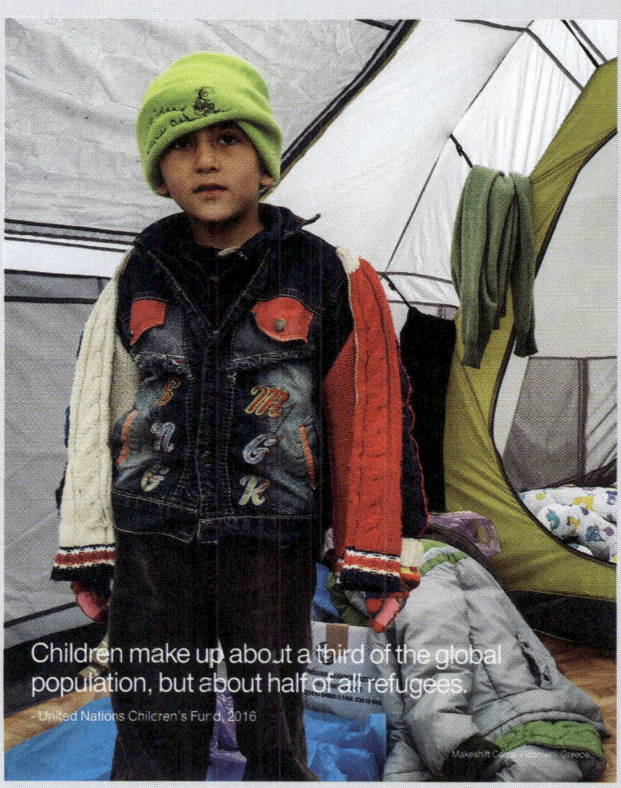

Good Neighbors 40, Makeshift Camp, Idomeni, Greece, 2016

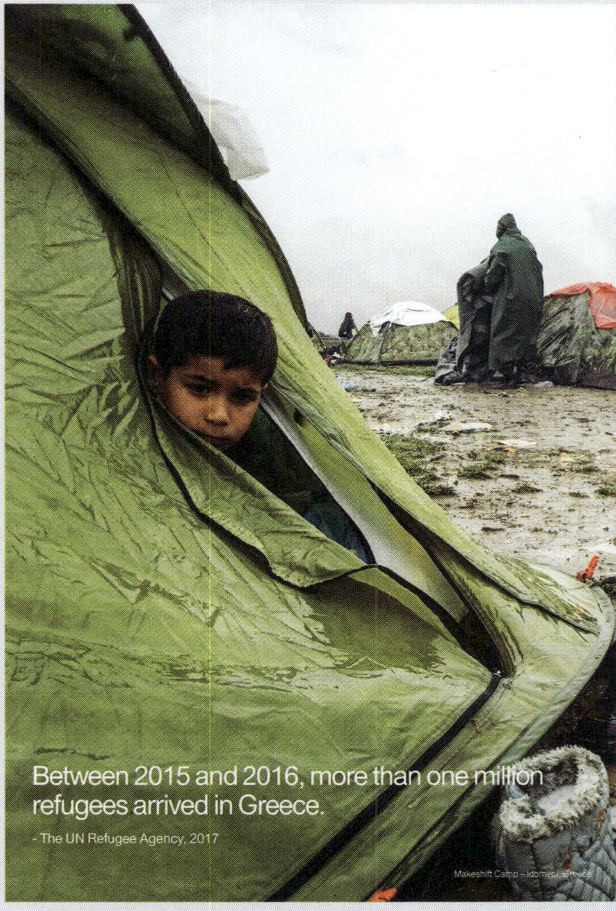

Good Neighbors 41, Makeshift Camp, Idomeni, Greece, 2016

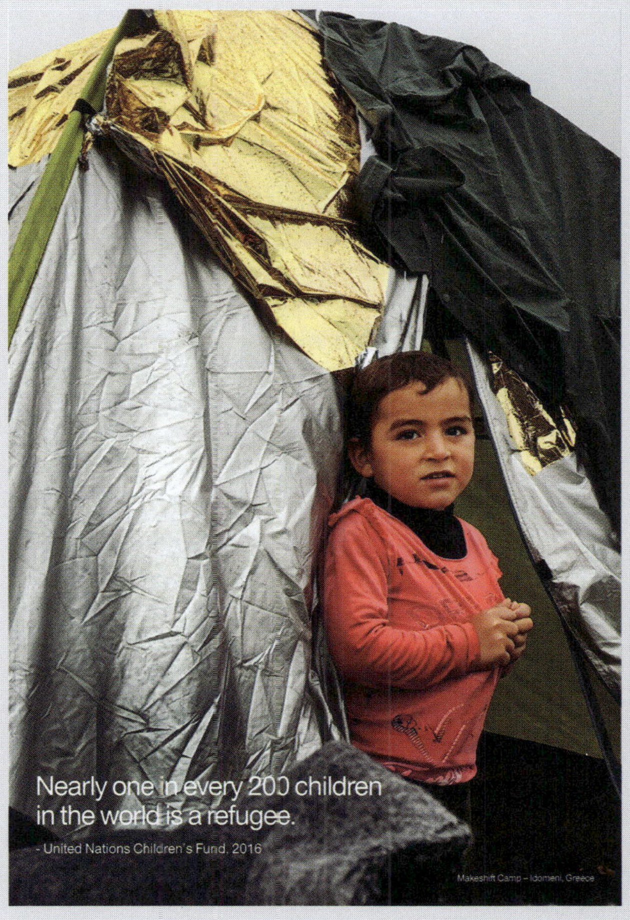

Good Neighbors 42, Makeshift Camp, Idomeni, Greece, 2016

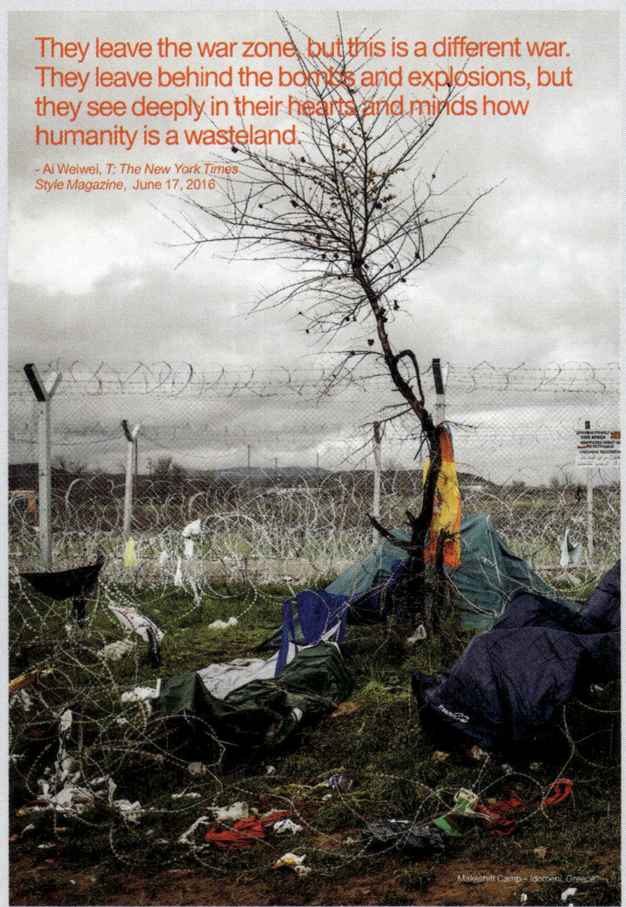

Good Neighbors 43, Makeshift Camp, Idomeni, Greece, 2016

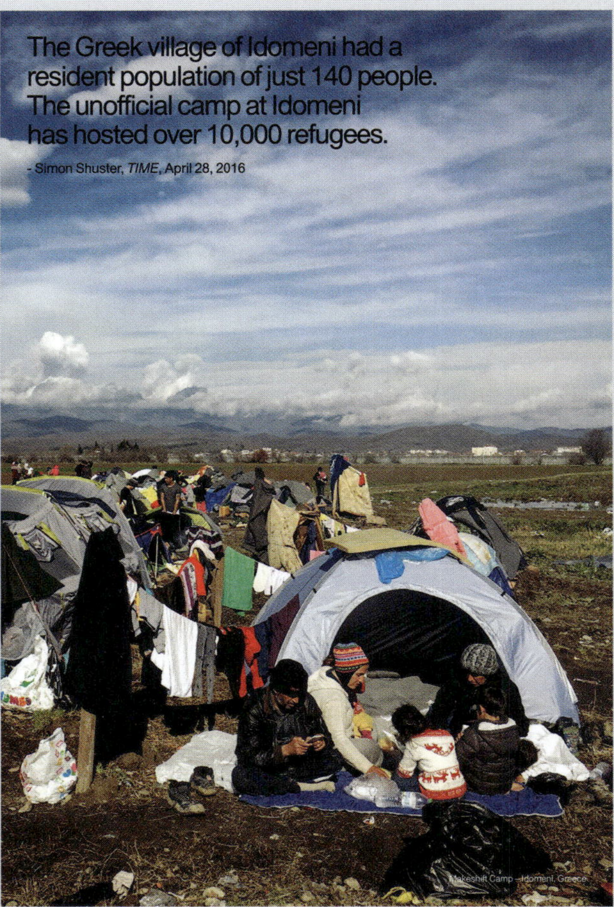

Good Neighbors 44, Makeshift Camp, Idomeni, Greece, 2016

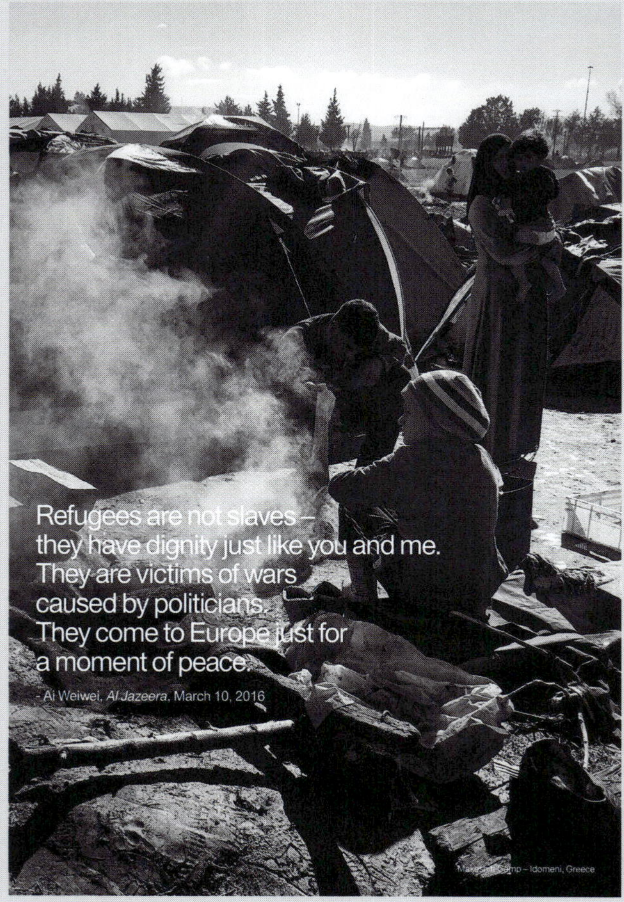

Good Neighbors 45, Makeshift Camp, Idomeni, Greece, 2016

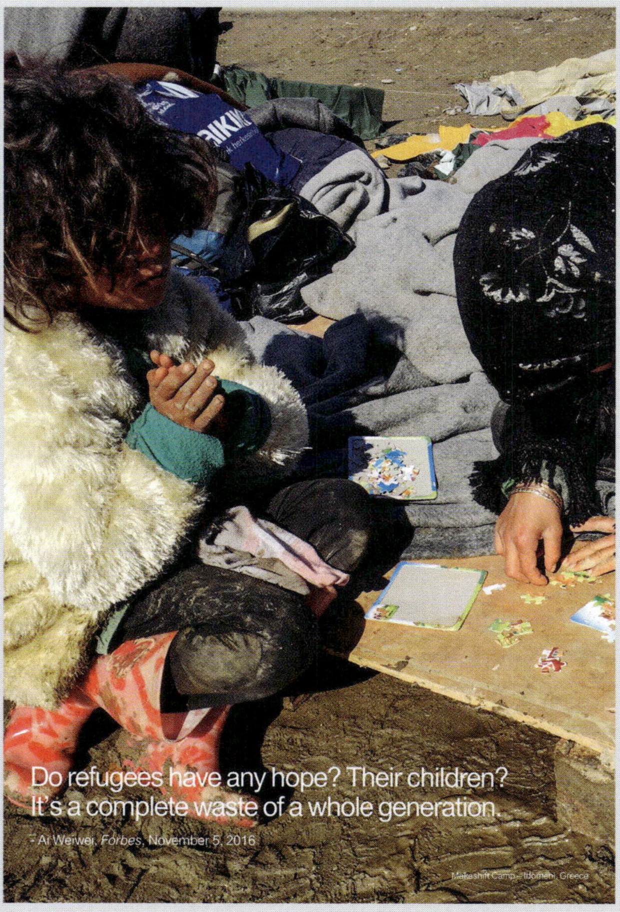

Good Neighbors 46, Makeshift Camp, Idomeni, Greece, 2016

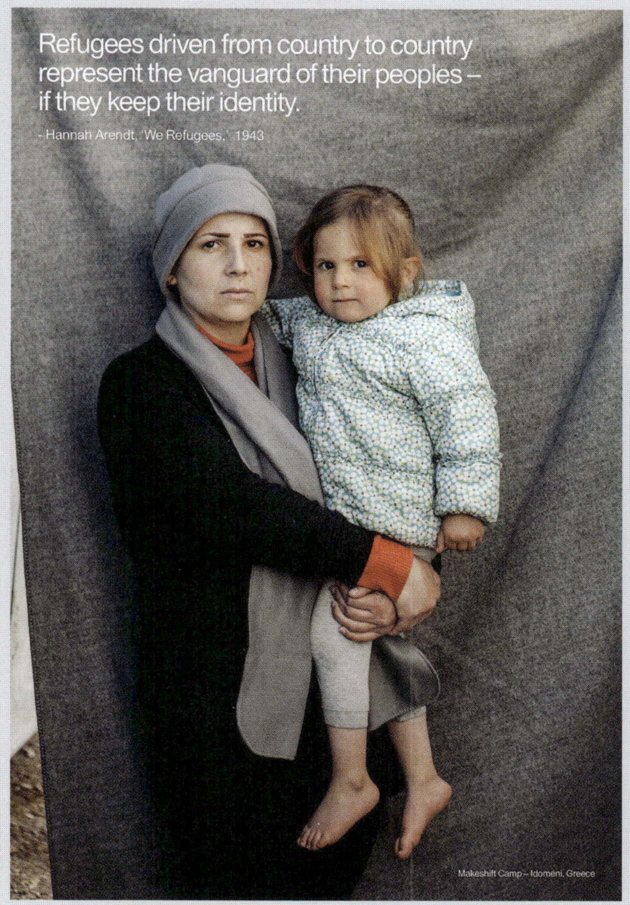

Good Neighbors 47, Makeshift Camp, Idomeni, Greece, 2016

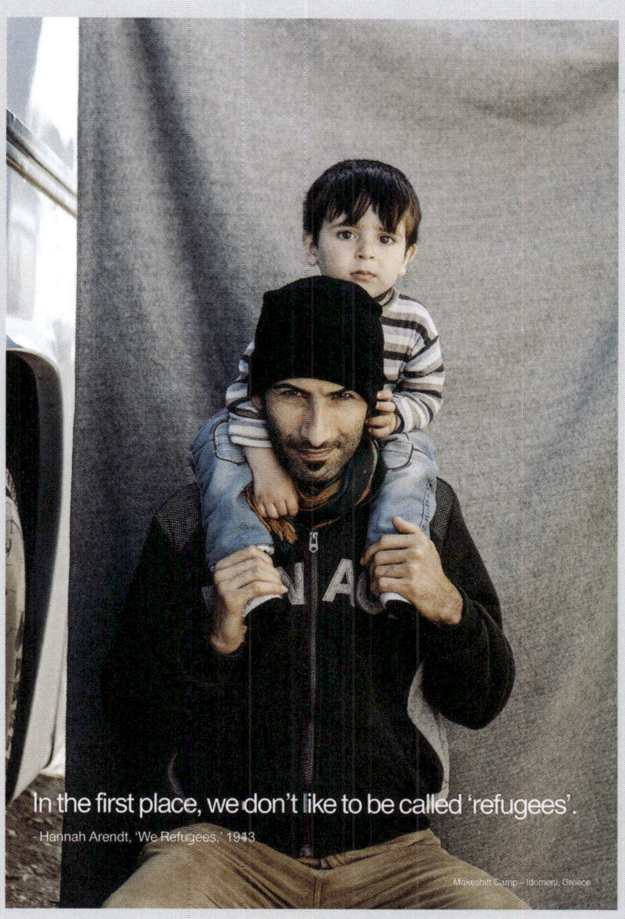

Good Neighbors 48, Makeshift Camp, Idomeni, Greece, 2016

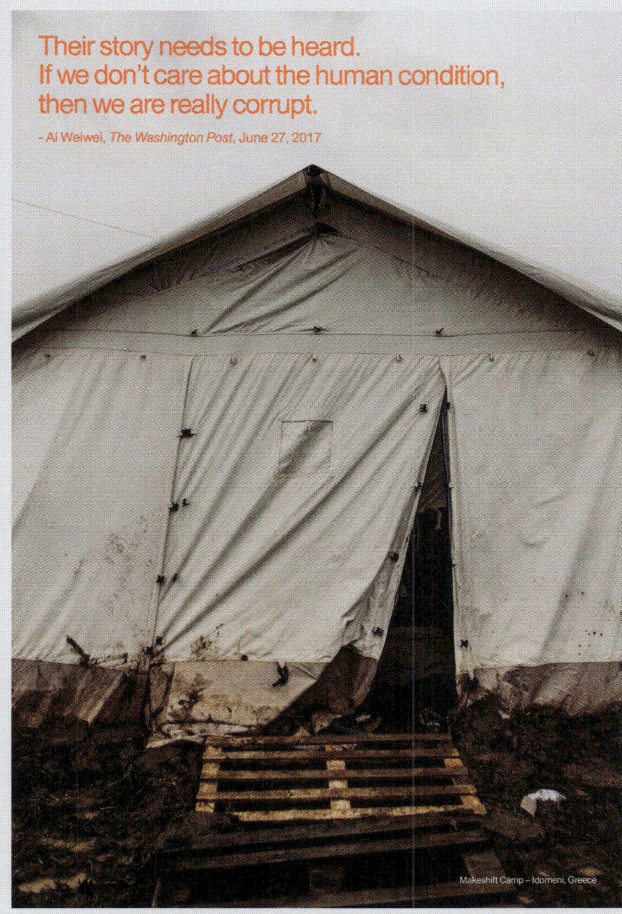

Good Neighbors 49, Makeshift Camp, Idomeni, Greece, 2016

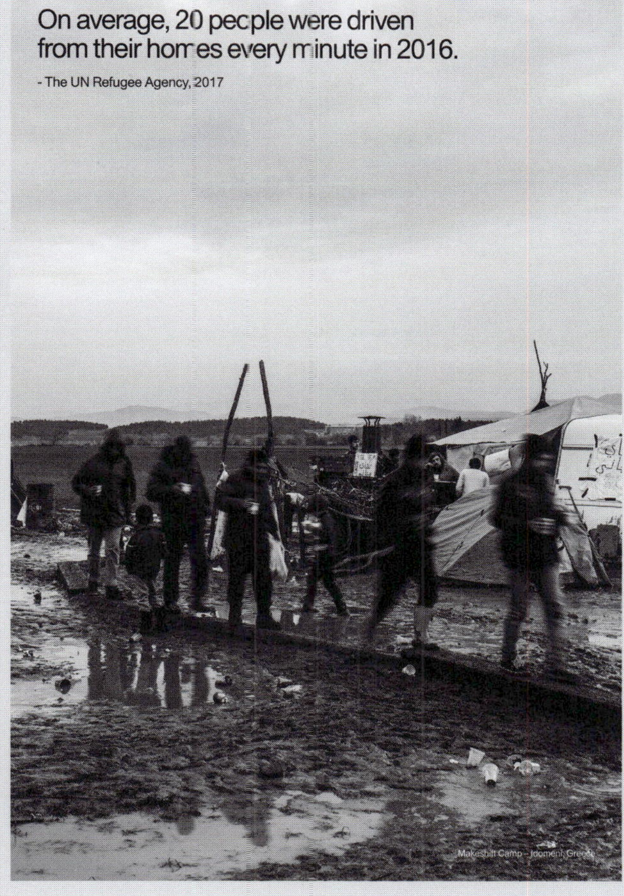

Good Neighbors 53, Makeshift Camp, Idomeni, Greece, 2016

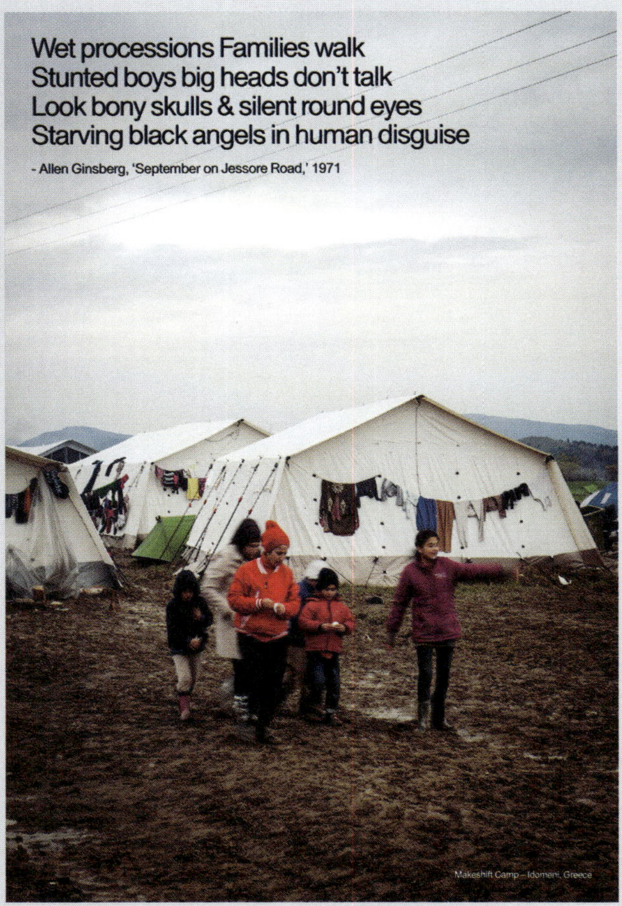

Good Neighbors 54, Makeshift Camp, Idomeni, Greece, 2016

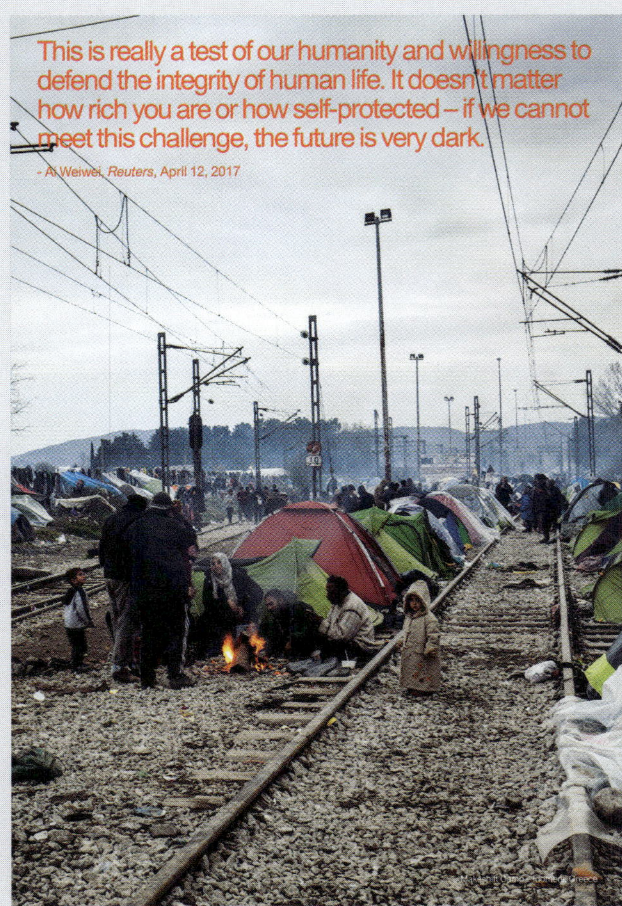

Good Neighbors 55, Makeshift Camp, Idomeni, Greece, 2016

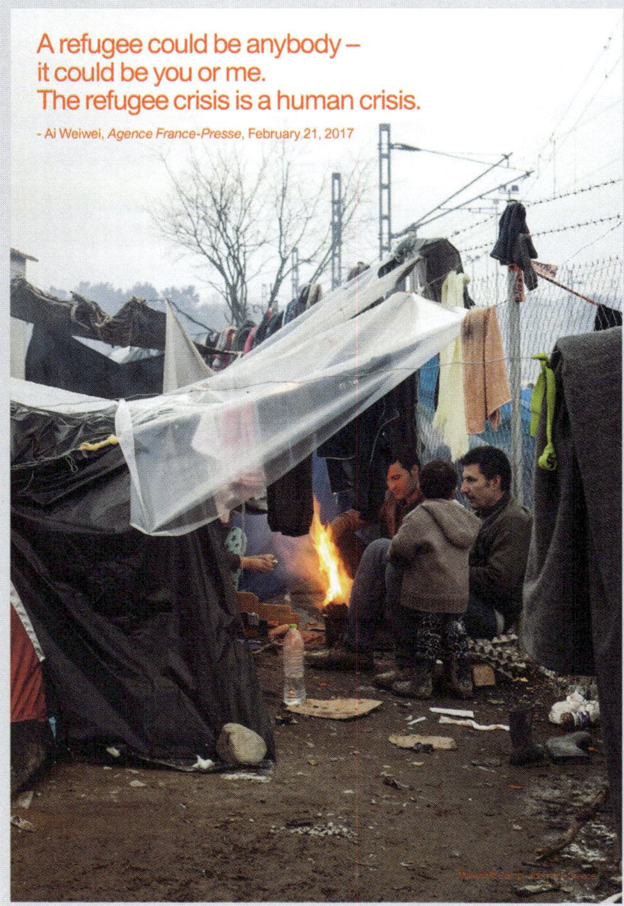

Good Neighbors 56, Makeshift Camp, Idomeni, Greece, 2016

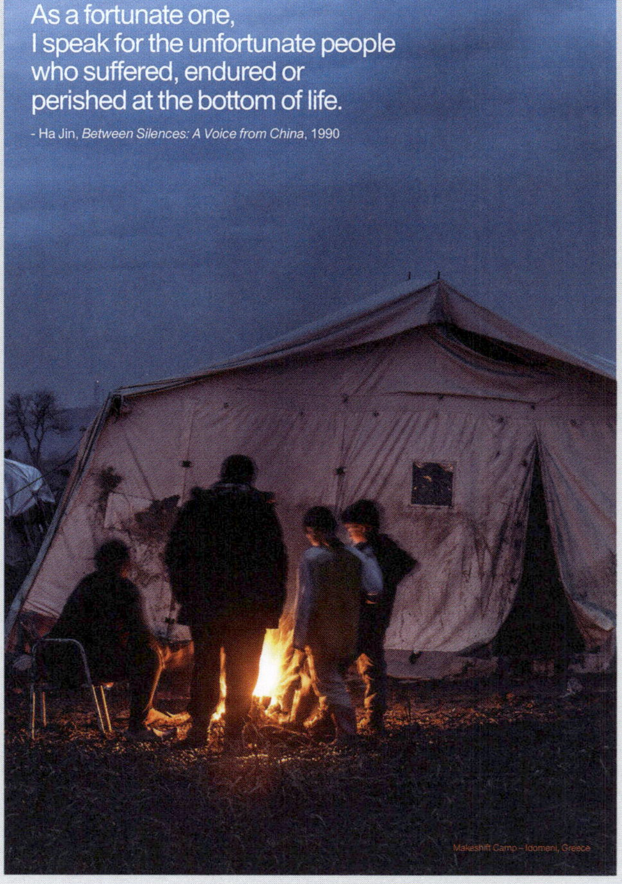

Good Neighbors 57, Makeshift Camp, Idomeni, Greece, 2016

This problem has such a long history – a human history. We are all refugees somehow, somewhere, and at some moment.

- Ai Weiwei, *The Guardian*, September 17, 2015

Makeshift Camp – Idomeni, Greece

Good Neighbors 58, Makeshift Camp, Idomeni, Greece, 2016

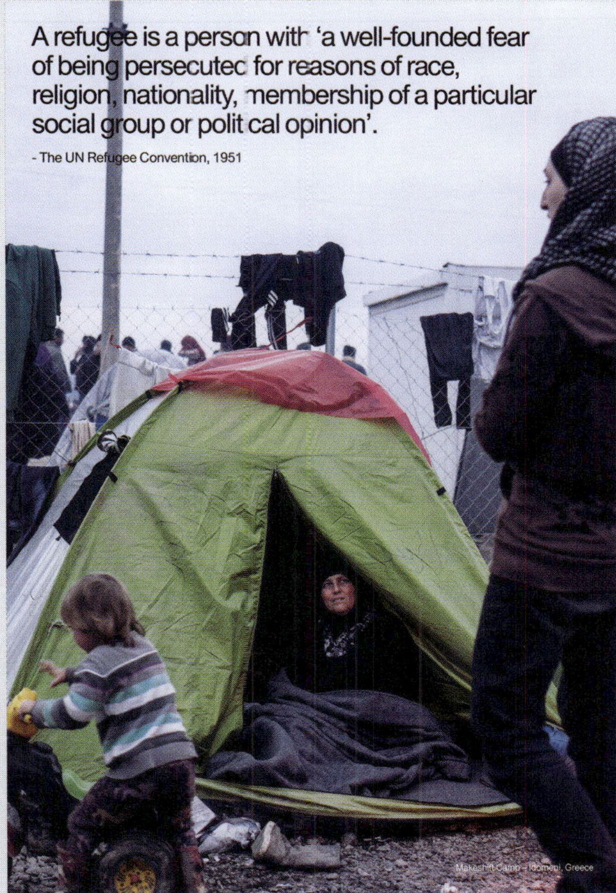

Good Neighbors 59, Makeshift Camp, Idomeni, Greece, 2016

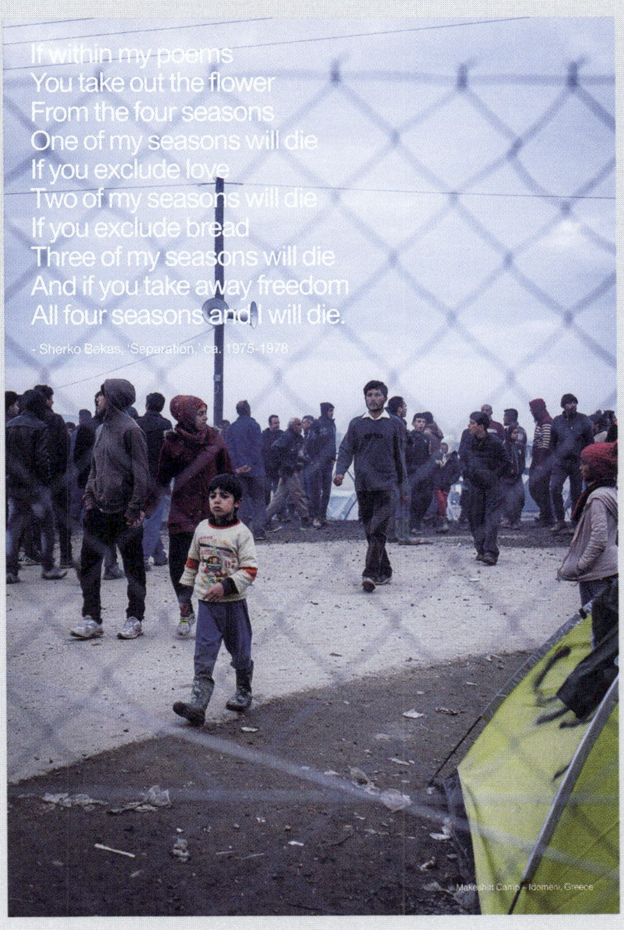

Good Neighbors 60, Makeshift Camp, Idomeni, Greece, 2016

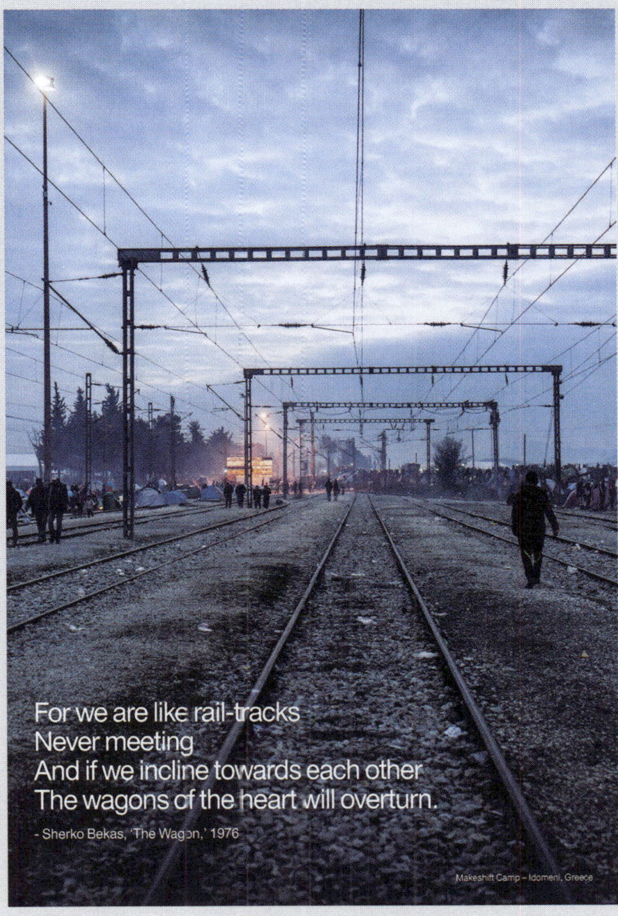

Good Neighbors 61, Makeshift Camp, Idomeni, Greece, 2016

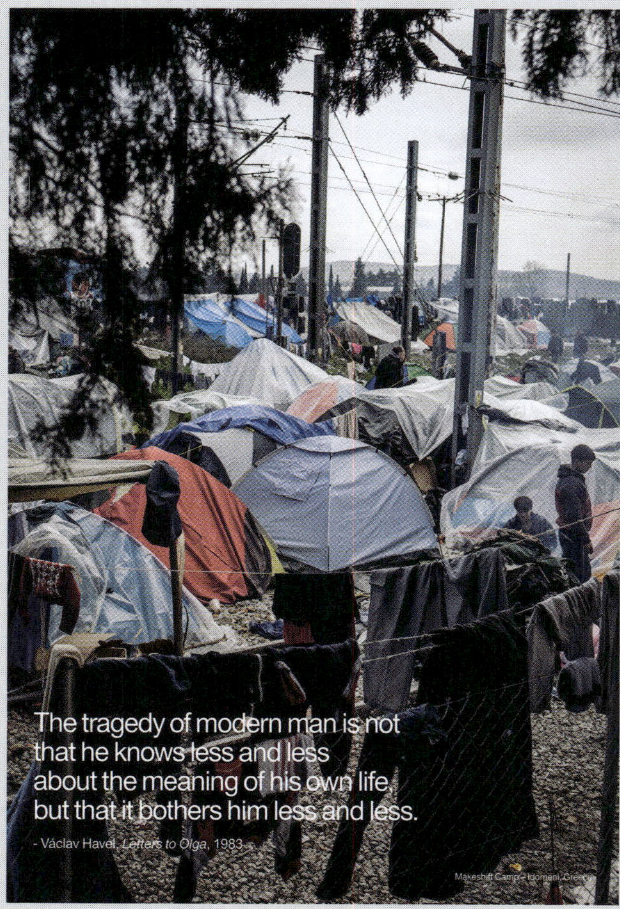

Good Neighbors 62, Makeshift Camp, Idomeni, Greece, 2016

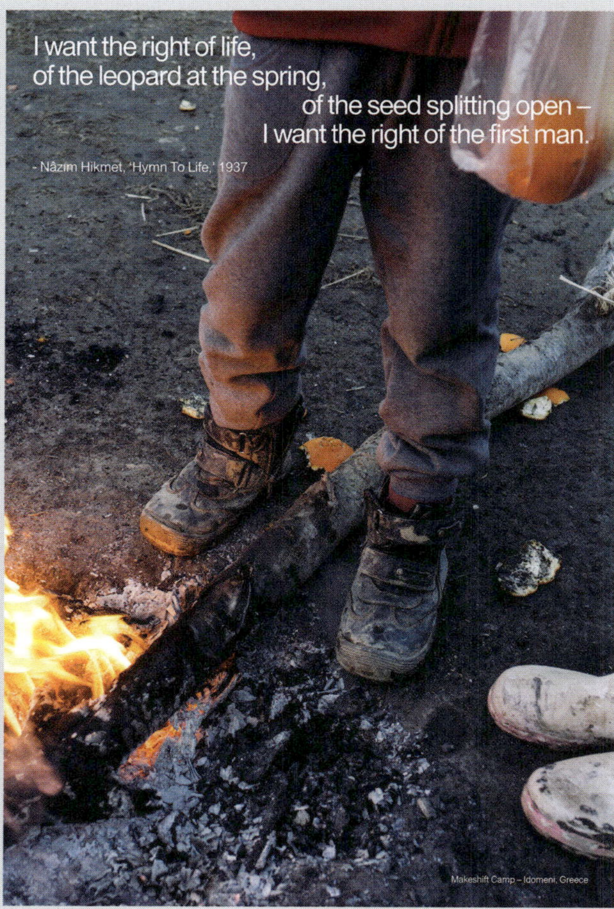

Good Neighbors 64, Makeshift Camp, Idomeni, Greece, 2016

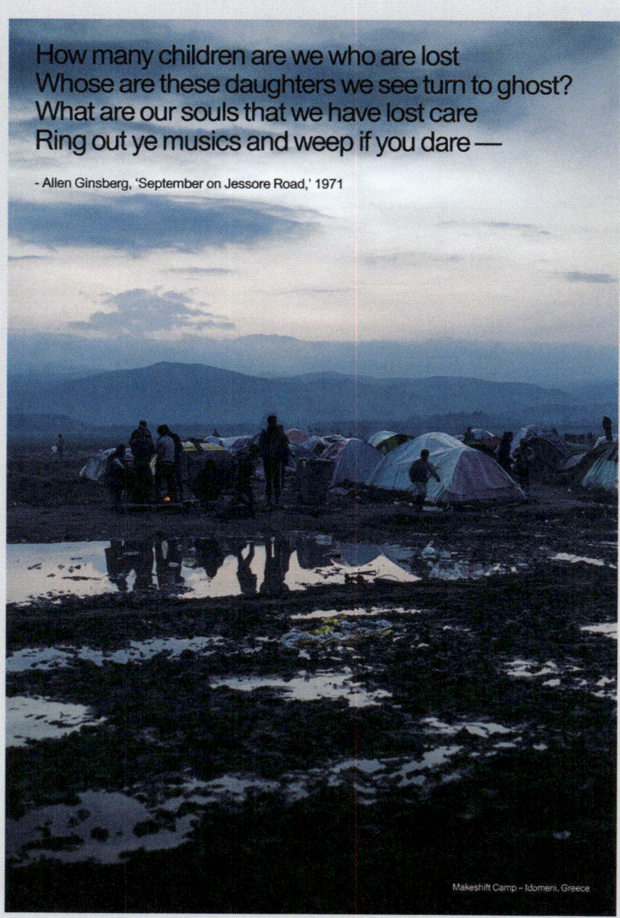

Good Neighbors 65, Makeshift Camp, Idomeni, Greece, 2016

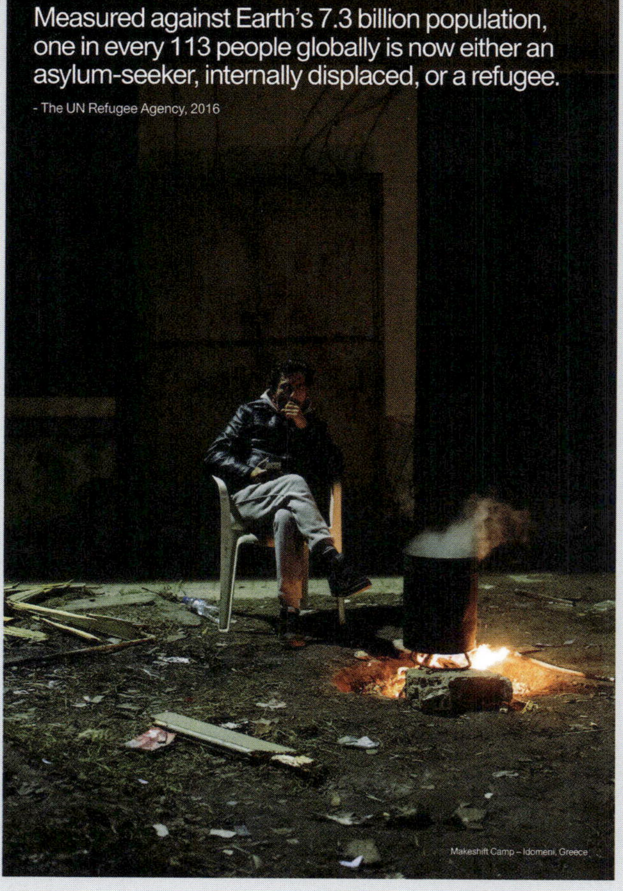

Good Neighbors 66, Makeshift Camp, Idomeni, Greece, 2016

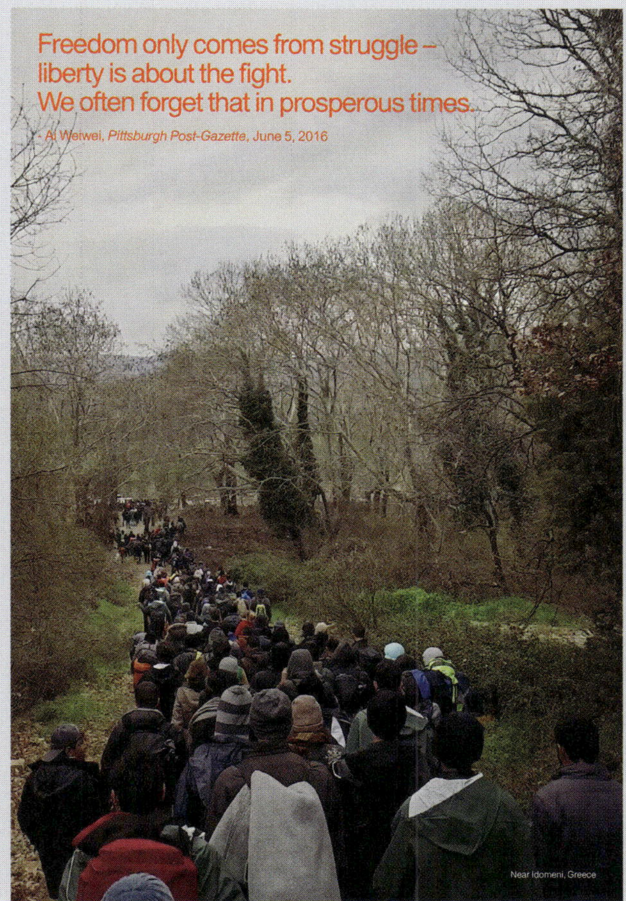

Good Neighbors 97, Near Idomeni, Greece, 2017

The salvation of this human world lies nowhere else than in the human heart, in the human power to reflect, in human meekness and human responsibility.

- Václav Havel, *International Herald Tribune*, February 21,1990

Good Neighbors 98, Makeshift Camp, Idomeni, Greece, 2017

Other Refugee Camps

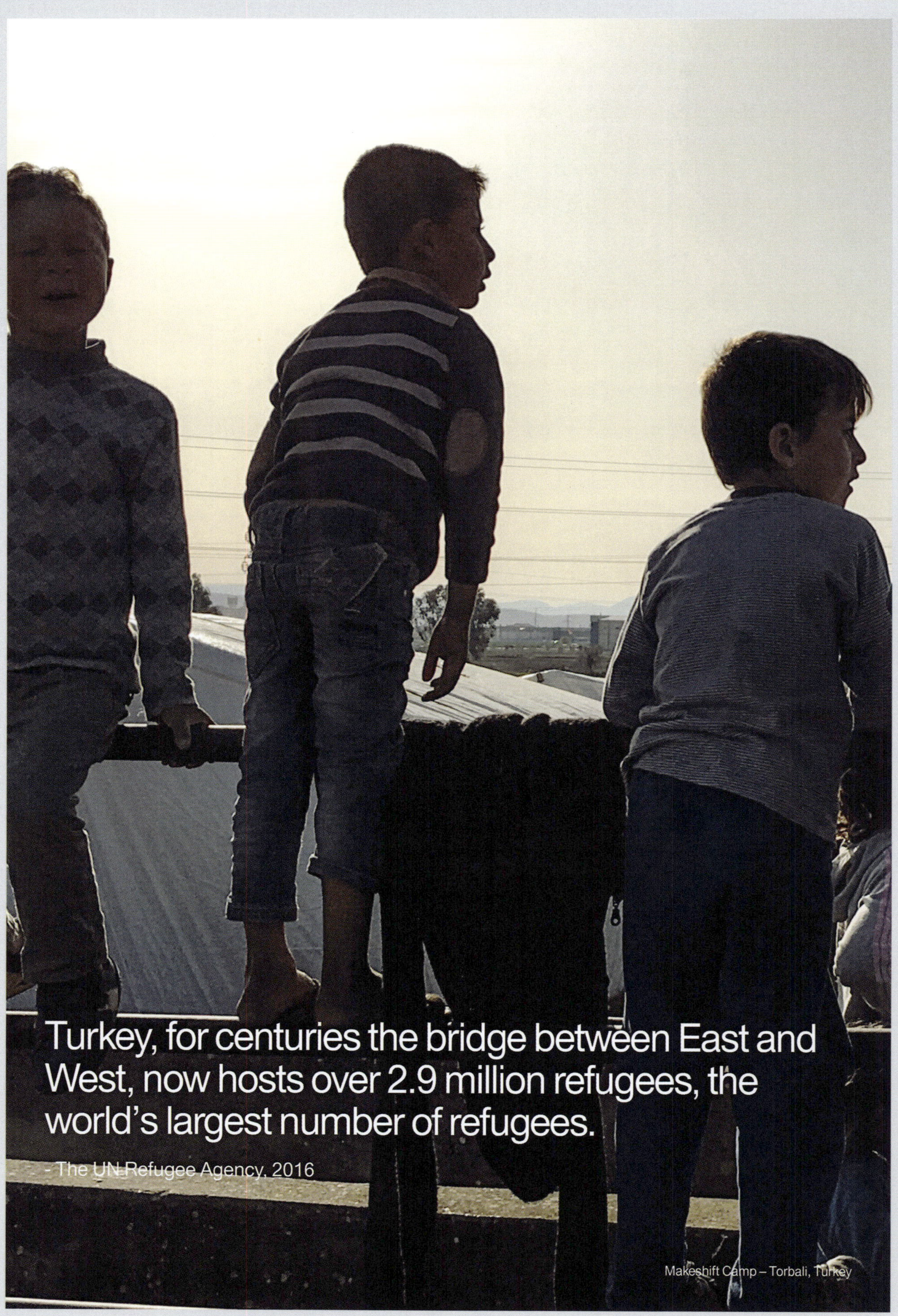

Good Neighbors 67, Makeshift Camp, Torbali, Turkey, 2016

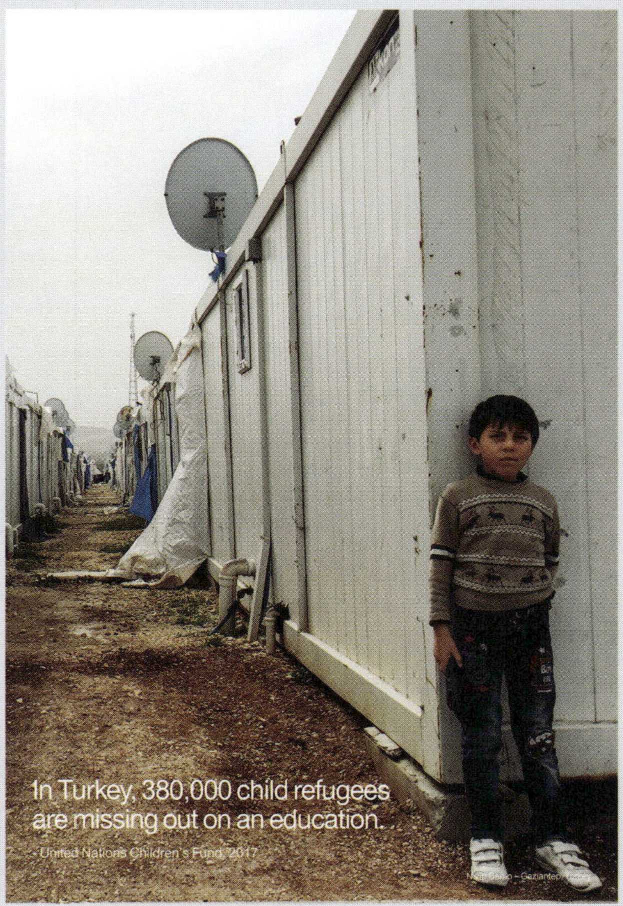

Good Neighbors 68, Nizip Camp, Gaziantep, Turkey, 2016

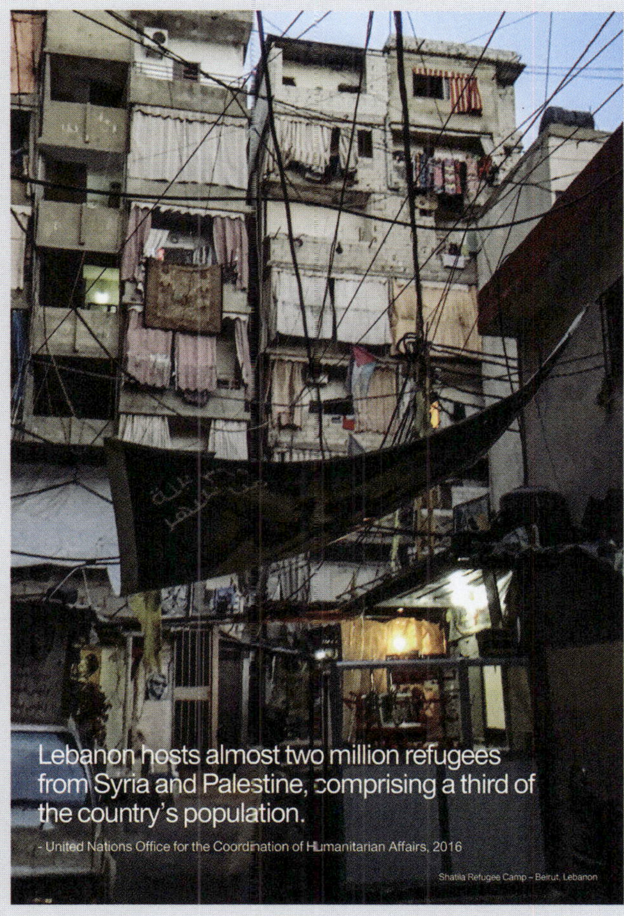

Good Neighbors 69, Shatila Refugee Camp, Beirut, Lebanon, 2016

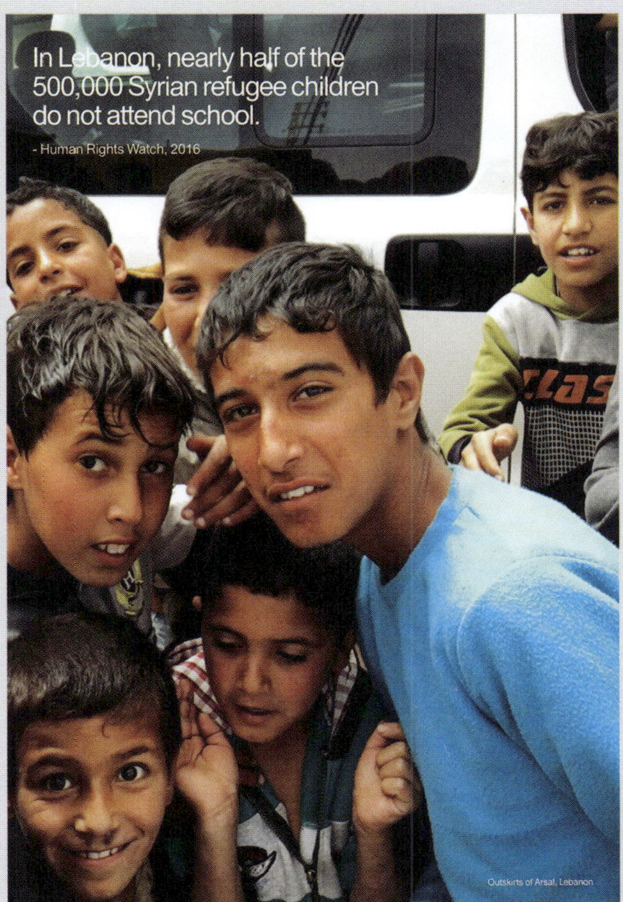

Good Neighbors 70, Outskirts of Arsal, Lebanon, 2016

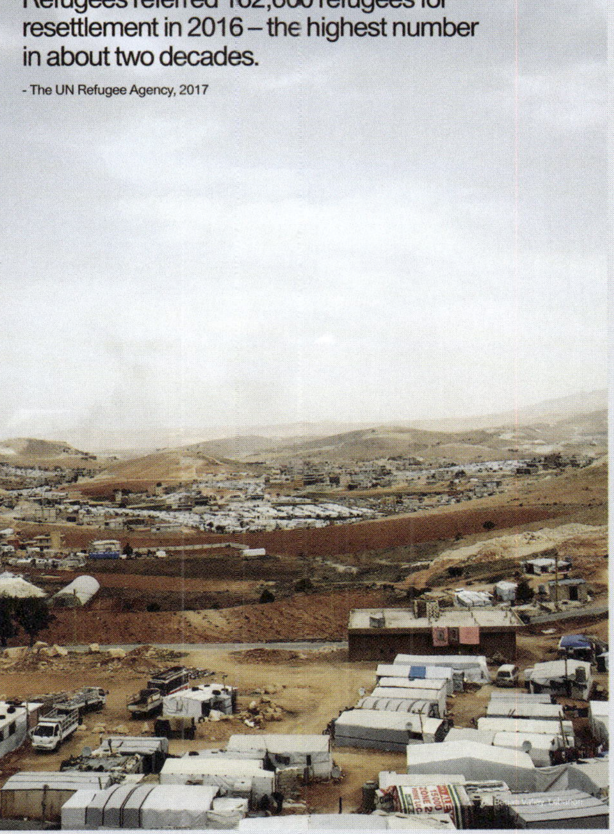

Good Neighbors 71, Beqaa Valley, Lebanon, 2016

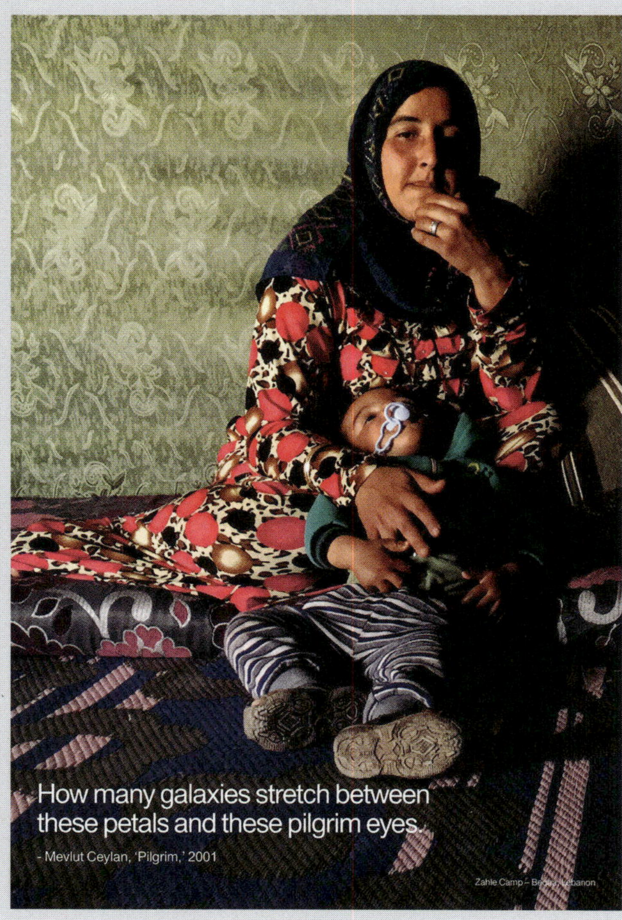

Good Neighbors 72, Zahle Camp, Beqaa, Lebanon, 2016

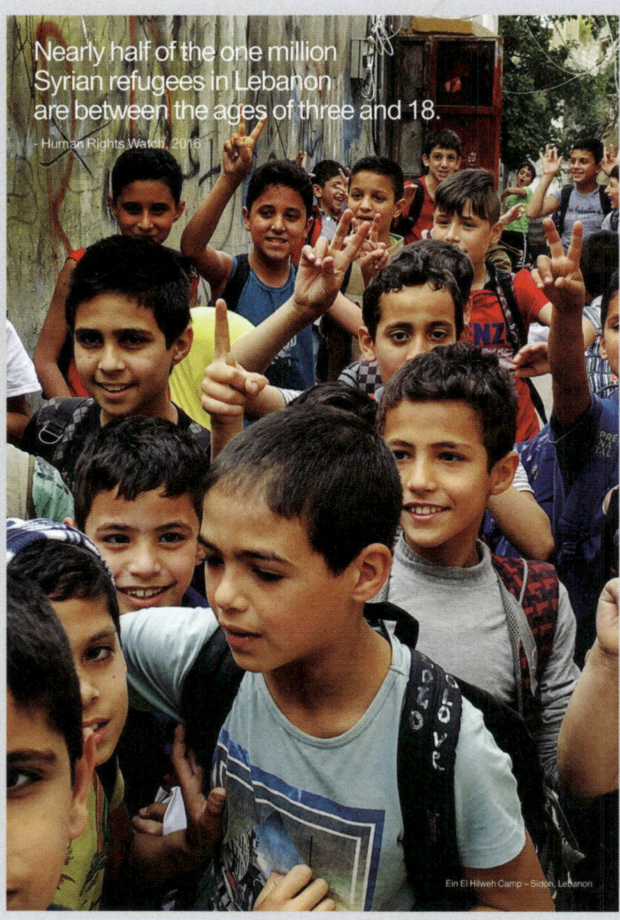

Good Neighbors 73, Ain al-Hilweh Camp, Sidon, Lebanon, 2016

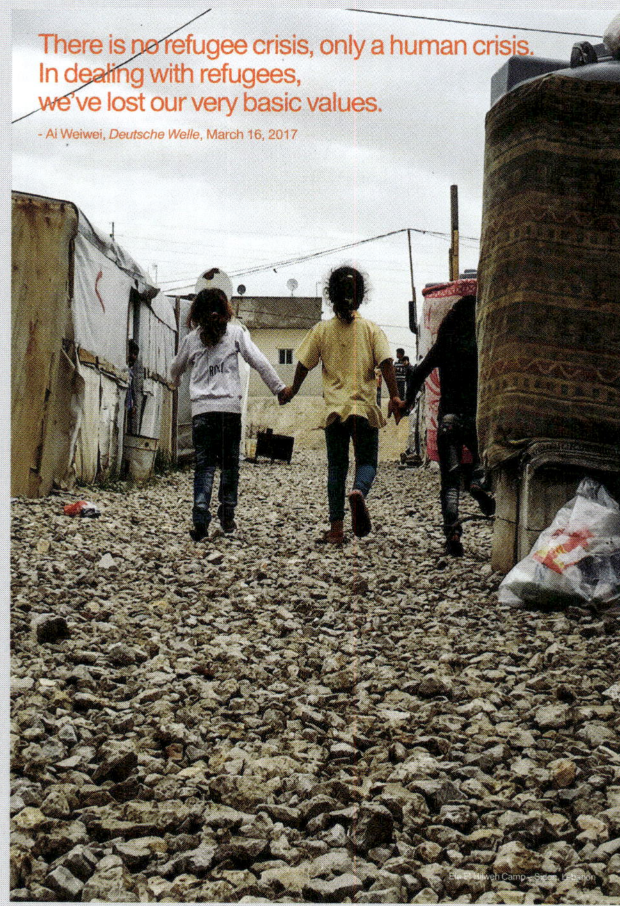

Good Neighbors 74, Ain al-Hilweh Camp, Sidon, Lebanon, 2016

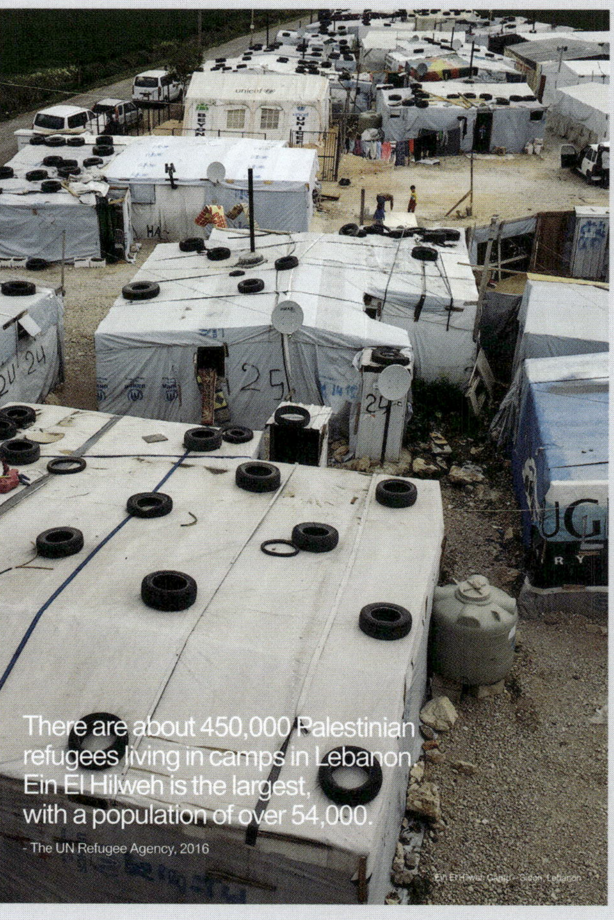

Good Neighbors 75, Ain al-Hilweh Camp, Sidon, Lebanon, 2016

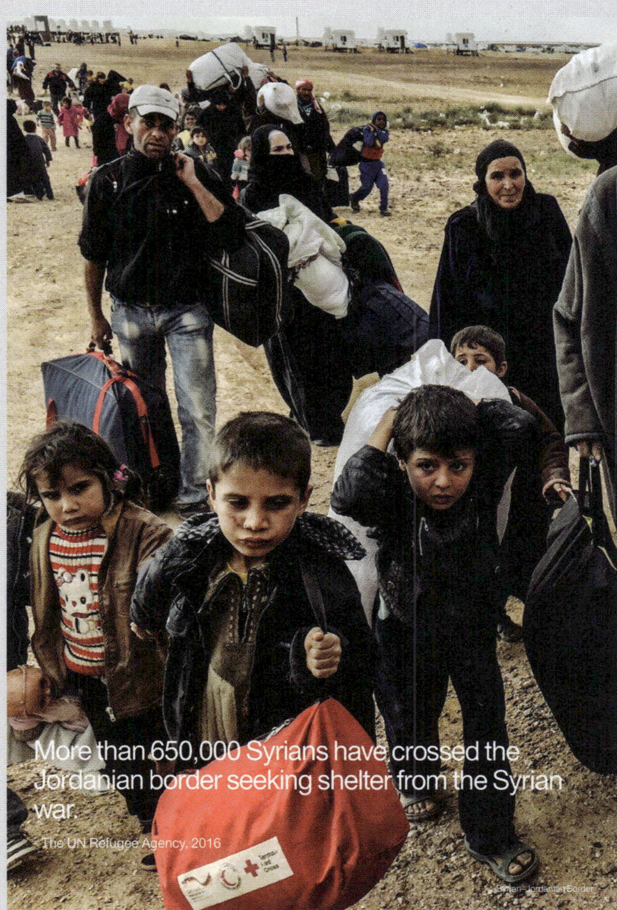

Good Neighbors 76, Syrian-Jordanian Border, 2016

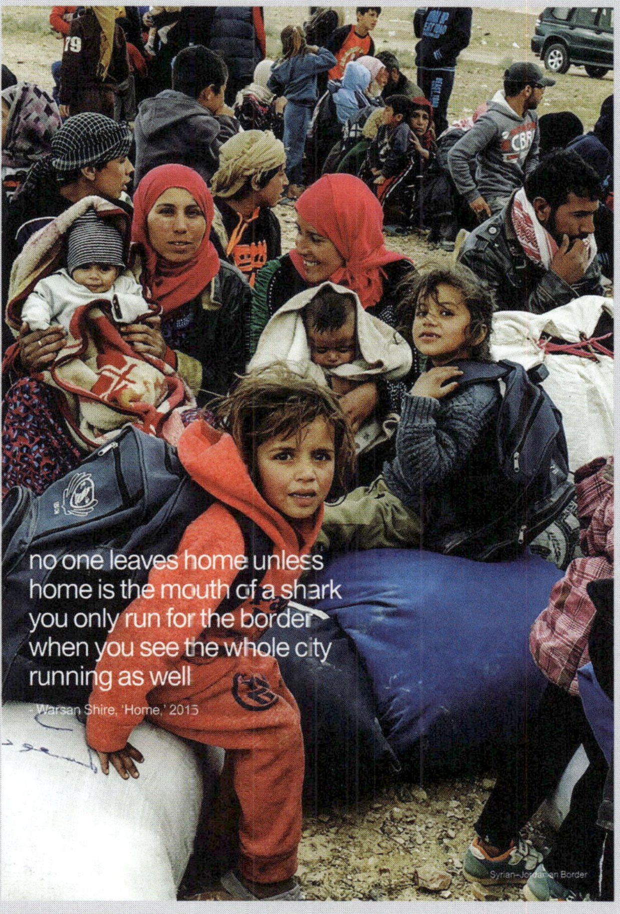

Good Neighbors 77, Syrian-Jordanian Border, 2016

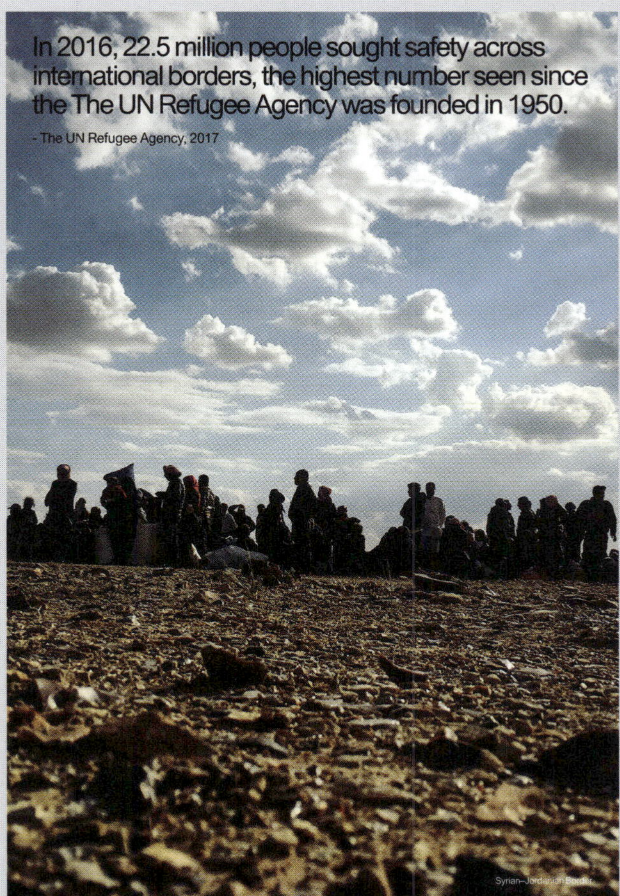

Good Neighbors 78, Syrian-Jordanian Border, 2016

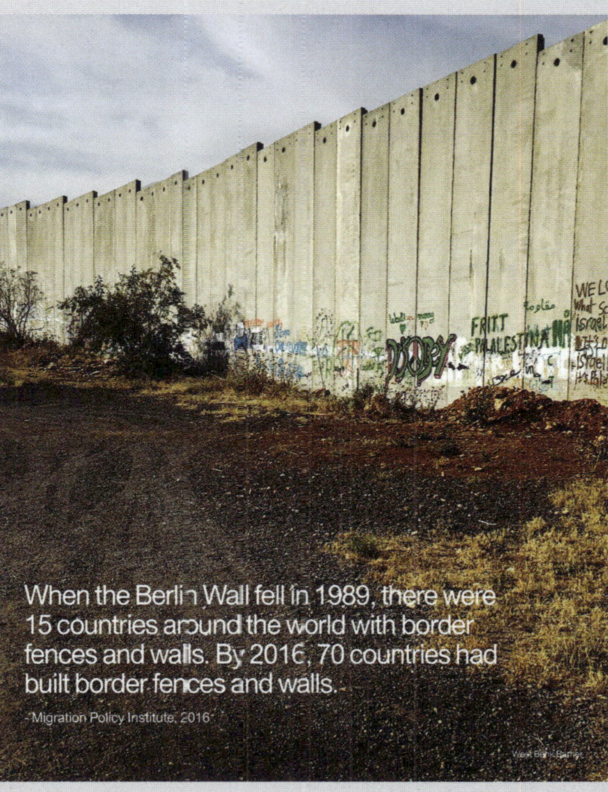

Good Neighbors 80, West Bank Barrier, 2016

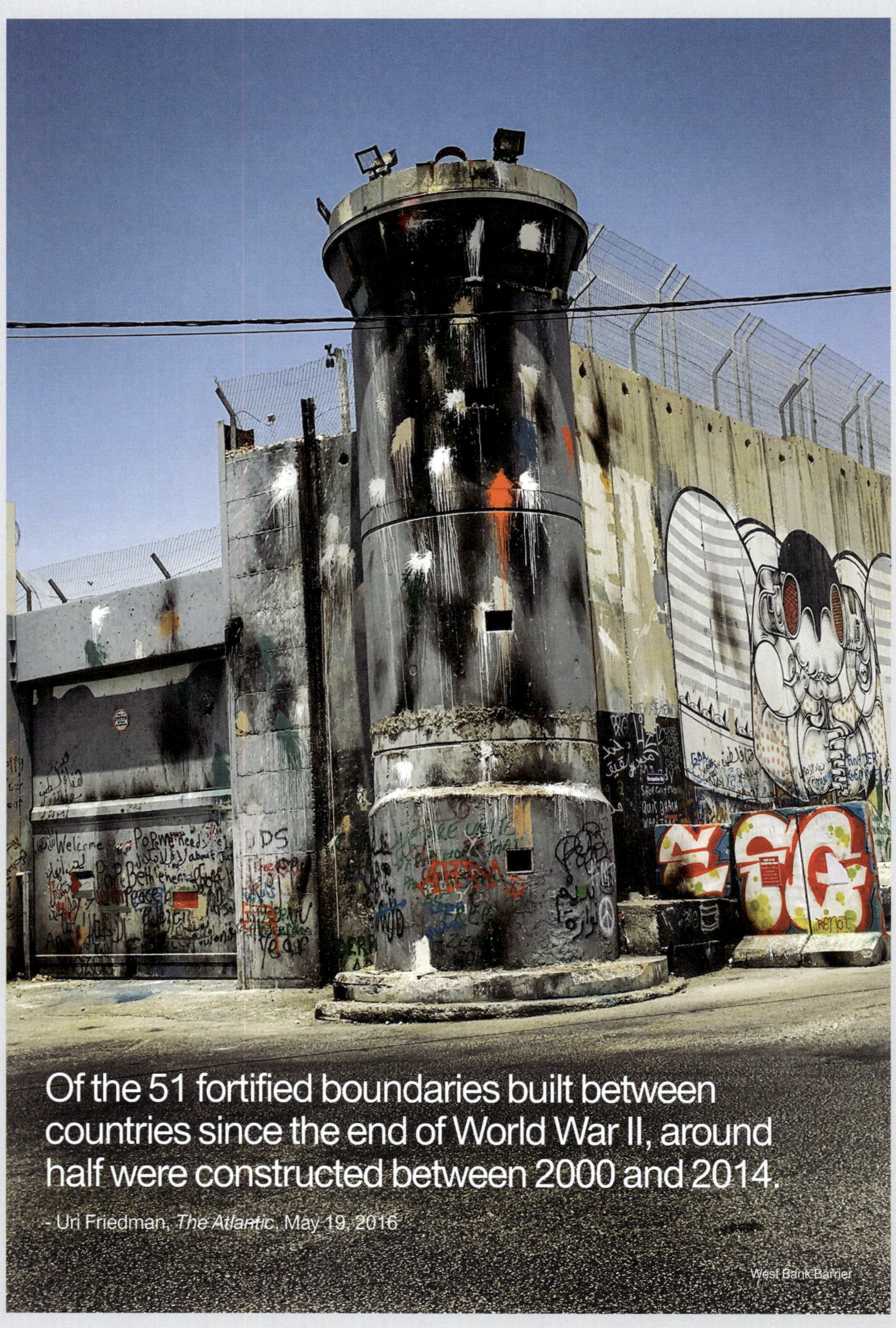

Good Neighbors 79, West Bank Barrier, 2016

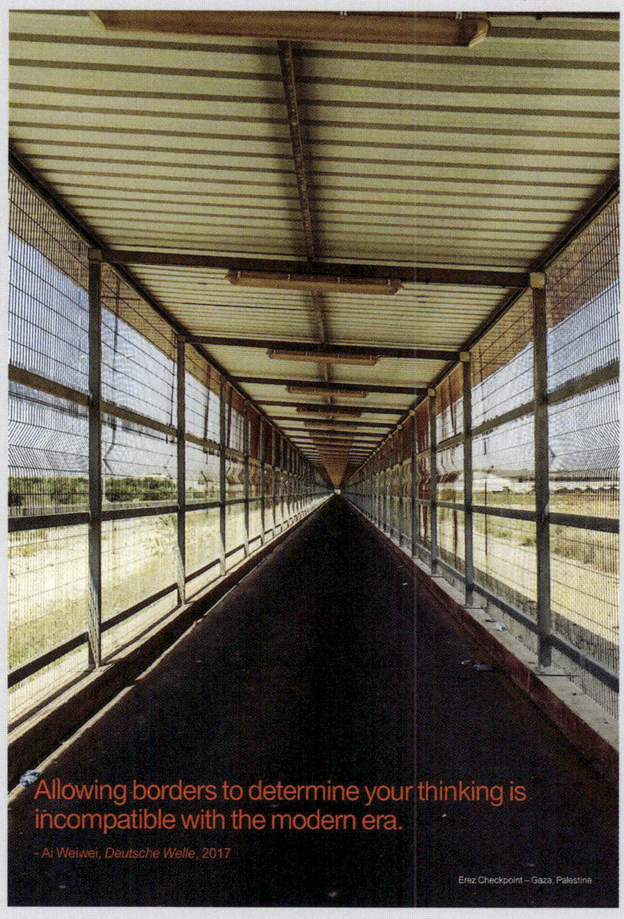

Good Neighbors 81, Erez Checkpoint, Gaza, Palestine, 2016

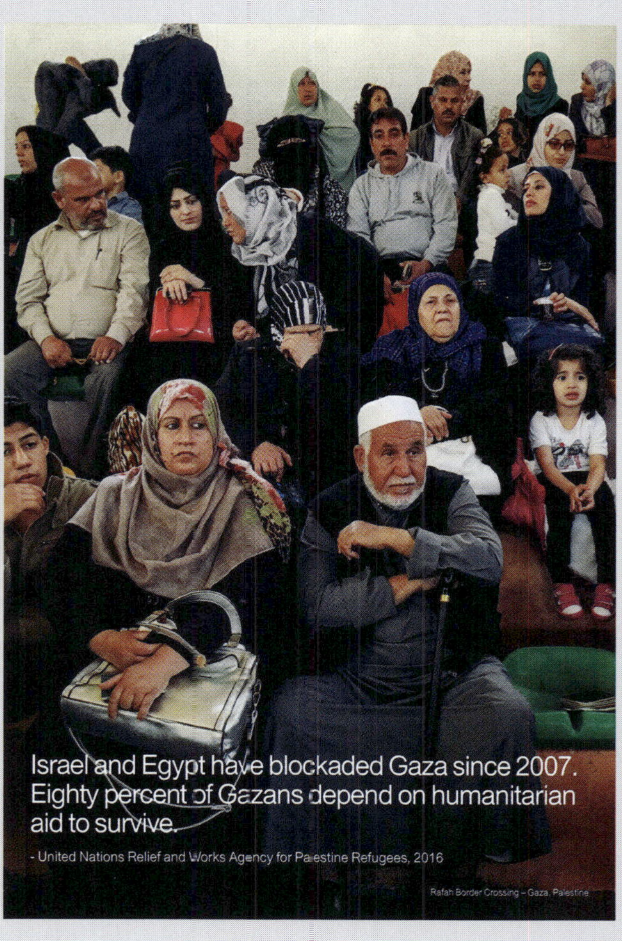

Good Neighbors 83, Rafah Border Crossing, Gaza, Palestine, 2016

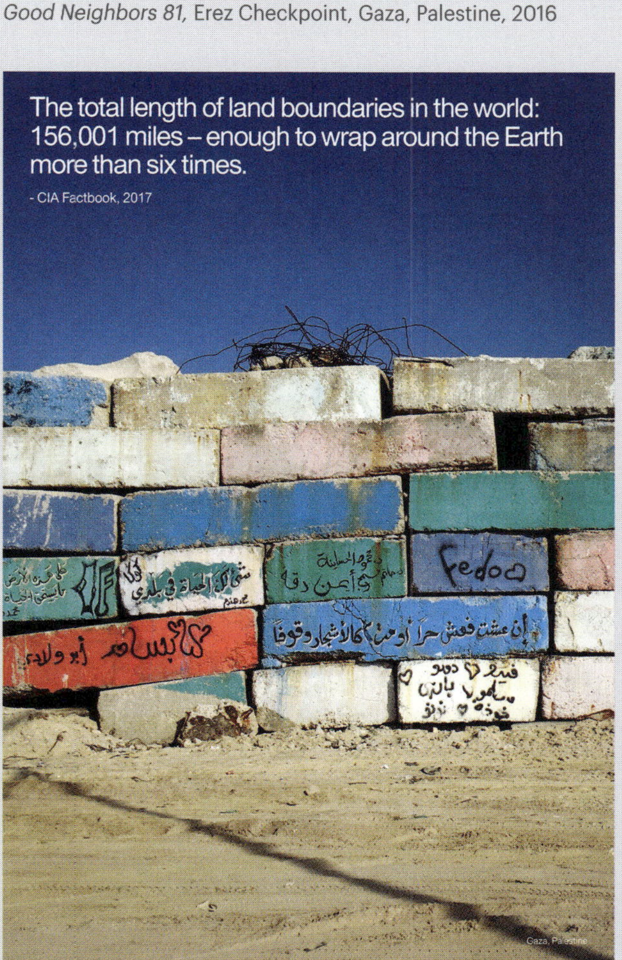

Good Neighbors 85, Gaza, Palestine, 2016

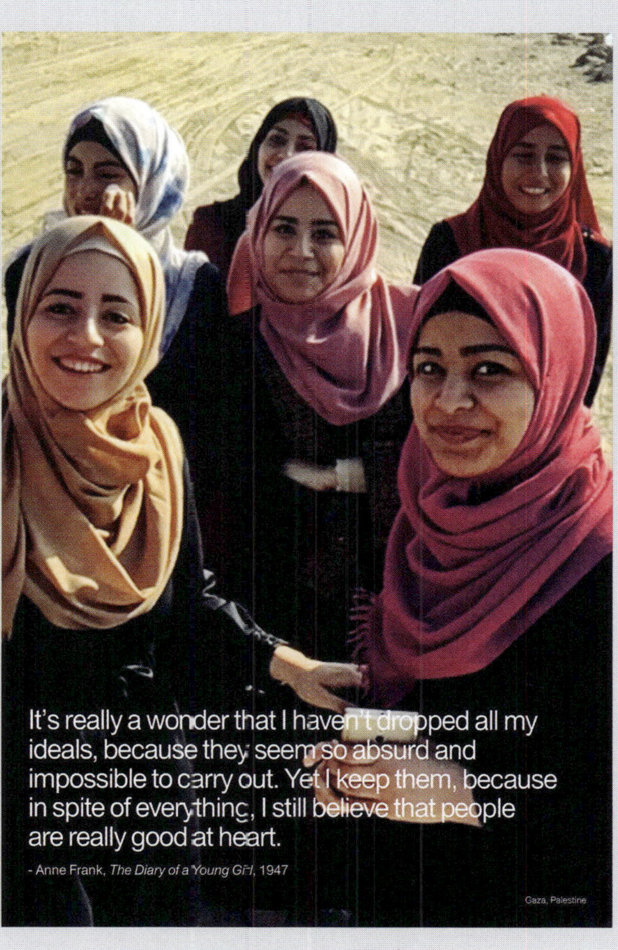

Good Neighbors 86, Gaza, Palestine, 2016

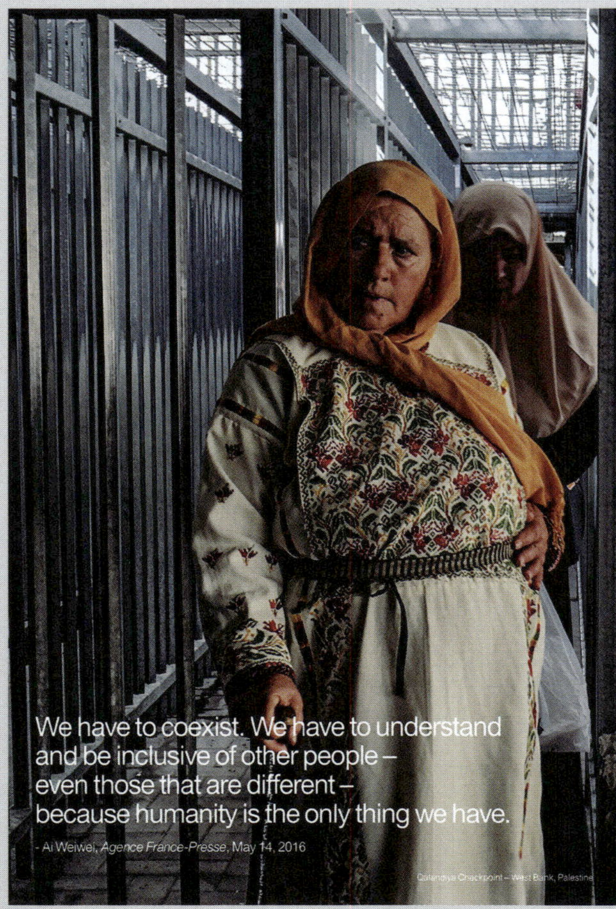

Good Neighbors 87, Qalandiya Checkpoint, West Bank, Palestine, 2016

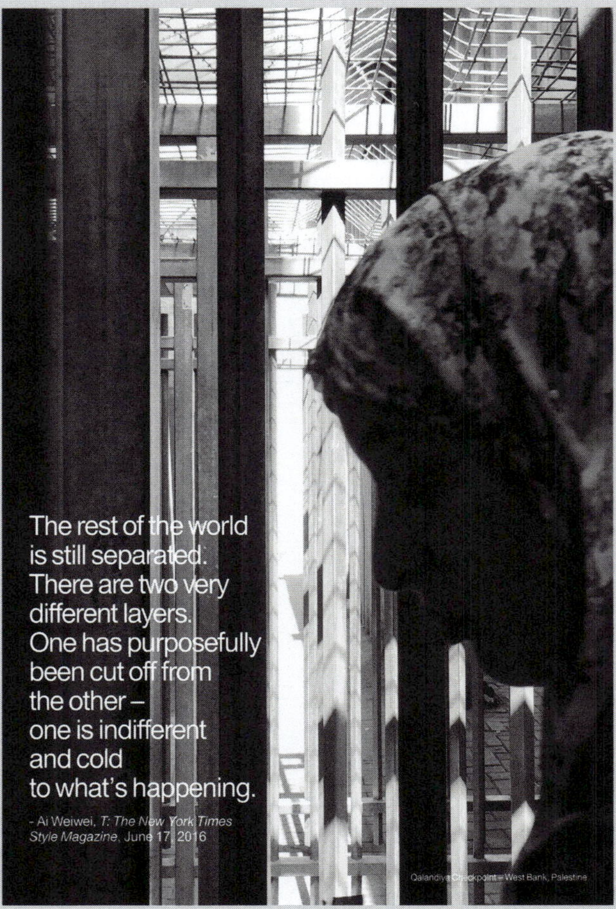

Good Neighbors 88, Qalandiya Checkpoint, West Bank, Palestine, 2016

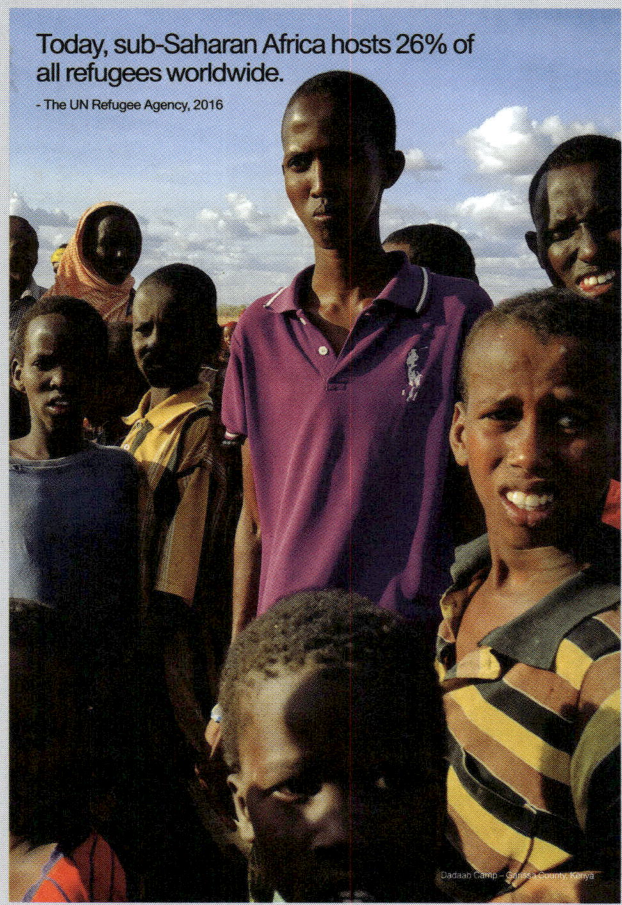

Good Neighbors 89, Dadaab Camp, Garissa County, Kenya, 2016

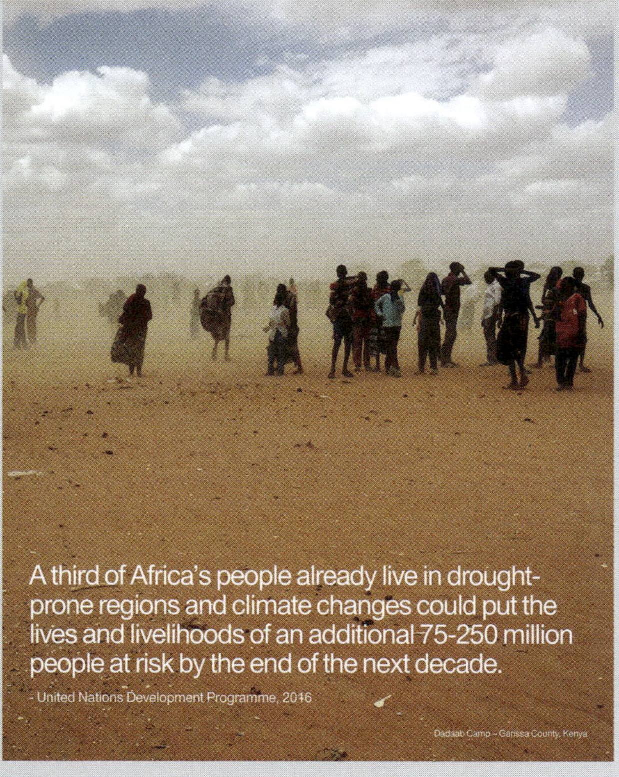

Good Neighbors 90, Dadaab Camp, Garissa County, Kenya, 2016

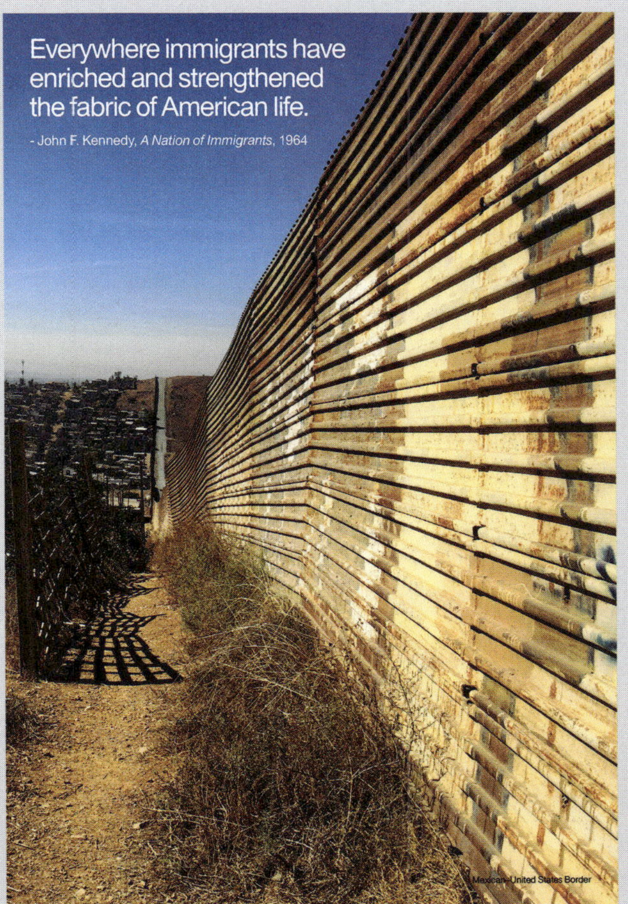

Good Neighbors 91, Mexican-United States Border, 2016

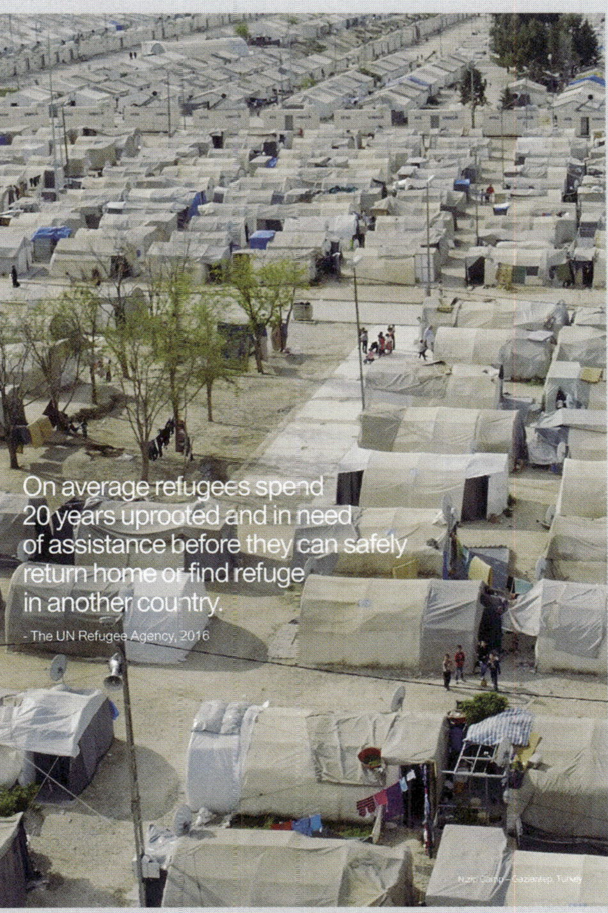

Good Neighbors 92 Nizip Camp, Gaziantep, Turkey, 2017

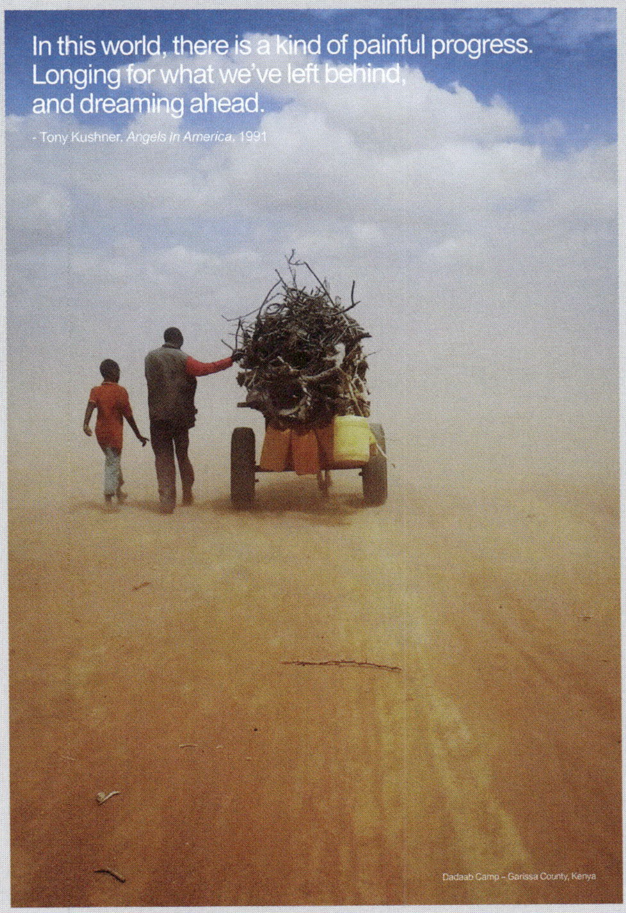

Good Neighbors 93, Dadaab Camp, Garissa County, Kenya, 2017

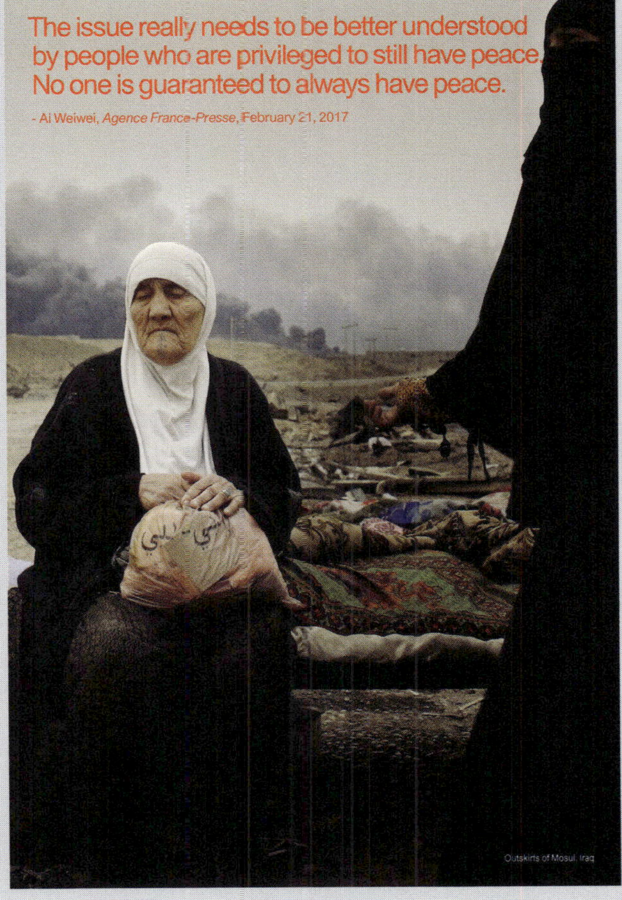

Good Neighbors 95, Outskirts of Mosul, Iraq, 2017

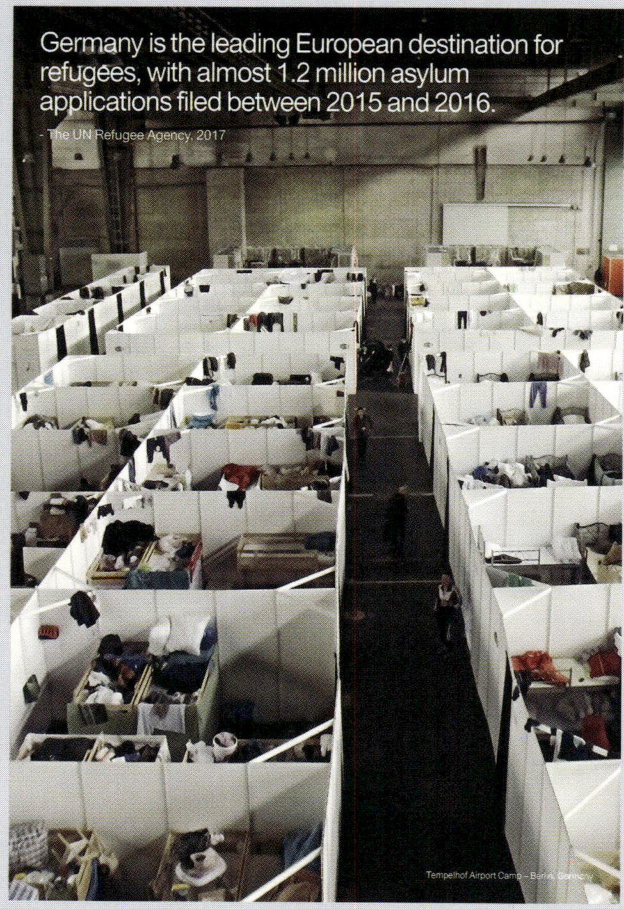

Good Neighbors 96, Tempelhof Airport Camp, Berlin, Germany, 2017

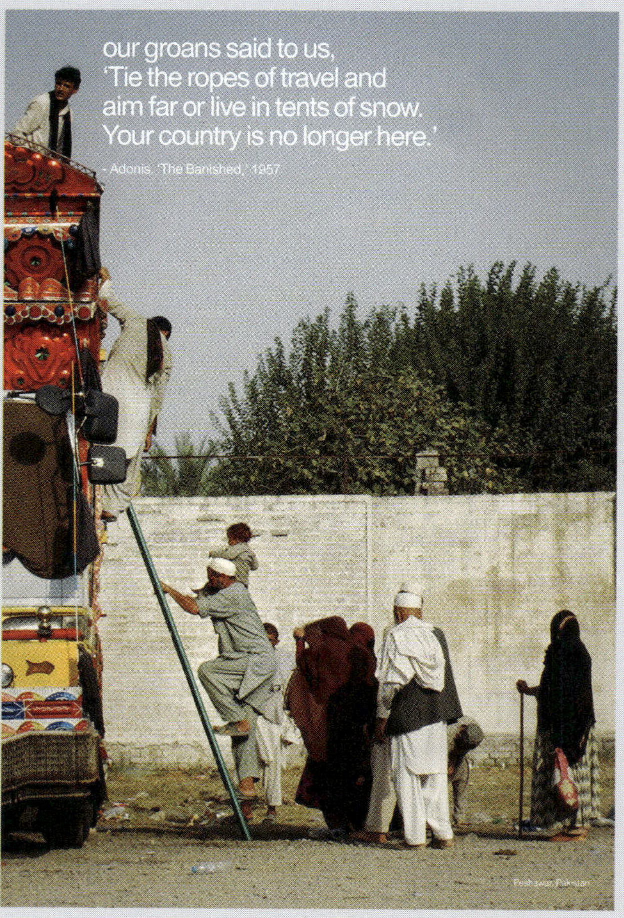

Good Neighbors 99, Peshawar, Pakistan, 2017

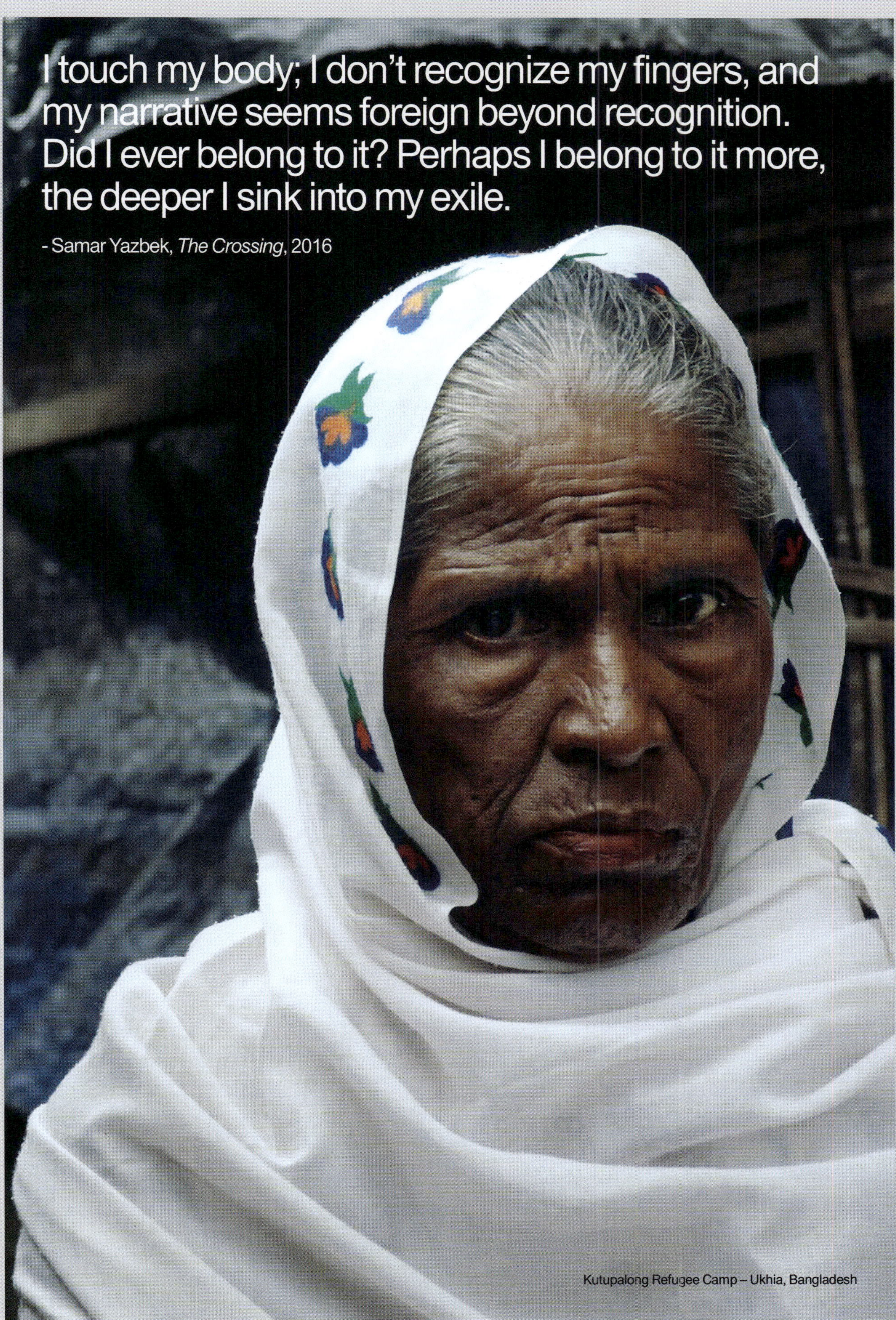

Good Neighbors 100, Kutupalong Refugee Camp, Ukhia, Bangladesh, 2017

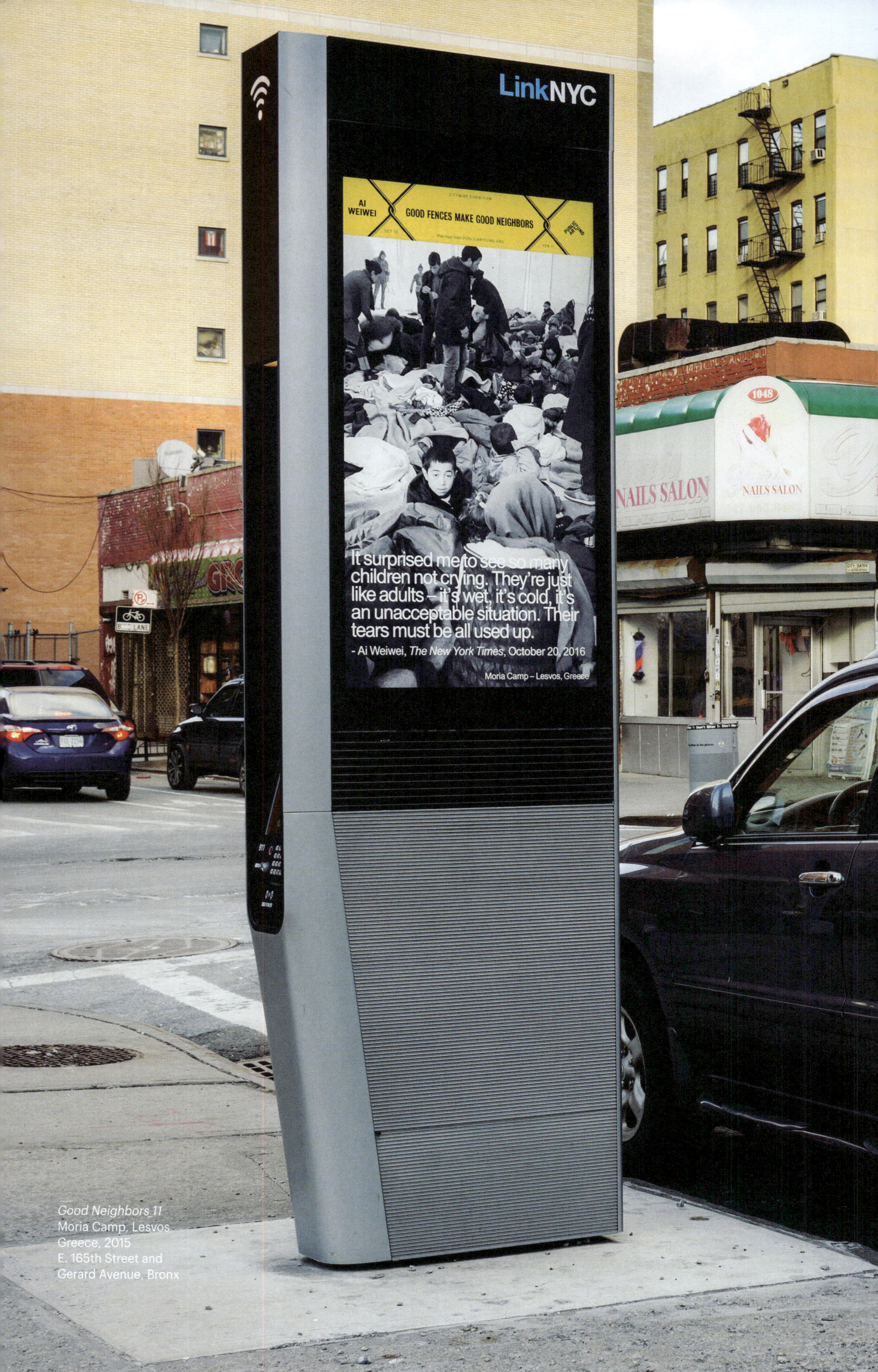

Good Neighbors 11
Moria Camp, Lesvos
Greece, 2015
E. 165th Street and
Gerard Avenue, Bronx

DOWNTOWN MANHATTAN

	Banners	91
	Exodus	1
	Good Neighbors	10
	Odyssey	3
	Structures	5

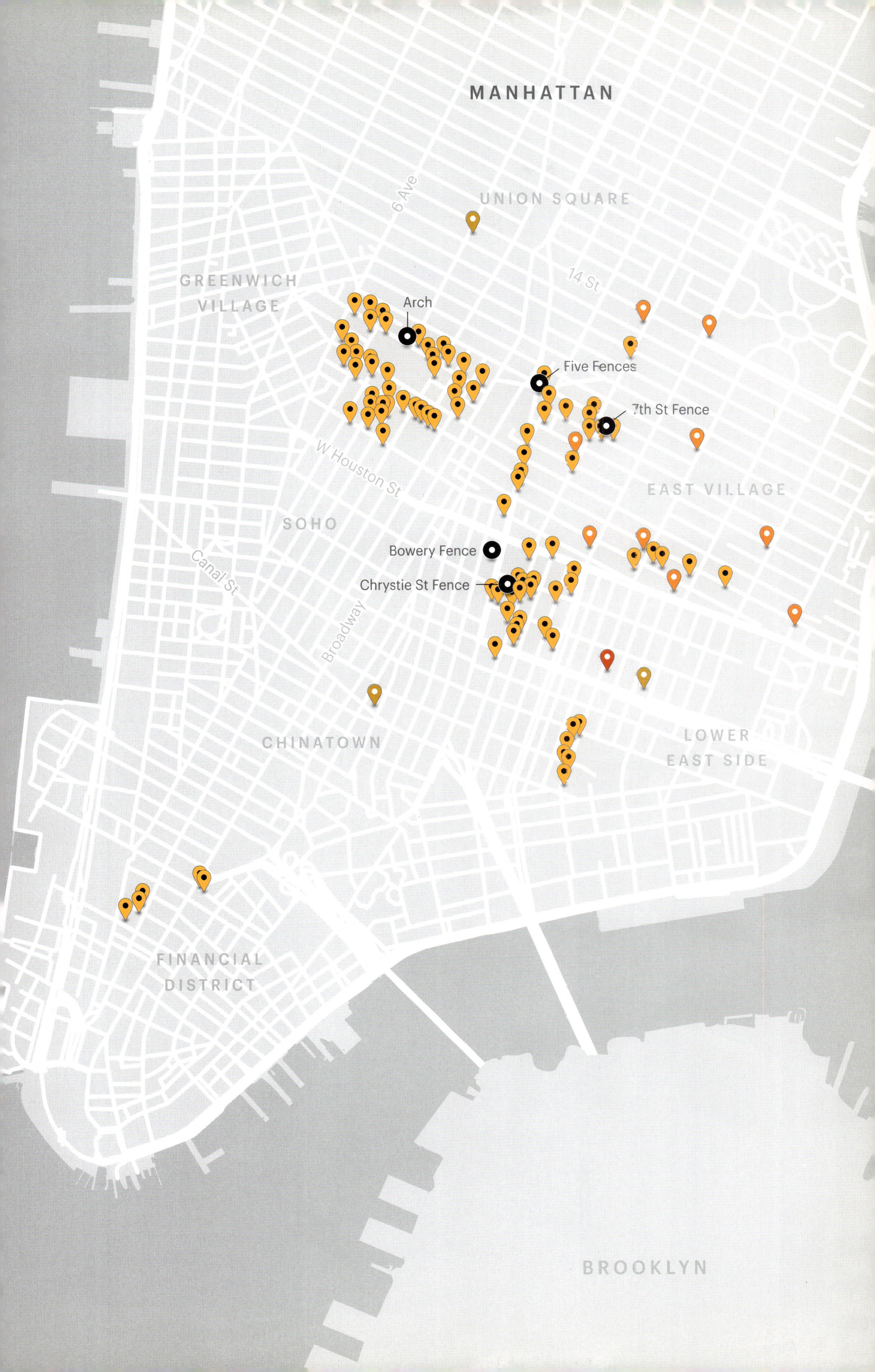

MANHATTAN

UNION SQUARE

6 Ave

14 St

GREENWICH VILLAGE

Arch

Five Fences

7th St Fence

W Houston St

EAST VILLAGE

SOHO

Bowery Fence

Chrystie St Fence

Canal St

Broadway

CHINATOWN

LOWER EAST SIDE

FINANCIAL DISTRICT

BROOKLYN

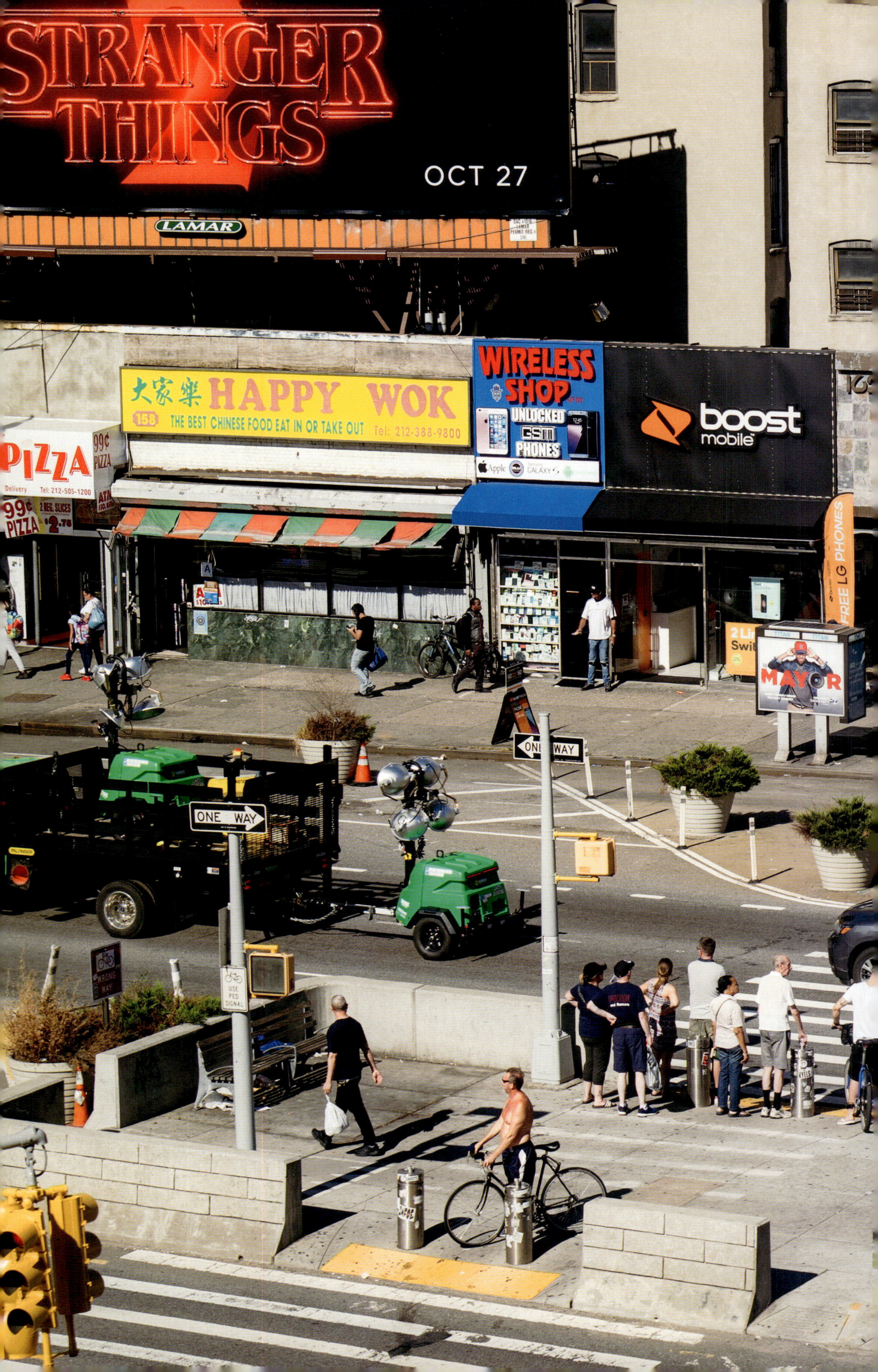
STRANGER THINGS
OCT 27
LAMAR
大家樂 HAPPY WOK
158 THE BEST CHINESE FOOD EAT IN OR TAKE OUT Tel: 212-388-9800
WIRELESS SHOP
UNLOCKED GSM PHONES
Apple
GALAXY
boost mobile
PIZZA
99¢ PIZZA
FREE LG PHONES
MAYOR
ONE WAY
ONE WAY
WRONG WAY
USE PED SIGNAL

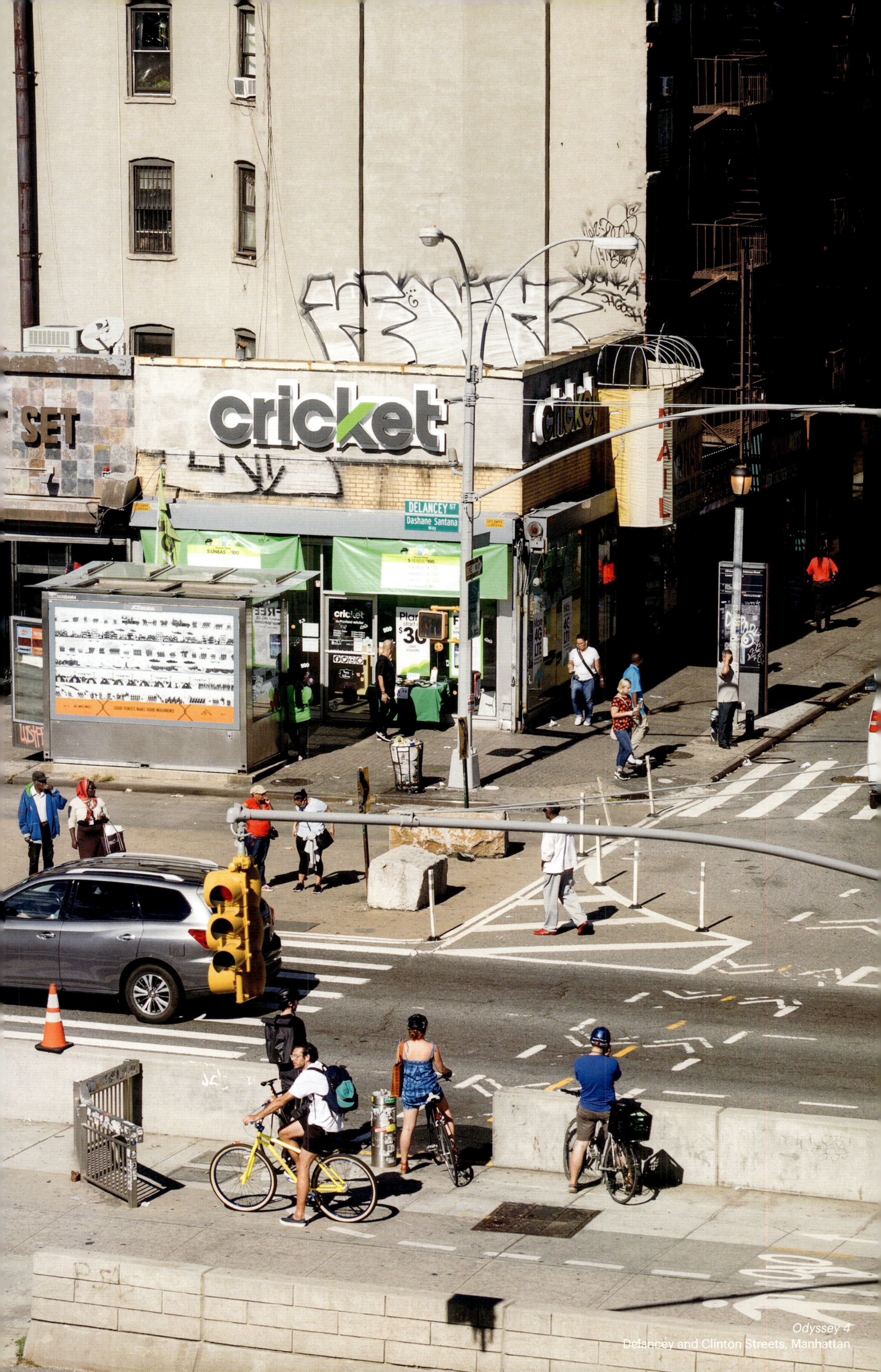

Odyssey 4
Delancey and Clinton Streets, Manhattan

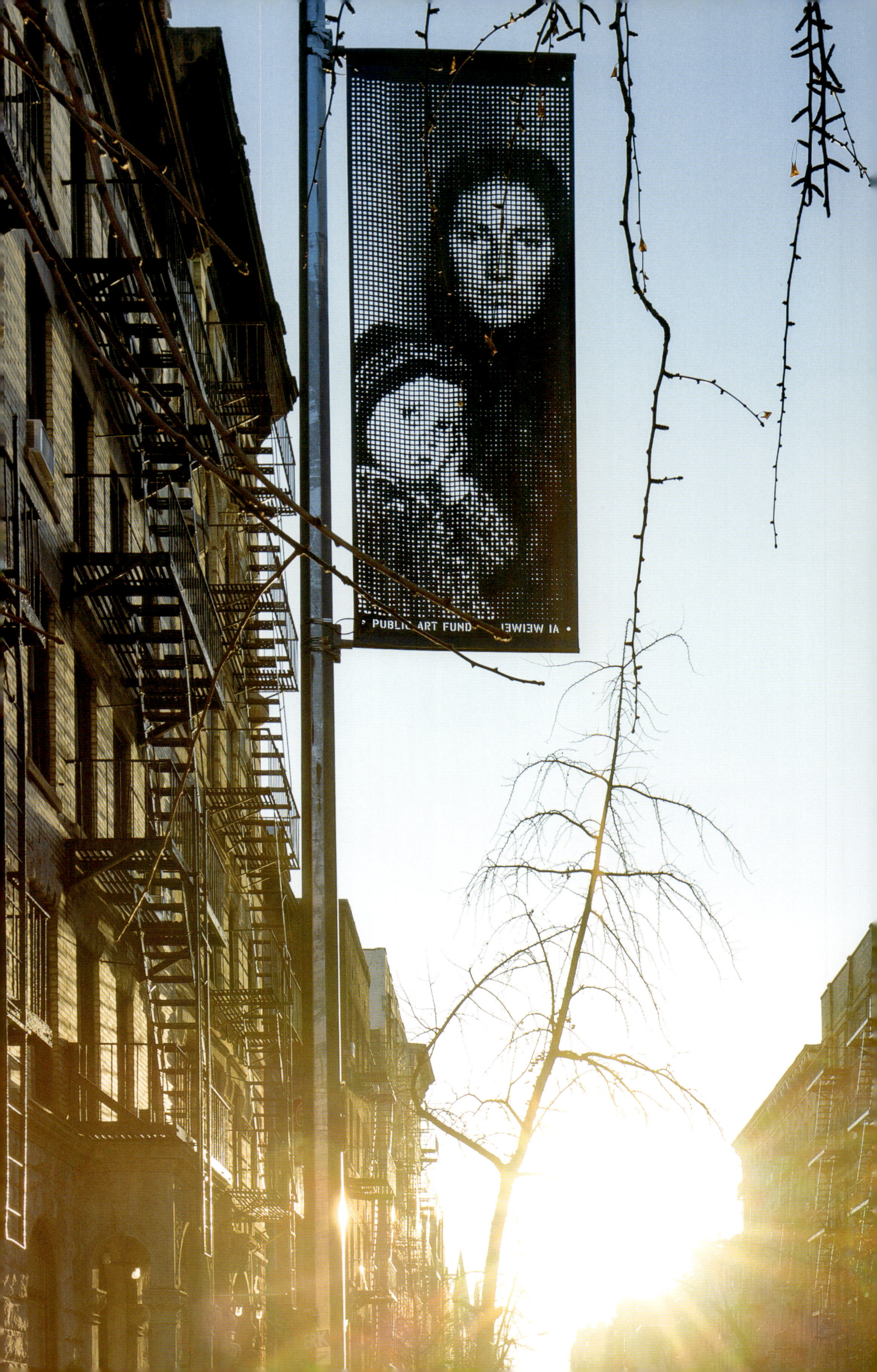
PUBLIC ART FUND
AI WEIWEI

Downtown Manhattan

Since the nineteenth century, many successive waves of immigrants who landed at Ellis Island settled on the Lower East Side, establishing it as a working-class neighborhood where residents lived in crowded tenements as they diligently worked to achieve their "American Dream." Although many of the ethnic groups who settled there initially retained their homogeneous enclaves, the vibrant streets and neighborhoods eventually became mixed, producing a thriving and vibrant symphony of cultures, tastes, colors, and sounds.

Having lived downtown for a time, Ai Weiwei has a significant personal connection to the dynamic array of streets and buildings that welcomed him and so many other immigrants. This varied cityscape motivated the artist's initial concept, which developed into this exhibition's rooftop fence installations—*Bowery Fence*, *Chrystie Street Fence*, and *7th Street Fence* (next to the basement apartment where the artist once lived)—that appear unexpectedly between buildings.

Upon his arrival, Weiwei enrolled as a student at Parsons (he recently joked he wasn't accepted to Cooper Union, the site of his *Five Fences* installation), but after dropping out, he continued to live in the area. Indeed, as a young immigrant-artist, he received an extraordinary education during these years from the artistic and intellectual circle of the scene that had long been established there. Weiwei's dialogue with figures such as Allen Ginsberg, Chinese artists and thinkers including Chen Kaige, Tan Dun, and Xu Bing among others, and his admiration for Andy Warhol encouraged his artistic and intellectual growth. Moreover, having witnessed the Tompkins Square Park riots firsthand, and the thriving public forum for politics and the arts at Washington Square Park—where *Arch* would eventually stand as a critical marker of the exhibition—the tense political climate at the time served to cultivate his belief in the power of artistic liberty and free speech.

Banner 22
Hungarian Family (detail), ca. 1905–1914
E. 2nd Street and 2nd Avenue, Manhattan
(opposite)

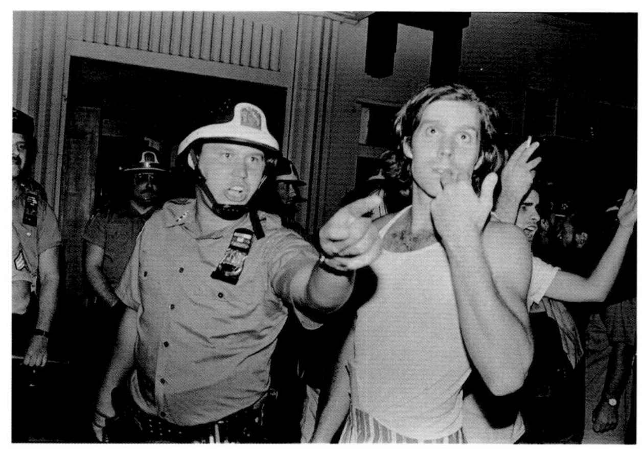

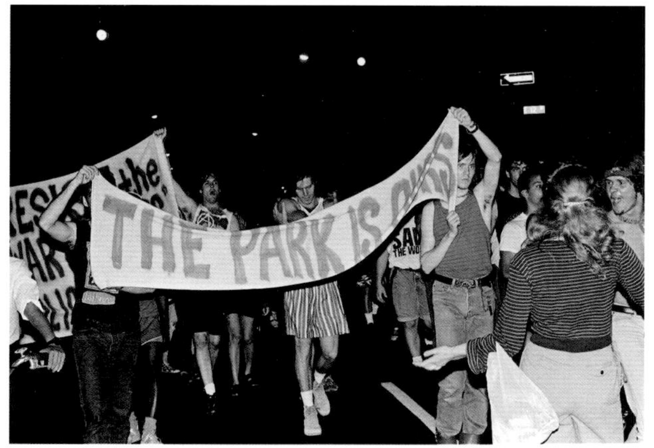

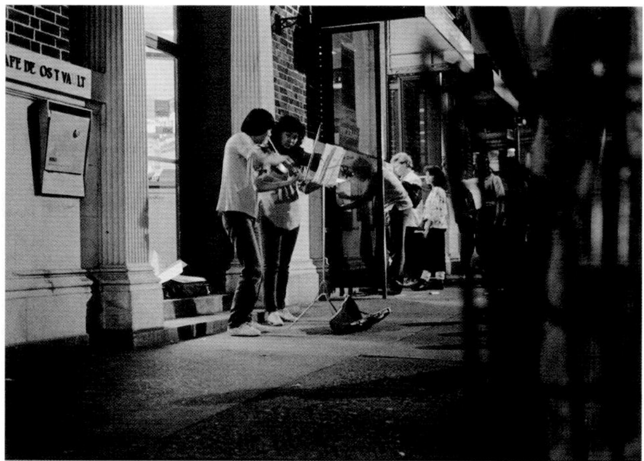

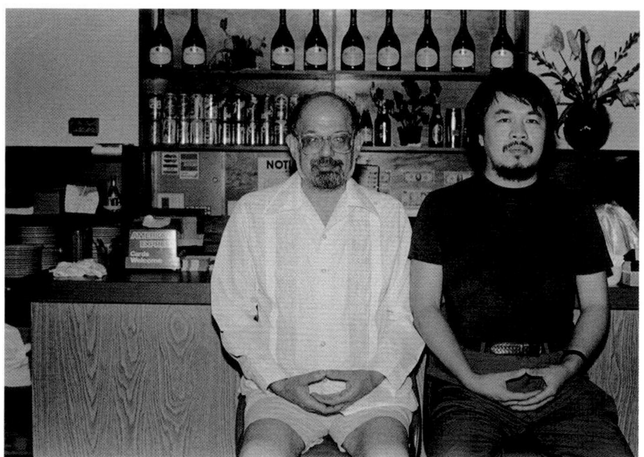

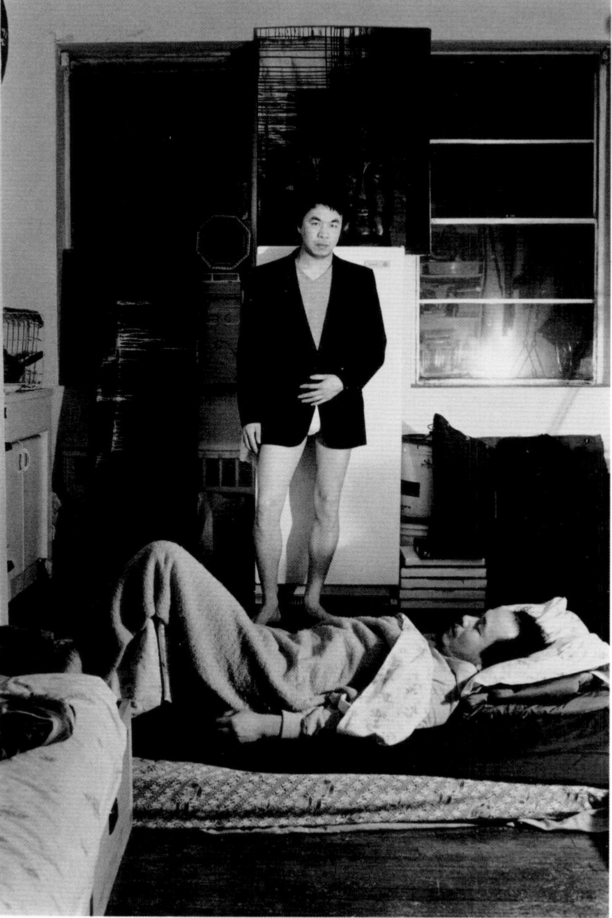

Washington Square Park Protest, 1988, from the series New York Photographs 1983–1993. Black-and-white photograph (top left)

Tompkins Square Park protests, 1988 (top right)

Hu Yongyan, Xu Weiling. Street Performance in Greenwich Village, 1986, from the series New York Photographs 1983–1993. Black-and-white photograph (center left)

Lower East Side Restaurant, 1988, from the series New York Photographs 1983–1993. Black-and-white photograph (bottom left)

Wang Keping and Ai Weiwei, 1987, from the series New York Photographs 1983–1993. Black-and-white photograph (bottom right)

Good Neighbors 1
Makeshift Camp, Idomeni, Greece, 2015. E. 13th Street and 1st Avenue, Manhattan (opposite)

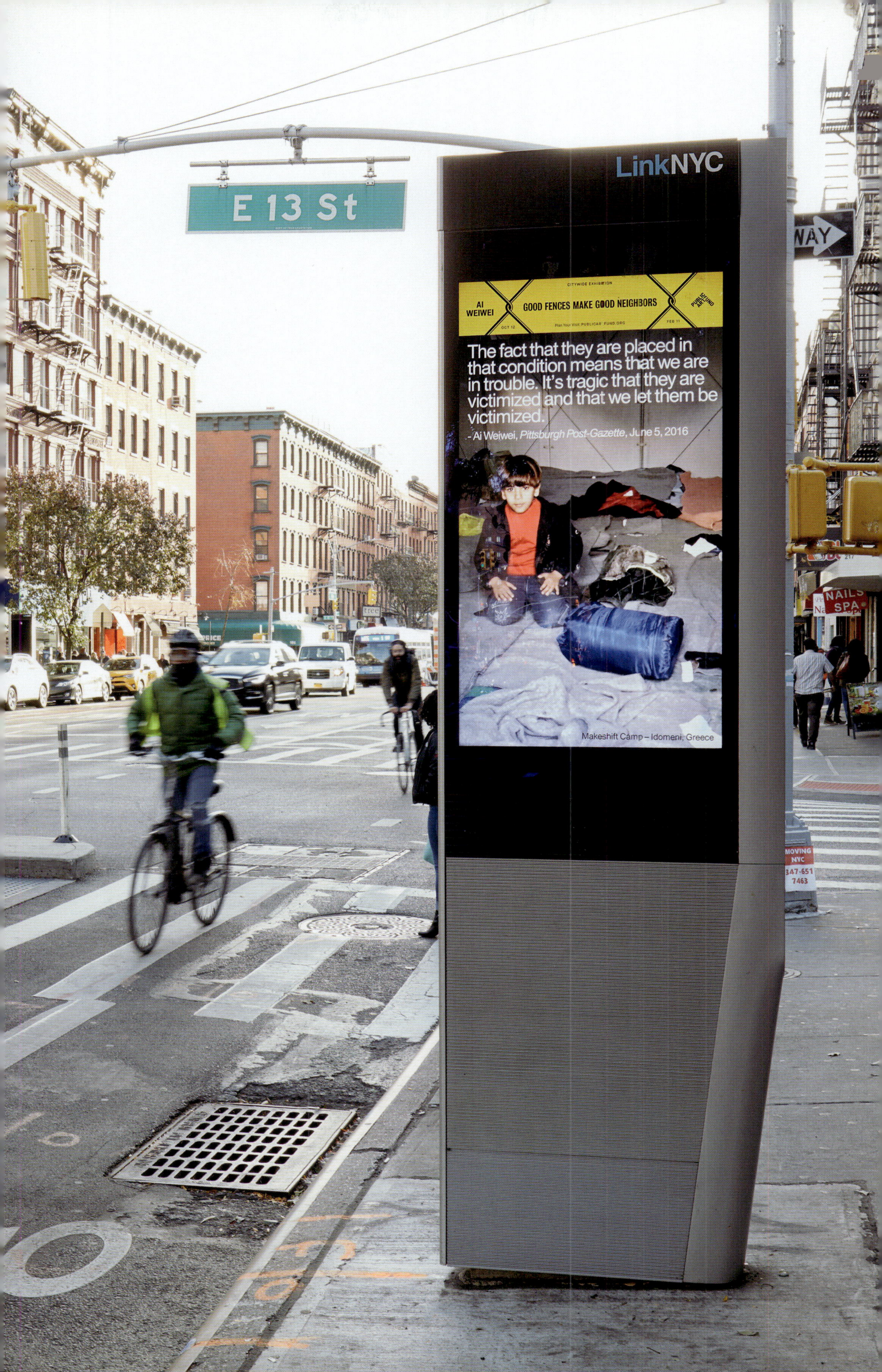
E 13 St
LinkNYC
WAY
AI
WEIWEI
CITYWIDE EXHIBITION
GOOD FENCES MAKE GOOD NEIGHBORS
PUBLIC ART FUND
OCT 12
Plan Your Visit: PUBLICARTFUND.ORG
FEB 11
The fact that they are placed in that condition means that we are in trouble. It's tragic that they are victimized and that we let them be victimized.
- Ai Weiwei, Pittsburgh Post-Gazette, June 5, 2016
Makeshift Camp – Idomeni, Greece
NAILS SPA
MOVING
NYC

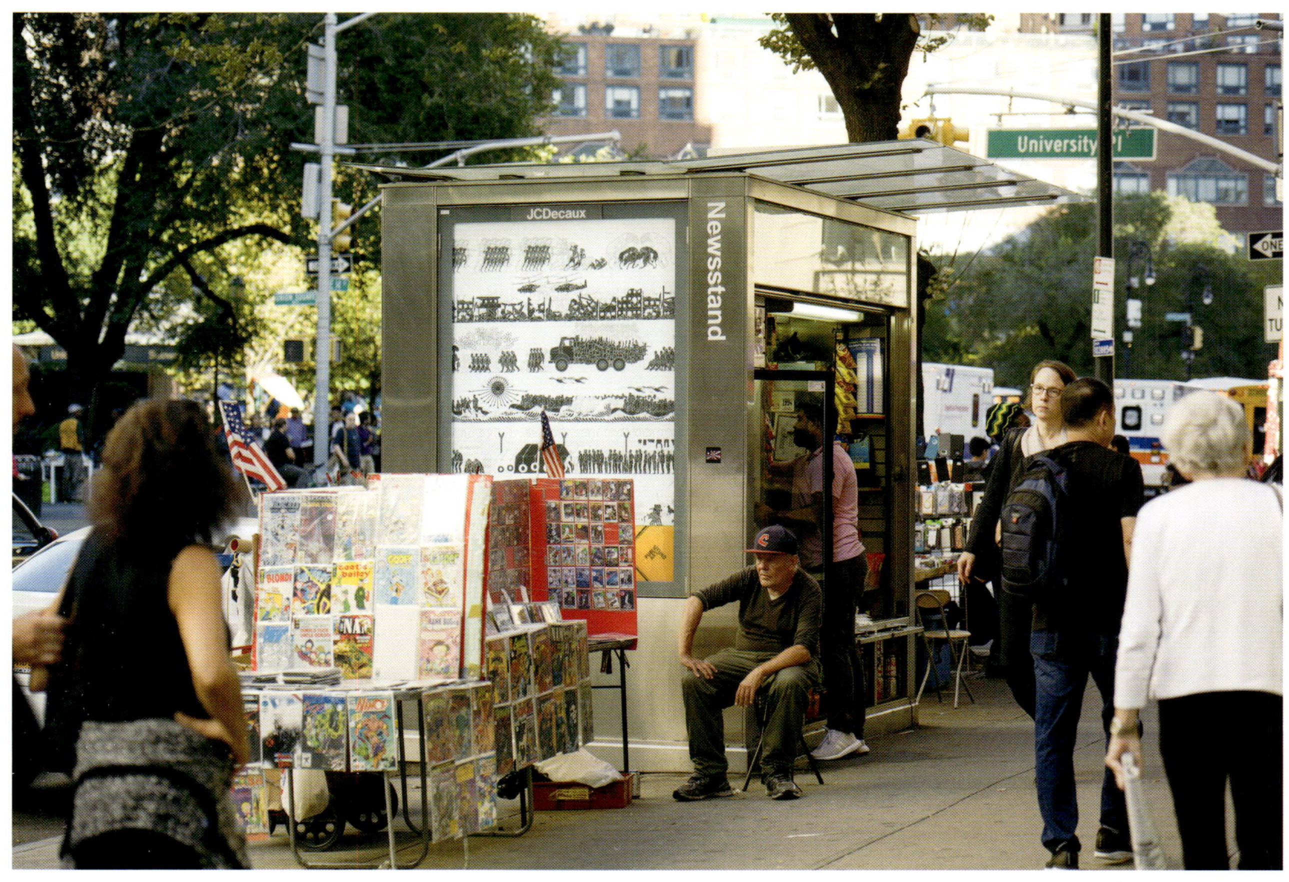

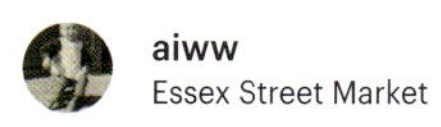

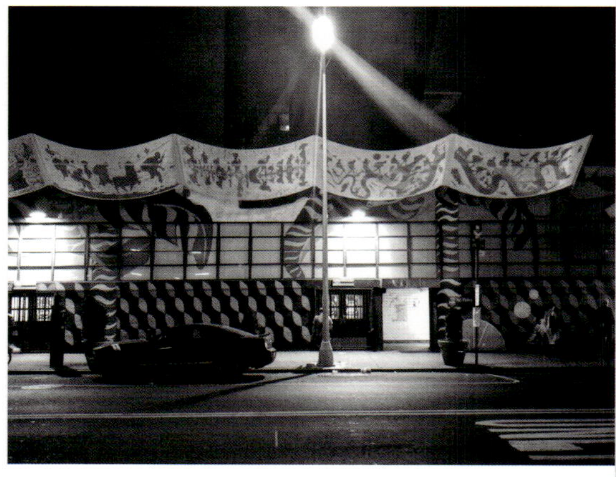

643 Likes

aiww @publicartfund #goodfences #humanflow @humanflowmovie

furryalligator

OCTOBER 8, 2017

Odyssey 3 (top)

Social media post, *Exodus* (bottom)

Banner 52
Walter Gropius, 1919 (opposite)

ELDRIDGE ST & STANTON ST

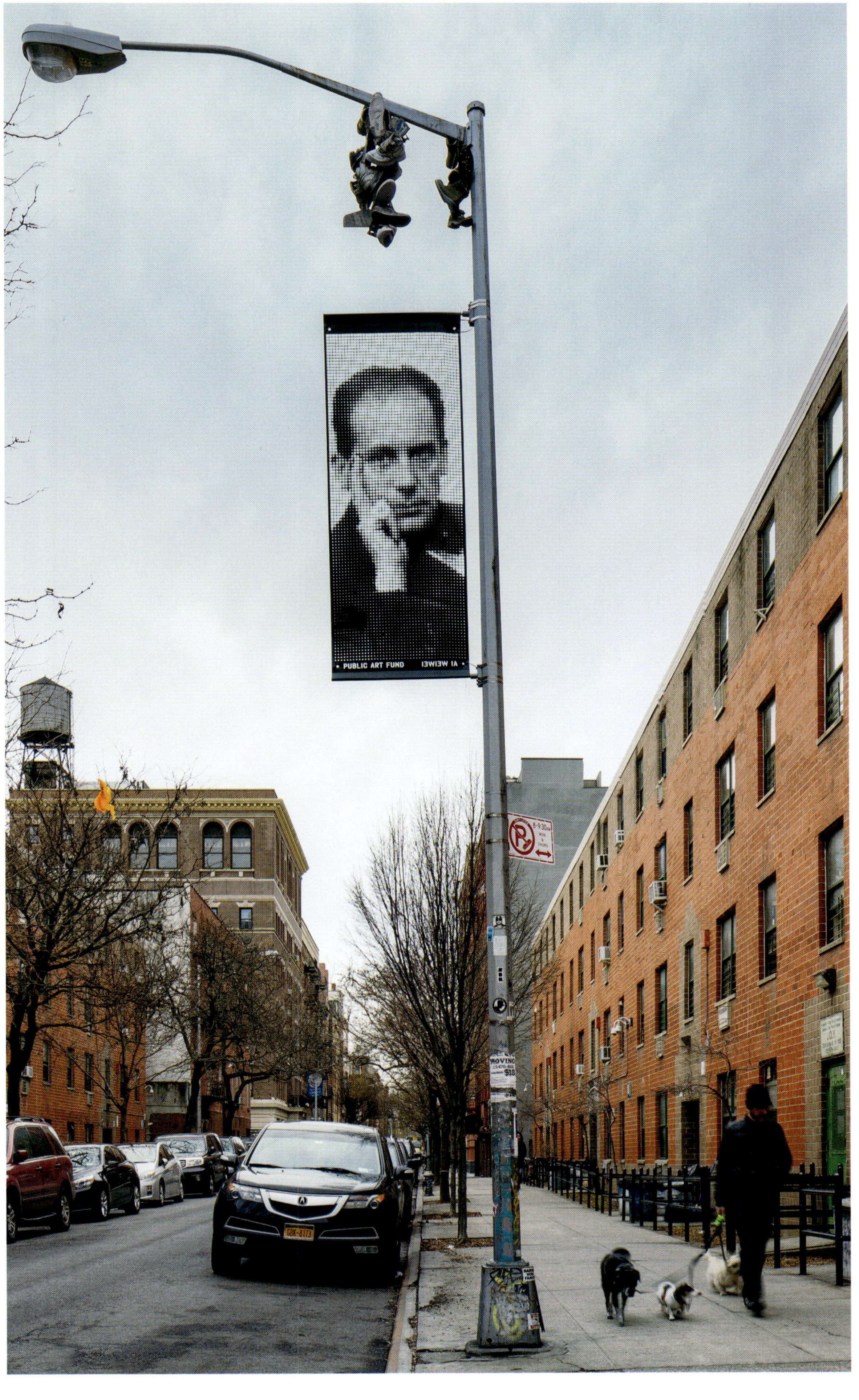

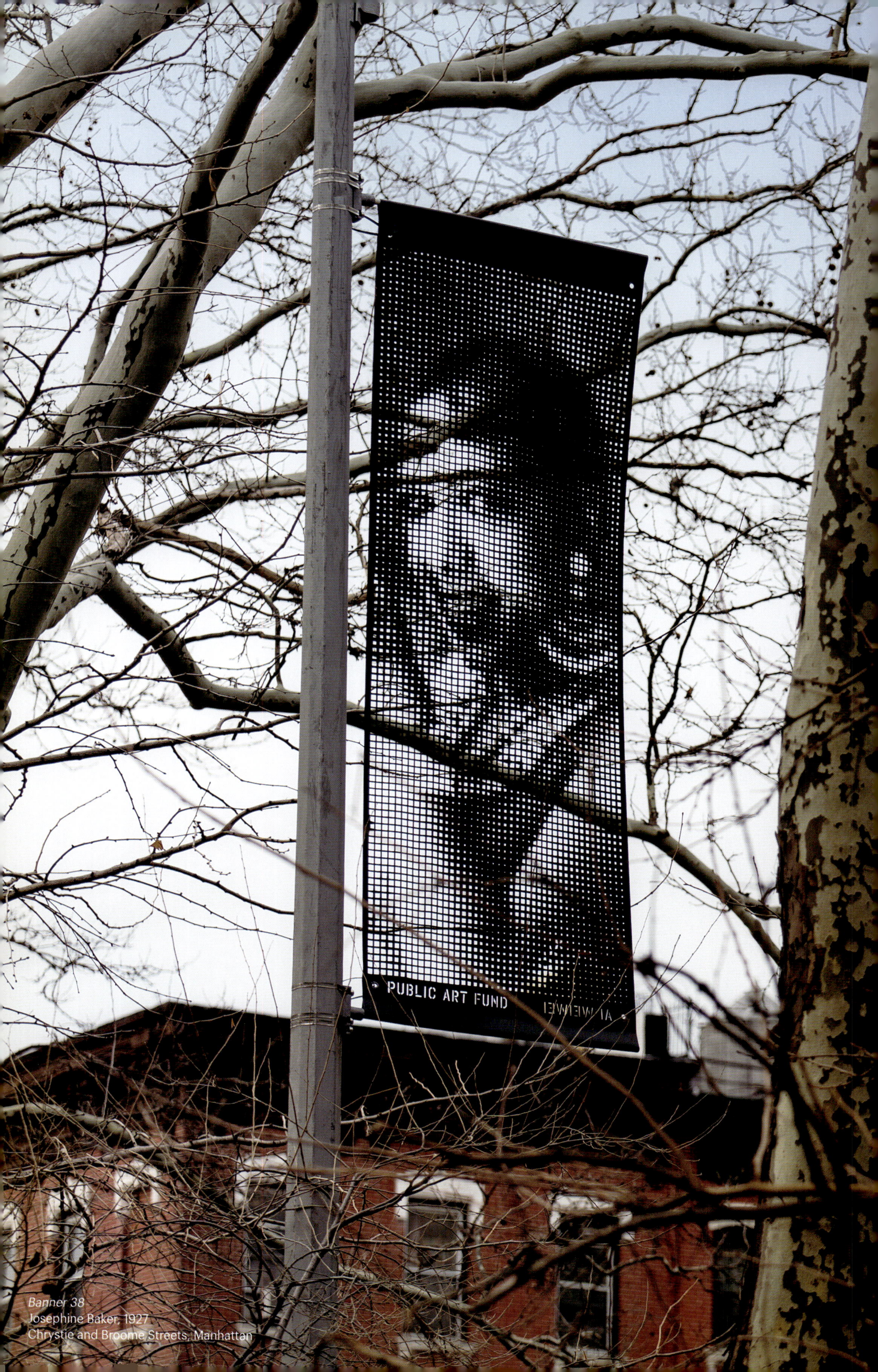

Banner 38
Josephine Baker, 1927
Chrystie and Broome Streets, Manhattan

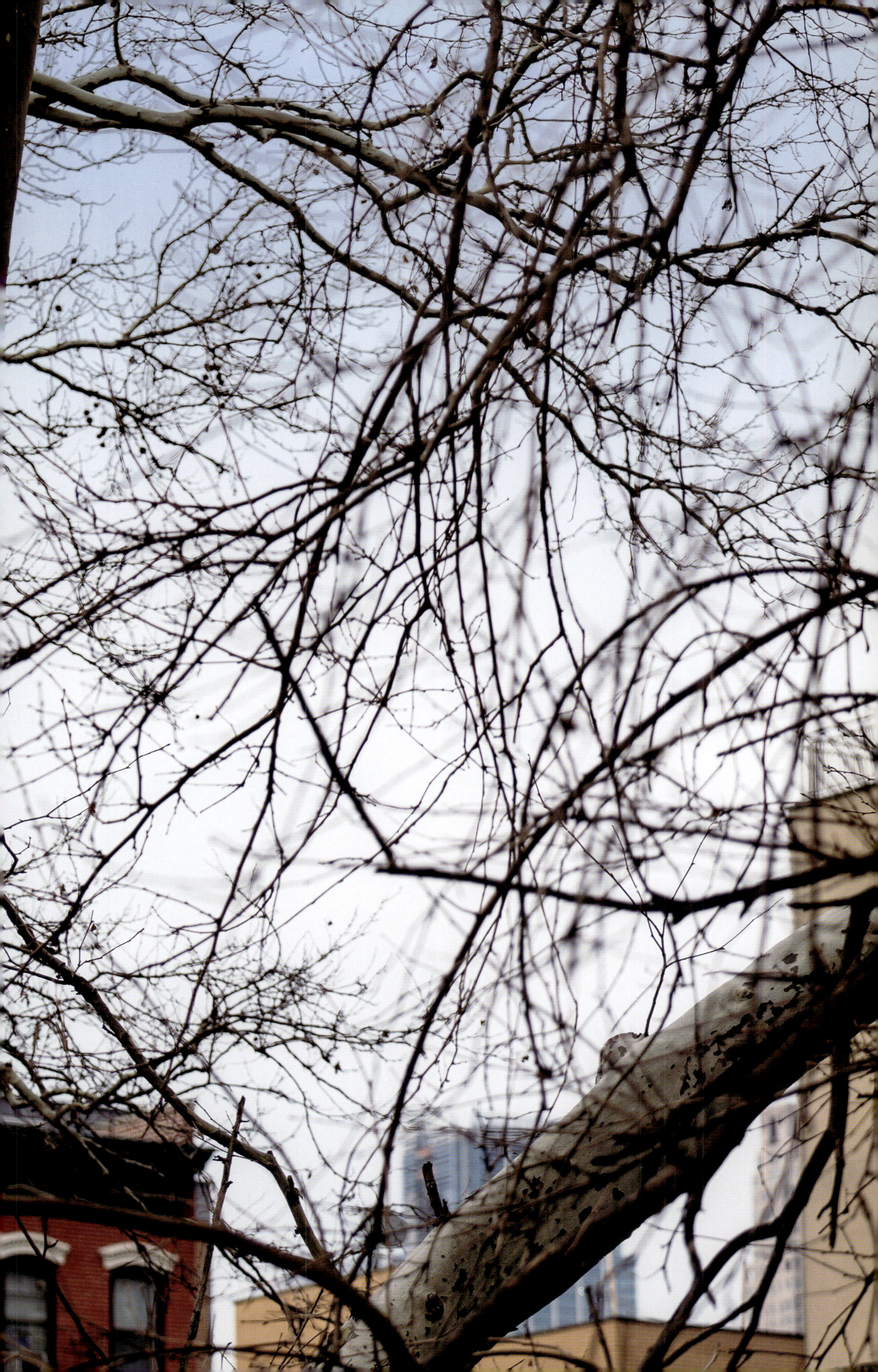

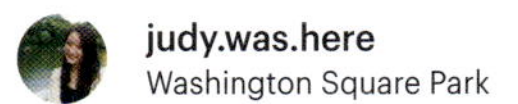

judy.was.here
Washington Square Park

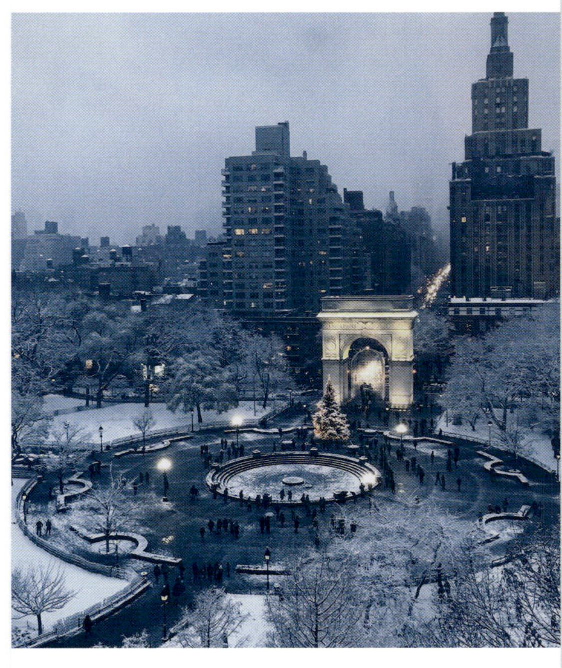

166 Likes

judy.was.here ❄

#hashtagnyu #nyu #newyork #newyorkcity

what_i_saw_in_nyc Awesome

mitzgami Awesome capture! Great POV. 👏👏👏👏

justine_nyc Beautiful shot

DECEMBER 9, 2017

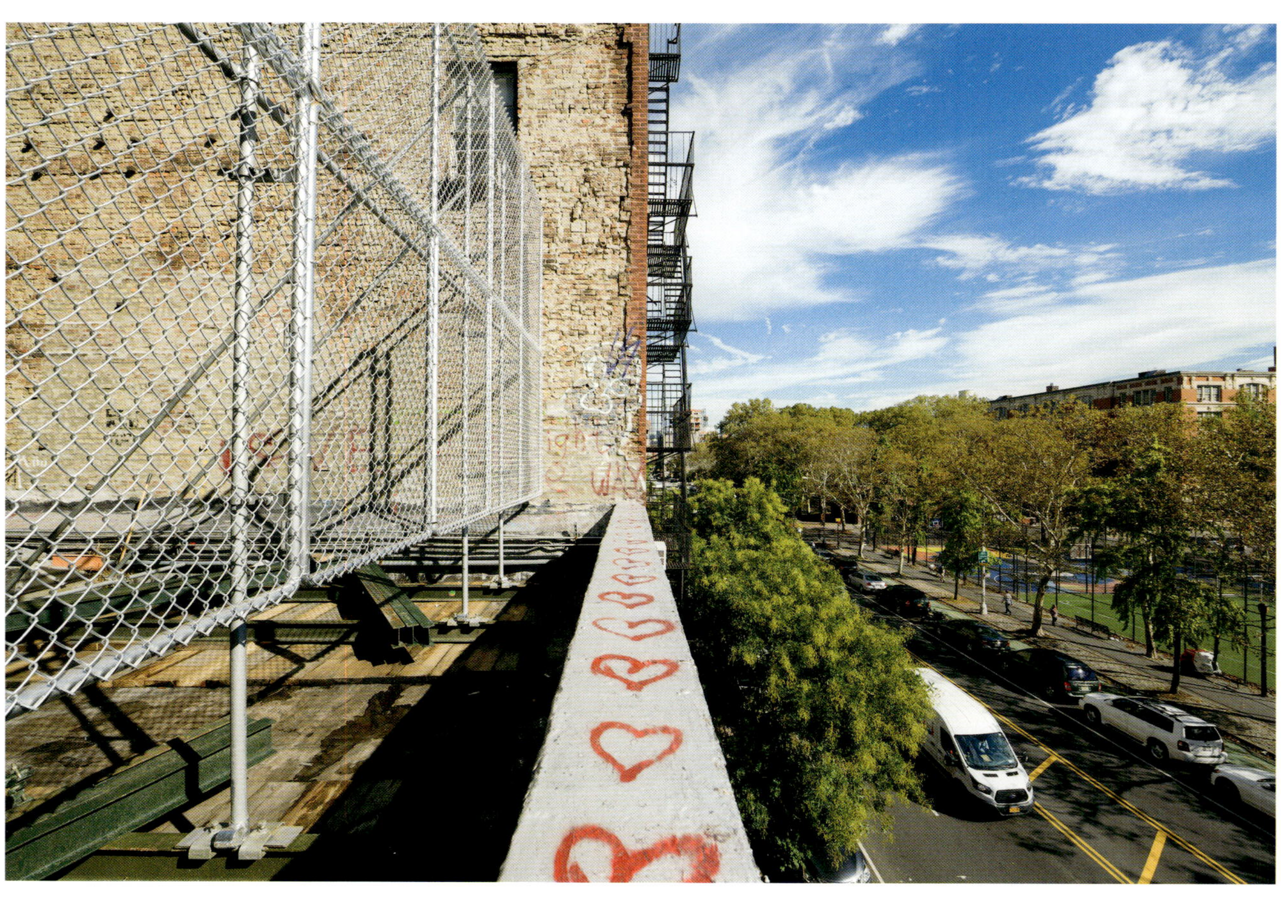

CHRYSTIE ST & E HOUSTON ST

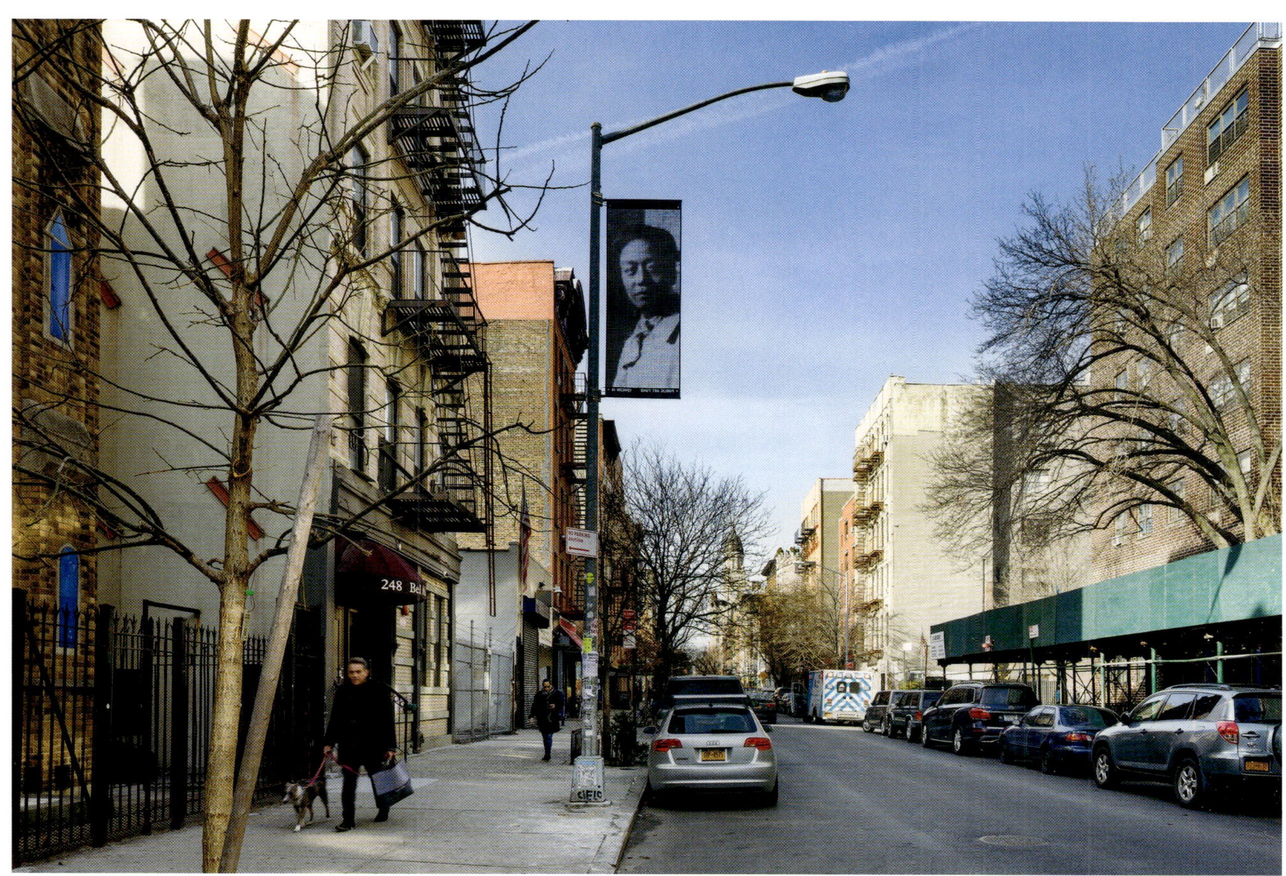

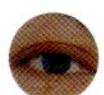

thesceneinnyc
East Village

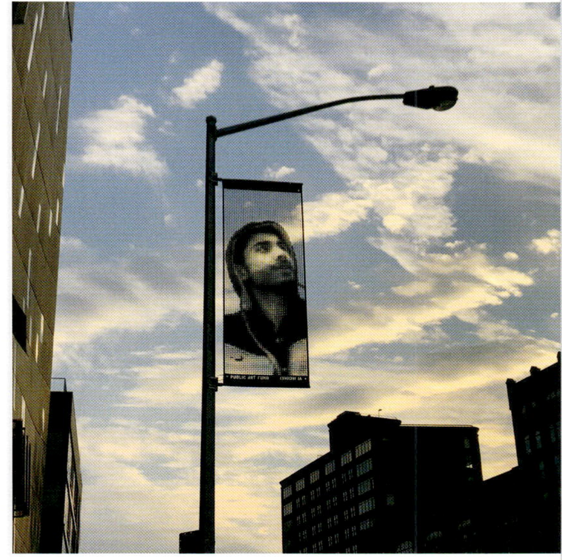

1,000 Likes

thesceneinnyc Cloud watching by @aiww #goodfencesmakegoodneighbors #goodfences @publicartfund

thesceneinnyc #aiweiwei #publicart #urbanart #streetart #thesceneinnyc #newyorkcity #ig_nyc #ig_nycity #igersofnyc #igersnyc #instanyc #instagramnyc #icapture_nyc #nycprimeshot #nycprime_ladies #imagesofnyc #newyork_ig #nypix #nbc4ny #abc7ny #cbsnewyork #timeoutnewyork

JANUARY 11, 2018

Social media post, *Arch* (opposite, top)

Chrystie Street Fence
189 Chrystie Street, Manhattan
(opposite, bottom)

Banner 69
Ai Qing, 1929 (top)

Social media post, *Banner 145*, Refugee, Ferry from Lesvos to Athens, Aegean Sea, Greece, 2016 (bottom)

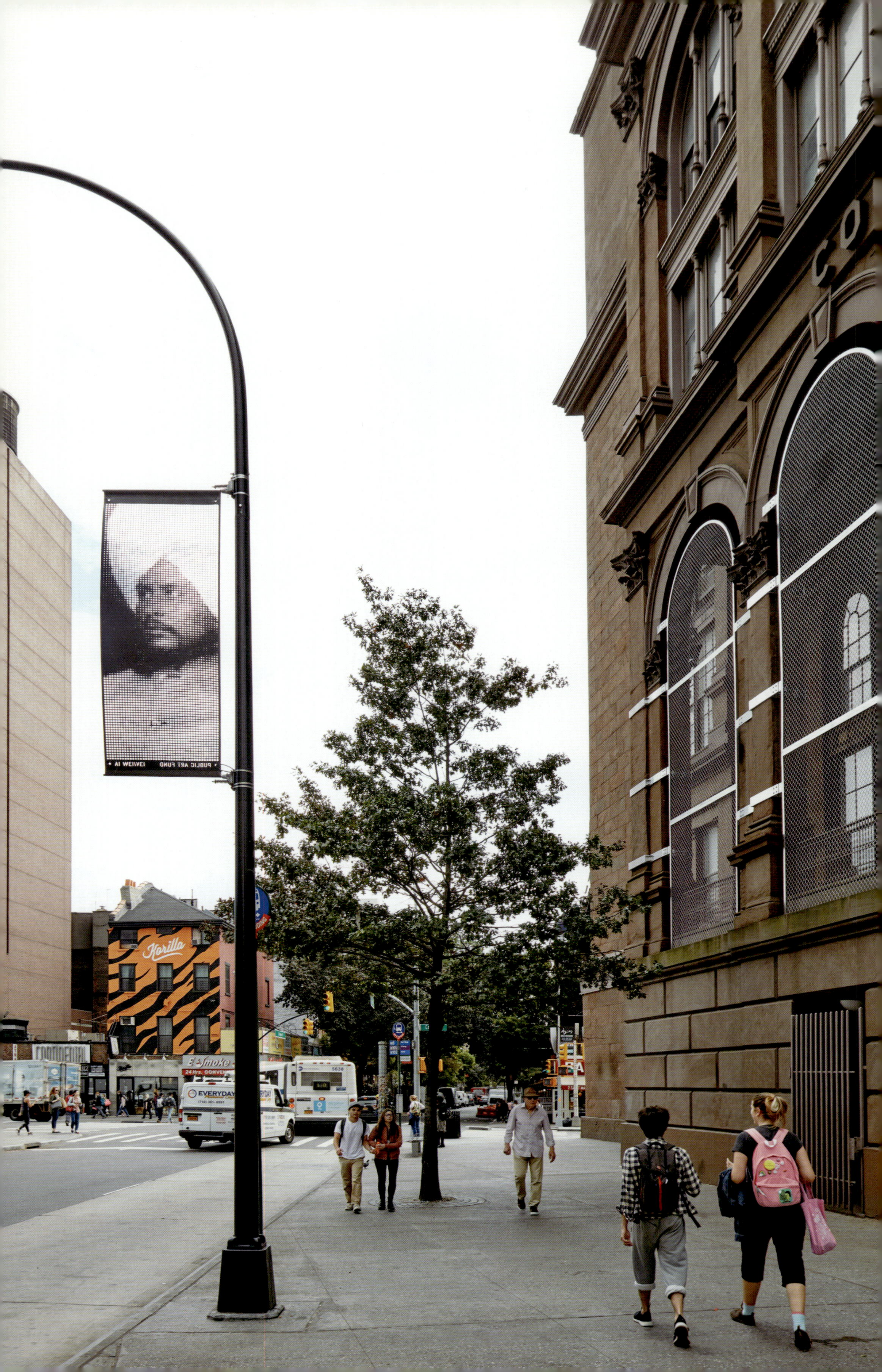
AI WEIWEI
PUBLIC ART FUND
Korilla
EVERYDAY
5638

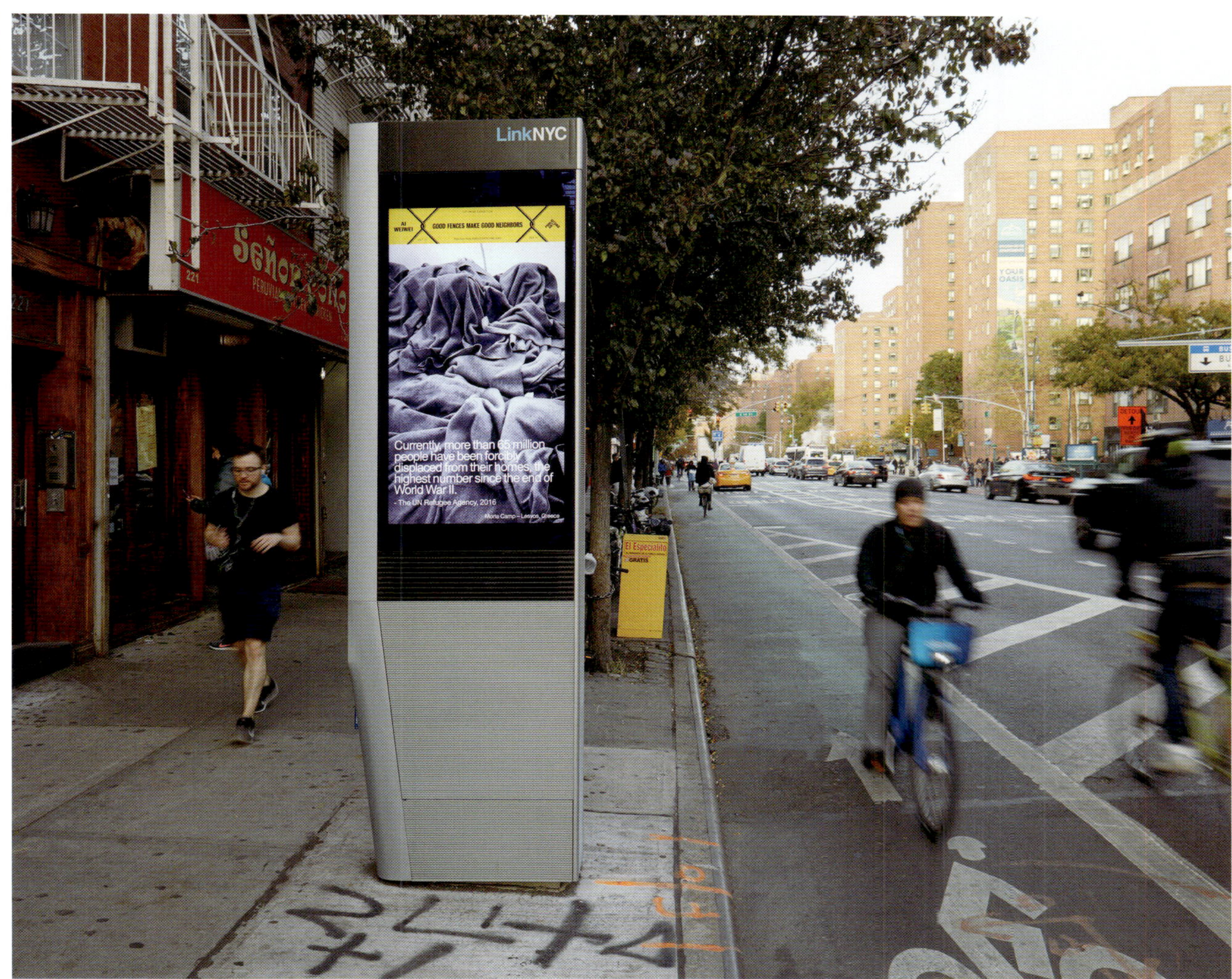

One of the great surprises of this citywide artistic outcry is that Ai Weiwei's obstructions—"very almost-art, but maybe, maybe not"—don't actually disrupt the city very much but plug into the urban fabric of New York with an ease I found disturbing.

Passengers waiting for the bus on 125th Street behind Ai Weiwei's barricades went right on with their commutes. Tourists in Corona Park were taking selfies with a fence in frame. At Cooper Union and in Washington Square Park, metal barriers from the NYPD echoed the artist's own barriers. Ai Weiwei's citywide checkpoints are a hundred muted bells that add up to a deafening alarm: We have accepted so many physical and political limits that new ones go unnoticed, and we may not protest our shrinking freedom until it's too late.

Jason Farago, Art Critic, *New York Times*

Five Fences and *Banner 32*
The Cooper Union for the Advancement of Science and Art, Foundation Building
7 E. 7th Street, Manhattan (opposite)

Good Neighbors 13
(top)

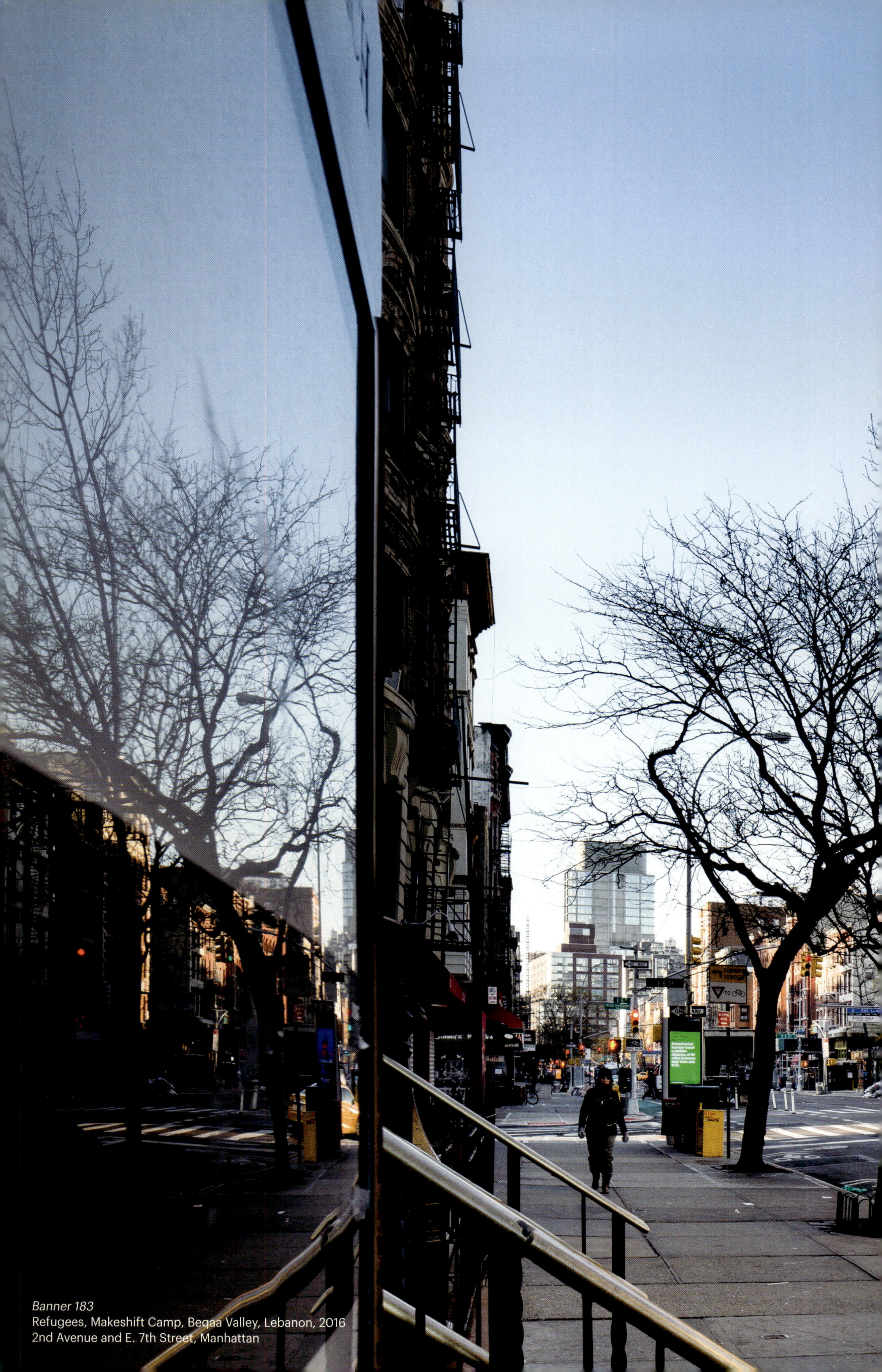

Banner 183
Refugees, Makeshift Camp, Beqaa Valley, Lebanon, 2016
2nd Avenue and E. 7th Street, Manhattan

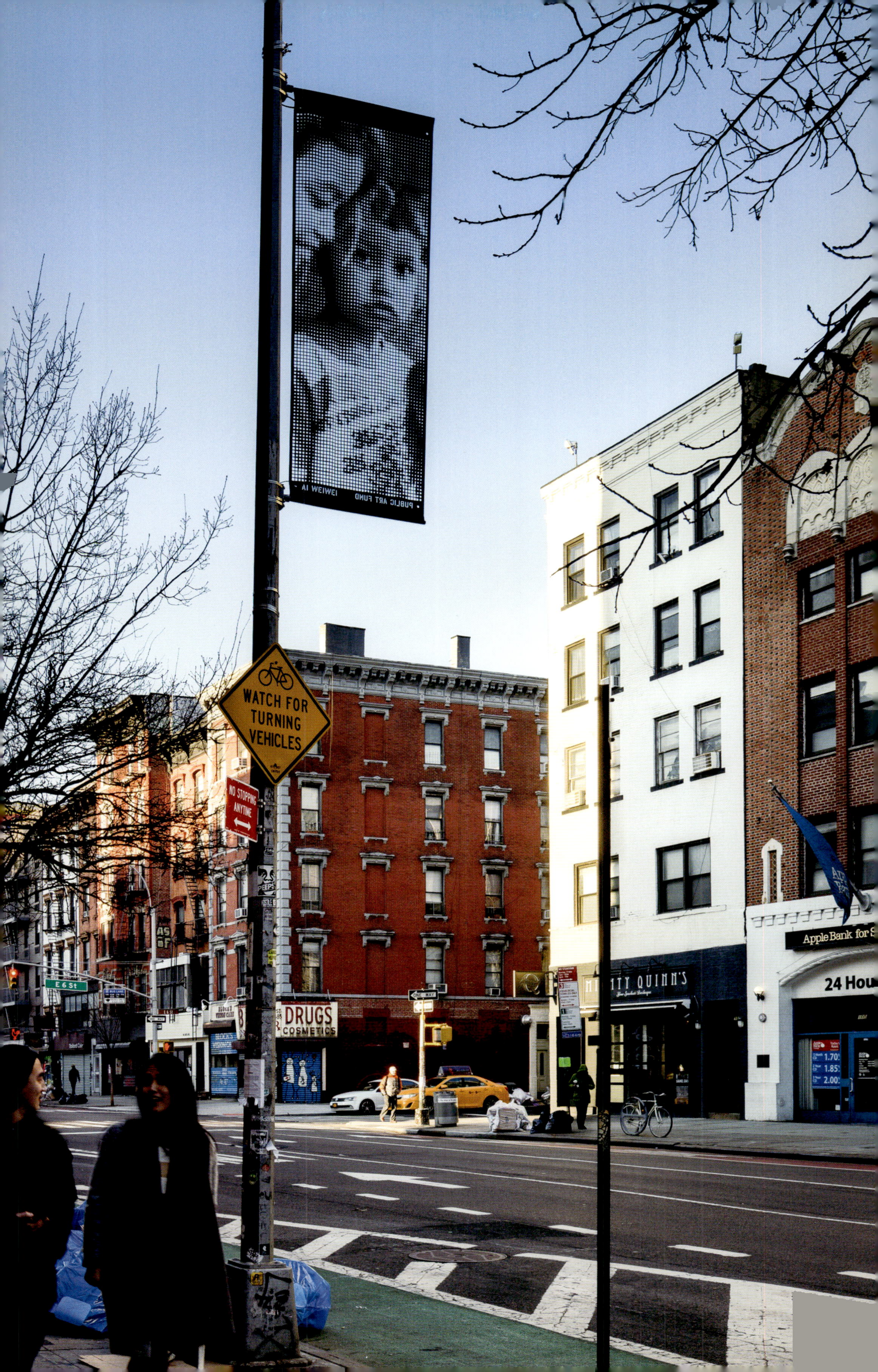
WATCH FOR TURNING VEHICLES
NO STOPPING ANYTIME
DRUGS
COSMETICS
E 6 St
Apple Bank for

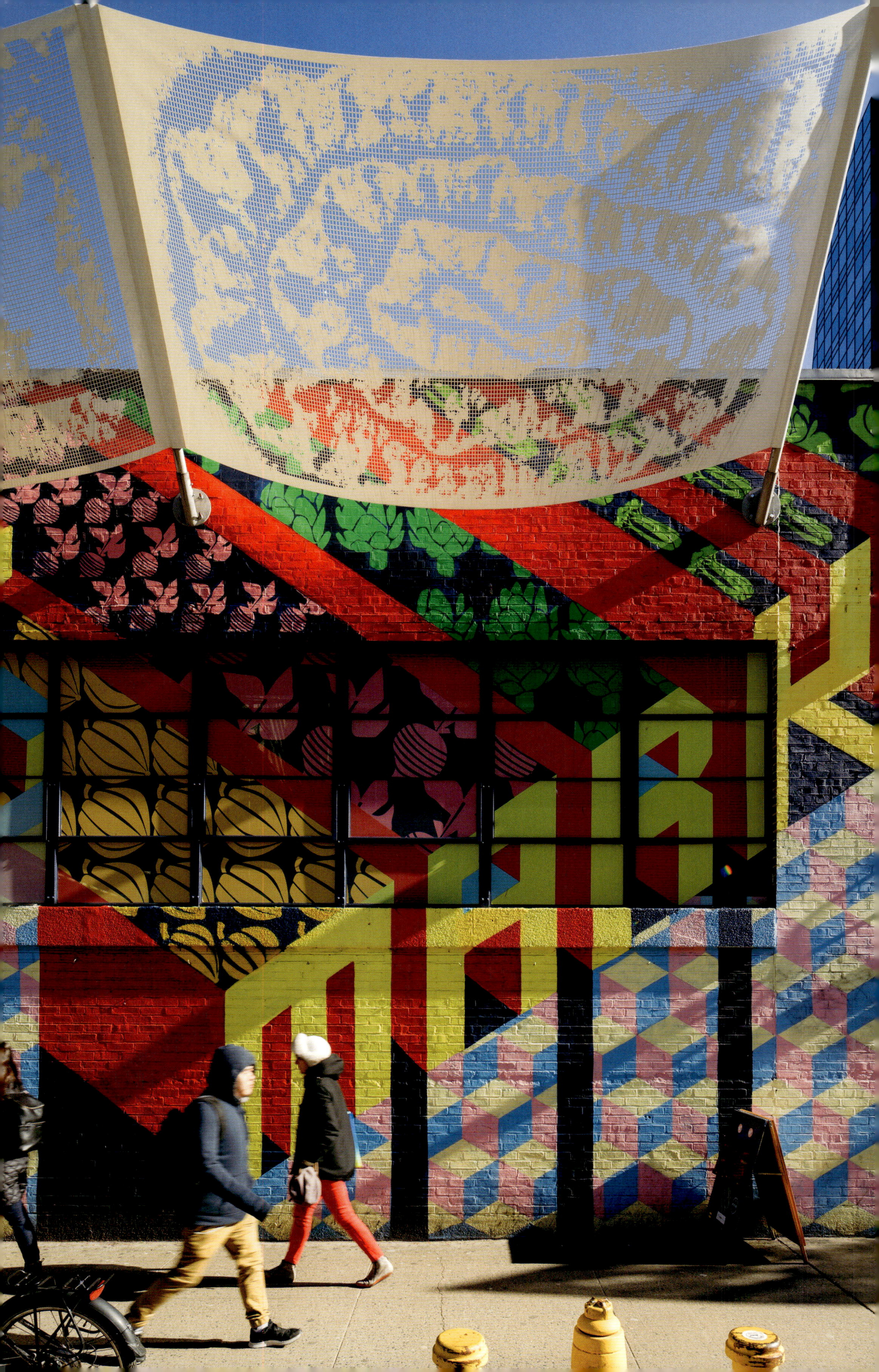

Exodus

120 Essex Street

Installed on the flagpoles of the historic Essex Street Market, *Exodus* was an epic narrative span of illustrated banners depicting refugee flight. The mode of display for this piece was based on the pole-mounted mesh tarps used for shade in the provisional markets that Ai Weiwei saw in Gaza City. This material was a continuation of the laser-cut industrial truck tarp that composed the exhibition's lamppost banners, here realized in white rather than black. Draped in this manner, its cutout forms cast strong shadows on the sidewalk below, in contrast to the building's colorful facade. This work's illustrations evoke the biblical tale of the exodus to suggest global departures of large groups of emigrants around the world, and we see the physical and mental stress of their journeys. They escape warfare and devastation, carrying what they can over vast distances, with children, the sick, and the elderly in their care. Despite constant threats to their survival, they are also driven by hope: flowers, birds, butterflies, and Chinese symbols such as clouds and dragons remind us just how indomitable nature and the human spirit can be. Subtle references to Ai Weiwei's opposition to the Chinese government's authoritarian nature are embedded in the designs, including the Twitter bird (alluding to the social media platform the artist uses extensively to communicate) and the cǎonímǎ, a Chinese internet meme of an alpaca-like creature widely used as a symbolic figure expressing defiance of censorship in China.

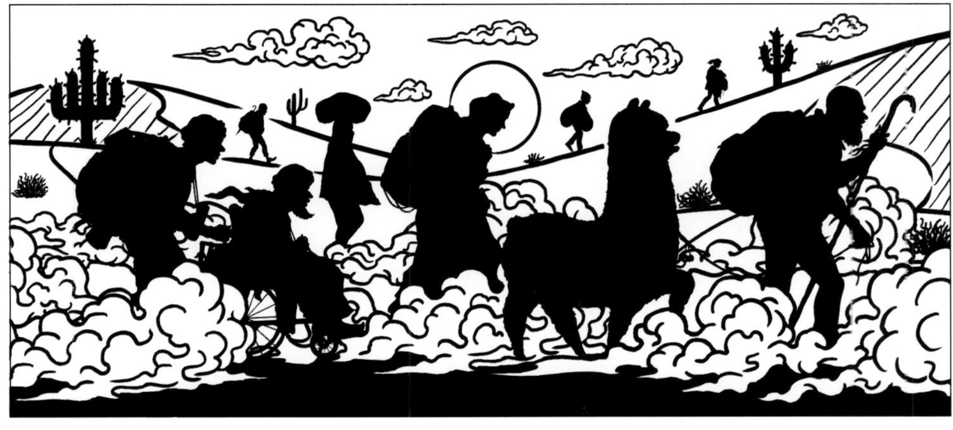

Original design for *Exodus* panel

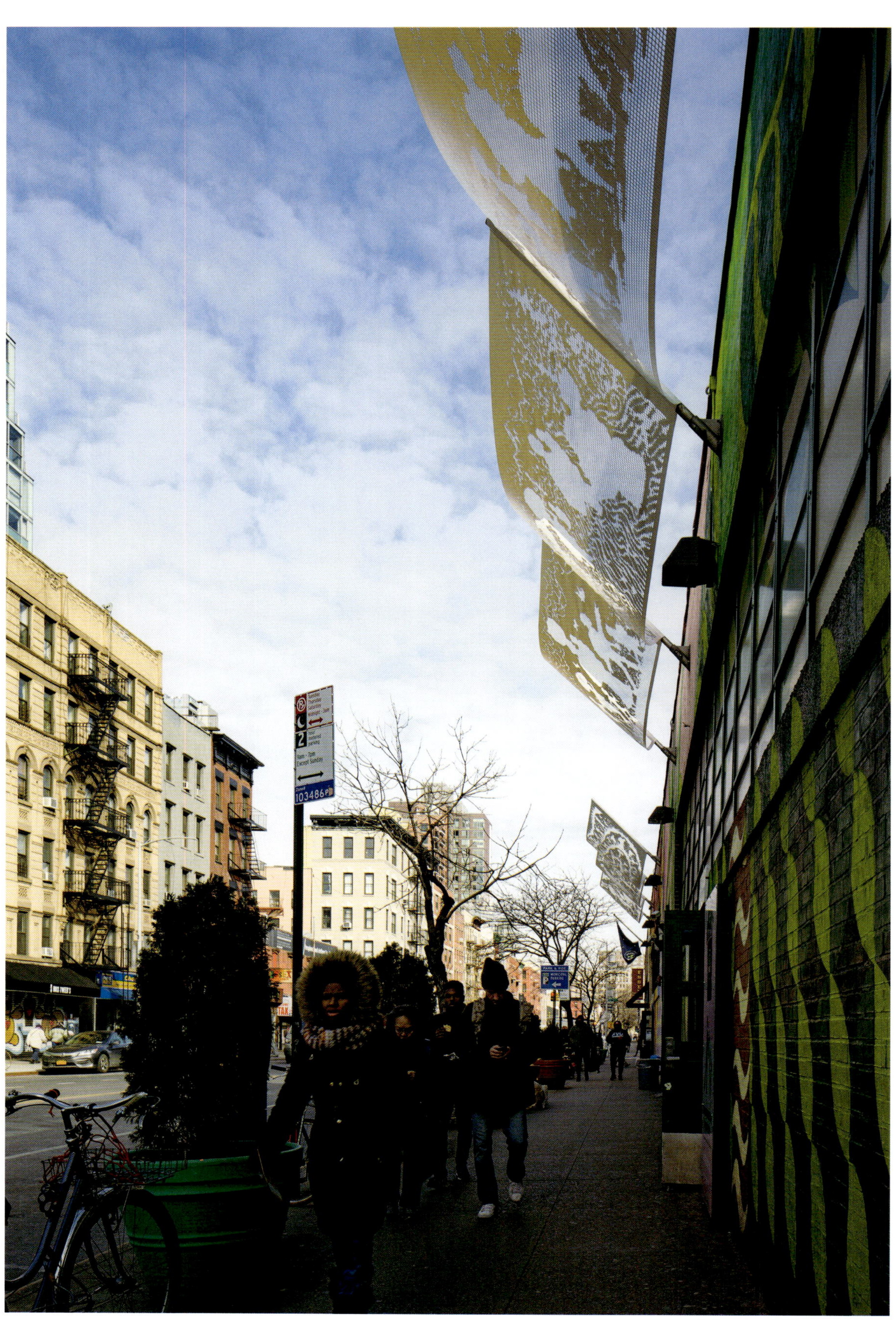

2
9am - 7pm
Except Sunday
103486

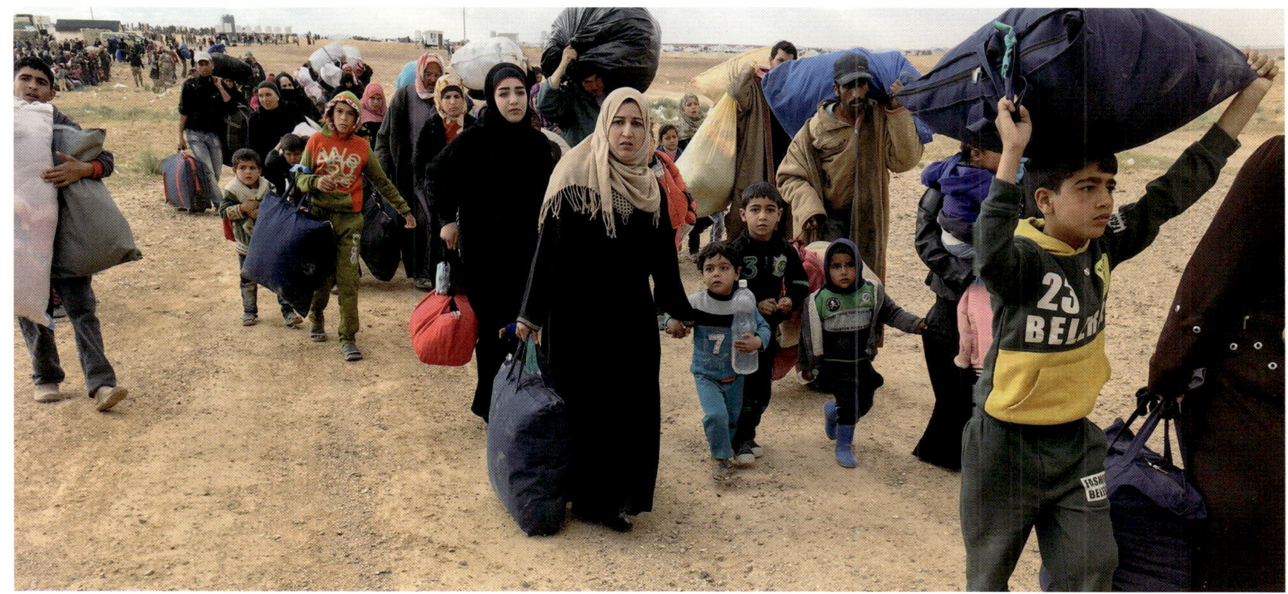

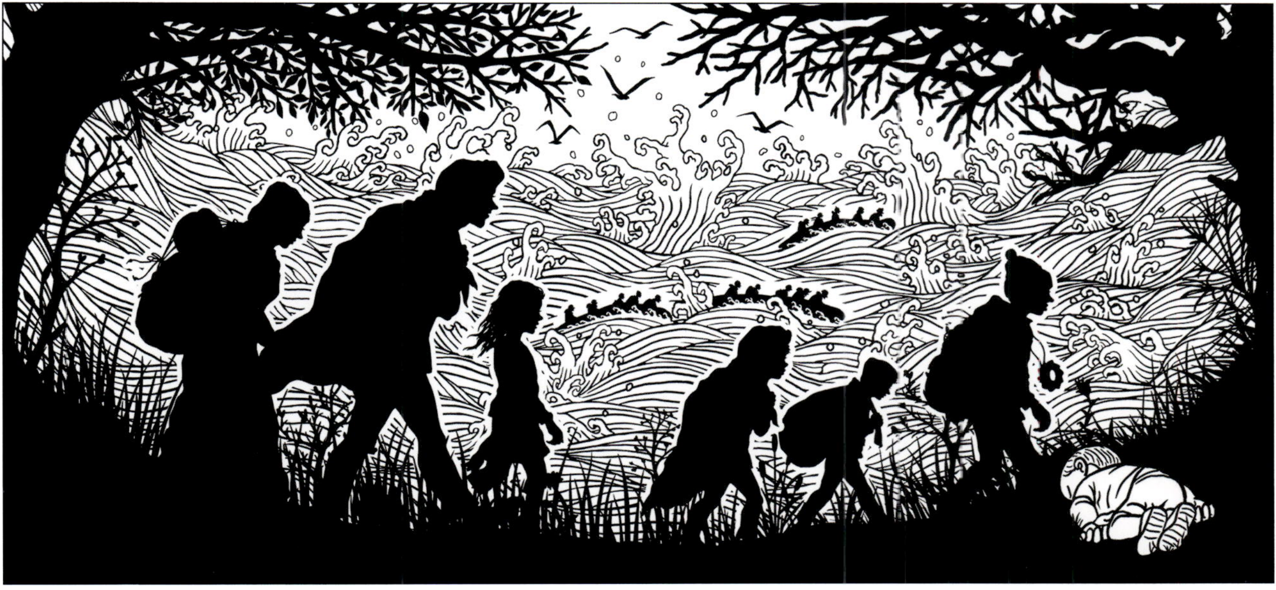

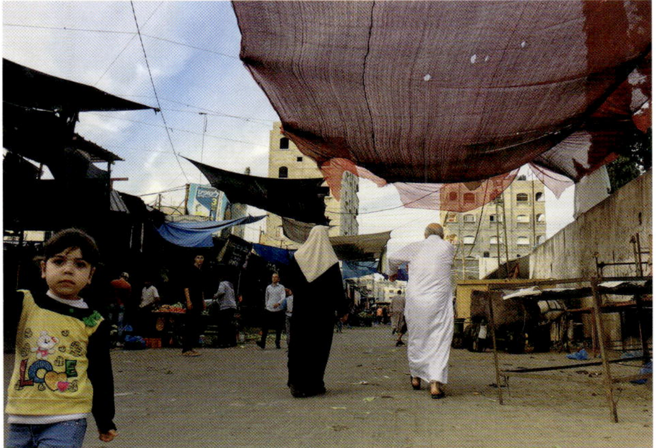

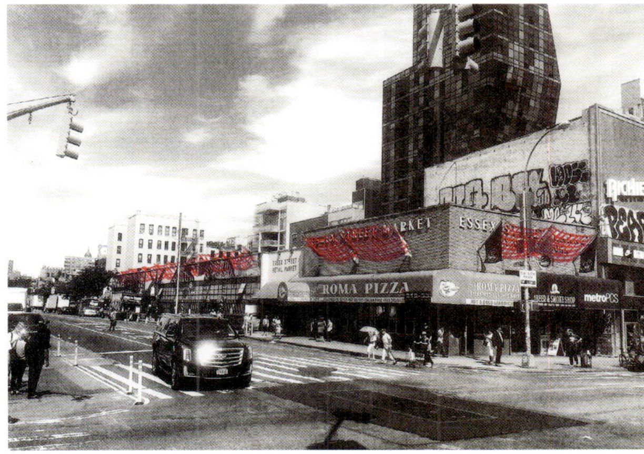

Refugees, Syria-Jordan border, 2016 (top)

Original design for *Exodus* panel (center)

Makeshift market with mesh shadecloth, Gaza City, 2016 (bottom left)

Essex Street Market, concept sketch (bottom right)

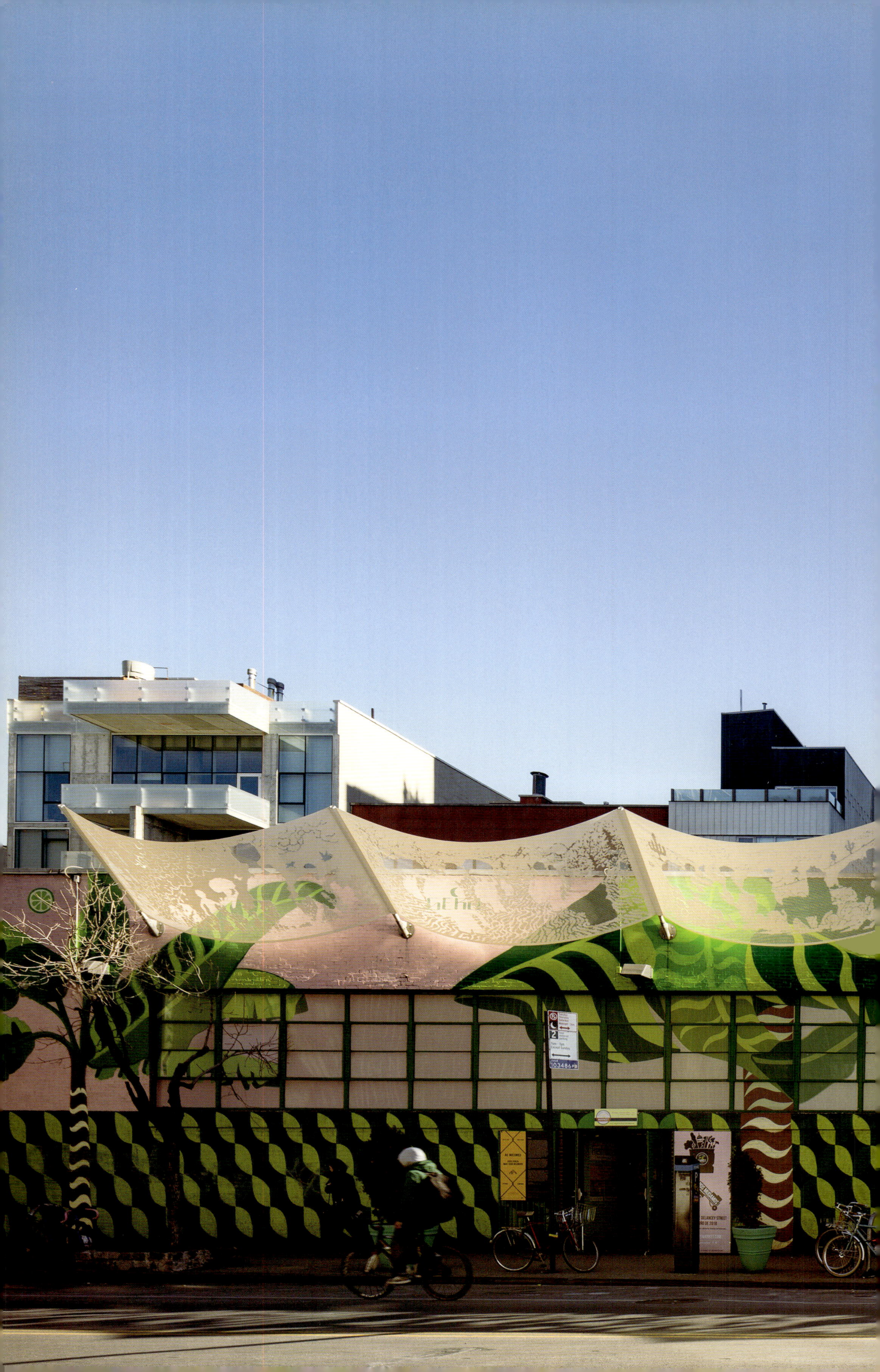

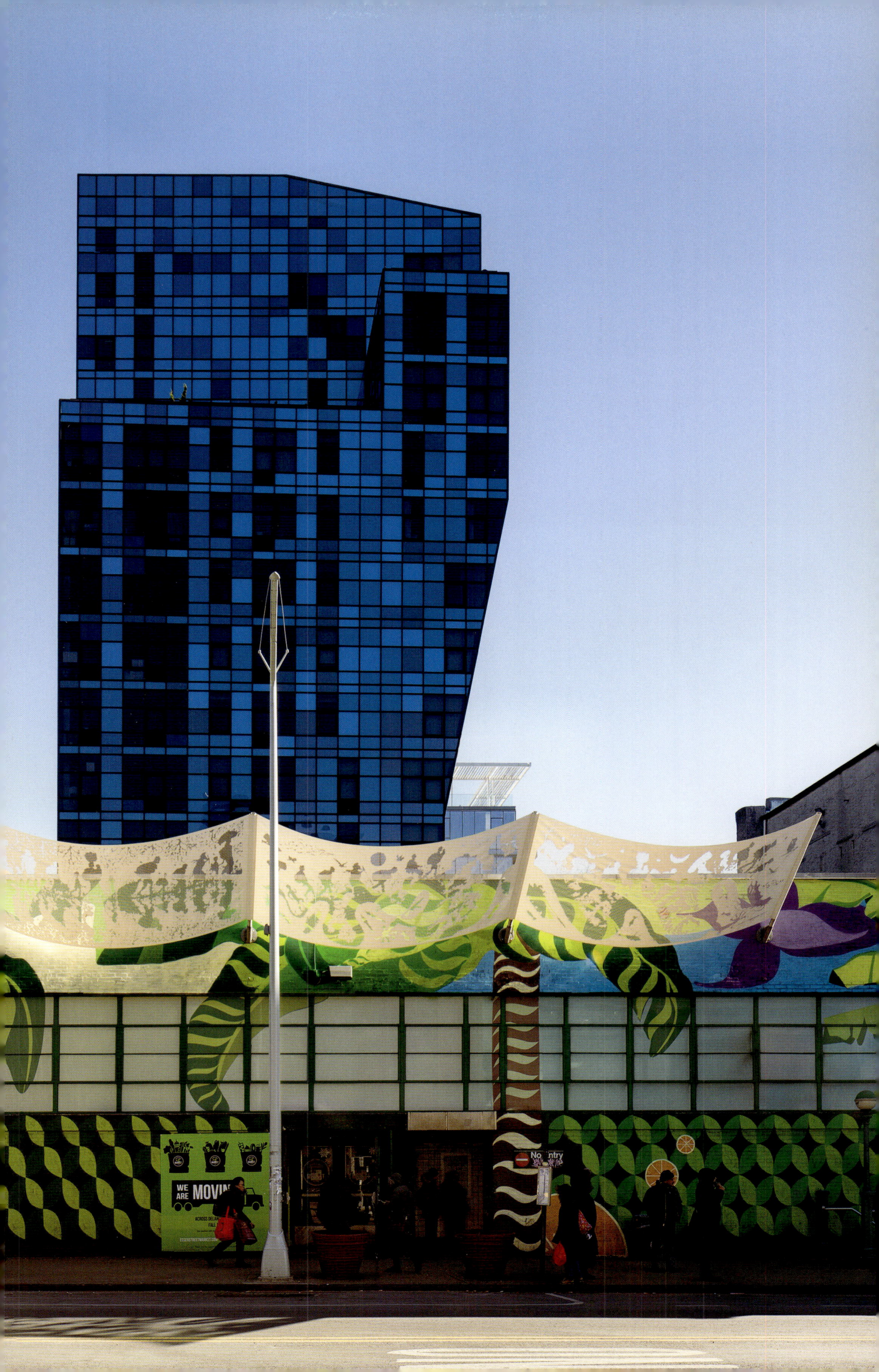
WE ARE MOVIN
No ntry

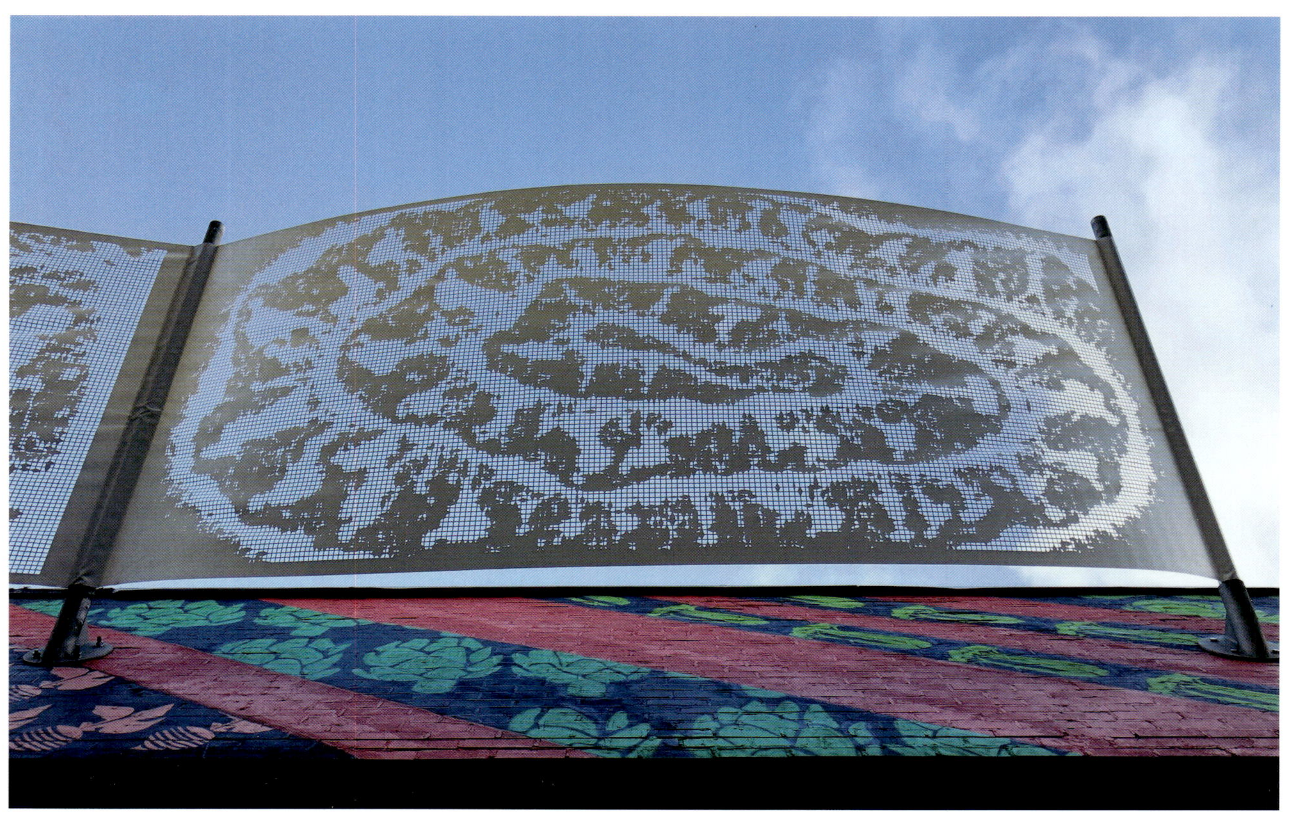

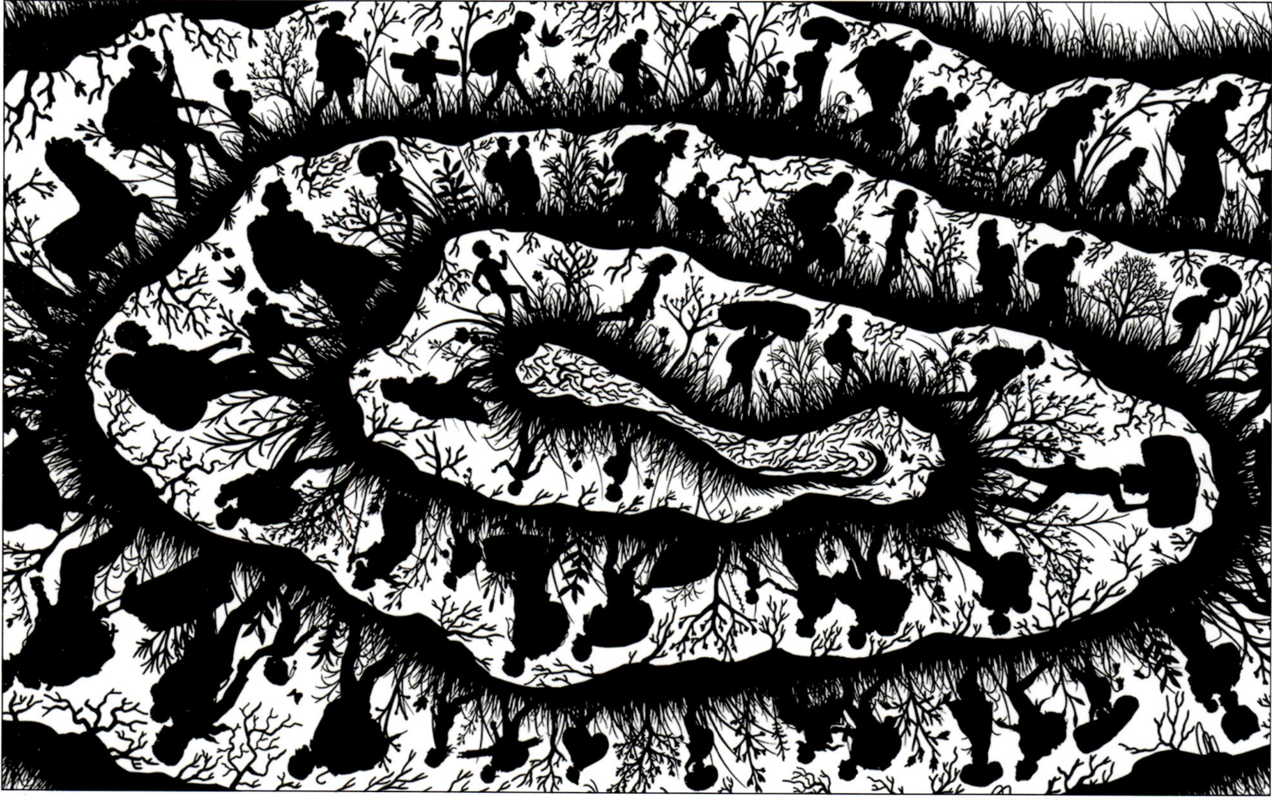

Exodus
Installation on Essex Street Market (top and opposite)

Original design for *Edoxus* panel (bottom)

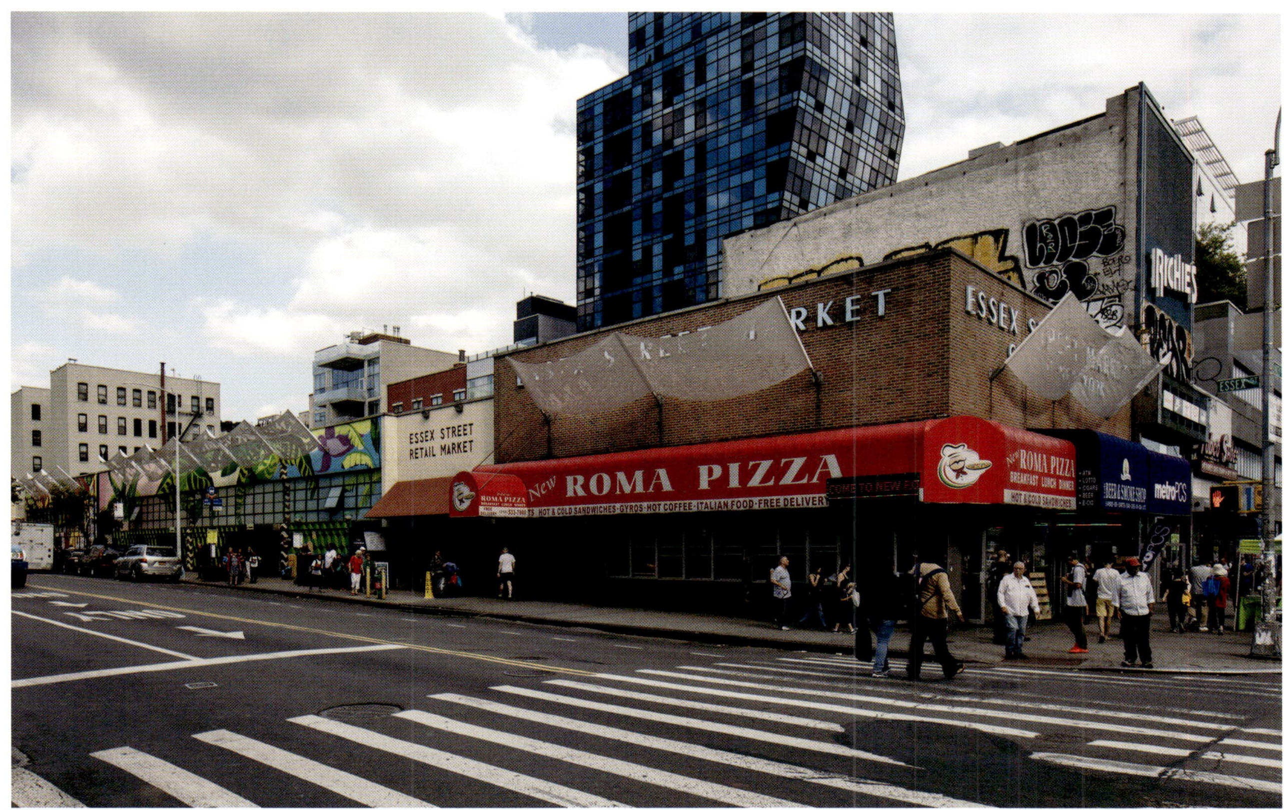

Ai Weiwei writes, "What's important to remember is that while barriers have been used to divide us as humans, we are all the same." This simple message obliterates the logic behind oppression and racism. If *Good Fences Make Good Neighbors* can facilitate a dialogue about how we as Americans can better install compassion and civic virtue into our national fabric, it couldn't come at a more necessary time.

Letitia James, New York Attorney General

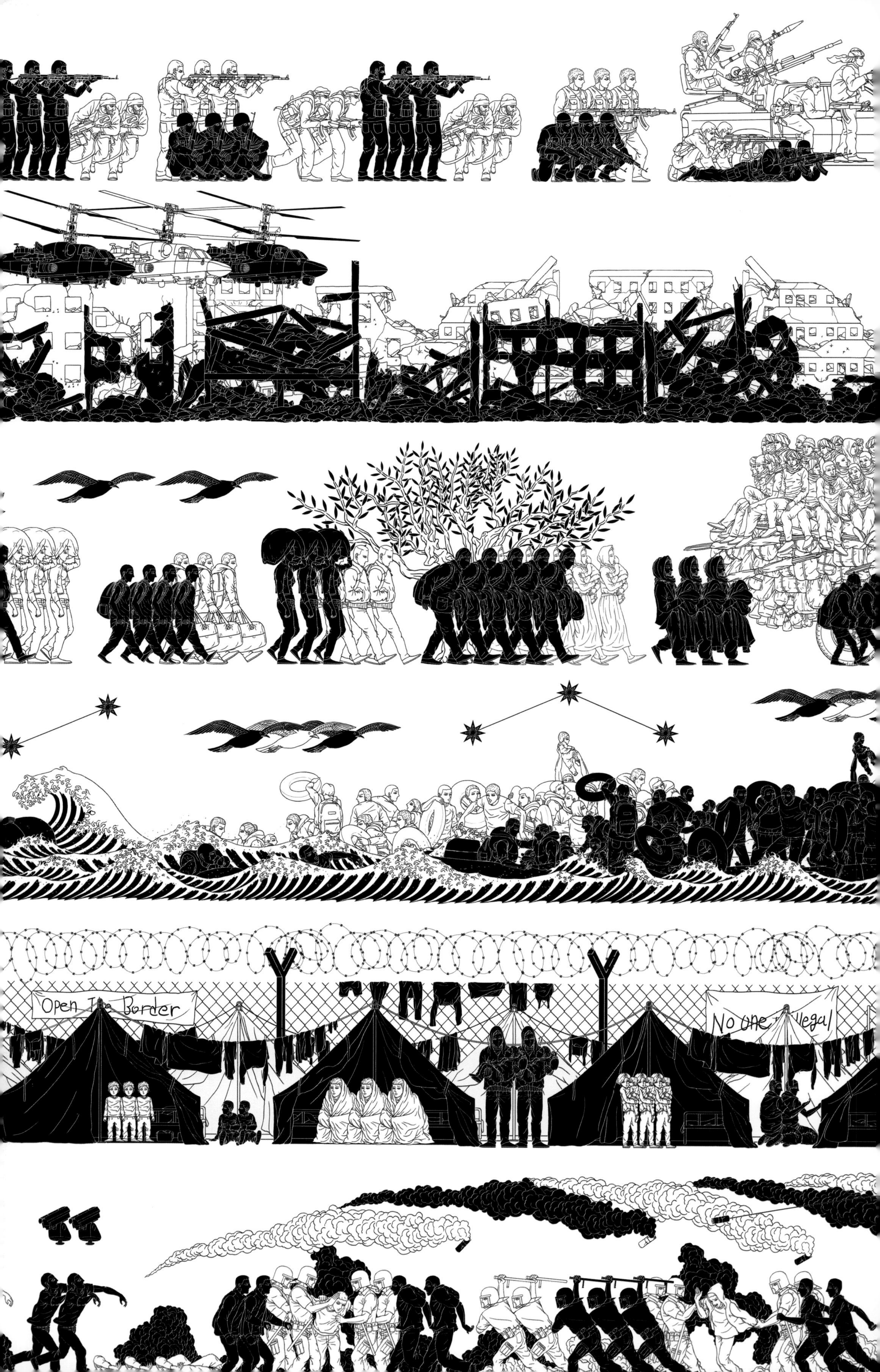
Open The Border
No one
llegal

Odyssey

Five Locations in Downtown and Midtown Manhattan

A classical, Greek-style frieze depicting the many forms of the contemporary global refugee crisis was displayed by the artist in spaces generally reserved for advertising on newsstands. In a mash-up of historical references, *Odyssey*'s stylized imagery evokes black-figure vase painting, ancient Egyptian symbolism, classical Chinese motifs, and Ai Weiwei's own iconic imagery to represent a contemporary epic of war, ruins, perilous journeys, sea crossings, refugee camps with restrictive fencing, and protest demonstrations. Borrowing its title from Homer's epic poem describing the hero's adventures on his ten-year journey home after the Trojan War, this artwork's compelling imagery highlights the struggle and stark conditions that millions of people worldwide face as they are uprooted and forced to flee their homes. The digital prints were exhibited on five newsstand kiosks in Manhattan between Canal and Forty-Sixth Street, and newsstand customers and pedestrians were able to view the arresting graphic images at eye level.

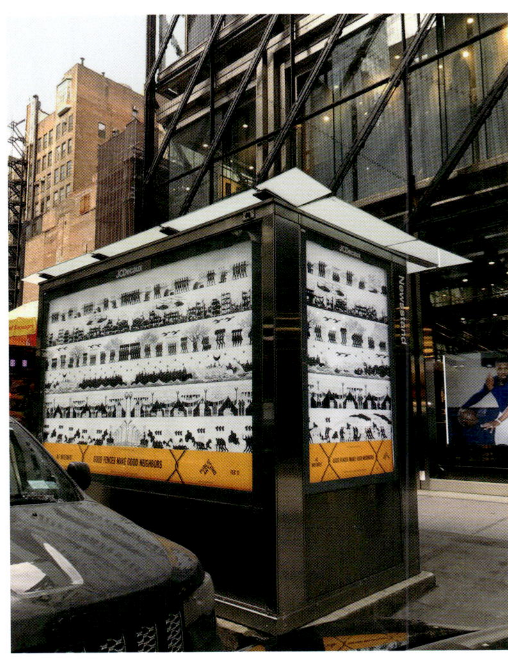

Odyssey 1 side panel (detail)
E. 46th Street and 5th
Avenue, Manhattan (opposite)

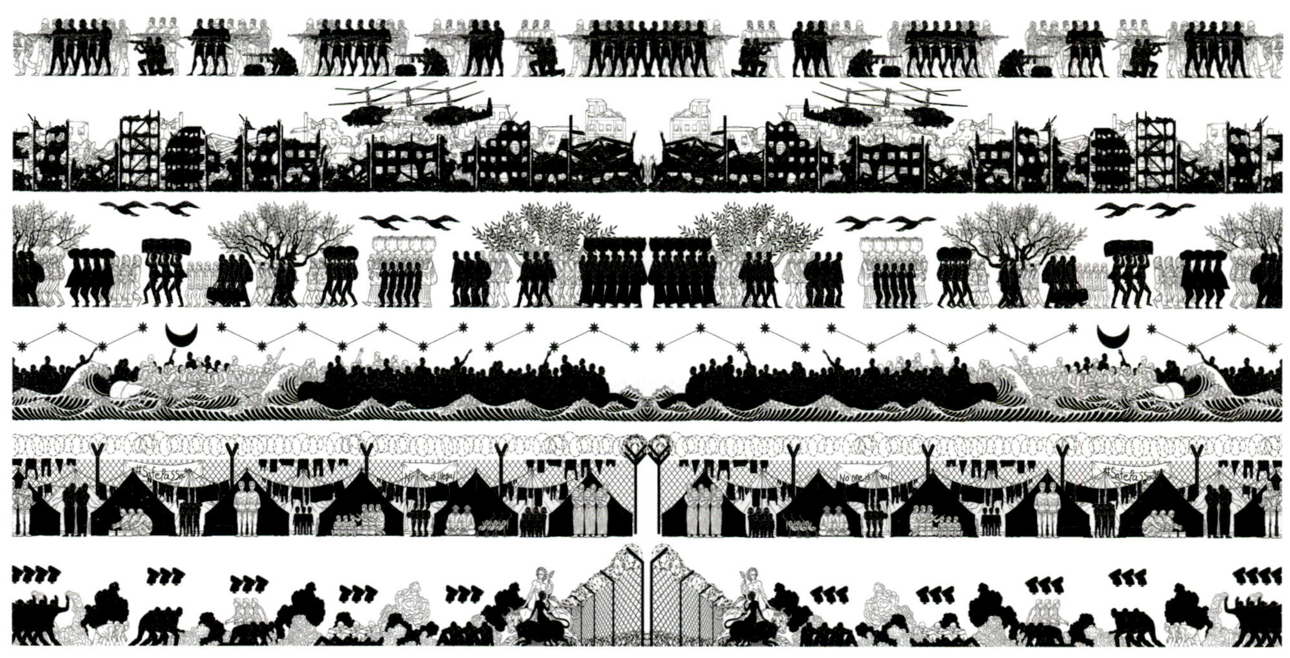

aiww
Canal Steet

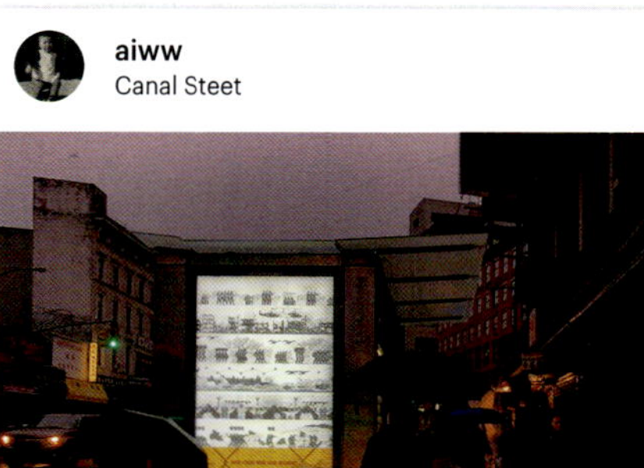

1,580 Likes

iampic2407 Looks just like NY! ★

willnyc Canal Street

anamariachin1 Reminds me of a painting in Paris by painter Gustavo Caillebotte.

albert_perez_studio ☺

aarooswa your pictures are rarely spectacular but always oddly beautiful and interesting. you definitely have a distinct style

JANUARY 18, 2018

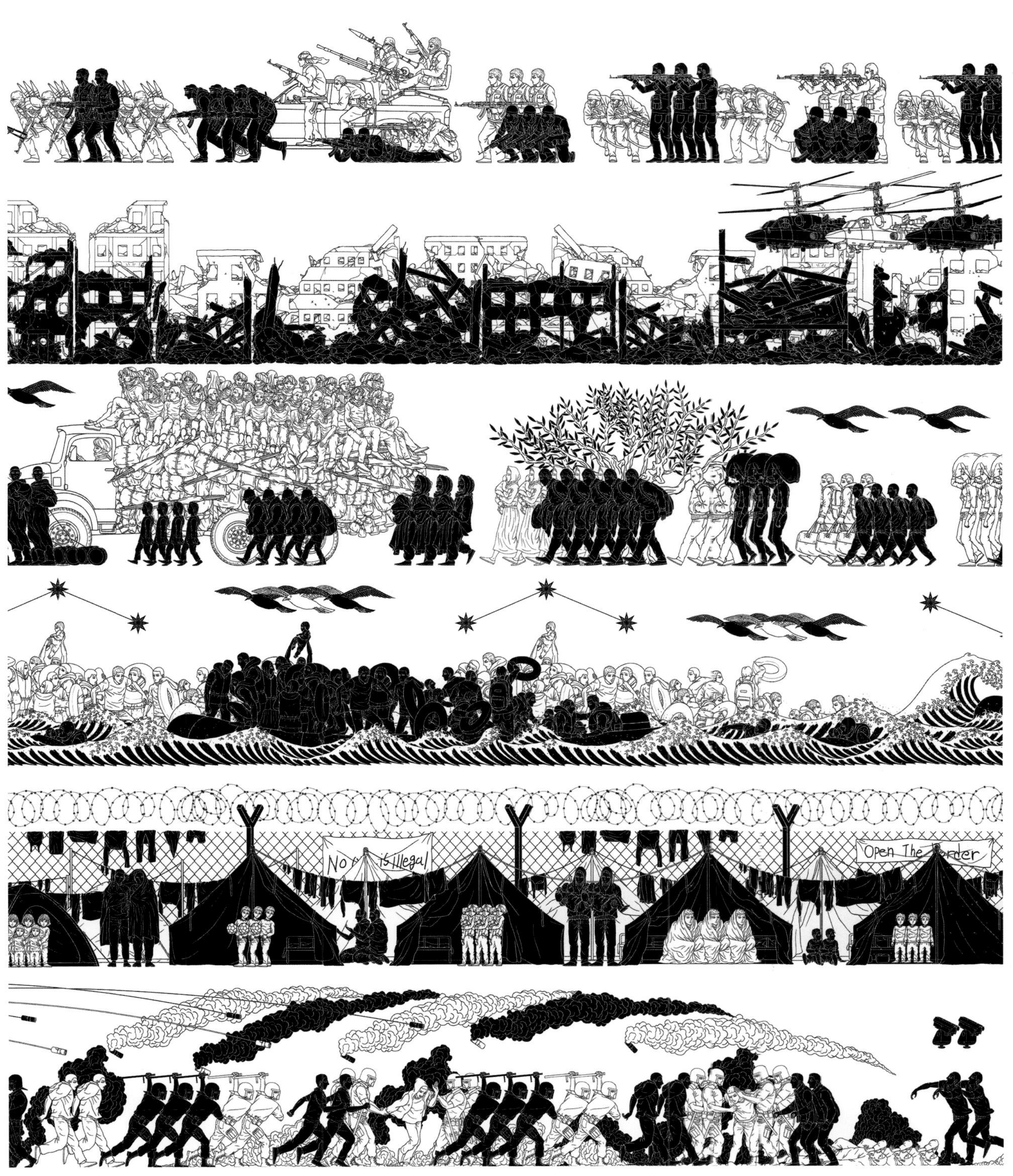

Odyssey 1, E. 46th Street and 5th Avenue, Manhattan (top)

Odyssey 2, E. 23rd Street and Park Avenue South, Manhattan (opposite, top)

Social media post, *Odyssey 5* (opposite, bottom)

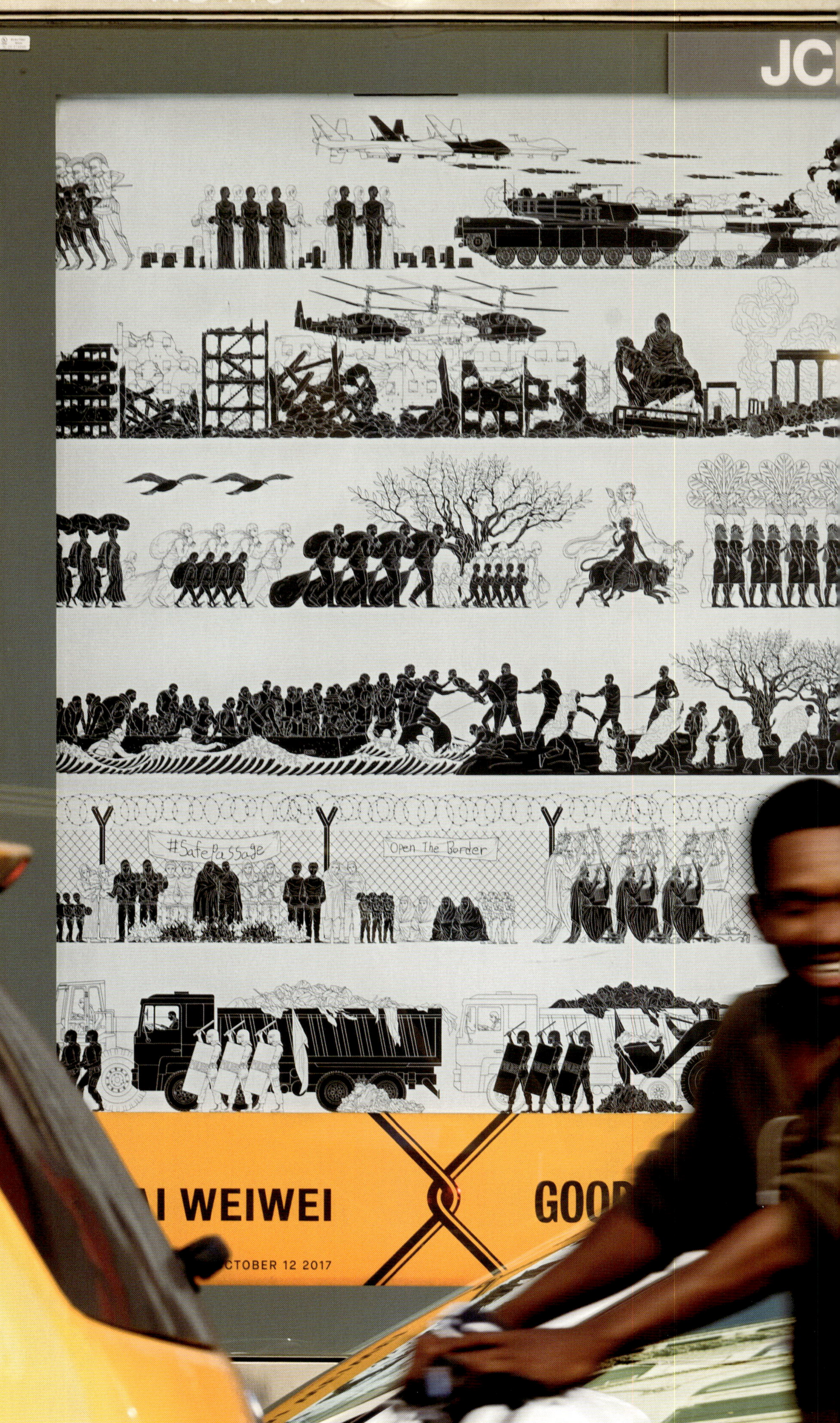

Odyssey 3
E. 14th Street and University Place, Manhattan

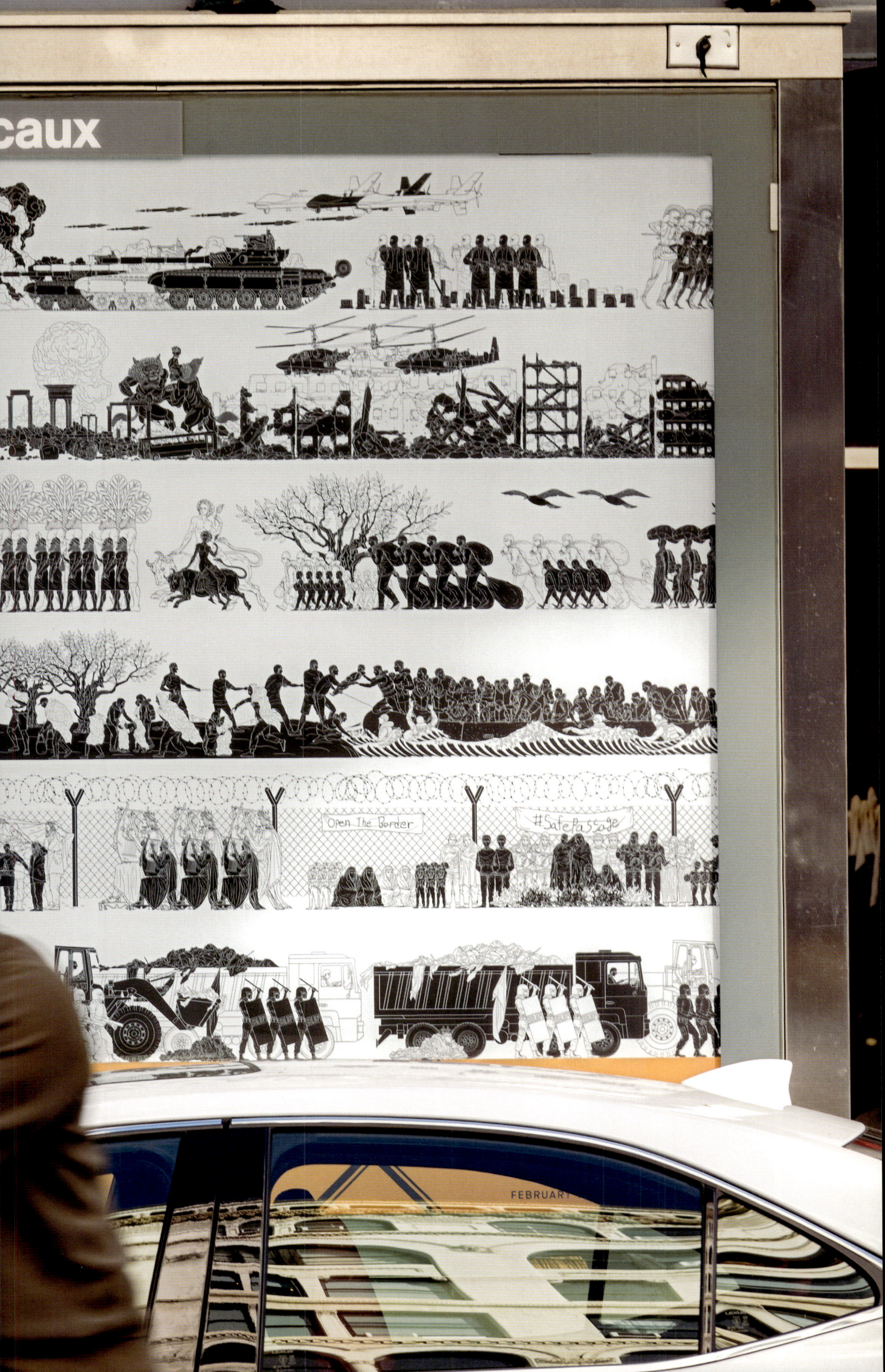

caux
Open The Border
#SafePassage
FEBRUARY

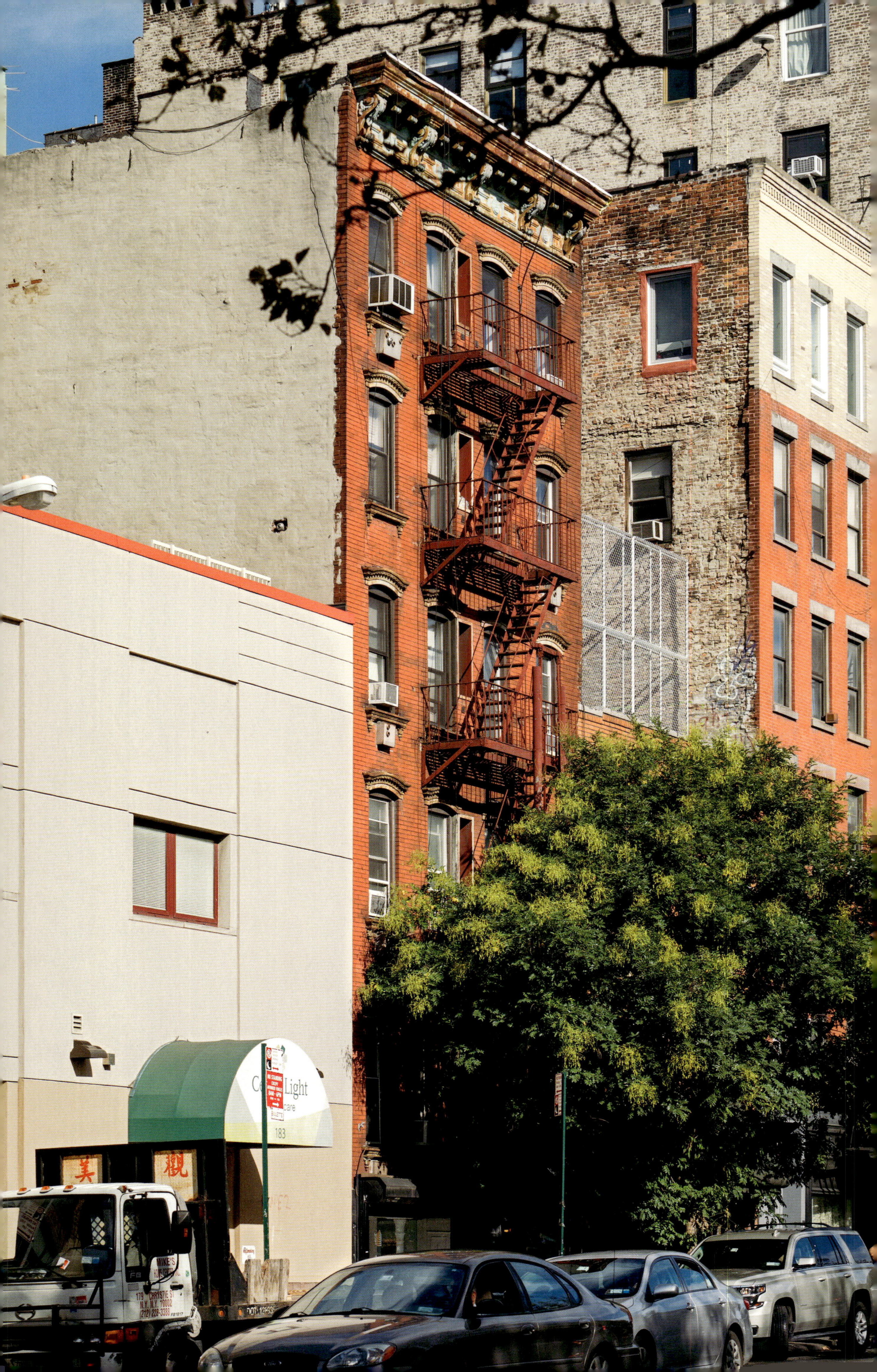
Light
care
183
NO STANDING
8AM - 6PM
美
觀

Chrystie Street Fence

189 Chrystie Street

This cityscape of Lower Manhattan constitutes the impetus for the artist's initial concept of using metal security fencing as an artistic symbol, blurring the line between art and function. Ai Weiwei's interventions grew out of the existing urban landscape, highlighting both the personal and the historical stories of these neighborhoods, as well as their continually evolving identities. Ai's subtle design refinements and modular panels for the fences on buildings adapted industrial materials and minimalist aesthetics that blended into the city's terrain. The artist selected this 1920s sign factory on Chrystie Street—now home to a nightclub—for its low cornice line and the taller buildings on either side. These custom-designed modular fence panels with curved edges and a mesh plane in front of the tubular structure filled the width of the rooftop span, glistening as a paradoxical symbol to the city below.

Preliminary drawing and installation of *Chrystie Street Fence*, October 2017

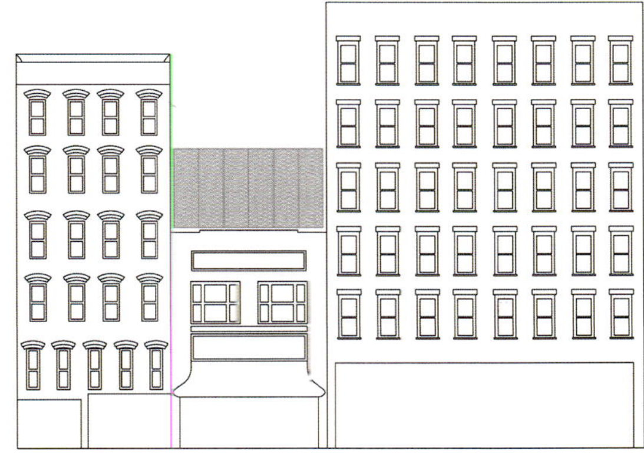

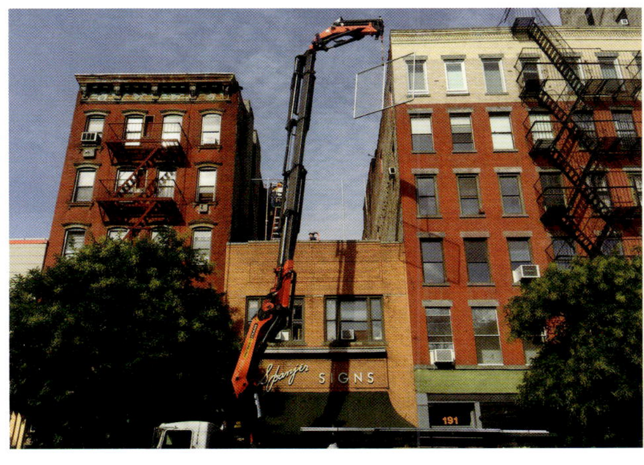

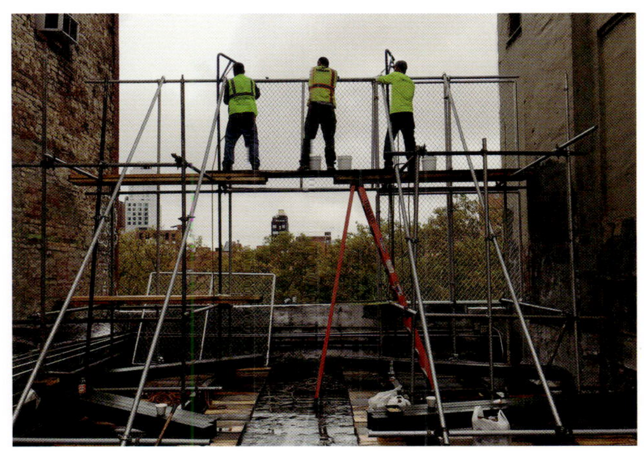

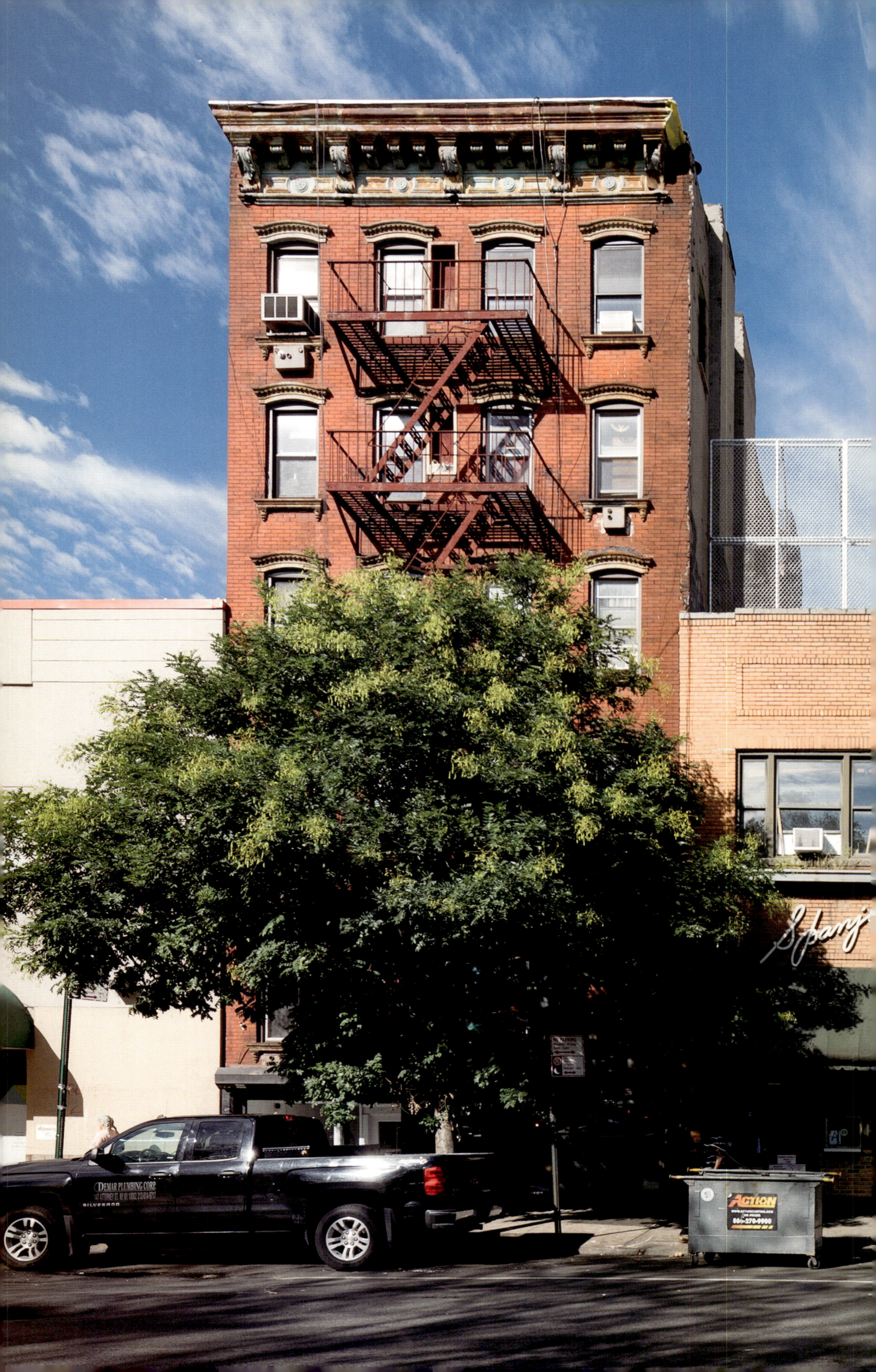
DEMAR PLUMBING CORP
ACTION

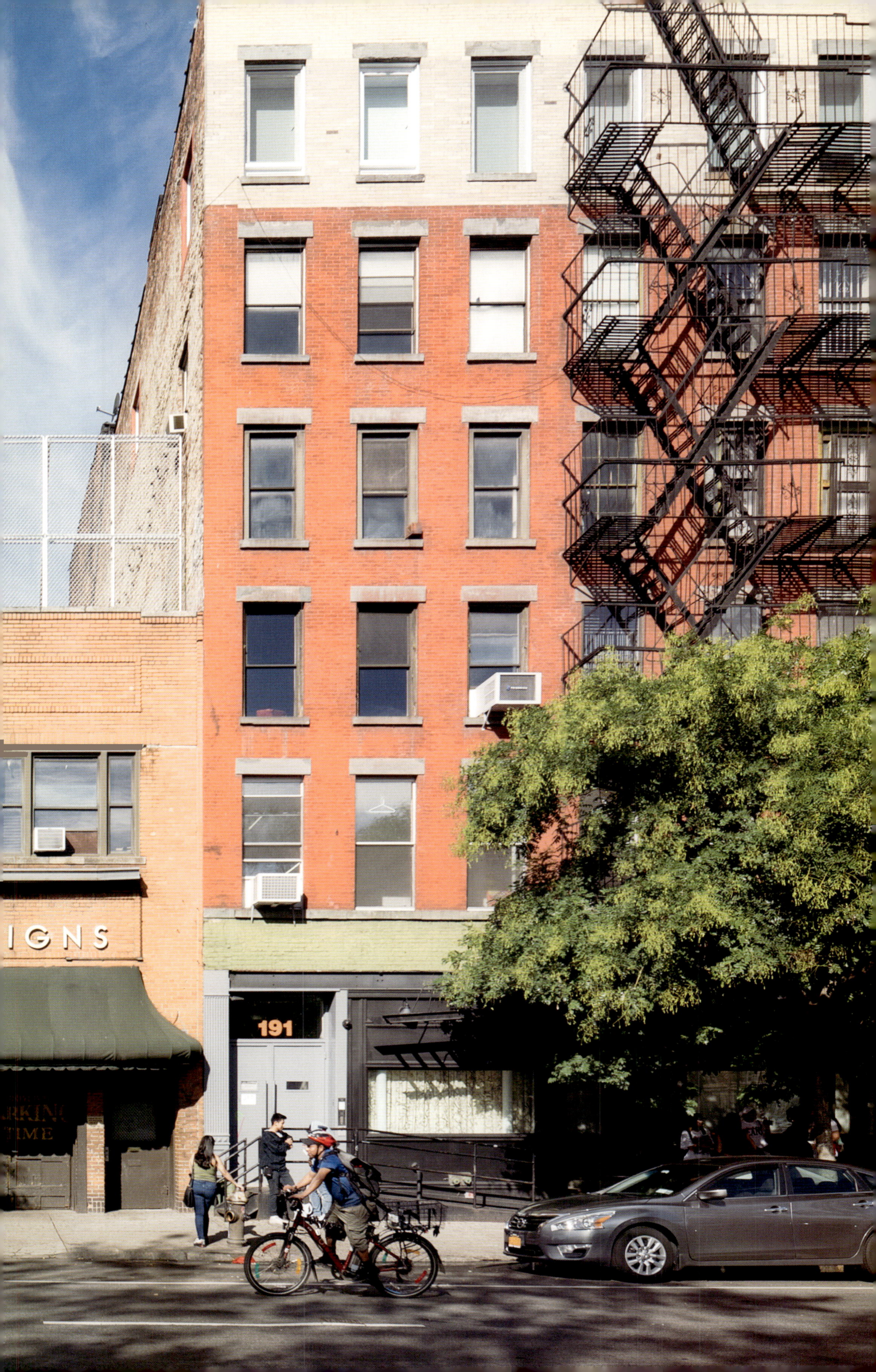
IGNS
191

Ai Weiwei pours his heart and soul into art that asks big questions and is not constrained by artistic and social traditions. With *Good Fences Make Good Neighbors*, he challenges us to think about the function and rationale for a common barrier. Given that the immigrant experience is at the core of what binds us as New Yorkers, the exhibition compels us to question the rhetoric and policies that seek to divide us.

Chirlane McCray, New York City First Lady

×

Good Fences Make Good Neighbors is a powerful, ambitious, and transformative project that truly exemplifies the force of art by elevating the ever-present metal security fence into a symbol that focuses our attention on the migration crisis. Taking over New York City, in locations known for large immigrant populations, Ai Weiwei illustrates a remarkable sensitivity for displaced people by creating artworks embedded in both landmarks and in more subtle and inconspicuous places. I was lucky enough to spend quite a bit of time with *Arch* in Washington Square Park and was moved by how people reacted and responded—walking through repeatedly, taking photos, reflecting, and marking the moment.

Agnes Gund, President Emerita of The Museum of Modern Art, philanthropist

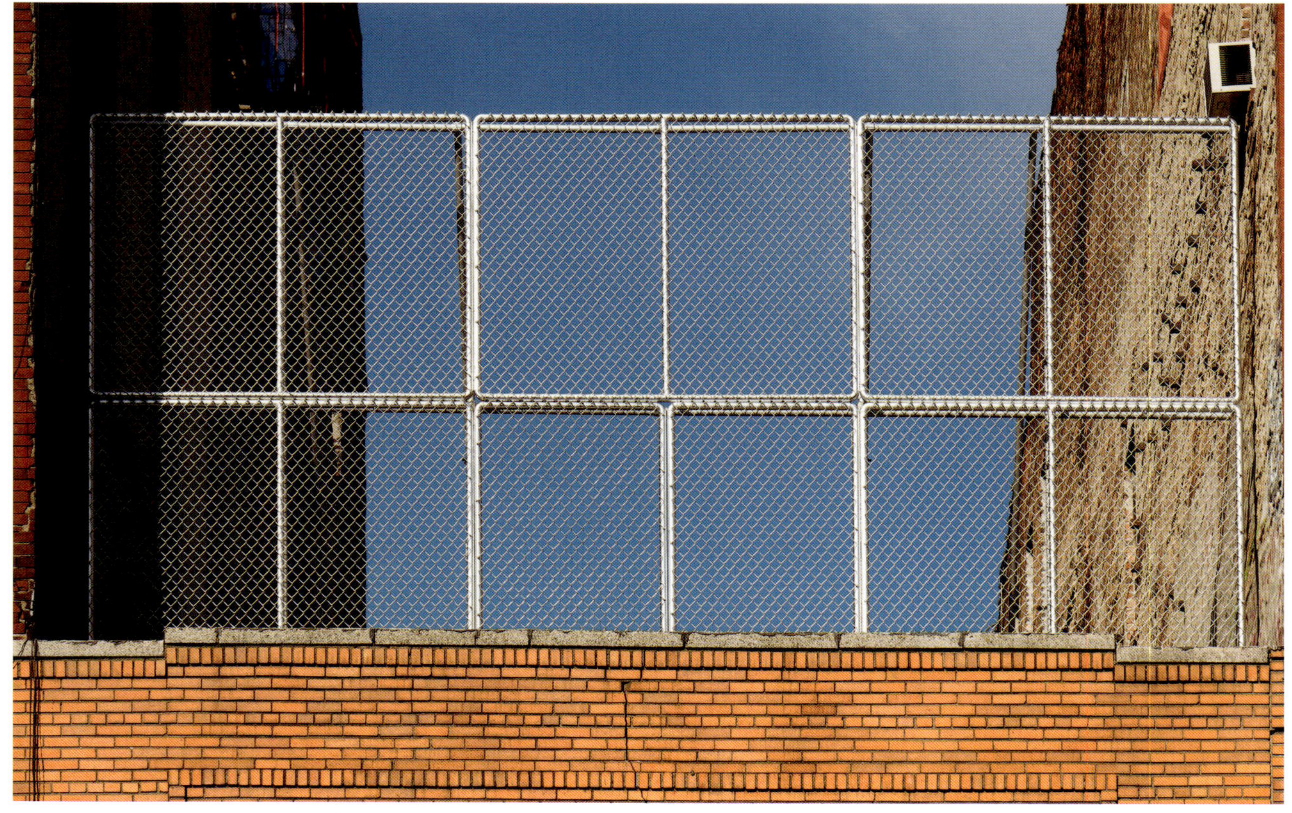

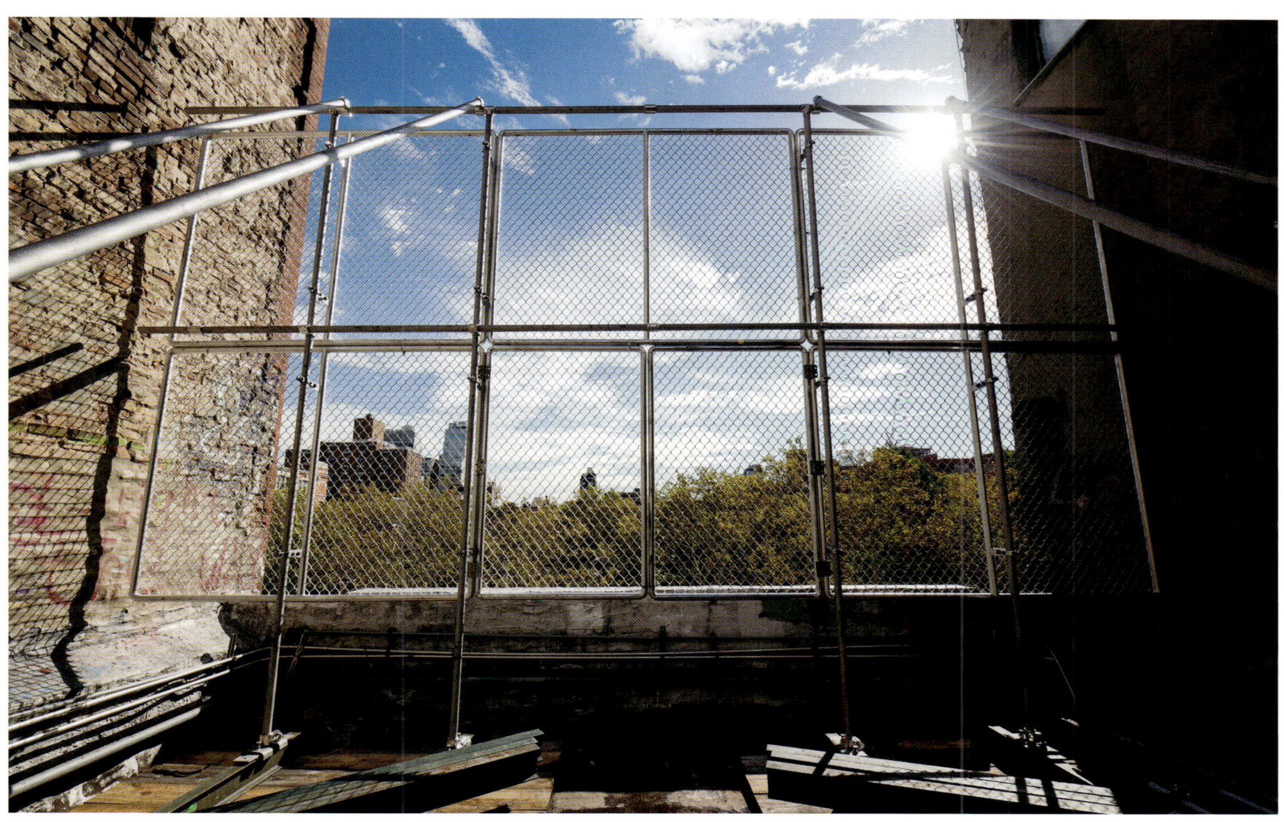

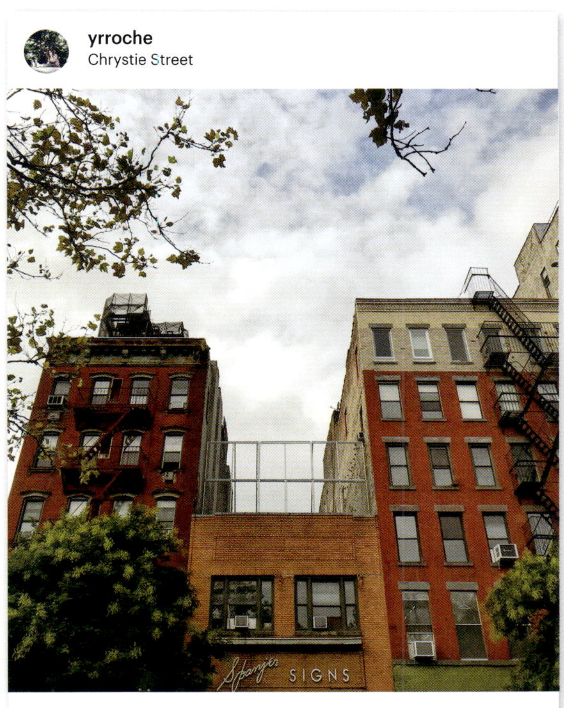

146 Likes

yrroche 189 Chrystie Street @aiww #goodfencesmakegoodneighbors

justynpikachu Lmao, what that fence in the middle?! Interesting choice for a fence...

OCTOBER 31, 2017

Social media post, *Chrystie Street Fence*

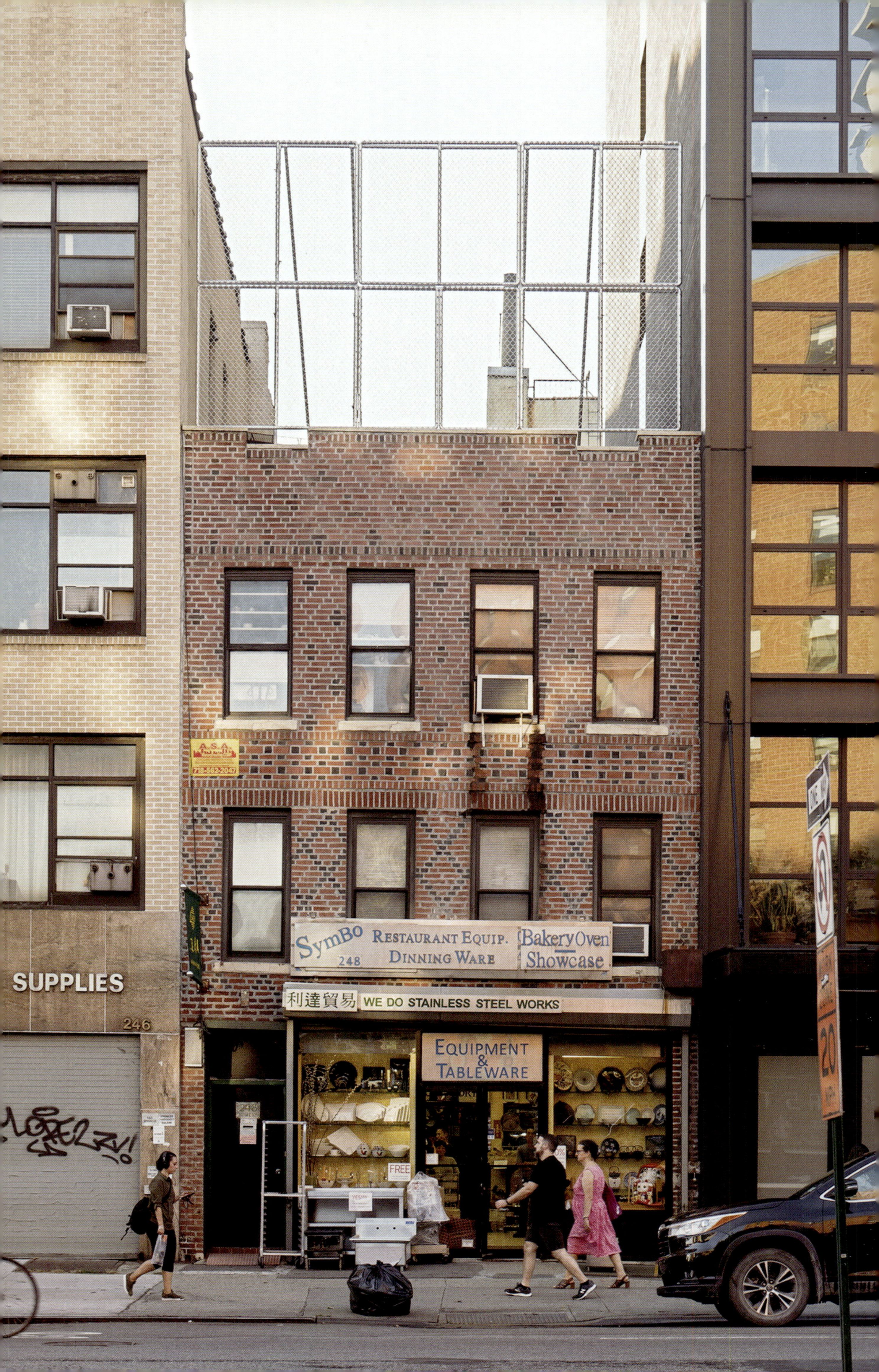
SymBo
248
RESTAURANT EQUIP.
DINNING WARE
Bakery Oven
Showcase
利達貿易
WE DO STAINLESS STEEL WORKS
EQUIPMENT
&
TABLEWARE
SUPPLIES
246
FREE
718-562-2047

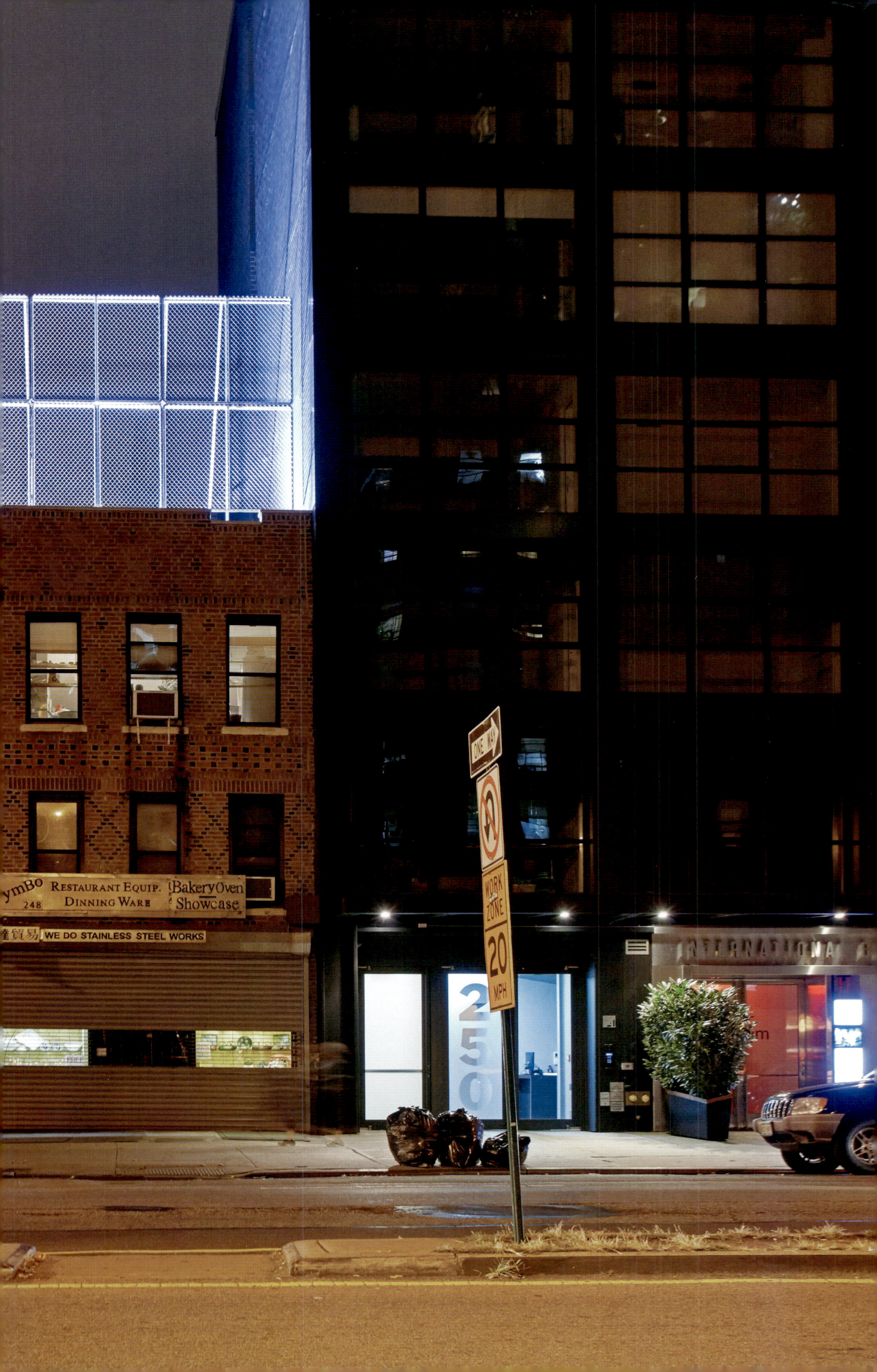

RESTAURANT EQUIP.
DINNING WARE
248
Bakery Oven
Showcase
WE DO STAINLESS STEEL WORKS
ONE WAY
WORK ZONE
20
MPH
250

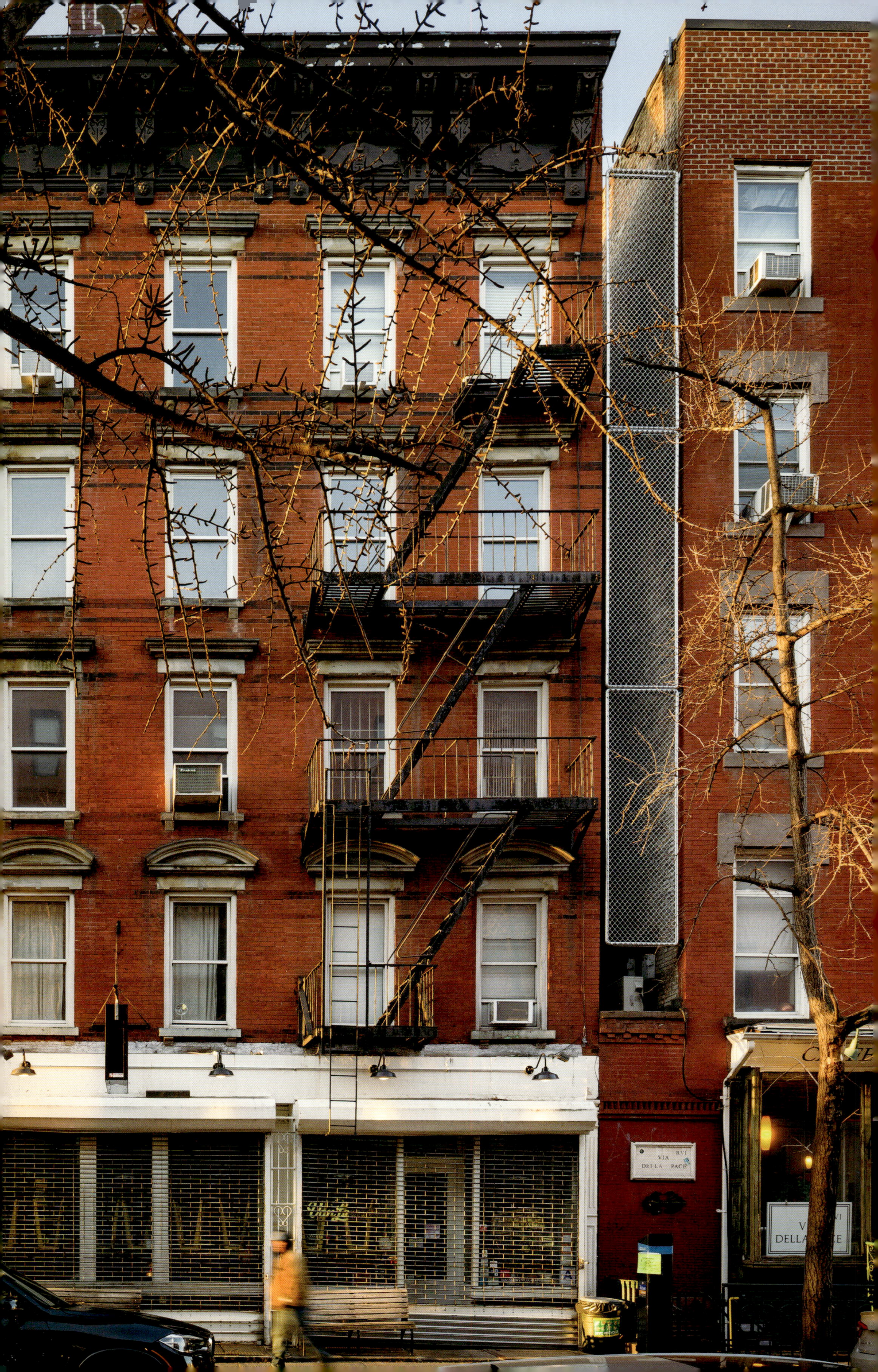

7th Street Fence

48 East 7th Street

Preliminary drawing for *7th Street Fence* (top)

Installation of *7th Street Fence*, October 2017 (bottom left and right)

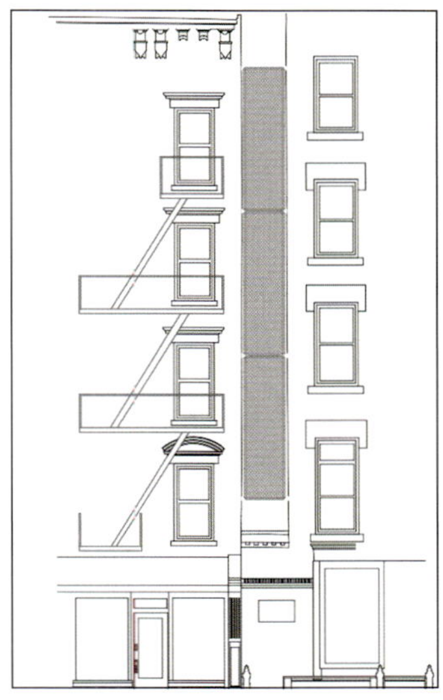

In contrast to both *Bowery Fence* and *Chrystie Street Fence*, which occupied rooftops between buildings, the installation at 48 East Seventh Street filled a 36-by-3-foot "sliver lot" between two adjoining residential buildings. Weaving his biography into the project, Ai Weiwei located the narrow three-panel structure on the street where he once lived in a basement apartment during his time in New York City in the early 1990s. Among the most elegant and subtle of the artist's urban interventions, this piece was a personal marker that also depended on the agreement of the current property owners, making the artwork doubly significant for the artist.

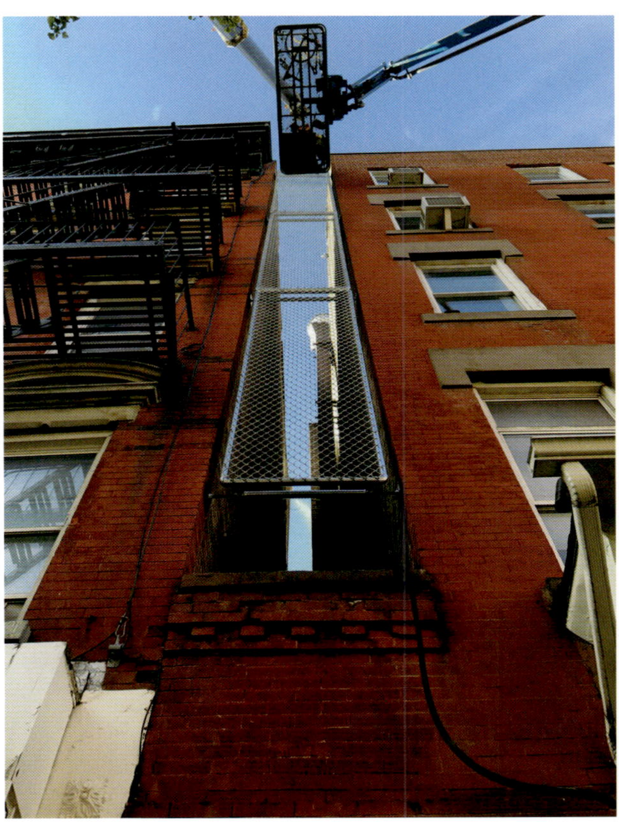

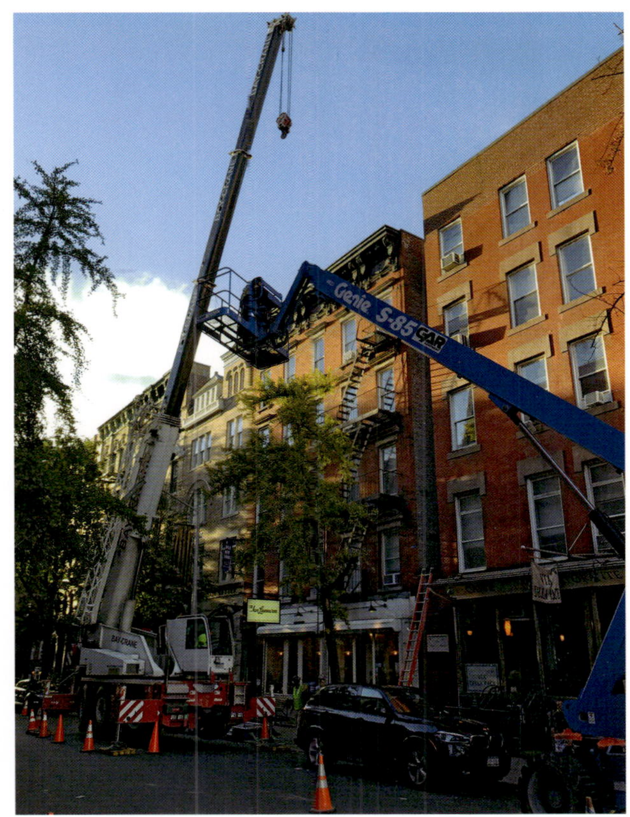

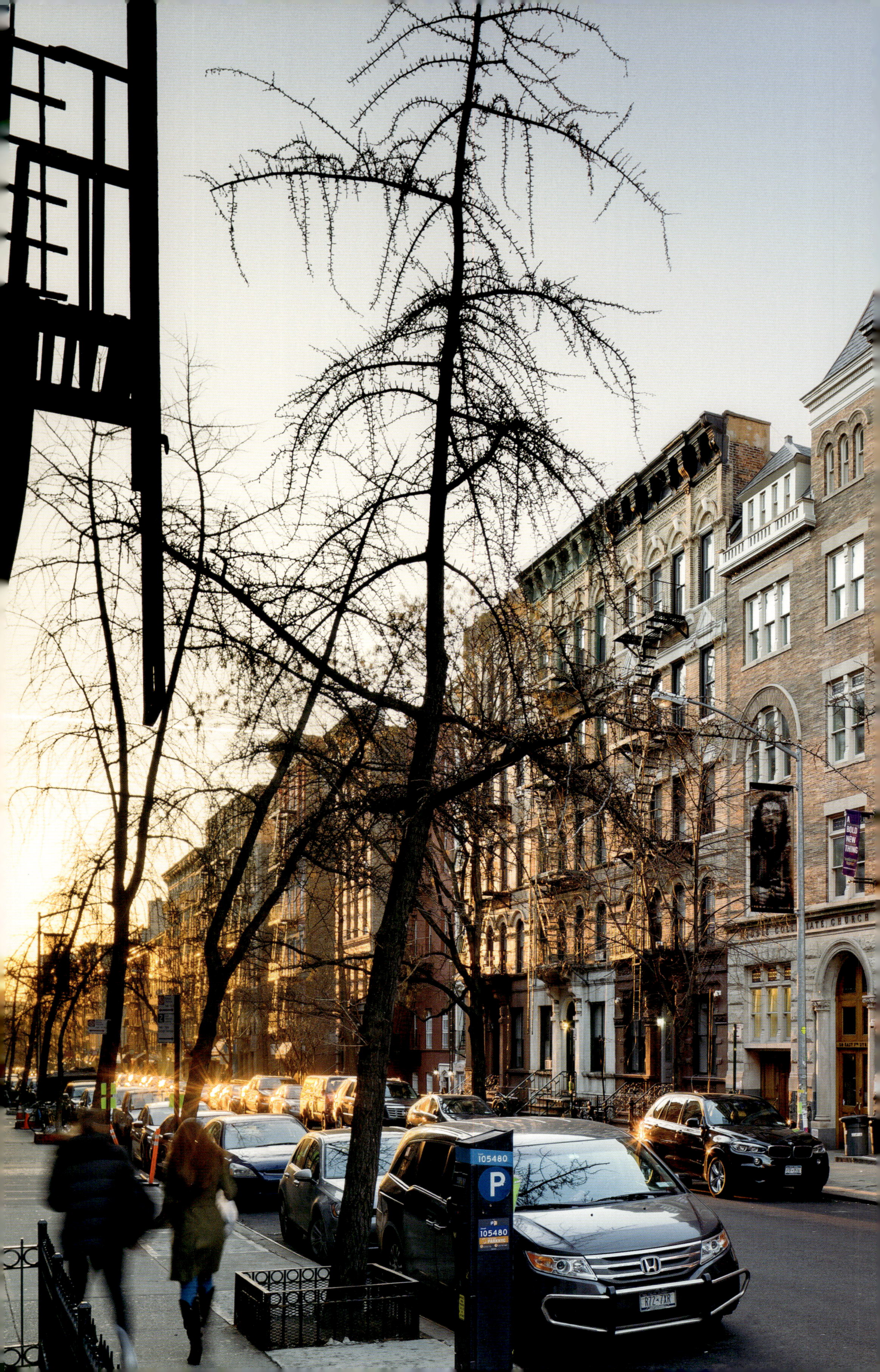
A BOLD NEW THING
CHURCH
105480
P
105480

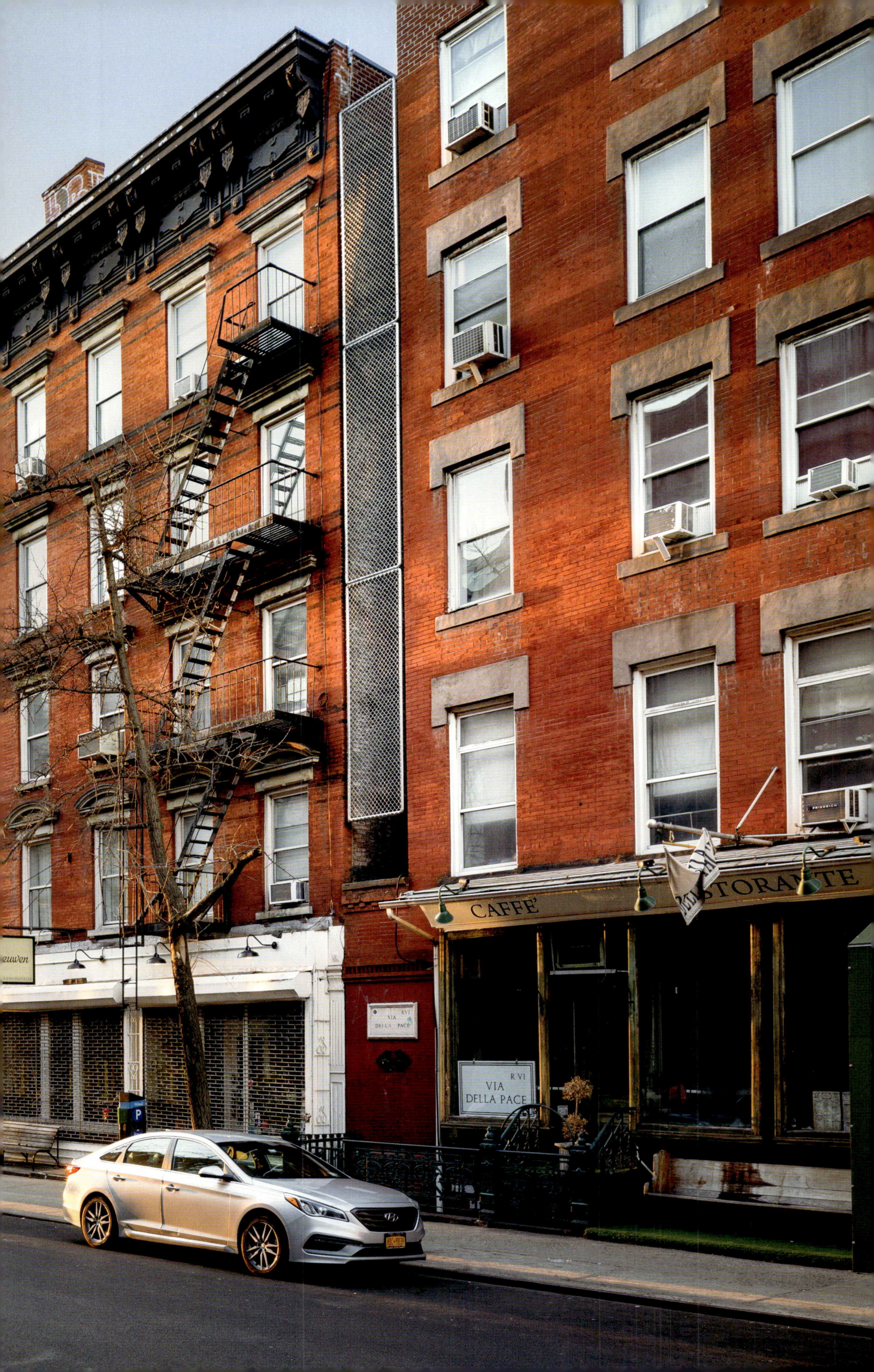
CAFFE'
R VI
VIA
DELLA PACE

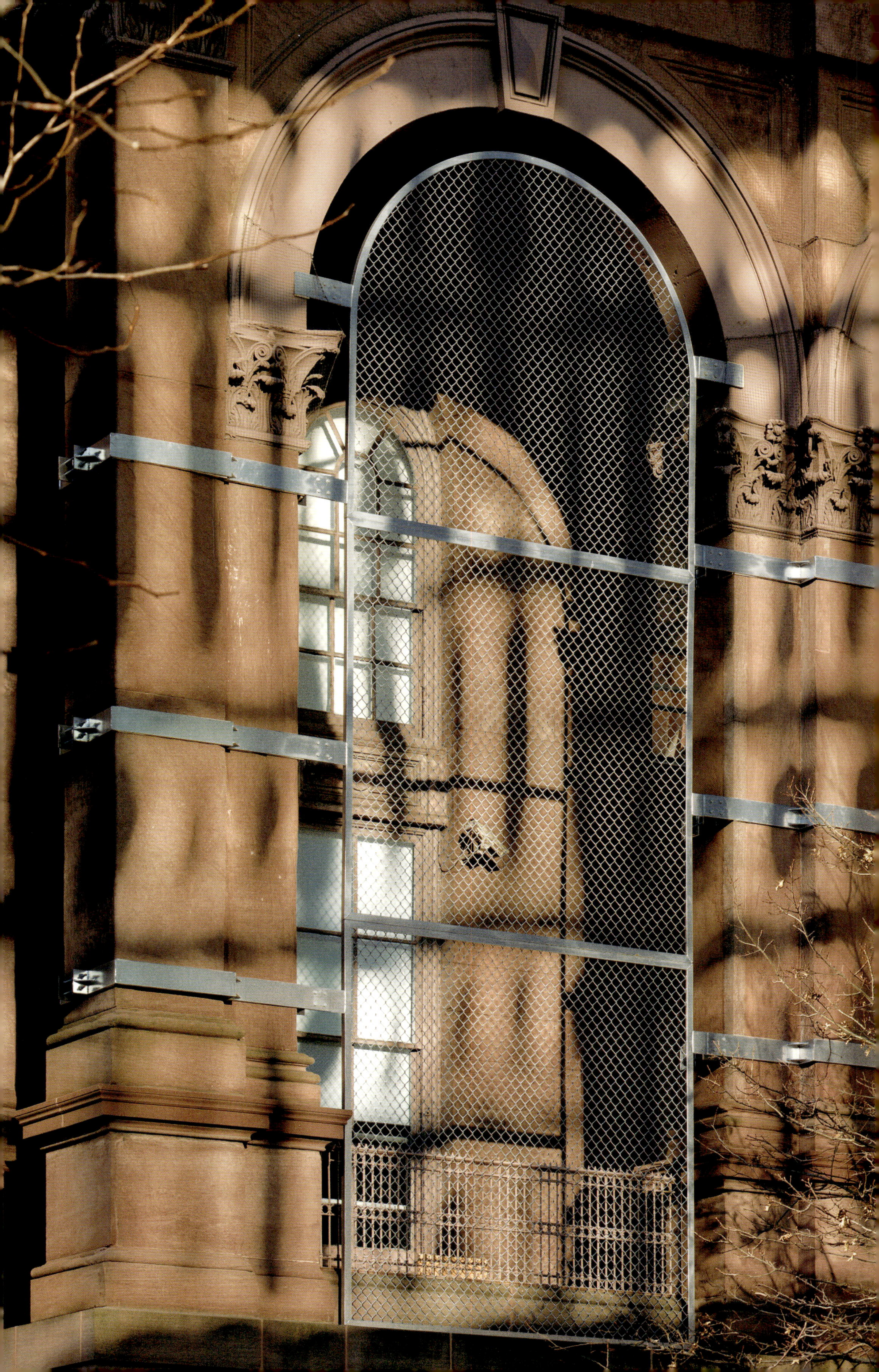

Five Fences

The Cooper Union for the Advancement of Science and Art

Elevation of Cooper Union, North view (top)

Fence panel sketch for Cooper Union's facade (middle)

Installation of *Five Fences*, October 2017 (bottom left and right)

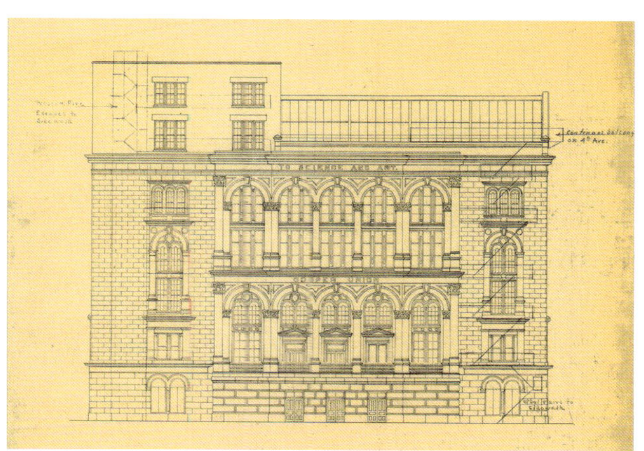

For more than 150 years, The Cooper Union for the Advancement of Science and Art has served as a beacon of democracy, free speech, equality, and educational rigor in New York City. The five arch-filling security fences installed at the iconic Foundation Building did not disrupt or restrict the customary use of the portico. Likewise, the large clamps required to adhere Ai Weiwei's sculptural intervention to the multifaceted columns and pilasters were fully reversible and did not puncture or damage the 158-year-old landmark building's delicate brownstone. While their arched silver mesh added a cool note of contrast to the warm stone of the historic facade, they did form a new physical—and metaphorical—barrier. *Five Fences* suggests that the logic of social division is often opportunistic and incremental, emerging from and adapting itself to existing conditions.

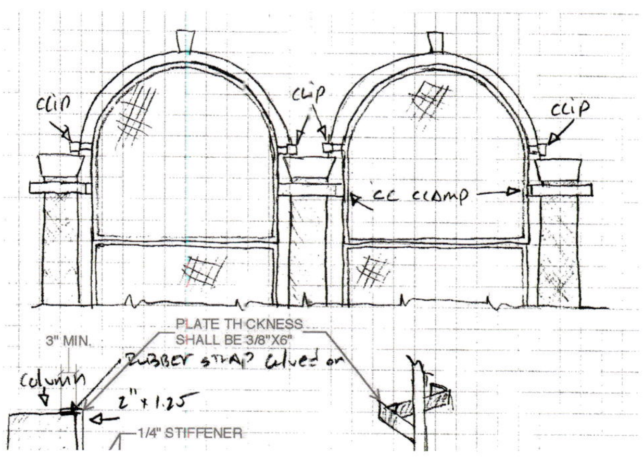

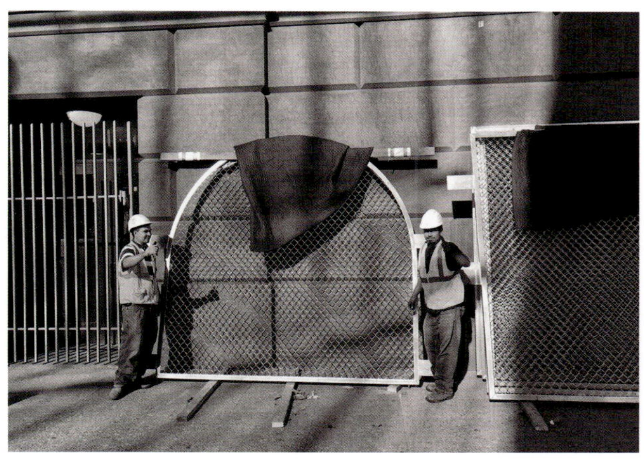

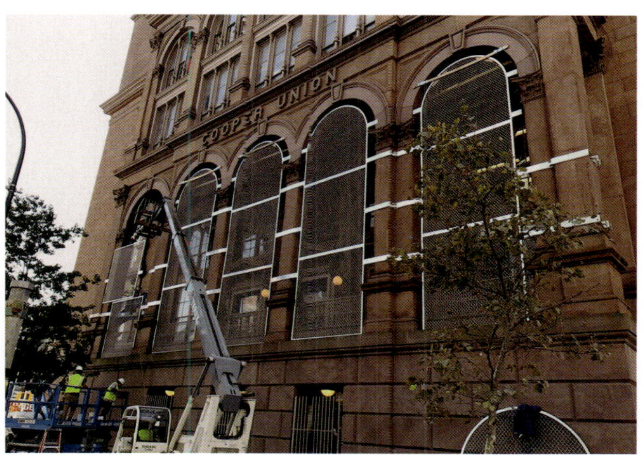

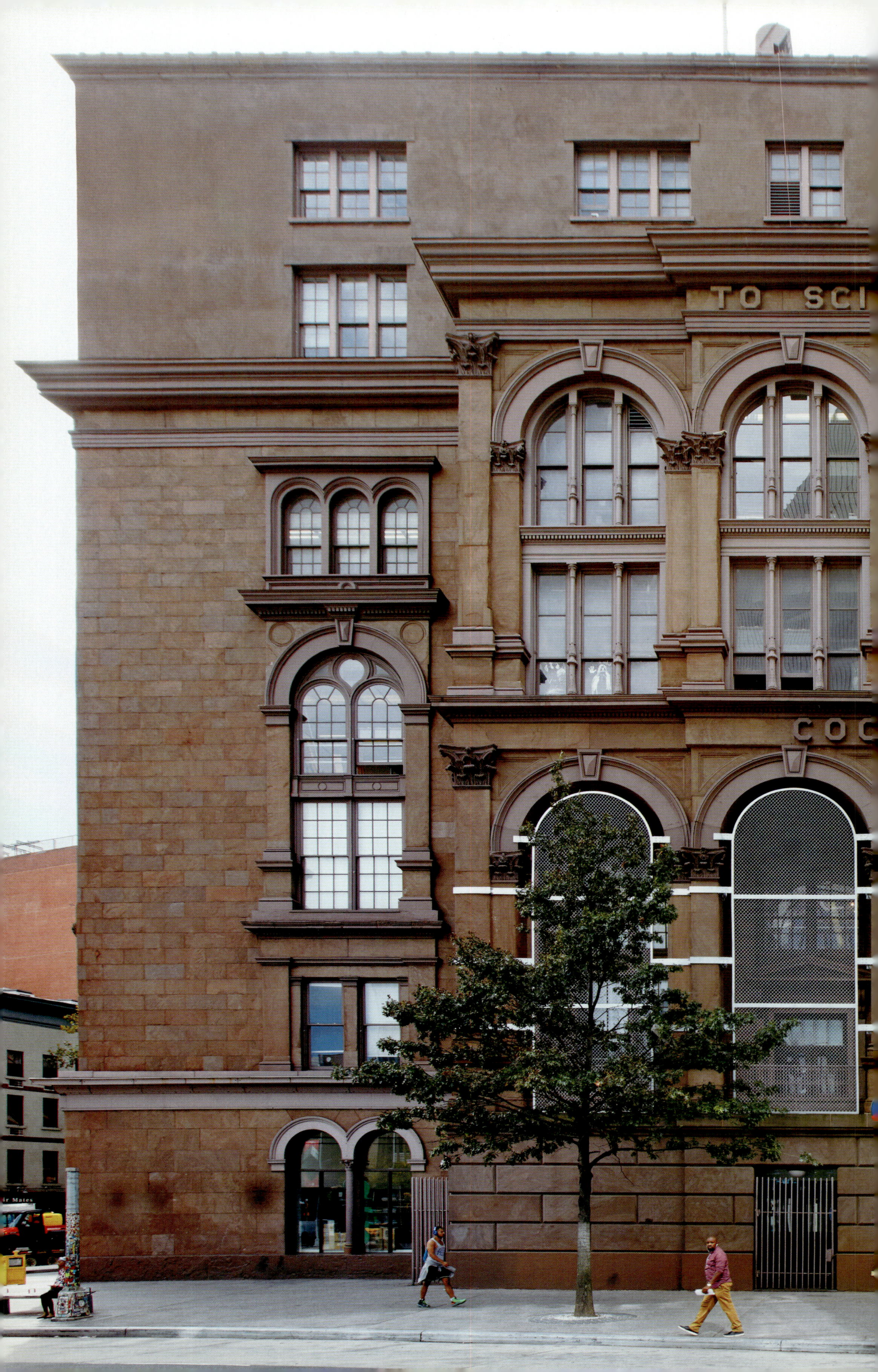
TO SCI

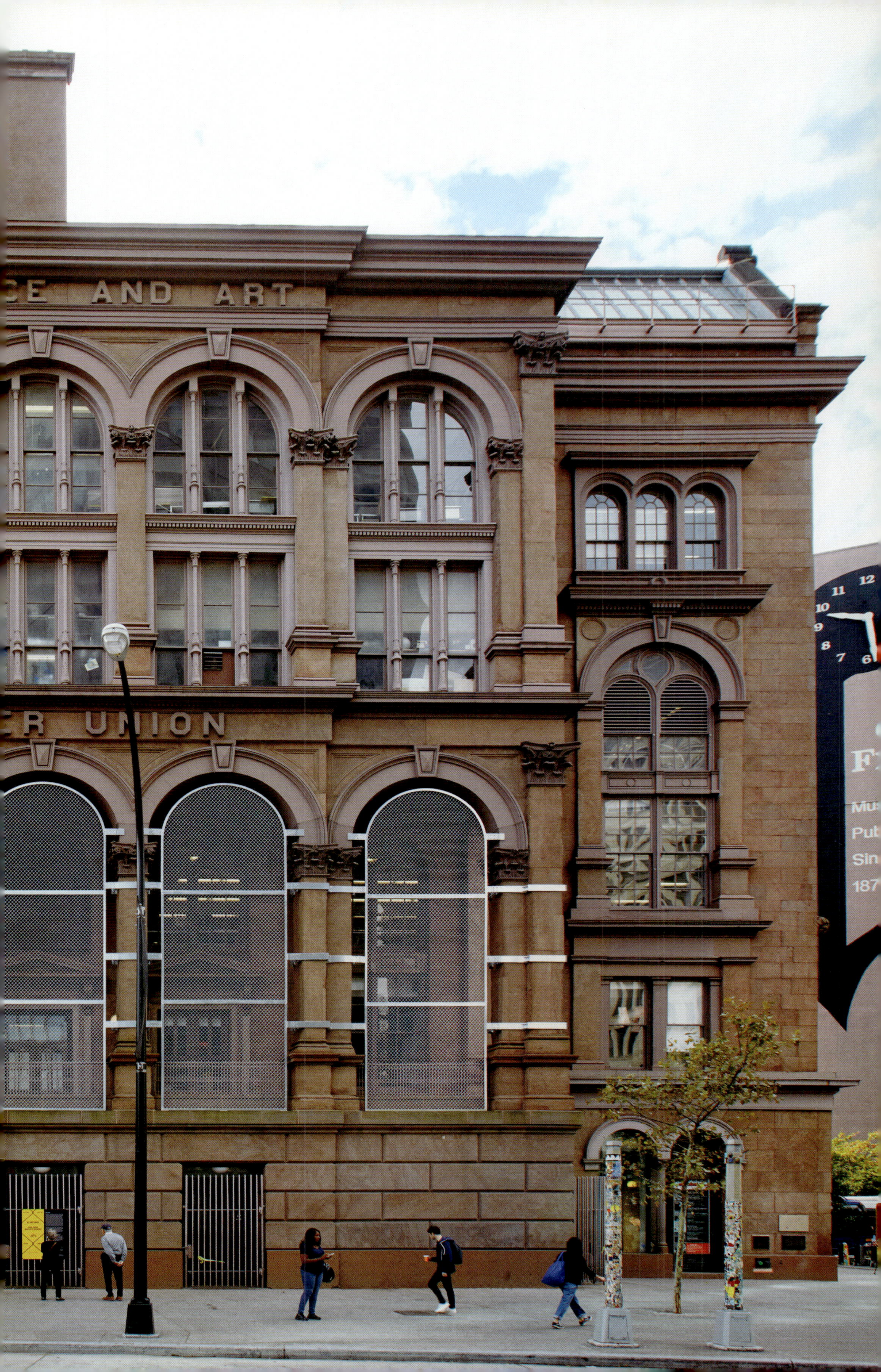
E AND ART
R UNION

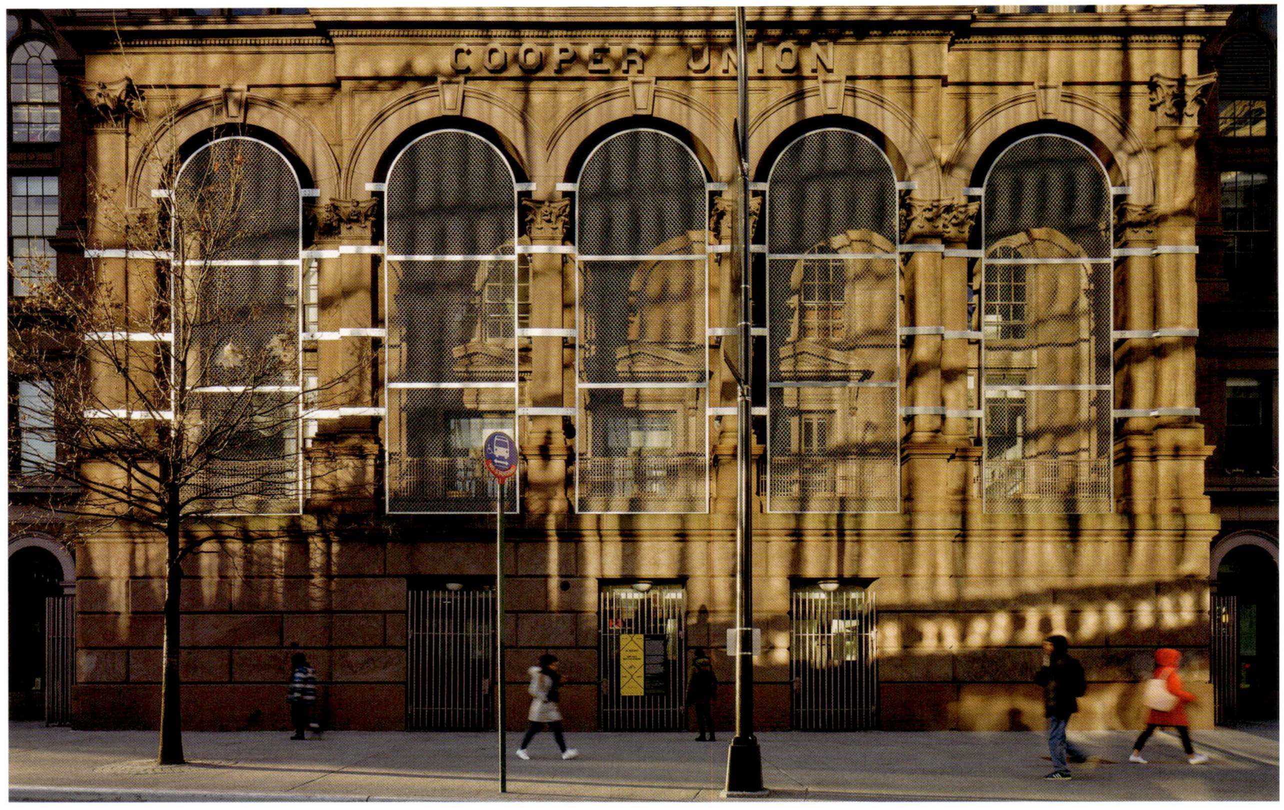

Ai Weiwei's deadpan objects—be they bicycles, seeds, or fences—seduce us into familiarity, but it is usually the startling aggregate effects of the work, and their requisite defamiliarizing impact, that transport the art to a collective imagination. He makes it effectively impossible to look at art without a deeper reading, mining out of our interpretive work the imperative to come to terms with the basic necessities of the human condition out of which the artwork emerges, calling on questions of equity, labor, or human rights as part of the baggage. It has been an immense pleasure to host Ai Weiwei at Cooper Union, not only because of the way in which *Good Fences Make Good Neighbors* redefines the public realm in New York—in our case, the portico of Cooper Union's Foundation Building—but as a personal gratitude for his generosity in opening the cultural doors of Beijing for me some twenty years ago.

Nader Tehrani, Dean, The Irwin S. Chanin School of Architecture at The Cooper Union for the Advancement of Science and Art

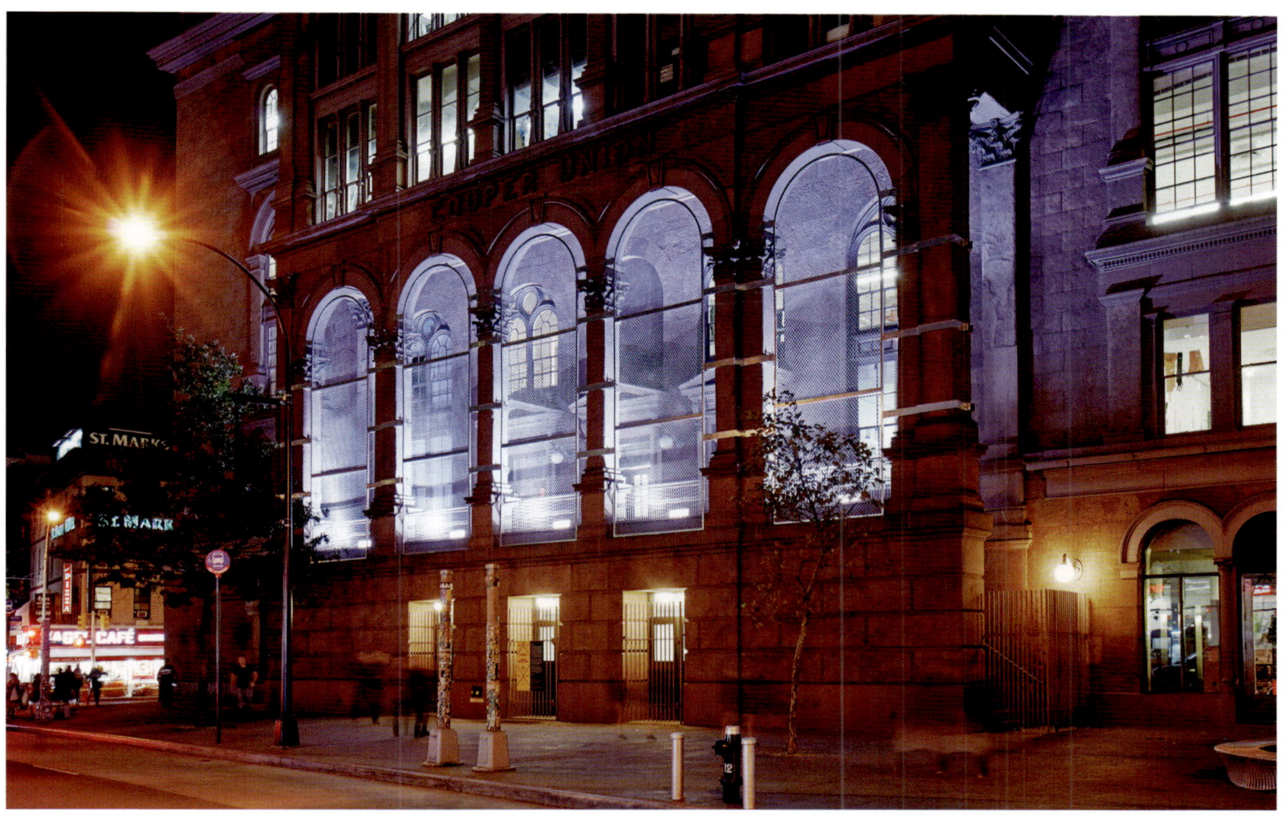

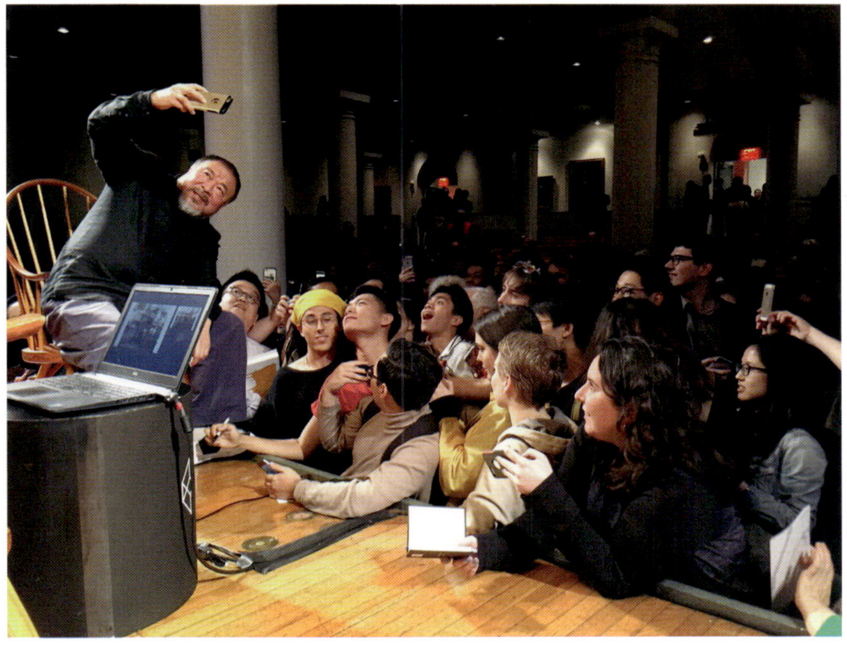

Ai Weiwei with audience members at his public talk, Cooper Union, October 12, 2017 (bottom)

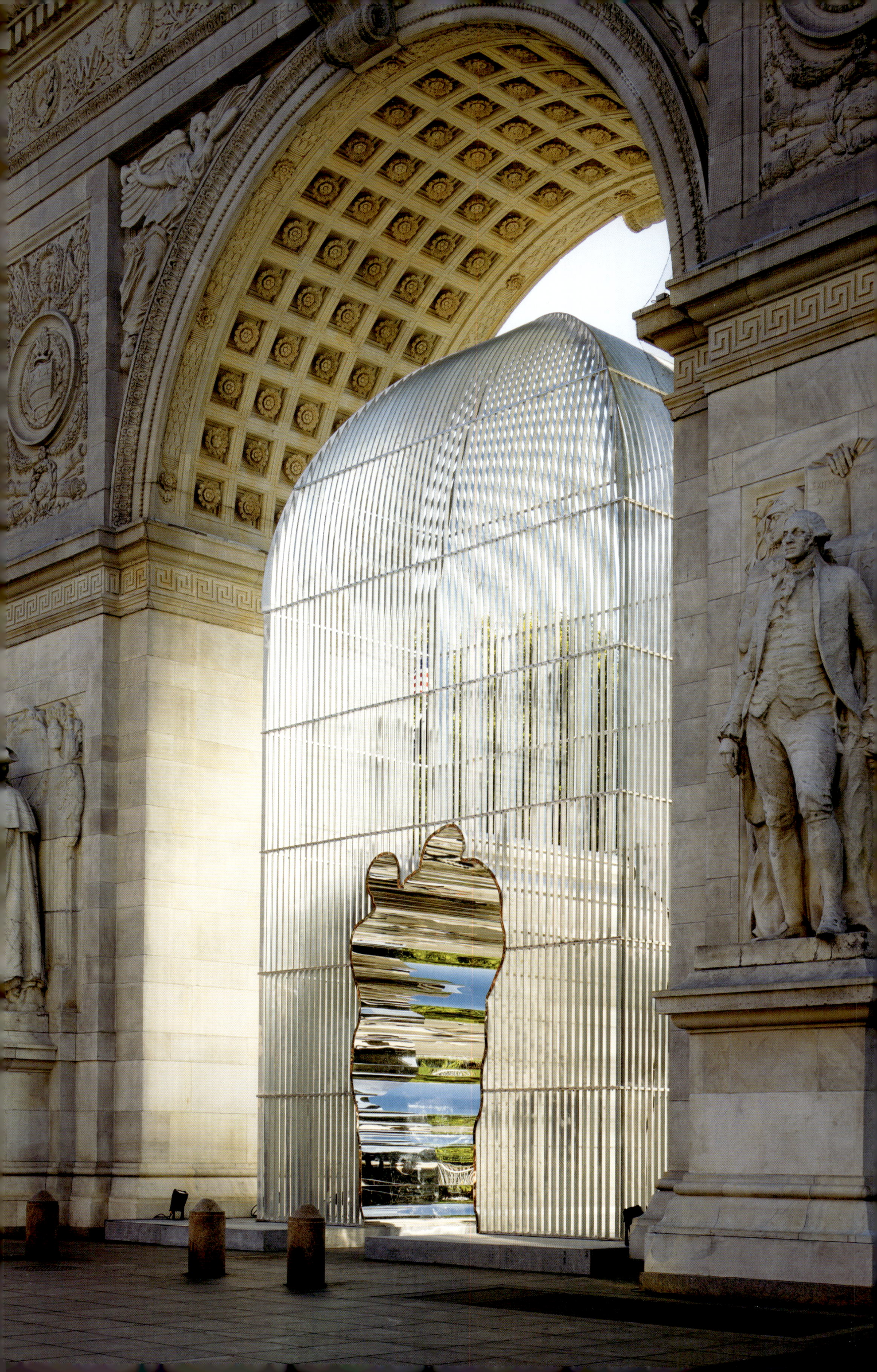
ERECTED BY THE

Arch

Washington Square Park

Ai Weiwei often visited Washington Square Park in the 1980s when he lived nearby, drawn to its vitality as a hub for creative and political expression. His thirty-seven-foot-tall steel cage echoed the iconic form of the marble arch, which commemorates George Washington leading the nation toward democracy. *Arch*, while seemingly an obstruction, provided a dynamic pathway for visitors through its center via the open silhouette of two united figures—their form borrowed from Marcel Duchamp's 1937 *Door for Gradiva*, created to frame the entrance to André Breton's art gallery in Paris—and viewers crossing through were surrounded by *Arch*'s undulating ribbon of polished stainless steel. The reflective steel enabled visitors to see themselves mirrored in the dual embracing silhouettes, transforming the concept of the "security fence" into a symbol of unity. The reference to the immigrant conceptual artist Duchamp is apt: he played chess in Washington Square Park and once notoriously climbed the arch with a group of other bohemian poets and artists. There, they spread out blankets, hung Chinese lanterns, tied red balloons to the arch's parapet, and declared it the "Free and Independent Republic of Washington Square." This subtle homage to Duchamp highlights just how influential he has been for Ai, who also often pilfers existing forms and materials for his artworks. It stands as a fitting tribute to a key figure who had an enormous impact on many immigrant artists in the years since who have in turn made New York the cultural hub that it is today.

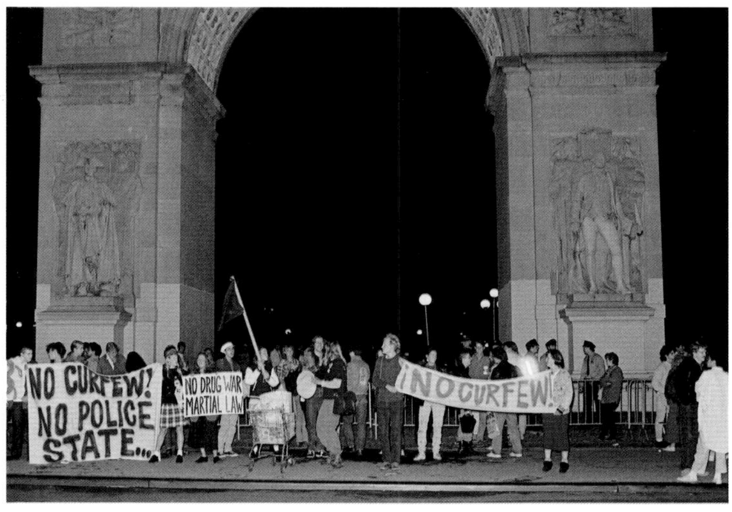

Washington Square Park protest, 1988

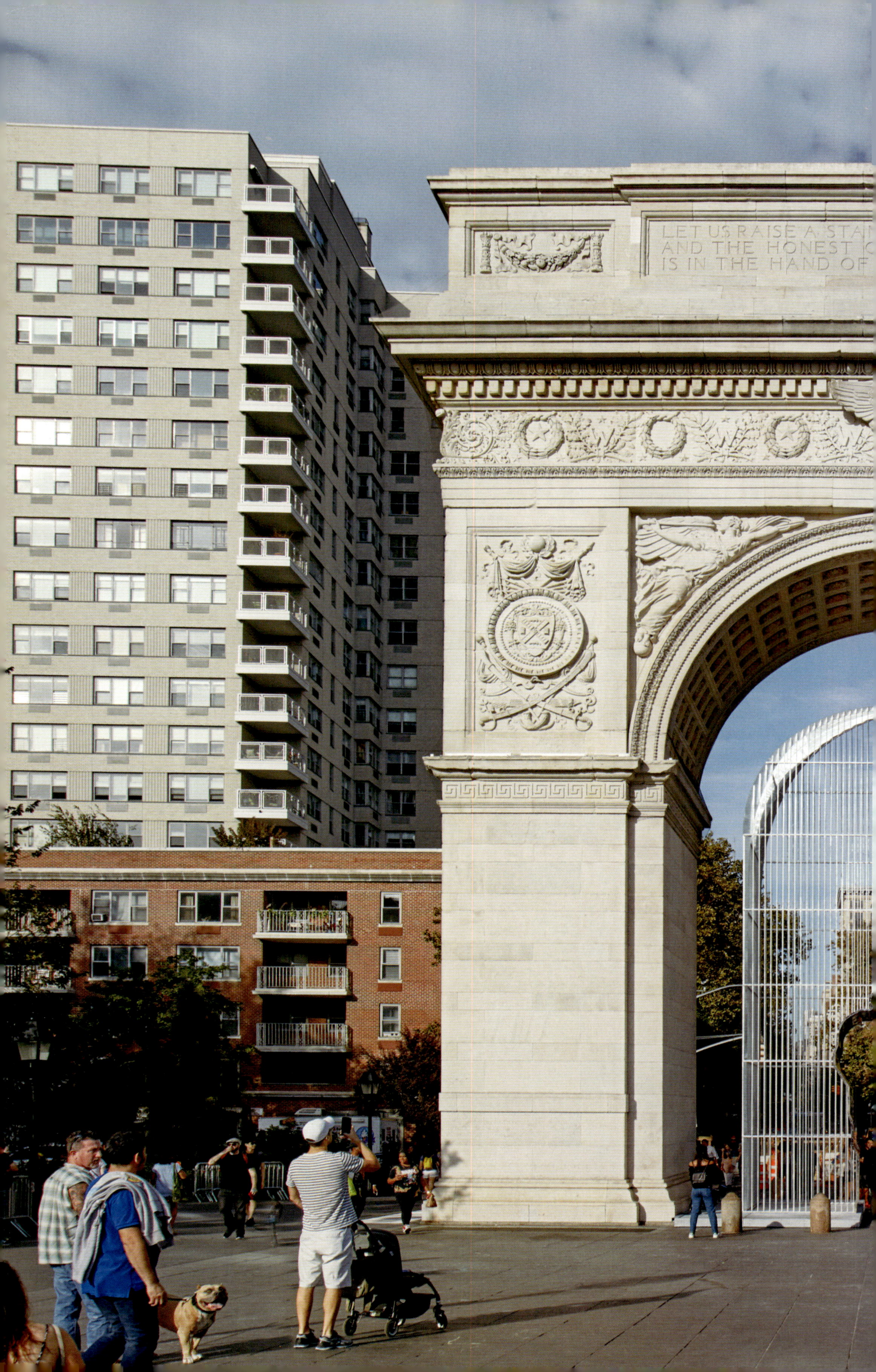
LET US RAISE A STA
AND THE HONEST
IS IN THE HAND OF

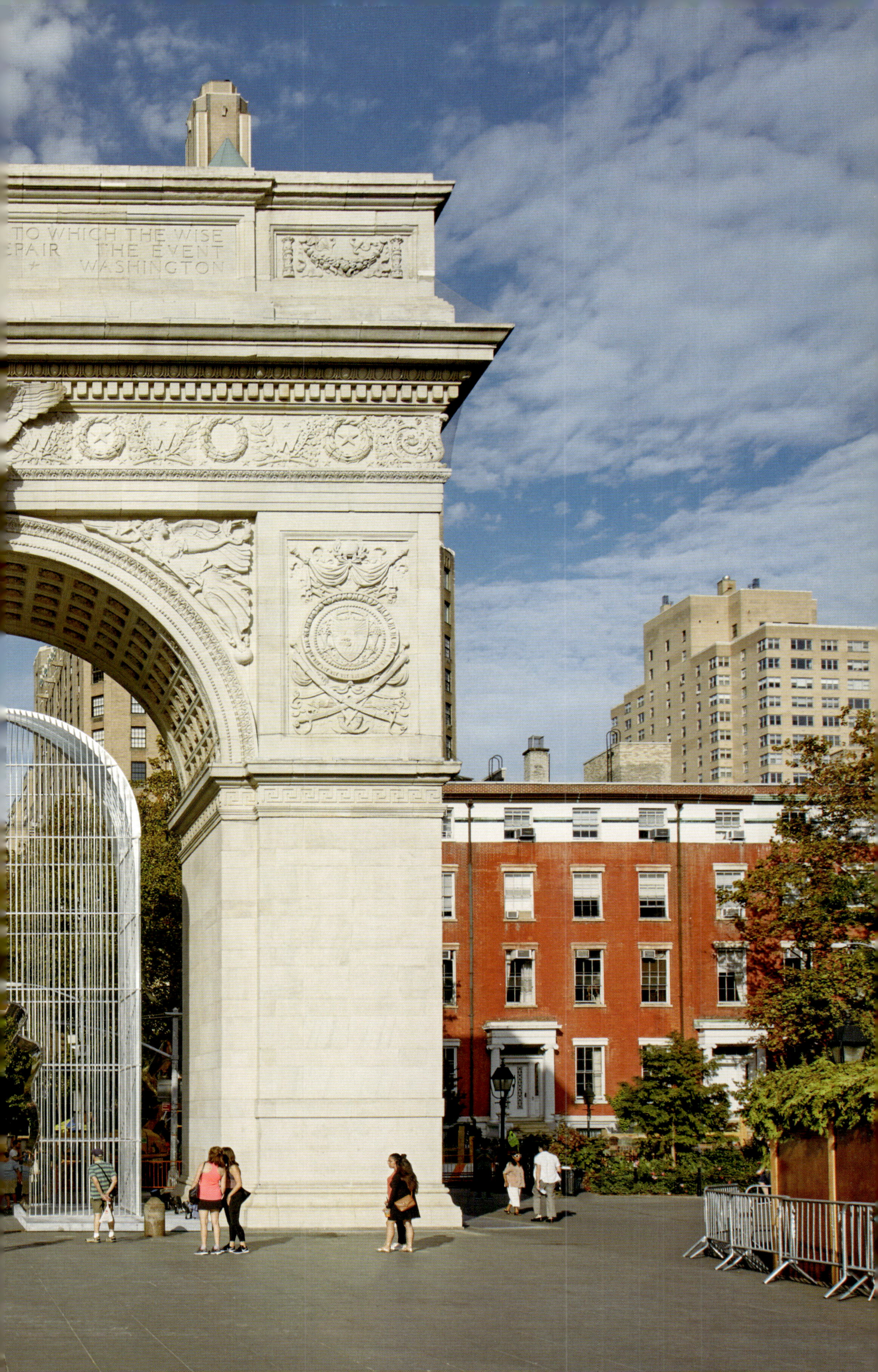
TO WHICH THE WISE
THE EVENT
WASHINGTON

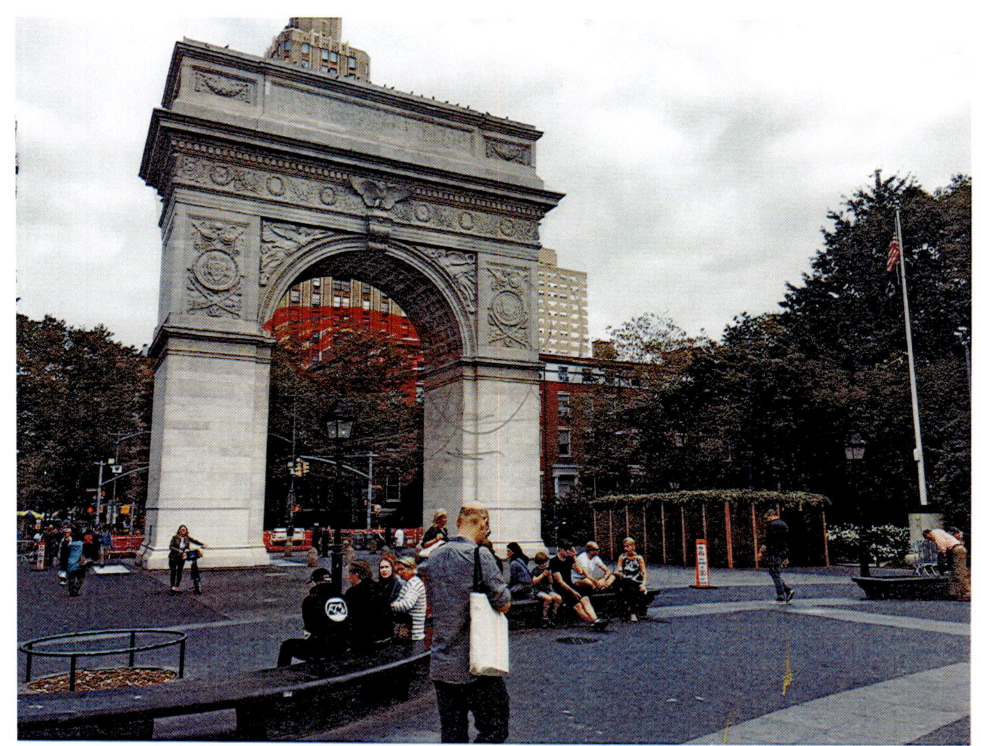

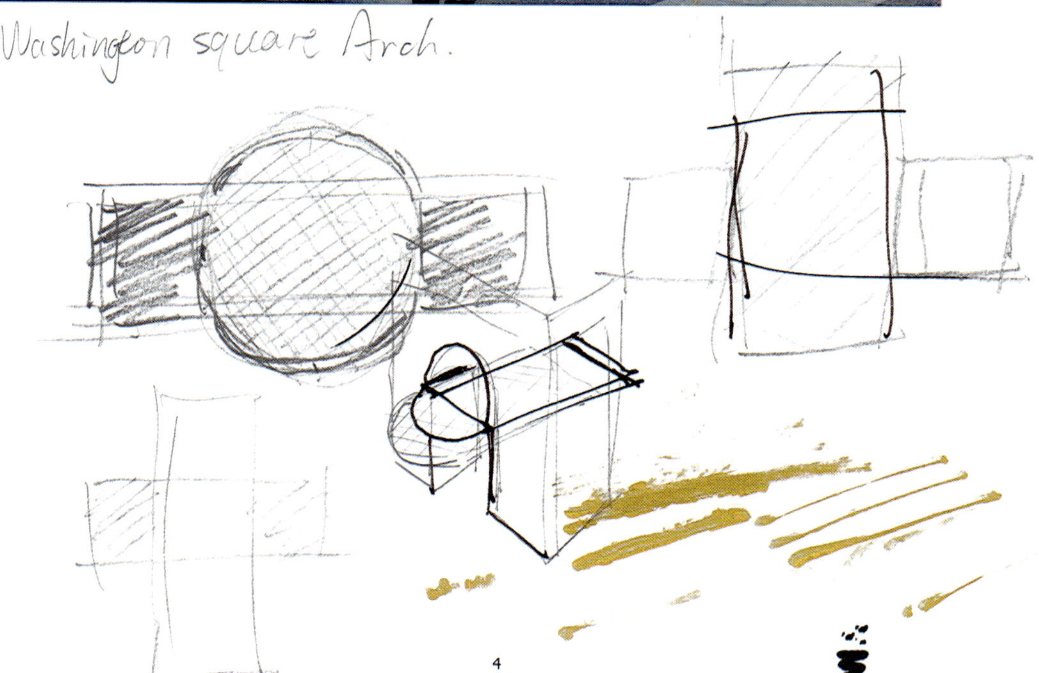
Washington square Arch.

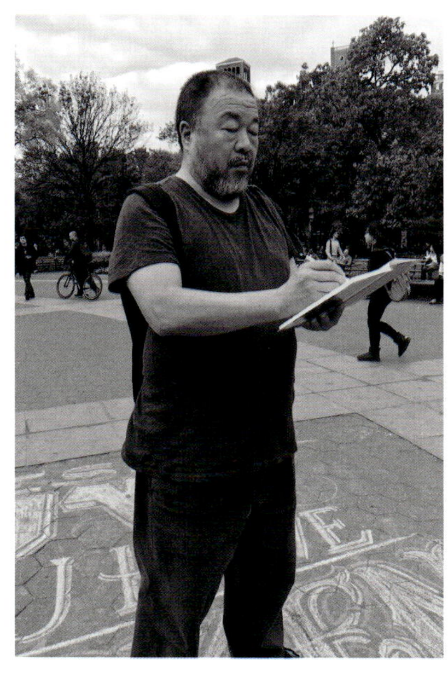

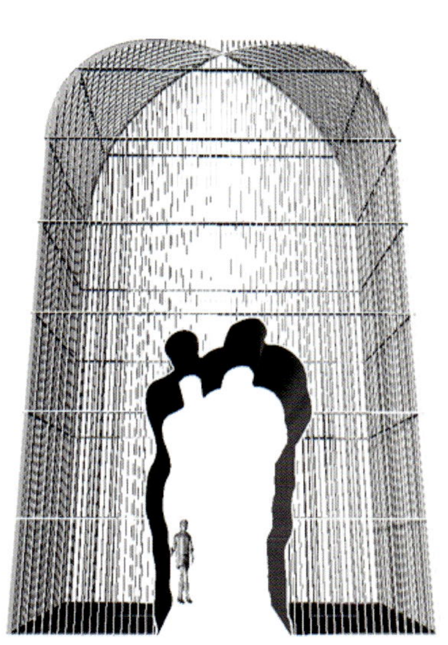

Although I was certainly not the only board member of Manhattan Community Board 2 of immigrant descent at the time of the discussion, I was the only Mexican American. I was thrilled to learn that the Ai Weiwei installation would be coming to our neighborhood. From my point of view, it was long overdue. Concerns voiced within our community about moving a holiday tree 150 feet from its regular position to allow for the greatest impact of the installation further highlighted the deep need to raise awareness within our community about how our country is treating immigrants today. Families are being torn apart, children do not know where their parents are or when they will see them again, and parents cannot protect their children. Yet somehow, yielding visual prominence in Washington Square Park to art that encourages everyone to think directly about these serious public policy issues and their impact on fellow human beings was being challenged. Perhaps that reaction itself most highlighted the need for this art.

Coral Juárez Ard Dawson, Board member, Manhattan Community Board 2

×

Few artists have demonstrated the courage and the creativity of Ai Weiwei. His recent *Good Fences Make Good Neighbors* project in New York City showed once again the ethical concerns that inflect and animate his work. The piece *Arch* in Washington Square made a monument newly monumental.

Richard Armstrong, Director, Solomon R. Guggenheim Museum and Foundation

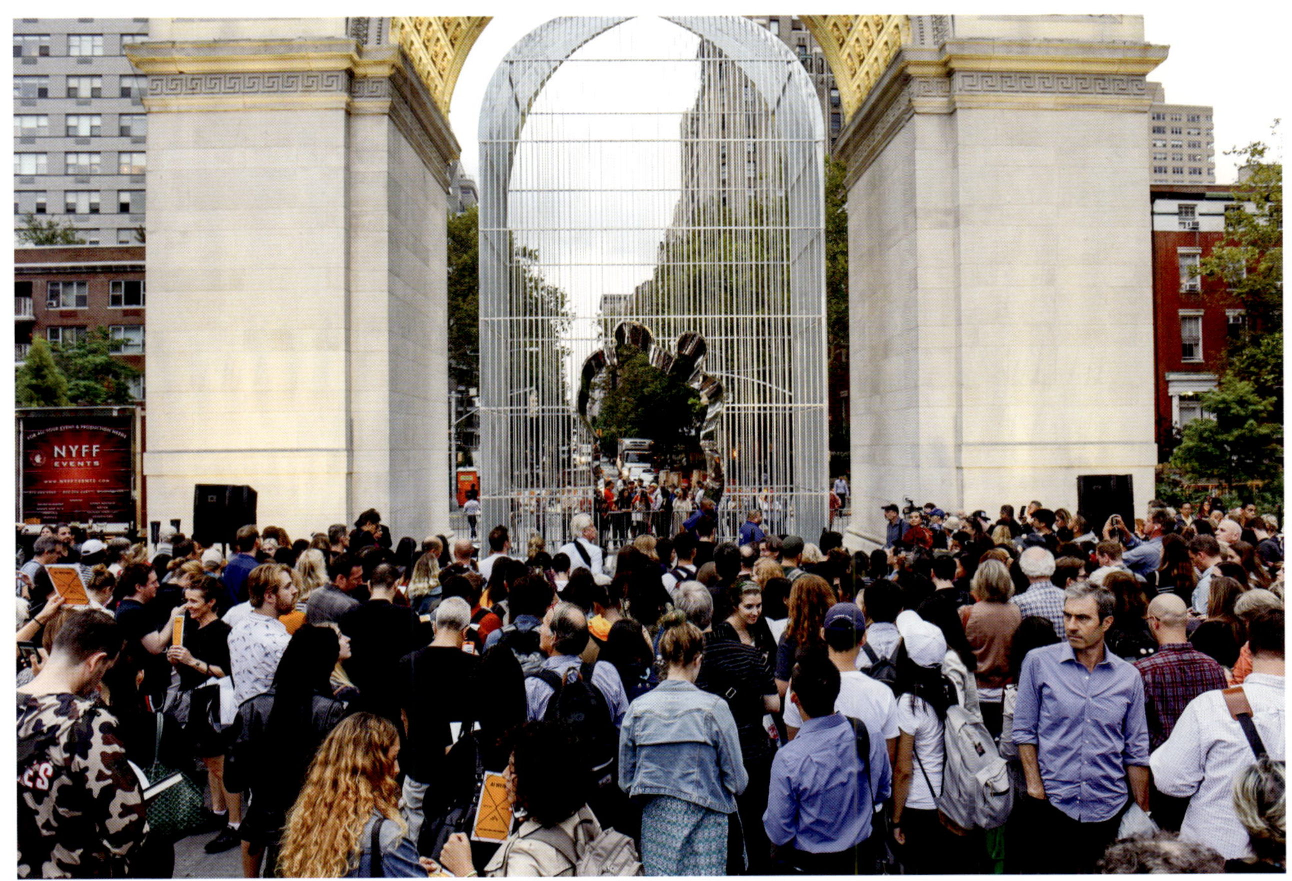

DOWNTOWN MANHATTAN

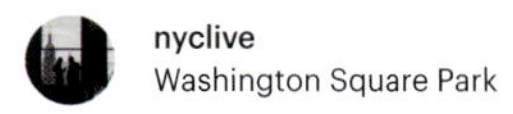

nyclive
Washington Square Park

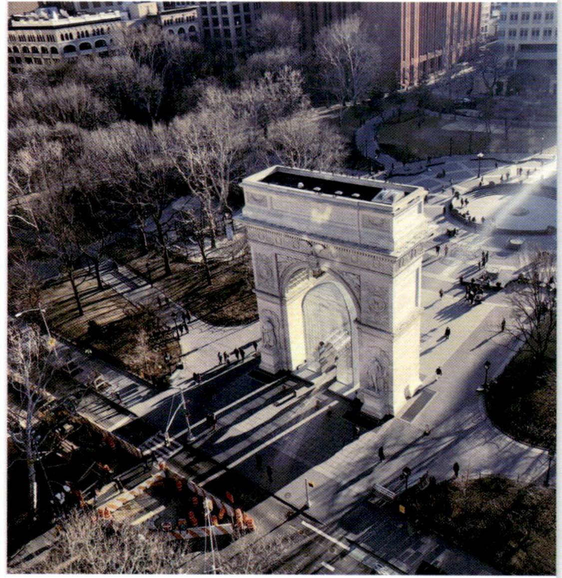

3,557 Likes

nyclive Not too crowded during the Winter. Revisit the first warm day of Spring. You'll be surprised ❀ photo by @eye_of_the_sixties #nyclives.

#nyc #people #newyork #arch #newyorker #manhattan #towers #wintervibes #building #nycparks #lifestyle #washingtonsquarepark #installationart #publicart #perspective #urban #goodfences #architecture

JANUARY 26, 2018

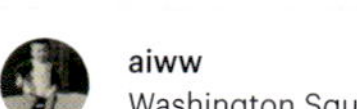

aiww
Washington Square Park

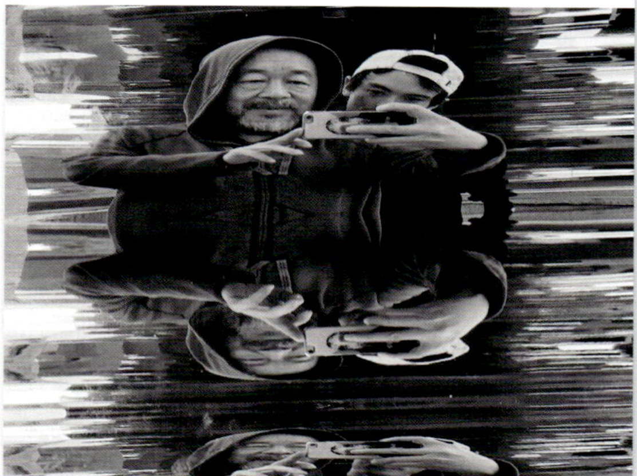

1,835 Likes

tilly2milly Hope you will post more about your NY installations ✶

annacarisma ⇧⇧⇧⇧

individualactivist Great shot!

sofiasuperlicious Proper selfie Mr Ai Weiwei ☺☺👌

nitin_shroff (::)

skangzz does anyone know how long will the installations be there for??

maryhh_dance God top ★

OCTOBER 12, 2017

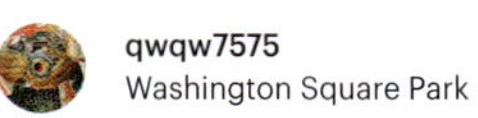

qwqw7575
Washington Square Park

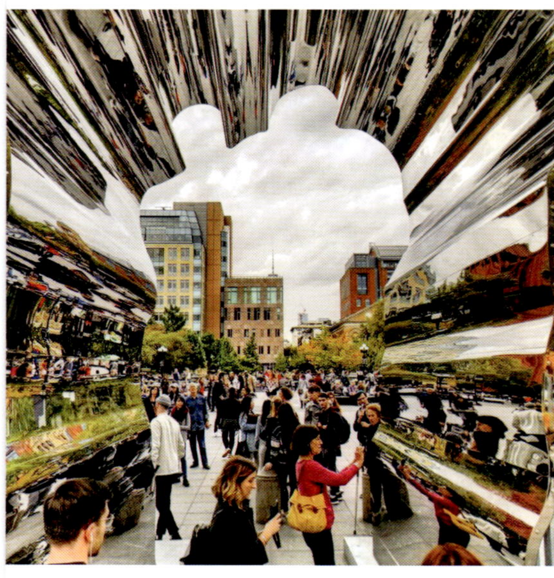

886 Likes

qwqw7575 Ai Weiwei's Controversial Washington Square Park Installation 'Good fences make good neighbors'
*

#aiweiwei #goodfencesmakegoodneighbors #art #artist #artists #artofvisuals #artartland #contemporaryart #artsanity #loveart #artiste #artgram #galleryart #abstractarts #artcollectors #cre8hype #multicolored #moodoflife #visualartist #kunstwerk #collageartist #instaarte #imagination

OCTOBER 25, 2017

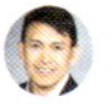

nyclovesnyc
Washington Square Park

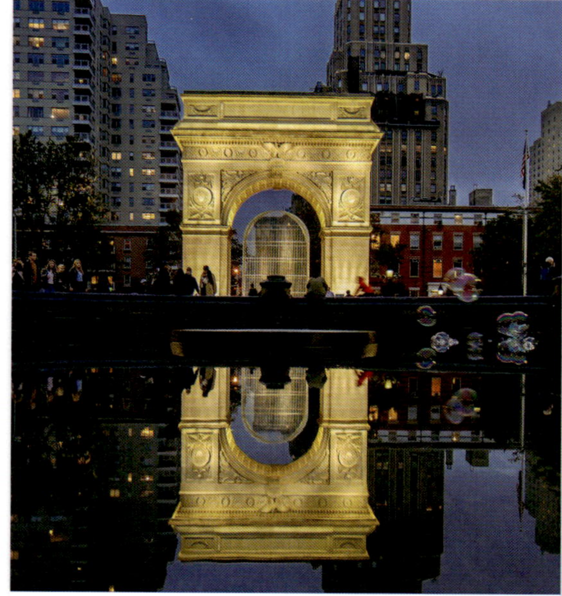

7,573 Likes

nyclovesnyc Reflecting on the issues surrounding the "international migration crisis." Washington Square Arch and Ai Wei Wei's "Good Fences Make Good Neighbors". Washington Square Park, Manhattan, New York City

#instagramnyc #total_newyork

NOVEMBER 7, 2017

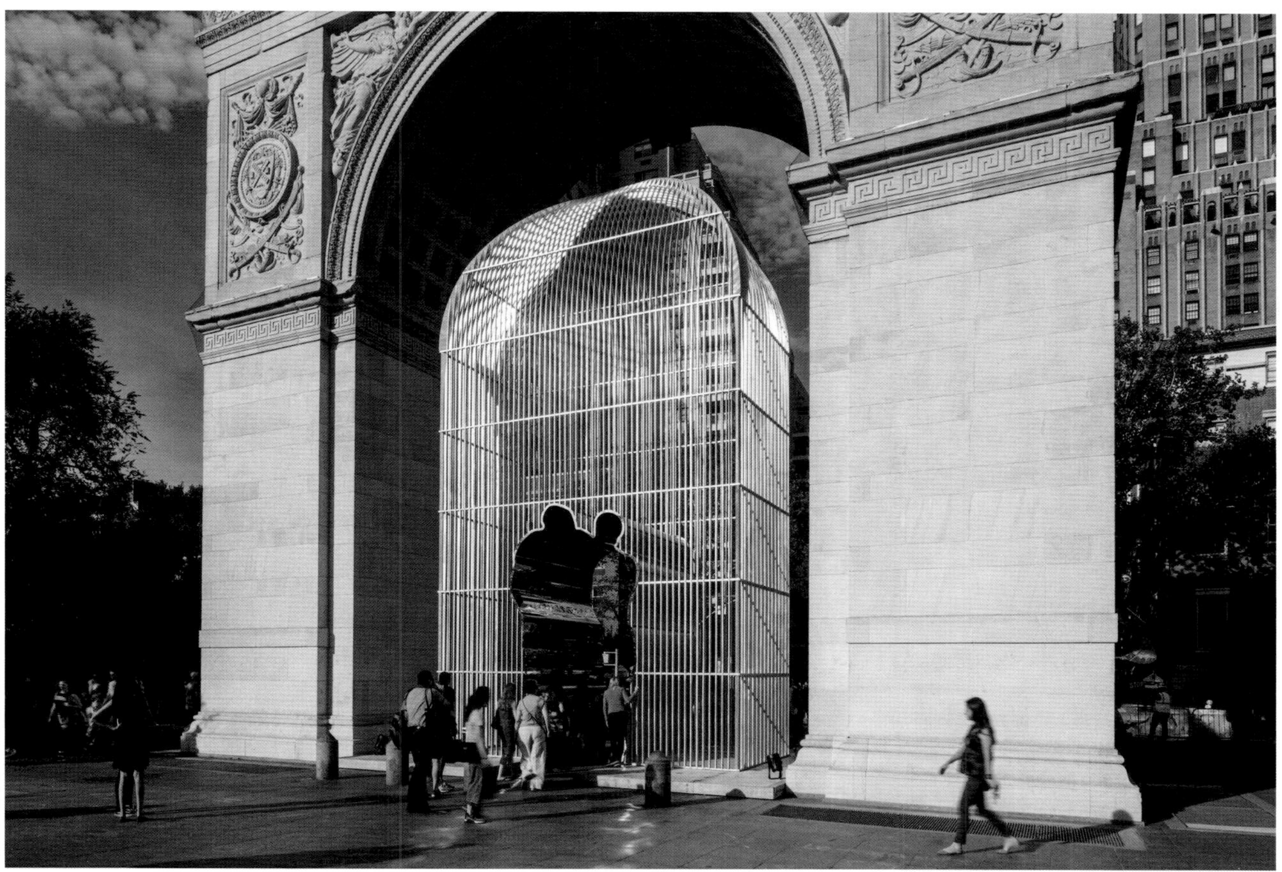

Ai Weiwei's voice now more than ever sparks both a universal and a local condition. And while I appreciate the desire, voiced by those who oppose the installation, to preserve the spirit of the Washington Square Arch, I would argue that this artwork is very much in the spirit of what the Arch and Washington Square represent. Now is the time to speak up, and where better than in New York City, where we have always listened to the powerful voices of art.

Billie Tsien, Tod Williams Billie Tsien Architects|Partners

×

I am accustomed to walking through Washington Square Park with frequency. The Arch sits in the northern part of the park. It is solely a decorative element. It possesses no life. Ai Weiwei's installation gave the Arch life. People—residents or tourists—consistently interacted with it and through it. It was indeed one of the most successful public art installations that I have had the privilege to engage with here in New York City. He continues to astonish me with his protean contemporary vision for what art can be for us in our daily lives.

Joseph V. Melillo, Executive Producer, BAM

Social media posts, *Arch* (opposite)

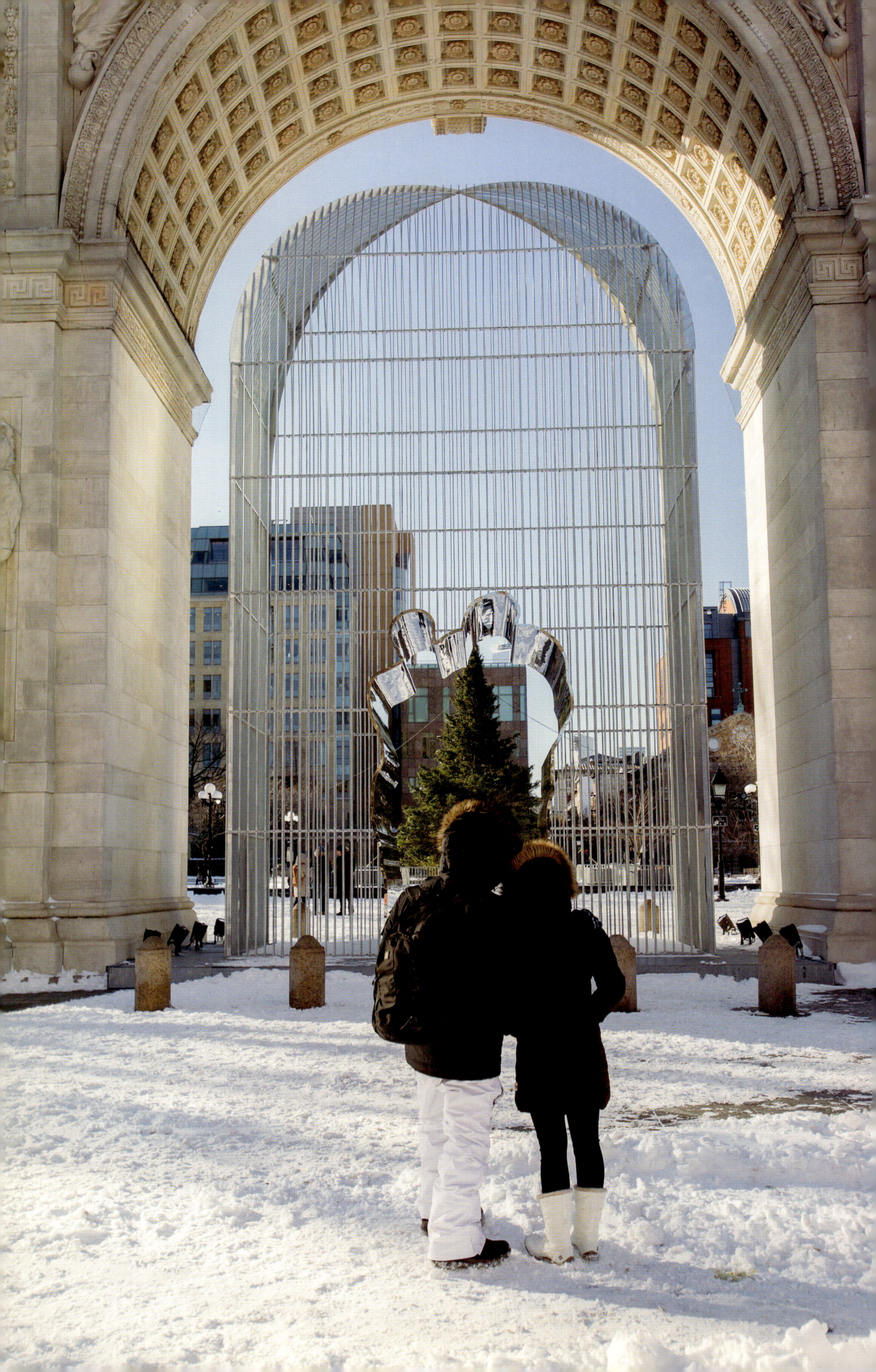

Mending Wall

Robert Frost, 1874–1963

Something there is that doesn't love a wall,
That sends the frozen-ground-swell under it,
And spills the upper boulders in the sun;
And makes gaps even two can pass abreast.
The work of hunters is another thing:
I have come after them and made repair
Where they have left not one stone on a stone,
But they would have the rabbit out of hiding,
To please the yelping dogs. The gaps I mean,
No one has seen them made or heard them made,
But at spring mending-time we find them there.
I let my neighbor know beyond the hill;
And on a day we meet to walk the line
And set the wall between us once again.
We keep the wall between us as we go.
To each the boulders that have fallen to each.
And some are loaves and some so nearly balls
We have to use a spell to make them balance:
"Stay where you are until our backs are turned!"
We wear our fingers rough with handling them.
Oh, just another kind of out-door game,
One on a side. It comes to little more:
There where it is we do not need the wall:
He is all pine and I am apple orchard.
My apple trees will never get across
And eat the cones under his pines, I tell him.
He only says, "Good fences make good neighbors."
Spring is the mischief in me, and I wonder
If I could put a notion in his head:
"*Why* do they make good neighbors? Isn't it
Where there are cows? But here there are no cows.
Before I built a wall I'd ask to know
What I was walling in or walling out,
And to whom I was like to give offence.
Something there is that doesn't love a wall,
That wants it down." I could say "Elves" to him,
But it's not elves exactly, and I'd rather
He said it for himself. I see him there
Bringing a stone grasped firmly by the top
In each hand, like an old-stone savage armed.
He moves in darkness as it seems to me,
Not of woods only and the shade of trees.
He will not go behind his father's saying,
And he likes having thought of it so well
He says again, "Good fences make good neighbors."

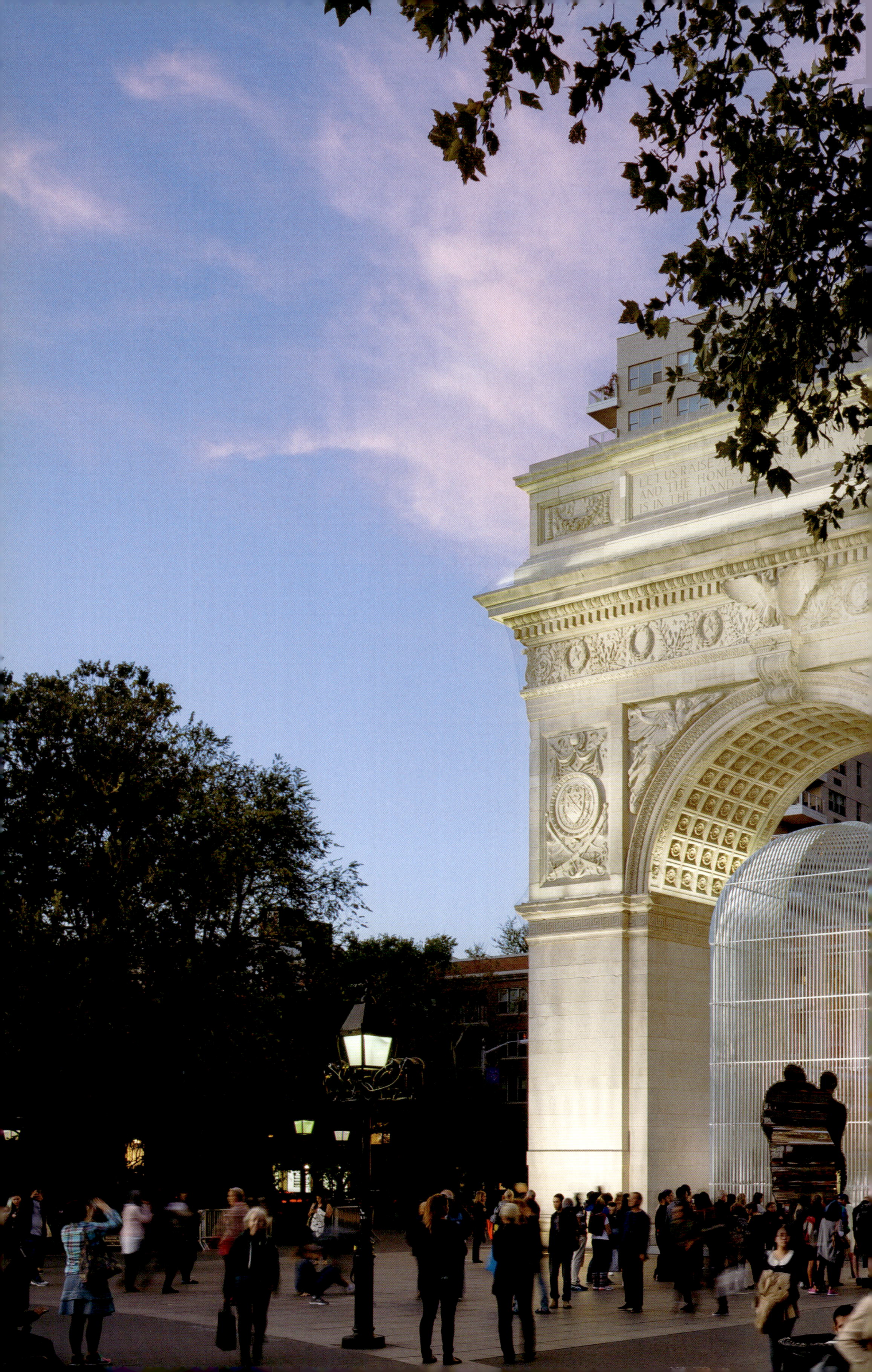
LET US RAISE
AND THE HONE
IS IN THE HAND

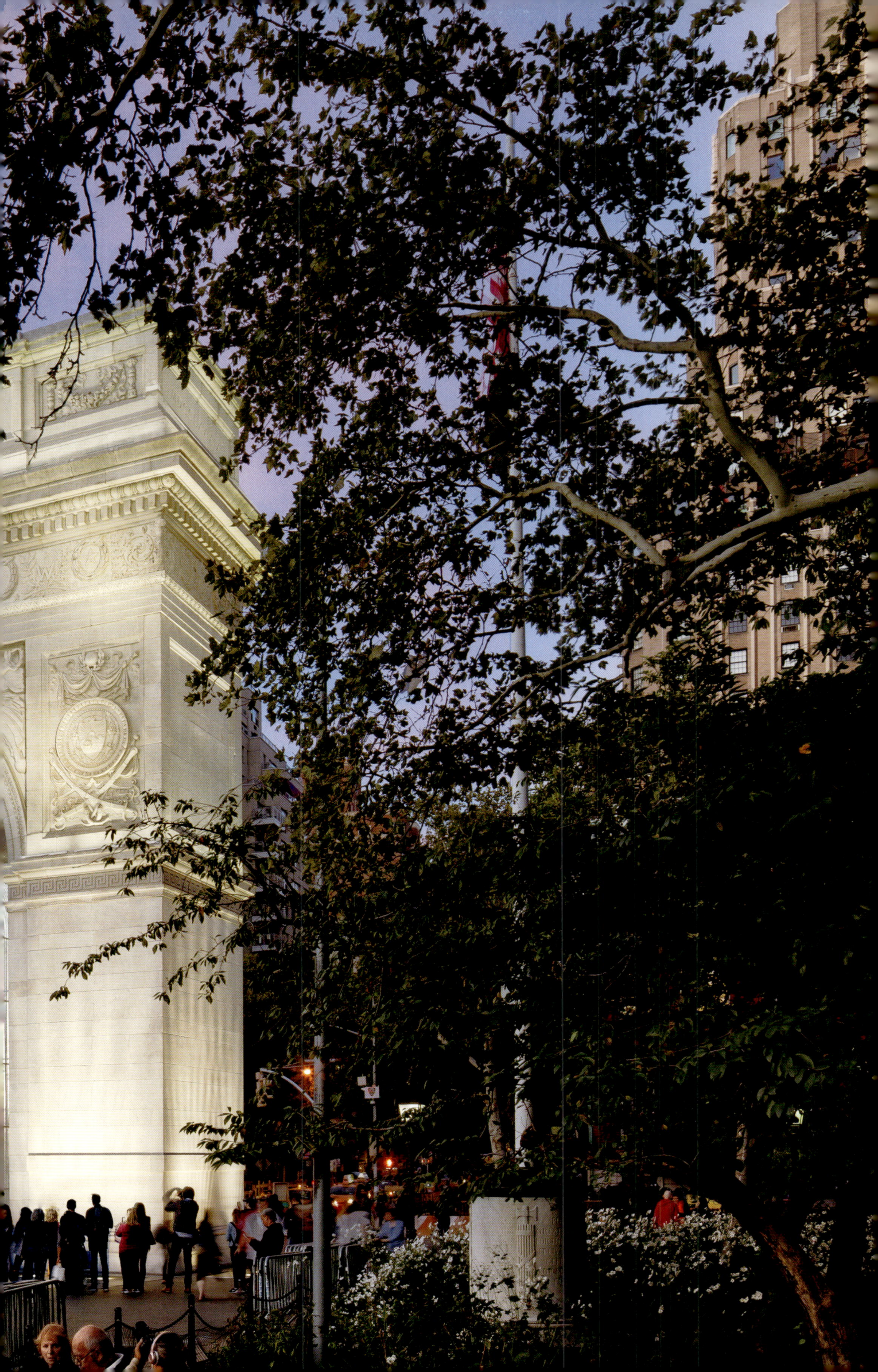

Checklist

All artworks, Ai Weiwei, 2017
All artworks and source photographs courtesy of the artist unless otherwise noted

Freestanding Installations

Arch
Galvanized mild steel, mirror-polished stainless steel
448 × 252 × 124 inches
Washington Square Park
Washington Square North and 5th Avenue, Manhattan
Courtesy Ai Weiwei Studio and Frahm & Frahm
Pages 282–86

Circle Fence
Powder-coated mild steel, polypropylene netting
64 × 76 × 12,480 inches (circumference)
Flushing Meadows Corona Park, Queens
Pages 154–163

Gilded Cage
Mild steel, paint
290 × 288 inches (diameter)
Doris C. Freedman Plaza, Central Park
60th Street and 5th Avenue, Manhattan
Courtesy Ai Weiwei Studio and Frahm & Frahm
Pages 58–71

Installations on Buildings

7th Street Fence
Steel, paint
432 × 36 × 2 inches
48 E. 7th Street, Manhattan
Pages 262–66

Bowery Fence
Steel, paint
144 × 252 × 2 inches
248 Bowery, Manhattan
Pages 256–261

Chrystie Street Fence
Steel, paint
144 × 276 × 2 inches
189 Chrystie Street, Manhattan
Pages 250–56

Exodus
CNC-cut vinyl polymer banner in thirteen elements
96 × 2,412 inches
Eight elements, each 96 × 186 inches
Two elements, each 96 × 180 inches
One element, 96 × 168 inches
One element, 96 × 192 inches
One element, 96 × 204 inches
Essex Street Market
120 Essex Street, Manhattan
Pages 236–243

Five Fences
Steel, paint
312 × 540 inches
Five elements, each 312 × 108 inches
The Cooper Union for the Advancement of Science and Art Foundation Building
7 E. 7th Street, Manhattan
Pages 266–271

Sculptural Installations for Bus Shelters

Pages 140–152
Unless otherwise noted, all works listed below are galvanized mild steel, 127 × 168 × 22 inches and were presented on JCDecaux bus shelters

Bronx Shelter 1
E. 163rd Street and 3rd Avenue, Bronx

Bronx Shelter 2
E. 163rd Street and 3rd Avenue, Bronx

Brooklyn Shelter 1
Boerum Place and Joralemon Street, Brooklyn

Brooklyn Shelter 2
Fulton and Smith Streets, Brooklyn

Brooklyn Shelter 3
Livingston and Smith Streets, Brooklyn

Brooklyn Shelter 4
127 × 338 × 22 inches
Fulton and Bond Streets, Brooklyn

Harlem Shelter 1
Central Park N. and Adam Clayton Powell Jr. Boulevard, Manhattan

Harlem Shelter 2
W. 122nd Street and Adam Clayton Powell Jr. Boulevard, Manhattan

Harlem Shelter 3
W. 125th Street and Frederick Douglass Boulevard, Manhattan

Harlem Shelter 4
W. 125th Street and 5th Avenue, Manhattan

Good Neighbors

Pages 184–216
One hundred *Good Neighbors* prints were exhibited at eighty-nine JCDecaux bus shelters in locations citywide. Ninety-eight of these were presented as printed posters and two as digital displays on 82-inch LCD monitors. In addition, ten of these were also displayed on digital LinkNYC kiosks at more than 1,000 locations. These ten digital works (15–30 seconds each) appeared on 45.5-by-27-inch monitors and are marked with an asterisk (*) below.

All printed works listed below are solvent-based pigment prints on GreenLight II Plus backlit matte paper with UV clear coat. 67 × 45.5 inches

Good Neighbors 1*
Source image: Makeshift Camp, Idomeni, Greece, 2016
Livingston and Smith Streets, Brooklyn

Good Neighbors 2*
Source image: Moria Camp, Lesvos, Greece, 2015
7th and Flatbush Avenues, Brooklyn

Good Neighbors 3*
Source image: Lesvos, Greece, 2015
Myrtle Avenue and Ashland Place, Brooklyn

Good Neighbors 4
Source image: Lesvos, Greece, 2015
Columbia and Carroll Streets, Brooklyn

Good Neighbors 5
Source image: Moria Camp, Lesvos, Greece, 2015
Brooklyn Shelter 3 (outside poster), Livingston Street and Gallatin Place, Brooklyn

Good Neighbors 6*
Source image: Moria Camp, Lesvos, Greece
Brooklyn Shelter 3 (inside poster), Livingston Street and Gallatin Place, Brooklyn

Good Neighbors 7
Source image: Moria Camp, Lesvos, Greece, 2015
Myrtle and N. Portland Avenues, Brooklyn

Good Neighbors 8*
Source image: Moria Camp, Lesvos, Greece, 2015
Prospect Park and Windsor Place, Brooklyn

Good Neighbors 9*
Source image: Moria Camp, Lesvos, Greece, 2015
5th Avenue and Bergen Street, Brooklyn

Good Neighbors 10*
Source image: Moria Camp, Lesvos, Greece, 2015
Vanderbilt Avenue and Plaza Street, Brooklyn

Good Neighbors 11*
Source image: Moria Camp, Lesvos, Greece, 2015
Brooklyn Shelter 4 (outside poster), Fulton and Bond Streets, Brooklyn

Good Neighbors 12*
Source image: Moria Camp, Lesvos, Greece, 2015
Brooklyn Shelter 4 (inside poster), Fulton and Bond Streets, Brooklyn

Good Neighbors 13*
Source image: Moria Camp, Lesvos, Greece, 2015
Digital display with *Good Neighbors 24*
Jamaica Avenue and Parsons Boulevard, Queens

Good Neighbors 14
Source image: Moria Camp, Lesvos, Greece, 2015
Brooklyn Shelter 2 (inside poster), Fulton and Smith Streets, Brooklyn

Good Neighbors 15
Source image: Moria Camp, Lesvos, Greece, 2015
Brooklyn Shelter 2 (outside poster), Fulton and Smith Streets, Brooklyn

Good Neighbors 16
Source image: Child Refugee Artwork, Lesvos, Greece, 2016
Brooklyn Shelter 4 (inside poster), Fulton and Bond Streets, Brooklyn

Good Neighbors 17
Source image: Lesvos, Greece, 2016
Brooklyn Shelter 4 (outside poster), Fulton and Bond Streets, Brooklyn

Good Neighbors 18
Source image: Lesvos, Greece, 2016
Sands and Pearl Streets, Brooklyn

Good Neighbors 19
Source image: Lesvos, Greece
Brooklyn Shelter 1 (inside poster), Boerum Place and Joralemon Street, Brooklyn

Good Neighbors 20
Source image: Lesvos, Greece, 2016
Brooklyn Shelter 1 (outside poster), Boerum Place and Joralemon Street, Brooklyn

Good Neighbors 21
Source image: Lesvos, Greece, 2016
Pelham Parkway and Williamsbridge Road, Bronx

Good Neighbors 22
Source image: Lesvos, Greece, 2016
Morris Avenue and E. 161st Street, Bronx

Good Neighbors 23
Source image: Lesvos, Greece, 2016
Grand Concourse and E. 161st Street, Bronx

Good Neighbors 24
Source image: Lesvos, Greece, 2016
Digital display with *Good Neighbors 13*
Jamaica Avenue and Parsons Boulevard, Queens

Good Neighbors 25
Source image: Moria Camp, Lesvos, Greece, 2016
Bronx Shelter 1 (inside poster), E. 163rd Street and 3rd Avenue, Bronx

Good Neighbors 26
Source image: Kara Tepe Camp, Lesvos, Greece, 2016
Bronx Shelter 1 (outside poster), E. 163rd Street and 3rd Avenue, Bronx

Good Neighbors 27
Source image: Lesvos, Greece, 2016
Bronx Shelter 2 (inside poster), E. 163rd Street and 3rd Avenue, Bronx

Good Neighbors 28
Source image: Lesvos, Greece, 2016
Bronx Shelter 2 (outside poster), E. 163rd Street and 3rd Avenue, Bronx

Good Neighbors 29
Source image: Mytilene Port, Lesvos, Greece, 2016
Morris Avenue and E. 158th Street, Bronx

Good Neighbors 30
Source image: Lesvos, Greece, 2016
Grand Concourse and E. 166th Street, Bronx

Good Neighbors 31
Source image: Lesvos, Greece, 2016
Morris Avenue and E. 158th Street, Bronx

Good Neighbors 32
Source image: Lesvos, Greece, 2016
Melrose Avenue and E. 162nd Street, Bronx

Good Neighbors 33
Source image: Lesvos, Greece, 2016
E. 161st Street and Melrose Avenue, Bronx

Good Neighbors 34*
Source image: Makeshift Camp, Idomeni, Greece, 2016
Melrose Avenue and E. 160th Street, Bronx

Good Neighbors 35
Source image: Makeshift Camp, Idomeni, Greece, 2016
E. 1st Street and 1st Avenue, Manhattan

Good Neighbors 36
Source image: Makeshift Camp, Idomeni, Greece, 2016
1st Avenue and E. 20th Street, Manhattan

Good Neighbors 37
Source image: Makeshift Camp, Idomeni, Greece, 2016
3rd Avenue and E. 106th Street, Manhattan

Good Neighbors 38
Source image: Makeshift Camp, Idomeni, Greece, 2016
W. 116th Street and Adam Clayton Powell Jr. Boulevard, Manhattan

Good Neighbors 39
Source image: West Bank Barrier, 2016
Harlem Shelter 1 (inside poster), Central Park N. and Lenox Avenue, Manhattan

Good Neighbors 40
Source image: Makeshift Camp, Idomeni, Greece, 2016
Avenue D and E. Houston Street, Manhattan

Good Neighbors 41
Source image: Makeshift Camp, Idomeni, Greece, 2016
Madison Avenue and E. 103rd Street, Manhattan

Good Neighbors 42
Source image: Makeshift Camp, Idomeni, Greece, 2016
Amsterdam Avenue and W. 131st Street, Manhattan

Good Neighbors 43
Source image: Makeshift Camp, Idomeni, Greece, 2016
E. Houston Street and Avenue B, Manhattan

Good Neighbors 44
Source image: Makeshift Camp, Idomeni, Greece, 2016
Avenue A and E. 3rd Street, Manhattan

Good Neighbors 45
Source image: Makeshift Camp, Idomeni, Greece, 2016
E. 116th Street and 3rd Avenue, Manhattan

Good Neighbors 46
Source image: Makeshift Camp, Idomeni, Greece, 2016
Frederick Douglass Boulevard and W. 130th Street, Manhattan

Good Neighbors 47
Source image: Makeshift Camp, Idomeni, Greece, 2016
Amsterdam Avenue and W. 143rd Street, Manhattan

Good Neighbors 48
Source image: Makeshift Camp, Idomeni, Greece, 2016
Riverside Drive and W. 158th Street, Manhattan

Good Neighbors 49
Source image: Makeshift Camp, Idomeni, Greece, 2016
2nd Avenue and E. 6th Street, Manhattan

Good Neighbors 50
Source image: Kara Tepe Camp, Lesvos, Greece, 2016
Manhattan Avenue and W. 114th Street, Manhattan

Good Neighbors 51
Source image: Kara Tepe Camp, Lesvos, Greece, 2016
Malcolm X Boulevard and W. 135th Street, Manhattan

Good Neighbors 52
Source image: Lesvos, Greece, 2016
Manhattan Avenue and W. 116th Street, Manhattan

Good Neighbors 53
Source image: Makeshift Camp, Idomeni, Greece, 2016
Avenue C and E. 6th Street, Manhattan

Good Neighbors 54
Source image: Makeshift Camp, Idomeni, Greece, 2016
2nd Avenue and E. 100th Street, Manhattan

Good Neighbors 55
Source image: Makeshift Camp, Idomeni, Greece, 2016
Central Park N. and W. 100th Street, Manhattan

Good Neighbors 56
Source image: Makeshift Camp, Idomeni, Greece, 2016
2nd Avenue and E. 13th Street, Manhattan

Good Neighbors 57
Source image: Makeshift Camp, Idomeni, Greece, 2016
W. 135th Street and Riverside Drive, Manhattan

Good Neighbors 58
Source image: Makeshift Camp, Idomeni, Greece, 2016
E. 125th Street and Lexington Avenue, Manhattan

Good Neighbors 59
Source image: Makeshift Camp, Idomeni, Greece, 2016
E. 125th Street and Madison Avenue, Manhattan

Good Neighbors 60
Source image: Makeshift Camp, Idomeni, Greece, 2016
Harlem Shelter 2 (inside poster), W. 122nd Street and Adam Clayton Powell Jr. Boulevard, Manhattan

Good Neighbors 61
Source image: Makeshift Camp, Idomeni, Greece, 2016
Harlem Shelter 2 (outside poster), W. 122nd Street and Adam Clayton Powell Jr. Boulevard, Manhattan

Good Neighbors 62
Source image: Makeshift Camp, Idomeni, Greece, 2016
E. 125th Street and 5th Avenue, Manhattan

Good Neighbors 63
Source image: Makeshift Camp, Idomeni, Greece, 2016
Amsterdam Avenue and W. 118th Street, Manhattan

Good Neighbors 64
Source image: Makeshift Camp, Idomeni, Greece, 2016
W. 125th Street and Amsterdam Avenue, Manhattan

Good Neighbors 65
Source image: Makeshift Camp, Idomeni, Greece, 2016
St. Nicholas Avenue and W. 135th Street, Manhattan

Good Neighbors 66
Source image: Makeshift Camp, Idomeni, Greece, 2016
Harlem Shelter 4 (inside poster), 125th Street and 5th Avenue, Manhattan

Good Neighbors 67
Source image: Makeshift Camp, Torbali, Turkey, 2016
Harlem Shelter 4 (outside poster), 125th Street and 5th Avenue, Manhattan

Good Neighbors 68
Source image: Nizip Camp, Gaziantep, Turkey, 2016
Adam Clayton Powell Jr. Boulevard and W. 126th Street, Manhattan

Good Neighbors 69
Source image: Shatila Refugee Camp, Beirut, Lebanon, 2016
W. 125th Street and Adam Clayton Powell Jr. Boulevard, Manhattan

Good Neighbors 70
Source image: Outskirts of Arsal, Lebanon, 2016
Harlem Shelter 3 (inside poster), W. 125th Street and Frederick Douglass Boulevard, Manhattan

Good Neighbors 71
Source image: Beqaa Valley, Lebanon, 2016
Harlem Shelter 3 (outside poster), W. 125th Street and Frederick Douglass Boulevard, Manhattan

Good Neighbors 72
Source image: Zahle Camp, Beqaa, Lebanon, 2016
W. 125th Street and Frederick Douglass Boulevard, Manhattan

Good Neighbors 73
Source image: Ain al-Hilweh Camp, Sidon, Lebanon, 2016
W. 145th Street and Frederick Douglass Boulevard, Manhattan

Good Neighbors 74
Source image: Ain al-Hilweh Camp, Sidon, Lebanon, 2016
Broadway and W. 133rd Street, Manhattan

Good Neighbors 75
Source image: Ain al-Hilweh Camp, Sidon, Lebanon, 2016
Broadway and W. 108th Street, Manhattan

Good Neighbors 76
Source image: Syrian-Jordanian Border, 2016
E. 14th Street and Avenue A, Manhattan

Good Neighbors 77
Source image: Syrian-Jordanian Border, 2016
Avenue A and E. 9th Street, Manhattan

Good Neighbors 78
Source image: Syrian-Jordanian Border, 2016
Broadway and LaSalle Street, Manhattan

Good Neighbors 79
Source image: West Bank Barrier, 2016
5th Avenue and W. 139th Street, Manhattan

Good Neighbors 80
Source image: West Bank Barrier, 2016
W. 5th Avenue and 116th Street, Manhattan

Good Neighbors 81
Source image: Erez Checkpoint, Gaza, Palestine, 2016
Harlem Shelter 1 (outside poster), Central Park N. and Adam Clayton Powell Jr. Boulevard, Manhattan

Good Neighbors 82
Source image: Kuba District, Gaza, Palestine, 2016
108th Street and Martense Avenue, Queens

Good Neighbors 83
Source image: Rafah Border Crossing, Gaza, Palestine, 2016
Corona Avenue and 104th Street, Queens

Good Neighbors 84
Source image: Rafah Border Crossing, Gaza, Palestine, 2016
108th Street and 51st Avenue, Queens

Good Neighbors 85
Source image: Gaza, Palestine, 2016
57th Avenue and 99th Street, Queens

Good Neighbors 86
Source image: Gaza, Palestine, 2016
Corona Avenue and 104th Street, Queens

Good Neighbors 87
Source image: Qalandiya Checkpoint, West Bank, Palestine, 2016
Corona Avenue and 102nd Street, Queens

Good Neighbors 88
Source image: Qalandiya Checkpoint, West Bank, Palestine, 2016
108th Street and Martense Avenue, Queens

Good Neighbors 89
Source image: Dadaab Camp, Garissa County, Kenya, 2016
Corona Avenue and 102nd Street, Queens

Good Neighbors 90
Source image: Dadaab Camp, Garissa County, Kenya, 2016
99th Street and 58th Avenue, Queens

Good Neighbors 91
Source image: Mexican-United States Border, 2017
99th Street and Lewis Avenue, Queens

Good Neighbors 92
Source image: Nizip Camp, Gaziantep, Turkey, 2017
Richmond Terrace and Shuyler Street, Staten Island

Good Neighbors 93
Source image: Dadaab Camp, Garissa County, Kenya, 2017
Richmond Terrace and Jersey Street, Staten Island

Good Neighbors 94
Source image: Mediterranean Sea, 2017
Victory Boulevard and Montgomery Avenue, Staten Island

Good Neighbors 95
Source image: Outskirts of Mosul, Iraq, 2017
Clove Road and Cheshire Place, Staten Island

Good Neighbors 96
Source image: Tempelhof Airport Camp, Berlin, Germany, 2017
Forest Avenue and Oxford Place, Staten Island

Good Neighbors 97
Source image: Near Idomeni, Greece, 2017
Richmond Terrace and Jersey Street, Staten Island

Good Neighbors 98
Source image: Makeshift Camp, Idomeni, Greece, 2017
Victory Boulevard and Eddy Street, Staten Island

Good Neighbors 99
Source image: Peshawar, Pakistan, 2017
Richmond Terrace and Nicholas Street, Staten Island

Good Neighbors 100
Source image: Kutupalong Refugee Camp, Ukhia, Bangladesh, 2017
Richmond Terrace and Franklin Avenue, Staten Island

Odyssey

Pages 244–49
Works listed below are solvent-based pigment prints on DuraPrint polyester film with UV clear coat
72 × 144 inches (rear poster)
804 × 45.5 inches (side poster)

Odyssey 1
E. 46th Street and 5th Avenue, Manhattan

Odyssey 2
E. 23rd Street and Park Avenue South, Manhattan

Odyssey 3
E. 14th Street and University Place, Manhattan

Odyssey 4
Delancey and Clinton Streets, Manhattan

Odyssey 5
Canal and Baxter Streets, Manhattan

Banners

Pages 72–104
Works listed below are made from CNC-cut vinyl polymer
96 × 36 inches

Banner 1
Albanian Soldier, ca. 1905–1914
Source photographer: Augustus Sherman
3rd Avenue and E. 7th Street, Manhattan

Banner 2
Algerian Man, ca. 1905–1914
Source photographer: Augustus Sherman
E. 56th Street and 5th Avenue, Manhattan

Banner 3
Girl from Alsace-Lorraine, 1906
Source photographer: Augustus Sherman
E. 161st Street and Melrose Avenue, Bronx

Banner 4
Bavarian Man, ca. 1905–1914
Source photographers: Augustus Sherman and Wilhelm Schleich
Bleeker and Sullivan Streets, Manhattan

Banner 5
Borana Family from Southern Ethiopia (detail), ca. 1905–1914
Source photographer: Augustus Sherman
Sullivan and W. 3rd Streets, Manhattan

Banner 6
Cantonese Woman, ca. 1905–1914
Source photographer: Augustus Sherman
Rivington and Chrystie Streets, Manhattan

Banner 7
Lapland Children (detail), ca. 1905–1914
Source photographer: Augustus Sherman
2nd Avenue and Avenue A, Manhattan

Banner 8
Cossack Immigrants, ca. 1905–1914
Source photographer: Augustus Sherman
Richmond Terrace and Nicholas Street, Staten Island

Banner 9
Dutch Siblings from the Island of Marken Holding Religious Tracts (detail), ca. 1905–1914
Source photographer: Augustus Sherman
Bleeker and Sullivan Streets, Manhattan

Banner 10
Mother from the Netherlands, ca. 1905–1914
Source photographer: Augustus Sherman
Richmond Terrace and St. Peter's Place, Staten Island

Banner 11
Protestant Woman from the Netherlands, ca. 1905–1914
Source photographer: Augustus Sherman
Grand Street and Bedford Avenue, Brooklyn

Banner 12
Eleazar Kaminetzko, Russian Hebrew, Hamburg, 1914
Source photographer: Augustus Sherman
Bleeker and Thompson Streets, Manhattan

Banner 13
English Jew, ca. 1905–1914
Source photographer: Augustus Sherman
Waverly Place and Greene Street, Manhattan

Banner 14
Finnish Family, ca. 1905–1914
Source photographer: Augustus Sherman
Grand Army Plaza and Doris C. Freedman Plaza West, Manhattan

Banner 15
Finnish Girl, ca. 1905–1914
Source photographer: Augustus Sherman
W. 116th Street and Adam Clayton Powell Jr. Boulevard, Manhattan

Banner 16
German Stowaway, 1911
Source photographer: Augustus Sherman
Metropolitan Avenue and Lorimer Street, Brooklyn

Banner 17
Swedish Girl, ca. 1905–1914
Source photographer: Augustus Sherman
Bowery and E. 1st Street, Manhattan

Banner 18
Reverend Joseph Valison, ca. 1905–1914
Source photographer: Augustus Sherman
7th Avenue and W. 116th Street, Manhattan

Banner 19
Greek Woman, 1909
Source photographer: Augustus Sherman
Malcolm X Boulevard and W. 124th Street, Manhattan

Banner 20
Roman Family (detail), ca. 1905–1914
Source photographer: Augustus Sherman
Thompson Street and W. 3rd Street, Manhattan

Banner 21
Thumbu Sammy, 1911
Source photographer: Augustus Sherman
Chrystie and Rivington Streets, Manhattan

Banner 22
Hungarian Family (detail), ca. 1905–1914
Source photographer: Augustus Sherman
E. 7th Street and 2nd Avenue, Manhattan

Banner 23
Italian Woman, ca. 1905–1914
Source photographer: Augustus Sherman
Park Avenue and E. 86th Street, Manhattan

Banner 24
Italian Woman, ca. 1905–1914
Source photographer: Augustus Sherman
Sullivan and W. 3rd Streets, Manhattan

Banner 25
Laplander, 1910
Source photographer: Augustus Sherman
37th Road and 75th Street, Queens

Banner 26
Moroccan Men and Boy (detail), ca. 1905–1914
Source photographer: Augustus Sherman
7th Avenue and W. 124th Street, Manhattan

Banner 27
Moroccan Men and Boy (detail), ca. 1905–1914
Source photographer: Augustus Sherman
W. 18th Street and 10th Avenue, Manhattan

Banner 28
Romanian Shepherd, 1906
Source photographer: Augustus Sherman
2nd Avenue and E. 7th Street, Manhattan

Banner 29
Romanian Woman, ca. 1905–1914
Source photograph: Ain al-Hilweh Camp, Sidon, Lebanon
Thompson and Bleeker Streets, Manhattan

Banner 30
Ruthenian Woman, 1906
Source photographer: Augustus Sherman
Elton Avenue and E. 163rd Street, Bronx

Banner 31
Scottish Girls in Kilts (detail), ca. 1905–1914
Source photographer: Augustus Sherman
Broadway and Fulton Street, Manhattan

Banner 32
Sikh from India, ca. 1905–1914
Source photographer: Augustus Sherman
E. 8th Street and Cooper Square, Manhattan

Banner 33
Slovakian Mother and Her Children (detail), ca. 1905–1914
Source photographer: Augustus Sherman
Washington Square North and Washington Square East, Manhattan

Banner 34
Slovakian Woman, ca. 1905–1914
Source photographer: Augustus Sherman
Rivington and Chrystie Streets, Manhattan

Banner 35
Swedish Woman, ca. 1905–1914
Source photographer: Augustus Sherman
Bleeker and Sullivan Streets, Manhattan

Banner 36
Turkish Bank Guard, John Postanzi, 1912
Source photographer: Augustus Sherman
Lenox Avenue and W. 124th Street, Manhattan

Banner 37
Blank
Livingston and Nevins Streets, Brooklyn

Banner 38
Josephine Baker, 1927
Source photographer: Lucien Waléry
Chrystie and Broome Streets, Manhattan

Banner 39
Béla Bartók, 1927
Source photographer unknown
Park Avenue and E. 82nd Street, Manhattan

Banner 40
Max Born
Source photographer unknown
Graham and Metropolitan Avenues, Brooklyn

Banner 41
Joseph Brodsky, 1972–1973
Source photograph: University of Michigan Yearbook
Washington Place and Greene Street, Manhattan

Banner 42
Robert Capa, 1937
Source photographer: Gerda Taro
Rodney and S. 4th Streets, Brooklyn

Banner 43
Marc Chagall, 1920
Source photographer: Pierre Choumoff
5th Avenue and E. 19th Street, Manhattan

Banner 44
Frédéric Chopin, 1849
Source photographer: Louis-Auguste Bisson
7th Avenue and W. 121st Street, Manhattan

Banner 45
Joseph Conrad, 1904
Source photographer: George Charles Beresford
W. 116th Street and Adam Clayton Powell Jr. Boulevard, Manhattan

Banner 46
The Dalai Lama, 2014
Source photographer: Pete Souza
Elton Avenue and E. 161st Street, Bronx

Banner 47
Marlene Dietrich, 1932
Source photographer: Don English
Church and Liberty Streets, Manhattan

Banner 48
Albert Einstein, 1920
Source photographer Unknown
Brook and 3rd Avenues, Bronx

Banner 49
Anne Frank, 1940
Source photographer unknown
37th Road and 75th Street, Queens

Banner 50
Sigmund Freud, ca. 1921
Source photographer: Max Halberstadt
W. 3rd Street and LaGuardia Place, Manhattan

Banner 51
Emma Goldman, mugshot, 1901
Source photographer: Bain News Service
E. 7th Street and 2nd Avenue, Manhattan

Banner 52
Walter Gropius, 1919
Source photographer: Louis Held
Eldridge and Stanton Streets, Manhattan

Banner 53
Victor Hugo, 1876
Source photographer: Étienne Carjat
Washington Square East and 5th Avenue, Manhattan

Banner 54
Wassily Kandinsky, 1913
Source photographer unknown
Park Avenue and E. 86th Street, Manhattan

Banner 55
André Kertész, 1975
Source photographer: Wien Wolfgang H
W. 18th Street and 5th Avenue, Manhattan

Banner 56
Thomas Mann, 1937
Source photographer: Carl Van Vechten
Rodney and S. 4th Streets, Brooklyn

Banner 57
Karl Marx, ca. 1875
Source photographer: John Habez Edwin Mayal
W. 56th Street and 5th Avenue, Manhattan

Banner 58
Tina Modotti, 1921
Source photographer: Edward Weston
Washington Place and Washington Square West, Manhattan

Banner 59
László Moholy-Nagy, 1938
Source photographer unknown
Bowery and E. 4th Street, Manhattan

Banner 60
Piet Mondrian, 1926
Source photographer: André Kertész
Essex and Hester Streets, Manhattan

Banner 61
Pablo Neruda, 1963
Source photographer: Mondadori Publishers
Richmond Terrace and Nicholas Street, Staten Island

Banner 62
Oscar Niemeyer, ca. 1950
Source photographer unknown
2nd Avenue and St. Mark's Place, Manhattan

Banner 63
Arnold Schoenberg, 1948
Source photographer: Florence Homolka
Church and Liberty Streets, Manhattan

Banner 64
Nina Simone, 1969
Source photographer: Gerrit de Bruin
E. 53rd Street and 5th Avenue, Manhattan

Banner 65
Blank
E. 161st Street and Melrose Avenue, Bronx

Banner 66
Leon Trotsky, 1920
Source photographer: Isaac McBride
W. 3rd Street and LaGuardia Place, Manhattan

Banner 67
Elie Wiesel, 1987
Source photographer: Erling Mandelmann
37th Avenue and 76th Street, Queens

Banner 68
Billy Wilder, ca. 1950
Source photographer unknown
Essex and Canal Streets, Manhattan

Banner 69
Ai Qing, 1929
Source photographer unknown
E. 3rd Street and Avenue B, Manhattan

Banner 70
Refugee, Shariya Camp, Iraq, 2015
Sullivan and W. 3rd Streets, Manhattan

Banner 71
Refugee, Shariya Camp, Iraq, 2015
W. 4th Street and 6th Avenue, Manhattan

Banner 72
Refugee, Shariya Camp, Iraq, 2015
37th Avenue and 75th Street, Queens

Banner 73
Refugee, Shariya Camp, Iraq, 2015
2nd Avenue and E. 11th Street, Manhattan

Banner 74
Refugee, Shariya Camp, Iraq, 2015
Grand and Berry Streets, Brooklyn

Banner 75
Refugee, Shariya Camp, Iraq, 2015
Amsterdam Avenue and W. 93rd Street, Manhattan

Banner 76
Refugee, Shariya Camp, Iraq, 2015
W. 18th Street and 10th Avenue, Manhattan

Banner 77
Refugee, Shariya Camp, Iraq, 2015
W. 30th Street and 6th Avenue, Manhattan

Banner 78
Refugee, Shariya Camp, Iraq, 2015
Greene and W. 4th Streets, Manhattan

Banner 79
Refugee, Shariya Camp, Iraq, 2015
W. 56th Street and 5th Avenue, Manhattan

Banner 80
Refugee, Shariya Camp, Iraq, 2015
Livingston Street and Hanover Place, Brooklyn

Banner 81
Refugee, Shariya Camp, Iraq, 2015
MacDougal Street and Washington Square North, Manhattan

Banner 82
Refugee, Shariya Camp, Iraq, 2015
W. 116th Street and Adam Clayton Powell Jr. Boulevard, Manhattan

Banner 83
Refugee, Shariya Camp, Iraq, 2015
W. 116th Street and Adam Clayton Powell Jr. Boulevard, Manhattan

Banner 84
Refugee, Shariya Camp, Iraq, 2015
Forsyth and Rivington Streets, Manhattan

Banner 85
Refugee, Shariya Camp, Iraq, 2015
Forsyth and E. Houston Streets, Manhattan

Banner 86
Refugee, Shariya Camp, Iraq, 2015
Chrystie and Rivington Streets, Manhattan

Banner 87
Refugee, Shariya Camp, Iraq, 2015
Amsterdam Avenue and W. 92nd Street, Manhattan

Banner 88
Refugee, Shariya Camp, Iraq, 2015
Forsyth and Rivington Streets, Manhattan

Banner 89
Refugee, Shariya Camp, Iraq, 2015
37th Avenue and 74th Street, Queens

Banner 90
Refugee, Shariya Camp, Iraq, 2015
Chrystie and Rivington Streets, Manhattan

Banner 91
Refugee, Shariya Camp, Iraq, 2015
W. 4th and Mercer Streets, Manhattan

Banner 92
Refugee, Shariya Camp, Iraq, 2015
Tito Puente Way and Madison Avenue, Manhattan

Banner 93
Refugee, Shariya Camp, Iraq, 2015
E. 19th Street and 5th Avenue, Manhattan

Banner 94
Refugee, Shariya Camp, Iraq, 2015
Elton Avenue and E. 161st Street, Bronx

Banner 95
Refugee, Shariya Camp, Iraq, 2015
Grand Concourse and E. 165th Street, Bronx

Banner 96
Refugee, Shariya Camp, Iraq, 2015
3rd Avenue and St. Ann's Avenue, Bronx

Banner 97
Refugee, Shariya Camp, Iraq, 2015
Essex and Hester Streets, Manhattan

Banner 98
Refugee, Shariya Camp, Iraq, 2015
Chrystie and Rivington Streets, Manhattan

Banner 99
Refugee, Shariya Camp, Iraq, 2015
Amsterdam Avenue and W. 69th Street, Manhattan

Banner 100
Refugee, Shariya Camp, Iraq, 2015
3rd Avenue and Weiher Court, Bronx

Banner 101
Refugee, Shariya Camp, Iraq, 2015
W. 18th Street and 9th Avenue, Manhattan

Banner 102
Refugee, Shariya Camp, Iraq, 2015
Bowery and E. 2nd Street, Manhattan

Banner 103
Refugee, Shariya Camp, Iraq, 2015
University Place and Washington Square North, Manhattan

Banner 104
Refugee, Shariya Camp, Iraq, 2015
Greene and W. 4th Streets, Manhattan

Banner 105
Refugee, Shariya Camp, Iraq, 2015
7th Avenue and W. 120th Street, Manhattan

Banner 106
Refugee, Shariya Camp, Iraq, 2015
Washington Place and Broadway, Manhattan

Banner 107
Refugee, Shariya Camp, Iraq, 2015
Doris C. Freedman Plaza, 60th Street and 5th Avenue, Manhattan

Banner 108
Refugee, Shariya Camp, Iraq, 2015
Grand and Berry Streets, Brooklyn

Banner 109
Refugee, Shariya Camp, Iraq, 2015
Havemeyer and Metropolitan Streets, Brooklyn

Banner 110
Refugee, Moria Camp, Lesvos, Greece, 2015
Madison Avenue and Tito Puente Way, Manhattan

Banner 111
Refugee, Moria Camp, Lesvos, Greece, 2015
Chrystie and Rivington Streets, Manhattan

Banner 112
Refugee, Moria Camp, Lesvos, Greece, 2015
Grand Army Plaza, Manhattan

Banner 113
Refugee, Moria Camp, Lesvos, Greece, 2015
Lorimer Street and Metropolitan Avenue, Brooklyn

Banner 114
Refugee, Northern Shores, Lesvos, Greece, 2015
Bowery and E. 2nd Street, Manhattan

Banner 115
Refugee, Moria Camp, Lesvos, Greece, 2015
W. 3rd Street and LaGuardia Place, Manhattan

Banner 116
Refugee, Moria Camp, Lesvos, Greece, 2015
3rd Avenue and E. 165th Street, Bronx

Banner 117
Refugee, Moria Camp, Lesvos, Greece, 2015
2nd Avenue and E. 13th Street, Manhattan

Banner 118
Refugee, Moria Camp, Lesvos, Greece, 2015
3rd Avenue and St. Ann's Avenue, Bronx

Banner 119
Refugee, Moria Camp, Lesvos, Greece, 2015
Washington Square North and 5th Avenue, Manhattan

Banner 120
Refugee, Moria Camp, Lesvos, Greece, 2015
Park Avenue and E. 81st Street, Manhattan

Banner 121
Refugee, Moria Camp, Lesvos, Greece, 2015
Park Avenue and E. 82nd Street, Manhattan

Banner 122
Refugee, Molyvos, Lesvos, Greece, 2015
Avenue A and E. 2nd Street, Manhattan

Banner 123
Refugee, Northern Shores, Lesvos, Greece, 2015
Washington Square East and University Place, Manhattan

Banner 124
Refugee, Port of Mytilene, Lesvos, Greece, 2015
Forsyth and Delancey Streets, Manhattan

Banner 125
Refugees, Northern Shores, Lesvos, Greece, 2016
Grand Concourse and 156th Street, Bronx

Banner 126
Refugee, Northern Shores, Lesvos, Greece, 2016
Chrystie and E. Houston Streets, Manhattan

Banner 127
Refugee, Lesvos, Greece, 2016
W. 3rd and MacDougal Streets, Manhattan

Banner 128
Refugee, Northern Shores, Lesvos, Greece, 2016
W. 4th and MacDougal Streets, Manhattan

Banner 129
Refugee, Eastern Shores, Lesvos, Greece, 2016
Elton Avenue and E. 161st Street, Bronx

Banner 130
Refugee, Eastern Shores, Lesvos, Greece, 2016
Park Avenue and E. 89th Street, Manhattan

Banner 131
Refugee, Tempelhof Airport, Berlin, Germany, 2016
E. 163rd Street and 3rd Avenue, Bronx

Banner 132
Refugee, Tempelhof Airport, Berlin, Germany, 2016
7th Avenue and N. 110th Street, Manhattan

Banner 133
Refugee, Eastern Shores, Lesvos, Greece, 2016
Essex and Canal Streets, Manhattan

Banner 134
Refugee, Port of Mytilene, Lesvos, Greece, 2016
Tito Puente Way and Duke Ellington Circle, Manhattan

Banner 135
Refugee, Eastern Shores, Lesvos, Greece, 2016
E. 57th Street and Madison Avenue, Manhattan

Banner 136
Refugee, Eastern Shores, Lesvos, Greece, 2016
5th Avenue and W. 18th Street, Manhattan

Banner 137
Refugee, Eastern Shores, Lesvos, Greece, 2016
Avenue B and E. 2nd Street, Manhattan

Banner 138
Refugee, Eastern Shores, Lesvos, Greece, 2016
Washington Square East and Washington Place, Manhattan

Banner 139
Refugee, Eastern Shores, Lesvos, Greece, 2016
Forsyth and Delancey Streets, Manhattan

Banner 140
Refugee, "Refugee Graveyard," Lesvos, Greece, 2016
Metropolitan Avenue and Union Street, Brooklyn

Banner 141
Refugee, Port of Mytilene, Lesvos, Greece, 2016
Metropolitan Avenue and Lorimer Street, Brooklyn

Banner 142
Refugee, Ferry from Lesvos to Athens, Aegean Sea, 2016
Allen and Rivington Streets, Manhattan

Banner 143
Refugees, Ferry from Lesvos to Athens, Aegean Sea, 2016
Waverly Place and Mercer Street, Manhattan

Banner 144
Refugee, Ferry from Lesvos to Athens, Aegean Sea, 2016
7th Avenue and 110th Street, Manhattan

Banner 145
Refugee, Ferry from Lesvos to Athens, Aegean Sea, 2016
3rd Avenue and E. 6th Street, Manhattan

Banner 146
Refugees, Idomeni Makeshift Camp, Idomeni, Greece, 2016
N. 7th Street and Driggs Avenue, Manhattan

Banner 147
Refugee, Idomeni Makeshift Camp, Idomeni, Greece, 2016
Richmond Terrace and Nicholas Street, Staten Island

Banner 148
Refugee, Idomeni Makeshift Camp, Idomeni, Greece, 2016
E. 7th Street and 2nd Avenue, Manhattan

Banner 149
Refugee, Idomeni Makeshift Camp, Idomeni, Greece, 2016
Bowery and E. 3rd Street, Manhattan

Banner 150
Refugee, Idomeni Makeshift Camp, Idomeni, Greece, 2016
Stanton and Allen Streets, Manhattan

Banner 151
Refugee, Idomeni Makeshift Camp, Idomeni, Greece, 2016
Washington Square North and 5th Avenue, Manhattan

Banner 152
Refugee, Idomeni Makeshift Camp, Idomeni, Greece, 2016
Grand Concourse and E. 156th Street, Bronx

Banner 153
Refugee, Idomeni Makeshift Camp, Idomeni, Greece, 2016
Park Avenue and E. 89th Street, Manhattan

Banner 154
Refugee, Idomeni Makeshift Camp, Idomeni, Greece, 2016
Amsterdam Avenue and W. 68th Street, Manhattan

Banner 155
Refugee, Idomeni Makeshift Camp, Idomeni, Greece, 2016
74th Street and 37th Road, Queens

Banner 156
Refugee, Idomeni Makeshift Camp, Idomeni, Greece, 2016
Amsterdam Avenue and W. 68th Street, Manhattan

Banner 157
Refugee, Idomeni Makeshift Camp, Idomeni, Greece, 2016
7th Avenue and W. 121st Street, Manhattan

Banner 158
Refugee, Idomeni Makeshift Camp, Idomeni, Greece, 2016
Park Avenue and E. 83rd Street, Manhattan

Banner 159
Refugee, Idomeni Makeshift Camp, Idomeni, Greece, 2016
Park Avenue and E. 84th Street, Manhattan

Banner 160
Refugee, Idomeni Makeshift Camp, Idomeni, Greece, 2016
Richmond Terrace and Nicholas Street, Staten Island

Banner 161
Refugees, Kara Tepe Camp, Lesvos, Greece, 2016
W. 3rd Street and LaGuardia Place, Manhattan

Banner 162
Refugee, Port of Mytilene, Lesvos, Greece, 2016
Waverly Place and Greene Street, Manhattan

Banner 163
Refugee, Idomeni Makeshift Camp, Idomeni, Greece, 2016
Washington Place and Washington Square West, Manhattan

Banner 164
Refugee, Idomeni Makeshift Camp, Idomeni, Greece, 2016
Amsterdam Avenue and W. 94th Street, Manhattan

Banner 165
Refugee, Idomeni Makeshift Camp, Idomeni, Greece, 2016
Grand Concourse and E. 158th Street, Bronx

Banner 166
Refugee, Istanbul, Turkey, 2016
Park Avenue and E. 86th Street, Manhattan

Banner 167
Refugee, Makeshift Camp, Torbali, Izmir, Turkey, 2016
Broadway and E. 18th Street, Manhattan

Banner 168
Refugee, Nizip Camp, Gaziantep, Turkey, 2016
Madison Avenue and E. 109th Street, Manhattan

Banner 169
Refugee, Nizip Camp, Gaziantep, Turkey, 2016
E. 18th Street and Broadway, Manhattan

Banner 170
Refugee, Nizip Camp, Gaziantep, Turkey, 2016
Fulton Street and Broadway, Manhattan

Banner 171
Refugee, Nizip Camp, Gaziantep, Turkey, 2016
Madison Avenue and E. 107th Street, Manhattan

Banner 172
Refugee, Nizip Camp, Gaziantep, Turkey, 2016
E. 163rd Street and 3rd Avenue, Bronx

Banner 173
Refugee, Nizip Camp, Gaziantep, Turkey, 2016
Essex and Hester Streets, Manhattan

Banner 174
Refugee, Shatila Camp, Beirut, Lebanon, 2016
Bleeker Street and LaGuardia Place, Manhattan

Banner 175
Refugee, Shatila Camp, Beirut, Lebanon, 2016
Amsterdam Avenue and W. 90th Street, Manhattan

Banner 176
Refugee, Shatila Camp, Beirut, Lebanon, 2016
W. 18th Street and 10th Avenue, Manhattan

Banner 177
Refugee, Arsal Camp, Arsal, Lebanon, 2016
Grand Concourse and 156th Street, Bronx

Banner 178
Refugees, Arsal Camp, Arsal, Lebanon, 2016
W. 3rd and MacDougal Streets, Manhattan

Banner 179
Refugee, Arsal Camp, Arsal, Lebanon, 2016
Amsterdam Avenue and W. 89th Street, Manhattan

Banner 180
Refugee, Arsal Camp, Arsal, Lebanon, 2016
Cedar Street and Trinity Place, Manhattan

Banner 181
Refugee, Ain al-Hilweh Camp, Sidon, Lebanon, 2016
7th Avenue and W. 120th Street, Manhattan

Banner 182
Refugee, Ain al-Hilweh Camp, Sidon, Lebanon, 2016
Thompson and Bleeker Streets, Manhattan

Banner 183
Refugees, Makeshift Camp, Beqaa Valley, Lebanon, 2016
2nd Avenue and E. 7th Street, Manhattan

Banner 184
Refugee, Makeshift Camp, Beqaa Valley, Lebanon, 2016
Eldridge and Rivington Streets, Manhattan

Banner 185
Refugee, Syrian-Jordanian Border, 2016
Washington Square West and Wavery Place, Manhattan

Banner 186
Refugee, Syrian-Jordanian Border, 2016
Forsyth and Delancey Streets, Manhattan

Banner 187
Refugees, Syrian-Jordanian Border, 2016
7th and St. Nicholas Avenues, Manhattan

Banner 188
Refugee, Syrian-Jordanian Border, 2016
MacDougal and W. 3rd Streets, Manhattan

Banner 189
Refugee, Syrian-Jordanian Border, 2016
Essex and Canal Streets, Manhattan

Banner 190
Refugee, Syrian-Jordanian Border, 2016
Richmond Terrace and Nicholas Street, Staten Island

Banner 191
Refugee, Syrian-Jordanian Border, 2016
Grand Concourse and E. 165th Street, Bronx

Banner 192
Refugee, Syrian-Jordanian Border, 2016
S. 4th and Rodney Streets, Brooklyn

Banner 193
Refugees, Israeli West Bank Barrier, 2016
Park Avenue and E. 85th Street, Manhattan

Banner 194
Refugee, Khan Yunis, Gaza Strip, 2016
W. 3rd Street and LaGuardia Place, Manhattan

Banner 195
Refugee, Rafah Crossing, Gaza Strip, 2016
Allen and E. Houston Streets, Manhattan

Banner 196
Refugee, Gaza Strip, 2016
Broadway and W. 31st Street, Manhattan

Banner 197
Refugee, Qalandiya Checkpoint, West Bank, 2016
S. 5th and Rodney Streets, Brooklyn

Banner 198
Refugee, Qalandiya Checkpoint, West Bank, 2016
N. 7th Street and Driggs Avenue, Brooklyn

Banner 199
Refugee, Dadaab Camp, Kenya, 2016
Grand Concourse and Concourse Village West, Bronx

Banner 200
Refugee, Dadaab Camp, Kenya, 2016
2nd Avenue and E. 4th Street, Manhattan

Acknowledgments

New York is universally recognized as a global city, perhaps *the* global city. Presenting artists from around the world is naturally a core component of Public Art Fund's program. With Ai Weiwei's *Good Fences Make Good Neighbors*, that engagement intensified with the international refugee crisis as the central focus of this monumental citywide exhibition. Through the unflinching lens of Ai's art, we were drawn to reflect on both individual experiences and power structures: the struggles of our fellow human beings and the global forces that shape them.

Such an ambitious undertaking depended on the extraordinary trust and generosity of many partners, from city government to philanthropic individuals and foundations to an international network of skilled fabricators, not to mention Ai Weiwei's remarkable studio team and Public Art Fund's own brilliant board and staff.

In particular, I would like to thank and acknowledge the exhibition's most generous and committed supporters, including the visionary brothers Nicolai Frahm and Michael Frahm; our devoted Board Chair, Jill Kraus, and her husband, Peter Kraus; Jennifer and Matthew Harris; and Fotene Demoulas and Tom Coté. I am also deeply grateful to the Horace W. Goldsmith Foundation; the Charina Endowment Fund/Richard and Ronay Menschel; Kathleen McDonough and Edward Berman; Glenn and Amanda Fuhrman, and the Stavros Niarchos Foundation for their major support.

A project of this scope would not have been possible without the additional generous support of Elizabeth Fearon Pepperman and Richard C. Pepperman II; Susan and Jonathan Bram; Jeffrey Deitch; Jennifer and Jason New; neugerriemschneider, Berlin; the Red Crane Foundation; the Silverweed Foundation; Marcia Dunn and Jonathan Sobel; Robert Soros; Sheryl and Dan Tishman; Wendy Fisher; Patricia and Howard Silverstein; Lisson Gallery; Espolòn Tequila; Shari and Jeff Aronson; Elise and Andrew Brownstein; Meg and Bennett Goodman; Holly and Jonathan Lipton; Linda Lennon and Stuart Baskin; Heidi and Richard Rieger; Marcia Riklis; Anne and Joel Ehrenkranz; Bridgitt and Bruce Evans; Andrew and Linda R. Safran; Rachel and Sam Shikiar; and the Consulate General of the Federal Republic of Germany, New York. Our great thanks also go to the team at eBay, who generously partnered with us on fundraising edition sales.

Ai Weiwei's long history with New York City provided fertile ground for the development of this exhibition, which engaged the city more broadly and intensively than any other in our history. The support and cooperation of city government was indispensable, and I am particularly grateful to Mayor Bill de Blasio and First Lady Chirlane McCray for their belief in the importance of this project from its inception. They and their resourceful team at City Hall, including Gabrielle Fialkoff, Peter Hatch, and Terri Richardson, were essential to the realization of this project, together with citywide leadership, in particular Manhattan Borough President Gale Brewer, Brooklyn Borough President Eric Adams, and Queens Borough President Melinda Katz. Our thanks also go to members of the New York City Council, in particular Margaret Chin; Julissa Ferreras-Copeland; former Council Member Daniel Garodnick; Speaker Corey Johnson; Mark Levine; and Deputy Leader Jimmy Van Bramer.

Leaders of numerous New York City agencies shared their expertise, and we thank all of them for their partnership and support: Cultural Affairs Commissioner Tom Finkelpearl; Commissioner of the Mayor's Office for Immigrant Affairs Bitta Mostafi; Department of Transportation Assistant Commissioner, Urban Design + Art + Wayfinding Wendy Feuer and DOT Art Director Emily Colasacco; Economic Development Corporation Chief of Staff James Katz, Executive Vice President, Asset Management Revenue Matthew Kwatinetz and Vice President-Executive Director of Markets David Hughes; Fire Department Chief Thomas Pigott; Department of Buildings Commissioner Elizabeth Skowronek; Former Citywide Event Coordination and Management Executive Director Michael Carey; Department of Citywide Administrative Services Commissioner Lisette Camilo; Department of Environmental Protection Commissioner Vincent Sapienza; former Landmarks Preservation Commission Chair Meenakshi Srinivasan; and NYC & Company President and CEO Fred Dixon and COO and General Counsel Bryan Grimaldi.

I would especially like to recognize our longtime friends and collaborators at the New York City Department of Parks and Recreation, in particular Commissioner Mitchell J. Silver, and his team including former Senior Advisor Kate Spellman, Director of Art and Antiquities Jonathan Kuhn, Deputy Director of Public Art Jennifer Lantzas, Flushing Meadows Corona Park Administrator Janice Melnick, and Washington Square Park Administrator George Vellonakis. Each year we work together to bring major art installations to millions of people across our city, and it was a privilege to present some of the exhibition's most prominent works in NYC Parks. Similarly, our thanks go to Douglas Blonsky, former President and CEO of the Central Park Conservancy.

In addition to the many New York City properties made available for the exhibition, a number of other organizations and individuals generously facilitated our use of their sites. We are enormously grateful to JCDecaux North America, led by Bernard Parisot, President and Co-CEO, and Gabrielle Brussel, Executive Vice President Business Development and Properties, which donated advertising space at bus shelters and newsstand kiosks citywide; Ruth Fasoldt, Director of External Affairs at Intersection, which provided use of LinkNYC digital kiosks; President Laura Sparks, Dean Nader Tehrani, and colleagues Stephen Hillyer and Kim Newman at The Cooper Union for the Advancement of Science and Art; and enlightened private property owners Mechele Flaume, Felix Fung, and Javier Vivas.

It is truly remarkable that Ai Weiwei was able to channel his energies toward conceiving these powerful, original artworks for all of these many sites so quickly and efficiently. Supporting every aspect of his work is a studio team of rare talent and dedication. Our tremendous thanks go to each member of his project crew: Cui Xing, Gui Nuo, Kang Sunkoo, Lucas Lai, Ken Lee, Darryl Leung, Liang Zhipeng, Max Logsdail, Jennifer Ng, Fuyuka Sato, Jennifer Schmachtenberg, Nadine Stenke, Kimberly Sung, Wibke Tiarks, Luitgard Wagner, Xie Zhenwei, and Inserk Yang.

Production of the artworks in the exhibition was a monumental task; we succeeded thanks to a team of brilliantly talented designers, engineers, and fabricators who worked around the clock to realize Ai's vision. My talented Australian friends and the founding principals of UAP, Daniel and Matthew Tobin, rose to the occasion, fabricating two of Ai Weiwei's most ambitious works, *Arch* and *Gilded Cage*. Our thanks to their team, including Kevin Davey, Jamie Perrow, and Brant Underwood. Thanks must also go to Isaac Zal and 4th State Metals; CAN-USA; Guy and Dean Torsilieri; and for banner production in Germany, the Laser Unit division of dGTecs, and Wolther Planen.

Vital engineering support was generously provided by Eli Gottlieb and Stanley King of Thornton Tomasetti; the insights and architectural expertise of FXCollaborative's Guy Geier, Silvia Smith, and David Wallance were invaluable; AECOM Tishman provided key advice early in the project; Emil Lissauer at Capalino + Company's Agency Resolution and Permitting Group secured our permits; Suri Kasirer and team at Kasirer provided valuable strategic advice, as did Evan Korn and team at iDEKO. Our thanks also go to Manhattan Community Board 2, particularly to Chair Terri Cude, Rich Caccappolo, and Robin Rothstein.

For more than forty years, Public Art Fund has been in the extraordinary business of doing things that have never been done before. That takes a bold spirit of adventure and experimentation, as well as a tremendous foundation of experience and expertise. Our distinguished President, Susan K. Freedman, my steadfast partner throughout this project, contributed in countless ways to its realization. I am deeply grateful to have such a generous mentor and guide. Inspired by our collective mission and Ai Weiwei's art, every staff member of Public Art Fund moved mountains to realize *Good Fences Make Good Neighbors*. My warmest thanks go to each of them.

Drawing on his broad experience, Sam Rauch, Director of Creative Partnerships, expertly led the exhibition's project management, juggling innumerable demands and solving many of the complex puzzles that this logistically unprecedented project entailed. Daniel S. Palmer, Associate Curator, was a key collaborator on the curatorial development and delivery of the exhibition and this publication, generating numerous insightful ideas that immensely enhanced the project. Kellie Honeycutt, Director of Institutional Advancement, astutely guided every aspect of our fundraising and communications, both of which achieved unprecedented success. Jesse Hamerman, Director of Exhibitions, brought his unmatched experience and technical expertise to bear on the project from beginning to end while also overseeing the project management team. Significant additional responsibilities were very adeptly handled by Nora Gomez-Strauss, Director of Digital Strategies; and Allegra Thoresen, Associate Director of Communications. Every team member played an integral role, and I would like to recognize Devon Caranicas, Associate Director of Patron Programs; Seth Cohen, Project Manager; Vaness Haddox, Associate Director of Individual Giving; Courtney Knights, Associate Director of Institutional Giving; Sydney Krassen, Development Associate; M.C. Madrigal, Associate Project Manager; Christina Martin, Executive Assistant; Sandrine Milet, Communications Manager; and Joni Todd, Senior Manager of Finance and Human Resources.

With so many sites around the city, the exhibition's graphic identity required conceptual strength and high visibility. This was skillfully accomplished by Anh Tuan Pham and team at For Office Use Only, including Victoire Coyon, Claudine Eriksson, and Louis Walch. Anh Tuan's beautiful and inventive design for this complex publication extends their exceptional work, providing a new and enduring way to experience the exhibition. Katerina Stathopoulou, Assistant Curator, adroitly coordinated every aspect of this comprehensive catalogue, which mirrors the exhibition in its wide reach and multiple layers. The book contains a multitude of powerful voices, and we are tremendously grateful to each contributor for their personal insights.

Donna Wingate and Marc Joseph Berg of Artist and Publisher Services have been indispensable collaborators in the book's development and production, the execution of which has been expertly managed by Adrian Lucia and colleagues at Lucia|Marquand. We are indebted to the work of a very talented group of photographers, including Nicholas Knight, Liz Ligon, Eric Gregory Powell, Timothy Schenck, Jason Wyche, as well as to many members of the public who granted permission to use of their social media posts. We are delighted to again partner with Yale University Press, and grateful for the enthusiastic support of Amy Canonico, Editor, Art and Architecture.

The opportunity to work closely with Ai Weiwei has been an extraordinary experience for all of us at Public Art Fund. His inspired realization of *Good Fences Make Good Neighbors* had a profound and lasting impact on many levels. He created this exhibition with deep passion and commitment, and in doing so exceeded even our highest hopes. We remain ever thankful for his great friendship, generosity, indomitable spirit, humanitarian activism, and transformational art.

Nicholas Baume
Director and Chief Curator, Public Art Fund

Biographies

Ai Weiwei was born in Beijing in 1957 and has lived and worked in Berlin since 2015. He is the recipient of the 2015 Ambassador of Conscience Award from Amnesty International and the 2012 Václav Havel International Prize for Creative Dissent from the Human Rights Foundation. The artist's first feature-length documentary, *Human Flow*, premiered in competition at the 74th Venice Film Festival in 2017.

Ai is internationally renowned for artworks and gestures that assert pointed aesthetic statements, the timely and lasting effects of which reverberate strongly in our geopolitical world. He deploys a wide range of mediums and platforms, including architecture, photography, sculpture, installations, direct actions, social media, and documentary films. The long arc of his projects has established myriad ways for audiences to experience representations of our present-day society—its mechanisms, power structures, and values. Recent exhibitions include *Fan-Tan* at the Mucem in Marseille (2018); *Inoculation* at Fundación Proa in Buenos Aires (2018); *Ai Weiwei on Porcelain* at the Sakip Sabanci Museum in Istanbul (2017); *Ai Weiwei: Trace at Hirshhorn* at the Hirshhorn Museum and Sculpture Garden in Washington, DC (2017); *Maybe, Maybe Not* at the Israel Museum in Jerusalem (2017); *Law of the Journey* at the National Gallery Prague (2017); and *Ai Weiwei: Libero* at Palazzo Strozzi in Florence (2016).

Nicholas Baume joined Public Art Fund as Director and Chief Curator in 2009. His career began in his native Australia at Kaldor Public Art Projects and continued with his appointment as Curator of Public Programs at Museum of Contemporary Art, Sydney. From 1998 to 2003, he was Contemporary Curator at the Wadsworth Atheneum in Hartford, Connecticut, before joining the Institute of Contemporary Art, Boston, as Chief Curator. There he was responsible for shaping the artistic program from 2003 to 2009, as well as the establishment of a permanent collection in advance of the 2006 opening of the ICA's award-winning building by architects Diller Scofidio + Renfro.

Recent Public Art Fund exhibitions have included projects by Tauba Auerbach, Isa Genzken, Liz Glynn, Anselm Kiefer, Alicja Kwade, Mark Manders, Tony Oursler, Yinka Shonibare, Hank Willis Thomas, Tatiana Trouve, and Oscar Tuazon; the group exhibitions *Statuesque*, *Common Ground*, and *Lightness of Being*; the career survey *Sol LeWitt: Structures 1965–2006*; major installations for Rockefeller Center including Elmgreen & Dragset's *Van Gogh's Ear*, Ugo Rondinone's *Human Nature*, and Jeff Koons's colossal flowering *Split-Rocker*; Jeppe Hein's multi-work *Please Touch the Art*, Anish Kapoor's *Descension*, and Siah Armajani's *Bridge Over Tree* at Brooklyn Bridge Park; and the landmark *Tatzu Nishi: Discovering Columbus*. Baume is a frequent public speaker on contemporary art, the author of several major exhibition catalogues, and has contributed essays and interviews to numerous publications.

Public Art Fund Staff and Ai Weiwei Studio

Public Art Fund Staff

Claire Aichholzer
Development Assistant

Nicholas Baume
Director and Chief Curator

Rachael Buchwald
Manager of Creative Partnerships

Devon Caranicas
Associate Director, Patron Programs

Seth Cohen
Project Manager

Susan K. Freedman
President

Nora Gomez-Strauss
Director of Digital Strategies

Vanessa Hadox
Associate Director, Individual Giving

Jesse Hamerman
Director of Exhibitions

Walsh Hansen
Project Manager

Kellie Honeycutt
Director of Institutional Advancement

Sarah Jones
Graphic Designer

Varun Kelkar
Administrative Assistant, Finance and Human Resources

Courtney Knights
Associate Director, Institutional Giving

Sydney Krassen
Development Associate

MC Madrigal
Associate Project Manager

Christina Martin
Executive Assistant

Sandrine Milet
Communications Manager

Daniel S. Palmer
Associate Curator

Rashel Peddersen
Project Manager

Sam Rauch
Director of Creative Partnerships

Paige Schaefer
Manager, Events and Membership

Katerina Stathopoulou
Assistant Curator

Allegra Thoresen
Associate Director of Communications

Joni Todd
Senior Manager, Finance and Human Resources

Ai Weiwei Studio

Ai Weiwei

Cui Xing

Gui Nuo

Kang Sunkoo

Lucas Lai

Ken Lee

Darryl Leung

Liang Zhipeng

Max Logsdail

Jennifer Ng

Eric Gregory Powell

Fuyuka Sato

Jennifer Schmachtenberg

Nadine Stenke

Kimberly Sung

Wibke Tiarks

Luitgard Wagner

Xie Zhenwei

Inserk Yang

Public Art Fund Board of Directors

Photography Credits

Unless otherwise noted, all images © Ai Weiwei, courtesy Ai Weiwei Studio

Courtesy Public Art Fund, photos by Jason Wyche: inside cover, pp. 34, 108–109, 116 (top), 129 (top), 140, 143, 146–47, 150–52, 172–73, 176 (top), 186 (right), 225, 232–33, 260–61, 268–69, 271 (top), 274–75; Courtesy Public Art Fund, photos by Nicholas Knight: pp. 4–5, 8–9, 10–12, 21, 30, 46, 68, 105, 120–22, 126–28, 130 (top), 131, 134, 135 (top), 136 (top), 138–39, 148, 156–57, 166–68, 171, 174, 175 (bottom), 177–78, 179 (top), 180, 181 (bottom), 182–84, 216, 222, 227–29, 231 (top), 234–36, 238, 240–41, 262, 264–66, 270, 272, 279–81, 288–89; Courtesy Public Art Fund, photos by Timothy Schenck: pp. 2–3, 6–7, 50–51, 53, 55 (bottom), 56–57, 58, 64, 67, 70–71, 132–33, 154, 160, 161 (top), 162–63, 220–21, 226 (top), 230 (bottom), 248–49, 250 (bottom), 252–54, 255 (top), 256, 258–59, 260–61; photo by Jens Weber, p. 22; Courtesy Ai Weiwei and AW Asia, photos by Daniel Avila, Courtesy NYC Parks & Recreation: p. 23 (top); © 1982 Jenny Holzer, Artists Rights Society (ARS), photo © 1982 Lisa Kahane, p. 23 (bottom); Courtesy Public Art Fund, photos by Nicholas Baume, p. 27 (top), 32 (bottom), 124 (bottom left), 186 (left), 187 bottom left, 271 (bottom); © 2019 Barbara Moore / Licensed by VAGA at Artists Rights Society (ARS), NY, Courtesy Paula Cooper Gallery, New York, p. 27 (bottom); © The Estate of Gordon Matta-Clark / Artists Rights Society (ARS), New York; Courtesy The Estate of Gordon Matta-Clark and David Zwirner, p. 28 (top); © 2019 Richard Serra / Artists Rights Society (ARS), New York, photo: Peter Moore, p. 28 (bottom); UAP, pp. 32 (top), 62 (top right, center left and bottom left), p. 277 (top right, middle and bottom left, bottom right); Courtesy Public Art Fund, photos by Liz Ligon, pp. 36, 286; Courtesy Public Art Fund, photo by Sam Rauch, p. 40 (right); photo by Stuart Freeman, p. 43 (left); photo by Nomi Ellenson, p. 43 (right); Courtesy Public Art Fund, photos by Daniel S. Palmer, pp. 48 (bottom left), 124 (top left and right), 159 (top left), 276 (bottom left); Courtesy Public Art Fund, photos by Susan K. Freedman, pp. 110, 149, 245; photo by G. Scott Segler, p. 55 (top); Courtesy Public Art Fund, photos by Claudio Papapietro, pp. 63 (top), 65, 69 (bottom); photo by JC Garcia-Lavin, p. 66; courtesy @artworldnyc, photo by @nickshotit, p. 69 (top); photos by Augustus Sherman, pp. 76–77 (top left, bottom right); photo by Lucien Waléry, p. 82 (left), photo by John Jabez Edwin Mayall, p. 82 (top), photo by Pete Souza, p. 82 (bottom); photo by Max Halberstadt, p. 83 (top left); photo by Don English, p. 83 (bottom right); Courtesy Public Art Fund, photos by MC Madrigal, p. 159 (bottom right); photo by Outfront Media, p. 115 (top); photo by @sergarod, p. 115 (bottom); photo by Katie N. Ward, p. 116 (bottom); photo by Eng C. Lau, p. 125; photo by Ignacio Soltero, p. 129 (bottom); photo by Bob K. Cuk, p. 136 (bottom); photos by 4th State, p. 142 (top left and right, center left); Courtesy Public Art Fund, photos by Seth Cohen, pp. 142 (bottom left), 159 (middle left); photo by Roger Higgins, p. 155; photo by Brigid Pierce, p. 161 (bottom left); photo by Ron Meisel, p. 161 (bottom right); photo by Pamela Kerpius, p. 175 (top); photo by Jodi Imburgia, p. 179 (bottom); © REUTERS /Stoyan Nenov, p. 185; photo by Judith Moy, p. 230 (top); photo by Maria L. Chang, p. 231 (bottom); Courtesy Public Art Fund, photos by Jesse Hamerman, p. 251 (right), p. 263 (bottom), p. 267 (bottom); photo by Yurina Roche, p. 255 (bottom); photos by Torsilieri, Inc p. 257 (bottom); Cooper Union, p. 269 (top); © André Breton, p. 277 (top right); photo by Carol Porteous, p. 278; photos by Zach Hilty / BFA.com, pp. 282–83; photo by @nyclive, p. 284 (top left); photo by @qwqw7575, p. 284 (top right); photo: Noel Y. Calingasan, p. 284 (bottom right).

Every effort has been made to identify the photographers and copyright holders for images reproduced in this publication. Errors or omissions will be corrected in subsequent editions.

Front inside cover: *Arch*. Washington Square Park, Manhattan
Pages 2–3: *Chrystie Street Fence*. 189 Chrystie Street, Manhattan
Pages 4–5: *Circle Fence*. Flushing Meadows Corona Park, Queens
Pages 6–7: *Gilded Cage*. Doris C. Freedman Plaza, Central Park, Manhattan
Pages 8–9: *Good Neighbors 35*. Makeshift Camp, Idomeni, Greece, 2016. E. 1st Street and 1st Avenue, Manhattan
Pages 10–11: *Banner 190*. Refugee, Syrian-Jordanian Border, 2016. Richmond Terrace and Nicholas Street, Staten Island
Page 12: *7th Street Fence*. 48 E. 7th Street, Manhattan

All artworks, Ai Weiwei, 2017

This book documents the New York citywide exhibition, *Ai Weiwei: Good Fences Make Good Neighbors*, organized by Nicholas Baume, Director and Chief Curator, with the assistance of Daniel S. Palmer, Associate Curator, Public Art Fund, October 12, 2017–February 11, 2018

Distributed by
Yale University Press
302 Temple Street
P.O. Box 209040
New Haven, CT 06520-9040
yalebooks.com/art

Produced by
Lucia|Marquand, Seattle
luciamarquand.com

Editorial
Donna Wingate and Marc Joseph Berg
Artist and Publisher Services, New York

Publication Coordinator
Katerina Stathopoulou

Proofreading
Laura Iwasaki

Design
For Office Use Only, New York
Anh Tuan Pham and Claudine Eriksson

Color management
iocolor, Seattle

Printed and bound in
Singapore by Pristone

Typefaces
Graphik Narrow, Commercial Font
Suisse Works, Swiss Typefaces
Bureau Grotesque, Font Bureau

ISBN 978-0-300-24379-6

Library of Congress Cataloging-in-Publication Data

Names: Baume, Nicholas.
Title: Ai Weiwei : good fences make good neighbors / Nicholas Baume ; additional texts by Daniel S. Palmer and Katerina Stathopoulou.
Other titles: Ai WeiWei (Public Art Fund (New York, N.Y.))
Description: New York: Public Art Fund, 2019.
Identifiers: LCCN 2018060670 | ISBN 9780300243796 (hardback)
Subjects: LCSH: Ai, Weiwei—Criticism and interpretation. | Public art—New York (State)—New York. | Conceptual art—New York (State)—New York. | Installations (Art)—New York (State)—New York. | BISAC: ART / Individual Artists / Monographs. | ART / History / Contemporary (1945–). | ART / Asian. | ART / Collections, Catalogs, Exhibitions / General.
Classification: LCC N7349.A5 A855 2019 | DDC 709.2—dc23
LC record available at https://lccn.loc.gov/2018060670

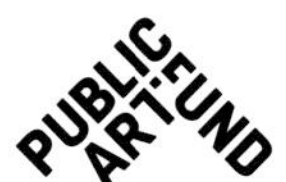

Public Art Fund
One East 53rd Street
New York, NY 10022
PublicArtFund.org